Haynes THE BOOK ®

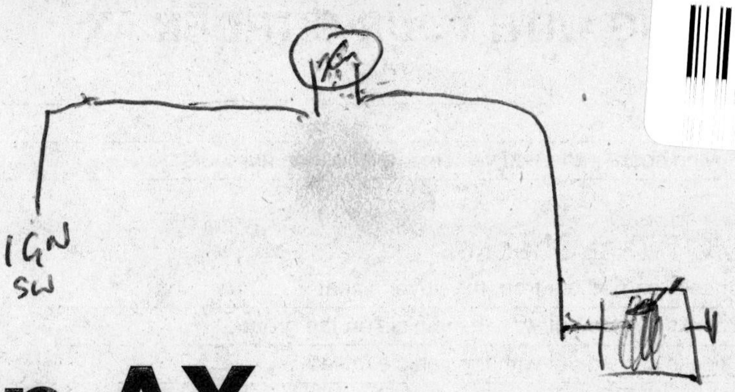

Citroën AX
Service and Repair Manual

A K Legg LAE MIMI

(3014-5AC2)

Models covered
Citroën AX models with petrol and Diesel engines, including special/limited editions
3- and 5-door Hatchback
954 cc, 1124 cc & 1360 cc
Covers most features of 1527 cc Diesel engine
Covers mechanical features of Van models

ABCDE

Printed in the USA

A book in the **Haynes Service and Repair Manual Series**

ISBN 1 85960 594 X

British Library Cataloguing in Publication Data
A catalogue record for this book is available from the British Library.

Haynes Publishing
Sparkford, Nr Yeovil, Somerset BA22 7JJ, England

Haynes North America, Inc
861 Lawrence Drive, Newbury Park, California 91320, USA

Editions Haynes S.A.
Tour Aurore - IBC, 18 Place des Reflets,
92975 Paris La Défense 2, Cedex, France

Haynes Publishing Nordiska AB
Box 1504, 751 45 Uppsala, Sverige

Contents

LIVING WITH YOUR CITROËN AX

MOT Test Checks

MAINTENANCE

Routine maintenance

Contents

REPAIRS & OVERHAUL

Engine and Associated Systems

Transmission

Brakes

Suspension and steering

Body Equipment

Electrical

Wiring diagrams

Reference

Index

Introduction to the Citroën AX

The Citroën AX was introduced in the UK in July 1987 (having being launched in France the previous September), the initial versions being three-door Hatchbacks. The five-door version was introduced in April 1988.

All engines are derived from the well-proven TU series engines which have appeared in many Peugeot and Citroën vehicles. The engine is of four-cylinder overhead camshaft design, mounted transversely, with the transmission mounted on the left-hand side. All models have a four- or five-speed manual transmission.

In early 1989, a 1.4 litre (1360 cc) Diesel engine was added to the range. In September 1991, the "second-generation" AX was introduced, with revised interior and exterior styling. A 1527 cc Diesel engine was introduced in July 1994 - however, at the time of writing, only limited technical information was available for this engine.

All models have fully-independent front and rear suspension. The rear suspension incorporates torsion bars and trailing arms.

A wide range of standard and optional equipment is available within the AX range to suit most tastes, including central locking and electric windows. An anti-lock braking system and air conditioning system are available as options on certain models.

Provided that regular servicing is carried out in accordance with the manufacturer's recommendations, the Citroën AX should prove reliable and very economical. The engine compartment is well-designed, and most of the items requiring frequent attention are easily accessible.

Citroën AX 11 TZX 5-door

Citroën AX GTi

About this manual

The aim of this manual is to help you get the best value from your vehicle. It can do so in several ways. It can help you decide what work must be done (even should you choose to get it done by a garage). It will also provide information on routine maintenance and servicing, and give a logical course of action and diagnosis when random faults occur. However, it is hoped that you will use the manual by tackling the work yourself. On simpler jobs it may even be quicker than booking the car into a garage and going there twice, to leave and collect it. Perhaps most important, a lot of money can be saved by avoiding the costs a garage must charge to cover its labour and overheads.

The manual has drawings and descriptions to show the function of the various components so that their layout can be understood. Tasks are described and photographed in a clear step-by-step sequence.

References to the "left" or "right" of the vehicle are in the sense of a person in the driving seat, facing forwards.

Acknowledgements

Thanks are due to Champion Spark Plug who supplied spark plug information. Certain illustrations are the copyright of Citroën Cars Ltd, and are used with their permission. Thanks are also due to Sykes-Pickavant, who provided many of the workshop tools, and all those at Sparkford who assisted in the production of this manual.

We take great pride in the accuracy of information given in this manual, but vehicle manufacturers make altera-tions and design changes during the production run of a particular vehicle of which they do not inform us. No liability can be accepted by the authors or publishers for loss, damage or injury caused by any errors in, or omissions from, the information given.

Working on your car can be dangerous. This page shows just some of the potential risks and hazards, with the aim of creating a safety-conscious attitude.

General hazards

Scalding

- Don't remove the radiator or expansion tank cap while the engine is hot.
- Engine oil, automatic transmission fluid or power steering fluid may also be dangerously hot if the engine has recently been running.

Burning

- Beware of burns from the exhaust system and from any part of the engine. Brake discs and drums can also be extremely hot immediately after use.

Crushing

- When working under or near a raised vehicle, always supplement the jack with axle stands, or use drive-on ramps. ***Never venture under a car which is only supported by a jack.***

- Take care if loosening or tightening high-torque nuts when the vehicle is on stands. Initial loosening and final tightening should be done with the wheels on the ground.

Fire

- Fuel is highly flammable; fuel vapour is explosive.
- Don't let fuel spill onto a hot engine.
- Do not smoke or allow naked lights (including pilot lights) anywhere near a vehicle being worked on. Also beware of creating sparks (electrically or by use of tools).
- Fuel vapour is heavier than air, so don't work on the fuel system with the vehicle over an inspection pit.
- Another cause of fire is an electrical overload or short-circuit. Take care when repairing or modifying the vehicle wiring.
- Keep a fire extinguisher handy, of a type suitable for use on fuel and electrical fires.

Electric shock

- Ignition HT voltage can be dangerous, especially to people with heart problems or a pacemaker. Don't work on or near the ignition system with the engine running or the ignition switched on.

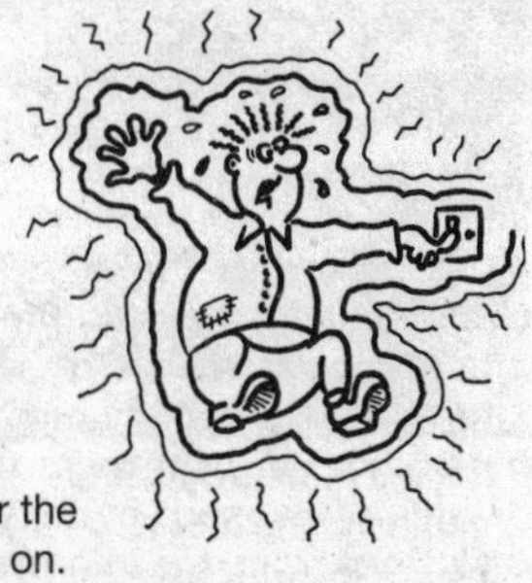

- Mains voltage is also dangerous. Make sure that any mains-operated equipment is correctly earthed. Mains power points should be protected by a residual current device (RCD) circuit breaker.

Fume or gas intoxication

- Exhaust fumes are poisonous; they often contain carbon monoxide, which is rapidly fatal if inhaled. Never run the engine in a confined space such as a garage with the doors shut.

- Fuel vapour is also poisonous, as are the vapours from some cleaning solvents and paint thinners.

Poisonous or irritant substances

- Avoid skin contact with battery acid and with any fuel, fluid or lubricant, especially antifreeze, brake hydraulic fluid and Diesel fuel. Don't syphon them by mouth. If such a substance is swallowed or gets into the eyes, seek medical advice.
- Prolonged contact with used engine oil can cause skin cancer. Wear gloves or use a barrier cream if necessary. Change out of oil-soaked clothes and do not keep oily rags in your pocket.
- Air conditioning refrigerant forms a poisonous gas if exposed to a naked flame (including a cigarette). It can also cause skin burns on contact.

Asbestos

- Asbestos dust can cause cancer if inhaled or swallowed. Asbestos may be found in gaskets and in brake and clutch linings. When dealing with such components it is safest to assume that they contain asbestos.

Special hazards

Hydrofluoric acid

- This extremely corrosive acid is formed when certain types of synthetic rubber, found in some O-rings, oil seals, fuel hoses etc, are exposed to temperatures above 400°C. The rubber changes into a charred or sticky substance containing the acid. *Once formed, the acid remains dangerous for years. If it gets onto the skin, it may be necessary to amputate the limb concerned.*
- When dealing with a vehicle which has suffered a fire, or with components salvaged from such a vehicle, wear protective gloves and discard them after use.

The battery

- Batteries contain sulphuric acid, which attacks clothing, eyes and skin. Take care when topping-up or carrying the battery.
- The hydrogen gas given off by the battery is highly explosive. Never cause a spark or allow a naked light nearby. Be careful when connecting and disconnecting battery chargers or jump leads.

Air bags

- Air bags can cause injury if they go off accidentally. Take care when removing the steering wheel and/or facia. Special storage instructions may apply.

Diesel injection equipment

- Diesel injection pumps supply fuel at very high pressure. Take care when working on the fuel injectors and fuel pipes.

Warning: Never expose the hands, face or any other part of the body to injector spray; the fuel can penetrate the skin with potentially fatal results.

Remember...

DO

- Do use eye protection when using power tools, and when working under the vehicle.
- Do wear gloves or use barrier cream to protect your hands when necessary.
- Do get someone to check periodically that all is well when working alone on the vehicle.
- Do keep loose clothing and long hair well out of the way of moving mechanical parts.
- Do remove rings, wristwatch etc, before working on the vehicle – especially the electrical system.
- Do ensure that any lifting or jacking equipment has a safe working load rating adequate for the job.

DON'T

- Don't attempt to lift a heavy component which may be beyond your capability – get assistance.
- Don't rush to finish a job, or take unverified short cuts.
- Don't use ill-fitting tools which may slip and cause injury.
- Don't leave tools or parts lying around where someone can trip over them. Mop up oil and fuel spills at once.
- Don't allow children or pets to play in or near a vehicle being worked on.

Buying spare parts

Spare parts are available from many sources; for example, Citroën garages, other garages and accessory shops, and motor factors. Our advice regarding spare part sources is as follows.

Officially-appointed Citroën garages - This is the best source for parts which are peculiar to your car, and are not generally available (eg complete cylinder heads, internal gearbox components, badges, interior trim etc). It is also the only place at which you should buy parts if the vehicle is still under warranty. To be sure of obtaining the correct parts, it will be necessary to give the storeman your car's vehicle identification number, and if possible, take the old parts along for positive identification. Many parts are available under a factory exchange scheme - any parts returned should always be clean. It obviously makes good sense to go straight to the specialists on your car for this type of part, as they are best equipped to supply you.

Other garages and accessory shops - These are often very good places to buy materials and components needed for the maintenance of your car (eg oil filters, spark plugs/glow plugs, bulbs, drivebelts, oils and greases, touch-up paint, filler paste, etc). They also sell general accessories, usually have convenient opening hours, charge lower prices, and can often be found not far from home.

Motor factors - Good factors will stock all the more important components which wear out comparatively quickly (eg exhaust systems, brake pads, seals and hydraulic parts, clutch components, bearing shells, pistons, valves etc). Motor factors will often provide new or reconditioned components on a part-exchange basis - this can save a considerable amount of money.

Vehicle identification numbers

Modifications are a continuing and unpublicised process in vehicle manufacture, quite apart from major model changes. Spare parts lists are compiled upon a numerical basis, the individual vehicle identification numbers being essential to correct identification of the component concerned.

When ordering spare parts, always give as much information as possible. Quote the car model, year of manufacture, body and engine numbers, as appropriate **(see illustrations)**.

The *Vehicle Identification Number (VIN)* plate is located on the right-hand front wheel arch/wing valance on models manufactured up to June 1988 - on models manufactured from June 1988 onwards it is on the left-hand side or attached to the crossmember at the front of the engine compartment. The plate can be viewed once the bonnet is open. The plate carries the VIN and vehicle weight information.

The *chassis number* is stamped into the body, along the top inner edge of the right-hand wing, and can be viewed with the bonnet open **(see illustration)**. On some models, the chassis number may also be etched into the windscreen and window glass.

The *engine number* is situated on the left-hand end of the front face of the cylinder block. On models with an aluminium cylinder block, the number is stamped on a plate which is riveted to the block **(see illustration)**; on models with a cast-iron cylinder block, the number is stamped on a machined surface on the cylinder block, at the flywheel end. The first part of the engine number gives the engine code - eg "H1A".

The *paint code* is stamped onto the right-hand front suspension turret.

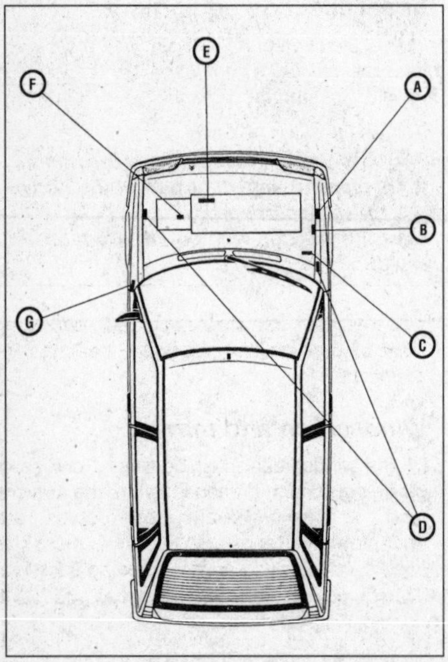

Identification plate locations (later models)

A VIN location
B Paint code
C Replacement parts identification number
D Chassis number
E Engine number
F Transmission number
G Build code (date) stamped mark

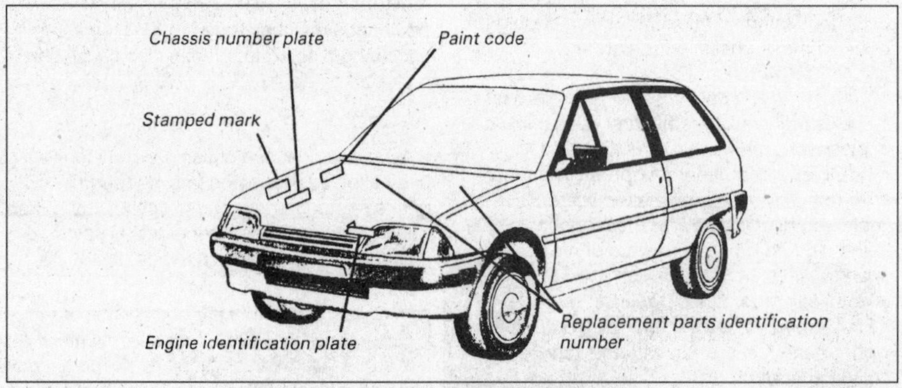

Identification plate locations (early models)

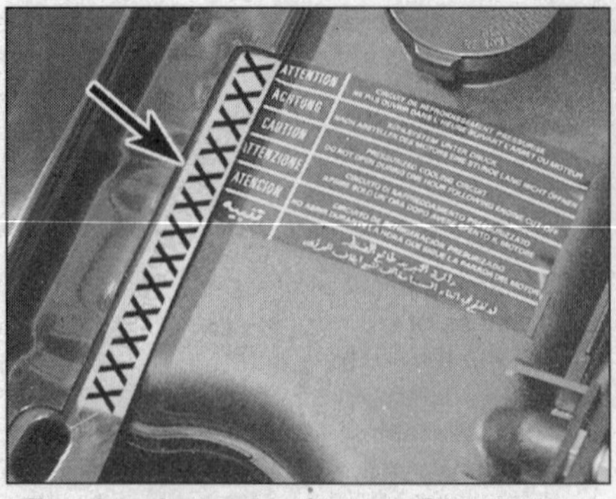

The chassis number (arrowed) is stamped into the top inner edge of the right-hand wing

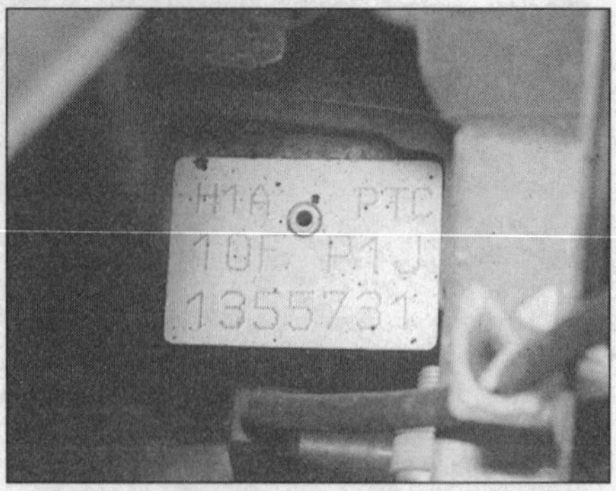

Engine number location - aluminium block engines. The first three letters of the plate indicate the engine code (H1A engine shown)

This is a guide to getting your vehicle through the MOT test. Obviously it will not be possible to examine the vehicle to the same standard as the professional MOT tester. However, working through the following checks will enable you to identify any problem areas before submitting the vehicle for the test.

Where a testable component is in borderline condition, the tester has discretion in deciding whether to pass or fail it. The basis of such discretion is whether the tester would be happy for a close relative or friend to use the vehicle with the component in that condition. If the vehicle presented is clean and evidently well cared for, the tester may be more inclined to pass a borderline component than if the vehicle is scruffy and apparently neglected.

It has only been possible to summarise the test requirements here, based on the regulations in force at the time of printing. Test standards are becoming increasingly stringent, although there are some exemptions for older vehicles. For full details obtain a copy of the Haynes publication Pass the MOT! (available from stockists of Haynes manuals).

An assistant will be needed to help carry out some of these checks.

The checks have been sub-divided into four categories, as follows:

1 Checks carried out **FROM THE DRIVER'S SEAT**

2 Checks carried out **WITH THE VEHICLE ON THE GROUND**

3 Checks carried out **WITH THE VEHICLE RAISED AND THE WHEELS FREE TO TURN**

4 Checks carried out on **YOUR VEHICLE'S EXHAUST EMISSION SYSTEM**

1 Checks carried out FROM THE DRIVER'S SEAT

Handbrake

☐ Test the operation of the handbrake. Excessive travel (too many clicks) indicates incorrect brake or cable adjustment.

☐ Check that the handbrake cannot be released by tapping the lever sideways. Check the security of the lever mountings.

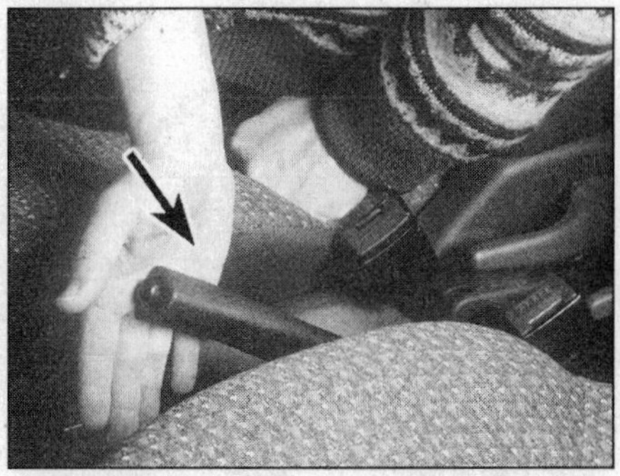

Footbrake

☐ Depress the brake pedal and check that it does not creep down to the floor, indicating a master cylinder fault. Release the pedal, wait a few seconds, then depress it again. If the pedal travels nearly to the floor before firm resistance is felt, brake adjustment or repair is necessary. If the pedal feels spongy, there is air in the hydraulic system which must be removed by bleeding.

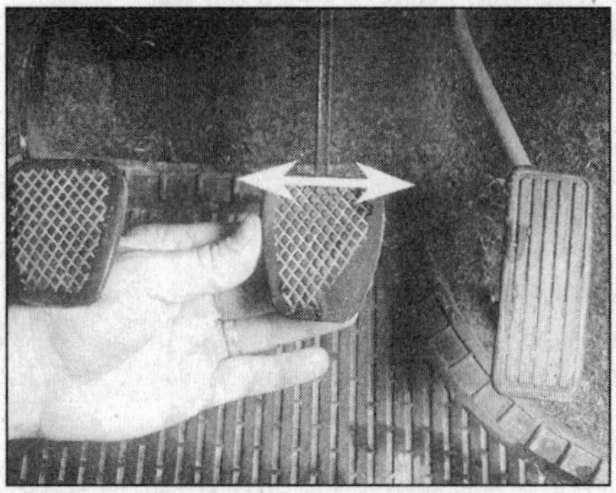

☐ Check that the brake pedal is secure and in good condition. Check also for signs of fluid leaks on the pedal, floor or carpets, which would indicate failed seals in the brake master cylinder.

☐ Check the servo unit (when applicable) by operating the brake pedal several times, then keeping the pedal depressed and starting the engine. As the engine starts, the pedal will move down slightly. If not, the vacuum hose or the servo itself may be faulty.

Steering wheel and column

☐ Examine the steering wheel for fractures or looseness of the hub, spokes or rim.

☐ Move the steering wheel from side to side and then up and down. Check that the steering wheel is not loose on the column, indicating wear or a loose retaining nut. Continue moving the steering wheel as before, but also turn it slightly from left to right.

☐ Check that the steering wheel is not loose on the column, and that there is no abnormal

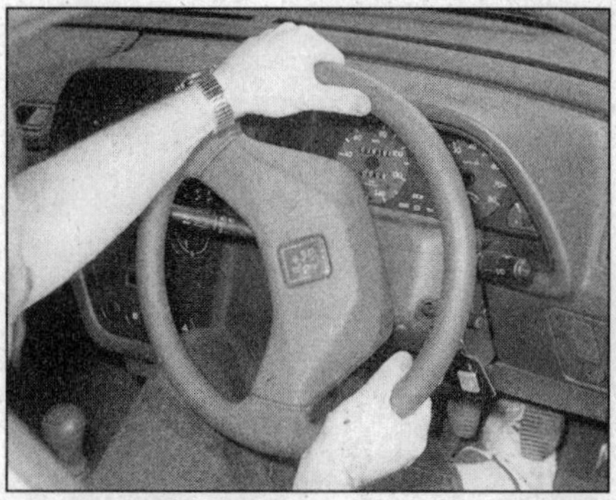

movement of the steering wheel, indicating wear in the column support bearings or couplings.

Windscreen and mirrors

☐ The windscreen must be free of cracks or other significant damage within the driver's field of view. (Small stone chips are acceptable.) Rear view mirrors must be secure, intact, and capable of being adjusted.

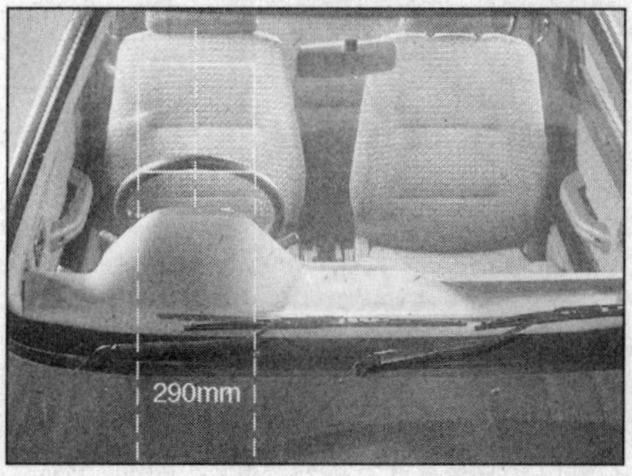

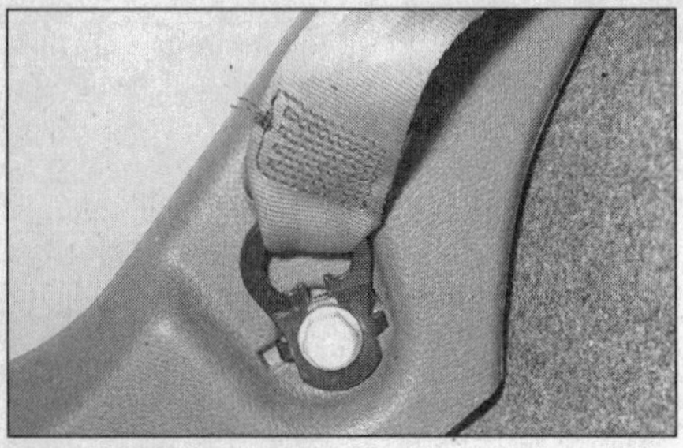

Seat belts and seats

Note: *The following checks are applicable to all seat belts, front and rear.*

☐ Examine the webbing of all the belts (including rear belts if fitted) for cuts, serious fraying or deterioration. Fasten and unfasten each belt to check the buckles. If applicable, check the retracting mechanism. Check the security of all seat belt mountings accessible from inside the vehicle.

☐ The front seats themselves must be securely attached and the backrests must lock in the upright position.

Doors

☐ Both front doors must be able to be opened and closed from outside and inside, and must latch securely when closed.

2 Checks carried out WITH THE VEHICLE ON THE GROUND

Vehicle identification

☐ Number plates must be in good condition, secure and legible, with letters and numbers correctly spaced – spacing at (A) should be twice that at (B).

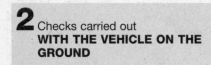

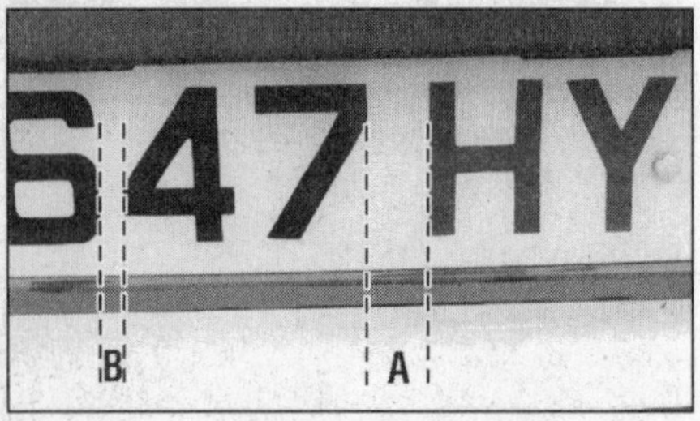

☐ The VIN plate (A) and homologation plate (B) must be legible.

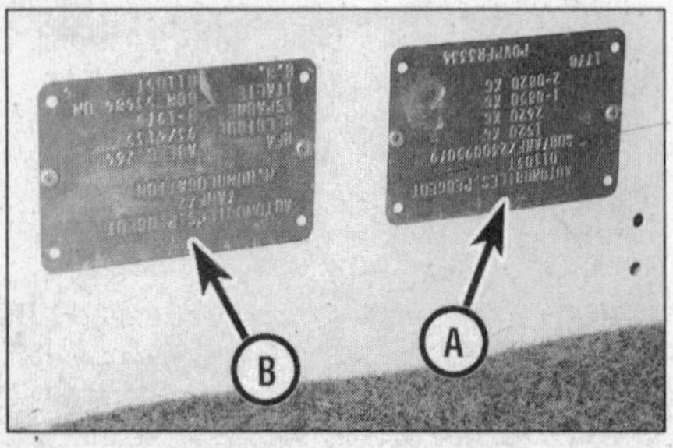

Electrical equipment

☐ Switch on the ignition and check the operation of the horn.

☐ Check the windscreen washers and wipers, examining the wiper blades; renew damaged or perished blades. Also check the operation of the stop-lights.

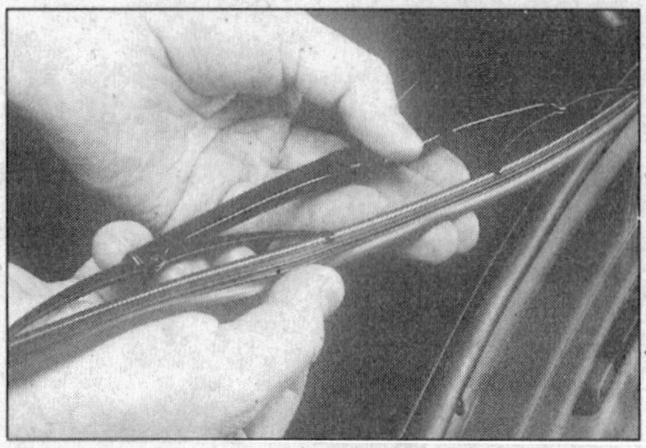

☐ Check the operation of the sidelights and number plate lights. The lenses and reflectors must be secure, clean and undamaged.

☐ Check the operation and alignment of the headlights. The headlight reflectors must not be tarnished and the lenses must be undamaged.

☐ Switch on the ignition and check the operation of the direction indicators (including the instrument panel tell-tale) and the hazard warning lights. Operation of the sidelights and stop-lights must not affect the indicators - if it does, the cause is usually a bad earth at the rear light cluster.

☐ Check the operation of the rear foglight(s), including the warning light on the instrument panel or in the switch.

Footbrake

☐ Examine the master cylinder, brake pipes and servo unit for leaks, loose mountings, corrosion or other damage.

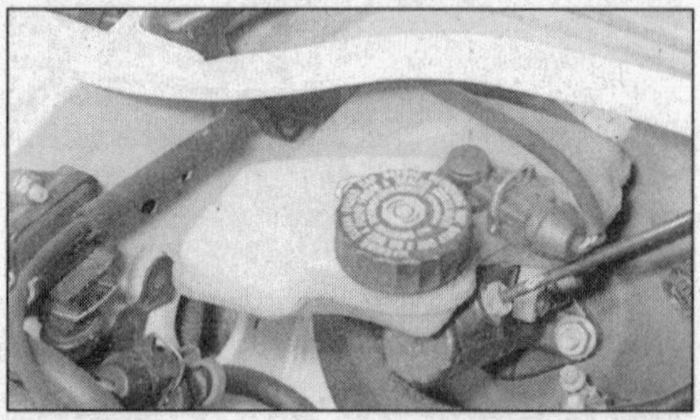

☐ The fluid reservoir must be secure and the fluid level must be between the upper (**A**) and lower (**B**) markings.

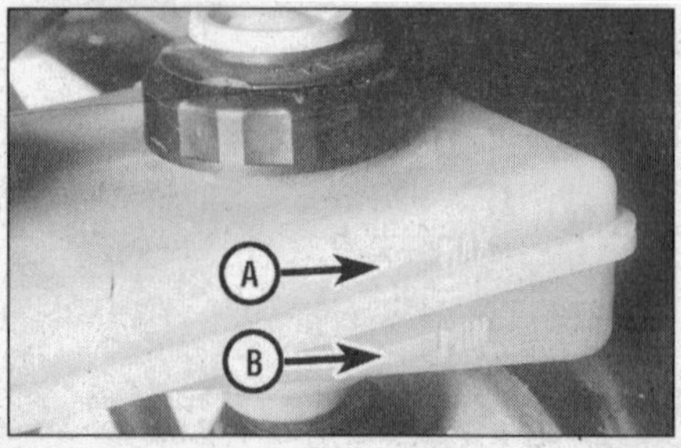

☐ Inspect both front brake flexible hoses for cracks or deterioration of the rubber. Turn the steering from lock to lock, and ensure that the hoses do not contact the wheel, tyre, or any part of the steering or suspension mechanism. With the brake pedal firmly depressed, check the hoses for bulges or leaks under pressure.

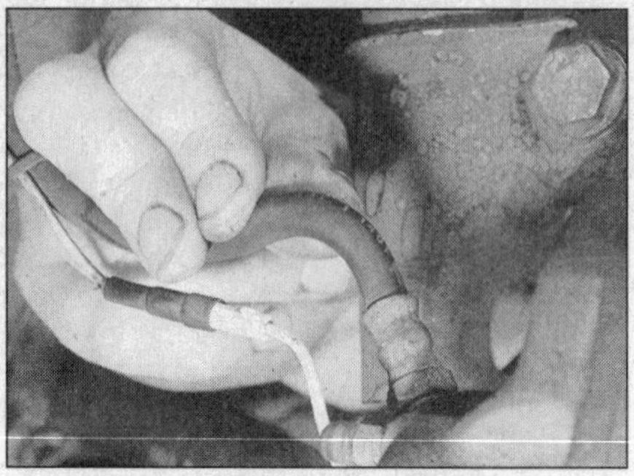

Steering and suspension

☐ Have your assistant turn the steering wheel from side to side slightly, up to the point where the steering gear just begins to transmit this movement to the roadwheels. Check for excessive free play between the steering wheel and the steering gear, indicating wear or insecurity of the steering column joints, the column-to-steering gear coupling, or the steering gear itself.

☐ Have your assistant turn the steering wheel more vigorously in each direction, so that the roadwheels just begin to turn. As this is done, examine all the steering joints, linkages, fittings and attachments. Renew any component that shows signs of wear or damage. On vehicles with power steering, check the security and condition of the steering pump, drivebelt and hoses.

☐ Check that the vehicle is standing level, and at approximately the correct ride height.

Shock absorbers

☐ Depress each corner of the vehicle in turn, then release it. The vehicle should rise and then settle in its normal position. If the vehicle continues to rise and fall, the shock absorber is defective. A shock absorber which has seized will also cause the vehicle to fail.

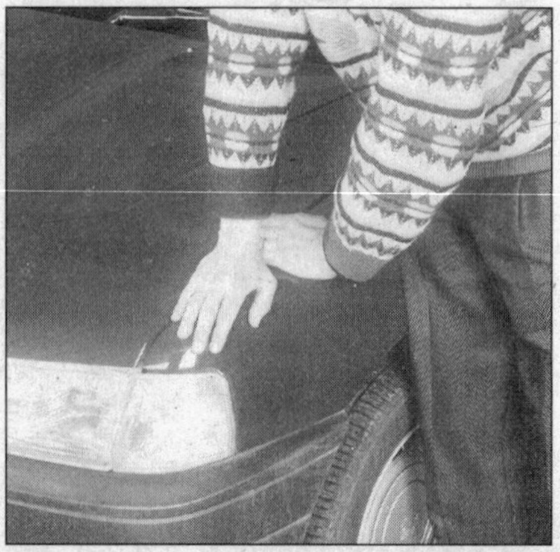

Exhaust system

☐ Start the engine. With your assistant holding a rag over the tailpipe, check the entire system for leaks. Repair or renew leaking sections.

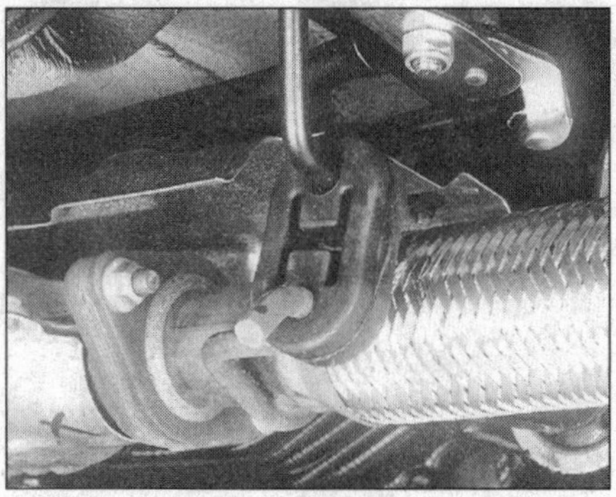

3 Checks carried out
WITH THE VEHICLE RAISED AND THE WHEELS FREE TO TURN

Jack up the front and rear of the vehicle, and securely support it on axle stands. Position the stands clear of the suspension assemblies. Ensure that the wheels are clear of the ground and that the steering can be turned from lock to lock.

Steering mechanism

☐ Have your assistant turn the steering from lock to lock. Check that the steering turns smoothly, and that no part of the steering mechanism, including a wheel or tyre, fouls any brake hose or pipe or any part of the body structure.

☐ Examine the steering rack rubber gaiters for damage or insecurity of the retaining clips. If power steering is fitted, check for signs of damage or leakage of the fluid hoses, pipes or connections. Also check for excessive stiffness or binding of the steering, a missing split pin or locking device, or severe corrosion of the body structure within 30 cm of any steering component attachment point.

Front and rear suspension and wheel bearings

☐ Starting at the front right-hand side, grasp the roadwheel at the 3 o'clock and 9 o'clock positions and shake it vigorously. Check for free play or insecurity at the wheel bearings, suspension balljoints, or suspension mountings, pivots and attachments.

☐ Now grasp the wheel at the 12 o'clock and 6 o'clock positions and repeat the previous inspection. Spin the wheel, and check for roughness or tightness of the front wheel bearing.

☐ If excess free play is suspected at a component pivot point, this can be confirmed by using a large screwdriver or similar tool and levering between the mounting and the component attachment. This will confirm whether the wear is in the pivot bush, its retaining bolt, or in the mounting itself (the bolt holes can often become elongated).

☐ Carry out all the above checks at the other front wheel, and then at both rear wheels.

Springs and shock absorbers

☐ Examine the suspension struts (when applicable) for serious fluid leakage, corrosion, or damage to the casing. Also check the security of the mounting points.

☐ If coil springs are fitted, check that the spring ends locate in their seats, and that the spring is not corroded, cracked or broken.

☐ If leaf springs are fitted, check that all leaves are intact, that the axle is securely attached to each spring, and that there is no deterioration of the spring eye mountings, bushes, and shackles.

☐ The same general checks apply to vehicles fitted with other suspension types, such as torsion bars, hydraulic displacer units, etc. Ensure that all mountings and attachments are secure, that there are no signs of excessive wear, corrosion or damage, and (on hydraulic types) that there are no fluid leaks or damaged pipes.

☐ Inspect the shock absorbers for signs of serious fluid leakage. Check for wear of the mounting bushes or attachments, or damage to the body of the unit.

Driveshafts (fwd vehicles only)

☐ Rotate each front wheel in turn and inspect the constant velocity joint gaiters for splits or damage. Also check that each driveshaft is straight and undamaged.

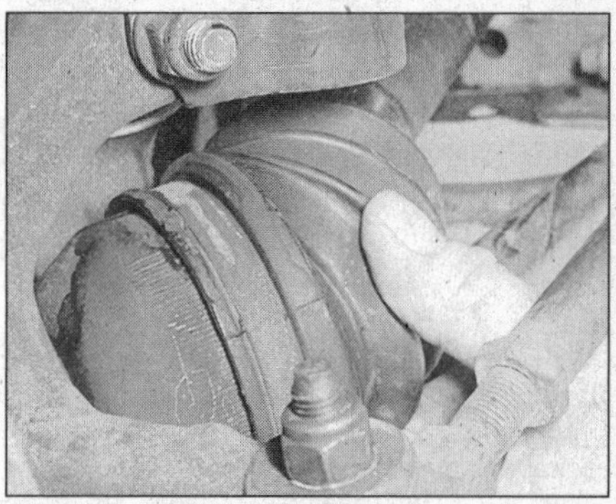

Braking system

☐ If possible without dismantling, check brake pad wear and disc condition. Ensure that the friction lining material has not worn excessively, (A) and that the discs are not fractured, pitted, scored or badly worn (B).

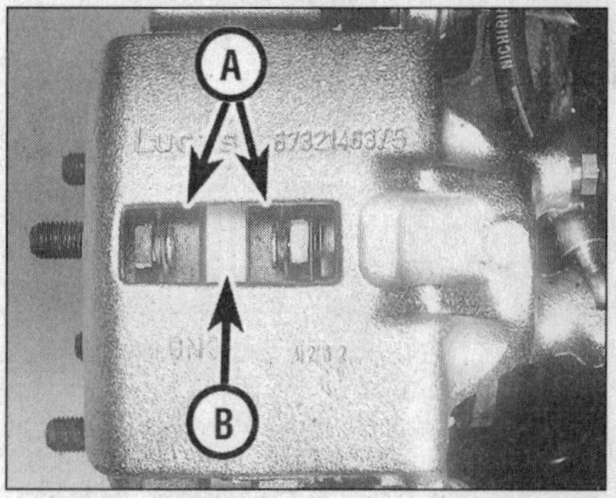

☐ Examine all the rigid brake pipes underneath the vehicle, and the flexible hose(s) at the rear. Look for corrosion, chafing or insecurity of the pipes, and for signs of bulging under pressure, chafing, splits or deterioration of the flexible hoses.

☐ Look for signs of fluid leaks at the brake calipers or on the brake backplates. Repair or renew leaking components.

☐ Slowly spin each wheel, while your assistant depresses and releases the footbrake. Ensure that each brake is operating and does not bind when the pedal is released.

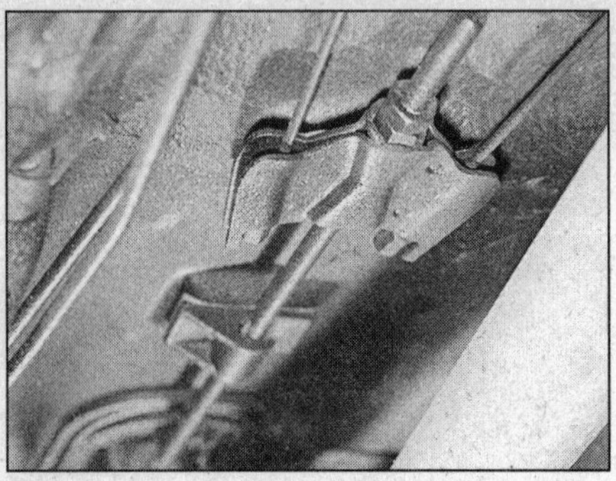

☐ Examine the handbrake mechanism, checking for frayed or broken cables, excessive corrosion, or wear or insecurity of the linkage. Check that the mechanism works on each relevant wheel, and releases fully, without binding.

☐ It is not possible to test brake efficiency without special equipment, but a road test can be carried out later to check that the vehicle pulls up in a straight line.

Fuel and exhaust systems

☐ Inspect the fuel tank (including the filler cap), fuel pipes, hoses and unions. All components must be secure and free from leaks.

☐ Examine the exhaust system over its entire length, checking for any damaged, broken or missing mountings, security of the retaining clamps and rust or corrosion.

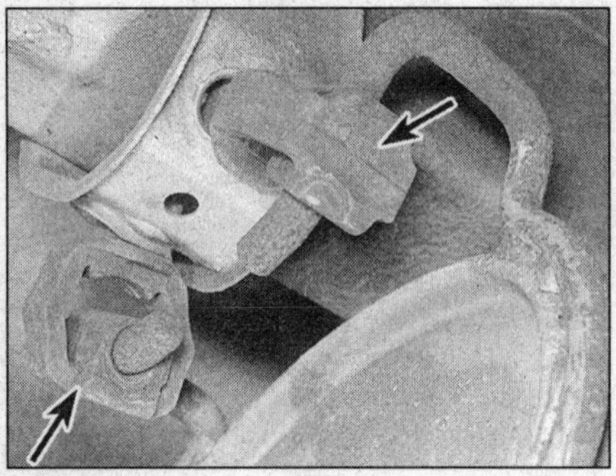

Wheels and tyres

☐ Examine the sidewalls and tread area of each tyre in turn. Check for cuts, tears, lumps, bulges, separation of the tread, and exposure of the ply or cord due to wear or damage. Check that the tyre bead is correctly seated on the wheel rim, that the valve is sound and

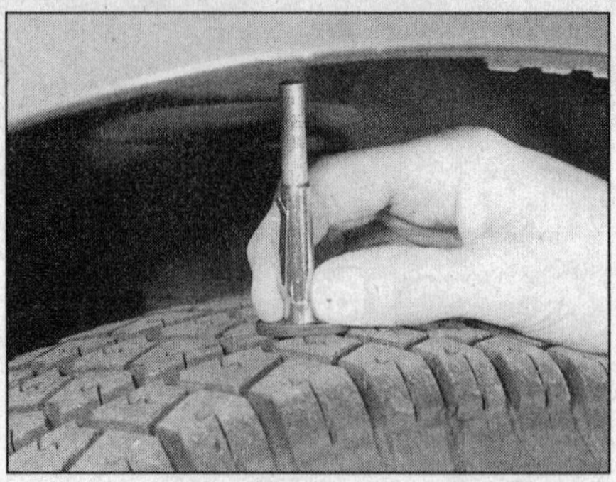

properly seated, and that the wheel is not distorted or damaged.

☐ Check that the tyres are of the correct size for the vehicle, that they are of the same size and type on each axle, and that the pressures are correct.

☐ Check the tyre tread depth. The legal minimum at the time of writing is 1.6 mm over at least three-quarters of the tread width. Abnormal tread wear may indicate incorrect front wheel alignment.

Body corrosion

☐ Check the condition of the entire vehicle structure for signs of corrosion in load-bearing areas. (These include chassis box sections, side sills, cross-members, pillars, and all suspension, steering, braking system and seat belt mountings and anchorages.) Any corrosion which has seriously reduced the thickness of a load-bearing area is likely to cause the vehicle to fail. In this case professional repairs are likely to be needed.

☐ Damage or corrosion which causes sharp or otherwise dangerous edges to be exposed will also cause the vehicle to fail.

4 Checks carried out on **YOUR VEHICLE'S EXHAUST EMISSION SYSTEM**

Petrol models

☐ Have the engine at normal operating temperature, and make sure that it is in good tune (ignition system in good order, air filter element clean, etc).

☐ Before any measurements are carried out, raise the engine speed to around 2500 rpm, and hold it at this speed for 20 seconds. Allow the engine speed to return to idle, and watch for smoke emissions from the exhaust tailpipe. If the idle speed is obviously much too high, or if dense blue or clearly-visible black smoke comes from the tailpipe for more than 5 seconds, the vehicle will fail. As a rule of thumb, blue smoke signifies oil being burnt (engine wear) while black smoke signifies unburnt fuel (dirty air cleaner element, or other carburettor or fuel system fault).

☐ An exhaust gas analyser capable of measuring carbon monoxide (CO) and hydrocarbons (HC) is now needed. If such an instrument cannot be hired or borrowed, a local garage may agree to perform the check for a small fee.

CO emissions (mixture)

☐ At the time or writing, the maximum CO level at idle is 3.5% for vehicles first used after August 1986 and 4.5% for older vehicles. From January 1996 a much tighter limit (around 0.5%) applies to catalyst-equipped vehicles first used from August 1992. If the CO level cannot be reduced far enough to pass the test (and the fuel and ignition systems are otherwise in good condition) then the carburettor is badly worn, or there is some problem in the fuel injection system or catalytic converter (as applicable).

HC emissions

☐ With the CO emissions within limits, HC emissions must be no more than 1200 ppm (parts per million). If the vehicle fails this test at idle, it can be re-tested at around 2000 rpm; if the HC level is then 1200 ppm or less, this counts as a pass.

☐ Excessive HC emissions can be caused by oil being burnt, but they are more likely to be due to unburnt fuel.

Diesel models

☐ The only emission test applicable to Diesel engines is the measuring of exhaust smoke density. The test involves accelerating the engine several times to its maximum unloaded speed.

Note: *It is of the utmost importance that the engine timing belt is in good condition before the test is carried out.*

☐ Excessive smoke can be caused by a dirty air cleaner element. Otherwise, professional advice may be needed to find the cause.

General dimensions and weights

Note: *All figures are approximate, and may vary according to model. Refer to manufacturer's data for exact figures.*

Dimensions

Overall length:	
All models except AX GT/AX Forté and GTi	3525 mm
AX GT/AX Forté and GTi models	3517 mm
Overall width:	
All models except AX GT/AX Forté and GTi	1555 mm
AX GT/AX Forté and GTi models	1596 mm
Overall height (unladen):	
All models except AX GT/AX Forté and GTi	1355 mm
AX GT/AX Forté models	1344 mm
AX GTi models	1340 mm
Wheelbase	2280 mm
Front track:	
AX 10, AX 11 and AX Diesel models	1380 mm
AX 14 models	1370 mm
AX GT/AX Forté models	1392 mm
AX GTi models	1390 mm
Rear track:	
AX 10, AX 11 and AX Diesel models	1300 mm
AX 14 models	1290 mm
AX GT/AX Forté models	1312 mm
AX GTi models	1331 mm

Weights

Kerb weight	655 to 795 kg*
Maximum gross vehicle weight**	1110 to 1240 kg*
Maximum roof rack load	50 kg
Maximum towing weight**:	
Braked trailer	500 to 700 kg*
Unbraked trailer	325 to 395 kg*
Maximum trailer nose weight	45 to 50 kg*

**Depending on model and specification.*

**Refer to Citroën dealer for exact recommendations.

Booster battery (jump) starting

When jump-starting a car using a booster battery, observe the following precautions.

a) Before connecting the booster battery, make sure that the ignition is switched off.

b) Ensure that all electrical equipment (lights, heater, wipers, etc) is switched off.

c) Make sure that the booster battery is the same voltage as the discharged one in the vehicle.

d) If the battery is being jump-started from the battery in another vehicle, the two vehicles MUST NOT TOUCH each other.

e) Make sure that the transmission is in neutral.

f) Take note of any special precautions printed on the battery case.

Connect one jump lead between the positive (+) terminals of the two batteries. Connect the other jump lead first to the negative (-) terminal of the booster battery, and then to a good earthing point on the vehicle to be started, such as a bolt or bracket on the engine block, at least 45 cm (18 in) from the battery if possible **(see illustration)**. Make sure that the jump leads will not come into contact with the fan, drivebelts or other moving parts of the engine.

Start the engine using the booster battery, and run it at idle speed. Switch on the lights, rear window demister and heater blower motor, then disconnect the jump leads in the reverse order of connection. Turn off the lights, etc.

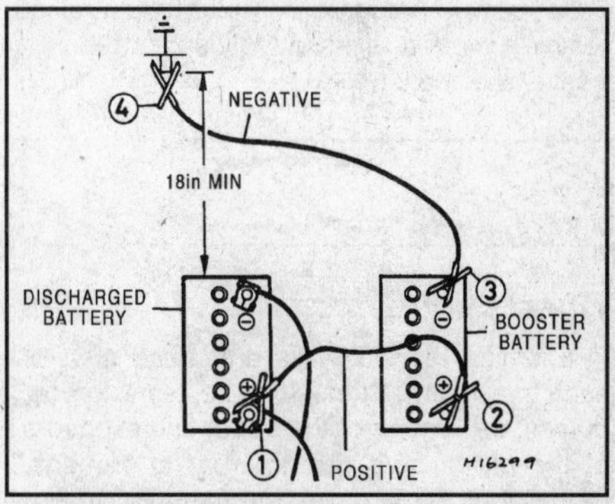

Jump start lead connections for negative-earth vehicles – connect leads in order shown

Radio/cassette unit anti-theft system - precaution

On later models, the radio/cassette unit fitted as standard equipment by Citroën is equipped with a built-in security code, to deter thieves. If the power source to the unit is cut, the anti-theft system will activate. Even if the power source is immediately reconnected, the radio/cassette unit will not function until the correct security code has been entered. Therefore, if you do not know the correct security code for the radio/cassette unit, **do not** disconnect the battery negative terminal of the battery, or remove the radio/cassette unit from the vehicle.

To enter the correct security code, follow the instructions provided with the radio/cassette player handbook.

If an incorrect code is entered, the unit will become locked, and cannot be operated.

If this happens, or if the security code is lost or forgotten, seek the advice of your Citroën dealer.

Jacking

The jack supplied with the vehicle tool kit should only be used for changing the roadwheels - see *"Wheel changing"* later in this Section. When carrying out any other kind of work, raise the vehicle using a hydraulic (or "trolley") jack, and always supplement the jack with axle stands positioned under the vehicle jacking points **(see illustration)**.

To raise the front of the vehicle, locate a beam transversely under the inboard mounting points of the front suspension arms, and position a trolley jack centrally beneath the beam **(see illustration)**. **Do not** jack the vehicle under the sump, or any of the steering or suspension components.

To raise the rear of the vehicle, position the jack head underneath the rear crossmember **(see illustration)**.

The jack supplied with the vehicle locates in the jacking points positioned centrally on the body sills on each side of the car. Ensure that the jack head is correctly engaged before attempting to raise the vehicle.

Never work under, around, or near a raised vehicle, unless it is adequately supported in at least two places.

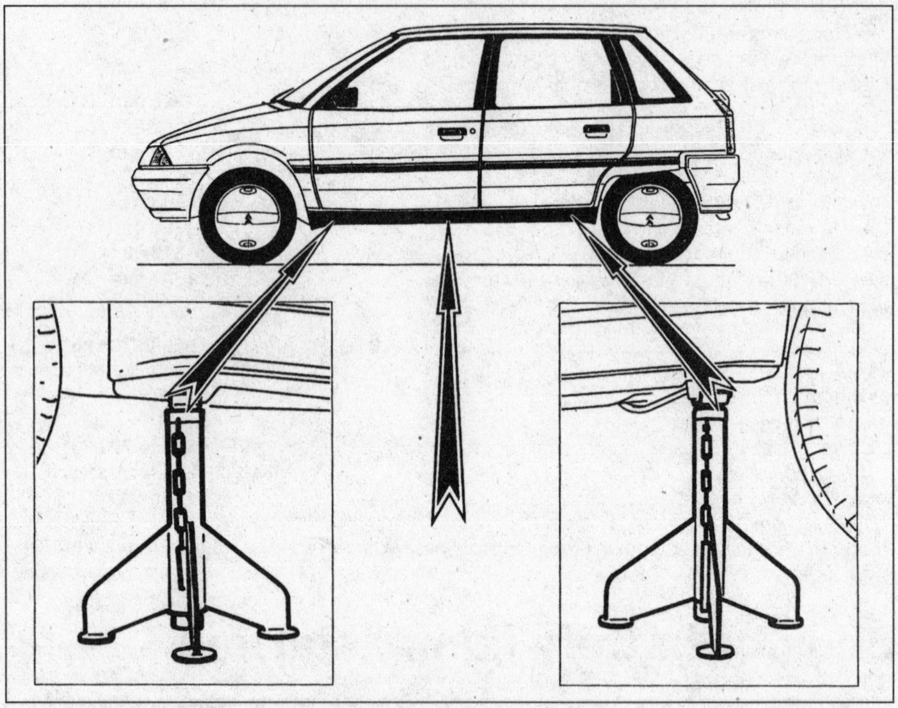

Location points for axle stands

Centre arrow indicates position for vehicle jack

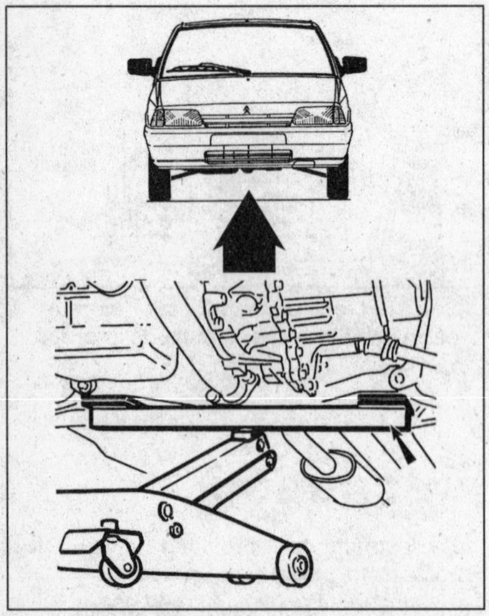

When raising the front of the vehicle, locate a beam (arrowed) transversely under the inboard mounting points of the front suspension arms

When raising the rear of the vehicle, position the jack head (arrowed) underneath the rear crossmember

Towing

Towing eyes are fitted to the front and rear of the vehicle for attachment of a tow rope. On early models, the towing eyes are located beneath the front or rear bumpers **(see illustration)**. On later models, they are located behind a plastic cover in the relevant bumper. Always turn the ignition key to position "M" when the vehicle is being towed, so that the steering lock is released, and that the direction indicator and brake lights will work.

Before being towed, release the handbrake, and select neutral on the transmission. Note that greater-than-usual pedal pressure will be required to operate the brakes, since the vacuum servo unit (or vacuum pump, on Diesel models) is only operational with the engine running.

Wheel changing

The spare wheel is located in a cradle under the rear of the vehicle. On early models, the brace and jack are located on the right-hand side of the engine compartment **(see illustration)**. On later models, the brace is located behind a cover on the right-hand side of the luggage compartment, and the jack is located in the spare wheel itself. For access to the spare wheel, proceed as follows:

a) Loosen the cradle securing bolt in the load area floor, using the end of the wheel brace.
b) Lift the cradle sufficiently to disengage it from the latch.
c) Lower the cradle, and lift out the spare wheel.

To change a wheel, remove the spare wheel, jack and wheel brace, as described previously, then proceed as follows.

Apply the handbrake, and place chocks at the front and rear of the wheel diagonally opposite the one to be changed. Select first or reverse gear, and make sure that the vehicle is located on firm, level ground. Prise off, and remove, the wheel trim where applicable **(see illustration)**. Slightly loosen the wheel bolts with the brace provided. Locate the jack head in the jacking point in the centre of the sill on the relevant side, and raise the jack by turning the handle **(see illustration)**. When the wheel is clear of the ground, remove the bolts and lift off the wheel. Remove the hub embellisher, where applicable, and fit it to the spare wheel. Fit the spare wheel, and moderately tighten the bolts. Lower the vehicle, and then tighten the bolts fully in a diagonal sequence. Refit the wheel trim, where applicable. If possible, check the tyre pressure on the spare wheel, and adjust as necessary. Remove the chocks, and stow the jack, tools and the punctured tyre in the luggage compartment. Hook the cradle back onto the latch, and raise the cradle back into position. Have the punctured tyre repaired, or renew it, as soon as possible.

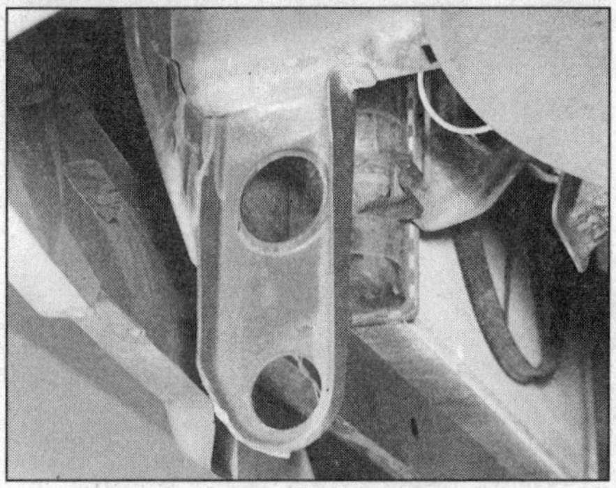

Front towing eye on early models

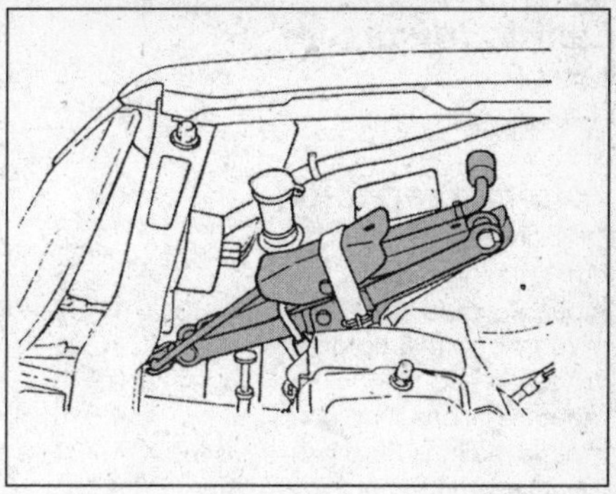

Jack location on early models

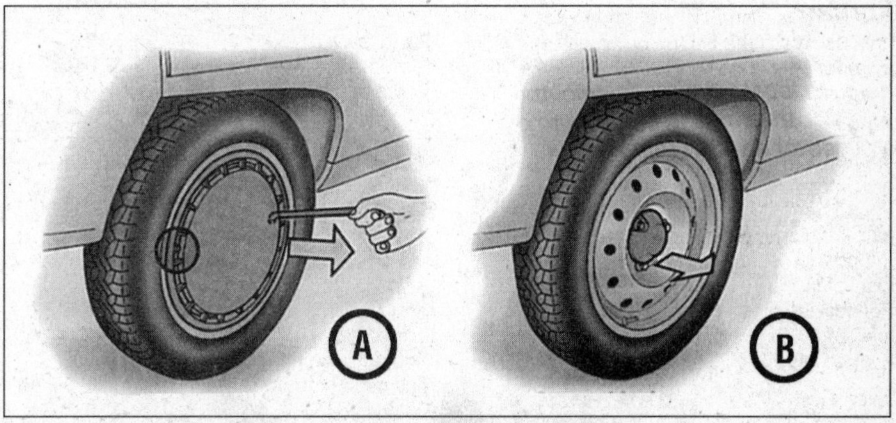

Wheel trim (A) and hub embellisher (B) removal. Note that (B) is removed when wheel bolts are slackened

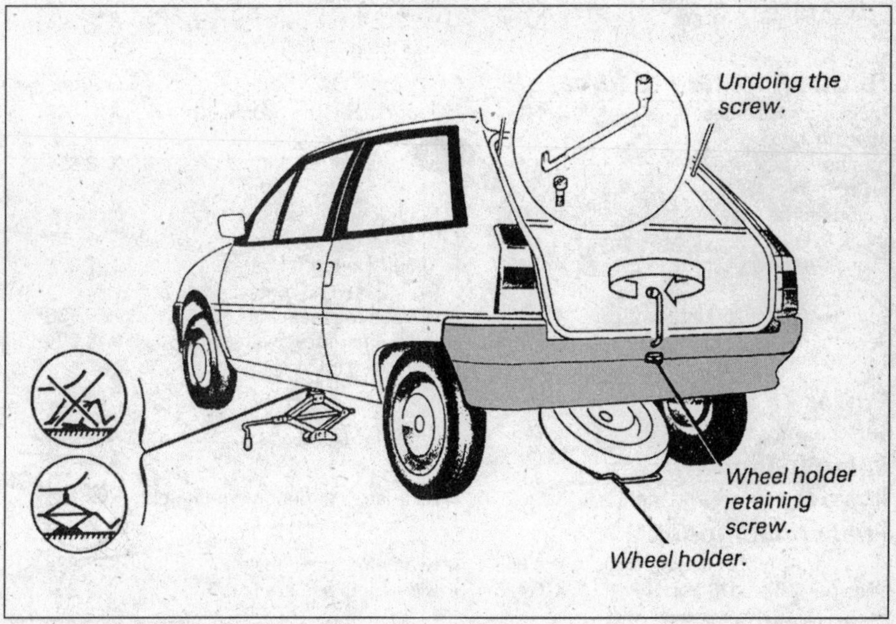

View showing jack location under body sill and spare wheel location/removal

Conversion Factors

Length (distance)

Inches (in)	X 25.4	= Millimetres (mm)	X 0.0394	= Inches (in)
Feet (ft)	X 0.305	= Metres (m)	X 3.281	= Feet (ft)
Miles	X 1.609	= Kilometres (km)	X 0.621	= Miles

Volume (capacity)

Cubic inches (cu in; in3)	X 16.387	= Cubic centimetres (cc; cm3)	X 0.061	= Cubic inches (cu in; in3)
Imperial pints (Imp pt)	X 0.568	= Litres (l)	X 1.76	= Imperial pints (Imp pt)
Imperial quarts (Imp qt)	X 1.137	= Litres (l)	X 0.88	= Imperial quarts (Imp qt)
Imperial quarts (Imp qt)	X 1.201	= US quarts (US qt)	X 0.833	= Imperial quarts (Imp qt)
US quarts (US qt)	X 0.946	= Litres (l)	X 1.057	= US quarts (US qt)
Imperial gallons (Imp gal)	X 4.546	= Litres (l)	X 0.22	= Imperial gallons (Imp gal)
Imperial gallons (Imp gal)	X 1.201	= US gallons (US gal)	X 0.833	= Imperial gallons (Imp gal)
US gallons (US gal)	X 3.785	= Litres (l)	X 0.264	= US gallons (US gal)

Mass (weight)

Ounces (oz)	X 28.35	= Grams (g)	X 0.035	= Ounces (oz)
Pounds (lb)	X 0.454	= Kilograms (kg)	X 2.205	= Pounds (lb)

Force

Ounces-force (ozf; oz)	X 0.278	= Newtons (N)	X 3.6	= Ounces-force (ozf; oz)
Pounds-force (lbf; lb)	X 4.448	= Newtons (N)	X 0.225	= Pounds-force (lbf; lb)
Newtons (N)	X 0.1	= Kilograms-force (kgf; kg)	X 9.81	= Newtons (N)

Pressure

Pounds-force per square inch (psi; lbf/in²; lb/in²)	X 0.070	= Kilograms-force per square centimetre (kgf/cm²; kg/cm²)	X 14.223	= Pounds-force per square inch (psi; lbf/in²; lb/in²)
Pounds-force per square inch (psi; lbf/in²; lb/in²)	X 0.068	= Atmospheres (atm)	X 14.696	= Pounds-force per square inch (psi; lbf/in²; lb/in²)
Pounds-force per square inch (psi; lbf/in²; lb/in²)	X 0.069	= Bars	X 14.5	= Pounds-force per square inch (psi; lbf/in²; lb/in²)
Pounds-force per square inch (psi; lbf/in²; lb/in²)	X 6.895	= Kilopascals (kPa)	X 0.145	= Pounds-force per square inch (psi; lbf/in²; lb/in²)
Kilopascals (kPa)	X 0.01	= Kilograms-force per square centimetre (kgf/cm²; kg/cm²)	X 98.1	= Kilopascals (kPa)
Millibar (mbar)	X 100	= Pascals (Pa)	X 0.01	= Millibar (mbar)
Millibar (mbar)	X 0.0145	= Pounds-force per square inch (psi; lbf/in²; lb/in²)	X 68.947	= Millibar (mbar)
Millibar (mbar)	X 0.75	= Millimetres of mercury (mmHg)	X 1.333	= Millibar (mbar)
Millibar (mbar)	X 0.401	= Inches of water (inH_2O)	X 2.491	= Millibar (mbar)
Millimetres of mercury (mmHg)	X 0.535	= Inches of water (inH_2O)	X 1.868	= Millimetres of mercury (mmHg)
Inches of water (inH_2O)	X 0.036	= Pounds-force per square inch (psi; lbf/in²; lb/in²)	X 27.68	= Inches of water (inH_2O)

Torque (moment of force)

Pounds-force inches (lbf in; lb in)	X 1.152	= Kilograms-force centimetre (kgf cm; kg cm)	X 0.868	= Pounds-force inches (lbf in; lb in)
Pounds-force inches (lbf in; lb in)	X 0.113	= Newton metres (Nm)	X 8.85	= Pounds-force inches (lbf in; lb in)
Pounds-force inches (lbf in; lb in)	X 0.083	= Pounds-force feet (lbf ft; lb ft)	X 12	= Pounds-force inches (lbf in; lb in)
Pounds-force feet (lbf ft; lb ft)	X 0.138	= Kilograms-force metres (kgf m; kg m)	X 7.233	= Pounds-force feet (lbf ft; lb ft)
Pounds-force feet (lbf ft; lb ft)	X 1.356	= Newton metres (Nm)	X 0.738	= Pounds-force feet (lbf ft; lb ft)
Newton metres (Nm)	X 0.102	= Kilograms-force metres (kgf m; kg m)	X 9.804	= Newton metres (Nm)

Power

Horsepower (hp)	X 745.7	= Watts (W)	X 0.0013	= Horsepower (hp)

Velocity (speed)

Miles per hour (miles/hr; mph)	X 1.609	= Kilometres per hour (km/hr; kph)	X 0.621	= Miles per hour (miles/hr; mph)

Fuel consumption*

Miles per gallon, Imperial (mpg)	X 0.354	= Kilometres per litre (km/l)	X 2.825	= Miles per gallon, Imperial (mpg)
Miles per gallon, US (mpg)	X 0.425	= Kilometres per litre (km/l)	X 2.352	= Miles per gallon, US (mpg)

Temperature

Degrees Fahrenheit = (°C x 1.8) + 32

Degrees Celsius (Degrees Centigrade; °C) = (°F - 32) x 0.56

** It is common practice to convert from miles per gallon (mpg) to litres/100 kilometres (l/100km), where mpg (Imperial) x l/100 km = 282 and mpg (US) x l/100 km = 235*

Chapter 1
Routine maintenance and servicing

Contents

Degrees of difficulty

Easy, suitable for novice with little experience	**Fairly easy,** suitable for beginner with some experience	**Fairly difficult,** suitable for competent DIY mechanic	**Difficult,** suitable for experienced DIY mechanic	**Very difficult,** suitable for expert DIY or professional

Lubricants and fluids

Engine (petrol)	Multigrade engine oil, viscosity SAE 10W/40, 15W/40 or 15W/50, to API SG/CD *(Duckhams QXR Premium Petrol Engine Oil, or Duckhams Hypergrade Petrol Engine Oil)*
Engine (diesel)	Multigrade engine oil, viscosity SAE 10W/40, 15W/40 or 15W/50, to API SG/CD *(Duckhams QXR Premium Diesel Engine Oil, or Duckhams Hypergrade Diesel Engine Oil)*
Cooling system	Ethylene glycol-based antifreeze *(Duckhams Antifreeze and Summer Coolant)*
Manual transmission	Total transmission oil BV 75W/80W *(Duckhams Hypoid Gear Oil 75W-80W GL-5)*
Braking system	Universal brake fluid to DOT 4 *(Duckhams Universal Brake and Clutch Fluid)*
General greasing	Multi-purpose lithium-based grease *(Duckhams LB 10)*

Choosing your engine oil

Engines need oil, not only to lubricate moving parts and minimise wear, but also to maximise power output and to improve fuel economy. By introducing a simplified and improved range of engine oils, Duckhams has taken away the confusion and made it easier for you to choose the right oil for your engine.

HOW ENGINE OIL WORKS

• *Beating friction*

Without oil, the moving surfaces inside your engine will rub together, heat up and melt, quickly causing the engine to seize. Engine oil creates a film which separates these moving parts, preventing wear and heat build-up.

• *Cooling hot-spots*

Temperatures inside the engine can exceed 1000° C. The engine oil circulates and acts as a coolant, transferring heat from the hot-spots to the sump.

• *Cleaning the engine internally*

Good quality engine oils clean the inside of your engine, collecting and dispersing combustion deposits and controlling them until they are trapped by the oil filter or flushed out at oil change.

OIL CARE - FOLLOW THE CODE

To handle and dispose of used engine oil safely, always:

OIL CARE
FOLLOW THE CODE
OIL BANK LINE
0800 66 33 66

• Avoid skin contact with used engine oil. Repeated or prolonged contact can be harmful.

• Dispose of used oil and empty packs in a responsible manner in an authorised disposal site. Call 0800 663366 to find the one nearest to you. Never tip oil down drains or onto the ground.

Capacities

Engine oil

Excluding filter:	
954 cc, 1124 cc and 1360 cc petrol models	3.2 litres
1360 cc Diesel models	3.5 litres
1527 cc Diesel models	4.5 litres
Including filter:	
954 cc, 1124 cc and 1360 cc petrol models	3.5 litres
1360 cc Diesel models	3.75 litres
1527 cc Diesel models	4.75 litres
Difference between MAX and MIN dipstick marks:	
954 cc, 1124 cc and 1360 cc petrol and Diesel models	1.4 litres
1527 cc Diesel models	2.0 litres

Cooling system (approximate) .... 4.8 litres

Transmission .... 2.0 litres

Fuel tank

Early 954 cc models	36 litres
Later 954 cc models, and all other models	43 litres

Washer reservoirs

Windscreen washers only	1.5 litres
Windscreen and tailgate washers	2.8 litres

Citroën AX maintenance schedule

1 The maintenance intervals in this manual are provided with the assumption that you will be carrying out the work yourself. These are the minimum maintenance intervals rec-ommended by the manufacturer for vehicles driven daily. If you wish to keep your vehicle in peak condition at all times, you may wish to perform some of these procedures more often. We encourage frequent maintenance, because it enhances the efficiency, performance and resale value of your vehicle.

2 If the vehicle is driven in dusty areas, used to tow a trailer, or driven frequently at slow speeds (idling in traffic) or on short journeys, more frequent maintenance intervals are recommended. Citroën actually recommend that the service intervals are halved for vehicles which are used under these conditions.

3 When the vehicle is new, it should be serviced by a factory-authorised dealer service department, in order to preserve the factory warranty.

Every 250 miles (400 km) or weekly

- ☐ Check the engine oil level (Section 3).
- ☐ Check the engine coolant level (Section 3).
- ☐ Check the brake fluid level (Section 3).
- ☐ Check the windscreen/tailgate washer fluid level (Section 3).
- ☐ Visually examine the tyres for tread depth, and wear or damage (Section 4).
- ☐ Check and adjust the tyre pressures (Section 4).
- ☐ Check the condition of the battery (Section 6).
- ☐ Check the operation of the horn, all lights, and the wipers and washers (Sections 5 and 7).

Every 6000 (10 000 km) (or 12 months – whichever comes first)

In addition to all the items listed above, carry out the following:

- ☐ Renew the engine oil and filter (Section 8).
- ☐ Check all underbonnet components and hoses for fluid leaks (Section 9).
- ☐ Renew the fuel filter - Diesel models (Section 10).
- ☐ Check the steering and suspension components for condition and security (Section 11).
- ☐ Check the condition of the driveshaft rubber gaiters (Section 12).

Every 12 000 (20 000 km)

In addition to all the items listed above, carry out the following:

- ☐ Check the condition of the air conditioning system refrigerant - where applicable (see Section 13).
- ☐ Renew the spark plugs (Section 14).
- ☐ Renew the fuel filter - carburettor models (Section 15).
- ☐ Drain any water from the fuel filter - Diesel models (Section 16).
- ☐ Check the ignition system and ignition timing - petrol models (Section 17).
- ☐ Check the idle speed and mixture adjustment - petrol models (Section 18).
- ☐ Check the idle speed and anti-stall speed - Diesel models (Section 19).
- ☐ Check the condition of the emission control system hoses and components (Section 20).
- ☐ Check the condition of the auxiliary drivebelt, and renew if necessary (Section 21).
- ☐ Check the clutch adjustment (Section 22).
- ☐ Lubricate the clutch control mechanism (Section 22).
- ☐ Check the condition of the front brake pads, and renew if necessary (Section 23).
- ☐ Check the operation of the handbrake (Section 24).
- ☐ Carry out a road test (Section 25).

Every 18 000 (30 000 km)

In addition to all the items listed above, carry out the following:

- ☐ Lubricate all hinges and locks (Section 26).

Every 24 000 (40 000 km)

In addition to all the items listed above, carry out the following:

- ☐ Renew the air filter (Section 27).
- ☐ Check the condition of the rear brake shoes, and renew if necessary (Section 28).
- ☐ Renew the brake fluid (Section 29).

Every 36 000 (60 000 km)

In addition to all the items listed above, carry out the following:

- ☐ Check the manual transmission oil level, and top-up if necessary (Section 30).

Every 48 000 (80 000 km)

In addition to all the items listed above, carry out the following:

- ☐ Renew the fuel filter - fuel-injected petrol models (Section 31).

Every 72 000 (120 000 km)

In addition to all the items listed above, carry out the following:

- ☐ Renew the timing belt (Section 32).

Note: *Citroën recommend that the timing belt renewal interval is halved to 36 000 miles (60 000 km) on vehicles which are subjected to intensive use, ie. mainly short journeys or a lot of stop-start driving. The actual belt renewal interval is therefore very much up to the individual owner. That being said, it is highly recommended to err on the side of safety, and renew the belt at this earlier interval, bearing in mind the drastic consequences resulting from belt failure.*

Every 2 years (regardless of mileage)

In addition to all the items listed above, carry out the following:

- ☐ Lubricate all hinges and locks (Section 26).

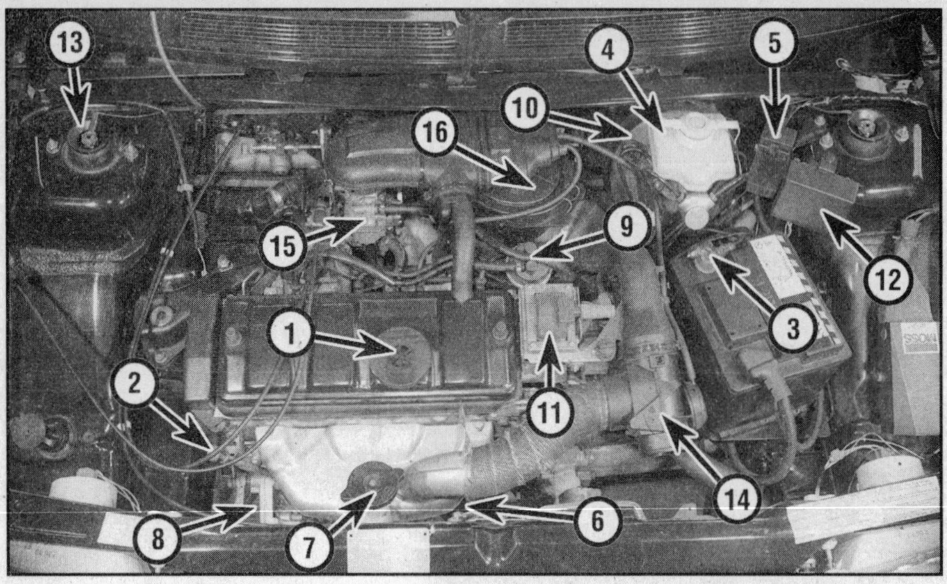

Underbonnet view of an 1124 cc (H1A engine) carburettor model

1 Engine oil filler cap
2 Engine oil dipstick
3 Battery earth (negative) terminal
4 Master cylinder/brake fluid reservoir
5 Auxiliary fusebox
6 Engine oil filter
7 Radiator filler cap
8 Alternator
9 Fuel pump
10 Braking system vacuum servo unit
11 Ignition HT coil
12 Relay box
13 Suspension strut upper mounting
14 Air cleaner air temperature control valve
15 Carburettor
16 Air cleaner housing

Underbonnet view of an 1124 cc (HDY engine) single-point fuel-injected model

1 Engine oil filler cap
2 Engine oil dipstick
3 Battery earth (negative) terminal
4 Master cylinder/brake fluid reservoir
5 Auxiliary fusebox
6 Engine oil filter
7 Radiator filler cap
8 Alternator
9 Washer fluid reservoir filler cap
10 Braking system vacuum servo unit
11 Ignition HT coil
12 Plastic box containing fuel injection ECU, relay unit and injector resistor
13 Suspension strut upper mounting
14 Air cleaner air temperature control valve
15 Throttle body assembly
16 Air cleaner housing

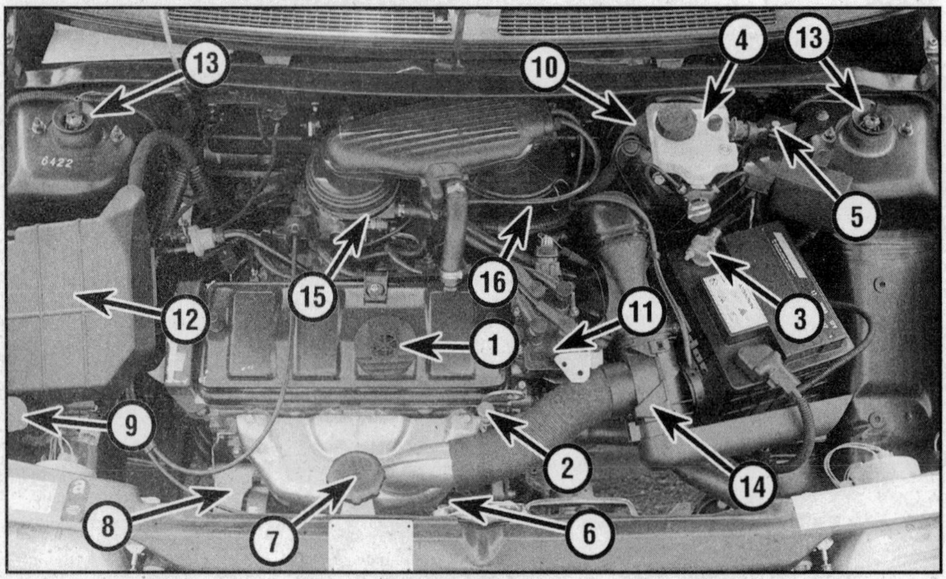

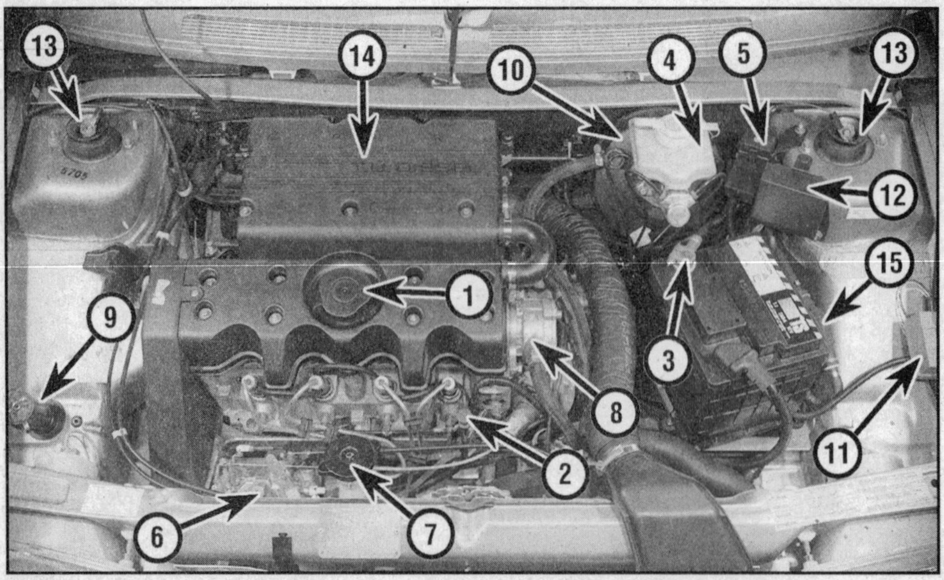

Underbonnet view of a 1360 cc (K9B engine) Diesel model

1 Engine oil filler cap
2 Engine oil dipstick
3 Battery earth (negative) terminal
4 Master cylinder/brake fluid reservoir
5 Auxiliary fusebox
6 Fuel injection pump
7 Radiator filler cap
8 Braking system vacuum pump
9 Washer fluid reservoir filler cap
10 Braking system vacuum servo unit
11 Preheating control unit
12 Relay box
13 Suspension strut upper mounting
14 Air cleaner housing
15 Fuel system priming bulb

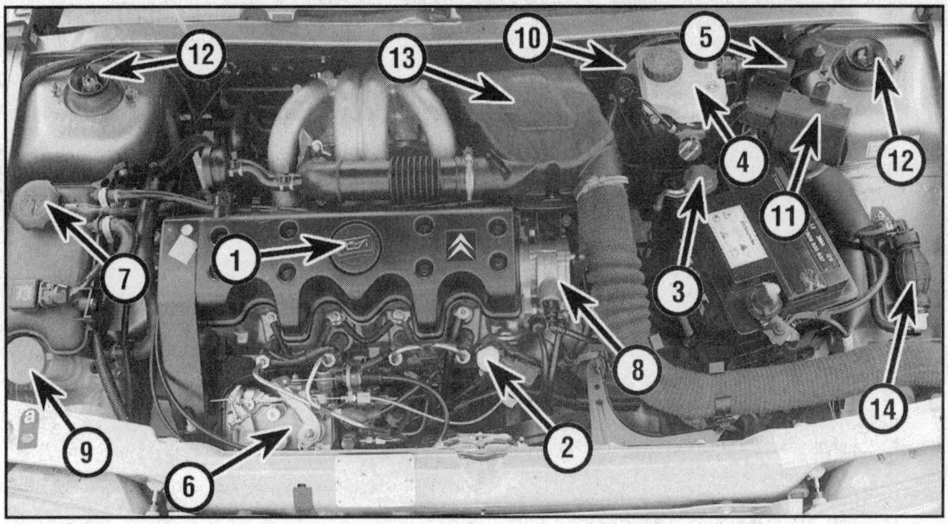

Underbonnet view of a 1527 cc (VJZ engine) Diesel model

1 Engine oil filler cap
2 Engine oil dipstick
3 Battery earth (negative) terminal
4 Master cylinder/brake fluid reservoir
5 Auxiliary fusebox
6 Fuel injection pump
7 Expansion tank filler cap
8 Braking system vacuum pump
9 Washer fluid reservoir filler cap
10 Braking system vacuum servo unit
11 Relay box
12 Suspension strut upper mounting
13 Air cleaner housing
14 Fuel system priming bulb

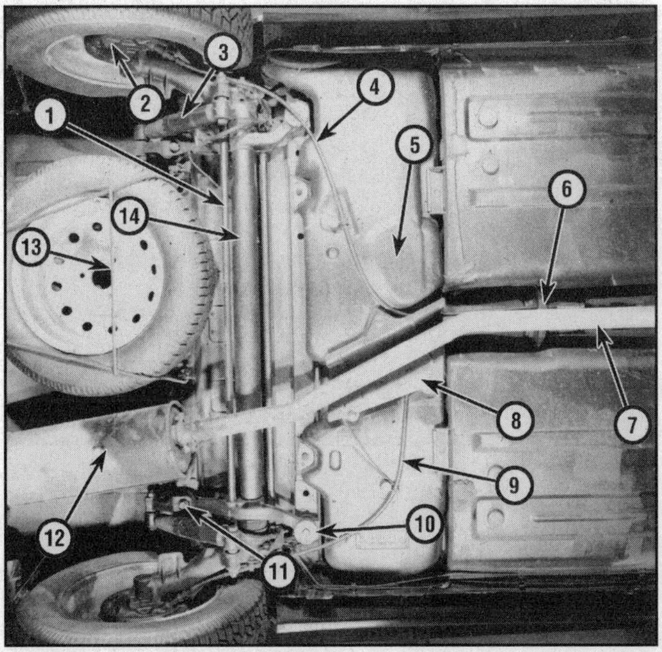

Rear underbody view - 1124 cc petrol model (Diesel models similar)

1 Torsion bar
2 Rear brake drum
3 Shock absorber
4 Handbrake cable (to right-hand rear brake)
5 Fuel tank
6 Handbrake cable equaliser
7 Exhaust pipe
8 Heat shield
9 Handbrake cable (to left-hand rear brake)
10 Rear axle mounting (front)
11 Rear axle mounting (rear)
12 Exhaust silencer
13 Spare wheel carrier
14 Rear axle

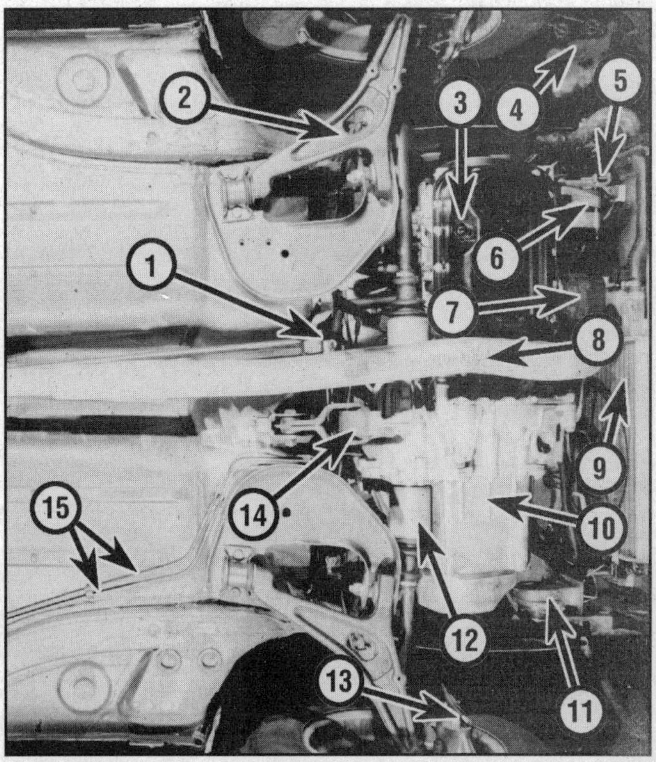

Front underbody view - 1124 cc petrol model (Diesel models similar)

1 Gearshift rod
2 Suspension arm
3 Engine sump drain plug
4 Windscreen/tailgate window washer reservoir
5 Alternator drivebelt adjuster
6 Alternator
7 Engine oil filter
8 Exhaust pipe
9 Radiator
10 Manual transmission
11 Horn
12 Driveshaft
13 Front brake caliper
14 Rear engine mounting link
15 Brake pipes

1 Introduction

1 This Chapter is designed to help the home mechanic maintain his/her vehicle for safety, economy, long life and peak performance.

2 The Chapter contains a master maintenance schedule, followed by Sections dealing specifically with each task in the schedule. Visual checks, adjustments, component renewal and other helpful items are included. Refer to the accompanying illustrations of the engine compartment and the underside of the vehicle for the locations of the various components.

3 Servicing your vehicle in accordance with the mileage/time maintenance schedule and the following Sections will provide a planned maintenance programme, which should result in a long and reliable service life. This is a comprehensive plan, so maintaining some items but not others at the specified service intervals, will not produce the same results.

4 As you service your vehicle, you will discover that many of the procedures can - and should - be grouped together, because of the particular procedure being performed, or because of the close proximity of two otherwise-unrelated components to one another. For example, if the vehicle is raised for any reason, the exhaust can be inspected at the same time as the suspension and steering components.

5 The first step in this maintenance programme is to prepare yourself before the actual work begins. Read through all the Sections relevant to the work to be carried out, then make a list and gather together all the parts and tools required. If a problem is encountered, seek advice from a parts specialist, or a dealer service department.

2 Intensive maintenance

1 If, from the time the vehicle is new, the routine maintenance schedule is followed closely, and frequent checks are made of fluid levels and high-wear items, as suggested throughout this manual, the engine will be kept in relatively good running condition, and the need for additional work will be minimised.

2 It is possible that there will be times when the engine is running poorly due to the lack of regular maintenance. This is even more likely if a used vehicle, which has not received regular and frequent maintenance checks, is purchased. In such cases, additional work may need to be carried out, outside of the regular maintenance intervals.

3 If engine wear is suspected, a compression test (refer to the relevant Part of Chapter 2) will provide valuable information regarding the overall performance of the main internal components. Such a test can be used as a basis to decide on the extent of the work to be carried out. If, for example, a compression test indicates serious internal engine wear, conventional maintenance as described in this Chapter will not greatly improve the performance of the engine, and may prove a waste of time and money, unless extensive overhaul work (Chapter 2C) is carried out first.

4 The following series of operations are those most often required to improve the performance of a generally poor-running engine:

Primary operations

a) Clean, inspect and test the battery (Section 6).
b) Check all the engine-related fluids (Section 3).
c) Check the condition and tension of the auxiliary drivebelt (Section 21).
d) Renew the spark plugs - petrol models (Section 14).
e) Inspect the distributor cap, rotor arm and HT - petrol models, as applicable (Section 17).
f) Check the condition of the air filter, and renew if necessary (Section 27).
g) Check the fuel filter (Section 10, 15, 16, or 31, as applicable).
h) Check the condition of all hoses, and check for fluid leaks (Section 9).
i) Check the idle speed, anti-stall, and mixture settings, as applicable (Section 18 or 19).

5 If the above operations do not prove fully effective, carry out the following secondary operations:

Secondary operations

All items listed under "Primary operations", plus the following:

a) Check the charging system (Chapter 5A).
b) Check the ignition system - petrol models (Chapter 5B).
c) Check the preheating system - Diesel models (Chapter 5C).
d) Check the fuel system (Chapter 4).
e) Renew the distributor cap and rotor arm - petrol models, as applicable (Section 17).
f) Renew the ignition HT leads - petrol models (Section 17).

Weekly Checks

3 Fluid level checks

Engine oil

1 The engine oil level is checked with a dipstick that extends through the dipstick tube and into the sump at the bottom of the engine. The dipstick is located at the front of the engine. On later models, the dipstick top is brightly-coloured (usually blue or yellow) for easy identification.

2 The oil level should be checked with the vehicle standing on level ground, with the engine switched off. Check the level before the vehicle is driven, or wait at least 5 minutes after the engine has been switched off.

3 Withdraw the dipstick from the tube, and wipe all the oil from the end with a clean rag or paper towel. Insert the clean dipstick back into the tube as far as it will go, then withdraw it once more. Note the oil level on the end of the dipstick. Add oil as necessary until the level is between the upper ("MAX") mark and lower ("MIN") mark on the dipstick **(see illustration)**. Note that approximately 1.4 litres (2.0 litres on the 1527 cc Diesel engine) of oil will be required to raise the level from the lower mark to the upper mark.

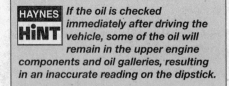

HAYNES HiNT ***If the oil is checked immediately after driving the vehicle, some of the oil will remain in the upper engine components and oil galleries, resulting in an inaccurate reading on the dipstick.***

4 Always maintain the level between the two dipstick marks. If the level is allowed to fall below the lower mark, oil starvation may result, which could lead to severe engine damage. If the engine is overfilled by adding too much oil, this may result in oil leaks or oil seal failures.

5 Oil is added to the engine via the filler cap on the cylinder head cover. Unscrew the cap and top-up the level **(see illustration)**; an oil can spout or funnel may help to reduce spillage. Always use the correct grade and type of oil, as shown in *"Lubricants fluids and capacities"*.

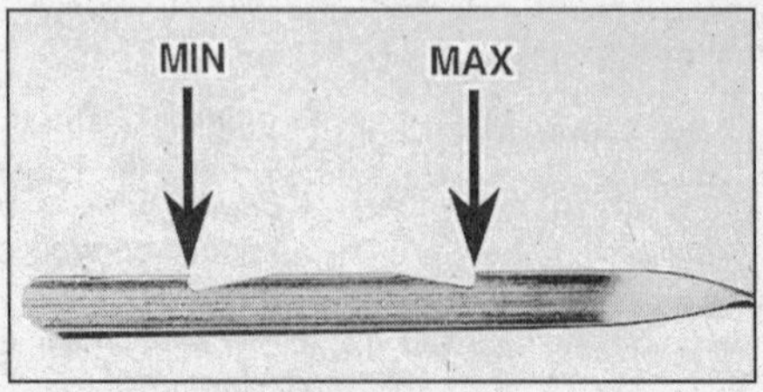

3.3 Engine oil level dipstick markings

3.5 Topping-up the engine oil - Diesel engine shown

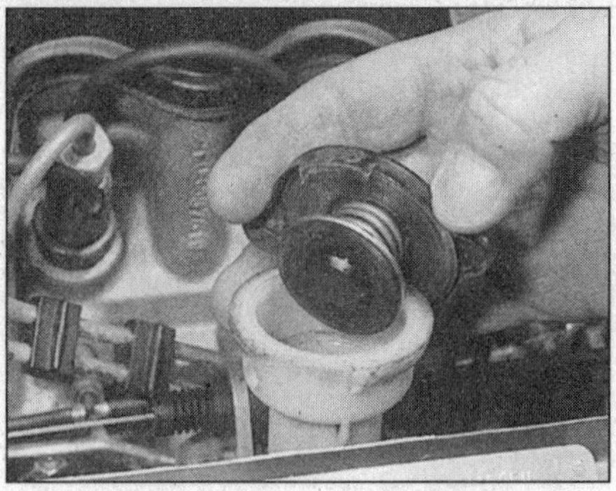

3.8 Removing the pressure cap from the expansion tank/radiator

3.9 Topping-up the coolant level - later Diesel engine shown

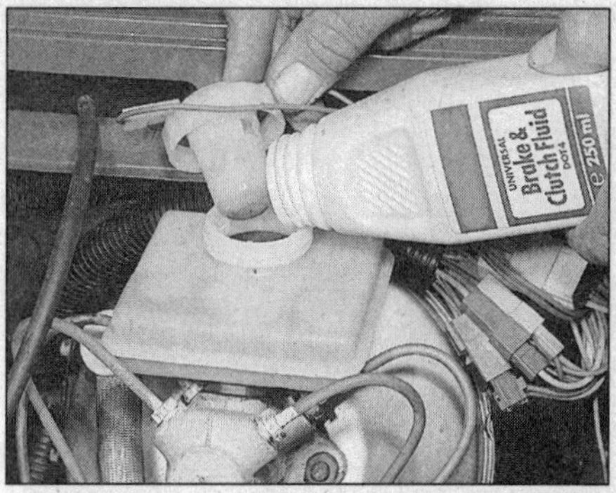

3.12 Topping-up the brake fluid level

Coolant

Warning: DO NOT attempt to remove the radiator/expansion tank pressure cap when the engine is hot, as there is a very great risk of scalding.

6 All vehicles covered by this manual have a pressurised cooling system. An expansion tank is incorporated in cooling system. On all petrol models and early Diesel models, the tank is incorporated into the side of the radiator; on later Diesel models, a separate expansion tank is located on the right-hand side of the engine compartment. As engine temperature increases, the coolant expands, and the level in the expansion tank rises. As the engine cools, the coolant is automatically drawn back into the system, to maintain the correct level.

7 The coolant level in the expansion tank should be checked regularly. The level in the tank varies with the temperature of the engine. When the engine is cold, the coolant level should be between the "MIN" and "MAX" marks on the side of the tank. When the engine is hot, the level may rise slightly above the "MAX" mark. Note that on later Diesel engine models, the maximum coolant level is indicated by a red marker, visible inside the expansion tank when the pressure cap has been removed.

8 If topping-up is necessary, wait until the engine is cold, then turn the pressure cap on the expansion tank anti-clockwise until it reaches the first stop. Wait until any pressure remaining in the system is released, then push the cap down, turn it anti-clockwise to the second stop and lift off **(see illustration)**.

9 Add a mixture of water and antifreeze (see Section 33) through the expansion tank filler neck **(see illustration)** until the coolant is approximately halfway between the two level marks, or just below the red marker on later Diesel models. Refit the cap, turning it clockwise as far as it will go to secure.

10 With a sealed type cooling system like this, the addition of coolant should only be necessary at very infrequent intervals. If frequent topping-up is required, it is likely there is a leak in the system. Check the radiator, all hoses and joint faces for any sign of staining or actual wetness, and rectify as necessary. If no leaks can be found, it is advisable to have the pressure cap and the entire system pressure-tested by a dealer or suitably-equipped garage, as this will often show up a small leak not previously apparent.

Brake fluid

11 The brake master cylinder and fluid reservoir is mounted on the front of the vacuum servo unit (or directly on the bulkhead where no servo is fitted) in the engine compartment. The maximum and minimum marks are indicated on the side of the reservoir, and the fluid level should be maintained between these marks at all times.

12 If topping-up is necessary, first wipe the area around the filler cap with a clean rag before removing the cap. When adding fluid, pour it carefully into the reservoir, to avoid spilling it on surrounding painted surfaces **(see illustration)**. Be sure to use only the specified brake hydraulic fluid, since mixing different types of fluid can cause damage to the system. See *"Lubricants fluids and capacities"* at the beginning of this Chapter.

Warning: Brake hydraulic fluid can harm your eyes and damage painted surfaces, so use extreme caution when handling and pouring it. Do not use fluid that has been standing open for some time, as it absorbs moisture from the air. Excess moisture can cause a dangerous loss of braking effectiveness.

13 When adding fluid, it is a good idea to inspect the reservoir for contamination. The system should be drained and refilled if deposits, dirt particles or contamination are seen in the fluid.

14 After filling the reservoir to the correct level, make sure that the cap is refitted securely, to avoid leaks and the entry of foreign matter.

15 The fluid level in the master cylinder reservoir will drop slightly as the brake pads and shoes wear down during normal operation. If the reservoir requires repeated replenishment to maintain the proper level, this is an indication of a hydraulic leak somewhere in the system, which should be investigated immediately.

3.16 Topping-up the washer fluid level

Washer fluid

16 The windscreen/tailgate washer fluid reservoir filler is located at the front right-hand corner of the engine compartment, behind the headlight unit **(see illustration)**.

17 When topping-up the reservoir(s), a screenwash additive should be added in the quantities recommended on the bottle.

4 Tyre checks

1 The original-equipment tyres have tread wear safety bands, which will appear when the tread depth reaches approximately 1.6 mm. Tread wear can be monitored with a simple, inexpensive device known as a tread depth indicator gauge **(see illustration)**.

2 Wheels and tyres should give no real problems in use, provided that a close eye is kept on them with regard to excessive wear or damage. To this end, the following points should be noted.

3 Ensure that the tyre pressures are checked regularly and maintained correctly **(see illustration)**. Checking should be carried out with the tyres cold, not immediately after the vehicle has been in use. If the pressures are checked with the tyres hot, an apparently-high reading will be obtained, owing to heat

4.1 Checking the tyre tread depth with a depth gauge

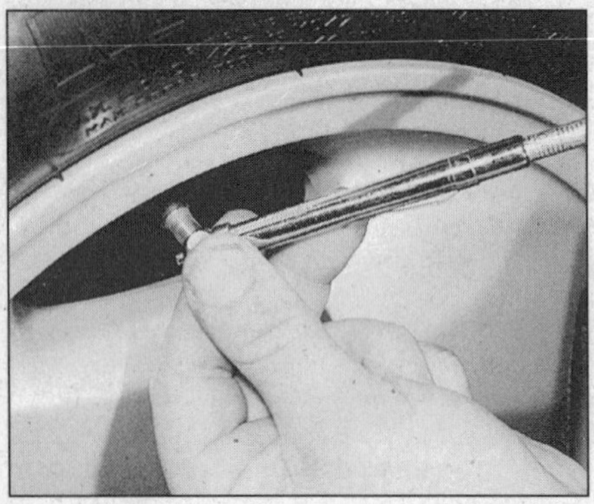

4.3 Checking the tyre pressure with a pressure gauge

expansion. **Under no circumstances** should an attempt be made to reduce the pressures to the quoted cold reading in this instance, or effective under-inflation will result.

4 Note any abnormal tread wear. Tread pattern irregularities such as feathering, flat spots, and more wear on one side than the other, are indications of front wheel alignment and/or balance problems. If any of these conditions are noted, they should be rectified as soon as possible.

5 Under-inflation will cause overheating of the tyre, owing to excessive flexing of the casing, and the tread will not sit correctly on the road surface. This will cause excessive wear, not to mention the danger of sudden tyre failure due to heat build-up.

6 Over-inflation will cause rapid wear of the centre part of the tyre tread, coupled with reduced adhesion, harsher ride, and the danger of shock damage occurring in the tyre casing.

7 Regularly check the tyres for damage in the form of cuts or bulges, especially in the sidewalls. Remove any nails or stones embedded in the tread, before they penetrate the tyre to cause deflation. If removal of a nail does reveal that the tyre has been punctured, refit the nail so that its point of penetration is marked. Then immediately change the wheel, and have the tyre repaired by a tyre dealer. **Do not** drive on a tyre in such a condition. If in any doubt as to the possible consequences of any damage found, consult your local tyre dealer for advice.

8 Periodically remove the wheels, and clean any dirt or mud from the inside and outside surfaces. Examine the wheel rims for signs of rusting, corrosion or other damage. Light alloy wheels are easily damaged by "kerbing" whilst parking, and similarly steel wheels may become dented or buckled. Renewal of the wheel is very often the only course of remedial action possible.

9 The balance of each wheel and tyre assembly should be maintained to avoid excessive wear, not only to the tyres but also to the steering and suspension components. Wheel imbalance is normally signified by vibration through the vehicle's bodyshell, although in many cases it is particularly noticeable through the steering wheel. Conversely, it should be noted that wear or damage in suspension or steering components may cause excessive tyre wear. Out-of-round or out-of-true tyres, damaged wheels, and wheel bearing wear also fall into this category. Balancing will not usually cure vibration caused by such wear.

10 Wheel balancing may be carried out with the wheel either on or off the vehicle. If balanced on the vehicle, ensure that the wheel-to-hub relationship is marked in some way prior to subsequent wheel removal, so that it may be refitted in its original position.

11 General tyre wear is influenced to a large degree by driving style - harsh braking and acceleration, or fast cornering, will all produce more rapid tyre wear. Interchanging of tyres may result in more even wear. However, if this

Tyre Tread Wear Patterns

Shoulder Wear

Underinflation (wear on both sides)
Check and adjust pressures

Incorrect wheel camber (wear on one side)
Repair or renew suspension parts

Hard cornering
Reduce speed!

Centre Wear

Overinflation
Check and adjust pressures

If you sometimes have to inflate your car's tyres to the higher pressures specified for maximum load or sustained high speed, don't forget to reduce the pressures to normal afterwards.

Toe Wear

Incorrect toe setting
Adjust front wheel alignment

Note: The feathered edge of the tread which characterises toe wear is best checked by feel.

Uneven Wear

Incorrect camber or castor
Repair or renew suspension parts

Malfunctioning suspension
Repair or renew suspension parts

Unbalanced wheel
Balance tyres

Out-of-round brake disc/drum
Machine or renew

is completely effective, the added expense is incurred of replacing all four tyres at once, which may prove financially-restrictive for many owners.

12 Front tyres may wear unevenly as a result of wheel misalignment. The front wheels should always be correctly aligned according to the settings specified by the vehicle manufacturer (see Chapter 10).

13 Legal restrictions apply to many aspects of tyre fitting and usage, and in the UK this information is contained in the Motor Vehicle Construction and Use Regulations. It is suggested that a copy of these regulations is obtained from your local police if in doubt as to current legal requirements with regard to tyre type and condition, minimum tread depth, etc.

5 Electrical system check

1 Check the operation of all the electrical equipment, ie lights, direction indicators, horn, washers, etc. Refer to the appropriate Sections of Chapter 12 for details if any of the circuits are found to be inoperative.

2 Stop-light switch adjustment is described in Chapter 9.

3 Visually check all accessible wiring connectors, harnesses and retaining clips for security, and for signs of chafing or damage. Rectify any faults found.

6 Battery check

Caution: Before carrying out any work on the vehicle battery, read through the precautions given in "Safety first!" at the beginning of this manual.

1 The battery is located on the left-hand side of the engine compartment. The exterior of the battery should be inspected periodically for damage such as a cracked case or cover.

2 Check the tightness of the battery cable clamps to ensure good electrical connections, and check the entire length of each cable for cracks or frayed conductors.

3 If corrosion (visible as white, fluffy deposits) is evident, remove the cables from the battery terminals, clean them with a small wire brush, then refit them.

Warning: These deposits are highly-caustic - take care not to get any on your skin, or in your eyes. Wear eye protection and gloves during cleaning.

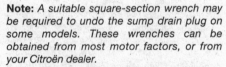

HAYNES HiNT ***Corrosion can be kept to a minimum by applying a layer of petroleum jelly to the clamps and terminals after they are reconnected.***

4 Make sure that the battery insulation plate (where fitted) is in good condition, and that the retaining clamp is tight.

5 Corrosion on the insulation plate, retaining clamp or the battery itself can be removed with a solution of water and baking soda (refer to the warning in paragraph 3 above). Thoroughly rinse all cleaned areas with plain water.

6 Any metal parts of the vehicle damaged by corrosion should be covered with a zinc-based primer, then painted.

7 Periodically (approximately every three months), check the charge condition of the battery as described in Chapter 5A.

8 Further information on the battery, charging and jump-starting can be found in Chapter 5, and in the preliminary sections of this manual.

7 Wiper blade check

1 Check the condition of the wiper blades; if they are cracked or show any signs of deterioration, or if the glass swept area is smeared, renew them. For maximum clarity of vision, wiper blades should be renewed annually, as a matter of course.

2 To remove a wiper blade, pull the arm fully away from the glass until it locks. Swivel the blade through 90°, press the locking tab(s) with your fingers, and slide the blade out of the arm's hooked end **(see illustration)**. On refitting, ensure that the blade locks securely into the arm.

1

Every 6000 miles / 10 000 km

8 Engine oil and filter renewal

Note: *On petrol models, the manufacturer specifies that the oil filter should be renewed at the first 6000 mile or 6 month service. After that, they recommend filter renewal at 12 000-mile or 12-monthly intervals, with only the oil being drained and renewed every 6000 miles or 6 months. Owners of high-mileage vehicles, or those who do a lot of stop-start driving, may prefer to carry out filter renewal at every oil change as a precautionary task.*

Note: *A suitable square-section wrench may be required to undo the sump drain plug on some models. These wrenches can be obtained from most motor factors, or from your Citroën dealer.*

1 Frequent oil and filter changes are the most important preventative maintenance procedures which can be undertaken by the DIY owner. As engine oil ages, it becomes diluted and contaminated, which leads to premature engine wear.

2 Before starting this procedure, gather together all the necessary tools and materials. Also make sure that you have plenty of clean rags and newspapers handy, to mop up any spills. Ideally, the engine oil should be warm, as it will drain better, and more built-up sludge will be removed with it. Take care, however, not to touch the exhaust or any other hot parts of the engine when working under the vehicle. To avoid any possibility of scalding, and to protect yourself from possible skin irritants and other harmful contaminants in used engine oils, it is advisable to wear gloves when carrying out this work. Access to the underside of the vehicle will be greatly improved if it can be raised on a lift, driven onto ramps, or jacked up and supported on

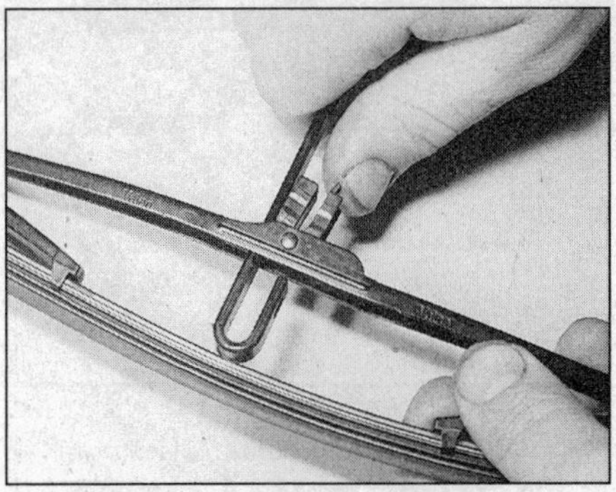

7.2 Removing a wiper blade from the wiper arm

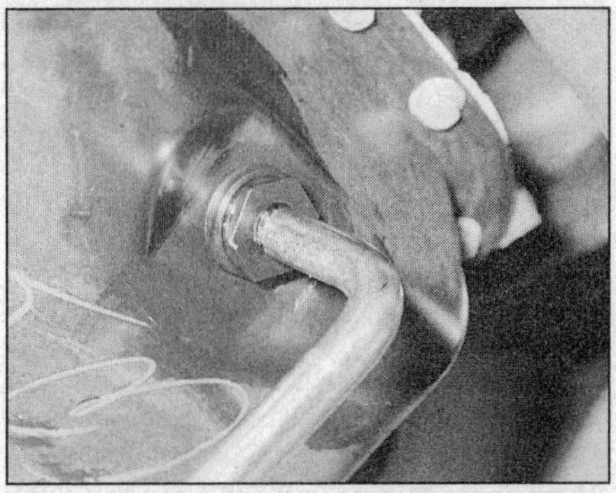

8.3 Slackening the sump drain plug with a square-section wrench

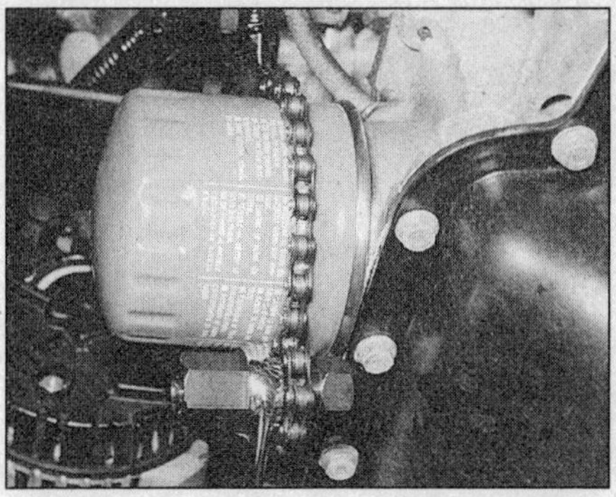

8.7 Using an oil filter removal tool (chain or strap wrench) to slacken the oil filter

axle stands (see "Jacking, towing and wheel changing"). Whichever method is chosen, make sure that the vehicle remains level, or if it is at an angle, that the drain plug is at the lowest point.

3 Slacken the drain plug about half a turn; on some models, a square-section wrench may be needed to slacken the plug **(see illustration)**. Position the draining container under the drain plug, then remove the plug completely. If possible, try to keep the plug pressed into the sump while unscrewing it by hand the last couple of turns. As the plug releases from the threads, move it away sharply, so that the stream of oil issuing from the sump runs into the container, not up your sleeve! Recover the sealing ring from the drain plug.

4 Allow some time for the old oil to drain, noting that it may be necessary to reposition the container as the oil flow slows to a trickle.

5 After all the oil has drained, wipe off the drain plug with a clean rag, and fit a new sealing washer. Clean the area around the drain plug opening, and refit the plug. Tighten the plug securely.

6 If the filter is also to be renewed, move the container into position under the oil filter, which is located on the front side of the cylinder block (below the inlet manifold on petrol engines, or below the injection pump on Diesel engines).

7 Using an oil filter removal tool if necessary, slacken the filter initially, then unscrew it by hand the rest of the way **(see illustration)**. Empty the oil in the old filter into the container.

8 Use a clean rag to remove all oil, dirt and sludge from the filter sealing area on the engine.

HAYNES HiNT ***Check the old filter to make sure that the rubber sealing ring hasn't stuck to the engine. If it has, carefully remove it.***

9 Apply a light coating of clean engine oil to the sealing ring on the new filter, then screw it into position on the engine. Tighten the filter firmly by hand only - **do not** use any tools.

10 Remove the old oil and all tools from under the car, then lower the car to the ground (if applicable).

11 Remove the dipstick, then unscrew the oil filler cap from the cylinder head cover. Fill the engine, using the correct grade and type of oil (see "Lubricants fluids and capacities"). An oil can spout or funnel may help to reduce spillage. Pour in half the specified quantity of oil first, then wait a few minutes for the oil to fall to the sump. Continue adding oil a small quantity at a time until the level is up to the lower mark on the dipstick. Adding a further 1.4 litres (2.0 litres on 1527 cc Diesel engines) will bring the level up to the upper mark on the dipstick. Refit the filler cap.

12 Start the engine and run it for a few minutes; check for leaks around the oil filter seal and the sump drain plug. Note that there may be a delay of a few seconds before the oil pressure warning light goes out when the engine is first started, as the oil circulates through the engine oil galleries and the new oil filter (where fitted) before the pressure builds up.

13 Switch off the engine, and wait a few minutes for the oil to settle in the sump once more. With the new oil circulated and the filter completely full, recheck the level on the dipstick, and add more oil as necessary.

14 Dispose of the used engine oil safely, with reference to *"General repair procedures"* in the preliminary Sections of this manual.

9 Hose and fluid leak check

1 Visually inspect the engine joint faces, gaskets and seals for any signs of water or oil leaks. Pay particular attention to the areas around the camshaft cover, cylinder head, oil filter and sump joint faces. Bear in mind that, over a period of time, some very slight seepage from these areas is to be expected - what you are really looking for is any indication of a serious leak. Should a leak be found, renew the offending gasket or oil seal by referring to the appropriate Chapters in this manual.

2 Also check the security and condition of all the engine-related pipes and hoses. Ensure that all cable ties or securing clips are in place and in good condition. Clips which are broken or missing can lead to chafing of the hoses, pipes or wiring, which could cause more serious problems in the future.

3 Carefully check the radiator hoses and heater hoses along their entire length. Renew any hose which is cracked, swollen or deteriorated. Cracks will show up better if the hose is squeezed. Pay close attention to the hose clips that secure the hoses to the cooling system components. Hose clips can pinch and puncture hoses, resulting in cooling system leaks. If the original Citroën crimped-type hose clips are used, it may be a good idea to replace them with standard worm-drive clips.

4 Inspect all the cooling system components (hoses, joint faces etc.) for leaks. A leak in the cooling system will usually show up as white- or rust-coloured deposits on the area adjoining the leak. Where any problems of this nature are found on system components, renew the component or gasket with reference to Chapter 3.

5 With the vehicle raised, inspect the fuel tank and filler neck for punctures, cracks and other damage. The connection between the filler neck and tank is especially critical. Sometimes, a rubber filler neck or connecting hose will leak due to loose retaining clamps or deteriorated rubber.

6 Carefully check all rubber hoses and metal fuel lines leading away from the fuel tank. Check for loose connections, deteriorated hoses, crimped lines, and other damage. Pay particular attention to the vent pipes and hoses, which often loop up around the filler neck and can become blocked or crimped. Follow the lines to the front of the vehicle, carefully inspecting them all the way. Renew damaged sections as necessary.

7 From within the engine compartment, check the security of all fuel hose attachments and pipe unions, and inspect the fuel hoses and vacuum hoses for kinks, chafing and deterioration.

10 Fuel filter renewal - Diesel models

Note: *On Diesel models, the manufacturer specifies that the fuel filter should be renewed at the first 6000-mile or 6-month service. After that, they recommend fuel filter renewal at 12 000-mile or 12-monthly intervals, with water being bled from the filter at the intermediate 6000-mile/6-month service.*

1 The fuel filter is screwed onto the underside of the filter/thermostat housing on the left-hand end of the cylinder head. To improve access to the filter, remove the battery as described in Chapter 5A and the inlet ducting with reference to Chapter 4D.

2 Cover the clutch bellhousing with a piece of plastic sheeting, to protect the clutch from fuel spillage.

3 Position a suitable container under the end of the fuel filter drain hose. Open the drain screw on the base of the filter, and allow the fuel to drain completely.

4 When the filter has drained, close the bleed screw and unscrew the filter. In the absence of the special fuel filter socket (Purflux no. F76, a shaped socket that fits the base of the filter), the filter can be unscrewed using a suitable strap or chain wrench **(see illustration)**.

5 Remove the filter, and dispose of it safely. Ensure that the sealing ring comes away with the filter, and does not stick to the filter/thermostat housing mating surface.

6 Apply a smear of clean diesel oil to the filter sealing ring, and wipe clean the housing mating surface. Screw the filter on until its sealing ring lightly contacts the housing

10.4 On Diesel models, if necessary, a chain wrench can be used to unscrew the fuel filter

mating surface, then tighten it through a further three-quarters of a turn.
7 Prime the fuel system as described in Chapter 4D.
8 Open the drain screw until clean fuel flows from the hose, then close the drain screw and withdraw the container from under the hose.
9 Refit the battery and ducting, and start the engine. If difficulty is encountered bleed the fuel system as described in Chapter 4D.

11 Steering and suspension check

Front suspension and steering

1 Raise the front of the vehicle, and securely support it on axle stands.
2 Visually inspect the balljoint dust covers and the steering rack-and-pinion gaiters for splits, chafing or deterioration. Any wear of these components will cause loss of lubricant, together with dirt and water entry, resulting in rapid deterioration of the balljoints or steering gear.
3 Grasp the roadwheel at the 12 o'clock and 6 o'clock positions, and try to rock it. Very slight free play may be felt, but if the movement is appreciable, further investigation is necessary to determine the source. Continue rocking the wheel while an assistant depresses the footbrake. If the movement is now eliminated or significantly reduced, it is likely that the hub bearings are at fault. If the free play is still evident with the footbrake depressed, then there is wear in the suspension joints or mountings.
4 Now grasp the wheel at the 9 o'clock and 3 o'clock positions, and try to rock it as before. Any movement felt now may again be caused by wear in the hub bearings or the steering track-rod balljoints. If the inner or outer balljoint is worn, the visual movement will be obvious.
5 Using a large screwdriver or flat bar, check for wear in the suspension mounting bushes by levering between the relevant suspension component and its attachment point. Some movement is to be expected, as the mountings are made of rubber, but excessive wear should be obvious. Also check the condition of any visible rubber bushes, looking for splits, cracks or contamination of the rubber.
6 With the car standing on its wheels, have an assistant turn the steering wheel back and forth about an eighth of a turn each way. There should be very little, if any, lost movement between the steering wheel and roadwheels. If this is not the case, closely observe the joints and mountings previously described, but in addition, check the steering column universal joints for wear, and the rack-and-pinion steering gear itself.

Suspension strut/shock absorber

7 Check for any signs of fluid leakage around the suspension strut/shock absorber body, or from the rubber gaiter around the piston rod. Should any fluid be noticed, the suspension strut/shock absorber is defective internally, and should be renewed. **Note:** *Suspension struts/shock absorbers should always be renewed in pairs on the same axle.*
8 The efficiency of the suspension strut/shock absorber may be checked by bouncing the vehicle at each corner. Generally speaking, the body will return to its normal position and stop after being depressed. If it rises and returns on a rebound, the suspension strut/shock absorber is probably suspect. Examine also the suspension strut/shock absorber upper and lower mountings for any signs of wear.

12 Driveshaft gaiter check

1 With the vehicle raised and securely supported on stands, turn the steering onto full lock, then slowly rotate the roadwheel. Inspect the condition of the outer constant velocity (CV) joint rubber gaiters, squeezing the gaiters to open out the folds. Check for signs of cracking, splits or deterioration of the rubber, which may allow the grease to escape, and lead to water and grit entry into the joint. Also check the security and condition of the retaining clips. Repeat these checks on the inner CV joints. If any damage or deterioration is found, the gaiters should be renewed as described in Chapter 8.
2 At the same time, check the general condition of the CV joints themselves by first holding the driveshaft and attempting to rotate the wheel. Repeat this check by holding the inner joint and attempting to rotate the driveshaft. Any appreciable movement indicates wear in the joints, wear in the driveshaft splines, or a loose driveshaft retaining nut.

Every 12 000 miles / 20 000 km

13 Air conditioning system refrigerant check

Warning: *Do not attempt to open the refrigerant circuit. Refer to the precautions given in Chapter 3.*

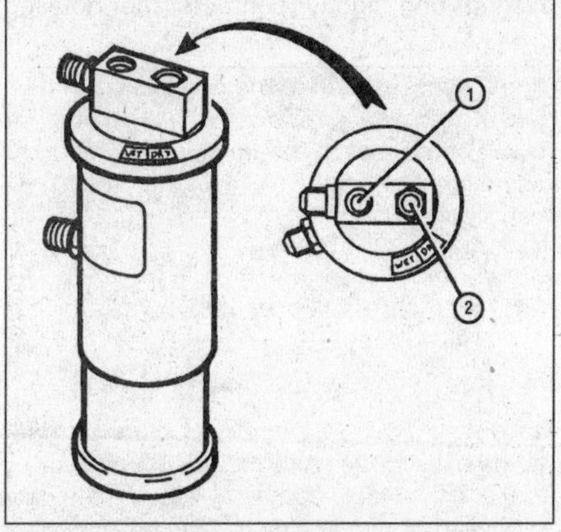

13.1 Air conditioning drier bottle sight glass (1) and humidity indicator (2)

1 In order to check the condition of the refrigerant, a humidity indicator and a sight glass are provided on top of the drier bottle, located in the engine compartment **(see illustration)**.

Refrigerant humidity check

2 Check the colour of the humidity indicator. Blue indicates that the condition of the refrigerant is satisfactory. Red indicates that the refrigerant is saturated with humidity. If the indicator shows red, the system should be drained and recharged, and a new drier bottle should be fitted. **Note:** *The system should be drained and recharged only by a Citroën dealer or air conditioning specialist.* ***Do not*** *attempt to carry out the work yourself, as the refrigerant is a highly-dangerous substance (refer to Chapter 3, Section 10).*

Refrigerant flow check

3 Run the engine, and switch on the air conditioning.
4 After a few minutes, inspect the sight glass, and check the fluid flow. Clear fluid should be visible - if not, the following will help to diagnose the problem:

a) Clear fluid flow - the system is functioning correctly.
b) No fluid flow - have the system checked for leaks by a Citroën dealer or air conditioning specialist.
c) Continuous stream of clear air bubbles in fluid - refrigerant level low - have the system recharged by a Citroën dealer or air conditioning specialist.
d) Milky air bubbles visible - high humidity (see paragraph 2).

14 Spark plug renewal - petrol models

1 The correct functioning of the spark plugs is vital for the correct running and efficiency of the engine. It is essential that the plugs fitted are appropriate for the engine (a suitable type is specified at the beginning of this Chapter). If this type is used and the engine is in good condition, the spark plugs should not need attention between scheduled replacement intervals. Spark plug cleaning is rarely necessary, and should not be attempted unless specialised equipment is available, as damage can easily be caused to the firing ends.

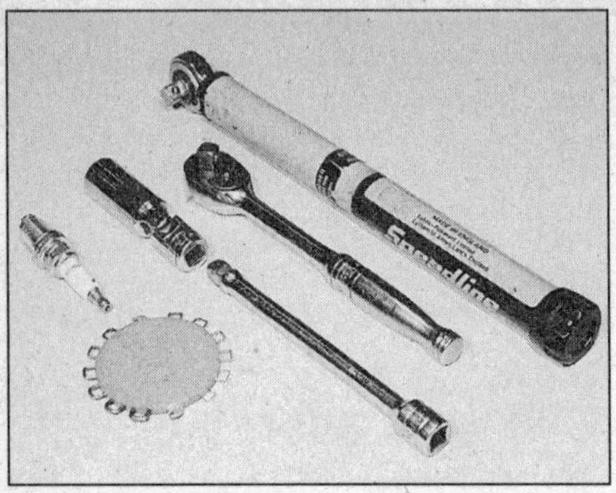

14.4 Tools required for spark plug removal, gap adjustment and refitting

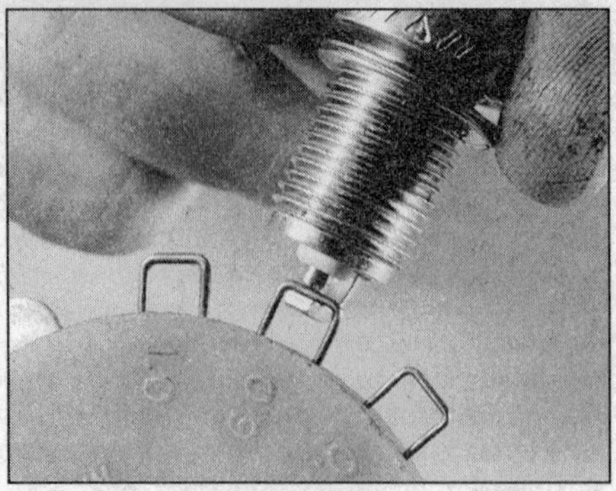

14.9a Measuring the spark plug gap with a wire gauge

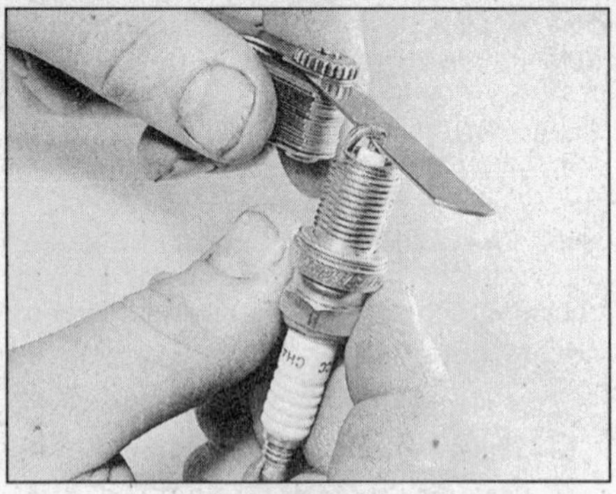

14.9b Measuring the spark plug gap with a feeler blade

2 If the marks on the original-equipment spark plug (HT) leads cannot be seen, mark the leads "1" to "4", to correspond to the cylinder the lead serves (No 1 cylinder is at the transmission end of the engine). Pull the leads from the plugs by gripping the end fitting, not the lead, otherwise the lead connection may be fractured.

3 It is advisable to remove the dirt from the spark plug recesses using a clean brush, vacuum cleaner or compressed air before removing the plugs, to prevent dirt dropping into the cylinders.

4 Unscrew the plugs using a spark plug spanner, suitable box spanner or a deep socket and extension bar **(see illustration)**. Keep the socket aligned with the spark plug - if it is forcibly moved to one side, the ceramic insulator may be broken off. As each plug is removed, examine it as follows.

5 Examination of the spark plugs will give a good indication of the condition of the engine. If the insulator nose of the spark plug is clean and white, with no deposits, this is indicative of a weak mixture or too hot a plug (a hot plug transfers heat away from the electrode slowly, a cold plug transfers heat away quickly).

6 If the tip and insulator nose are covered with hard black-looking deposits, then this is indicative that the mixture is too rich. Should the plug be black and oily, then it is likely that the engine is fairly worn, as well as the mixture being too rich.

7 If the insulator nose is covered with light tan to greyish-brown deposits, then the mixture is correct and it is likely that the engine is in good condition.

8 The spark plug electrode gap is of considerable importance as, if it is too large or too small, the size of the spark and its efficiency will be seriously impaired. The gap should be set to the value given in the Specifications at the beginning of this Chapter.

9 To set the gap, measure it with a feeler blade or wire gauge and then bend open, or close, the outer plug electrode until the correct gap is achieved **(see illustrations)**. The centre electrode should never be bent, as this will crack the insulator and cause plug failure, if nothing worse. If using feeler blades, the gap is correct when the appropriate-size blade is a firm sliding fit.

10 Special spark plug electrode gap adjusting tools are available from most motor accessory shops, or from some spark plug manufacturers.

11 Before fitting the spark plugs, check that the threaded connector sleeves are tight, and that the plug exterior surfaces and threads are clean.

12 It is very often difficult to insert spark plugs into their holes without cross-threading them. To avoid this possibility, fit a short length of 5/16 inch internal diameter rubber hose over the end of the spark plug. The flexible hose acts as a universal joint to help align the plug with the plug hole. Should the plug begin to cross-thread, the hose will slip on the spark plug, preventing thread damage to the aluminium cylinder head. Remove the rubber hose, and tighten the plug to the specified torque using the spark plug socket and a torque wrench. Refit the remaining spark plugs in the same manner.

13 Connect the HT leads in their correct order, and refit any components removed for access.

15 Fuel filter renewal - carburettor petrol models

Warning: Before carrying out the following operation, refer to the precautions given in "Safety first!" at the beginning of this manual, and follow them implicitly. Petrol is a highly-dangerous and volatile liquid, and the precautions necessary when handling it cannot be overstressed.

1 The in-line fuel filter is situated on the left-hand side of the engine compartment, between the vacuum servo unit and the wheel arch.

2 To remove the filter from the fuel line, first note its direction of fitting, then separate the filter from the hoses each side. Be prepared for fuel leakage as the hoses are detached, and plug the hose ends to prevent a continuous loss of fuel if the new filter is not being fitted immediately.

3 When fitting the new filter, ensure that it is correctly orientated as noted during removal, and if necessary renew the hose clips. On completion, restart the engine and check for any signs of leakage from the filter hose connections.

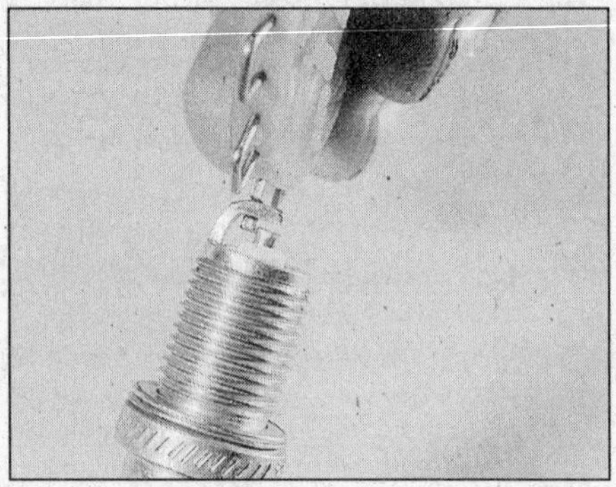

14.9c Adjusting the gap using a special adjusting tool

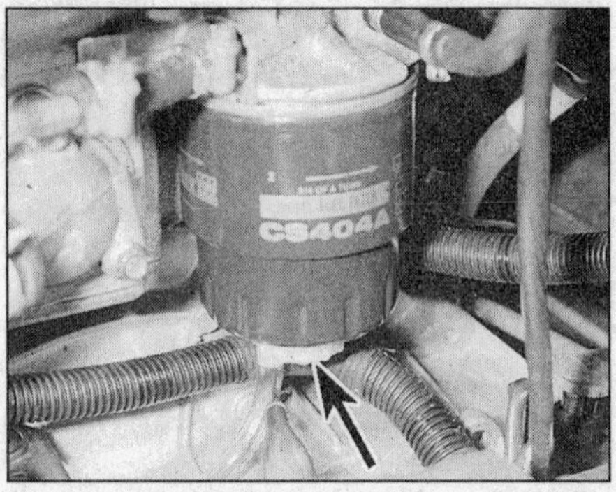

16.1 Fuel filter drain screw (arrowed) - Diesel models - battery removed for clarity

16 Fuel filter water draining - Diesel models

1 A water drain screw and tube are provided at the base of the fuel filter **(see illustration)**.

2 Place a suitable container beneath the drain tube, and cover the clutch bellhousing.

3 Open the drain screw by turning it anti-clockwise, and allow fuel and water to drain until fuel, free from water, emerges from the end of the tube. Close the drain screw and tighten it securely.

4 Dispose of the drained fuel safely.

5 Start the engine. If difficulty is experienced, bleed the fuel system as described in Chapter 4D.

17 Ignition system check - petrol models

Warning: Voltages produced by an electronic ignition system are considerably higher than those produced by conventional ignition systems. Extreme care must be taken when working on the system with the ignition switched on. Persons with surgically-implanted cardiac pacemaker devices should keep well clear of the ignition circuits, components and test equipment.

1 The ignition system components should be checked for damage or deterioration as described under the relevant sub-heading.

Ignition systems incorporating a distributor

General component check

2 The spark plug (HT) leads should be checked whenever new spark plugs are fitted.

3 Ensure that the leads are numbered before removing them, to avoid confusion when refitting (see Section 14).

HAYNES HiNT ***Pull the leads from the plugs by gripping the end fitting, not the lead, otherwise the lead connection may be fractured.***

4 Check inside the end fitting for signs of corrosion, which will look like a white crusty powder. Push the end fitting back onto the spark plug, ensuring that it is a tight fit on the plug. If not, remove the lead again and use pliers to carefully crimp the metal connector inside the end fitting until it fits securely on the end of the spark plug.

5 Using a clean rag, wipe the entire length of the lead to remove any built-up dirt and grease. Once the lead is clean, check for burns, cracks and other damage. Do not bend the lead excessively, nor pull the lead lengthwise - the conductor inside might break.

6 Disconnect the other end of the lead from the distributor cap. Again, pull only on the end fitting. Check for corrosion and a tight fit, in the same manner as the spark plug end. If an ohmmeter is available, check the resistance of the lead by connecting the meter between the spark plug end of the lead and the segment inside the distributor cap - if the resistance is not similar to that given in the Specifications, the lead should be renewed. Refit the lead securely on completion.

7 Check the remaining leads one at a time, in the same way.

8 If new spark plug (HT) leads are required, purchase a set for your specific car and engine.

9 Unscrew its retaining screws and remove the distributor cap. Wipe it clean, and carefully inspect it inside and out for signs of cracks, black carbon tracks (tracking) and worn, burned or loose contacts; check that the cap's carbon brush is unworn, free to move against spring pressure, and making good contact with the rotor arm. Also inspect the cap seal for signs of wear or damage, and renew if necessary. Remove the rotor arm from the distributor shaft, and inspect the rotor arm **(see illustration)**. It is common practice to renew the cap and rotor arm whenever new spark plug (HT) leads are fitted. When fitting a new cap, remove the leads from the old cap one at a time, and fit them to the new cap in the exact same location - do not simultaneously remove all the leads from the old cap, or firing order confusion may occur. When refitting, ensure that the arm is securely pressed onto the shaft, and tighten the cap retaining screws securely.

10 Even with the ignition system in first-class condition, some engines may still occasionally experience poor starting, attributable to damp ignition components. To disperse moisture, a water-dispersant aerosol can be very effective.

Ignition timing - check and adjustment

11 Check the ignition timing as described in Chapter 5B.

Static (distributorless) ignition systems

General component check

12 Check the condition of the HT leads as described above in paragraphs 3 to 8.

Ignition timing - check and adjustment

13 Refer to Chapter 5B.

18 Idle speed and mixture check and adjustment - petrol models

1 Before checking the idle speed and mixture setting, always check the following first:

a) Check the ignition timing (Chapter 5B).
b) Check that the spark plugs are in good condition and correctly gapped (Section 14).
c) Check that the accelerator cable and, on carburettor models, the choke cable is correctly adjusted (see relevant Part of Chapter 4).
d) Check that the crankcase breather hoses are secure, with no leaks or kinks (Section 20).
e) Check that the air cleaner filter element is clean (Section 27).

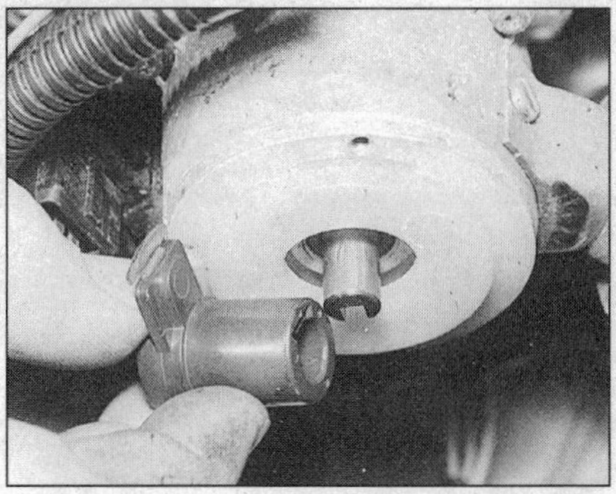

17.9 The rotor arm is a push fit on the distributor shaft (1360 cc model shown)

f) Check that the exhaust system is in good condition (see relevant Part of Chapter 4).
g) If the engine is running very roughly, check the compression pressures and valve clearances as described in Chapter 2A.
h) On fuel-injected models, check that the fuel injection/ignition system warning light is not illuminated (see relevant Part of Chapter 4).

2 Take the car on a journey of sufficient length to warm it up to normal operating temperature. Proceed as described under the relevant sub-heading. **Note:** *Adjustment should be completed within two minutes of return, without stopping the engine. If this cannot be achieved, or if the radiator electric cooling fan operates, first wait for the cooling fan to stop. Clear any excess fuel from the inlet manifold by racing the engine two or three times to between 2000 and 3000 rpm, then allow it to idle again.*

Carburettor models

3 Ensure all electrical loads are switched off and the choke lever is pushed fully in; if the car does not have a tachometer (rev counter), connect one to the engine, following its manufacturer's instructions. Note the idle speed, and compare it with that specified.

4 The idle speed adjusting screw is on the throttle linkage on the carburettor. On some models, it may be necessary to remove a retaining clip and plastic cover to gain access to the carburettor. Using a suitable flat-bladed screwdriver, turn the idle screw in or out as necessary to obtain the specified speed **(see illustrations)**.

5 The idle mixture (exhaust gas CO level) is set at the factory, and should require no further adjustment. If, due to a change in engine characteristics (carbon build-up, bore wear etc) or after a major carburettor overhaul, the mixture setting is lost, it can be reset. Note, however, that an exhaust gas analyser (CO meter) will be required to check the mixture, in order to set it with the necessary standard of accuracy; if this is not available, the car must be taken to a Citroën dealer for the work to be carried out.

6 If an exhaust gas analyser is available,

1

18.4a Idle speed adjustment screw (arrowed) - Solex 32 PBISA carburettor (954 cc, 1124 cc and 1360 cc engines)

18.4b Idle speed adjustment screw (A) - early Weber 32 IBSH carburettor (954 cc engine)

18.4c Idle speed adjustment screw (arrowed) - later Weber 32 IBSH carburettor (954 cc engine)

follow its manufacturer's instructions to check the exhaust gas CO level. If adjustment is required, it is made by turning the mixture adjustment screw. The screw may be covered with a tamperproof plug to prevent unnecessary adjustment. To gain access to the screw, use a sharp instrument to hook out the plug.

7 Using a suitable flat-bladed screwdriver, turn the mixture adjustment screw (in very small increments) until the CO level is correct. Turning the screw in (clockwise) weakens the mixture and reduces the CO level, turning it out will richen the mixture and increase the CO level **(see illustrations)**.

8 When adjustments are complete, disconnect any test equipment used, and fit a new tamperproof plug to the mixture adjustment screw. Recheck the idle speed and, if necessary, readjust.

Fuel-injected models

1360 cc (K6B engine) models without a catalytic converter

9 The idle speed is under full control of the engine management (fuel injection/ignition) ECU, and is not adjustable (see paragraph 13). However, the idle speed mixture content can be adjusted as follows.

10 The idle mixture is set at the factory, and should require no further adjustment. If, due to a change in engine characteristics (carbon build-up, bore wear etc) or after a major overhaul, the mixture setting is lost, it can be reset. Note, however, that an exhaust gas analyser (CO meter) will be required to check the mixture, in order to set it with the necessary standard of accuracy; if this is not available, the car must be taken to a Citroën dealer for the work to be carried out.

11 If an exhaust gas analyser is available, follow its manufacturer's instructions to check the exhaust gas CO level. Adjustment is made using the screw on the mixture adjustment potentiometer, which is situated on the right-hand side of the engine compartment, on the underside of the ECU bracket. Using a suitable flat-bladed screwdriver, turn the screw (in very small increments) until the level is correct.

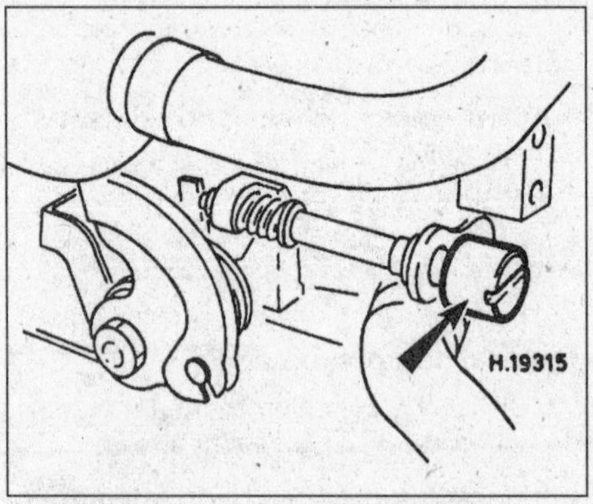

18.4d Idle speed adjustment screw (arrowed) - Weber 34 TLP carburettor (1360 cc engine)

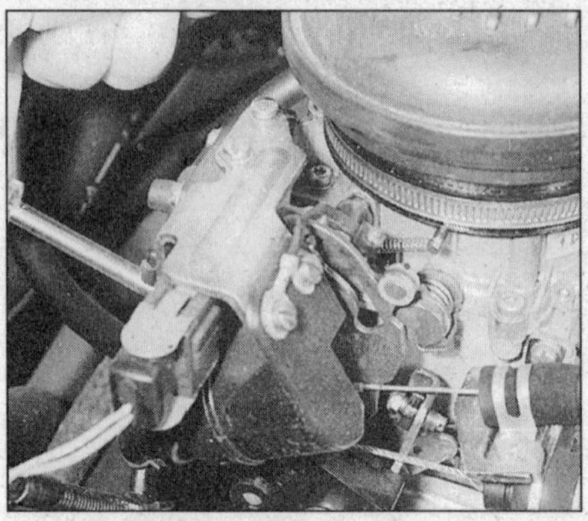

18.4e Adjusting the Idle speed - Solex 32-34 Z2 PSA carburettor (1360 cc engine)

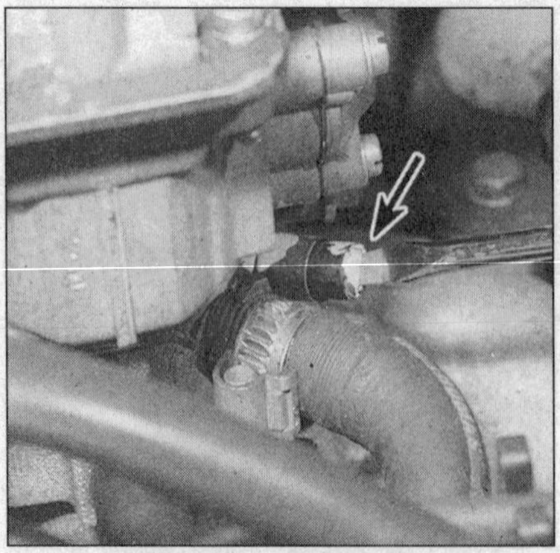

18.7a Mixture adjustment screw (arrowed) - Solex 32 PBISA carburettor (954 cc, 1124 cc and 1360 cc engines)

18.7b Mixture adjustment screw (B) - early Weber 32 IBSH carburettor (954 cc engine)

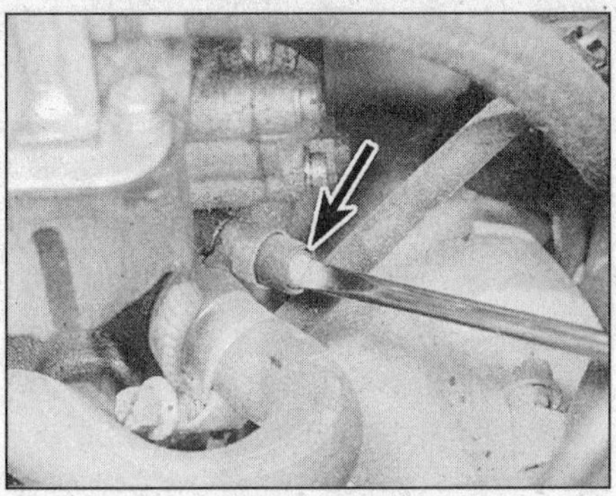

18.7c Mixture adjustment screw (arrowed) - later Weber 32 IBSH carburettor (954 cc engine)

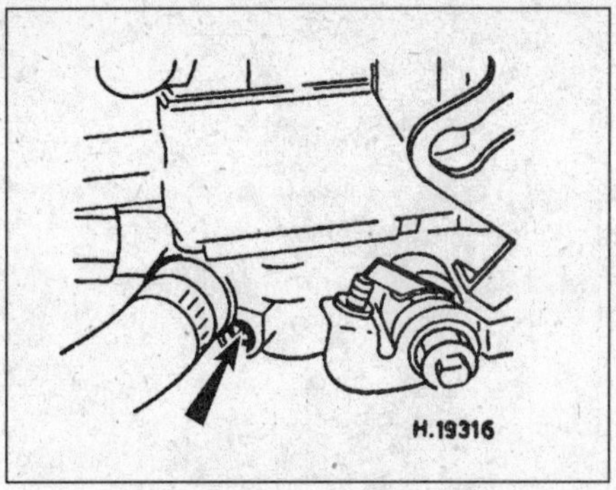

18.7d Mixture adjustment screw (arrowed) - Weber 34 TLP carburettor (1360 cc engine)

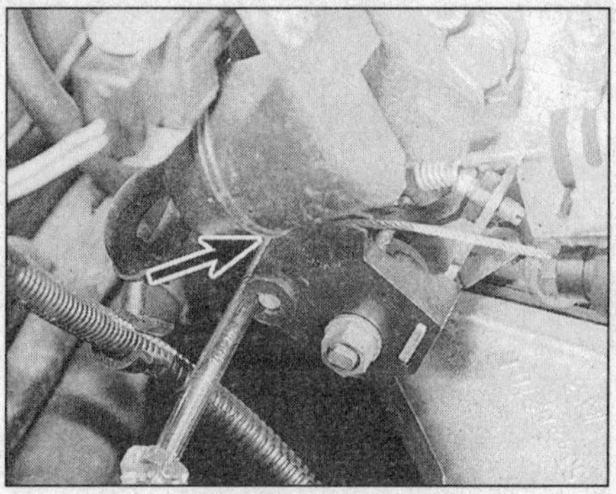

18.7e Adjusting the mixture (screw arrowed) - Solex 32-34 Z2 PSA carburettor (1360 cc engine)

12 When adjustments are complete, disconnect any test equipment.

All other models

13 Experienced home mechanics with a considerable amount of skill and equipment (including a good-quality tachometer and a good-quality, carefully-calibrated exhaust gas analyser) may be able to *check* the exhaust CO level and the idle speed. However, if these are found to be in need of *adjustment*, the car **must** be taken to a suitably-equipped Citroën dealer.

14 On later (July 1992-on) 1124 cc models, fitted with a Magneti Marelli G6 engine management (fuel injection/ignition) system, adjustment of the mixture setting (exhaust gas CO level) is possible, but adjustments can only be made by reprogramming the engine management ECU, using special electronic test equipment which is connected to the diagnostic wiring connector (see Chapter 4B).

15 On all other vehicles, adjustments are not possible. If the idle speed and/or exhaust gas CO level is incorrect, there must be a fault in the engine management system, and the vehicle should be taken to a Citroën dealer for testing (see relevant Part of Chapter 4).

19 Idle speed and anti-stall speed check and adjustment - Diesel models

1 The usual type of tachometer (rev counter), which works from ignition system pulses, cannot be used on Diesel engines. A diagnostic socket is provided for the use of Citroën test equipment, but this will not normally be available to the home mechanic. If it is not felt that adjusting the idle speed "by ear" is satisfactory, it will be necessary to purchase or hire an appropriate tachometer, or else leave the task to a Citroën dealer or other suitably-equipped specialist.

2 Before making adjustments, warm up the engine to normal operating temperature. Make sure that the accelerator cable is correctly adjusted (see Chapter 4D).

Idle speed - check and adjustment

3 Check that the engine idles at the specified speed. If necessary, adjustments can be made using the idle speed adjustment screw on the injection pump.

4 Loosen the locknut, then adjust the screw (as necessary) until the position is found where the engine is idling at the specified speed **(see illustrations)**. Once the screw is correctly positioned, securely tighten the locknut.

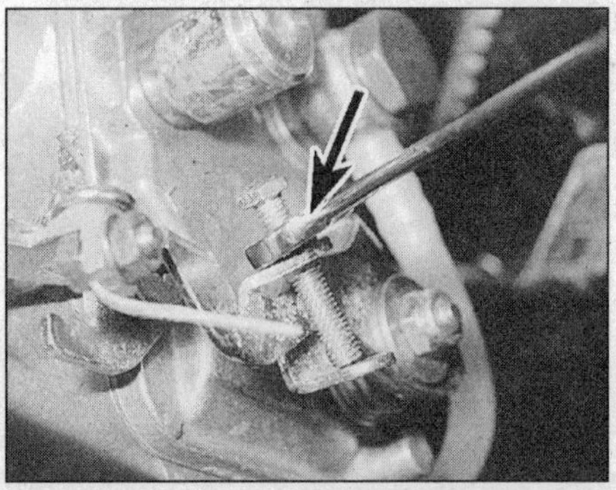

19.4a On Diesel models with the Lucas/CAV injection pump, slacken the locknut (location arrowed) . . .

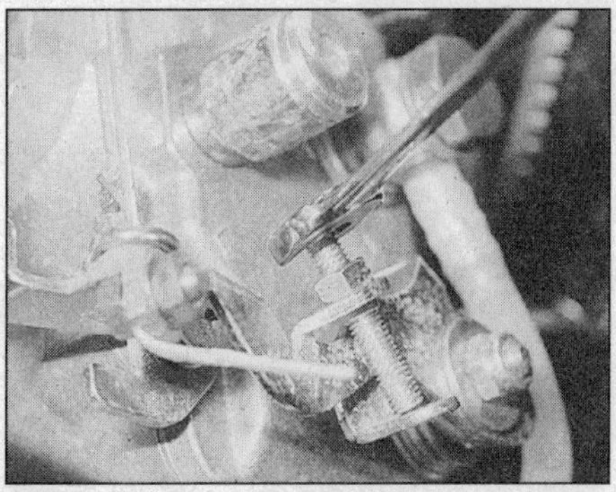

19.4b . . . then turn the idle speed screw as necessary

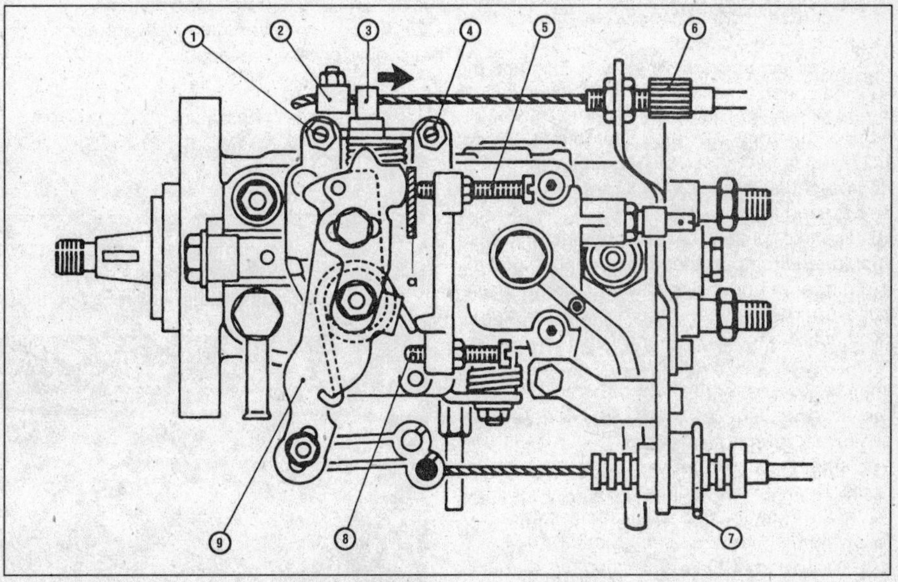

19.4c Bosch fuel injection pump adjustment points

1 Fast idle adjustment screw
2 Cable end fitting
3 Fast idle lever
4 Idle speed adjustment screw
5 Anti-stall adjustment screw
6 Fast idle cable adjustment ferrule
7 Accelerator cable adjustment ferrule
8 Maximum speed adjustment screw
9 Control (accelerator) lever
a Shim for anti-stall adjustment

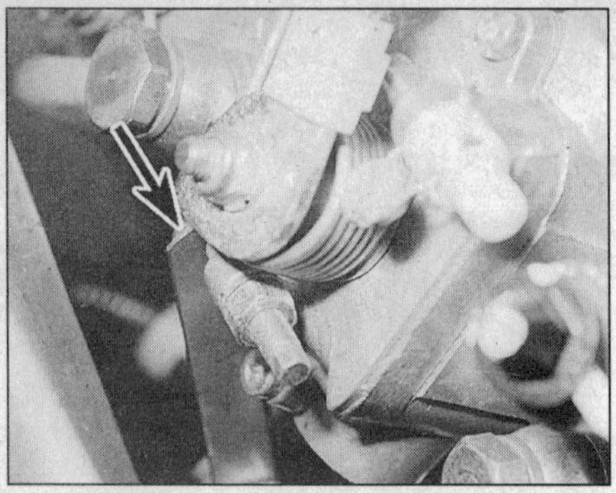

19.7 On the Lucas/CAV injection pump, insert a feeler blade of the required thickness (arrowed) between the anti-stall adjustment screw and the accelerator lever . . .

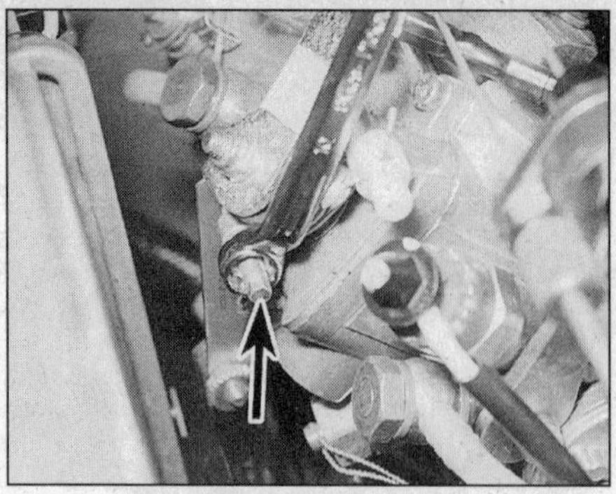

19.9 . . . then slacken the locknut and turn the screw (arrowed) to set the anti-stall speed

5 Check the anti-stall adjustment as described below.

Anti-stall - check and adjustment

Lucas/CAV injection pump

6 Adjust the idle speed as described in paragraphs 3 and 4, then switch off the engine.
7 Insert a shim or feeler blade, of the correct thickness (see Specifications), between the pump accelerator lever and the anti-stall adjustment screw **(see illustration)**.
8 Start the engine and allow it to idle. The engine should now run at the specified anti-stall speed (see Specifications).
9 If adjustment is necessary, loosen the locknut, and turn the anti-stall adjustment screw as required, until the anti-stall speed is correct **(see illustration)**. Hold the screw in this position, and securely tighten the locknut.
10 Remove the shim or feeler blade, then recheck the idle speed.
11 Move the accelerator lever to increase the engine speed to approximately 3000 rpm, then quickly release the lever. The deceleration period should be between 2.5 and 3.5 seconds, and the engine speed should drop to approximately 50 rpm below idle.
12 If the deceleration is too fast and the engine stalls, screw the anti-stall adjustment screw in a quarter of a turn towards the accelerator lever. If the deceleration is too slow, resulting in poor engine braking, unscrew it a quarter of a turn away from the lever. Adjust as necessary, then securely retighten the locknut.
13 Recheck the idle speed and, if necessary, adjust as described above.
14 With the engine idling, check the operation of the manual stop control by turning the stop lever anti-clockwise. The engine must stop instantly.
15 Where applicable, disconnect the tachometer on completion.

Bosch injection pump

16 Adjust the idle speed as described in paragraphs 3 and 4, then switch off the engine.
17 Insert a shim or feeler blade, of the correct thickness (see Specifications), between the pump accelerator lever and the anti-stall adjustment screw.
18 Start the engine and allow it to idle. The engine should now run at the specified anti-stall speed (see Specifications).
19 If adjustment is necessary, loosen the locknut and turn the anti-stall adjustment screw as required. Retighten the locknut.
20 Remove the shim or feeler blade and allow the engine to idle.
21 Move the fast idle lever fully towards the flywheel end of the engine, and check that the engine speed increases to the fast idle speed (see Chapter 4D). If necessary, loosen the locknut and turn the fast idle adjusting screw as required, then retighten the locknut.
22 With the engine idling, check the operation of the manual stop control by turning the stop lever. The engine must stop instantly.
23 Where applicable, disconnect the tachometer on completion.

20 Emission control systems check

1 Details of the emission control system components are given in Chapter 4E.
2 Checking consists simply of a visual check for obvious signs of damaged or leaking hoses and joints.
3 Detailed checking and testing of the evaporative and/or exhaust emission systems (as applicable) should be entrusted to a Citroën dealer.

21 Auxiliary drivebelt check and renewal

1 On all models, only one auxiliary drivebelt is fitted. The belt drives the alternator and (where fitted) the air conditioning compressor.

Checking the auxiliary drivebelt condition

2 Apply the handbrake, then jack up the front of the car and support it on axle stands. Remove the right-hand front roadwheel. Where necessary, undo the retaining nut, and free the coolant hoses from the retaining clip to improve access to the crankshaft sprocket bolt.
3 Using a suitable socket and extension bar fitted to the crankshaft sprocket bolt, rotate the crankshaft so that the entire length of the drivebelt can be examined. Examine the drivebelt for cracks, splitting, fraying, or other damage. Check also for signs of glazing (shiny patches) and for separation of the belt plies. Renew the belt if worn or damaged.
4 If the condition of the belt is satisfactory, check the drivebelt tension as described below under the relevant sub-heading.

Auxiliary drivebelt (models without air conditioning) - removal, refitting and tensioning

Removal

5 If not already done, carry out the operations described in paragraph 2.
6 Disconnect the battery negative lead.
7 Slacken both the alternator upper and lower mounting bolts, and the bolt securing the adjuster strap to the mounting bracket.
8 Back off the adjuster bolt to relieve the tension in the drivebelt, then slip the drivebelt from the pulleys **(see illustrations)**.

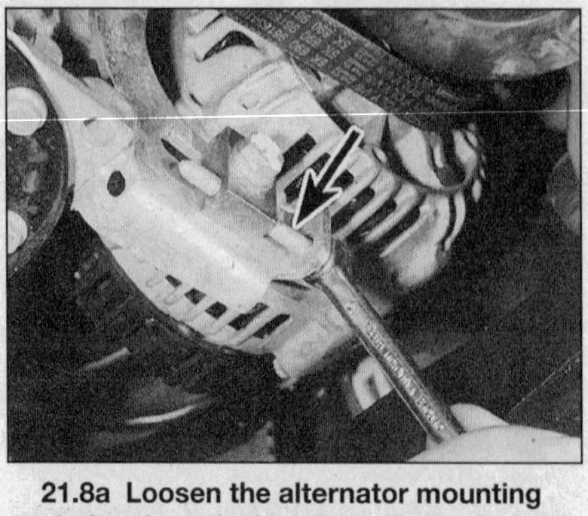

21.8a Loosen the alternator mounting bolts, then slacken the adjuster bolt (arrowed) . . .

21.8b . . . and slip the drivebelt off its pulleys

Refitting

9 Fit the belt around the pulleys, ensuring that the belt is of the correct type if it is being renewed, and take up the slack in the belt by tightening the adjuster bolt.
10 Tension the drivebelt as described in the following paragraphs.

Tensioning

11 If not already done, carry out the operations described in paragraph 2.
12 Correct tensioning of the drivebelt will ensure that it has a long life. Beware, however, of overtightening, as this can cause wear in the alternator bearings.
13 The belt should be tensioned so that, under firm thumb pressure, there is approximately 5.0 mm of free movement at the mid-point between the pulleys, on the longest belt run.
14 To adjust, with the upper mounting bolt just holding the alternator firm, and the lower mounting bolt loosened, turn the adjuster bolt until the correct tension is achieved. Rotate the crankshaft through two complete turns, then recheck the tension. When the tension is correct, securely tighten both the alternator mounting bolts and, where necessary, the bolt securing the adjuster strap to its mounting bracket.
15 Reconnect the battery negative lead.
16 Clip the coolant hoses in position, and secure them with the retaining nut (where removed). Refit the roadwheel, and lower the vehicle to the ground.

Auxiliary drivebelt (models with air conditioning) - removal, refitting and tensioning

Removal

17 If not already done, carry out the operations described in paragraph 2.
18 Disconnect the battery negative lead.
19 Slacken the two bolts securing the tensioner pulley assembly to the engine, and the lower alternator mounting bolt.
20 Rotate the adjuster bolt to move the tensioner pulley away from the drivebelt, until there is sufficient slack for the drivebelt to be removed from the pulleys.

Refitting

21 Fit the belt around the pulleys, ensuring that the belt is of the correct type if it is being renewed, and take up the slack in the belt by tightening the adjuster bolt.
22 Tension the drivebelt as described in the following paragraphs.

Tensioning

23 If not already done, carry out the operations described in paragraph 2.
24 Correct tensioning of the drivebelt will ensure that it has a long life. Beware, however, of overtightening, as this can cause wear in the alternator bearings.
25 The belt should be tensioned so that, under firm thumb pressure, there is approximately 5.0 mm of free movement at the mid-point between the pulleys, on the longest belt run.
26 To adjust the tension, with the two tensioner pulley assembly retaining bolts and the lower alternator mounting bolt slackened, rotate the adjuster bolt until the correct tension is achieved. Once the belt is correctly tensioned, rotate the crankshaft through two complete turns, and recheck the tension.
27 When the belt is correctly tensioned, securely tighten the tensioner pulley assembly retaining bolts, and the lower alternator mounting bolt.
28 Reconnect the battery negative lead.
29 Clip the coolant hoses back in position, and secure with the retaining nut (where removed). Refit the roadwheel, and lower the vehicle to the ground.

22 Clutch adjustment check and control mechanism lubrication

1 Check that the clutch pedal moves smoothly and easily through its full travel, and that the clutch itself functions correctly, with no trace of slip or drag.
2 Adjust the clutch cable as described in Chapter 6.
3 If excessive effort is required to operate the clutch, check first that the cable is correctly routed and undamaged, then remove the pedal and check that its pivot is properly greased. Refer to Chapter 6 for further information.

23 Front brake pad check

1 Firmly apply the handbrake, then jack up the front of the car and support it securely on axle stands (see "Jacking, towing and wheel changing"). Remove the front roadwheels.
2 For a quick check, the thickness of friction material remaining on each brake pad can be measured through the aperture in the caliper body **(see illustration)**. If any pad's friction material is worn to the specified thickness or less, *all four pads must be renewed as a set.*
3 For a comprehensive check, the brake pads should be removed and cleaned. The operation of the caliper can then also be checked, and the condition of the brake disc itself can be fully examined on both sides. Refer to Chapter 9 for further information.

23.2 Brake pad friction material thickness (arrowed) can be checked with the pads in place - ATE type caliper shown

24 Handbrake check and adjustment

1 Chock the front wheels, then jack up the rear of the vehicle, and support securely on axle stands (see "Jacking, towing and wheel changing").
2 Apply the footbrake firmly several times to establish correct shoe-to-drum clearance, then apply and release the handbrake several times to ensure that the self-adjust mechanism has compensated fully for any wear in the linings.
3 Fully release the handbrake, and check that the rear wheels rotate freely, without binding. If not, check that all cables are routed correctly, and check that the cable components and levers move freely.

> **HAYNES HiNT** ***If the handbrake mechanism fails to operate, or appears to be seized on one side of the vehicle only, remove the relevant brake drum (see Chapter 9) and check the handbrake lever pivot on the trailing brake shoe - it is possible for the lever to seize due to corrosion. If necessary, remove the lever, and clean the contact faces of the lever, brake shoe, and pivot.***

4 If all components are free to move, but the wheels still bind when rotated, adjustment is required as follows.
5 Again, apply the footbrake several times to settle the shoes.
6 Ensure that the handbrake is fully released, then working under the vehicle, slacken the locknut and back off the adjuster ferrule on each outer cable where it enters the rear brake backplate. Back off the adjustment until the drums are free to rotate. To ensure correct operation of the handbrake, the ferrules should be in the same position on each rear brake backplate.
7 Inside the vehicle, apply the handbrake so that the lever is on its 4th notch up from the "off" position.
8 Tighten the adjuster ferrules equally on each outer cable until the brake shoes just rub on the drums (slight resistance as the wheels are rotated).
9 Check that there is a total handbrake lever travel of between 4 and 7 notches (the wheels should lock fully after a maximum 7 notches of handbrake lever movement).
10 Check that both the left- and right-hand rear cables move together when the handbrake is operated.
11 Fully release the handbrake, and check that both rear wheels turn freely by hand.

12 Tighten both locknuts and recheck the adjustment again.

13 Check that the handbrake warning light illuminates from approximately the 4th notch of handbrake lever travel.

14 On completion, lower the vehicle to the ground.

25 Road test

Instruments and electrical equipment

1 Check the operation of all instruments and electrical equipment.

2 Make sure that all instruments read correctly, and switch on all electrical equipment in turn to check that it functions properly.

Steering and suspension

3 Check for any abnormalities in the steering, suspension, handling or road "feel".

4 Drive the vehicle, and check that there are no unusual vibrations or noises.

5 Check that the steering feels positive, with no excessive "sloppiness", or roughness, and check for any suspension noises when cornering, or when driving over bumps.

Drivetrain

6 Check the performance of the engine, clutch, transmission and driveshafts.

7 Listen for any unusual noises from the engine, clutch and transmission.

8 Make sure that the engine runs smoothly when idling, and that there is no hesitation when accelerating.

9 Check that the clutch action is smooth and progressive, that the drive is taken up smoothly, and that the pedal travel is correct. Also listen for any noises when the clutch pedal is depressed.

10 Check that all gears can be engaged smoothly, without noise, and that the gear lever action is not abnormally vague or "notchy".

11 Listen for a metallic clicking sound from the front of the vehicle, as the vehicle is driven slowly in a circle with the steering on full lock. Carry out this check in both directions. If a clicking noise is heard, this indicates wear in a driveshaft joint, in which case, the complete driveshaft must be renewed (see Chapter 8).

Check the operation and performance of the braking system

12 Make sure that the vehicle does not pull to one side when braking, and that the wheels do not lock prematurely when braking hard.

13 Check that there is no vibration through the steering when braking.

14 Check that the handbrake operates correctly, without excessive movement of the lever, and that it holds the vehicle stationary on a slope.

15 Test the operation of the brake servo unit (where fitted) as follows. With the engine off, depress the footbrake four or five times to exhaust the vacuum. Start the engine, holding the brake pedal depressed. As the engine starts, there should be a noticeable "give" in the brake pedal as vacuum builds up. Allow the engine to run for at least two minutes, and then switch it off. If the brake pedal is depressed now, it should be possible to detect a hiss from the servo as the pedal is depressed. After about four or five applications, no further hissing should be heard.

Every 18 000 miles / 30 000 km

26 Hinge and lock lubrication

1 Work around the vehicle, and lubricate the hinges of the bonnet, doors and tailgate with a light machine oil.

2 Lightly lubricate the bonnet release mechanism and exposed section of inner cable with a smear of grease.

3 Check carefully the security and operation of all hinges, latches and locks, adjusting them where required. Check the operation of the central locking system (if fitted).

4 Check the condition and operation of the tailgate struts, renewing them if either is leaking or no longer able to support the tailgate securely when raised.

Every 24 000 miles / 40 000 km

27 Air filter renewal

Carburettor models

1 Slacken the retaining clips (where fitted) and disconnect the vacuum and breather hoses from the front of the air cleaner housing-to-carburettor duct. Where crimped-type hose clips or ties are fitted, cut and discard them; replace them with standard worm-drive hose clips or new cable ties on refitting.

2 Slacken the retaining clips, then lift the duct off the top of the carburettor and air cleaner housing. Disconnect the air temperature control valve hose from the end of the duct, and remove the duct from the engine compartment **(see illustration)**. Recover the rubber sealing ring(s) from the top of the carburettor and/or air cleaner housing (as applicable).

3 Release the retaining clips securing the lid to the top of the air cleaner housing. Lift the lid away from the housing, and recover the sealing ring. On some models, the air cleaner element is attached to the cover **(see illustration)**; on other models it will be necessary to twist the lid to release it. Inspect the sealing ring for signs of damage or deterioration, and renew if necessary.

4 Where the air filter element is not an integral part of the cover, lift the element out of the housing **(see illustration)**. Fit the new element, making sure it is correctly positioned in the housing.

5 Fit the sealing ring to the housing, then refit the cover and secure it in position with the retaining clips.

27.2 Removing the air cleaner duct assembly

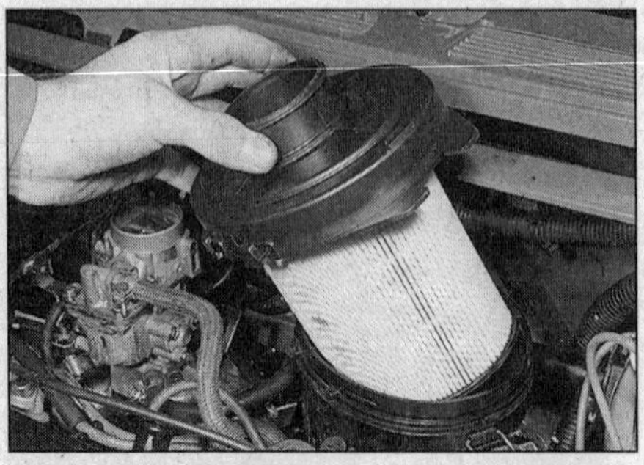

27.3 Removing the air cleaner cover - type with integral element

27.4 Removing the air cleaner element - type separate from the cover

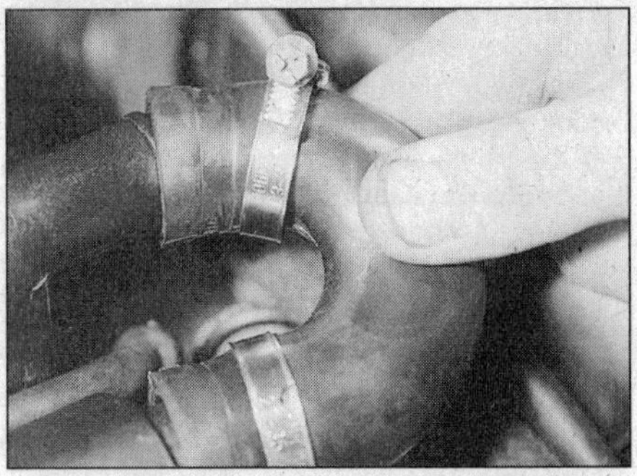
27.15 On 1360 cc Diesel models, slacken the retaining clip and disconnect the breather hose from the air cleaner cover

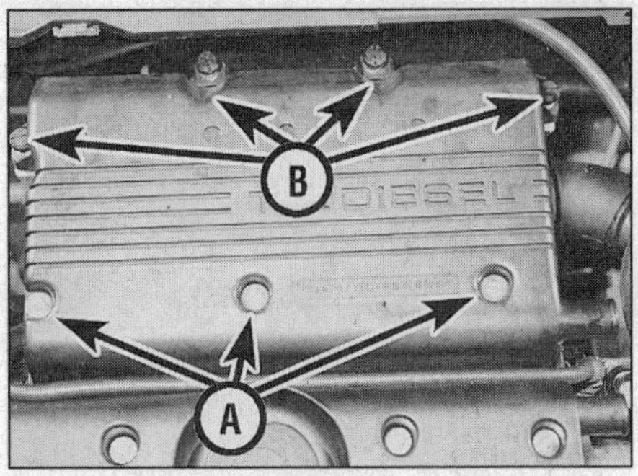

27.16a Air cleaner cover retaining screws (A) and quick-release fasteners (B)

27.16b Lift off the cover . . .

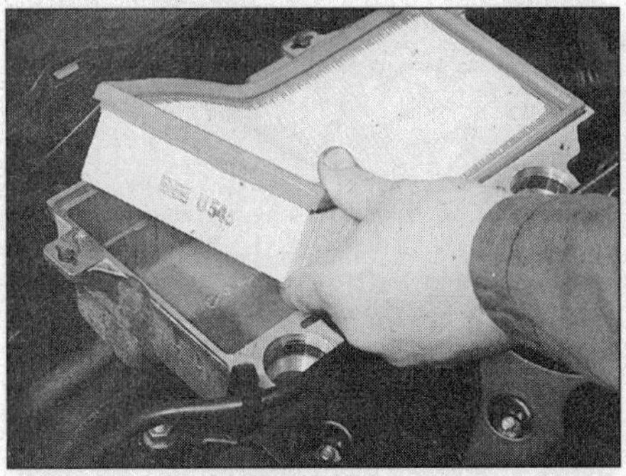
27.17a . . . and withdraw the element from the inlet manifold

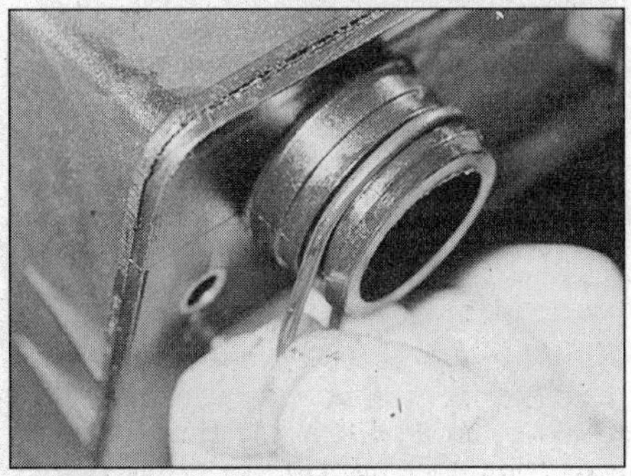
27.17b Check the air cleaner cover O-rings for signs of damage, and renew if necessary

6 Refit the air cleaner-to-carburettor duct assembly. Ensure that the duct is correctly seated on its sealing rings, and securely tighten its retaining clips.
7 Reconnect the vacuum and breather hoses to the duct, and secure them in position with the retaining clips (where fitted).

Single-point petrol injection models

8 Refer to the information given in paragraphs 1 to 7.

Multi-point petrol injection models

9 Slacken the retaining clip, and disconnect the intake duct from the air cleaner housing lid.
10 Release the retaining clips (where fitted), then unclip the lid and position it clear of the housing.
11 Recover the sealing ring from the top of the filter housing, and lift the element out of the housing. Inspect the sealing ring for signs of damage or deterioration, and renew if necessary.
12 Fit the new element, making sure it is correctly seated in the housing.
13 Refit the sealing ring to the top of the housing, and securely refit the housing lid. Where necessary, secure the lid in position with its retaining clips.
14 Reconnect the intake duct, and securely tighten its retaining clip.

1360 cc Diesel models

15 Slacken the retaining clip, and disconnect the breather hose from the left-hand end of the air cleaner cover **(see illustration)**.
16 Slacken and remove the three retaining screws from the front of the air cleaner housing cover. Work around the cover, undoing all its quick-release fasteners, then lift off the cover, noting the four sealing rings **(see illustrations)**.
17 Lift out the filter element, noting which way around it is fitted. Inspect the cover sealing rings for signs of damage or deterioration, and renew as necessary **(see illustrations)**.
18 Fit the new filter element, ensuring that it is correctly seated in the inlet manifold.
19 Ensure that each sealing ring is correctly seated in its recess in the cover, then refit the cover to the manifold.
20 Secure the cover in position with its quick-release fasteners, then refit the three retaining screws and tighten them securely.

1527 cc Diesel models

21 At the time of writing, no information was available.

28 Rear brake shoe check

1 Remove the rear brake drums, and check the brake shoes for signs of wear or contamination. At the same time, also inspect the wheel cylinders for signs of leakage, and the brake drum for signs of wear. Refer to the relevant Sections of Chapter 9 for further information.

29 Brake fluid renewal

Warning: Brake hydraulic fluid can harm your eyes and damage painted surfaces, so use extreme caution when handling and pouring it. Do not use fluid that has been standing open for some time, as it absorbs moisture from the air. Excess moisture can cause a dangerous loss of braking effectiveness.

1 The procedure is similar to that for bleeding the hydraulic system as described in Chapter 9, except that allowance should be made for all the old fluid to be expelled when bleeding a section of the circuit.
2 The brake fluid reservoir should first be emptied of old fluid by syphoning, using a clean poultry baster, syringe, or similar, then refilled with fresh fluid. Do not operate the brakes while the reservoir is being emptied, or air will be drawn into the system.
3 Working as described in Chapter 9, open the first bleed screw in the sequence, and pump the brake pedal gently until nearly all the fluid has been emptied from the reservoir. Top-up to the "MAX" level with new fluid, and continue pumping until only new fluid can be seen emerging from the bleed screw. Old hydraulic fluid is invariably much darker in colour than the new, making it easy to distinguish the two. Tighten the screw, and top the reservoir level up to the "MAX" level line.
4 Work through all the remaining bleed screws in the sequence until new fluid can be seen at all of them. Be careful to keep the master cylinder reservoir topped-up to above the "MIN" level at all times, or air may enter the system and greatly increase the length of the task.
5 When the operation is complete, check that all bleed screws are securely tightened, and that their dust caps are refitted. Wash off all traces of spilt fluid, and recheck the master cylinder reservoir fluid level.
6 Check the operation of the brakes before taking the car on the road.

Every 36 000 miles / 60 000 km

30 Manual transmission oil level check

Note: *A suitable square-section wrench may be required to undo the transmission filler/level plug on some models. These wrenches can be obtained from most motor factors, or from your Citroën dealer.*

1 Park the car on a level surface.

2 Wipe clean the area around the filler/level plug, which is situated on the left-hand end of the transmission **(see illustration)**. Unscrew the plug and clean it; discard the sealing washer.

3 The oil level should reach the lower edge of the filler/level hole. A certain amount of oil will have gathered behind the filler/level plug, and will trickle out when it is removed; this does **not** necessarily indicate that the level is correct.

HAYNES HiNT

To ensure that a true level is established, wait until the initial trickle has stopped, then add oil as necessary until a trickle of new oil can be seen emerging. The level will be correct when the flow ceases; use only good-quality oil of the specified type.

4 Filling the transmission with oil is an extremely awkward operation; above all, allow plenty of time for the oil level to settle properly before checking it.

5 If the transmission has been overfilled so that oil flows out as soon as the filler/level plug is removed, check that the car is completely level (front-to-rear and side-to-side), and allow the surplus to drain off into a suitable container.

6 When the level is correct, fit a new sealing washer to the filler/level plug. Refit the plug, tightening it to the specified torque wrench setting. Wash off any spilt oil.

Every 48 000 miles / 80 000 km

31 Fuel filter renewal - fuel-injected petrol models

Warning: Before carrying out the following operation, refer to the precautions given in "Safety first!" at the beginning of this manual, and follow them implicitly. Petrol is a highly-dangerous and volatile liquid, and the precautions necessary when handling it cannot be overstressed.

1 The fuel filter is located underneath the rear of the vehicle, on the left-hand side of the fuel tank. To gain access to the filter, chock the front wheels, then jack up the rear of the vehicle and support it on axle stands.

2 Depressurise the fuel system, with reference to Chapter 4B or 4C as applicable.

3 Unclip the filter retaining strap from the underbody or left-hand side of the fuel tank as applicable **(see illustration)**.

4 Noting the direction of the fuel flow arrow marked on the filter body, release the retaining clips and disconnect the fuel hoses from the filter **(see illustration)**. Where the original Citroën crimped-type clips are still fitted, cut and discard them; replace them with standard worm-drive hose clips on installation.

5 Remove the filter from the vehicle. Dispose safely of the old filter; it will be highly inflammable, and may explode if thrown on a fire.

6 Slide the new filter into position, ensuring that the arrow on the filter body is pointing in the direction of the fuel flow, as noted when removing the old filter. The flow direction can otherwise be determined by tracing the fuel hoses back along their length.

7 Connect the fuel hoses to the filter, securing them in position with their retaining clips, then clip the filter strap back onto the fuel tank or underbody as applicable.

8 Start the engine, check the filter hose connections for leaks, then lower the vehicle to the ground.

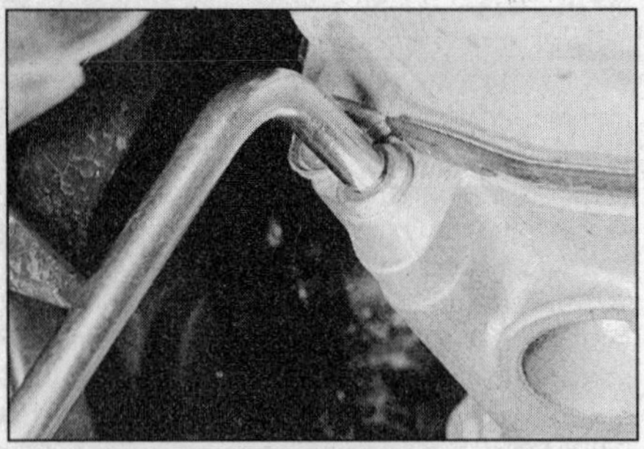

30.2 Using the square-section wrench to unscrew the transmission filler/level plug

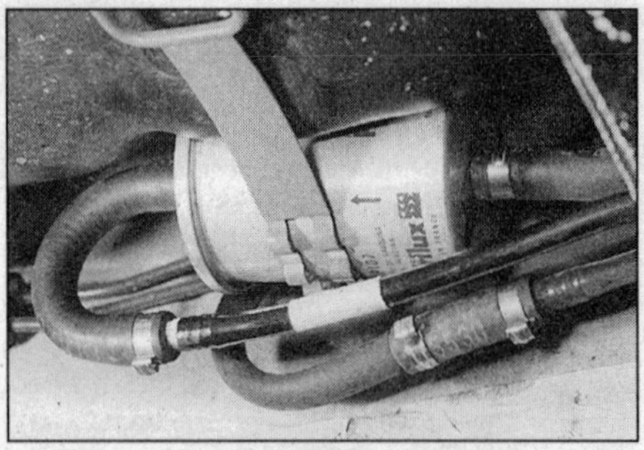

31.3 Fuel filter location on the side of the fuel tank

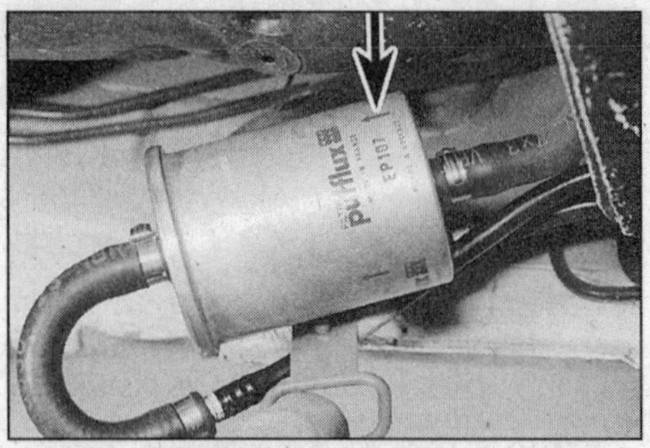

31.4 Release the strap and disconnect the hoses to remove the fuel filter. Note the direction of the arrow on the filter body (arrowed)

Every 72 000 miles / 120 000 km

32 Timing belt renewal

Refer to the relevant Part of Chapter 2.

Every 2 years

33 Coolant renewal

Warning: Wait until the engine is cold before starting this procedure. Do not allow antifreeze to come in contact with your skin, or with the painted surfaces of the vehicle. Rinse off spills immediately with plenty of water. Never leave antifreeze lying around in an open container, or in a puddle in the driveway or on the garage floor. Children and pets are attracted by its sweet smell, but antifreeze can be fatal if ingested.

Cooling system draining

1 With the engine completely cold, remove the expansion tank filler cap. Turn the cap anti-clockwise until it reaches the first stop. Wait until any pressure remaining in the system is

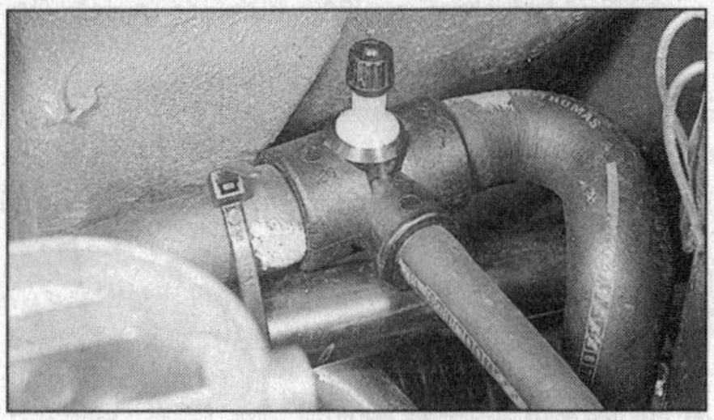

33.4a Bleed screw location in the heater hose connector near the engine compartment bulkhead on an early 1124 cc (H1A engine) carburettor model

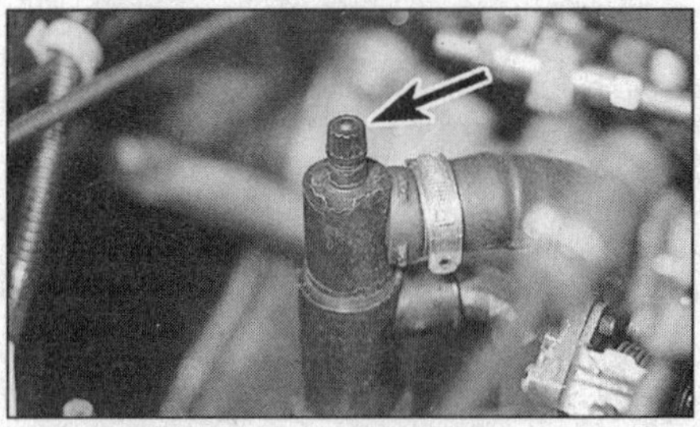

33.4b Bleed screw location (arrowed) in the heater return hose on a later 1124 cc (H1A engine) carburettor model

33.6 Cylinder block drain plug location (arrowed)

released, then push the cap down, turn it anti-clockwise to the second stop, and lift it off.

2 Position a suitable container beneath the lower left-hand side of the radiator.

3 Loosen the radiator drain plug (where applicable) and allow the coolant to drain into the container. On models not fitted with a drain plug, it will be necessary to disconnect the bottom hose from the radiator.

4 To assist draining, open the cooling system bleed screws. These are located in the top of the left-hand radiator tank (except Diesel models), in the heater hose connector near the engine compartment bulkhead **(see illustrations)**, and on the thermostat housing at the left-hand end of the cylinder head. Refer to the illustrations in Chapter 3 for the exact location of the bleed points. On some models, it may be necessary to unscrew the temperature sender from the top of the thermostat housing.

5 When the flow of coolant stops, reposition the container below the cylinder block drain plug, located at the front left-hand corner of the cylinder block.

6 Remove the drain plug, and allow the coolant to drain into the container **(see illustration)**.

7 If the coolant has been drained for a reason other than renewal, then provided it is clean and less than two years old, it can be re-used.

8 Refit the radiator bottom hose or drain plug (as applicable), and the cylinder block drain plug on completion of draining.

Cooling system flushing

9 If coolant renewal has been neglected, or if the antifreeze mixture has become diluted, then in time, the cooling system may gradually lose efficiency, as the coolant passages become restricted due to rust, scale deposits, and other sediment. The cooling system efficiency can be restored by flushing the system clean.

10 The radiator should be flushed independently of the engine, to avoid unnecessary contamination.

Radiator flushing

11 To flush the radiator, first tighten the radiator drain plug and the radiator bleed screw, as applicable.

12 Disconnect the top and bottom hoses from the radiator. On models with a remote expansion tank, also disconnect the expansion tank hose from the right-hand side of the radiator.

13 Insert a garden hose into the radiator top inlet. Direct a flow of clean water through the radiator, and continue flushing until clean water emerges from the radiator bottom outlet.

14 If after a reasonable period, the water still does not run clear, the radiator can be flushed with a good proprietary cleaning agent. It is important that their manufacturer's instructions are followed carefully. If the contamination is particularly bad, remove the radiator, then insert the hose in the radiator bottom outlet, and reverse-flush the radiator.

Engine flushing

15 To flush the engine, first refit the cylinder block drain plug, and tighten the cooling system bleed screws.

16 Remove the thermostat as described in Chapter 3, then temporarily refit the thermostat cover.

17 With the top and bottom hoses disconnected from the radiator, insert a garden hose into the radiator top hose. Direct a clean flow of water through the engine, and continue flushing until clean water emerges from the radiator bottom hose.

18 On completion of flushing, refit the thermostat and reconnect the hoses with reference to Chapter 3.

Cooling system filling

19 Before attempting to fill the cooling system, make sure that all hoses and clips are in good condition, and that the clips are tight. Note that an antifreeze mixture must be used all year round, to prevent corrosion of the engine components (see following sub-Section). Also check that the radiator and cylinder block drain plugs are in place and tight.

20 Remove the expansion tank filler cap.

21 Open all the cooling system bleed screws (see paragraph 4).

22 Some of the cooling system hoses are positioned at a higher level than the top of the radiator expansion tank. It is therefore necessary to use a "header tank" when refilling the cooling system, to eliminate the possibility of air being trapped in the system.

> **HAYNES HiNT** ***Although Citroën dealers use a special header tank, the same effect can be achieved by using a suitable bottle or plastic container sealed to the expansion tank filler neck.***

23 Fit the "header tank" to the expansion tank. Slowly fill the system. Coolant will emerge from each of the bleed screws in turn, starting with the lowest screw. As soon as coolant free from air bubbles emerges from the lowest screw, tighten that screw, and watch the next bleed screw in the system. Repeat the procedure on the remaining bleed screws. Note that the bleed screws should be tightened in the following order:

a) Radiator bleed screw (petrol models only).
b) Thermostat housing bleed screw.
c) Heater hose bleed screw.

24 Ensure that the "header tank" is full (at least 0.5 litres of coolant). Start the engine, and run it at a fast idle speed (do not exceed 2000 rpm) until the cooling fan cuts in, and then cuts out. Stop the engine.

25 Remove the "header tank", taking great care not to scald yourself with the hot coolant, then fit the expansion tank cap.

26 Allow the engine to cool, then check the coolant level with reference to Section 3 of this Chapter. Top-up the level if necessary.

Antifreeze mixture

27 The antifreeze should always be renewed at the specified intervals. This is necessary not only to maintain the antifreeze properties, but also to prevent corrosion which would otherwise occur as the corrosion inhibitors become progressively less effective.

28 Always use an ethylene-glycol based antifreeze which is suitable for use in mixed-metal cooling systems. The quantity of antifreeze and levels of protection are indicated in the Specifications.

29 Before adding antifreeze, the cooling system should be completely drained, preferably flushed, and all hoses checked for condition and security.

30 After filling with antifreeze, a label should be attached to the expansion tank filler neck, stating the type and concentration of antifreeze used, and the date installed. Any subsequent topping-up should be made with the same type and concentration of antifreeze.

31 Do not use engine antifreeze in the windscreen/tailgate washer system, as it will cause damage to the vehicle paintwork. Instead, a screenwash additive should be added to the washer system in the quantities stated on the bottle.

Cooling system

Antifreeze mixture:	
28% antifreeze	Protection down to -15°C (5°F)
50% antifreeze	Protection down to -30°C (-22°F)

Note: *Refer to antifreeze manufacturer for latest recommendations.*

Fuel system - petrol models

Idle speed:	
Carburettor models	750 rpm
Fuel-injected models*:	
Single-point injection models	850 ± 50 rpm (not adjustable - controlled by ECU)
Multi-point injection models	880 ± 50 rpm (not adjustable - controlled by ECU)
Idle mixture CO content:	
Carburettor models*:	
954 and 1124 cc models	0.8 to 1.2 %
1360 cc models	0.5 to 2.0 %
Fuel-injected models*:	
1360 cc (K6B engine) models	1.0 ± 0.5 % (adjustable via mixture potentiometer)
All other models	Less than 1.0 % (not adjustable - controlled by ECU)

***Note:** *See the relevant Part of Chapter 4 for further information.*

Fuel system - Diesel models

Idle speed	775 ± 25 rpm
Anti-stall speed (with 1 mm shim/feeler blade inserted)	1600 ± 50 rpm

Ignition system - petrol models

Ignition timing	Refer to Chapter 5B	
Spark plugs:	**Type**	**Electrode gap***
954 cc models to July 1995, and all 1124 cc models	Champion RC9YCC	0.8 mm
954 cc models from July 1995 onwards	Champion RC10DMC	Not adjustable
1360 cc models except GT/GTi	Champion RC9YCC	0.8 mm
1360 cc GT models	Champion RC7YCC	0.8 mm
1360 cc GTi models	Champion RC7BMC	Not adjustable
Ignition HT lead resistance	Approximately 600 ohms per 100 mm length	

**The spark plug gap quoted is that recommended by Champion for their specified plugs listed above. If spark plugs of any other type are to be fitted, refer to their manufacturer's recommendations.*

Brakes

Brake pad friction material minimum thickness	2.0 mm
Brake shoe friction material minimum thickness	1.0 mm

Tyres

Tyre size (depending on model)	135/70 R 13 T, 145/70 R 13 S, 145/70 R 13 T, 155/70 R 13 S, 155/70 R 13 T, 165/65 R 13 S, 165/65 R 13 H, 165/65 R 13 T or 185/60 R 13 H	
Pressures (tyres cold) - psi (bar):	**Front**	**Rear**
135/70 R 13 T (Except Entreprise)	29 (2.0)	29 (2.0)
135/70 R 13 T (Entreprise)	33 (2.3)	38 (2.6)
145/70 R 13 S	30 (2.1)	30 (2.1)
145/70 R 13 T (Except Entreprise)	29 (2.0)	29 (2.0)
145/70 R 13 T (Entreprise)	30 (2.1)	33 (2.3)
155/70 R 13 S (carburettor models)	29 (2.0)	29 (2.0)
155/70 R 13 S (fuel-injected models)	31 (2.1)	31 (2.1)
155/70 R 13 T	29 (2.0)	29 (2.0)
165/65 R 13 S	29 (2.0)	29 (2.0)
165/65 R 13 H	28 (1.9)	28 (1.9)
165/65 R 13 T	28 (1.9)	29 (2.0)
185/60 R 13 H	28 (1.9)	28 (1.9)

Note: *Pressures apply only to original-equipment tyres, and may vary if any other make or type is fitted; check with the tyre manufacturer or supplier for correct pressures if necessary. Pressures should be increased by apporximately 3.0 psi (0.2 bars) on long journeys with 5 persons.*

Torque wrench settings

	Nm	**lbf ft**
Spark plugs	25	18
Transmission filler/level and drain plugs	25	18
Roadwheel bolts	90	66

Chapter 2 Part A: Petrol engine in-car repair procedures

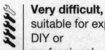

Contents

Degrees of difficulty

Easy, suitable for novice with little experience	**Fairly easy,** suitable for beginner with some experience	**Fairly difficult,** suitable for competent DIY mechanic	**Difficult,** suitable for experienced DIY mechanic	**Very difficult,** suitable for expert DIY or professional

Specifications

General

Designation:	
954 cc engine	TU9
1124 cc engine	TU1
1360 cc engine	TU3
Engine codes*:	
954 cc carburettor engine	C1A
954 cc fuel-injected engine	CDZ and CDY
1124 cc carburettor engine	H1A and H1B
1124 cc fuel-injected engine	HDZ and HDY
1360 cc carburettor engine	K1A, K1G, K2A and K2D (TU3 F/2/K)
1360 cc fuel-injected engine with a distributor	KDY and KDZ
1360 cc fuel-injected engine with distributorless ignition system	KDX
1360 cc fuel-injected engine with DME Motronic system (GTi)	K6B (TU3 FJ2/K) and KFZ (TU3 FJ2/Z)
No 1 cylinder location	Flywheel/transmission end of block
Direction of crankshaft rotation	Clockwise (viewed from right-hand side of vehicle)
Firing order	1-3-4-2
Bore:	
954 cc engine	70.00 mm
1124 cc engine	72.00 mm
1360 cc engine	75.00 mm
Stroke:	
954 cc engine	62.00 mm
1124 cc engine	69.00 mm
1360 cc engine	77.00 mm

Compression ratio:	
954 cc engine	9.4 : 1
1124 cc engine	9.4 : 1
1360 cc engine	9.3 : 1
1360 cc engine (GTi)	9.6 : 1
Maximum power (DIN):	
954 cc engine	50 bhp (37.3 kW) @ 6000 rpm
1124 cc engine	60 bhp (44.1 kW) @ 6200 rpm
1360 cc engine (except GT/Forté and GTi)	75 bhp (55 kW) @ 5800 rpm
1360 cc engine (GT/Forté)	85 bhp (63 kW) @ 6400 rpm
1360 cc engine (GTi)	100 bhp (75 kW) @ 6800 rpm
Maximum torque (DIN):	
954 cc engine	74 Nm (54.6 lbf ft) @ 3700 rpm
1124 cc engine	90 Nm (66.4 lbf ft) @ 3800 rpm
1360 cc engine (except GT/Forté and GTi)	113 Nm (83.4 lbf ft) @ 3400 rpm
1360 cc engine (GT/Forté)	115 Nm (85 lbf ft) @ 3800 rpm
1360 cc engine (GTi)	123 Nm (90.4 lbf ft) @ 4200 rpm

**The engine code is situated on the left-hand end of the cylinder block, either stamped on a plate which is riveted to the block (aluminium block engines) or stamped directly on the cylinder block (cast-iron block engines). The code given in brackets is the factory identification number, and is not often referred to by Citroën or this manual.*

Camshaft

Drive method	Toothed belt
Number of bearings	5
Camshaft bearing journal diameter (outside diameter):	
No 1	36.950 to 36.925 mm
No 2	40.650 to 40.625 mm
No 3	1.250 to 41.225 mm
No 4	1.850 to 41.825 mm
No 5	2.450 to 42.425 mm
Cylinder head bearing journal diameter (inside diameter):	
No 1	7.000 to 37.039 mm
No 2	0.700 to 47.739 mm
No 3	1.300 to 41.339 mm
No 4	1.900 to 41.939 mm
No 5	2.500 to 42.539 mm

Valve clearances (engine cold)

Inlet valves	0.20 mm
Exhaust valves	0.40 mm

Lubrication system

Oil pump type	Gear-type, chain-driven off the crankshaft
Minimum oil pressure at 90°C	4 bars at 4000 rpm
Oil pressure warning switch operating pressure	0.5 bars

Torque wrench settings

	Nm	lbf ft
Cylinder head cover nuts	16	12
Timing belt cover bolts	8	6
Crankshaft pulley retaining bolts	8	6
Timing belt tensioner pulley nut	23	17
Camshaft sprocket retaining bolt	80	59
Crankshaft sprocket retaining bolt	110	81
Camshaft thrust fork retaining bolt	16	12
Cylinder head bolts (aluminium block engine):		
Stage 1	20	15
Stage 2	Angle-tighten through 240°	Angle-tighten through 240°
Cylinder head bolts (cast-iron block engine):		
Stage 1	20	15
Stage 2	Angle-tighten through 120°	Angle-tighten through 120°
Stage 3	Angle-tighten through 120°	Angle-tighten through 120°
Sump drain plug	30	22
Sump retaining nuts and bolts	8	6
Oil pump retaining bolts	8	6
Flywheel retaining bolts	65	48
Big-end bearing cap nuts	40	30

Main bearing ladder casting (aluminium block engine):		
11 mm bolts:		
Stage 1	20	15
Stage 2	Angle-tighten through 45°	Angle-tighten through 45°
6 mm bolts	8	6
Main bearing cap bolts (cast-iron block engine):		
Stage 1	20	15
Stage 2	Angle-tighten through 45°	Angle-tighten through 45°
Engine/transmission right-hand mounting:		
Mounting bracket retaining nuts to bracket on rear of cylinder block:		
Aluminium block engine	50	37
Cast-iron block engine	45	33
Mounting bracket retaining nut-to-body:		
Aluminium block engine	35	26
Cast-iron block engine	70	52
Engine/transmission left-hand mounting:		
Mounting bracket-to-transmission nuts	18	13
Mounting bracket-to-body bolts	17	13
Centre bolt	50	37
Engine/transmission rear mounting:		
Mounting assembly-to-block bolts	40	30
Mounting bracket-to-mounting bolt	60	44
Mounting bracket-to-subframe bolt	90	66

1 General information

How to use this Chapter

This Part of Chapter 2 describes those repair procedures that can reasonably be carried out on the TU series petrol engine while it remains in the car. If the engine has been removed from the car and is being dismantled as described in Part C, any preliminary dismantling procedures can be ignored.

Note that, while it may be possible physically to overhaul items such as the piston/connecting rod assemblies while the engine is in the car, such tasks are not normally carried out as separate operations. Usually, several additional procedures (not to mention the cleaning of components and of oilways) have to be carried out. For this reason, all such tasks are classed as major overhaul procedures, and are described in Part C of this Chapter.

Part C describes the removal of the engine/transmission unit from the vehicle, and the full overhaul procedures that can then be carried out.

Engine description

The TU series engine is a well-proven engine which has been fitted to many previous Citroën and Peugeot vehicles. The engine is of the in-line four-cylinder, overhead camshaft (OHC) type, mounted transversely at the front of the car **(see illustration)**. The clutch and transmission are attached to its left-hand end. The AX range is fitted with 954 cc, 1124 cc and 1360 cc versions of the engine, with either carburettor or fuel injection. The 1360 cc engine is available in both aluminium and cast-iron cylinder block versions.

The crankshaft runs in five main bearings. Thrustwashers are fitted to No 2 main bearing (upper half) to control crankshaft endfloat.

The connecting rods rotate on horizontally-split bearing shells at their big-ends. The pistons are attached to the connecting rods by gudgeon pins, which are an interference fit in the connecting rod small-end eyes. The aluminium-alloy pistons are fitted with three piston rings - two compression rings and an oil control ring.

On aluminium block engines, the cylinder bores have replaceable wet liners. Sealing O-rings are fitted at the base of each liner, to prevent the escape of coolant into the sump.

On 1360 cc cast-iron block engines (K2D, K6B and KFZ) the cylinder bores are an integral part of the cylinder block. On this type of engine, the cylinder bores are sometimes referred to as having "dry liners".

The inlet and exhaust valves are each closed by coil springs, and operate in guides pressed into the cylinder head; the valve seat inserts are also pressed into the cylinder head, and can be renewed separately if worn.

The camshaft is driven by a toothed timing belt, and operates the eight valves via rocker arms. Valve clearances are adjusted by a screw-and-locknut arrangement. The camshaft rotates directly in the cylinder head. The timing belt also drives the coolant pump.

Lubrication is by means of an oil pump, which is driven (via a chain and sprocket) off the right-hand end of the crankshaft. It draws oil through a strainer located in the sump, and then forces it through an externally-mounted filter into galleries in the cylinder block/crankcase. From there, the oil is distributed to the crankshaft (main bearings)

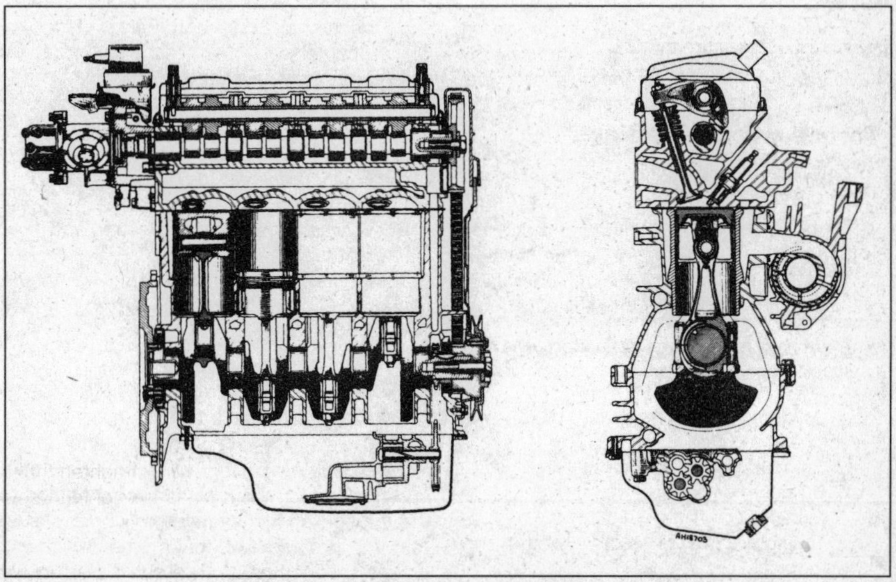

1.4 Sectional views of a typical TU petrol engine

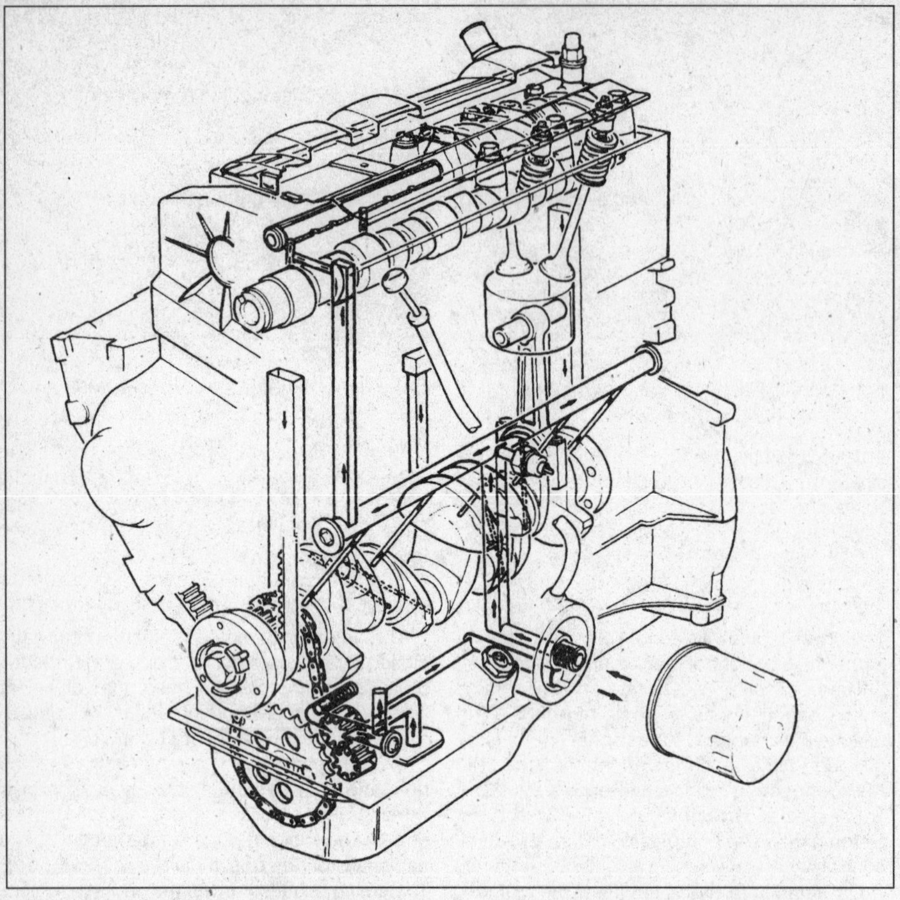

1.11 Lubrication system of the TU series engine (aluminium block type shown)

1.12 Engine code is stamped on a plate (arrowed) attached to the front of the aluminium cylinder block

and camshaft. The big-end bearings are supplied with oil via internal drillings in the crankshaft, while the camshaft bearings also receive a pressurised supply. The camshaft lobes and valves are lubricated by splash, as are all other engine components **(see illustration)**.

Throughout this manual, it is often necessary to identify the engines not only by their capacity, but also by their engine code. This can be found on the left-hand end of the front face of the cylinder block. On models with an aluminium cylinder block, the code is stamped on a plate which is riveted to the block; on models with a cast-iron cylinder block, the number is stamped on a machined surface on the cylinder block, at the flywheel end. The first part of the engine number gives the engine code - eg "KDY" **(see illustration)**.

Repair operations possible with the engine in the car

The following work can be carried out with the engine in the car:

a) Compression pressure - testing.
b) Cylinder head cover - removal and refitting.
c) Timing belt covers - removal and refitting.
d) Timing belt - removal, refitting and adjustment.
e) Timing belt tensioner and sprockets - removal and refitting.
f) Camshaft oil seal - renewal.
g) Camshaft and rocker arms - removal, inspection and refitting.*
h) Cylinder head - removal and refitting.
i) Cylinder head and pistons - decarbonising (refer to Part C of this Chapter).
j) Sump - removal and refitting.
k) Oil pump - removal, inspection and refitting.
l) Crankshaft oil seals - renewal.
m) Engine/transmission mountings - inspection and renewal.
n) Flywheel - removal, inspection and refitting.

**The cylinder head must be removed for the successful completion of this work. Refer to Section 10 for details.*

2 Compression test - description and interpretation

1 When engine performance is down, or if misfiring occurs which cannot be attributed to the ignition or fuel systems, a compression test can provide diagnostic clues as to the engine's condition. If the test is performed regularly, it can give warning of trouble before any other symptoms become apparent.

2 The engine must be fully warmed-up to normal operating temperature, the battery must be fully charged, and all the spark plugs must be removed (Chapter 1). The aid of an assistant will also be required.

3 On models with a distributor, disable the ignition system by disconnecting the ignition HT coil lead from the distributor cap and earthing it on the cylinder block. Use a jumper lead or similar wire to make a good connection.

4 On models with a static (distributorless) ignition system, disable the ignition system by disconnecting the LT wiring connector from the ignition HT coil(s), referring to Chapter 5B for further information.

5 Fit a compression tester to the No 1 cylinder spark plug hole - the type of tester which screws into the plug thread is to be preferred. No 1 cylinder is at the transmission end of the block.

6 Have the assistant hold the throttle wide open, and crank the engine on the starter motor. After one or two revolutions, the compression pressure should build up to a maximum figure, and then stabilise. Record the highest reading obtained.

7 Repeat the test on the remaining cylinders, recording the pressure in each.

8 All cylinders should produce very similar pressures; a difference of more than 2 bars between any two cylinders indicates a fault. Note that the compression should build up quickly in a healthy engine; low compression on the first stroke, followed by gradually-increasing pressure on successive strokes, indicates worn piston rings. A low compression reading on the first stroke, which does not build up during successive strokes, indicates leaking valves or a blown head gasket (a cracked head could also be the cause). Deposits on the undersides of the valve heads can also cause low compression.

9 Although Citroën do not specify exact compression pressures, as a guide, any cylinder pressure of below 10 bars can be considered as less than healthy. Refer to a Citroën dealer or other specialist if in doubt as to whether a particular pressure reading is acceptable.

10 If the pressure in any cylinder is low, carry out the following test to isolate the cause.

Introduce a teaspoonful of clean oil into that cylinder through its spark plug hole, and repeat the test.

11 If the addition of oil temporarily improves the compression pressure, this indicates that bore or piston wear is responsible for the pressure loss. No improvement suggests that leaking or burnt valves, or a blown head gasket, may be to blame.

12 A low reading from two adjacent cylinders is almost certainly due to the head gasket having blown between them; the presence of coolant in the engine oil, or vice-versa, will confirm this.

13 If one cylinder is about 20 percent lower than the others and the engine has a slightly rough idle, a worn camshaft lobe could be the cause.

14 If the compression reading is unusually high, the combustion chambers are probably coated with carbon deposits. If this is the case, the cylinder head should be removed and decarbonised.

15 On completion of the test, refit the spark plugs and reconnect the ignition system.

3 Top dead centre (TDC) for No 1 piston - locating

Note: *Do not attempt to rotate the engine whilst the crankshaft/camshaft are locked in position. If the engine is to be left in this state for a long period of time, it is a good idea to place warning notices inside the vehicle, and in the engine compartment. This will reduce the possibility of the engine being accidentally cranked on the starter motor, which is likely to cause damage with the locking tools in place.*

1 On all models, timing holes are drilled in the camshaft sprocket and in the flywheel. The holes are used to ensure that the crankshaft and camshaft are correctly positioned when assembling the engine (to prevent the possibility of the valves contacting the pistons when refitting the cylinder head), or when refitting the timing belt. When the timing holes are aligned with access holes in the cylinder head and the front of the cylinder block, suitable diameter tools can be inserted to lock both the camshaft and crankshaft in position, preventing them from rotating. Proceed as follows. **Note:** *With the timing holes aligned, No 1 cylinder is at TDC on its compression stroke. No 1 cylinder is at the transmission end of the cylinder block.*

3.4 Insert a 6 mm bolt (arrowed) through hole in cylinder block flange and into timing hole in the flywheel . . .

2 Remove the timing belt upper cover, as described in Section 5.

3 The crankshaft must now be turned until the timing hole in the camshaft sprocket is aligned with the corresponding hole in the cylinder head. The holes are aligned when the camshaft sprocket hole is in the 2 o'clock position, when viewed from the right-hand end of the engine. The crankshaft can be turned by using a spanner on the crankshaft sprocket bolt, noting that it should always be rotated in a clockwise direction (viewed from the right-hand end of the engine).

HAYNES HiNT *Turning the crankshaft will be much easier if the spark plugs are removed first (see Chapter 1).*

4 With the camshaft sprocket hole correctly positioned, insert a 6 mm diameter bolt, or drill bit, through the hole in the front, left-hand flange of the cylinder block, and locate it in the timing hole in the flywheel **(see illustration)**. Note that it may be necessary to rotate the crankshaft slightly, to get the holes to align.

3.5 . . . then insert a 10 mm bolt through the camshaft sprocket timing hole, and locate it in the cylinder head

5 With the flywheel correctly positioned, insert a 10 mm diameter bolt, or drill bit, through the timing hole in the camshaft sprocket, and locate it in the hole in the cylinder head **(see illustration)**.

6 The crankshaft and camshaft are now locked in position, preventing unnecessary rotation.

4 Cylinder head cover - removal and refitting

Removal

1 Disconnect the battery negative lead.

2 Where necessary, undo the bolts securing the HT lead retaining clips to the rear of the cylinder head cover, and position the clips clear of the cover.

3 Slacken the retaining clip, and disconnect the breather hose from the left-hand end of the cylinder head cover **(see illustration)**. Where the original crimped-type Citroën hose clip is fitted, cut it off and discard it. Use a standard worm-drive clip on refitting.

4 Undo the two retaining nuts, and remove the washer from each of the cylinder head cover studs **(see illustration)**.

5 Lift off the cylinder head cover, and remove it along with its rubber seal **(see illustration)**. Examine the seal for signs of damage and deterioration, and if necessary, renew it.

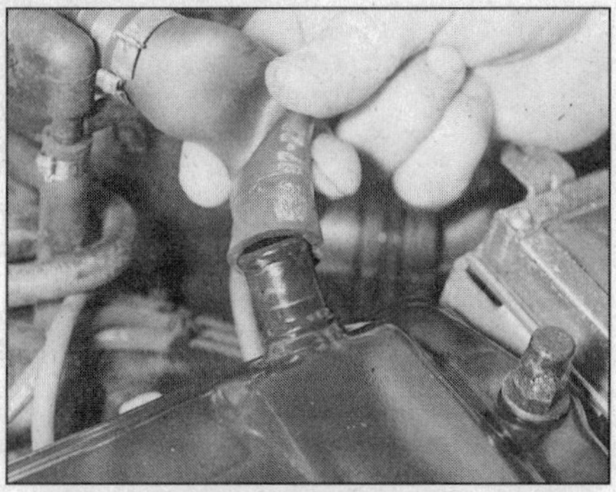

4.3 Disconnect the breather hose from the cylinder head cover . . .

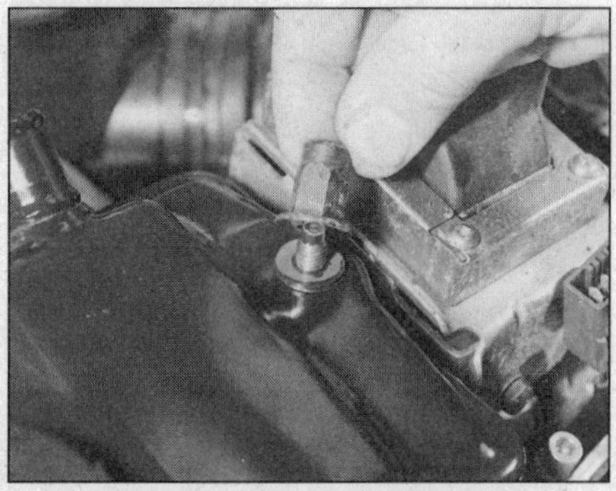

4.4 . . . then slacken and remove the cover retaining nuts and washers . . .

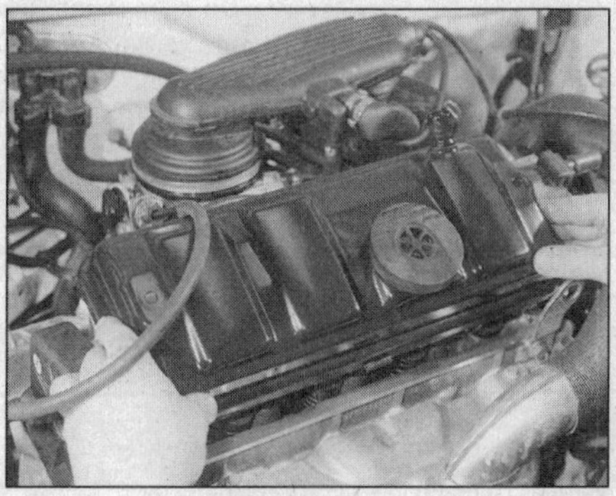

4.5 . . . and lift off the cylinder head cover

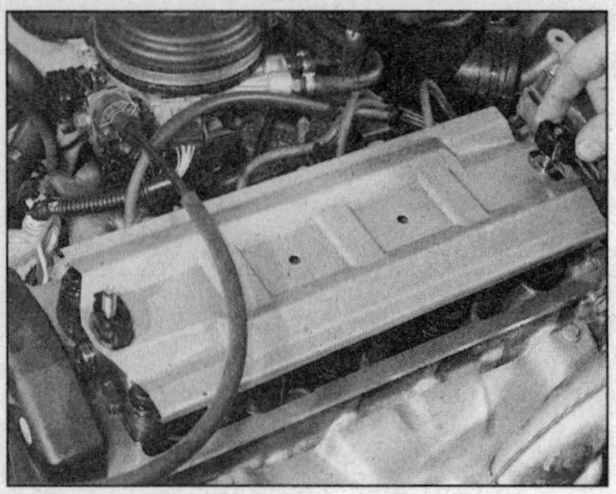

4.6a Lift off the spacers . . .

4.6b . . . and remove the oil baffle plate

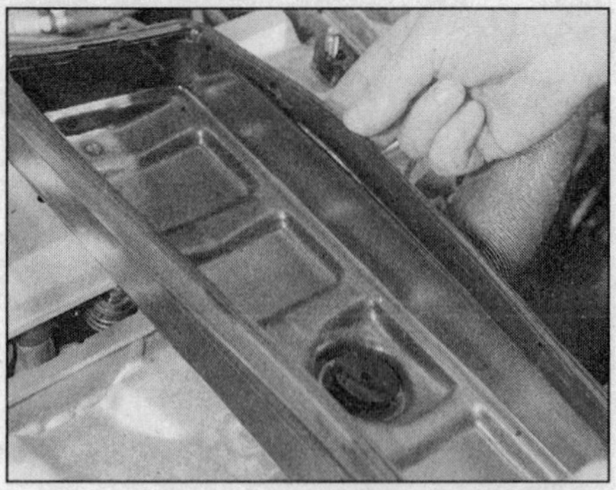

4.8 On refitting, ensure that the rubber seal is correctly located on the cylinder head cover

6 Remove the spacer from each stud, and lift off the oil baffle plate **(see illustrations)**.

Refitting

7 Carefully clean the cylinder head and cover mating surfaces, and remove all traces of oil.

8 Fit the rubber seal over the edge of the cylinder head cover, ensuring that it is correctly located along its entire length **(see illustration)**.

9 Refit the oil baffle plate to the engine, and locate the spacers in their recesses in the baffle plate.

10 Carefully refit the cylinder head cover to the engine, taking great care not to displace the rubber seal.

11 Check that the seal is correctly located, then refit the washers and cover retaining nuts, and tighten them to the specified torque.

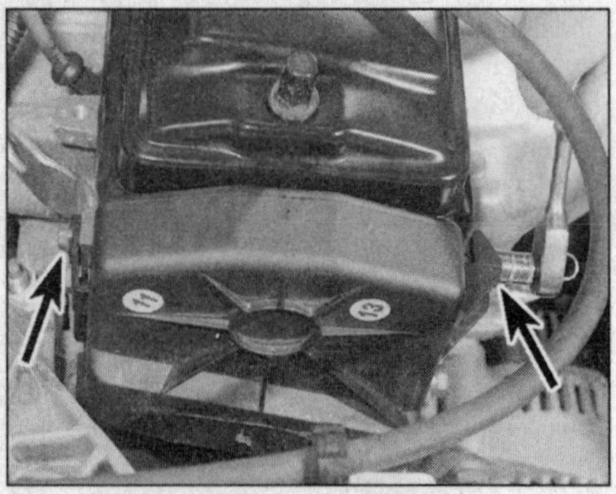

5.1a Undo the two retaining bolts (arrowed) . . .

12 Where necessary, refit the HT lead clips to the rear of the head cover, and securely tighten their retaining bolts.

13 Reconnect the breather hose to the cylinder head cover, securely tightening its retaining clip, and reconnect the battery negative lead.

5 Timing belt covers - removal and refitting

Removal

Upper cover

1 Slacken and remove the two retaining bolts (one at the front and one at the rear), and remove the upper timing cover from the cylinder head **(see illustrations)**.

Centre cover

2 Remove the upper cover as described in paragraph 1, then free the wiring from its retaining clips on the centre cover **(see illustration)**.

3 Slacken and remove the retaining bolts, and manoeuvre the centre cover out from the engine compartment **(see illustration)**.

Lower cover

4 Remove the auxiliary drivebelt as described in Chapter 1.

5 Remove the upper and centre covers as described in paragraphs 1 to 3.

6 Undo the three crankshaft pulley retaining bolts and remove the pulley, noting which way round it is fitted **(see illustrations)**.

7 Slacken and remove the single retaining bolt, and slide the lower cover off the end of the crankshaft **(see illustration)**.

Refitting

Upper cover

8 Refit the cover, ensuring that it is correctly located with the centre cover, and tighten its retaining bolts.

Centre cover

9 Manoeuvre the centre cover back into position, ensuring it is correctly located with the lower cover, and tighten its retaining bolts.

10 Clip the wiring loom into its retaining clips on the front of the centre cover, then refit the upper cover as described in paragraph 8.

Lower cover

11 Locate the lower cover over the timing belt sprocket, and tighten its retaining bolt.

12 Fit the pulley to the end of the crankshaft, ensuring that it is fitted the correct way round,

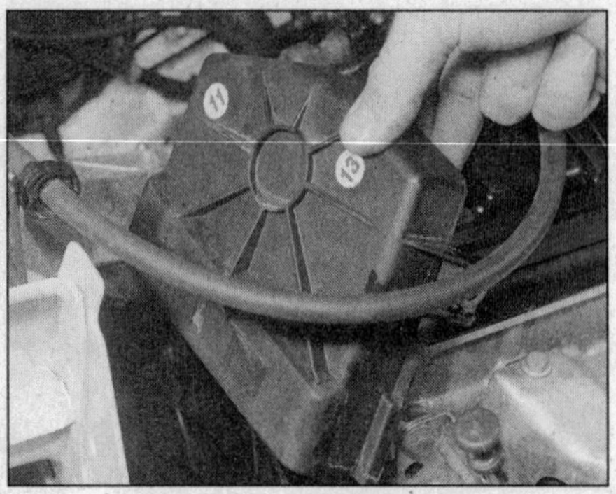

5.1b . . . and remove the upper timing belt cover

5.2 Free the wiring loom from its retaining clips . . .

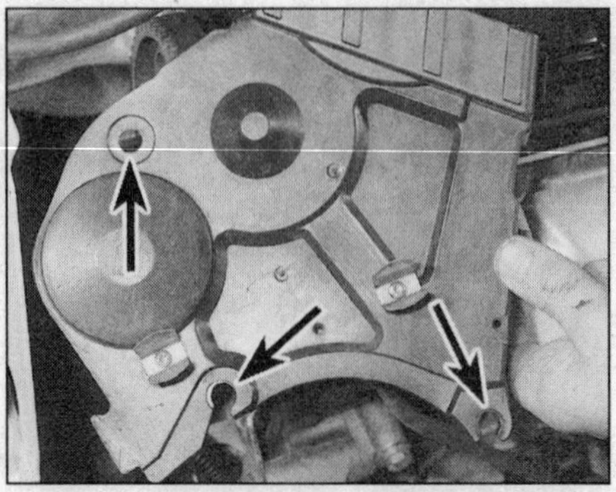

5.3 . . . then undo the retaining bolts (locations arrowed) and remove the centre timing belt cover

5.6a Undo the three retaining bolts (arrowed) . . .

5.6b . . . and remove the crankshaft pulley

5.7 Undo the retaining bolt and remove the lower timing belt cover

and tighten its retaining bolts to the specified torque.

13 Refit the centre and upper covers as described above, then refit and tension the auxiliary drivebelt as described in Chapter 1.

6 Timing belt - general information, removal and refitting

General information

1 The timing belt drives the camshaft and coolant pump from a toothed sprocket on the front of the crankshaft. If the belt breaks or slips in service, the pistons are likely to hit the valve heads, resulting in extensive (and expensive) damage.

2 The timing belt should be renewed at the specified intervals (see Chapter 1), or earlier if it is contaminated with oil, or if it is at all noisy in operation (a "scraping" noise due to uneven wear).

3 If the timing belt is being removed, it is a wise precaution to check the condition of the coolant pump at the same time (check for signs of coolant leakage). This may avoid the need to remove the timing belt again at a later stage, should the coolant pump fail.

Removal

4 Disconnect the battery negative terminal.

5 Align the engine assembly/valve timing holes as described in Section 3, and lock both the camshaft sprocket and the flywheel in position. *Do not* attempt to rotate the engine whilst the locking tools are in position.

6 Remove the timing belt centre and lower covers as described in Section 5.

7 Loosen the timing belt tensioner pulley retaining nut. Pivot the pulley in a clockwise direction, using a square-section key fitted to the hole in the pulley hub, then retighten the retaining nut.

8 If the timing belt is to be re-used, use white paint or similar to mark the direction of rotation on the belt (if markings do not already exist) **(see illustration)**. Slip the belt off the sprockets.

9 Check the timing belt carefully for any signs of uneven wear, splitting, or oil contamination. Pay particular attention to the roots of the teeth. If signs of oil contamination are found, trace the source of the oil leak, and rectify it. Wash down the engine timing belt area and all related components, to remove all traces of oil.

> **HAYNES HiNT** ***Renew the belt if there is the slightest doubt about its condition. If the engine is undergoing an overhaul, and has covered more than 36 000 miles (60 000 km) with the existing belt fitted, renew the belt as a matter of course, regardless of its apparent condition. The cost of a new belt is nothing when compared to the cost of repairs, should the belt break in service.***

Refitting

10 Prior to refitting, thoroughly clean the timing belt sprockets. Check that the tensioner pulley rotates freely, without any sign of roughness. If necessary, renew the tensioner pulley as described in Section 7. Make sure that the locking tools are still in place, as described in Section 3.

11 Manoeuvre the timing belt into position, ensuring that the arrows on the belt are pointing in the direction of rotation (clockwise when viewed from the right-hand end of the engine).

6.8 Mark the direction of rotation on the belt, if it is to be re-used

12 Do not twist the timing belt sharply while refitting it. Fit the belt over the crankshaft and camshaft sprockets. Make sure that the "front run" of the belt is taut - ie, ensure that any slack is on the tensioner pulley side of the belt. Fit the belt over the water pump sprocket and tensioner pulley. Ensure that the belt teeth are seated centrally in the sprockets.

13 Loosen the tensioner pulley retaining nut. Pivot the pulley anti-clockwise to remove all free play from the timing belt, then retighten the nut.

14 Citroën dealers use a special tool to tension the timing belt **(see illustration)**. A similar tool may be fabricated using a suitable square-section bar attached to an arm; a hole should be drilled in the arm at a distance of 80 mm from the centre of the square-section bar. Fit the tool to the hole in the tensioner pulley, keeping the tool arm as close to the horizontal as possible, and hang a 1.5 kg (3.3 lb) weight (aluminium block engine) or 2.0 kg (4.4 lb) weight (cast-iron block engine) from the hole in the tool. In the absence of an object of the specified weight, a spring balance can be used

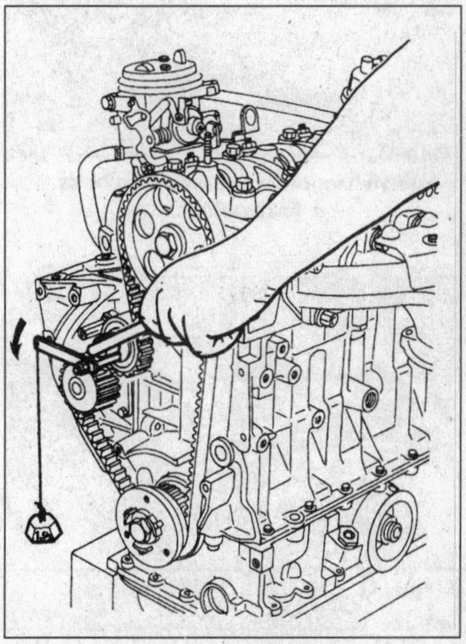

6.14 Using the Citroën special tool to tension the timing belt

to exert the required force, ensuring that the spring balance is held at 90° to the tool arm. Slacken the pulley retaining nut, allowing the weight or force exerted (as applicable) to push the tensioner pulley against the belt, then retighten the pulley nut.

15 If the special tool is not available, an approximate setting may be achieved as follows. Slacken the pulley retaining nut, and pivot the tensioner pulley anti-clockwise until it is just possible to twist the timing belt through 90° by finger and thumb, midway between the crankshaft and camshaft sprockets. The square hole in the tensioner pulley hub should be directly below the retaining nut, and the deflection of the belt at the mid-point between the sprockets should be approximately 6.0 mm. If this method is used, the belt tension should be checked by a Citroën dealer at the earliest possible opportunity.

16 Remove the locking tools from the camshaft sprocket and flywheel.

17 Using a socket and extension bar on the crankshaft sprocket bolt, rotate the crankshaft through four complete rotations in a clockwise direction (viewed from the right-hand end of the engine). *Do not* at any time rotate the crankshaft anti-clockwise.

18 Slacken the tensioner pulley nut, re-tension the belt using one of the methods just described, then tighten the tensioner pulley nut to the specified torque.

7.10 Use the fabricated tool shown to lock flywheel ring gear and prevent the crankshaft rotating

19 Rotate the crankshaft through a further two turns clockwise, and check that both the camshaft sprocket and flywheel timing holes are still correctly aligned.

20 If all is well, refit the timing belt covers as described in Section 5, and reconnect the battery negative terminal.

7 Timing belt tensioner and sprockets - removal, inspection and refitting

Removal

Note: *This Section describes the removal and refitting of the components concerned as individual operations. If more than one of them is to be removed at the same time, start by removing the timing belt as described in Section 6; remove the actual component as described below, ignoring the preliminary dismantling steps.*

1 Disconnect the battery negative terminal.

2 Position the engine assembly/valve timing holes as described in Section 3, and lock both the camshaft sprocket and flywheel in position. *Do not* attempt to rotate the engine whilst the locking tools are in position.

Camshaft sprocket

3 Remove the upper and centre timing belt covers as described in Section 5. Also, where fitted on cast-iron block engines, remove the electronic control unit.

4 Loosen the timing belt tensioner pulley retaining nut. Rotate the pulley in a clockwise direction, using a square-section key fitted to the hole in the pulley hub, then retighten the retaining nut.

5 Disengage the timing belt from the sprocket, and move the belt clear, taking care not to bend or twist it sharply. Remove the locking tool from the camshaft sprocket.

6 Slacken the camshaft sprocket retaining bolt and remove it, along with its washer. To prevent the camshaft rotating as the bolt is slackened, a sprocket-holding tool will be required. *Do not* attempt to use the locking tool to prevent the sprocket from rotating whilst the bolt is slackened.

7 With the retaining bolt removed, slide the sprocket off the end of the camshaft. If the locating peg is a loose fit in the rear of the sprocket, remove it for safe-keeping. Examine the camshaft oil seal for signs of oil leakage and, if necessary, renew it as described in Section 8.

> **HAYNES HiNT** *In the absence of the special Citroën tool to prevent the camshaft rotating, an acceptable substitute can be fabricated as follows. Use two lengths of steel strip (one long, the other short), and three nuts and bolts; one nut and bolt forms the pivot of a forked tool, with the remaining two nuts and bolts at the tips of the "forks" to engage with the sprocket spokes as shown (see illustration 7.18).*

Crankshaft sprocket

8 Remove the centre and lower timing belt covers as described in Section 5.

9 Loosen the timing belt tensioner pulley retaining nut. Rotate the pulley in a clockwise direction, using a square-section key fitted to the hole in the pulley hub, then retighten the retaining nut.

10 To prevent crankshaft rotation whilst the sprocket retaining bolt is slackened, select top gear, and have an assistant apply the brakes firmly. If the engine has been removed from the vehicle, lock the flywheel ring gear, using an arrangement similar to that shown **(see illustration)**. *Do not* be tempted to use the flywheel locking tool to prevent the crankshaft from rotating; temporarily remove the locking tool from the rear of the flywheel prior to slackening the pulley bolt, then refit it once the bolt has been slackened.

11 Unscrew the retaining bolt and washer, then slide the sprocket off the end of the crankshaft **(see illustrations)**. Refit the locking tool through the timing hole into the rear of the flywheel.

12 If the Woodruff key is a loose fit in the crankshaft, remove it and store it with the sprocket for safe-keeping. If necessary, also slide the flanged spacer off the end of the crankshaft **(see illustration)**. Examine the crankshaft oil seal for signs of oil leakage and, if necessary, renew as described in Section 14.

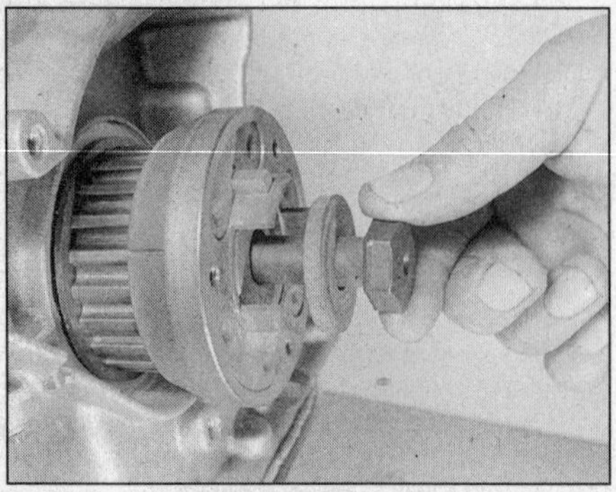

7.11a Remove the crankshaft sprocket retaining bolt . . .

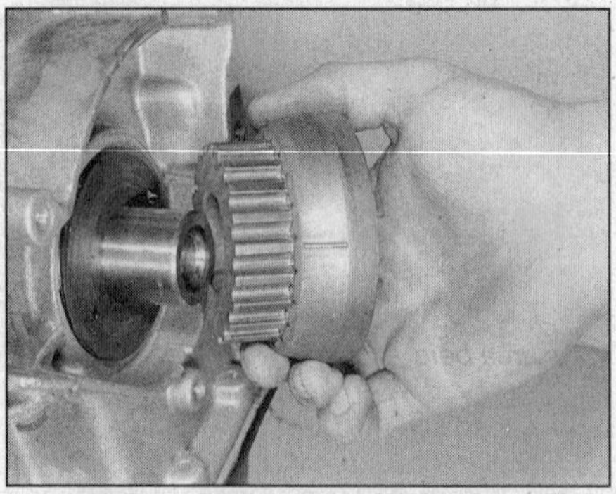

7.11b . . . then slide off the sprocket

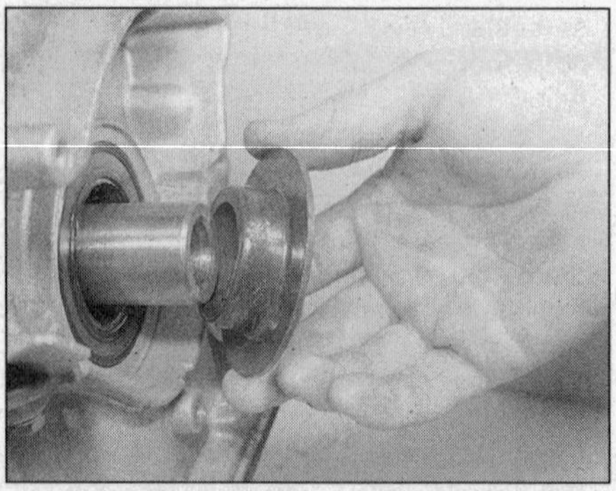

7.12 Remove the flanged spacer if necessary

7.18 Using a home-made tool to hold the camshaft sprocket stationary whilst the retaining bolt is tightened (shown with the cylinder head on the bench)

Tensioner pulley

13 Remove the centre timing belt cover as described in Section 5.

14 Slacken and remove the timing belt tensioner pulley retaining nut, and slide the pulley off its mounting stud. Examine the mounting stud for signs of damage and, if necessary, renew it.

Inspection

15 Clean the sprockets thoroughly, and renew any that show signs of wear, damage or cracks.

16 Clean the tensioner assembly, but do not use any strong solvent which may enter the pulley bearing. Check that the pulley rotates freely about its hub, with no sign of stiffness or of free play. Renew the tensioner pulley if there is any doubt about its condition, or if there are any obvious signs of wear or damage.

Refitting

Camshaft sprocket

17 Refit the locating peg (where removed) to the rear of the sprocket, then locate the sprocket on the end of the camshaft. Ensure that the locating peg is correctly engaged with the cut-out in the camshaft end.

18 Refit the sprocket retaining bolt and washer. Tighten the bolt to the specified torque, whilst retaining the sprocket with the tool used on removal **(see illustration)**.

19 Realign the timing hole in the camshaft sprocket (see Section 3) with the corresponding hole in the cylinder head, and refit the locking tool.

20 Refit the timing belt to the camshaft sprocket. Ensure that the "front run" of the belt is taut - ie, ensure that any slack is on the tensioner pulley side of the belt. Do not twist the belt sharply while refitting it, and ensure that the belt teeth are seated centrally in the sprockets.

21 Loosen the tensioner pulley retaining nut. Rotate the pulley anti-clockwise to remove all free play from the timing belt, then retighten the nut.

22 Tension the belt as described in paragraphs 14 to 19 of Section 6.

23 Refit the timing belt covers as described in Section 5, and reconnect the battery negative terminal.

Crankshaft sprocket

24 Where removed, locate the Woodruff key in the crankshaft end, then slide on the flanged spacer, aligning its slot with the Woodruff key.

25 Align the crankshaft sprocket slot with the Woodruff key, and slide it onto the end of the crankshaft.

26 Temporarily remove the locking tool from the rear of the flywheel, then refit the crankshaft sprocket retaining bolt and washer. Tighten the bolt to the specified torque, whilst preventing crankshaft rotation using the method employed on removal. Refit the locking tool to the rear of the flywheel.

27 Relocate the timing belt on the crankshaft sprocket. Ensure that the "front run" of the belt is taut - ie, ensure that any slack is on the tensioner pulley side of the belt. Do not twist the belt sharply while refitting it, and ensure that the belt teeth are seated centrally in the sprockets.

28 Loosen the tensioner pulley retaining nut. Rotate the pulley anti-clockwise to remove all free play from the timing belt, then retighten the nut.

29 Tension the belt as described in paragraphs 14 to 19 of Section 6.

30 Refit the timing belt covers as described in Section 5, and reconnect the battery negative terminal.

Tensioner pulley

31 Refit the tensioner pulley to its mounting stud, and fit the retaining nut.

32 Ensure that the "front run" of the belt is taut - ie, ensure that any slack is on the pulley side of the belt. Check that the belt is centrally located on all its sprockets. Rotate the pulley anti-clockwise to remove all free play from the timing belt, then tighten the pulley retaining nut securely.

33 Tension the belt as described in paragraphs 14 to 19 of Section 6.

34 Refit the timing belt covers as described in Section 5, and reconnect the battery negative terminal.

8 Camshaft oil seal - renewal

Note: *If the camshaft oil seal is to be renewed with the timing belt still in place, check first that the belt is free from oil contamination. (Renew the belt as a matter of course if signs of oil contamination are found; see Section 6.) Cover the belt to protect it from oil contamination while work is in progress. Ensure that all traces of oil are removed from the area before the belt is refitted.*

1 Remove the camshaft sprocket as described in Section 7.

2 Punch or drill two small holes opposite each other in the oil seal. Screw a self-tapping screw into each, and pull on the screws with pliers to extract the seal.

3 Clean the seal housing, and polish off any burrs or raised edges, which may have caused the seal to fail in the first place.

4 Lubricate the lips of the new seal with clean engine oil, and drive it into position until it seats on its locating shoulder.

> HAYNES HiNT ***Use a tubular drift, such as a socket, which bears only on the hard outer edge of the seal. Take care not to damage the seal lips during fitting. Note that the seal lips should face inwards.***

5 Refit the camshaft sprocket as described in Section 7.

9 Valve clearances - checking and adjustment

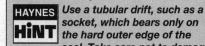

Note: *The valve clearances must be checked and adjusted only when the engine is cold.*

1 The importance of having the valve clearances correctly adjusted cannot be overstressed, as they vitally affect the performance of the engine. If the clearances are too big, the engine will be noisy (characteristic rattling or tapping noises) and engine efficiency will be reduced, as the valves open too late and close too early. A more serious problem arises if the clearances are too small, however. If this is the case, the valves may not close fully when the engine is hot, resulting in serious damage to the engine (eg. burnt valve seats and/or cylinder head warping/cracking). The clearances are checked and adjusted as follows.

2A

2 Remove the cylinder head cover as described in Section 4.

3 The engine can now be turned using a socket and extension bar fitted to the crankshaft sprocket/pulley bolt. It will be easier if the spark plugs are removed first - see Chapter 1.

4 It is important that the clearance of each valve is checked and adjusted only when the valve is fully closed, with the rocker arm resting on the heel of the cam (directly opposite the peak). This can be ensured by carrying out the adjustments in the following sequence, noting that No 1 cylinder is at the transmission end of the engine. The correct valve clearances are given in the Specifications at the start of this Chapter. The valve locations can be determined from the position of the manifolds.

Valve fully open	Adjust valves
No 1 exhaust	*No 3 inlet and No 4 exhaust*
No 3 exhaust	*No 4 inlet and No 2 exhaust*
No 4 exhaust	*No 2 inlet and No 1 exhaust*
No 2 exhaust	*No 1 inlet and No 3 exhaust*

5 With the relevant valve fully open, check the clearances of the two valves specified. Clearances are checked by inserting a feeler

9.5 Adjusting a valve clearance

gauge of the correct thickness between the valve stem and the rocker arm adjusting screw. The feeler gauge should be a light, sliding fit. If adjustment is necessary, slacken the adjusting screw locknut, and turn the screw as necessary. Once the correct clearance is obtained, hold the adjusting screw and securely tighten the locknut **(see illustration)**. Recheck the valve clearance, and adjust again if necessary.

6 Rotate the crankshaft until the next valve in the sequence is fully open, and check the clearances of the next two specified valves.

7 Repeat the procedure until all eight valve clearances have been checked (and if necessary, adjusted), then refit the cylinder head cover as described in Section 4.

10 Camshaft and rocker arms - removal, inspection and refitting

General information

1 The rocker arm assembly is secured to the top of the cylinder head by the cylinder head bolts. Although in theory it is possible to undo the head bolts and remove the rocker arm assembly without removing the head, in practice, this is not recommended. Once the bolts have been removed, the head gasket will be disturbed, and the gasket will almost certainly leak or blow after refitting. For this reason, removal of the rocker arm assembly cannot be done without removing the cylinder head and renewing the head gasket.

2 The camshaft is slid out of the right-hand end of the cylinder head, and therefore it cannot be removed without first removing the cylinder head, due to a lack of clearance.

Removal

Rocker arm assembly

3 Remove the cylinder head as described in Section 11.

4 To dismantle the rocker arm assembly, carefully prise off the circlip from the right-hand end of the rocker shaft; retain the rocker pedestal, to prevent it being sprung off the end of the shaft. Slide the various components off the end of the shaft, keeping all components in their correct fitted order. Make a note of each component's correct fitted position/orientation as it is removed, to ensure that it is fitted correctly on reassembly **(see illustration)**.

5 To separate the left-hand pedestal and shaft, first unscrew the cylinder head cover retaining stud from the top of the pedestal; this can be achieved using a stud extractor, or two nuts locked together. With the stud removed, unscrew the grub screw from the top of the pedestal, and withdraw the rocker shaft **(see illustrations)**.

Camshaft

6 Remove the cylinder head as described in Section 11.

7 With the head on a bench, remove the locking tool, then remove the camshaft sprocket as described in paragraphs 6 and 7 of Section 7.

8 Undo the retaining bolt, and remove the camshaft thrust fork from the cylinder head **(see illustration)**.

9 Using a large flat-bladed screwdriver, carefully prise the oil seal out of the right-hand end of the cylinder head, then slide out the camshaft **(see illustrations)**. Discard the seal - a new one must be used on refitting.

Inspection

Rocker arm assembly

10 Examine the rocker arm bearing surfaces which contact the camshaft lobes for wear ridges and scoring. Renew any rocker arms on

10.4 Remove the circlip, and slide the components off the end of the rocker arm

10.5a To remove the left-hand pedestal, lock two nuts together and unscrew the stud . . .

10.5b . . . then remove the grub screw

10.8 Undo the retaining bolt, and remove the camshaft thrust fork (arrowed) . . .

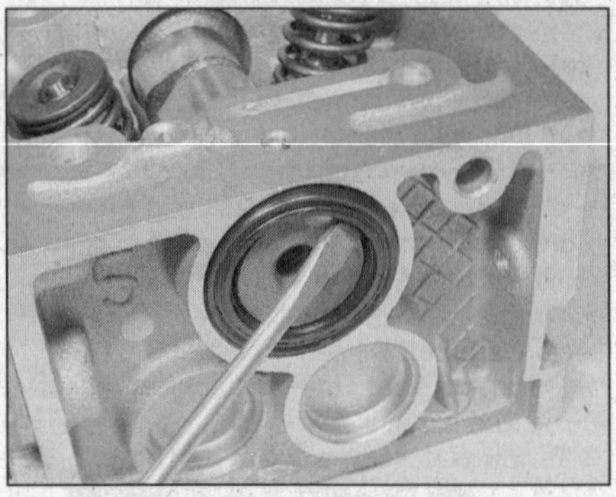

10.9a . . . prise out the oil seal . . .

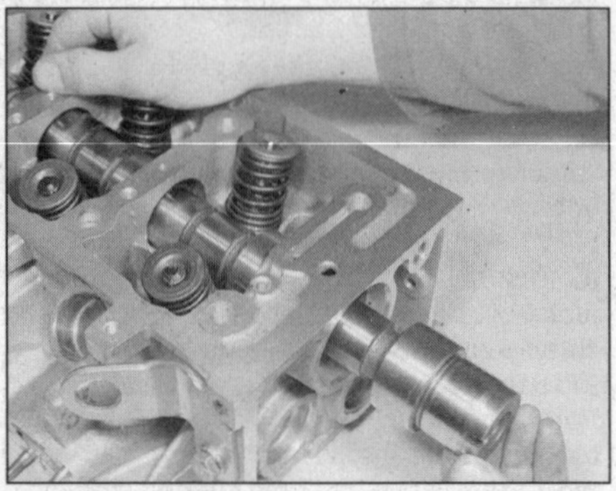

10.9b . . . and slide out the camshaft

which these conditions are apparent. Renew worn components as necessary. The rocker arm assembly can be dismantled as described in paragraphs 4 and 5.

> **HAYNES HiNT** *If a rocker arm bearing surface is badly scored, also examine the corresponding lobe on the camshaft for wear, as it is likely that both will be worn*

11 Inspect the ends of the (valve clearance) adjusting screws for signs of wear or damage, and renew as required.
12 If the rocker arm assembly has been dismantled, examine the rocker arm and shaft bearing surfaces for wear ridges and scoring. If there are obvious signs of wear, the relevant rocker arm(s) and/or the shaft must be renewed.

Camshaft

13 Examine the camshaft bearing surfaces and cam lobes for signs of wear ridges and scoring. Renew the camshaft if any of these conditions are apparent. Examine the condition of the bearing surfaces, both on the camshaft journals and in the cylinder head. If the head bearing surfaces are worn excessively, the cylinder head will need to be renewed. If the necessary measuring equipment is available, camshaft bearing journal wear can be checked by direct measurement, noting that No 1 journal is at the transmission end of the head.
14 Examine the thrust fork for signs of wear or scoring, and renew as necessary.

Refitting

Rocker arm assembly

15 If the rocker arm assembly was dismantled, refit the rocker shaft to the left-hand pedestal, aligning its locating hole with the pedestal threaded hole. Refit the grub screw, and tighten it securely. With the grub screw in position, refit the cylinder head cover mounting stud to the pedestal, and tighten it securely. Apply a smear of clean engine oil to the shaft, then slide on all removed components, ensuring each is correctly fitted in its original position. Once all components are in position on the shaft, compress the right-hand pedestal and refit the circlip. Ensure that the circlip is correctly located in its groove on the shaft.
16 Refit the cylinder head and rocker arm assembly as described in Section 11.

Camshaft

17 Ensure that the cylinder head and camshaft bearing surfaces are clean, then liberally oil the camshaft bearings and lobes. Slide the camshaft back into position in the cylinder head.
18 Locate the thrust fork with the left-hand end of the camshaft. Refit the fork retaining bolt, tightening it to the specified torque setting.

> **HAYNES HiNT** *On carburettor engines, take care that the fuel pump operating lever is not trapped by the camshaft as it is slid into position. To prevent, this remove the fuel pump before refitting the camshaft, then refit it afterwards .*

19 Lubricate the lips of the new seal with clean engine oil, then drive it into position until it seats on its locating shoulder. Use a tubular drift, such as a socket, which bears only on the hard outer edge of the seal. Take care not to damage the seal lips during fitting. Note that the seal lips should face inwards.
20 Refit the camshaft sprocket as described in paragraphs 17 to 19 of Section 7.
21 Refit the cylinder head as described in Section 11.

11 Cylinder head - removal and refitting

Removal

1 Disconnect the battery negative lead.
2 Drain the cooling system as described in Chapter 1.
3 Remove the cylinder head cover as described in Section 4.
4 Align the engine assembly/valve timing holes as described in Section 3, and lock both the camshaft sprocket and flywheel in position. *Do not* attempt to rotate the engine whilst the locking tools are in position.
5 Note that the following text assumes that the cylinder head will be removed with both inlet and exhaust manifolds attached; this is easier, but makes it a bulky and heavy assembly to handle. If it is wished to remove the manifolds first, proceed as described in Chapter 4.
6 Working as described in Chapter 4, disconnect the exhaust system front pipe from the manifold. On models with a catalytic converter, disconnect or release the lambda sensor wiring, so that it is not strained by the weight of the exhaust.
7 Remove the air cleaner housing and intake duct assembly as described in Chapter 4.
8 On carburettor engines, disconnect the following from the carburettor and inlet manifold as described in Chapter 4:

a) Fuel feed hose from the pump, and the return hose from the anti-percolation chamber (plug all openings, to prevent loss of fuel and the entry of dirt into the system).
b) Accelerator cable.
c) Choke cable.
d) Carburettor coolant hoses where applicable
e) Carburettor heating element and idle cut-off solenoid wiring connector(s) where applicable
f) Vacuum servo unit vacuum hose, coolant hose and all other relevant breather/vacuum hoses from the manifold.

9 On fuel injection engines, carry out the following operations as described in Chapter 4:

a) Depressurise the fuel system, and disconnect the fuel feed and return hoses from the throttle body (plug all openings, to prevent loss of fuel and the entry of dirt into the system).
b) Disconnect the accelerator cable.
c) On single-point injection models, disconnect the relevant electrical connectors from the throttle body.
d) On multi-point injection models, disconnect the relevant electrical connectors from the throttle housing, fuel injectors and (where necessary) the idle speed auxiliary air valve.
e) Disconnect the vacuum servo unit vacuum hose, coolant hose(s) and all the other relevant vacuum/breather hoses from the inlet manifold.

10 Remove the centre and upper timing belt covers as described in Section 5.
11 Loosen the timing belt tensioner pulley retaining nut. Pivot the pulley in a clockwise direction, using a square-section key fitted to the hole in the pulley hub, then retighten the retaining nut.
12 Disengage the timing belt from the camshaft sprocket, and position the belt clear of the sprocket. Ensure that the belt is not bent or twisted sharply, if it is to be re-used.
13 Slacken the retaining clips, and disconnect the coolant hoses from the thermostat housing (on the left-hand end of the cylinder head).
14 Depress the retaining clip(s), and disconnect the wiring connector(s) from the electrical switch and/or sensor(s) which are screwed into the thermostat housing (as appropriate). Also (where necessary) release the TDC connector from its support on the distributor bracket on the left-hand end of the cylinder head.

Models with a distributor

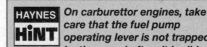

15 Disconnect the LT wiring connectors from the distributor and HT coil. Release the TDC sensor wiring connector from the side of the coil mounting bracket, and disconnect the vacuum pipe from the distributor vacuum diaphragm unit. If the cylinder head is to be dismantled for overhaul, remove the distributor and ignition HT coil as described in Chapter 5; disconnect the HT leads from the spark plugs, and remove the distributor cap and lead assembly.

> **HAYNES HiNT** *If the cylinder numbers are not already marked on the HT leads, number each lead, to avoid the possibility of the leads being incorrectly connected on refitting .*

Models with a distributorless ignition system

16 Disconnect the wiring connector from the ignition HT coil. If the cylinder head is to be dismantled for overhaul, remove the ignition

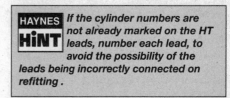

2A

HT coil as described in Chapter 5. Note that the HT leads should be disconnected from the spark plugs instead of the coil, and the coil and leads removed as an assembly. If the cylinder numbers are not already marked on the HT leads, number each lead, to avoid the possibility of the leads being incorrectly connected on refitting.

All models

17 Slacken and remove the bolt securing the engine oil dipstick tube to the cylinder head, and withdraw the tube from the cylinder block.
18 Working in the reverse of the sequence shown in illustration 11.38a, progressively slacken the ten cylinder head bolts by half a turn at a time, until all bolts can be unscrewed by hand.
19 With all the cylinder head bolts removed, lift the rocker arm assembly off the cylinder head. Note the locating pins which are fitted to the base of each rocker arm pedestal. If any pin is a loose fit in the head or pedestal, remove it for safe-keeping.
20 On engines with a cast-iron cylinder block, lift the cylinder head away; seek assistance if possible, as it is a heavy assembly, especially if it is removed complete with the manifolds.
21 On engines with an aluminium cylinder block, the joint between the cylinder head and gasket and the cylinder block/crankcase must now be broken without disturbing the wet liners. To break the joint, obtain two L-shaped metal bars which fit into the cylinder head bolt holes. Gently "rock" the cylinder head free towards the front of the car **(see illustration)**. Do not try to swivel the head on the cylinder block/crankcase; it is located by dowels, as well as by the tops of the liners. **Note:** *If care is not taken and the liners are moved, there is also a possibility of the bottom seals being disturbed, causing leakage after refitting the head.* When the joint is broken, lift the cylinder head away; seek assistance if possible, as it is a heavy assembly, especially if it is removed complete with the manifolds.
22 On all models, remove the gasket from the top of the block, noting the two locating dowels. If the locating dowels are a loose fit, remove them and store them with the head for safe-keeping. Do not discard the old gasket yet - on some models, it will be needed to ensure that the correct new gasket is obtained (see paragraphs 28 and 29).
23 Note: *On aluminium block engines, do not attempt to rotate the crankshaft with the cylinder head removed, otherwise the wet liners may be displaced. Operations that require the rotation of the crankshaft (eg cleaning the piston crowns), should only be carried out once the cylinder liners are firmly clamped in position.*

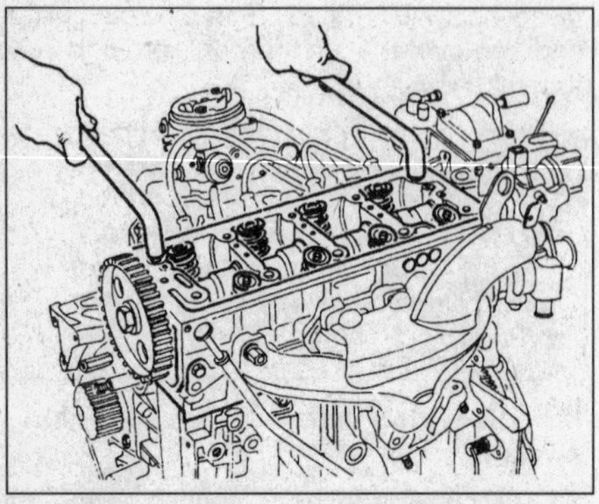

11.21 Using two angled metal rods to free the cylinder head from the block

HAYNES HiNT ***In the absence of the special Citroën liner clamps, the liners can be clamped in position using large flat washers positioned underneath suitable-length bolts. Alternatively, the original head bolts could be temporarily refitted, with spacers fitted to their shanks.***

24 If the cylinder head is to be dismantled for overhaul, remove the camshaft as described in Section 10, then refer to Part C of this Chapter.

Preparation for refitting

25 The mating faces of the cylinder head and cylinder block/crankcase must be perfectly clean before refitting the head. Use a hard plastic or wood scraper to remove all traces of gasket and carbon; also clean the piston crowns. Refer to paragraph 23 before turning the crankshaft on aluminium block engines. Take particular care during the cleaning operations, as the soft aluminium alloy is damaged easily. Also, make sure that the carbon is not allowed to enter the oil and water passages - this is particularly important for the lubrication system, as carbon could block the oil supply to the engine's components. Using adhesive tape and paper, seal the water, oil and bolt holes in the cylinder block/crankcase. To prevent carbon entering the gap between the pistons and bores, smear a little grease in the gap. After cleaning each piston, use a small brush to remove all traces of grease and carbon from the gap, then wipe away the remainder with a clean rag. Clean all the pistons in the same way.
26 Check the mating surfaces of the cylinder block/crankcase and the cylinder head for nicks, deep scratches and other damage. If slight, they may be removed carefully with a file, but if excessive, machining may be the only alternative to renewal.

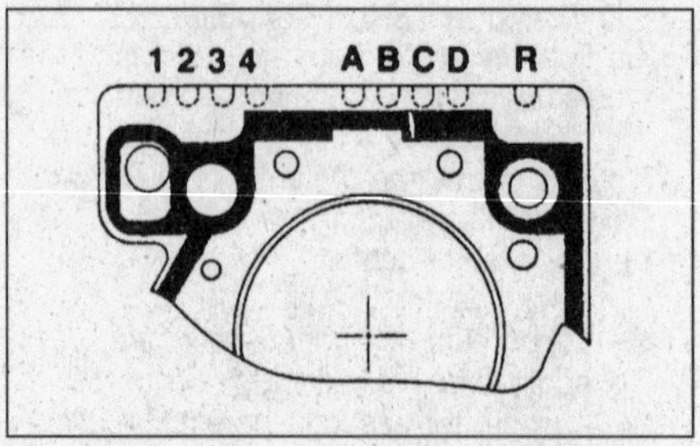

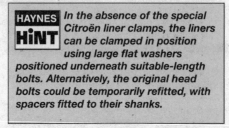

11.29 TU engine gasket markings

1, 2, 3, 4 Engine type identification cut-outs
A, B, C, D Gasket manufacturer and asbestos content identification cut-outs
R Gasket thickness identification cut-out

27 If warpage of the cylinder head gasket surface is suspected, use a straight-edge to check it for distortion. Refer to Part C of this Chapter if necessary.
28 When purchasing a new cylinder head gasket, it is essential that a gasket of the correct thickness is obtained. There are two different thicknesses available - the standard gasket which is fitted at the factory, and a slightly thicker gasket (+ 0.2 mm), for use once the head gasket face has been machined. If the cylinder head has been machined, it should have the letter "R" stamped adjacent to the No 3 exhaust port, and the gasket should also have the letter "R" stamped adjacent to No 3 cylinder on its front upper face. The gaskets can also be identified as described in the following paragraph, using the cut-outs on the left-hand end of the gasket.
29 With the gasket fitted the correct way up on the cylinder block, there is a single cut-out at the rear of the left-hand side (position 1) on all engines except the C1A - on the C1A there is no cut-out at all **(see illustration)**. On cast-iron block engines (K2D, K6B and KFZ) there is also a cut-out at position 3. In the centre of the gasket, there is another series of up to four cut-outs identifying the manufacturer of the gasket, and whether or not it contains asbestos (these cut-outs are of little importance). The important cut-out location is at the front of the gasket. On the standard-thickness gasket, there will be no cut-out in this position; on the thicker, "repair" gasket, there will be a single cut-out. Identify the gasket type, and ensure that the new gasket obtained is of the correct thickness. If there is any doubt as to which gasket is fitted, take the old gasket along to your Citroën dealer, and have the dealer confirm the gasket type.
30 Check the condition of the cylinder head bolts, and particularly their threads, whenever they are removed. Wash the bolts in suitable solvent, and wipe them dry. Check each for any sign of visible wear or damage, renewing any bolt if necessary. Measure the length of each bolt, to check for stretching (although this is not a conclusive test, in the event that all ten bolts have stretched by the same amount). Although Citroën do not actually specify that the bolts must be renewed, it is strongly recommended that the bolts should be renewed as a complete set whenever they are disturbed.
31 On aluminium block engines, prior to refitting the cylinder head, check the cylinder liner protrusion as described in Part C of this Chapter.

Refitting

32 Wipe clean the mating surfaces of the cylinder head and cylinder block/crankcase. Check that the two locating dowels are in position at each end of the cylinder block/crankcase surface and, if necessary, remove the cylinder liner clamps.

11.33 Locate the cylinder head gasket on the block . . .

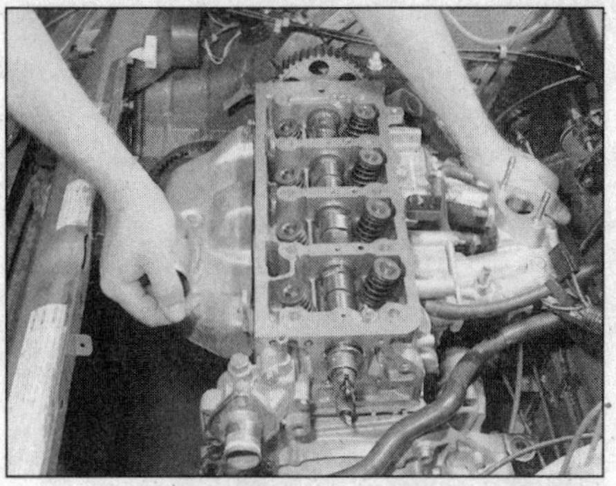

11.34 . . . then lower the cylinder head into position . . .

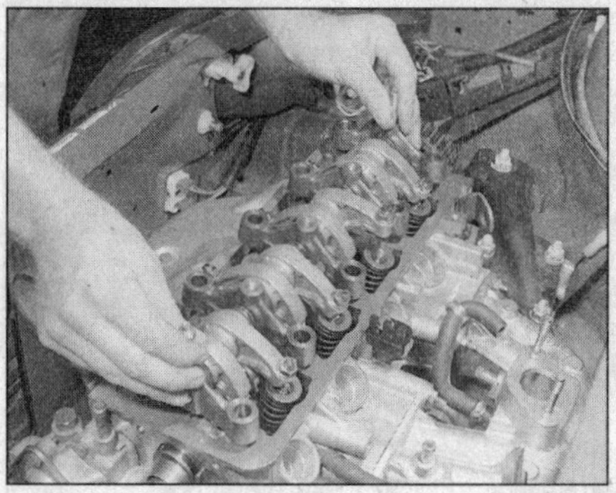

11.35 . . . and refit the rocker arm assembly

33 Position a new gasket on the cylinder block/crankcase surface **(see illustration)**, ensuring that its identification cut-outs are at the left-hand end of the gasket.

34 Check that the flywheel and camshaft sprocket are still correctly locked in position with their respective locking tools. With the aid of an assistant, carefully refit the cylinder head assembly to the block, aligning it with the locating dowels **(see illustration)**.

35 Ensure that the locating pins are in position in the base of each rocker pedestal, then refit the rocker arm assembly to the cylinder head **(see illustration)**.

36 Apply a smear of grease to the threads, and to the underside of the heads, of the cylinder head bolts. Citroën recommend the use of Molykote G Rapid Plus grease (available from your Citroën dealer - a sachet is supplied with the head gasket set); in the absence of the specified grease, a good-quality high-melting-point grease may be used.

37 Carefully enter each bolt into its relevant hole (*do not drop them in*) and screw in, by hand only, until finger-tight.

38 Working progressively and in the sequence shown, tighten the cylinder head bolts to their Stage 1 torque setting, using a torque wrench and socket **(see illustrations)**.

39 Once all the bolts have been tightened to their Stage 1 setting, working again in the given sequence, angle-tighten the bolts through the specified Stage 2 angle, using a socket and extension bar. It is recommended that an angle-measuring gauge is used during this stage of the tightening, to ensure accuracy **(see illustration)**. If a gauge is not available, use white paint to make alignment marks between the bolt head and cylinder head prior to tightening; the marks can then be used to check that the bolt has been rotated through the correct angle during tightening.

40 On cast-iron block engines, it will then be necessary to tighten the bolts through the specified Stage 3 angle setting.

41 With the cylinder head bolts correctly tightened, refit the dipstick tube to the engine, and securely tighten its retaining bolt.

42 Refit the timing belt to the camshaft sprocket. Ensure that the "front run" of the belt is taut - ie, ensure that any slack is on the tensioner pulley side of the belt. Do not twist the belt sharply while refitting it, and ensure that the belt teeth are seated centrally in the sprockets.

43 Loosen the tensioner pulley retaining nut. Pivot the pulley anti-clockwise to remove all free play from the timing belt, then retighten the nut.

44 Tension the belt as described in paragraphs 14 to 19 of Section 6, then refit the centre and upper timing belt covers as described in Section 5.

Models with a distributor

45 If the head was stripped for overhaul, refit the distributor and HT coil as described in Chapter 5, ensuring that the HT leads are correctly reconnected. If the head was not stripped, reconnect the wiring connector and vacuum pipe to the distributor, and the HT lead to the coil; clip the TDC sensor wiring connector onto the coil bracket.

Models with a distributorless ignition system

46 If the head was stripped for overhaul, refit the ignition HT coil and leads as described in Chapter 5, ensuring that the leads are correctly reconnected. If the head was not stripped, simply reconnect the wiring connector to the HT coil.

All models

47 Reconnect the wiring connector(s) to the coolant switch/sensor(s) on the left-hand end of the head.

48 Reconnect the coolant hoses to the thermostat housing, securely tightening their retaining clips.

49 Working as described in the relevant Part of Chapter 4, carry out the following tasks:

a) Refit all disturbed wiring, hoses and control cable(s) to the inlet manifold and fuel system components.
b) On carburettor models, reconnect and adjust the choke and accelerator cables.
c) On fuel injection models, reconnect and adjust the accelerator cable.
d) Reconnect the exhaust system front

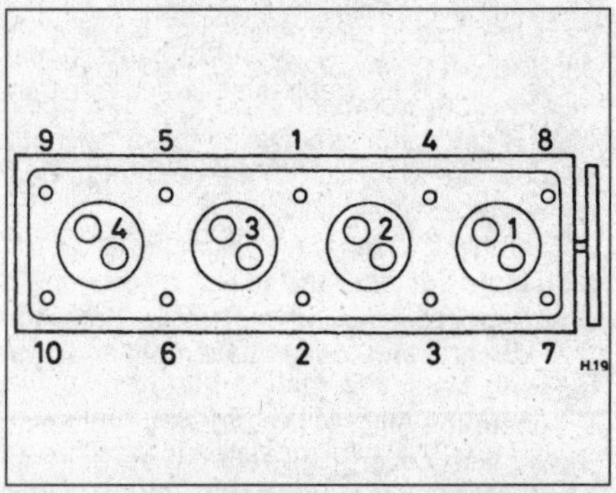

11.38a Cylinder head bolt tightening sequence (cylinder numbering also shown)

11.38b Working in the sequence shown, tighten the head bolts first to the Stage 1 torque setting . . .

11.39 . . . then through the angle specified for Stage 2

12.4 Slacken and remove the sump retaining nuts and bolts . . .

12.5 . . . then remove the sump from the engine

13.2 Oil pump is retained by three bolts

pipe to the manifold. Where applicable, reconnect the lambda sensor wiring connector.

e) Refit the air cleaner housing and intake duct.

50 Check and, if necessary, adjust the valve clearances as described in Section 9, then refit the cylinder head cover as described in Section 4.

51 On completion, reconnect the battery, and refill the cooling system as described in Chapter 1.

12 Sump - removal and refitting

Removal

1 Firmly apply the handbrake, then jack up the front of the vehicle and support it on axle stands. Disconnect the battery negative lead.

2 Drain the engine oil, then clean and refit the engine oil drain plug, tightening it to the specified torque. If the engine is nearing its service interval when the oil and filter are due for renewal, it is recommended that the filter is also removed, and a new one fitted. After reassembly, the engine can then be refilled with fresh oil. Refer to Chapter 1 for further information.

3 Remove the exhaust system front pipe as described in Chapter 4.

4 Progressively slacken and remove all the sump retaining nuts and bolts **(see illustration)**.

5 Break the joint by striking the sump with the palm of your hand, then lower the sump and withdraw it from underneath the vehicle **(see illustration)**.

6 While the sump is removed, take the opportunity to check the oil pump pick-up/strainer for signs of clogging or splitting. If necessary, remove the pump as described in Section 13, and clean or renew the strainer.

Refitting

7 Clean all traces of sealant from the mating surfaces of the cylinder block/crankcase and sump, then use a clean rag to wipe out the sump and the engine's interior.

8 Ensure that the sump and cylinder block/crankcase mating surfaces are clean and dry, then apply a coating of suitable sealant to the sump mating surface. Citroën recommend the use of Auto-Joint E10 sealant (available from your Citroën dealer); in the absence of the specified sealant, any good-quality sealant may be used.

9 Offer up the sump, locating it on its retaining studs, and refit its retaining nuts and bolts. Tighten the nuts and bolts evenly and progressively to the specified torque.

10 Refit the exhaust front pipe as described in Chapter 4.

11 Replenish the engine oil as described in Chapter 1.

13 Oil pump - removal, inspection and refitting

Removal

1 Remove the sump as described in Section 12.

2 Slacken and remove the three bolts securing the oil pump to the base of the main bearing ladder (aluminium block engine) or crankcase (cast-iron block engine) **(see illustration)**. Disengage the pump sprocket from the chain, and remove the oil pump. If the pump locating dowel is a loose fit, remove and store it with the retaining bolts for safe-keeping.

3 If it is required to remove the oil pump drive chain, the crankshaft right-hand oil seal must be removed as described in Section 14, then the spacer removed from the front of the crankshaft. The oil pump drive sprocket must then be removed from the key on the crankshaft after lifting the chain over its teeth. With the sprocket removed, the chain can be withdrawn upwards through the aperture in the front of the cylinder block, and over the nose of the crankshaft.

HAYNES HiNT ***On cast-iron block engines (K2D, K6B and KFZ) it should not be necessary to unbolt the oil seal housing from the block, but this will give increased room to remove the chain .***

Inspection

4 Examine the oil pump sprocket for signs of damage and wear, such as chipped or missing teeth. If the sprocket is worn, the pump assembly must be renewed, since the sprocket is not available separately. It is also recommended that the chain and drive sprocket, fitted to the crankshaft, be renewed at the same time.

5 Slacken and remove the five bolts securing the strainer cover to the pump body, then lift off the strainer cover. Remove the relief valve piston and spring (and guide pin - cast-iron block engines only), noting which way round they are fitted.

6 Examine the pump rotors and body for signs of wear ridges and scoring. If worn, the complete pump assembly must be renewed.

7 Examine the relief valve piston for signs of wear or damage, and renew if necessary. The condition of the relief valve spring can only be measured by comparing it with a new one; if there is any doubt about its condition, it should also be renewed. Both the piston and spring are available individually.

8 Thoroughly clean the oil pump strainer with a suitable solvent, and check it for signs of clogging or splitting. If the strainer is damaged, the strainer and cover assembly must be renewed.

9 Locate the relief valve spring and piston in the strainer cover, then refit the cover to the pump body. Align the relief valve piston with its bore in the pump. Refit the five cover retaining bolts, tightening them securely.

14.2 Using a screwdriver to lever out the crankshaft front oil seal

Refitting

10 Where necessary, fit the oil pump drive chain, sprocket and new oil seal to the right-hand end of the crankshaft, with reference to Section 14.

11 Ensure that the locating dowel is in position, then engage the pump sprocket with its drive chain. Seat the pump on the main bearing ladder or crankcase (as applicable). Refit the pump retaining bolts, and tighten them to the specified torque setting.

12 Refit the sump as described in Section 12.

13 Before running the engine, disconnect the ignition wiring harness to disable the ignition system, then spin the engine on the starter motor until oil pressure is restored and the oil pressure warning light is extinguished. Reconnect the wiring harness and start the engine to check for oil leaks.

14 Crankshaft oil seals - renewal

Right-hand oil seal

1 Remove the crankshaft sprocket and flanged spacer as described in Section 7. Secure the timing belt clear of the working area, so that it cannot be contaminated with oil. Make a note of the correct fitted depth of the seal in its housing.

2 Punch or drill two small holes opposite each other in the seal. Screw a self-tapping screw into each, and pull on the screws with pliers to extract the seal. Alternatively, the seal can be levered out of position using a flat-bladed screwdriver, taking great care not to damage the crankshaft shoulder or seal housing **(see illustration)**.

3 Clean the seal housing, and polish off any burrs or raised edges, which may have caused the seal to fail in the first place.

4 Lubricate the lips of the new seal with clean engine oil, and carefully locate the seal on the end of crankshaft. Note that its sealing lip must face inwards. Take care not to damage the seal lips during fitting.

5 Using a tubular drift (such as a socket) which bears only on the hard outer edge of the seal, tap the seal into position, to the same depth in the housing as the original was prior to removal. The inner face of the seal must end up flush with the inner wall of the crankcase.

6 Wash off any traces of oil, then refit the crankshaft sprocket as described in Section 7.

Left-hand oil seal

7 Remove the flywheel as described in Section 15.

8 Make a note of the correct fitted depth of the seal in its housing. Punch or drill two small holes opposite each other in the seal. Screw a self-tapping screw into each, and pull on the screws with pliers to extract the seal.

9 Clean the seal housing, and polish off any burrs or raised edges, which may have caused the seal to fail in the first place.

10 Lubricate the lips of the new seal with clean engine oil, and carefully locate the seal on the end of the crankshaft.

11 Using a tubular drift (such as a socket), which bears only on the hard outer edge of the seal, drive the seal into position, to the same depth in the housing as the original was prior to removal.

12 Wash off any traces of oil, then refit the flywheel as described in Section 15.

15 Flywheel - removal, inspection and refitting

Removal

1 Remove the transmission as described in Chapter 7, then remove the clutch assembly as described in Chapter 6.

2 Prevent the flywheel from turning by locking the ring gear teeth with a similar arrangement to that shown in illustration 7.10 (Section 7). Alternatively, bolt a strap between the flywheel and the cylinder block/crankcase. *Do not attempt to lock the flywheel in position using the locking tool described in Section 3.*

3 Slacken and remove the flywheel retaining bolts, and discard them; they must be renewed whenever they are disturbed.

4 Remove the flywheel. Do not drop it, as it is very heavy. If the locating dowel is a loose fit in the crankshaft end, remove and store it with the flywheel for safe-keeping.

Inspection

5 If the flywheel's clutch mating surface is deeply scored, cracked or otherwise damaged, the flywheel must be renewed. However, it may be possible to have it surface-ground; seek the advice of a Citroën dealer or engine reconditioning specialist.

6 If the ring gear is badly worn or has missing teeth, it must be renewed. This job is best left to a Citroën dealer or engine reconditioning specialist. The temperature to which the new ring gear must be heated for installation is critical and, if not done accurately, the hardness of the teeth will be destroyed.

Refitting

7 Clean the mating surfaces of the flywheel and crankshaft. Remove any remaining locking compound from the threads of the crankshaft holes, using the correct-size tap, if available.

> **TOOL TIP** *If a tap is not available, cut two slots into the threads of an old flywheel bolt and use the bolt to remove the locking compound from the threads.*

8 If the new flywheel retaining bolts are not supplied with their threads already pre-coated, apply a suitable thread-locking compound to the threads of each bolt. Citroën recommend the use of Frenetanch E3 (available from your Citroën dealer); in the absence of this, ensure that a good-quality locking compound is used.

9 Ensure that the locating dowel is in position. Offer up the flywheel, locating it on the dowel, and fit the new retaining bolts.

10 Lock the flywheel using the method employed on dismantling, and tighten the retaining bolts to the specified torque.

11 Refit the clutch as described in Chapter 6. Remove the locking tool, and refit the transmission as described in Chapter 7.

16 Engine/transmission mountings - inspection and renewal

2A

Inspection

1 If improved access is required, raise the front of the car and support it securely on axle stands.

2 Check the mounting rubber to see if it is cracked, hardened or separated from the metal at any point; renew the mounting if any such damage or deterioration is evident.

3 Check that all the mounting's fasteners are securely tightened; use a torque wrench to check if possible.

4 Using a large screwdriver or a crowbar, check for wear in the mounting by carefully levering against it to check for free play. Where this is not possible, enlist the aid of an assistant to move the engine/transmission unit back and forth, or from side to side, while you watch the mounting. While some free play is to be expected even from new components, excessive wear should be obvious. If excessive free play is found, check first that the fasteners are correctly secured, then renew any worn components as described below.

Renewal

Right-hand mounting

5 Disconnect the battery negative lead.

6 Place a jack beneath the engine, with a block of wood on the jack head. Raise the jack until it is supporting the weight of the engine.

7 Slacken and remove the nuts securing the right-hand engine mounting upper bracket to the bracket on the cylinder block. Remove the nut securing the bracket to the mounting rubber, and lift off the bracket.

8 Where applicable, lift the buffer plate off the mounting rubber stud, then unscrew the nut and remove the mounting rubber from the body.
9 Check carefully for signs of wear or damage on all components, and renew them where necessary.
10 On reassembly, tighten the nut securing the mounting rubber to the body.
11 Refit the buffer plate to the mounting rubber stud where applicable, then install the mounting bracket.
12 Tighten the mounting bracket retaining nuts to the specified torque setting.
13 Remove the jack from underneath the engine, and reconnect the battery negative lead.

Left-hand mounting

14 Remove the battery and its tray, as described in Chapter 5.
15 Place a jack beneath the transmission, with a block of wood on the jack head. Raise the jack until it is supporting the weight of the transmission.
16 Slacken and remove the mounting rubber centre bolt, and the two nuts securing the bracket to the body. Remove the mounting rubber.
17 Where necessary, unscrew the nuts and remove the bracket from the transmission.
18 Check carefully for signs of wear or damage on all components, and renew them where necessary.
19 Refit the bracket to the transmission, tightening its mounting nuts to the specified torque.
20 Refit the mounting rubber to the body, and tighten its retaining bolts to the specified torque. Refit the mounting centre bolt and tighten to the specified torque.
21 Remove the jack from underneath the transmission, then refit the battery and its tray as described in Chapter 5.

Rear mounting

22 If not already done, firmly apply the handbrake, then jack up the front of the vehicle and support it securely on axle stands.
23 Unscrew and remove the centre bolt securing the rear mounting link to the bracket on the rear of the transmission.
24 Remove the centre bolt securing the rear mounting link to the bracket on the underbody. Withdraw the link.
25 Unbolt the bracket from the rear of the transmission.
26 Check carefully for signs of wear or damage on all components, and renew them where necessary.
27 On reassembly, fit the rear mounting assembly to the rear of the transmission, and tighten its retaining bolts to the specified torque.
28 Refit the rear mounting link, and tighten the centre bolts to the specified torques.
29 Lower the vehicle to the ground.

Chapter 2 Part B: Diesel engine in-car repair procedures

Contents

Degrees of difficulty

Easy, suitable for novice with little experience	**Fairly easy,** suitable for beginner with some experience	**Fairly difficult,** suitable for competent DIY mechanic	**Difficult,** suitable for experienced DIY mechanic	**Very difficult,** suitable for expert DIY or professional

Specifications

General

Designation:	
1360 cc aluminium block engine	TUD3
1527 cc cast-iron block engine	TUD5
Engine codes*:	
1360 cc engine	K9A
1527 cc engine	VJZ and VJY
No 1 cylinder location	Flywheel/transmission end of block
Direction of crankshaft rotation	Clockwise (viewed from right-hand side of vehicle)
Firing order	1-3-4-2
Bore:	
1360 cc engine	75.00 mm
1527 cc engine	77.00 mm
Stroke:	
1360 cc engine	77.00 mm
1527 cc engine	82.00 mm
Compression ratio:	
1360 cc engine	22.0 : 1
1527 cc engine	23.0 : 1
Maximum power (DIN):	
1360 cc engine	53 hp (40 kW) at 5000 rpm
1527 cc engine:	
VJZ engine	58 hp (42 kW) at 5000 rpm
VJY engine	55 hp (40 kW) at 5000 rpm
Maximum torque (DIN):	
1360 cc engine	83 Nm (61 lbf ft) at 2500 rpm
1527 cc engine	95 Nm (70 lbf ft) at 2250 rpm

**The engine code is stamped on a plate attached to the front left-hand end of the cylinder block; this is the code most often used by Citroën. The code given in brackets is the factory identification number, and is not often referred to by Citroën or this manual.*

Camshaft

Drive method	Toothed belt
Number of bearings	3
Endfloat	0.025 to 0.114 mm

Valve clearances (engine cold)

Inlet valves (all engines)	0.15 ± 0.075 mm
Exhaust valves (all engines)	0.30 ± 0.075 mm

Lubrication system

Oil pump type	Gear-type, chain-driven off the crankshaft
Minimum oil pressure at 90°C	4 bars at 4000 rpm
Oil pressure warning switch operating pressure	0.5 bars

Torque wrench settings

Torque wrench settings	Nm	lbf ft
Cylinder head cover nuts	7	5
Timing belt cover bolts:		
Except upper cover-to-cylinder head cover	8	6
Upper cover-to-cylinder head cover	5	5
Timing belt tensioner pulley nut	23	17
Camshaft sprocket retaining bolt	80	59
Injection pump sprocket nut	50	37
Oil dipstick tube-to-cylinder head retaining bolt	16	12
Injector pipe union	20	15
Camshaft bearing cap	18	13
Crankshaft pulley-to-sprocket	16	12
Crankshaft sprocket retaining bolt	110	81
Sump-to-cylinder block	8	6
Sump drain plug	30	22
Oil pump retaining bolts	8	6
Flywheel retaining bolts	65	48
Cylinder head bolts (aluminium block engine):		
Stage 1	60	44
Stage 2	Slacken all cylinder head bolts	
Stage 3	20	15
Stage 4	Angle-tighten through 160°	Angle-tighten through 160°
Stage 5	Angle-tighten a further 160°	Angle-tighten a further 160°
Cylinder head bolts (cast-iron block engine):		
Stage 1	40	30
Stage 2	Angle-tighten through 260°	Angle-tighten through 260°
Engine/transmission right-hand mounting:		
Mounting bracket retaining nuts-to-bracket on rear of cylinder block	45	33
Mounting bracket-to-body mounting nut	35	26
Mounting-to-body nut	35	26
Engine/transmission left-hand mounting:		
Mounting bracket-to-transmission nuts	30	22
Mounting bracket-to-body bolts	17	13
Centre bolt	50	37
Engine/transmission rear mounting:		
Mounting assembly-to-block bolts	40	30
Mounting bracket-to-mounting centre bolt	60	44
Mounting bracket-to-subframe bolt	90	66

1 General information

How to use this Chapter

This Part of Chapter 2 describes the repair procedures that can reasonably be carried out on the TUD Diesel engine while it remains in the vehicle. If the engine has been removed from the vehicle and is being dismantled as described in Part C, any preliminary dismantling procedures can be ignored.

Note that, while it may be possible physically to overhaul items such as the piston/connecting rod assemblies while the engine is in the car, such tasks are not usually carried out as separate operations. Usually, several additional procedures are required (not to mention the cleaning of components and of oilways); for this reason, all such tasks are classed as major overhaul procedures, and are described in Part C of this Chapter.

Part C describes the removal of the engine/transmission unit from the vehicle, and the full overhaul procedures that can then be carried out.

Engine description

The TUD engine is one of the smallest passenger car diesels in current production. This engine is well-proven, and has been fitted to many previous Citroën and Peugeot vehicles (the bottom end of the engine is very similar to that of the TU petrol engine covered in Part A). The aluminium block engine is of four-cylinder wet liner type, with a belt-driven overhead camshaft **(see illustration)**. The engine is mounted transversely, with the transmission on the left-hand side. The cast-iron block engine introduced in July 1994 has integral bores in the cylinder block - on this type of engine, the cylinder bores are sometimes referred to as having "dry liners".

The crankshaft runs in five main bearings of the usual shell type. Endfloat is controlled by thrustwashers either side of No 2 main bearing.

The connecting rods rotate on horizontally-split bearing shells at their big-ends. The pistons are attached to the connecting rods by gudgeon pins, which are fully-floating in the connecting rod small-end eyes, and retained by circlips in the pistons. The aluminium-alloy pistons are fitted with three piston rings - two compression rings and an oil control ring.

The aluminium block engine is fitted with replaceable cast-iron wet liners. Sealing O-rings are fitted at the base of each liner, to prevent the escape of coolant into the sump.

The inlet and exhaust valves are each closed by coil springs, and operate in guides pressed into the cylinder head; the valve seat inserts are also pressed into the cylinder head, and can be renewed separately if worn.

The camshaft is driven by a toothed timing belt, and operates the eight valves directly via bucket tappets. Valve clearance adjustment is by means of selective shims. The camshaft is supported by three bearings machined directly in the cylinder head.

Lubrication is by means of an oil pump, which is driven (via a chain and sprocket) off the right-hand end of the crankshaft. It draws oil through a strainer located in the sump, and

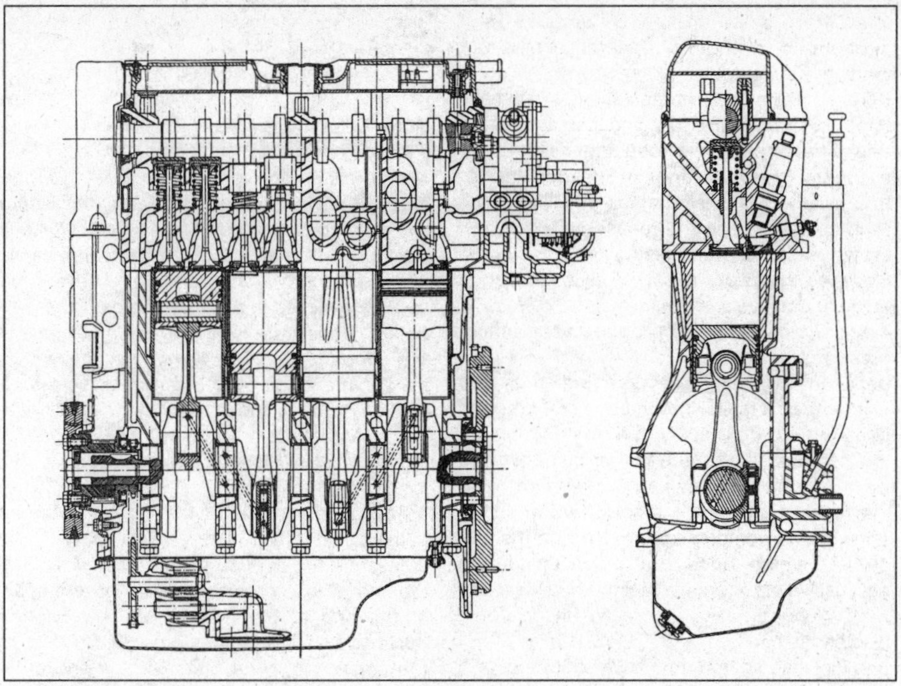

1.4 Sectional view of the aluminium block TUD Diesel engine - cast-iron block engine similar

then forces it through an externally-mounted filter into galleries in the cylinder block/crankcase. From there, the oil is distributed to the crankshaft (main bearings) and camshaft. The big-end bearings are supplied with oil via internal drillings in the crankshaft, while the camshaft bearings also receive a pressurised supply. The camshaft lobes and valves are lubricated by splash, as are all other engine components **(see illustration)**.

Throughout this manual, it is often necessary to identify the engines not only by their capacity, but also by their engine code. The engine code, which consists of three digits (eg. K9A), is stamped on a plate attached to the front left-hand end of the cylinder block **(see illustration)**.

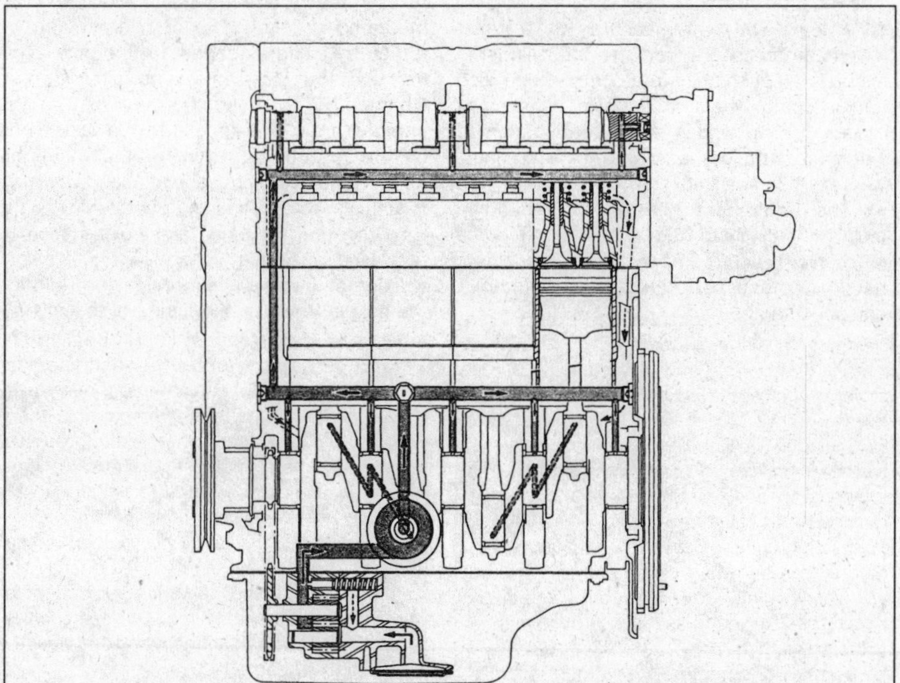

1.11 Lubrication system of the TUD Diesel engine (aluminium block engine shown)

Repair operations possible with the engine in the car

The following work can be carried out with the engine in the car:

a) Compression pressure and leakdown testing.
b) Cylinder head cover - removal and refitting.
c) Timing belt covers - removal and refitting.
d) Timing belt - removal, refitting and adjustment.
e) Timing belt tensioner and sprockets - removal and refitting.
f) Camshaft oil seal - renewal.
g) Camshaft and followers - removal, inspection and refitting.
h) Cylinder head - removal and refitting.
i) Cylinder head and pistons - decarbonising (refer to Part C of this Chapter).
j) Sump - removal and refitting.
k) Oil pump - removal, overhaul and refitting.
l) Crankshaft oil seals - renewal.
m) Engine/transmission mountings - inspection and renewal.
n) Flywheel - removal, inspection and refitting.

Note: *At the time of writing, only limited information was available on the cast-iron block Diesel engine introduced in July 1994. This information consists mainly of Specifications, and therefore the main Sections of this Chapter refer only to the aluminium block engine. There are many similarities between the petrol and Diesel iron-block engines, and procedures for the lower half of the engine are very similar to those for the petrol iron-block engine. The cylinder head is based on the aluminium block Diesel engine, although the locations of the injectors and glow plugs are reversed (ie the glow plugs are above the injectors).*

1.12 The engine code is stamped on a plate (arrowed) attached to the front of the cylinder block - viewed from above

2B

2 Compression and leakdown tests - description and interpretation

Compression test

Note: *A compression tester specifically designed for Diesel engines must be used for this test.*

1 When engine performance is down, or if misfiring occurs which cannot be attributed to the fuel system, a compression test can provide diagnostic clues as to the engine's condition. If the test is performed regularly, it can give warning of trouble before any other symptoms become apparent.

2 A compression tester specifically designed for Diesel engines must be used, because of the higher pressures involved. The tester is connected to an adapter which screws into the glow plug or injector hole **(see illustration).** It is unlikely to be worthwhile buying such a tester for occasional use, but it may be possible to borrow or hire one - if not, have the test performed by a garage.

3 Unless specific instructions to the contrary are supplied with the tester, observe the following points:

a) The battery must be in a good state of charge, the air filter must be clean, and the engine should be at normal operating temperature.
b) All the injectors or glow plugs should be removed before starting the test. If removing the injectors, also remove the flame shield washers, otherwise they may be blown out.
c) The stop solenoid must be disconnected, to prevent the engine from running or fuel from being discharged.

4 There is no need to hold the accelerator pedal down during the test, because the Diesel engine air inlet is not throttled.

5 The actual compression pressures measured are not so important as the balance between cylinders. Although Citroën do not specify exact compression pressures, as a guide, any cylinder pressure below 20 bars can be considered as less than healthy. Refer to a Citroën dealer or other Diesel specialist if in doubt as to whether a particular pressure reading is acceptable.

6 The cause of poor compression is less easy to establish on a Diesel engine than on a petrol one. The effect of introducing oil into the cylinders ("wet" testing) is not conclusive, because there is a risk that the oil will sit in the swirl chamber or in the recess on the piston crown instead of passing to the rings. However, the following can be used as a rough guide to diagnosis.

7 All cylinders should produce very similar pressures; any difference of more than 4 bars between any two cylinders indicates the existence of a fault. Note that the compression should build up quickly in a healthy engine; low compression on the first stroke, followed by gradually-increasing pressure on successive strokes, indicates worn piston rings. A low compression reading on the first stroke, which does not build up during successive strokes, indicates leaking valves or a blown head gasket (a cracked head could also be the cause).

8 A low reading from two adjacent cylinders is almost certainly due to the head gasket having blown between them; the presence of coolant in the engine oil, or vice-versa, will confirm this.

9 If the compression reading is unusually high, the cylinder head surfaces, valves and pistons are probably coated with carbon deposits. If this is the case, the cylinder head should be removed and decarbonised (see Chapter 2C, Section 7).

Leakdown test

10 A leakdown test measures the rate at which compressed air fed into the cylinder is lost. It is an alternative to a compression test, and in many ways it is better, since the escaping air provides easy identification of where pressure loss is occurring (piston rings, valves or head gasket).

11 The equipment needed for leakdown testing is unlikely to be available to the home mechanic. If poor compression is suspected, have the test performed by a suitably-equipped garage.

3 Top dead centre (TDC) for No 4 piston - locating

Note: *Refer to the note at the end of Section 1 if working on the cast-iron block engine.*

Note: *This engine is timed on No 4 cylinder. Three 8 mm diameter bolts and one 8 mm diameter rod or drill will be required for this procedure. Do not attempt to rotate the engine whilst the crankshaft, camshaft or injection pump are locked in position. If the engine is to be left in this state for a long period of time, it is a good idea to place warning notices inside the vehicle, and in the engine compartment. This will reduce the possibility of the engine being accidentally cranked on the starter motor, which is likely to cause damage with the locking tools in place.*

1 Top dead centre (TDC) is the highest point in the cylinder that each piston reaches as the crankshaft turns. Each piston reaches TDC at the end of the compression stroke, and again at the end of the exhaust stroke. For the purpose of timing this engine, TDC refers to the position of No 4 piston at the end of its compression stroke. On the TUD engine, No 1 piston is at the flywheel end of the engine, therefore No 4 piston is at the timing belt end of the engine.

2 Remove the upper and centre timing belt covers as described in Section 5.

3 The crankshaft must now be turned until the three bolt holes in the camshaft and injection pump sprockets (one hole in the camshaft sprocket, two holes in the injection pump sprocket) are aligned with the corresponding holes in the cylinder head and injection pump mounting bracket. The crankshaft can be turned by using a spanner on the pulley bolt (remove the glow plugs as described in Chapter 5C to make it easier to turn the engine). Improved access to the pulley bolt can be obtained by jacking up the front right-hand corner of the vehicle (see *"Jacking, towing and wheel changing"*) and removing the roadwheel and the wheel arch covers (secured by plastic clips).

4 Insert an 6 mm diameter rod or drill through the hole in the left-hand flange of the cylinder

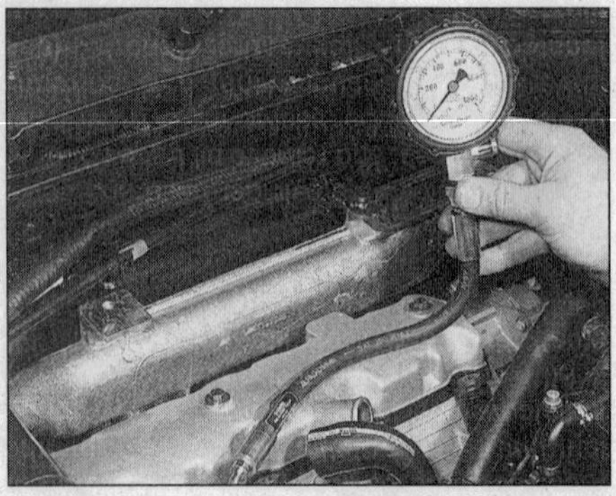

2.2 Performing a compression test

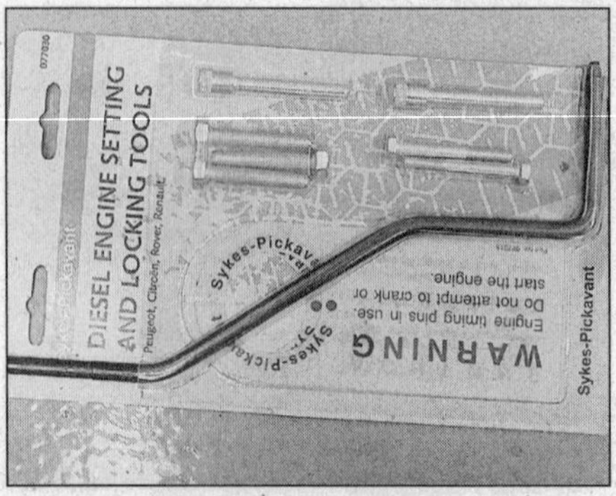

3.4a Suitable tools available for locking engine with No 4 piston at TDC

3.4b Insert a 6 mm bolt (arrowed) through the hole in the cylinder block flange and into timing hole in the flywheel

3.5a Insert an 8 mm bolt (arrowed) through the camshaft sprocket timing hole, and screw it into the cylinder head . . .

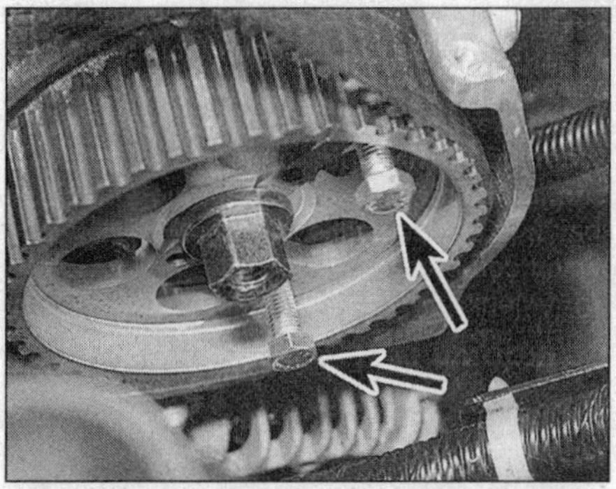

3.5b . . . then insert two 8 mm bolts (arrowed) into the injection pump sprocket holes, and screw them into the mounting bracket

3.7 Warning notice in place in (typical) engine compartment

block (just above the TDC sensor position); if necessary, carefully turn the crankshaft either way until the rod enters the TDC hole in the flywheel **(see illustrations)**.

5 Insert three M8 bolts through the holes in the camshaft and fuel injection pump sprockets, and screw them into the engine finger-tight **(see illustrations)**.

6 The crankshaft, camshaft and injection pump are now "locked" in position with No 4 piston at TDC.

7 If the engine is to be left in this state for a long period of time, it is a good idea to place suitable warning notices inside the vehicle, and in the engine compartment **(see illustration)**. This will reduce the possibility of the engine being accidentally cranked on the starter motor, which is likely to cause damage with the locking tools in place.

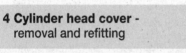

4 Cylinder head cover - removal and refitting

Note: *A new cylinder head cover rubber seal must be used on refitting.*

Removal

1 Disconnect the breather hose from the left-hand rear of the cylinder head cover **(see illustration)**.

2 Remove the timing belt upper cover as described in Section 5.

3 Unscrew the eight securing bolts, noting their locations as they are of two different lengths. Recover the washers from the bolts/cover **(see illustrations)**.

4 Lift off the cylinder head cover **(see illustration)**, and discard the rubber seal.

Refitting

5 Carefully clean the cylinder head and cover mating surfaces, and remove all traces of oil.

6 Fit the new rubber seal to the cylinder head cover groove, ensuring that it is correctly located along its entire length **(see illustration)**.

7 Carefully refit the cylinder head cover to the engine, taking great care not to displace the rubber seal.

8 Install the retaining bolts and washers, and tighten them to the specified torque setting.

9 Refit the upper timing belt cover as described in Section 5.

10 Reconnect the breather hose to the cylinder head cover, securely tightening its retaining clip, and reconnect the battery negative lead.

2B

4.1 Slacken the retaining clip and disconnect the breather hose from the left-hand end of the cylinder head cover

4.3a Unscrew the eight retaining bolts (arrowed) . . .

4.3b . . . and remove them along with their washers

4.4 Lift the cover away from the engine, and recover the rubber seal

4.6 Ensure the new rubber seal is correctly located in the cover groove prior to refitting

5.1 Removing the timing belt upper cover

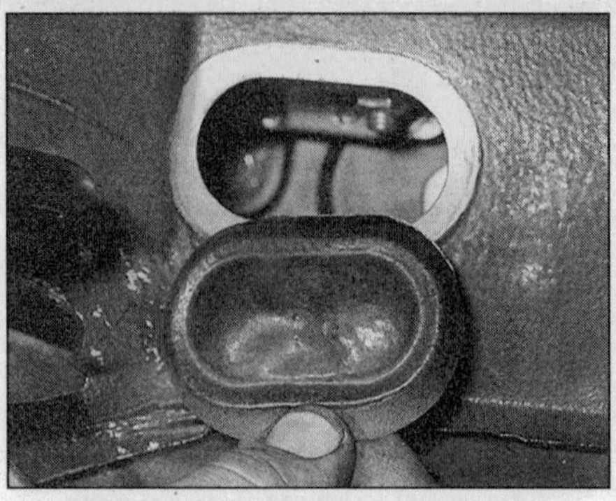

5.3a Remove the rubber plug from the right-hand wing valance . . .

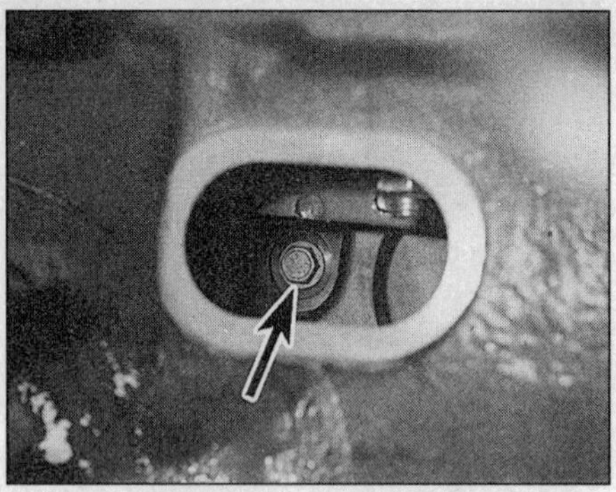

5.3b . . . to gain access to the timing belt centre cover bolt (arrowed)

5 Timing belt covers - removal and refitting

Removal

Upper cover

1 Slacken and remove the retaining bolts, and remove the upper timing cover from the cylinder head **(see illustration)**.

Centre cover

2 Remove the upper cover as described in paragraph 1.

3 Turn the wheels onto full right-hand lock, then prise out the rubber plug from underneath the right-hand front wheel arch. Unscrew the timing belt cover bolt which is accessible through the hole in the wing valance **(see illustrations)**.

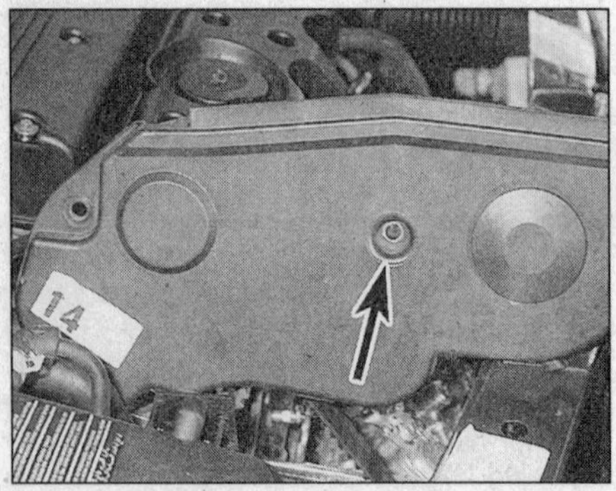

5.4 Unscrew the remaining bolt (location arrowed) and remove the centre cover

4 Unscrew the other retaining bolt from the centre of the cover, then manoeuvre the cover out of position **(see illustration)**.

Lower cover

5 Remove the auxiliary drivebelt as described in Chapter 1.

6 Remove the upper and centre covers as described in paragraphs 1 to 4.

7 Undo the crankshaft pulley retaining bolts and remove the pulley, noting which way round it is fitted **(see illustrations)**.

8 Slacken and remove the retaining bolts, and withdraw the lower cover over the crankshaft sprocket outer flange **(see illustration)**.

Refitting

Upper cover

9 Refit the cover, ensuring it is correctly located with the centre cover, and tighten its retaining bolts.

Centre cover

10 Manoeuvre the centre cover back into position, ensuring that it is correctly located with the cut-out in the lower cover, then tighten its retaining bolts. Refit the rubber plug to the wing valance.

11 Refit the upper cover as described above.

Lower cover

12 Locate the lower cover over the crankshaft sprocket outer flange, and tighten its retaining bolts.

13 Fit the pulley onto the crankshaft sprocket flange, ensuring that it is fitted the correct way round, and tighten its retaining bolts to the specified torque.

14 Refit the centre and upper covers as described above, then refit and tension the auxiliary drivebelt as described in Chapter 1.

6 Timing belt - general information, removal and refitting

Note: *Refer to the note at the end of Section 1 if working on the cast-iron block engine.*

General information

1 The timing belt drives the camshaft, injection pump, and coolant pump from a toothed sprocket on the front of the crankshaft. The belt also drives the brake vacuum pump indirectly via the rear ("flywheel") end of the camshaft. If the belt breaks or slips in service, the pistons are likely to hit the valve heads, resulting in extensive (and expensive) damage.

2 The timing belt should be renewed at the specified intervals, or earlier if it is

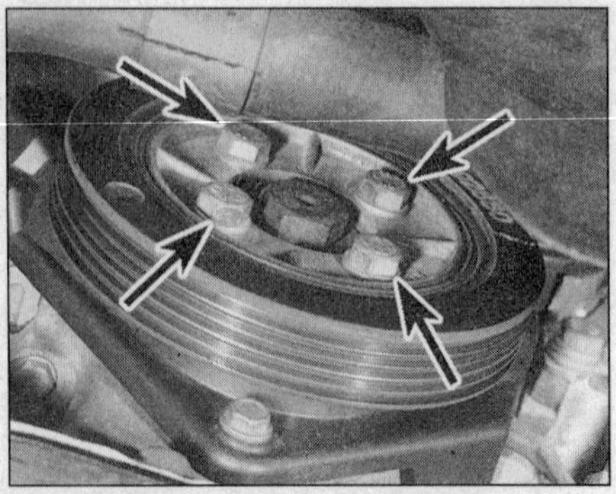

5.7a Undo the retaining bolts (arrowed) . . .

5.7b . . . and remove the crankshaft pulley from the engine

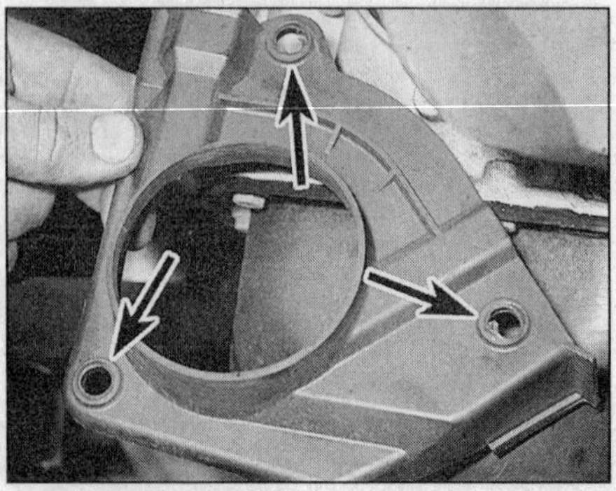

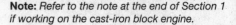

5.8 Undo the retaining bolts (locations arrowed) and remove the lower cover

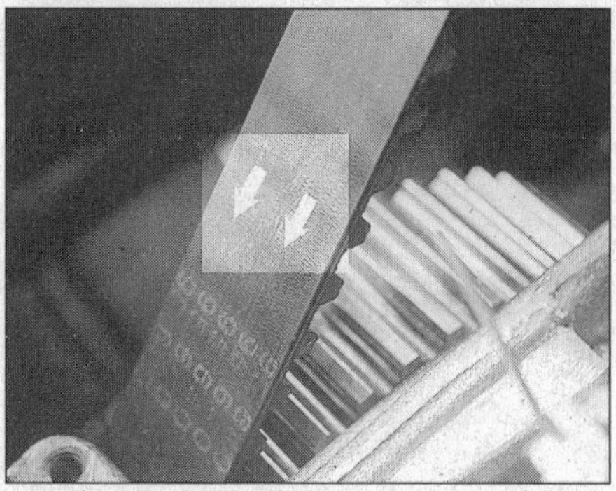

6.8 Mark the direction of rotation on the belt if it is to be re-used

6.13 Engage the timing belt with the sprockets as described in text

6.14 Remove all free play from the belt, then securely tighten the tensioner pulley retaining nut

contaminated with oil, or at all noisy in operation (a "scraping" noise due to uneven wear).

3 If the timing belt is being removed, it is a wise precaution to check the condition of the coolant pump at the same time (check for signs of coolant leakage). This may avoid the need to remove the timing belt again at a later stage, should the coolant pump fail.

Removal

4 Disconnect the battery negative terminal. For improved access, remove the right-hand headlight as described in Chapter 12.

5 Set No 4 piston to TDC, then lock the crankshaft, and the camshaft and fuel injection pump sprockets, in position as described in Section 3. *Do not* attempt to rotate the engine whilst the locking tools are in position.

6 Remove the timing belt covers as described in Section 5.

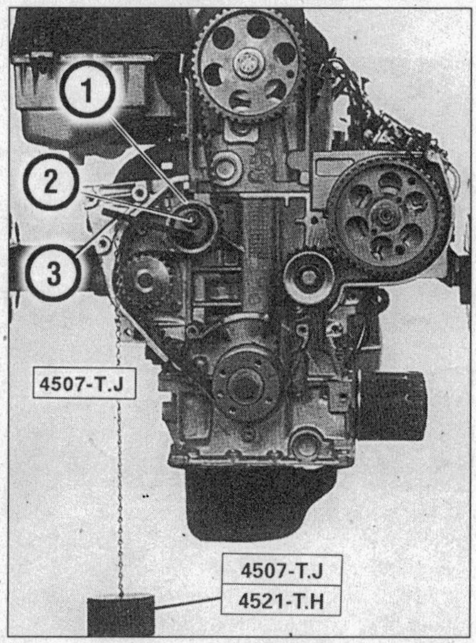

6.15a Using one of the Citroën special tools to tension the timing belt

1 Tensioner roller
2 Pulley retaining nut
3 Special tool fitted to tensioner roller

7 Loosen the timing belt tensioner pulley retaining nut. Pivot the pulley in a clockwise direction, using a square-section key fitted to the hole in the pulley hub, then retighten the retaining nut.

8 If the timing belt is to be re-used, use white paint or similar to mark the direction of rotation on the belt (if markings do not already exist) (see illustration).

9 Slip the belt off the sprockets, idler and tensioner.

10 Check the timing belt carefully for any signs of uneven wear, splitting, or oil contamination. Pay particular attention to the roots of the teeth. If signs of oil contamination are found, trace the source of the oil leak, and rectify it. Wash down the engine timing belt area and all related components, to remove all traces of oil.

HAYNES HiNT ***Renew the belt if there is the slightest doubt about its condition. If the engine is undergoing an overhaul, and has covered more than 36 000 miles (60 000 km) with the existing belt fitted, renew the belt as a matter of course, regardless of its apparent condition. The cost of a new belt is nothing when compared to the cost of repairs, should the belt break in service.***

6.15b Using a home-made special tool and spring balance to tension the timing belt

Refitting

11 Prior to refitting, thoroughly clean the timing belt sprockets. Check that the tensioner pulley rotates freely, without any sign of roughness. If necessary, renew the tensioner pulley as described in Section 7. Make sure that the locking tools are still in place, as described in Section 3.

12 Manoeuvre the timing belt into position, ensuring that the arrows on the belt are pointing in the direction of rotation (clockwise when viewed from the right-hand end of the engine).

13 Do not twist the timing belt sharply while refitting it. First locate the belt over the crankshaft sprocket, then feed it over the coolant pump sprocket, idler and injection pump sprocket, making sure that it is kept taut (see illustration). Locate the back of the belt under the tensioner roller, then engage it with the camshaft sprocket. Ensure that the belt teeth are seated centrally in the sprockets.

14 Loosen the tensioner pulley retaining nut. Pivot the pulley anti-clockwise to remove all free play from the timing belt, then retighten the nut (see illustration).

15 Citroën dealers use one of two special tools to tension the timing belt - one of these tools is fitted on the timing belt between the injection pump and camshaft sprockets - the belt is tensioned until the tool reads 25 units. The other tool consists of a bar and weight applied to the tensioner pulley (see illustration). A similar tool may be fabricated using a suitable square-section bar attached to an arm; a hole should be drilled in the arm at a distance of 80 mm from the centre of the square-section bar. Fit the tool to the hole in the tensioner pulley, keeping the tool arm as close to the horizontal as possible, and hang a 2.0 kg (4.4 lb) weight from the hole in the tool. In the absence of an object of the specified weight, a spring balance can be used to exert the required force, ensuring that the spring balance is held at 90° to the tool arm (see illustration). Slacken the pulley retaining nut, allowing the weight or force exerted (as applicable) to push the tensioner pulley against the belt, then retighten the pulley nut.

16 Remove the locking tools from the

camshaft sprocket and injection pump sprocket, and from the flywheel.

17 Using a suitable socket and extension bar on the crankshaft sprocket bolt, rotate the crankshaft through ten complete rotations in a clockwise direction (viewed from the right-hand end of the engine). *Do not* at any time rotate the crankshaft anti-clockwise.

18 Slacken the tensioner pulley nut, re-tension the belt using the method just described, then tighten the tensioner pulley nut to the specified torque.

19 Rotate the crankshaft through a further two turns clockwise, and check that both the camshaft sprocket and flywheel timing holes are correctly aligned once more.

20 If all is well, refit the timing belt covers as described in Section 5, and reconnect the battery negative terminal. If removed, refit the right-hand headlight.

7 Timing belt tensioner and sprockets - removal, inspection and refitting

Removal

Note: *This Section describes the removal and refitting of the components concerned as individual operations. If more than one of them is to be removed at the same time, start by removing the timing belt as described in Section 6; remove the actual component as described below, ignoring the preliminary dismantling steps.*

1 Disconnect the battery negative terminal.

2 Position the engine at top dead centre (TDC on No 4 cylinder) as described in Section 3, and lock the camshaft sprocket, injection pump sprocket and flywheel in position. *Do not* attempt to rotate the engine whilst the locking tools are in position.

Camshaft sprocket

3 Remove the upper and centre timing belt covers as described in Section 5.

4 Loosen the timing belt tensioner pulley retaining nut. Rotate the pulley in a clockwise direction, using a suitable square-section key fitted to the hole in the pulley hub, then retighten the retaining nut.

5 Disengage the timing belt from the sprocket, and move the belt clear, taking care not to bend or twist it sharply. Remove the locking tool from the camshaft sprocket.

6 Slacken the camshaft sprocket retaining bolt and remove it, along with its washer. To prevent the camshaft rotating as the bolt is slackened, a sprocket-holding tool will be required **(see illustration).** *Do not* attempt to use the sprocket locking tool (Section 3) to prevent the sprocket from rotating whilst the retaining bolt is slackened.

In the absence of the special Citroën tool, an acceptable substitute can be fabricated as follows. Use two lengths of steel strip (one long, the other short), and three nuts and bolts; one nut and bolt forms the pivot of a forked tool, with the remaining two nuts and bolts at the tips of the "forks" to engage with the sprocket spokes.

7 With the retaining bolt removed, slide the sprocket off the end of the camshaft. Note that the tab on the rear of the sprocket engages with a cut-out on the end of the camshaft. Examine the camshaft oil seal for signs of oil leakage and, if necessary, renew it as described in Section 8.

Crankshaft sprocket

8 Remove all of the timing belt covers as described in Section 5.

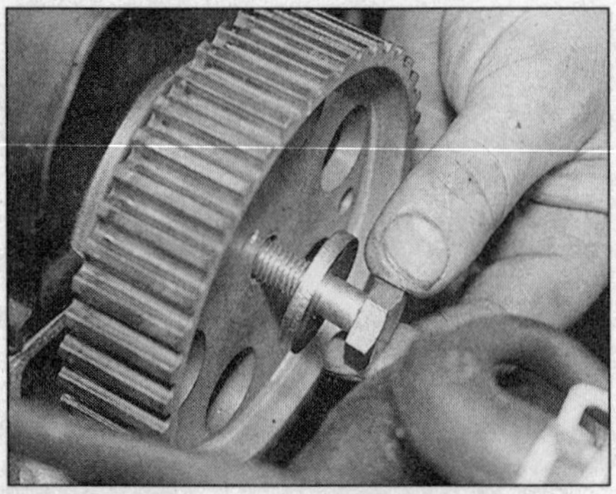

7.6 Remove the retaining bolt and washer, then remove the camshaft sprocket

7.11 The Citroën flywheel-locking tool inserted in the TDC sensor hole

9 Loosen the timing belt tensioner pulley retaining nut. Rotate the pulley in a clockwise direction, using a suitable square-section key fitted to the hole in the pulley hub, then retighten the retaining nut.

10 Disengage the timing belt from the crankshaft sprocket, and move the belt clear, taking care not to bend or twist it sharply.

11 To prevent crankshaft rotation whilst the sprocket retaining bolt is slackened, select top gear, and have an assistant apply the brakes firmly. Note that Citroën technicians use a special tool inserted through the TDC sensor hole, which is located near the locking tool hole in the cylinder block rear flange **(see illustration)** - if possible, obtain and use this tool. If the engine has been removed from the vehicle and the special tool is not available, lock the flywheel ring gear, using an arrangement similar to that shown in illustration 7.10 in Part A of this Chapter. *Do not* be tempted to use the locking tool described in Section 3 to prevent the crankshaft from rotating; temporarily remove this tool from the rear of the flywheel prior to slackening the pulley bolt, then refit it once the bolt has been slackened.

12 Unscrew the retaining bolt and washer, then slide the sprocket off the end of the crankshaft (see illustrations 7.11a and 7.11b in Part A of this Chapter). Refit the locking tool through the timing hole into the rear of the flywheel.

13 If the Woodruff key is a loose fit in the crankshaft, remove it and store it with the sprocket for safe-keeping. If necessary, also slide the flanged spacer off the end of the crankshaft (see illustration 7.12 in Part A of this Chapter). Examine the crankshaft oil seal for signs of oil leakage and, if necessary, renew as described in Section 14.

Fuel injection pump sprocket

14 Remove the upper and centre timing belt covers as described in Section 5.

15 Make alignment marks on the fuel injection pump sprocket and the timing belt, to ensure that the sprocket and timing belt are correctly aligned on refitting.

16 Loosen the timing belt tensioner pulley retaining nut. Rotate the pulley in a clockwise direction, using a suitable square-section key fitted to the hole in the pulley hub, then retighten the retaining nut.

17 Disengage the timing belt from the injection pump sprocket, and move the belt clear, taking care not to bend or twist it sharply.

18 Remove the locking tools securing the fuel injection pump sprocket in the TDC position.

19 On some engines, the sprocket may be fitted with a flanged nut over which the Citroën puller may be fitted. The puller consists of a plate which is bolted to the sprocket; when the nut is unscrewed, the sprocket is pulled off the injection pump shaft. On other engines, the sprocket is retained by a normal nut and washer, which must be removed before the Citroën puller and special flanged nut is

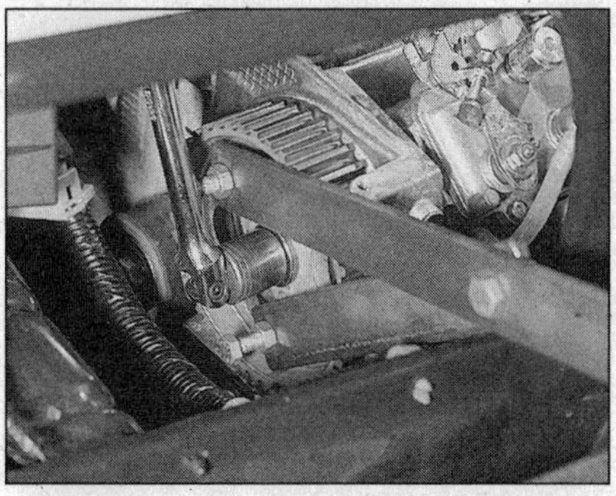

7.20 Using a home-made tool to hold the injection pump sprocket stationary whilst the retaining bolt is slackened - viewed through headlight aperture

7.22a Home-made injection pump sprocket removal tool in position on the sprocket

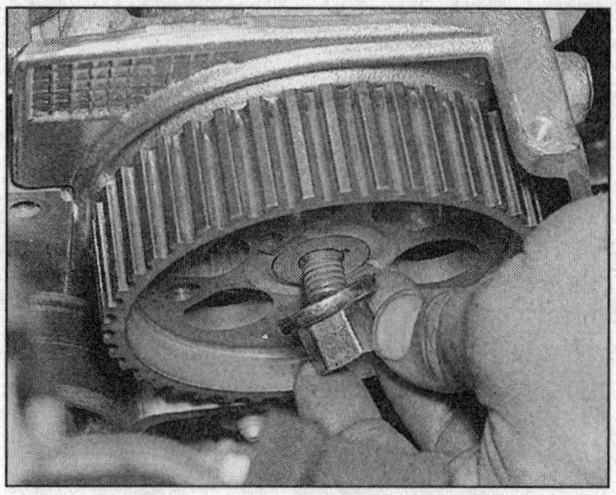

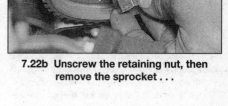

7.22b Unscrew the retaining nut, then remove the sprocket . . .

attached. If necessary, a suitable puller can be made up using a short length of bar, and two M7 bolts screwed into the holes provided in the sprocket. The bolts must be approximately 40 mm in length, and the holes in the bar 45 mm apart.

20 The fuel injection pump shaft must be prevented from turning as the sprocket nut is unscrewed, and this can be achieved using a tool similar to that shown in illustration 7.18 in Part A of this Chapter. Use the tool to hold the sprocket stationary by means of the holes in the sprocket **(see illustration).**

21 On engines with a flanged securing nut, bolt the puller to the sprocket, then unscrew the sprocket securing nut until the sprocket is freed from the taper on the pump shaft. Recover the Woodruff key from the end of the pump shaft, if it is loose. Unbolt the puller assembly from the sprocket by removing the two securing screws and washers.

22 On engines fitted with a normal nut and washer, first remove the nut and washer, then attach the puller tool and bolt it to the sprocket. Remove the sprocket as described in the previous paragraph. If an improvised puller is being used, partially unscrew the sprocket securing nut, then fit the puller, and tighten the two bolts (forcing the bar against the sprocket nut), until the sprocket is freed from the taper on the pump shaft. Withdraw the sprocket, and recover the Woodruff key from the end of the pump shaft if it is loose **(see illustrations).** Remove the puller from the sprocket.

Tensioner pulley

23 Remove the timing belt upper and centre covers as described in Section 5.

24 Slacken and remove the timing belt tensioner pulley retaining nut, and slide the pulley off its mounting stud (see illustration). Carefully tie the timing belt down so that it is kept in full engagement with the sprockets. Examine the mounting stud for signs of damage and, if necessary, renew it - it is removed by unscrewing it from the cylinder block.

Idler

25 Remove the timing belt upper and centre covers as described in Section 5.

26 Loosen the timing belt tensioner pulley retaining nut. Rotate the pulley in a clockwise direction, using a suitable square-section key fitted to the hole in the pulley hub, then retighten the retaining nut. In order to provide some slack in the timing belt between the crankshaft and injection pump sprockets, it will be necessary to remove the locking tool from the flywheel, and rotate the crankshaft slightly anti-clockwise. Make sure, however, that the timing belt remains in full contact with the crankshaft sprocket.

27 Unscrew the bolt retaining the idler to the cylinder block, and withdraw the idler (see illustration). Carefully tie the timing belt up, so that it is kept in full engagement with all of the sprockets.

Inspection

28 Clean the sprockets thoroughly, and renew any that show signs of wear, damage or cracks.

29 Clean the tensioner pulley and idler, but do not use any strong solvent which may enter the bearings. Check that each roller rotates freely about its hub, with no sign of stiffness or of free play. Renew the tensioner pulley or idler if there is any doubt about its condition, or if there are any obvious signs of wear or damage.

2B

Refitting

Camshaft sprocket

30 Locate the sprocket on the end of the camshaft. Ensure that the locating tab is correctly engaged with the cut-out in the camshaft end **(see illustration).**

31 Refit the sprocket retaining bolt and washer. Tighten the bolt to the specified torque, retaining the sprocket with the tool used on removal **(see illustration).**

32 Realign the timing hole in the camshaft sprocket (see Section 3) with the corresponding hole in the cylinder head, and refit the locking tool.

33 Refit the timing belt to the camshaft

7.22c . . . and recover the Woodruff key (arrowed) from the injection pump shaft

7.24 Timing belt tensioner pulley retaining nut (arrowed)

7.27 Timing belt idler pulley retaining bolt (arrowed)

7.30 On refitting, ensure that the camshaft sprocket key and camshaft slot are correctly aligned (arrowed)

7.31 Tighten the camshaft sprocket retaining bolt to the specified torque setting

7.46 Align the sprocket groove (arrowed) with the Woodruff key when refitting the injection pump sprocket

sprocket. Ensure that the "front run" of the belt is taut around the injection pump sprocket - ie, ensure that any slack is on the tensioner pulley side of the belt. Do not twist the belt sharply while refitting it, and ensure that the belt teeth are seated centrally in the sprockets.

34 Loosen the tensioner pulley retaining nut. Rotate the pulley anti-clockwise to remove all free play from the timing belt, then retighten the nut.

35 Tension the belt as described in paragraphs 15 to 19 of Section 6.

36 Refit the timing belt covers as described in Section 5.

37 Reconnect the battery negative terminal.

Crankshaft sprocket

38 Where removed, locate the Woodruff key in the crankshaft end, then slide on the flanged spacer, aligning its slot with the Woodruff key.

39 Align the crankshaft sprocket slot with the Woodruff key, and slide it onto the end of the crankshaft.

40 Temporarily remove the locking tool from the rear of the flywheel, then refit the crankshaft sprocket retaining bolt and washer. Tighten the bolt to the specified torque, preventing crankshaft rotation using the method employed on removal. Refit the locking tool to the rear of the flywheel.

41 Relocate the timing belt on the crankshaft sprocket. Ensure that the belt is taut between the crankshaft, injection pump and camshaft sprockets, and over the idler roller - ie, ensure that any slack is on the tensioner pulley side of the belt. Do not twist the belt sharply while refitting it, and ensure that the belt teeth are seated centrally in the sprockets.

42 Loosen the tensioner pulley retaining nut. Rotate the pulley anti-clockwise to remove all free play from the timing belt, then retighten the nut.

43 Tension the belt as described in paragraphs 15 to 19 of Section 6.

44 Refit the timing belt covers as described in Section 5.

Fuel injection pump sprocket

45 Where applicable, refit the Woodruff key to the pump shaft, ensuring that it is correctly located in its groove.

46 Locate the sprocket on the injection pump shaft, and engage it with the key **(see illustration).**

47 Tighten the securing nut to the specified torque, preventing the pump shaft from turning as during removal.

48 Make sure that the locking tools are fitted to the camshaft and fuel injection pump sprockets, and to the TDC hole in the flywheel.

49 Fit the timing belt around the fuel injection pump sprocket, ensuring that the marks made on the belt and sprocket before removal are aligned.

50 Tension the timing belt as described in paragraphs 15 to 19 of Section 6.

51 Refit the upper and centre timing belt covers as described in Section 5.

Tensioner pulley

52 Check that the mounting stud is tightened in the cylinder block.

53 While holding the timing belt down, locate the tensioner pulley on the stud and refit the retaining nut. Make sure that the rest of the timing belt is not displaced from the other sprockets.

54 Tension the timing belt as described in paragraphs 15 to 19 of Section 6.

55 Refit the upper and centre timing belt covers as described in Section 5.

Idler

56 While holding the timing belt up, locate the idler on the cylinder block, and refit the retaining bolt. Tighten the bolt securely.

57 Carefully turn the crankshaft clockwise until the locking tool can be inserted into the flywheel.

8.2 Removing the camshaft oil seal

58 Tension the timing belt as described in paragraphs 15 to 19 of Section 6.

59 Refit the upper and centre timing belt covers as described in Section 5.

8 Camshaft oil seal - renewal

Note: *If the camshaft oil seal is to be renewed with the timing belt still in place, check first that the belt is free from oil contamination. (Renew the belt as a matter of course if signs of oil contamination are found; see Section 6.) Cover the belt to protect it from oil contamination while work is in progress. Ensure that all traces of oil are removed from the area before the belt is refitted.*

1 Remove the camshaft sprocket as described in Section 7.

2 Punch or drill two small holes opposite each other in the oil seal. Screw a self-tapping screw into each, and pull on the screws with pliers to extract the seal **(see illustration).**

3 Clean the seal housing, and polish off any burrs or raised edges, which may have caused the seal to fail in the first place.

4 Lubricate the lips of the new seal with clean engine oil, and drive it into position until it seats on its locating shoulder. Take care not to damage the seal lips during fitting. Note that the seal lips should face inwards.

5 Refit the camshaft sprocket as described in Section 7.

TOOL TiP

Use a suitable tubular drift, such as a socket, which bears only on the hard outer edge of the seal.

9 Camshaft and followers - removal, inspection and refitting

Note: A *new oil seal must be used on refitting.*

Removal

1 Remove the cylinder head cover as described in Section 4.

2 Remove the camshaft sprocket as described in Section 7.

3 Unbolt the brake vacuum pump from the left-hand end of the cylinder head and move it to one side, with reference to Chapter 9. Recover the O-ring seal.

4 The camshaft bearing caps should be numbered 1 to 3, No 1 being at the transmission end of the engine **(see illustration).** If the caps are not already numbered, identify them accordingly.

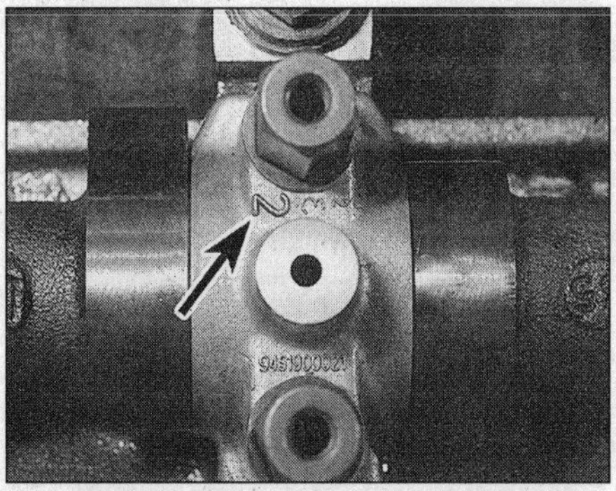

9.4 Identification numbers (arrowed) are cast onto the camshaft bearing caps

5 Progressively unscrew the nuts, then remove the bearing caps.

6 Lift the camshaft from the cylinder head. Remove the oil seal from the timing belt end of the camshaft.

7 Obtain eight small, clean plastic containers, and number them 1 to 8. Alternatively, divide a larger container into eight compartments. Using a rubber sucker, withdraw each shim and follower in turn, and place it in its respective container. Do not interchange the cam followers, or the rate of wear will be much increased.

Inspection

8 Examine the camshaft bearing surfaces and cam lobes for signs of wear ridges and scoring. Renew the camshaft if any of these conditions are apparent. Examine the condition of the bearing surfaces both on the camshaft journals and in the cylinder head/bearing caps. If the head bearing surfaces are worn excessively, the cylinder head will need to be renewed. Since no dimensions are given by Citroën, it is not possible to assess the amount of wear by direct measurement. Seek the advice of a Citroën dealer or engine overhaul specialist before condemning the camshaft or cylinder head.

Refitting

9 Liberally oil the cylinder head cam follower bores and the followers. Carefully refit the followers to the cylinder head, ensuring that each follower is refitted to its original bore **(see illustration)**. Some care will be required to enter the followers squarely into their bores.

10 Ensure all the shims are correctly seated in the top of each follower.

11 Liberally oil the camshaft bearing and lobe contact surfaces, then refit the camshaft to the cylinder head **(see illustration).** Temporarily refit the sprocket to the end of the shaft, and position it so that the sprocket timing hole is aligned with the threaded hole in the cylinder head. The tips of the cams 7 and 8 should be facing upwards (No 4 cylinder at TDC); the tips of cams 1 and 2 should be facing downwards and resting on the bucket tappets. Where applicable, the cast "DIST" marking on the camshaft must be at the timing belt end of the cylinder head, and the tab cut-out for the camshaft sprocket should be facing upwards at the 11 o'clock position. Also ensure that the crankshaft is still locked in position (see Section 3).

12 Ensure that the bearing cap and head mating surfaces are completely clean, unmarked and free from oil. Apply a smear of suitable sealant to Nos 1 and 3 bearing caps as shown **(see illustration).**

13 Refit the bearing caps, using the identification marks noted on removal to

2B

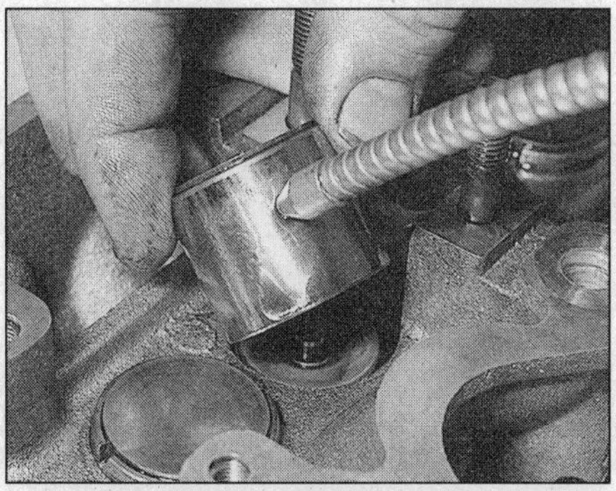

9.9 Oil the camshaft followers, and refit them to their original locations in the cylinder head

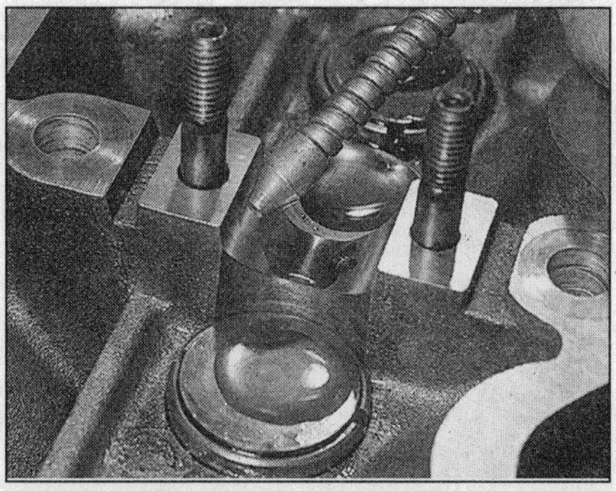

9.11 Thoroughly oil the camshaft bearing surfaces prior to installing the camshaft

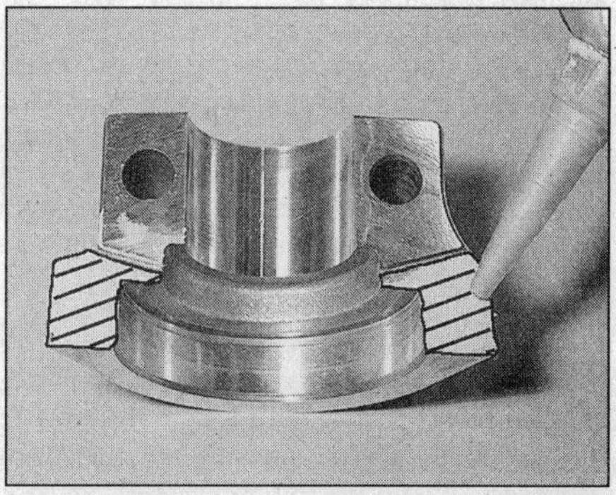

9.12 Apply sealant to the shaded areas of Nos 1 and 3 bearing caps

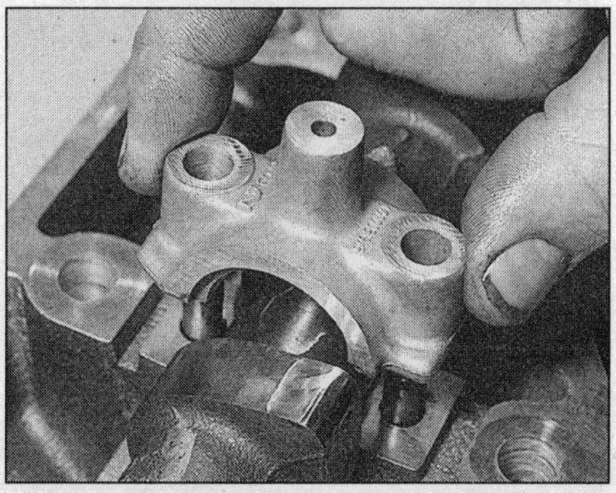

9.13 Install the bearings caps, using the identification markings to ensure they are correctly positioned . . .

9.14a . . . and refit the retaining nuts . . .

9.14b . . . tightening them evenly and progressively to the specified torque setting

ensure that each is installed correctly and in its original location **(see illustration).**

14 Insert the camshaft bearing cap nuts, then evenly and progressively tighten them by one turn at a time until the caps touch the cylinder head **(see illustrations).** Then go round again and tighten all the nuts to the specified torque setting. Work only as described, to impose the pressure of the valve springs gradually and evenly on the bearing caps.

15 Fit a new camshaft oil seal, using the information given in Section 8, then refit the camshaft sprocket as described in Section 7.

16 Check, and if necessary adjust, the valve clearances as described in Section 10.

17 Refit the braking system vacuum pump as described in Chapter 9.

18 Refit the cylinder head cover as described in Section 4, and reconnect the battery negative terminal.

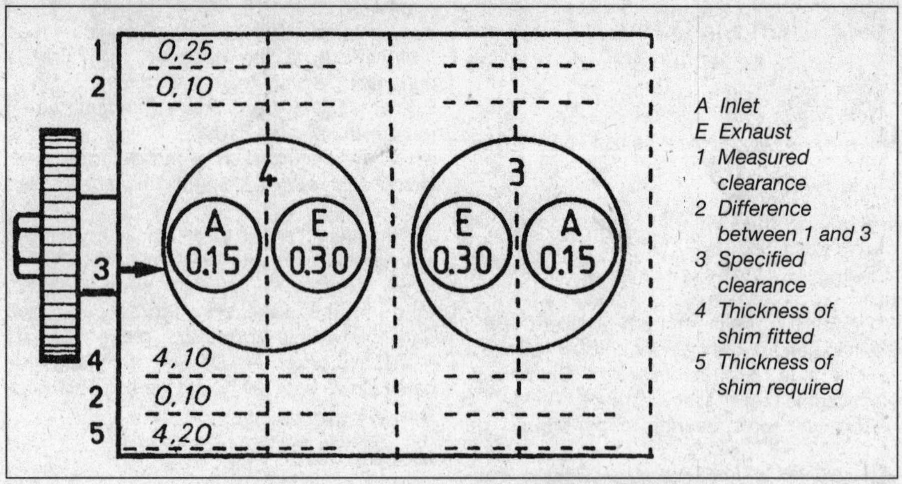

10.3 Example of valve shim thickness calculation

10 Valve clearances - checking and adjustment

Note: *This is not a routine operation. It should only be necessary at high mileage, after overhaul, or when investigating noise or power loss which may be attributable to the valvegear.*

Note: *Refer to the note at the end of Section 1 if working on the cast-iron block engine.*

Checking

1 During this procedure, the crankshaft must be turned to bring each valve in turn to a position where the clearance can be checked. This can be achieved by engaging 4th or 5th gear, applying the handbrake, then jacking up the front right-hand corner of the vehicle (support the vehicle securely on an axle stand - see *"Jacking, towing and wheel changing"*) and turning the roadwheel.

> **HAYNES HiNT** ***Turning the engine will be much easier if the glow plugs are removed first - see Chapter 5C.***

2 Remove the timing belt upper cover (Section 5) and the cylinder head cover (Section 4).

3 On a piece of paper, draw the outline of the engine, with the cylinders numbered from the flywheel end. Show the position of each valve, together with the specified valve clearance. Above each valve, draw two lines for noting (1) the actual clearance and (2) the amount of adjustment required **(see illustration)**.

4 Turn the crankshaft until the inlet valve of No 1 cylinder (nearest the flywheel) is fully closed, with the tip of the cam facing directly upwards away from the bucket tappet.

5 Using feeler gauges, measure the clearance between the base of the cam and the shim on top of the bucket tappet **(see illustration)**. Record the clearance on line (1).

6 Repeat the measurement for the other seven valves, turning the crankshaft as necessary so that the cam lobe in question is always facing directly away from the relevant bucket tappet.

7 Calculate the difference between each measured clearance and the desired value, and record it on line (2). Since the clearance is different for inlet and exhaust valves, make sure that you are aware which valve you are dealing with. The valve sequence from either end of the engine is:

Ex - In - Ex - In - In - Ex - In - Ex

8 If all the clearances are within tolerance, refit the cylinder head cover with reference to Section 4, and where applicable, lower the vehicle to the ground. If any clearance measured is outside the specified tolerance, adjustment must be carried out as described in the following paragraphs.

Adjustment

Note: *A micrometer will be required for this operation.*

9 Make sure that the relevant valve is fully closed as described in paragraph 4; the cam lobe must be facing directly upwards away from the bucket tappet. Depress the tappet with a C-spanner or similar tool, and extract the shim using long-nosed pliers.

> ***Warning: Do not depress a tappet with the piston for that cylinder at TDC, and do not turn the crankshaft while shims are removed from the tappets. In the first case, there is a risk of piston-to-valve contact; in the second case, the camshaft lobes may jam in the empty tappets.***

10 Clean the shim, and measure its thickness with a micrometer **(see illustrations).** The shims carry thickness markings, but wear may

10.5 Measuring a valve clearance using a feeler gauge

10.10a Shim thickness is stamped on the bottom face of the shim . . .

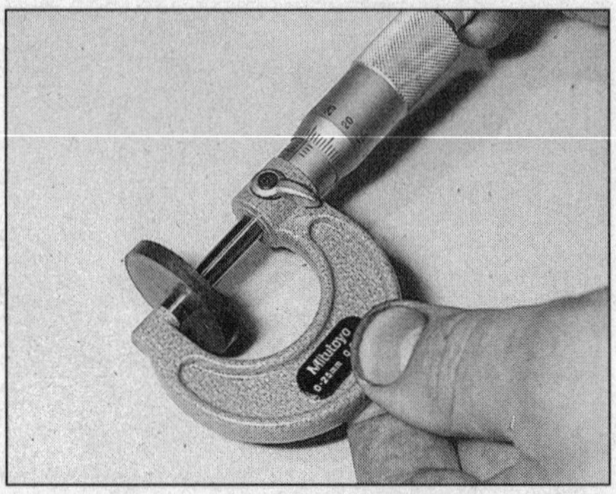

10.10b . . . however shims should be measured to determine their true thickness

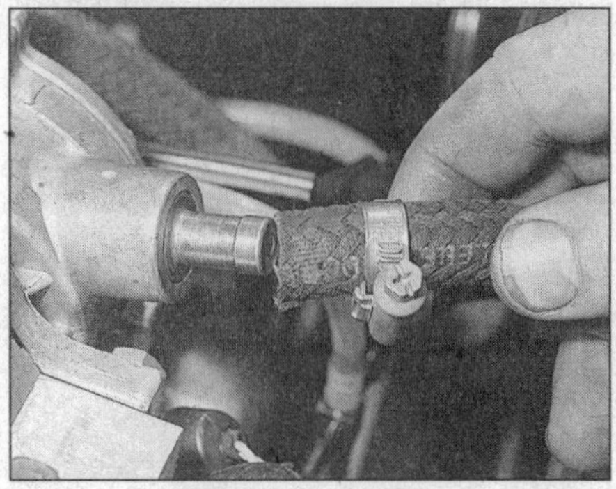

11.8 Slacken the retaining clip, and disconnect the hose from the braking system vacuum pump

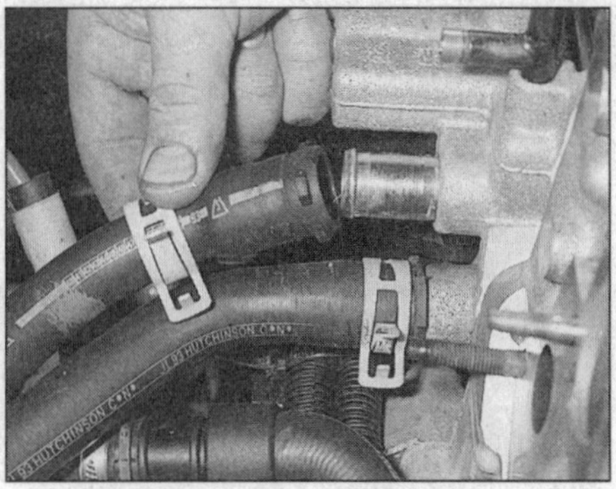

11.9 Disconnect the small coolant hoses from the fuel filter/thermostat housing

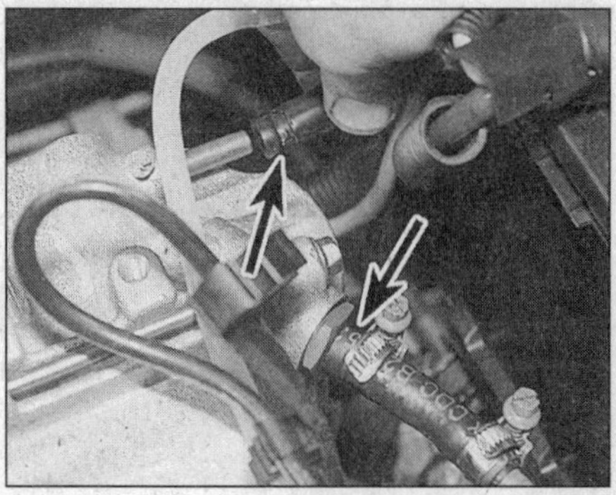

11.10 Disconnect the fuel supply and pump feed hoses (arrowed) from the fuel filter/thermostat housing

have reduced the original thickness, so be sure to check.

11 Refer to the clearance recorded for the valve concerned. If the clearance was more than that specified, the shim thickness must be increased by the difference recorded (2). If the clearance was less than that specified, the thickness of the shim must be decreased by the difference recorded (2).

12 Draw three more lines beneath each valve on the calculation paper (see illustration 10.3). On line (4) note the measured thickness of the shim, then add or deduct the difference from line (2) to give the final shim thickness required on line (5).

13 Shims are available in thicknesses between 3.20 mm and 4.90 mm. Clean new shims before measuring or fitting them. If a comprehensive selection of shims is available at this stage, proceed to paragraph 15; otherwise, proceed to paragraph 14 so that a list of shims required can be made.

14 Repeat the procedure given in paragraphs 9 to 12 on the remaining valves. Make sure that the original shims are refitted first before turning the engine to the next position.

15 With all of the new shims obtained, remove each original shim in turn, and fit the new one. Oil the new shim, and fit it in the recess on the bucket tappet, with the size marking face downwards.

16 When all the shims are in position, recheck the valve clearances before refitting the camshaft cover, to make sure they are correct.

11 Cylinder head - removal and refitting

Note: *This is an involved procedure, and it is suggested that the Section is read thoroughly before starting work. To aid refitting, make notes on the locations of all relevant brackets, and the routing of hoses and cables, before removal. A new cylinder head gasket must be used on refitting, and new cylinder head bolts may be required - see text.*

Note: *Refer to the note at the end of Section 1 if working on the cast-iron block engine.*

Removal

1 Disconnect the battery negative lead.

2 Drain the cooling system as described in Chapter 1.

3 Position the engine at top dead centre (TDC on No 4 cylinder) as described in Section 3, and lock the camshaft sprocket, injection pump sprocket and flywheel in position. *Do not* attempt to rotate the engine whilst the locking tools are in position.

4 If not already done, remove the upper and centre timing belt covers as described in Section 5.

5 Loosen the timing belt tensioner pulley retaining nut. Rotate the pulley in a clockwise direction, using a suitable square-section key fitted to the hole in the pulley hub, then retighten the retaining nut.

6 Disengage the timing belt from the camshaft sprocket, and move the belt clear, taking care not to bend or twist it sharply. Remove the locking bolt from the camshaft sprocket.

7 Loosen the clips and disconnect the air inlet pipe from the air cleaner and inlet manifold.

8 Loosen the clip and disconnect the vacuum pipe from the brake vacuum pump located on the left-hand end of the cylinder head **(see illustration).**

9 Disconnect the small coolant hoses from the fuel filter/thermostat housing, noting their fitted positions **(see illustration).**

10 Disconnect the fuel supply and pump feed hoses from the fuel filter housing **(see illustration).**

11 Disconnect the top hose from the thermostat housing on the left-hand side of the cylinder head **(see illustration).**

12 Disconnect the fast idle cable from the injection pump, with reference to Chapter 4D.

13 Unscrew the terminal nut on No 1 cylinder glow plug, and disconnect the feed cable. Recover the washers **(see illustration).**

14 Disconnect and remove the fuel injector leak-off hoses.

15 Unscrew the union nuts, and disconnect the injector fuel supply pipes from the injectors. Remove the pipes for Nos 3 and 4 cylinders completely from the injection pump as well. Refer to Chapter 4D if necessary.

16 Unscrew the bolt securing the engine oil dipstick tube to the front of the cylinder head **(see illustration).**

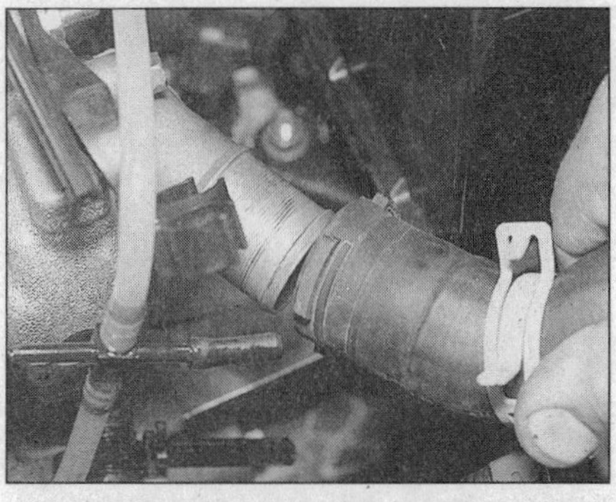

11.11 Disconnect the top hose from the thermostat housing

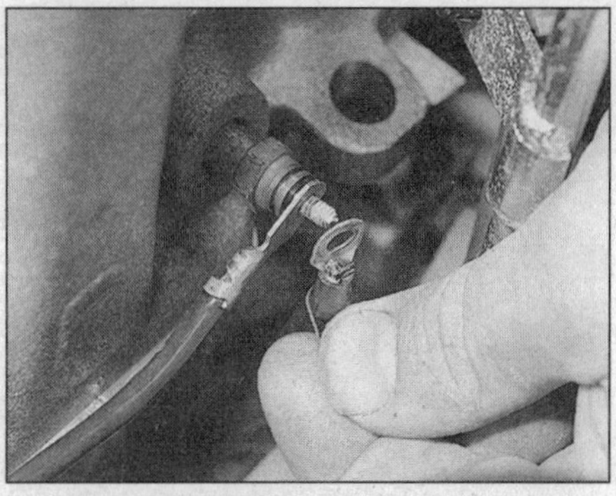

11.13 Slacken the retaining nut, and disconnect the feed wire from No 1 cylinder glow plug

11.16 Unscrew the dipstick tube retaining bolt (arrowed)

11.19 Disconnect the wiring connector from the temperature sender unit

17 Remove the air cleaner assembly as described in Chapter 4D.

18 Unscrew the nuts securing the exhaust downpipe to the exhaust manifold (refer to Chapter 4D if necessary). Also unbolt the bracket securing the exhaust pipe to the cylinder block.

19 Disconnect the wiring from the temperature sender located on the front left-hand end of the cylinder head **(see illustration).**

20 Remove the cylinder head cover as described in Section 4.

21 If required, the inlet and exhaust manifolds may be removed at this stage, with reference to Chapter 4D. However, they may be left in position if preferred.

22 Working in the reverse of the sequence shown in illustration 11.38a, progressively slacken the ten cylinder head bolts by half a turn at a time, until all bolts can be unscrewed by hand. Remove the washers.

23 The joint between the cylinder head and gasket and the cylinder block/crankcase must now be broken without disturbing the wet liners. Although these liners are better-located and sealed than on some other wet-liner engines, there is still a risk of coolant and foreign matter leaking into the sump if the cylinder head is lifted carelessly. If care is not taken and the liners are moved, there is also a possibility of the bottom seals being disturbed, causing leakage after refitting the head.

24 To break the joint, obtain two L-shaped metal bars which fit into the cylinder head bolt holes. Gently "rock" the cylinder head free towards the front of the car (see illustration 11.21 in Part A). Do not try to swivel the head on the cylinder block/crankcase; it is located by dowels, as well as by the tops of the liners.

25 When the joint is broken, lift the cylinder head away; seek assistance if possible, as it is a heavy assembly, especially if it is removed complete with the manifolds. Remove the gasket from the top of the block, noting the two locating dowels. If the locating dowels are a loose fit, remove them and store them with the head for safe-keeping. Do not discard the old gasket yet - it will be needed to ensure that the correct new gasket is obtained.

26 *Do not* attempt to rotate the crankshaft with the cylinder head removed, otherwise the wet liners may be displaced. Operations that require the rotation of the crankshaft (eg cleaning the piston crowns), should only be carried out once the cylinder liners are firmly clamped in position **(see illustration).**

11.26 The cylinder liners must be clamped in position before the crankshaft is rotated

> **HAYNES HiNT** *In the absence of the special Citroën liner clamps, the liners can be clamped in position using large flat washers positioned underneath suitable-length bolts. Alternatively, the original head bolts could be temporarily refitted, with suitable spacers fitted to their shanks.*

27 If the cylinder head is to be dismantled for overhaul, remove the camshaft as described in Section 9, then refer to Part C of this Chapter.

Preparation for refitting

Liner protrusion check

28 Check the protrusion of the liners above the cylinder block. Make sure that clamps are placed on each side of the liner being checked, in order to compress its seal and obtain a correct reading. If the Citroën liner clamps are being used, it will be necessary to remove the cylinder head locating dowels before clamping Nos 1 and 4 liners.

29 Position a dial test indicator (dial gauge) on the cylinder block, and zero it on the block face. Transfer the probe to the liner, and note the protrusion. The desired values are as follows:

Overall protrusion – 0.05 to 0.10 mm
Maximum difference between adjacent liners – 0.05 mm

30 If the liner protrusion is incorrect, the engine must be removed and dismantled for new base seals and/or new liners to be fitted. Refer to Part C of this Chapter.

Cylinder head face examination

31 The mating faces of the cylinder head and cylinder block/crankcase must be perfectly clean before refitting the head. Use a hard plastic or wood scraper to remove all traces of gasket and carbon; also clean the piston crowns. Refer to paragraph 26 before turning the crankshaft. Take particular care during the cleaning operations, as the soft aluminium alloy is damaged easily. Also, make sure that the carbon is not allowed to enter the oil and water passages - this is particularly important for the lubrication system, as carbon could block the oil supply to the engine's components. Using adhesive tape and paper, seal the water, oil and bolt holes in the cylinder block/crankcase. To prevent carbon entering the gap between the pistons and bores, smear a little grease in the gap. After cleaning each piston, use a small brush to remove all traces of grease and carbon from the gap, then wipe away the remainder with a clean rag. Clean all the pistons in the same way.

32 Check the mating surfaces of the cylinder block/crankcase and the cylinder head for nicks, deep scratches and other damage. If slight, they may be removed carefully with a file, but if excessive, machining may be the only alternative to renewal. If warpage of the cylinder head gasket surface is suspected, use a straight-edge to check it for distortion. Refer to Part C of this Chapter if necessary.

33 Check for any distortion of the cylinder head using a straight-edge. Full instructions are given in Part C of this Chapter.

Cylinder head bolt examination

34 The manufacturers recommend that the cylinder head bolts are measured, to determine whether renewal is necessary; however, some owners may wish to renew all the bolts as a matter of course. Measure the length of each bolt (without the washer fitted) from the underside of the head to the end of the thread. If all of the bolts are within the

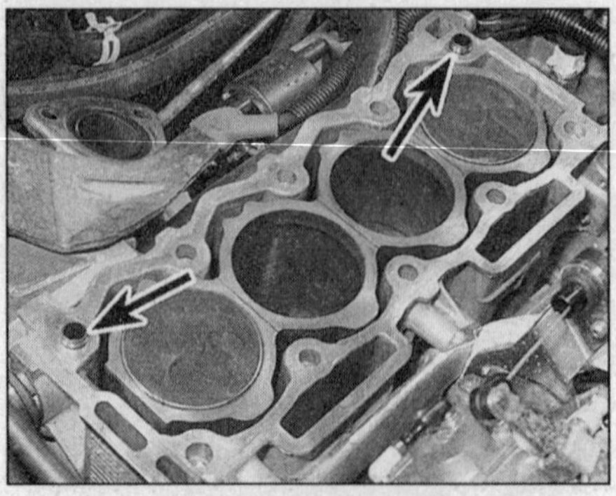

11.35a Ensure that the locating dowels (arrowed) are in position . . .

11.35b . . . and fit a new gasket

11.36 Ensure that all sprockets are correctly positioned, then refit the cylinder head assembly

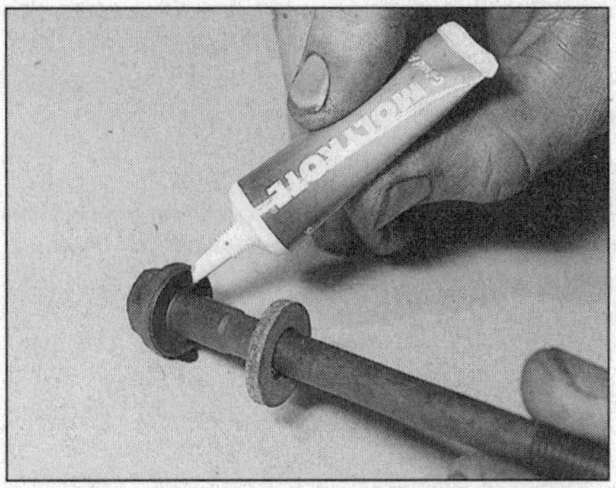

11.37a Apply a smear of the specified grease to the underside of the heads . . .

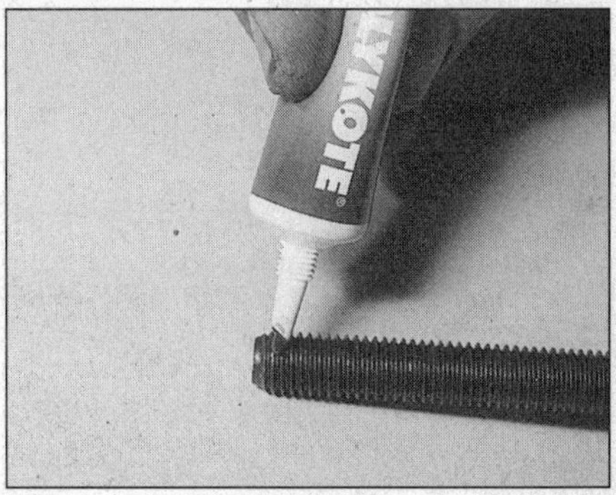

11.37b . . . and to the threads of all cylinder head bolts

11.37c Insert the head bolts into position

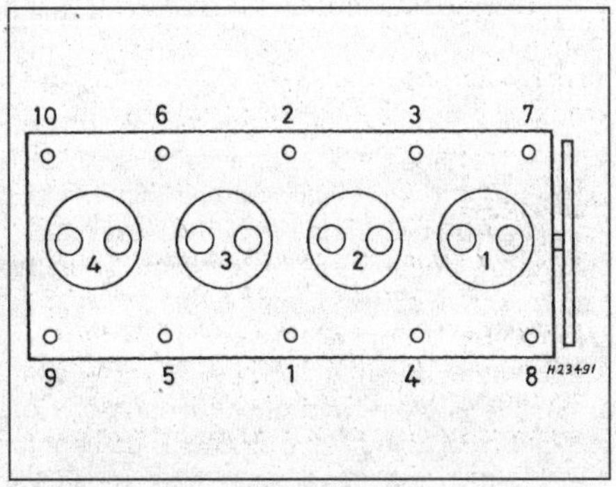

11.38a Cylinder head bolt tightening sequence (cylinder numbering also shown)

11.38b Tightening the head bolts with the torque wrench . . .

range 184.5 to 185.9 mm they may be re-used, but if any one bolt is greater than 185.9 mm in length, all of the bolts should be renewed.

Refitting

35 Make sure that Nos 1 and 4 pistons are at TDC, and the locking tool is located in the flywheel. Also check that the locking tool is located in the camshaft sprocket. Commence refitting by removing the liner clamps, refitting the cylinder head locating dowels (where removed), and placing a new gasket on the cylinder block, with the maker's name facing upwards **(see illustrations)**. Do not apply any sealant to the gasket.

36 Check that the flywheel, injection pump sprocket and camshaft sprocket are still correctly locked in position then, with the aid of an assistant, lower the cylinder head onto the block, making sure that it engages on the locating dowels (see illustration).

37 Grease the threads and contact faces of the cylinder head bolts, then insert them, together with their washers (lugs towards the cylinder head). Citroën recommend the use of Molykote G Rapid Plus grease (available from your Citroën dealer - a sachet is supplied with the head gasket set); in the absence of the specified grease, a good-quality high-melting-point grease may be used (see illustrations).

38 Tighten the cylinder head bolts in the order shown (see illustrations). Tighten the bolts in the five Stages given in the Specifications.

39 If removed, refit the inlet and exhaust manifolds with reference to Chapter 4D.

40 Refit the cylinder head cover as described in Section 4.

41 Reconnect the wiring to the temperature sender located on the front left-hand end of the cylinder head.

42 Reconnect the exhaust downpipe to the manifold, and refit the bracket to the cylinder block (refer to Chapter 4D if necessary).

43 Refit the air cleaner assembly as described in Chapter 4D.

44 Refit the engine oil dipstick tube to the front of the cylinder head, and tighten the bolt.

45 Refit the injector fuel supply pipes, and tighten the union nuts with reference to Chapter 4D.

46 Reconnect the fuel injector leak-off hoses.

47 Reconnect the feed cable to the terminal on No 1 cylinder glow plug.

48 Reconnect the fast idle cable to the injection pump, with reference to Chapter 4D.

49 Reconnect the top hose to the thermostat housing on the left-hand side of the cylinder head, and tighten the clip.

50 Reconnect the fuel supply and pump feed hoses to the fuel filter housing.

51 Reconnect the coolant hoses to the fuel filter/thermostat housing in their previously-noted positions.

52 Reconnect the vacuum pipe to the brake vacuum pump located on the left-hand end of the cylinder head, and tighten the clip.

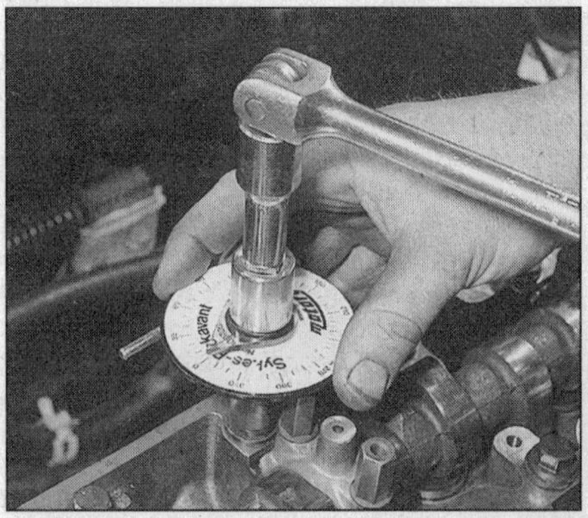

11.38c . . . and angle-tightening the bolts using a torque wrench and angle gauge

53 Reconnect the air inlet pipe to the air cleaner and inlet manifold, and tighten the clips.

54 Refit the timing belt to the camshaft sprocket, and tension it with reference to paragraphs 15 to 19 of Section 6.

55 Remove the locking tools from the sprockets and flywheel.

56 Refit the upper and centre timing belt covers as described in Section 5.

57 Refill the cooling system as described in Chapter 1.

58 Reconnect the battery negative lead.

59 Bleed the fuel system as described in Chapter 4D.

12 Sump - removal and refitting

Removal

1 Apply the handbrake, then jack up the front of the vehicle and support securely on axle stands (see *"Jacking, towing and wheel changing"*).
2 Position a suitable container beneath the engine. Unscrew the sump drain plug, using a suitable key, and allow the oil to drain into the container.
3 Wipe the drain plug clean, and refit it.
4 For improved access to some of the sump bolts, remove the exhaust front downpipe with reference to Chapter 4. However, this is not essential.
5 Unscrew the sump nuts and bolts. Leave one nut or bolt in position at opposite ends of the sump while the remaining bolts and nuts are being removed.
6 Remove the remaining nut/bolt, and remove the sump from the cylinder block. The sump will probably be stuck in position, in which case it will be necessary to cut it free using a thin knife.

Refitting

7 Commence refitting by cleaning the remains of the sealant from the sump and cylinder block, and wipe dry. Take care, however, not to cut into the aluminium block.
8 Apply sealing compound to the joint face on the sump. Citroën recommend Auto Joint E10; if possible, this should be obtained from a Citroën dealer.
9 Lift the sump into position, and refit the nuts and bolts.
10 Tighten the nuts and bolts progressively to the specified torque.
11 Refit the exhaust front downpipe with reference to Chapter 4.
12 Lower the vehicle to the ground, and refill the engine with the correct grade and quantity of oil (see Chapter 1).

13 Oil pump - removal, inspection and refitting

Removal

1 Remove the sump as described in Section 12.
2 Slacken and remove the three bolts securing the oil pump to the base of the main bearing ladder. Disengage the pump sprocket from the chain, and remove the oil pump. If the pump locating dowel is a loose fit, remove and store it with the retaining bolts for safe-keeping.
3 If it is required to remove the oil pump drive chain, the crankshaft right-hand oil seal must be removed as described in Section 14, then the spacer removed from the front of the crankshaft. The oil pump drive sprocket must then be removed from the key on the crankshaft, after lifting the chain over its teeth. With the sprocket removed, the chain can be withdrawn upwards through the aperture in the front of the cylinder block, over the nose of the crankshaft.

Inspection

4 Examine the oil pump sprocket for signs of damage and wear, such as chipped or missing teeth. If the sprocket is worn, the pump assembly must be renewed, since the sprocket is not available separately. It is also recommended that the chain and drive sprocket, fitted to the crankshaft, be renewed at the same time.
5 Slacken and remove the five bolts securing the strainer cover to the pump body, then lift off the strainer cover. Remove the relief valve piston and spring, noting which way round they are fitted.
6 Examine the pump rotors and body for signs of wear ridges and scoring. If worn, the complete pump assembly must be renewed.
7 Examine the relief valve piston for signs of wear or damage, and renew if necessary. The condition of the relief valve spring can only be measured by comparing it with a new one; if there is any doubt about its condition, it should also be renewed. Both the piston and spring are available individually.
8 Thoroughly clean the oil pump strainer with a suitable solvent, and check it for signs of clogging or splitting. If the strainer is damaged, the strainer and cover assembly must be renewed.
9 Oil the rotors and piston with clean engine oil, then locate the relief valve spring and piston in the strainer cover, and refit the cover to the pump body. Align the relief valve piston with its bore in the pump. Refit the five cover retaining bolts, tightening them securely.

Refitting

10 Where necessary, fit the oil pump drive chain, sprocket and new oil seal to the right-hand end of the crankshaft with reference to Section 14.
11 Ensure that the locating dowel is in position, then engage the pump sprocket with its drive chain. Seat the pump on the main bearing ladder. Refit the pump retaining bolts, and tighten them to the specified torque setting.
12 Refit the sump as described in Section 12.
13 Before running the engine, disconnect the wire from the stop solenoid on the injection pump. Spin the engine on the starter motor until oil pressure is restored and the oil pressure warning light is extinguished. Reconnect the wire, and start the engine to check for oil leaks.

14 Crankshaft oil seals - renewal

Right-hand oil seal

1 Remove the crankshaft sprocket and flanged spacer as described in Section 7. Secure the timing belt clear of the working area, so that it cannot be contaminated with oil. Make a note of the correct fitted depth of the seal in its housing.
2 Punch or drill two small holes opposite each other in the seal. Screw a self-tapping screw into each, and pull on the screws with pliers to extract the seal. Alternatively, the seal can be levered out of position using a suitable flat-bladed screwdriver, taking great care not to damage the crankshaft shoulder or seal housing.
3 Clean the seal housing, and polish off any burrs or raised edges, which may have caused the seal to fail in the first place.
4 Lubricate the lips of the new seal with clean engine oil, and carefully locate the seal on the end of crankshaft. Note that its sealing lip must face inwards. Take care not to damage the seal lips during fitting.
5 Using a suitable tubular drift (such as a socket) which bears only on the hard outer edge of the seal, tap the seal into position, to the same depth in the housing as the original was prior to removal. The inner face of the seal must end up flush with the inner wall of the crankcase.
6 Wash off any traces of oil, then refit the crankshaft sprocket as described in Section 7.

Left-hand oil seal

7 Remove the flywheel as described in Section 15.
8 Make a note of the correct fitted depth of the seal in its housing. Punch or drill two small holes opposite each other in the seal. Screw a self-tapping screw into each, and pull on the screws with pliers to extract the seal.
9 Clean the seal housing, and polish off any burrs or raised edges, which may have caused the seal to fail in the first place.
10 Lubricate the lips of the new seal with clean engine oil, and carefully locate the seal on the end of the crankshaft.
11 Using a suitable tubular drift which bears only on the hard outer edge of the seal, drive the seal into position, to the same depth in the housing as the original was prior to removal.
12 Wash off any traces of oil, then refit the flywheel as described in Section 15.

15 Flywheel - removal, inspection and refitting

Removal

1 Remove the transmission as described in Chapter 7, then remove the clutch assembly as described in Chapter 6.
2 Prevent the flywheel from turning by locking the ring gear teeth with a similar arrangement to that shown in illustration 7.10 in Part A. Alternatively, bolt a strap between the flywheel and the cylinder block/crankcase. *Do not attempt to lock the flywheel in position using the locking tool described in Section 3.*
3 Slacken and remove the flywheel retaining bolts, and discard them; they must be renewed whenever they are disturbed.

4 Remove the flywheel. Do not drop it, as it is very heavy. If the locating dowel is a loose fit in the crankshaft end, remove and store it with the flywheel for safe-keeping.

Inspection

5 If the flywheel's clutch mating surface is deeply scored, cracked or otherwise damaged, the flywheel must be renewed. However, it may be possible to have it surface-ground; seek the advice of a Citroën dealer or engine reconditioning specialist.

6 If the ring gear is badly worn or has missing teeth, it must be renewed. This job is best left to a Citroën dealer or engine reconditioning specialist. The temperature to which the new ring gear must be heated for installation is critical and, if not done accurately, the hardness of the teeth will be destroyed.

Refitting

7 Clean the mating surfaces of the flywheel and crankshaft. Remove any remaining locking compound from the threads of the crankshaft holes, using the correct-size tap, if available.

8 If the new flywheel retaining bolts are not supplied with their threads already pre-coated, apply a suitable thread-locking compound to the threads of each bolt. Citroën recommend the use of Frenetanch E3 (available from your Citroën dealer); in the absence of this, ensure that a good-quality locking compound is used.

9 Ensure that the locating dowel is in position. Offer up the flywheel, locating it on the dowel, and fit the new retaining bolts.

10 Lock the flywheel using the method employed on dismantling, and tighten the retaining bolts to the specified torque.

11 Refit the clutch as described in Chapter 6. Remove the locking tool, and refit the transmission as described in Chapter 7.

16 Engine/transmission mountings - inspection and renewal

Note: *Refer to the note at the end of Section 1 if working on the cast-iron block engine.*

Inspection

1 If improved access is required, raise the front of the car and support it securely on axle stands.

2 Check the mounting rubber to see if it is cracked, hardened or separated from the metal at any point; renew the mounting if any such damage or deterioration is evident.

3 Check that all the mounting's fasteners are securely tightened; use a torque wrench to check if possible.

4 Using a large screwdriver or a crowbar, check for wear in the mounting by carefully levering against it to check for free play. Where this is not possible, enlist the aid of an assistant to move the engine/transmission unit back and forth, or from side to side, while you watch the mounting. While some free play is to be expected even from new components, excessive wear should be obvious. If excessive free play is found, check first that the fasteners are correctly secured, then renew any worn components as described below.

Renewal

Right-hand mounting

5 Disconnect the battery negative lead.

6 Place a jack beneath the engine, with a block of wood on the jack head. Raise the jack until it is supporting the weight of the engine.

7 Slacken and remove the three nuts securing the right-hand engine mounting upper bracket to the bracket on the cylinder block. Remove the nut securing the bracket to the mounting rubber, and lift off the bracket.

8 Lift the buffer plate off the mounting rubber stud, then unscrew the nut and remove the mounting rubber from the body.

9 Check carefully for signs of wear or damage on all components, and renew them where necessary.

10 On reassembly, tighten the nut securing the mounting rubber to the body.

11 Refit the rubber buffer plate to the mounting rubber stud, and install the mounting bracket.

12 Tighten the mounting bracket retaining nuts to the specified torque setting.

13 Remove the jack from underneath the engine, and reconnect the battery negative lead.

Left-hand mounting

14 Remove the battery and the battery tray, as described in Chapter 5.

15 Place a jack beneath the transmission, with a block of wood on the jack head. Raise the jack until it is supporting the weight of the transmission.

16 Slacken and remove the mounting rubber centre bolt, and the two nuts securing the bracket to the body. Remove the mounting rubber.

17 Where necessary, unscrew the nuts and remove the bracket from the transmission.

18 Check carefully for signs of wear or damage on all components, and renew them where necessary.

19 Refit the bracket to the transmission, tightening its mounting nuts to the specified torque.

20 Refit the mounting rubber to the body, and tighten its retaining bolts to the specified torque. Refit the mounting centre bolt, and tighten it to the specified torque.

21 Remove the jack from underneath the transmission, then refit the battery and its tray as described in Chapter 5.

Rear mounting

22 If not already done, firmly apply the handbrake, then jack up the front of the vehicle and support it securely on axle stands.

23 Unscrew and remove the centre bolt securing the rear mounting link to the bracket on the rear of the transmission.

24 Remove the centre bolt securing the rear mounting link to the bracket on the underbody. Withdraw the link.

25 Unbolt the bracket from the rear of the transmission.

26 Check carefully for signs of wear or damage on all components, and renew them where necessary.

27 On reassembly, fit the rear mounting assembly to the rear of the transmission, and tighten its retaining bolts to the specified torque.

28 Refit the rear mounting link, and tighten the centre bolts to the specified torques.

29 Lower the vehicle to the ground.

Notes

Chapter 2 Part C: Engine removal and general engine overhaul procedures

Contents

Degrees of difficulty

Easy, suitable for novice with little experience	**Fairly easy,** suitable for beginner with some experience	**Fairly difficult,** suitable for competent DIY mechanic	**Difficult,** suitable for experienced DIY mechanic	**Very difficult,** suitable for expert DIY or professional

Specifications

Cylinder head

Maximum gasket face distortion	0.05 mm
Cylinder head height (nominal) - 1360 cc Diesel (K9A) engine only	136.4 ± 0.1 mm
Swirl chamber protrusion - 1360 cc Diesel (K9A) engine only	0 to 0.35 mm

Valves

Valve head diameter:	
Inlet:	
954 cc engine	34.7 mm
1124 cc and 1360 cc (K1A, K2A, K1G) engines	36.7 mm
1360 cc (K2D) engine	36.8 mm
1360 cc (K6B and KFZ) engines	39.5 mm
1360 cc (KDX, KDY and KDZ) engines	Not available
1360 cc Diesel (K9A) engine	35.5 mm
Exhaust:	
954 cc engine	27.7 mm
1124 cc and 1360 cc (K1A, K2A, K1G) engines	29.2 mm
1360 cc (K2D) engine	29.4 mm
1360 cc (K6B and KFZ) engines	31.4 mm
1360 cc (KDX, KDY and KDZ) engines	Not available
1360 cc Diesel (K9A) engine	30.5 mm
Valve stem diameter:	
Inlet:	
All except 1360 cc Diesel (K9A) engine	6.965 to 6.980 mm
1360 cc Diesel (K9A) engine	6.980 to 6.995 mm
1360 cc (KDX, KDY and KDZ) engines	Not available
Exhaust:	
954 cc engine	6.960 to 6.975 mm
1124 cc and 1360 cc (K1A, K2A, K1G) engines	6.945 to 6.960 mm
1360 cc (K2D, K6B, KFZ) engines	6.965 to 6.980 mm
1360 cc (KDX, KDY and KDZ) engine	Not available
1360 cc Diesel (K9A) engine	6.980 to 6.995 mm

Overall length:	
Inlet:	
954 cc, 1124 cc and 1360 cc (K1A, K2A, K1G) engines	112.76 mm
1360 cc (K2D) engine	112.76 ± 0.25 mm
1360 cc (K6B and KFZ) engines	111.70 ± 0.27 mm
1360 cc (KDX, KDY and KDZ) engines	Not available
1360 cc Diesel (K9A) engine	108.43 mm
Exhaust:	
954 cc, 1124 cc and 1360 cc (K1A, K2A, K1G) engines	112.56 mm
1360 cc (K2D) engine	112.56 ± 0.25 mm
1360 cc (K6B and KFZ) engines	111.48 ± 0.27 mm
1360 cc (KDX, KDY and KDZ) engines	Not available
1360 cc Diesel (K9A) engine	108.17 mm

Cylinder block

Note: *At the time of writing, specifications were only available on the following engines. Consult your Citroën dealer for further specifications on the TUD Diesel engine.*

Cylinder bore diameter:	
954 cc engine:	
Size group A	70.000 to 70.010 mm
Size group B	70.010 to 70.020 mm
Size group C	70.020 to 70.030 mm
1124 cc engine:	
Size group A	72.000 to 72.010 mm
Size group B	72.010 to 72.020 mm
Size group C	72.020 to 72.030 mm
1360 cc TU engine (aluminium block):	
Size group A	75.000 to 75.010 mm
Size group B	75.010 to 75.020 mm
Size group C	75.020 to 75.030 mm
Liner protrusion above block mating surface - aluminium block engine only:	
Standard:	
TU (petrol) engines	0.03 to 0.10 mm
TUD (Diesel) engine	0.05 to 0.10 mm
Maximum difference between any two liners	0.05 mm

Pistons

Piston diameter:

Note: *At the time of writing, specifications were only available on the following engines. Consult your Citroën dealer for specifications on other engines.*

954 cc engine:	
Size group A	69.960 to 69.970 mm
Size group B	69.970 to 69.980 mm
Size group C	69.980 to 69.990 mm
1124 cc engine:	
Size group A	71.960 to 71.970 mm
Size group B	71.970 to 71.980 mm
Size group C	71.980 to 71.990 mm
1360 cc TU engine (aluminium block):	
Size group A	74.960 to 74.970 mm
Size group B	74.970 to 74.980 mm
Size group C	74.980 to 74.990 mm
Maximum weight difference between any two pistons:	
954 cc, 1124 cc, 1360 cc (except K1G, K9A, K2D, K6B and KFZ) engines	2.0 g
1360 cc (K1G) engine	12 g
1360 cc Diesel (K9A) engine	10 g
1360 cc (K2D, K6B and KFZ) engines	3.0 g

Connecting rods

Maximum weight difference between any two connecting rods:	3.0 g

Crankshaft

Endfloat:	
All engines (except K2D, K6B and KFZ)	0.1 to 0.3 mm
K2D, K6B and KFZ	0.07 to 0.272 mm
Main bearing journal diameter:	
954 cc, 1124 cc and 1360 cc (except K2D, K6B and KFZ) engines:	
Standard	49.965 to 49.981 mm
Undersize	49.665 to 49.681 mm

Main bearing journal diameter (cont):	
K2D, K6B and KFZ engines:	
Standard	49.962 to 49.981 mm
Undersize	49.662 to 49.681 mm
Big-end bearing journal diameter:	
954 cc engine:	
Standard	38.000 ± 0.008 mm
Undersize	37.700 ± 0.008 mm
1124 cc and 1360 cc engines:	
Standard	44.975 to 44.991 mm
Undersize	44.675 to 44.691 mm
Maximum bearing journal out-of-round	0.007 mm
Main bearing running clearance (see note below):	
1124 cc and 1360 cc engines*:	
Pre-February 1992 models	0.023 to 0.083 mm
February 1992-on models	0.023 to 0.048 mm
Big-end bearing running clearance - all models**	0.025 to 0.050 mm

**On 1124 cc and 1360 cc models, the main bearing shells were modified in February 1992, resulting in a reduction in the specified running clearance - see text for further information.*

***These are suggested figures, typical for this type of engine - no exact values are stated by Citroën.*

Note: *At the time of writing, specifications were only available on 1124 cc and 1360 cc engines. Consult your Citroën dealer for specifications on other engines.*

Piston rings

End gaps:	
Top compression ring:	
954 cc and 1124 cc engines	0.25 to 0.45 mm
1360 cc petrol engine	0.30 to 0.50 mm
1360 cc Diesel (K9A) engine	0.20 to 0.40 mm
Second compression ring:	
954 cc and 1124 cc engines	0.25 to 0.45 mm
1360 cc petrol engine	0.30 to 0.50 mm
1360 cc Diesel (K9A) engine	0.15 to 0.35 mm
Oil control ring:	
954 cc, 1124 cc and 1360 cc (except K9A) engines	0.3 to 0.5 mm*
1360 cc Diesel (K9A) engine	0.25 to 0.50 mm

**These are suggested figures, typical for this type of engine - no exact values are stated by Citroën.*

Torque wrench settings

TU series petrol engine - 954 cc, 1124 cc and 1360 cc

Refer to Chapter 2A Specifications.

TU series Diesel engine - 1360 cc

Refer to Chapter 2B Specifications.

2C

1 General information

Included in this Part of Chapter 2 are details of removing the engine from the vehicle, and the general overhaul procedures for the cylinder head, cylinder block/crankcase and all other engine internal components.

The information given ranges from advice concerning preparation for an overhaul and the purchase of replacement parts, to detailed step-by-step procedures covering removal, inspection, renovation and refitting of engine internal components.

After Section 6, all instructions are based on the assumption that the engine has been removed from the vehicle. For information concerning in-car engine repair, as well as the removal and refitting of those external components necessary for full overhaul, refer to Part A or B of this Chapter (as applicable) and to Section 6. Ignore any preliminary dismantling operations described in Part A (petrol engine) or Part B (Diesel engine) that are no longer relevant once the engine has been removed from the vehicle.

Apart from torque wrench settings, which are given at the beginning of Part A or Part B, all specifications relating to engine overhaul are at the beginning of this Part of Chapter 2.

Note: *At the time of writing, only limited information was available on the cast-iron block 1527 cc Diesel engine introduced in July 1994. This information consists mainly of Specifications, and therefore the main Sections of this Chapter refer only to the aluminium block engine. There are similarities between the petrol and Diesel iron-block engines, and procedures for the lower half of the engine are very similar to those for the petrol iron-block engine. The cylinder head is based on the aluminium block Diesel engine, but the locations of the injectors and glow plugs are reversed (ie the glow plugs are above the injectors).*

2 Engine overhaul - general information

It is not always easy to determine when, or if, an engine should be completely overhauled, as a number of factors must be considered.

High mileage is not necessarily an indication that an overhaul is needed, while low mileage does not preclude the need for an overhaul. Frequency of servicing is probably the most important consideration. An engine which has had regular and frequent oil and filter changes, as well as other required maintenance, should give many thousands of miles of reliable service. Conversely, a neglected engine may require an overhaul very early in its life.

Excessive oil consumption is an indication that piston rings, valve seals and/or valve guides are in need of attention. Make sure that oil leaks are not responsible before deciding that the rings and/or guides are worn. Perform a compression test, as described in Part A of this Chapter, to determine the likely cause of the problem.

Check the oil pressure with a gauge fitted in place of the oil pressure switch, and compare it with that specified. If it is extremely low, the main and big-end bearings, and/or the oil pump, are probably worn out.

Loss of power, rough running, knocking or metallic engine noises, excessive valve gear noise, and high fuel consumption may also point to the need for an overhaul, especially if they are all present at the same time. If a complete service does not remedy the situation, major mechanical work is the only solution.

An engine overhaul involves restoring all internal parts to the specification of a new engine. During an overhaul, the cylinder liners (where applicable), the pistons and the piston rings are renewed. New main and big-end bearings are generally fitted; if necessary, the crankshaft may be renewed, to restore the journals. The valves are also serviced as well, since they are usually in less-than-perfect condition at this point. While the engine is being overhauled, other components, such as the distributor, starter and alternator, can be overhauled as well. The end result should be an as-new engine that will give many trouble-free miles.

Note: *Critical cooling system components such as the hoses, thermostat and water pump should be renewed when an engine is overhauled. The radiator should be checked carefully, to ensure that it is not clogged or leaking. Also, it is a good idea to renew the oil pump whenever the engine is overhauled.*

Before beginning the engine overhaul, read through the entire procedure, to familiarise yourself with the scope and requirements of the job. Overhauling an engine is not difficult if you carefully follow all of the instructions, have the necessary tools and equipment, and pay close attention to all specifications. It can, however, be time-consuming. Plan on the car being off the road for a minimum of two weeks, especially if parts must be taken to an engineering works for repair or reconditioning. Check on the availability of parts, and make sure that any necessary special tools and equipment are obtained in advance. Most work can be done with typical hand tools, although a number of precision measuring tools are required for inspecting parts to determine if they must be renewed. Often, the engineering works will handle the inspection of parts, and can offer advice concerning reconditioning and renewal.

Note: *Always wait until the engine has been completely dismantled, and until all components (especially the cylinder block/crankcase and the crankshaft) have been inspected, before deciding what service and repair operations must be performed by an engineering works. The condition of these components will be the major factor to consider when determining whether to overhaul the original engine, or to buy a reconditioned unit. Do not, therefore, purchase parts or have overhaul work done on other components until they have been thoroughly inspected.* As a general rule, time is the primary cost of an overhaul, so it does not pay to fit worn or sub-standard parts.

As a final note, to ensure maximum life and minimum trouble from a reconditioned engine, everything must be assembled with care, in a spotlessly-clean environment.

3 Engine removal - methods and precautions

If you have decided that the engine must be removed for overhaul or major repair work, several preliminary steps should be taken.

Locating a suitable place to work is extremely important. Adequate work space, along with storage space for the vehicle, will be needed. If a workshop or garage is not available, at the very least, a flat, level, clean work surface is required.

Cleaning the engine compartment and engine/transmission before beginning the removal procedure will help keep tools clean and organised.

An engine hoist or A-frame will also be necessary. Make sure that the equipment is rated in excess of the combined weight of the engine and transmission. Safety is of primary importance, considering the potential hazards involved in lifting the engine/transmission out of the vehicle.

If this is the first time you have removed an engine, an assistant should ideally be available. Advice and aid from someone more experienced would also be helpful. There are many instances when one person cannot simultaneously perform all of the operations required when lifting the engine out of the vehicle.

Plan the operation ahead of time. Before starting work, arrange for the hire of or obtain all of the tools and equipment you will need. Some of the equipment necessary to perform engine/transmission removal and installation safely and with relative ease (in addition to an engine hoist) is as follows: a heavy-duty trolley jack, complete sets of spanners and sockets as described in the front of this manual, wooden blocks, and plenty of rags and cleaning solvent for mopping-up spilled oil, coolant and fuel. If the hoist must be hired, make sure that you arrange for it in advance, and perform all of the operations possible without it beforehand. This will save you money and time.

Plan for the vehicle to be out of use for quite a while. An engineering works will be required to perform some of the work which the do-it-yourselfer cannot accomplish without special equipment. These places often have a busy schedule, so it would be a good idea to consult them before removing the engine, in order to accurately estimate the amount of time required to rebuild or repair components that may need work.

Always be extremely careful when removing and refitting the engine/transmission. Serious injury can result from careless actions. Plan ahead and take your time, and a job of this nature, although major, can be accomplished successfully.

The engine and transmission is removed from under the vehicle on all models described in this manual.

4 Engine and transmission - removal, separation and refitting

Removal

Note: *The engine can be removed from the car only as a complete unit with the transmission; the two are then separated for overhaul. The engine/transmission unit is lowered out of position. To allow adequate clearance underneath the vehicle to enable the unit to be withdrawn, there should be at least 75 cm between the front bumper and the ground when the vehicle is raised and supported.*

1 Park the vehicle on firm, level ground. Chock the rear wheels, then firmly apply the handbrake. Jack up the front of the vehicle, and securely support it on axle stands, bearing in mind the note at the start of this Section.

2 Remove both front roadwheels.

3 Remove the bonnet (Chapter 11) and remove the battery (Chapter 5).

4 Drain the cooling system (see Chapter 1), saving the coolant if it is fit for re-use. Although not essential, it may also be worth removing the radiator (Chapter 3), which is easily damaged during engine removal.

5 Drain the transmission oil as described in Chapter 7. Refit the drain and filler plugs, and tighten them to their specified torque settings.

6 If the engine is to be dismantled, working as described in Chapter 1, drain the oil and if required remove the oil filter. Clean and refit the drain plug, tightening it securely.

7 To give improved working room, remove the alternator as described in Chapter 5.

8 On models with air conditioning, unbolt the compressor and position it clear of the engine unit. Support the weight of the compressor by tying it to the vehicle body, to prevent any excess strain being placed on the compressor lines whilst the engine is removed. **Do not** disconnect the refrigerant lines from the compressor (refer to the warnings given in Chapter 3).

Petrol engine models

9 Remove the complete air cleaner housing and duct assembly, as described in the relevant Part of Chapter 4 **(see illustrations)**.

10 On early models, remove the jack and its support from the engine compartment.

11 On carburettor models, disconnect the choke cable with reference to Chapter 4.

12 Disconnect the fuel supply hose from the fuel pump on the left-hand end of the cylinder head on carburettor models. On fuel injection models, disconnect the fuel inlet and return hoses with reference to Chapter 4.

13 Disconnect the brake vacuum servo hose from the inlet manifold.

4.9a Remove the air cleaner housing . . .

4.9b . . . and intake duct

14 Disconnect the top hose and small expansion tank hose from the thermostat housing on the left-hand end of the cylinder head.

15 On fuel injection models, disconnect the wiring and vacuum hose from the ECU, as applicable (see Chapter 4).

16 Remove the exhaust front pipe completely, with reference to Chapter 4.

17 On fuel injection models, it will be necessary to remove the ECU from the right-hand engine mounting.

Diesel engine models

18 Remove the screws and disconnect the air inlet duct nozzle from the engine compartment front crossmember, then loosen the clip and disconnect the duct from the air cleaner assembly.

19 Disconnect the coolant hose from the thermostat/fuel filter housing on the left-hand end of the cylinder head.

20 Disconnect the brake vacuum servo hose from the vacuum pump on the left-hand end of the cylinder head.

21 Disconnect the fuel hoses from the fuel filter housing on the left-hand end of the cylinder head.

22 Disconnect the feed wire from the No 1 glow plug terminal.

23 Disconnect the exhaust intermediate section from the front pipe by unscrewing the flange bolts. Recover the springs and sealing ring. There is no need to remove the front pipe from the exhaust manifold.

24 Disconnect the starter motor cable from the starter motor.

All models

25 Disconnect the speedometer cable from the transmission.

26 Disconnect the clutch release cable from the transmission.

27 Loosen the clips and disconnect the heater hoses from the bulkhead at the rear of the engine compartment.

28 Disconnect the accelerator cable with reference to Chapter 4.

29 Unbolt the transmission earth cable from the body on the left-hand side of the engine compartment.

30 Locate and disconnect the engine wiring harness connector(s) on the left-hand side of the engine compartment **(see illustrations)**.

31 Where necessary, remove the anti-roll bar as described in Chapter 10.

32 Disconnect the front suspension lower arms from the swivel hubs with reference to Chapter 10. Note which way round the bolts are fitted, to ensure correct refitting.

33 Disconnect the driveshafts from each side of the transmission, with reference to Chapter 8. It is not necessary to completely remove the driveshafts - just disconnect their inner ends by pulling the front suspension struts outwards.

34 Unscrew and remove the centre bolt securing the rear engine mounting link to the transmission bracket. Loosen the remaining centre bolt, and swivel the link downwards.

35 Disconnect the three gearchange rods from the gearshift mechanism, and move them to one side.

36 Where necessary, release the radiator bottom hose from the clips on the right-hand side of the body.

37 Manoeuvre the engine hoist into position, and attach it to the lifting brackets bolted onto the cylinder head. Raise the hoist until it is supporting the weight of the engine.

38 Unscrew the nuts securing the left-hand engine mounting to the body, then unscrew and remove the centre bolt and remove the mounting.

39 Unscrew and remove the nuts securing the right-hand engine mounting upper bracket to the body mounting and bracket on the cylinder block. Withdraw the bracket.

40 Make a final check that any components which would prevent the removal of the engine/transmission from the car have been removed or disconnected. Ensure that components such as the gearchange selector rods are secured so that they cannot be damaged on removal.

41 If available, a low trolley should be placed under the engine/transmission assembly to facilitate its easy removal from under the vehicle. Lower the engine/transmission assembly, making sure that nothing is trapped or damaged. Enlist the help of an assistant during this procedure, as it may be necessary to tilt the assembly slightly to clear the body panels. Great care must also be taken to ensure that the radiator, if not removed, (and, on right-hand drive models, the braking system master cylinder reservoir) are not damaged during the removal procedure.

42 Withdraw the assembly from under the vehicle.

Separation

43 With the engine/transmission assembly removed, support the assembly on suitable blocks of wood, on a workbench (or failing that, on a clean area of the workshop floor).

44 Unscrew the retaining bolts, and remove the starter motor from the transmission. On cast-iron block engine models, unbolt and remove the lower cover from the transmission.

45 Disconnect the reversing light wire from the switch on the transmission.

4.30a Disconnecting the main engine/transmission wiring harness connector . . .

4.30b . . . then disconnect the harness leads . . .

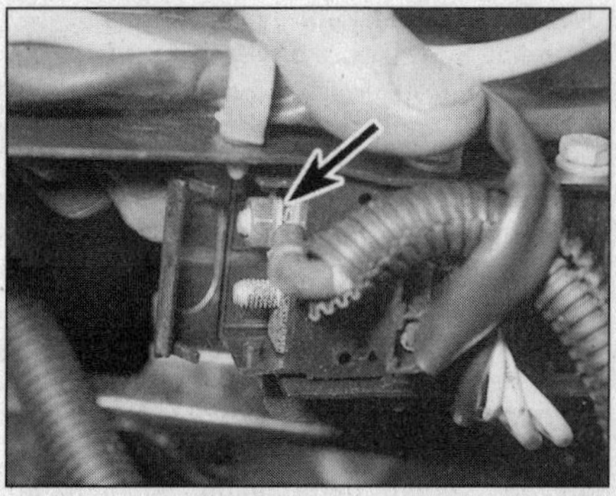

4.30c . . . and earth lead (arrowed) from the auxiliary fusebox

46 Ensure that both engine and transmission are adequately supported, then slacken and remove the bolts securing the transmission housing to the engine. Note the correct fitted positions of each bolt (and, where fitted, the relevant brackets) as they are removed, to use as a reference on refitting.

47 Carefully withdraw the transmission from the engine, ensuring that the weight of the transmission is not allowed to hang on the input shaft while it is engaged with the clutch friction disc.

48 If they are loose, remove the locating dowels from the engine or transmission, and keep them in a safe place.

Refitting

49 Apply a smear of high-melting-point grease to the splines of the transmission input shaft. Do not apply too much, otherwise there is a possibility of the grease contaminating the clutch friction plate.

50 Ensure that the locating dowels are correctly positioned in the engine or transmission.

51 Carefully offer the transmission to the engine, until the locating dowels are engaged. Ensure that the weight of the transmission is not allowed to hang on the input shaft as it is engaged with the clutch friction disc.

52 Refit the transmission housing-to-engine bolts, ensuring that all the necessary brackets are correctly positioned, and tighten them to the specified torque setting.

53 Check that the release fork and bearing are correctly engaged.

> HAYNES HiNT *If necessary, the clutch cable can be refitted at this stage and the clutch pedal depressed in order to check the operation of the release fork. Should there be any doubt that the clutch is working properly, the gearbox should be removed and the clutch checked for correct assembly.*

54 Reconnect the wire to the reversing light switch.

55 Refit the starter motor, and tighten the retaining bolts. On cast-iron block engine models, refit the lower cover to the transmission, and tighten the bolts.

56 Locate the engine/transmission assembly under the vehicle, then reconnect the hoist and lifting tackle to the engine lifting brackets.

57 With the aid of an assistant, lift the assembly up into the engine compartment, making sure that it clears the surrounding components. Again, take care not to damage the radiator or brake master cylinder reservoir, if applicable.

58 Refit the right-hand engine mounting upper bracket to the body mounting and bracket, and tighten the nuts to the specified torque.

59 Refit the left-hand engine mounting, and tighten the centre bolt and mounting nuts to the specified torques.

60 Where necessary, refit the radiator bottom hose to the clips on the right-hand side of the body.

61 Reconnect the three gearchange rods to the gearshift mechanism.

62 Swivel up the rear engine mounting link, then insert the centre bolt. Tighten both bolts to the specified torque.

63 Reconnect both driveshafts to the transmission, with reference to Chapter 8.

64 Reconnect the front suspension lower arms to the swivel hubs with reference to Chapter 10. Make sure that the bolts are fitted the correct way round.

65 Refit the anti-roll bar with reference to Chapter 10.

66 Reconnect the engine wiring harness connector(s) on the left-hand side of the engine compartment.

67 Refit the earth cable to the body on the left-hand side of the engine compartment, and tighten the bolt.

68 Reconnect the accelerator cable with reference to Chapter 4.

69 Reconnect the heater hoses to the bulkhead at the rear of the engine compartment.

70 Reconnect and adjust the clutch release cable with reference to Chapter 6.

71 Reconnect the speedometer cable to the transmission.

Diesel engine models

72 Reconnect the cable to the starter motor.

73 Reconnect the exhaust intermediate section to the front pipe with reference to Chapter 4.

74 Reconnect the feed wire to the No 1 glow plug terminal.

75 Reconnect the fuel hoses to the fuel filter housing on the left-hand end of the cylinder head.

76 Reconnect the brake vacuum servo hose to the vacuum pump on the left-hand end of the cylinder head.

77 Reconnect the coolant hose to the thermostat/fuel filter housing on the left-hand end of the cylinder head.

78 Refit the air inlet duct to the air cleaner assembly, and the nozzle to the engine compartment front crossmember.

Petrol engine models

79 On fuel injection models, refit the ECU to the left-hand end of the cylinder head.

80 Refit the exhaust front pipe with reference to Chapter 4.

81 On fuel injection models, reconnect the wiring and vacuum hose to the ECU, as applicable.

82 Reconnect the top hose and small expansion tank hose to the thermostat housing on the left-hand end of the cylinder head.

83 Reconnect the brake vacuum servo hose to the inlet manifold.

84 Reconnect the fuel supply hose to the fuel pump on the left-hand end of the cylinder head on carburettor models. On fuel injection models, reconnect he fuel inlet and return hoses.

85 On carburettor models, reconnect and adjust the choke cable with reference to Chapter 4.

86 On early models, refit the jack and its support into the engine compartment.

87 Refit the air cleaner housing and duct assembly with reference to Chapter 4.

All models

88 If applicable, refill the engine with the correct quantity and grade of oil.

89 Refill the transmission with the correct quantity and grade of oil.

90 If removed, refit the radiator.

91 If removed, refit the alternator.

92 Where applicable, refit the air conditioning compressor.

93 Refill the cooling system with coolant (see Chapter 1).

94 Refit the battery (Chapter 5) and the bonnet (Chapter 11).

95 Refit both front roadwheels, and tighten the bolts to the specified torque.

96 Ensure that all wiring has been reconnected and all nuts and bolts have been tightened.

5 Engine overhaul - dismantling sequence

1 It is much easier to dismantle and work on the engine if it is mounted on a portable engine stand. These stands can often be hired from a tool hire shop. Before the engine is mounted on a stand, the flywheel should be removed, so that the stand bolts can be tightened into the end of the cylinder block/crankcase.

2 If a stand is not available, it is possible to dismantle the engine with it blocked up on a sturdy workbench, or on the floor. Be extra-careful not to tip or drop the engine when working without a stand.

3 If you are going to obtain a reconditioned engine, all the external components must be removed first, to be transferred to the replacement engine (just as they will if you are doing a complete engine overhaul yourself). These components include the following:

a) Alternator mounting bracket (Chapter 5A).
b) On petrol engines, the distributor, HT leads and spark plugs (Chapters 1 and 5B).
c) On Diesel engines, the fuel injection pump and mounting bracket, the fuel injectors and glow plugs (see Chapter 4D).
d) Thermostat and housing, and coolant outlet chamber/elbow (Chapter 3). On Diesel engines, the housing also includes the fuel filter housing.
e) Where applicable, the dipstick tube.
f) On petrol engines, the carburettor/fuel injection system components (Chapter 4).
g) All electrical switches and sensors, and the engine wiring harness.
h) Inlet and exhaust manifolds (Chapter 4).

6.4a Compressing the valve spring using a spring compressor

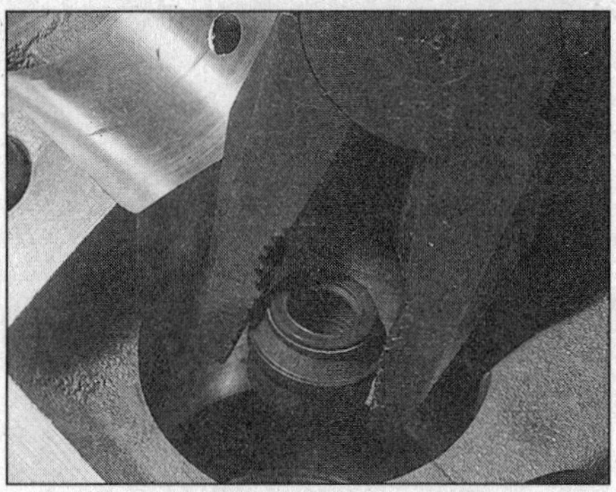

6.4b Remove the valve stem oil seal using a pair of pliers

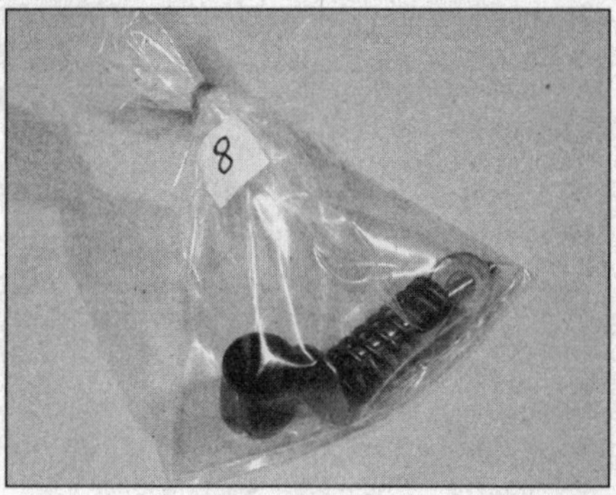

6.6 Place each valve and its associated components in a labelled polythene bag

i) Oil filter (Chapter 1).
j) On carburettor petrol engines, the fuel pump (Chapter 4A).
k) Engine mountings (Part A or B of this Chapter).
l) Flywheel (Part A or B of this Chapter).

Note: *When removing the external components from the engine, pay close attention to details that may be helpful or important during refitting. Note the fitted position of gaskets, seals, spacers, pins, washers, bolts, and other small items.*

4 If you are obtaining a "short" engine (which consists of the engine cylinder block/crankcase, crankshaft, pistons and connecting rods all assembled), then the cylinder head, sump, oil pump, and timing belt will have to be removed also.

5 If you are planning a complete overhaul, the engine can be dismantled, and the internal components removed, in the order given below, referring to Part A or B of this Chapter unless otherwise stated:

a) Inlet and exhaust manifolds (Chapter 4).
b) Timing belt, sprockets and tensioner.
c) Cylinder head.
d) Flywheel.
e) Sump.
f) Oil pump.
g) Piston/connecting rod assemblies (Section 9).
h) Crankshaft (Section 10).

6 Before beginning the dismantling and overhaul procedures, make sure that you have all of the correct tools necessary. Refer to *"Tools and working facilities"* at the beginning of this manual for further information.

6 Cylinder head - dismantling

Note: *New and reconditioned cylinder heads are available from the manufacturer, and from engine overhaul specialists. Be aware that some specialist tools are required for the dismantling and inspection procedures, and new components may not be readily available. It may therefore be more practical and economical for the home mechanic to purchase a reconditioned head, rather than dismantle, inspect and recondition the original head.*

1 Remove the cylinder head as described in Part A or B of this Chapter (as applicable).

2 Remove the inlet and exhaust manifolds with reference to Chapter 4 (if not already done).

3 Remove the camshaft (and the followers and shims on Diesel engines) as described in Part A or B of this Chapter.

4 Using a valve spring compressor, compress each valve spring in turn until the split collets can be removed. Release the compressor, and lift off the spring retainer, spring and spring seat. Using a pair of pliers, carefully extract the valve stem seal from the top of the guide **(see illustrations)**.

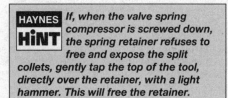

> **HAYNES HiNT** ***If, when the valve spring compressor is screwed down, the spring retainer refuses to free and expose the split collets, gently tap the top of the tool, directly over the retainer, with a light hammer. This will free the retainer.***

5 Withdraw the valve through the combustion chamber.

6 It is essential that each valve is stored together with its collets, retainer, spring, and spring seat. The valves should also be kept in their correct sequence, unless they are so badly worn that they are to be renewed. If they are going to be kept and used again, place each valve assembly in a labelled polythene bag or similar small container **(see illustration)**. Note that No 1 valve is nearest to the transmission (flywheel) end of the engine.

7 Cylinder head and valves - cleaning and inspection

1 Thorough cleaning of the cylinder head and valve components, followed by a detailed inspection, will enable you to decide how much valve service work must be carried out during the engine overhaul. **Note:** *If the engine has been severely overheated, it is best to assume that the cylinder head is warped - check carefully for signs of this.*

Cleaning

2 Scrape away all traces of old gasket material from the cylinder head.

3 Scrape away the carbon from the combustion chambers and ports, then wash the cylinder head thoroughly with paraffin or a suitable solvent.

4 Scrape off any heavy carbon deposits that may have formed on the valves, then use a power-operated wire brush to remove deposits from the valve heads and stems.

Inspection

Note: *Be sure to perform all the following inspection procedures before concluding that the services of a machine shop or engine overhaul specialist are required. Make a list of all items that require attention.*

Cylinder head

5 Inspect the head very carefully for cracks, evidence of coolant leakage, and other damage. If cracks are found, a new cylinder head should be obtained.

6 Use a straight-edge and feeler blade to check that the cylinder head surface is not distorted **(see illustration)**. If it is, it may be possible to have it machined, provided that the cylinder head is not reduced to less than the specified height. **Note:** *On Diesel engines, it is necessary to recut the combustion chambers*

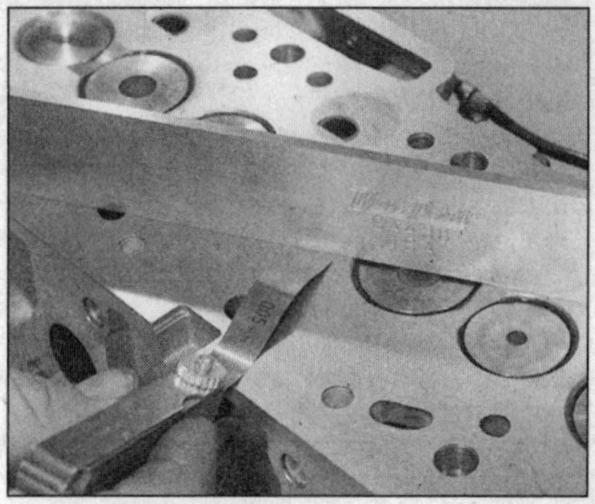

7.6 Checking the cylinder head gasket surface for distortion

7.10 Checking swirl chamber protrusion - Diesel engine

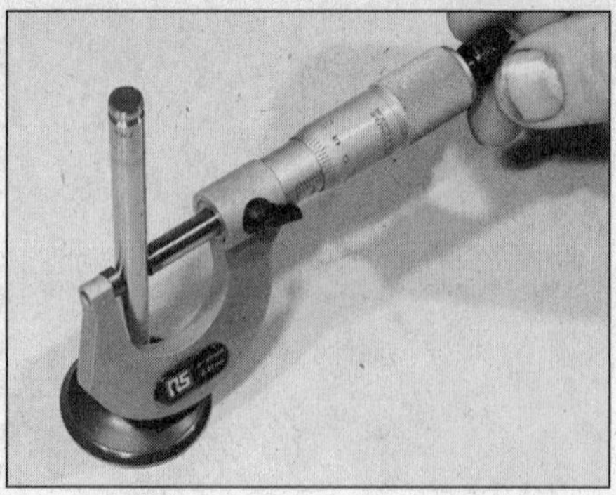

7.12 Measuring a valve stem diameter

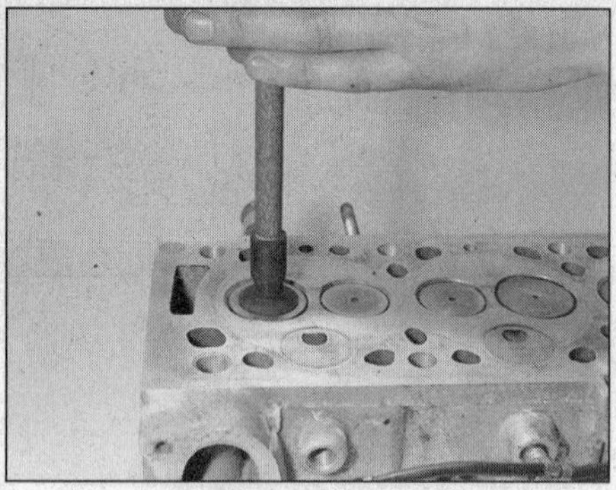

7.15 Grinding-in a valve

and valve seats if more than 0.1 mm has been machined off of the cylinder head. This is necessary in order to maintain the correct dimensions between the valve heads, valve guides and cylinder head gasket face.

7 Examine the valve seats in each of the combustion chambers. If they are severely pitted, cracked, or burned, they will need to be renewed or re-cut by an engine overhaul specialist. If they are only slightly pitted, this can be removed by grinding-in the valve heads and seats with fine valve-grinding compound, as described below.

8 Check the valve guides for wear by inserting the relevant valve, and checking for side-to-side motion of the valve. A very small amount of movement is acceptable. If the movement seems excessive, remove the valve. Measure the valve stem diameter (see below), and renew the valve if it is worn. If the valve stem is not worn, the wear must be in the valve guide, and the guide must be renewed. The renewal of valve guides is best carried out by a Citroën dealer or engine overhaul specialist, who will have the necessary tools available. Where no valve stem diameter is specified, seek the advice of a Citroën dealer on the best course of action.

9 If renewing the valve guides, the valve seats are to be re-cut or re-ground only *after* the guides have been fitted.

10 On Diesel models, inspect the swirl chambers for burning or damage such as cracking. Small cracks in the chambers are acceptable; renewal of the chambers will only be required if chamber tracts are badly burned and disfigured, or if they are no longer a tight fit in the cylinder head. If there is any doubt as to the swirl chamber condition, seek the advice of a Citroën dealer or a suitable repairer who specialises in Diesel engines. Swirl chamber renewal should be entrusted to a specialist. Using a dial test indicator, check that the swirl chamber protrusion is within the limits given in the Specifications **(see illustration)**. Zero the dial test indicator on the gasket surface of the cylinder head, then measure the protrusion of the swirl chamber. If the protrusion is not within the specified limits, the advice of a Citroën dealer or suitable repairer who specialises in Diesel engines should be sought.

Valves

11 Examine the head of each valve for pitting, burning, cracks, and general wear. Check the valve stem for scoring and wear ridges. Rotate the valve, and check for any obvious indication that it is bent. Look for pits and excessive wear on the tip of each valve stem. Renew any valve that shows any such signs of wear or damage.

12 If the valve appears satisfactory at this stage, measure the valve stem diameter at several points using a micrometer **(see illustration)**. Any significant difference in the readings obtained indicates wear of the valve stem. Should any of these conditions be apparent, the valve(s) must be renewed.

13 If the valves are in satisfactory condition, they should be ground (lapped) into their respective seats, to ensure a smooth, gas-tight seal. If the seat is only lightly pitted, or if it has been re-cut, fine grinding compound *only* should be used to produce the required finish. Coarse valve-grinding compound should *not* be used, unless a seat is badly burned or deeply pitted. If this is the case, the cylinder head and valves should be inspected by an expert, to decide whether seat re-cutting, or even the renewal of the valve or seat insert (where possible) is required.

14 Valve grinding is carried out as follows. Place the cylinder head upside-down on a bench.

15 Smear a trace of (the appropriate grade of) valve-grinding compound on the seat face, and press a suction grinding tool onto the valve head. With a semi-rotary action, grind the valve head to its seat, lifting the valve occasionally to redistribute the grinding compound **(see illustration)**. A light spring placed under the valve head will greatly ease this operation.

16 If coarse grinding compound is being used, work only until a dull, matt even surface is produced on both the valve seat and the valve, then wipe off the used compound, and repeat the process with fine compound. When a smooth unbroken ring of light grey matt finish is produced on both the valve and seat, the grinding operation is complete. *Do not* grind-in the valves any further than absolutely necessary, or the seat will be prematurely sunk into the cylinder head.

17 When all the valves have been ground-in, carefully wash off *all* traces of grinding compound using paraffin or a suitable solvent, before reassembling the cylinder head.

Valve components

18 Examine the valve springs for signs of damage and discoloration. No minimum free length is specified by Citroën, so the only way of judging valve spring wear is by comparison with a new component.

19 Stand each spring on a flat surface, and check it for squareness. If any of the springs are damaged, distorted or have lost their tension, obtain a complete new set of springs. It is normal to renew the valve springs as a matter of course if a major overhaul is being carried out.

20 Renew the valve stem oil seals regardless of their apparent condition.

8 Cylinder head - reassembly

1 Lubricate the stems of the valves, and insert the valves into their original locations **(see illustration)**. If new valves are being fitted, insert them into the locations to which they have been ground.

2 Refit the spring seat then, working on the first valve, dip the new valve stem seal in fresh engine oil. Carefully locate it over the valve and onto the guide. Take care not to damage the

8.1 Lubricate the valve stems prior to refitting the valves

8.2a Refit the spring seat . . .

8.2b . . . then fit a new valve stem oil seal, using a socket

8.3a Refit the valve spring . . .

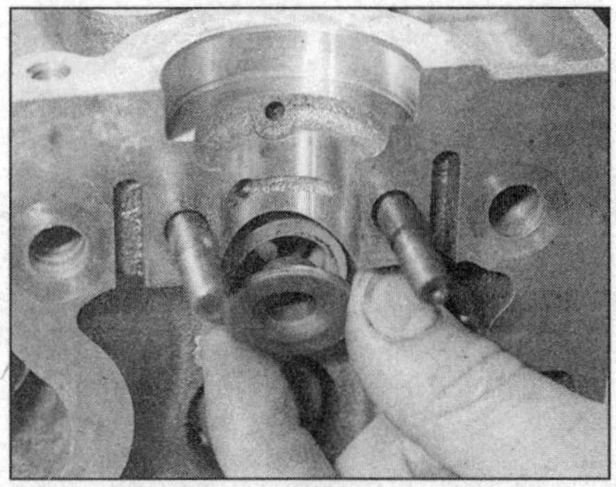

8.3b . . . and the spring retainer . . .

8.4a . . . and compress the spring with a spring compressor

8.4b Locate the collets on the valve, using a dab of grease to hold them in position

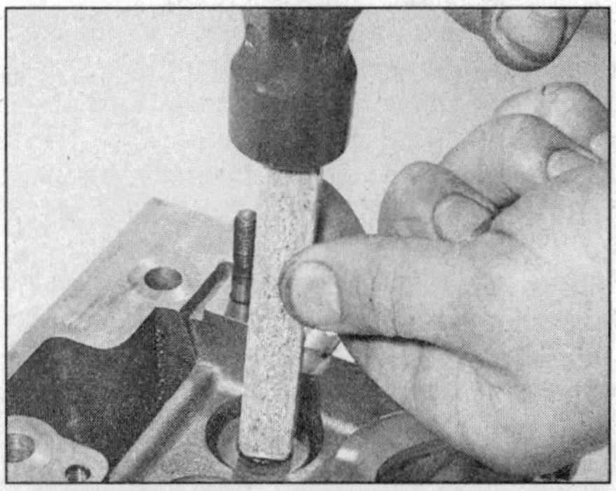

8.5 Remove the spring compressor, and tap the end of the valve to seat the collets in position

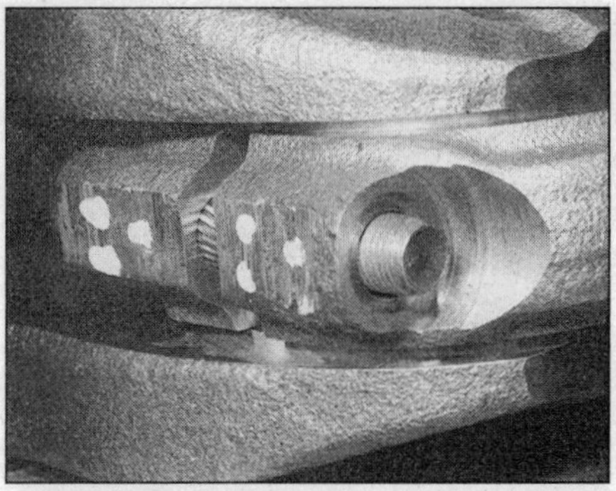

9.3 Connecting rod and big-end bearing cap marked for identification (No 3 cylinder shown)

seal as it is passed over the valve stem. Use a suitable socket or metal tube to press the seal firmly onto the guide **(see illustrations)**.

3 Locate the valve spring on top of its seat, then refit the spring retainer **(see illustrations)**.

4 Compress the valve spring, and locate the split collets in the recess in the valve stem. Release the compressor, then repeat the procedure on the remaining valves **(see illustrations)**.

HAYNES HiNT *Use a little dab of grease to hold the collets in position on the valve stem while the spring compressor is released.*

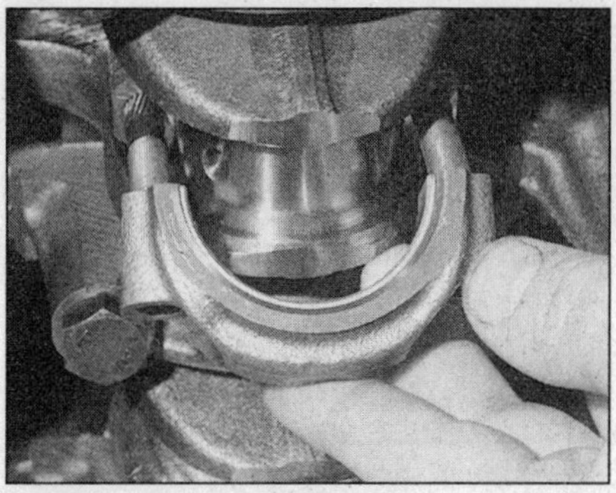

9.5 Removing a big-end bearing cap and shell

5 With all the valves installed, place the cylinder head flat on the bench and, using a hammer and interposed block of wood, tap the end of each valve stem to settle the components **(see illustration)**.

6 Refit the camshaft as described in Part A or B (as applicable).

7 Refit the inlet and exhaust manifolds with reference to Chapter 4.

8 The cylinder head may now be refitted as described in Part A or B of this Chapter (as applicable).

9 Piston/connecting rod assembly - removal

1 Remove the cylinder head, sump and oil pump as described in Part A or B of this Chapter (as applicable)

2 If there is a pronounced wear ridge at the top of any bore, it may be necessary to remove it with a scraper or ridge reamer, to avoid piston damage during removal. Such a ridge indicates excessive wear of the cylinder bore.

3 Using a hammer and centre-punch, paint or similar, mark each connecting rod big-end bearing cap with its respective cylinder number on the flat machined surface provided; if the engine has been dismantled before, note carefully any identifying marks made previously **(see illustration)**. Note that No 1 cylinder is at the transmission (flywheel) end of the engine.

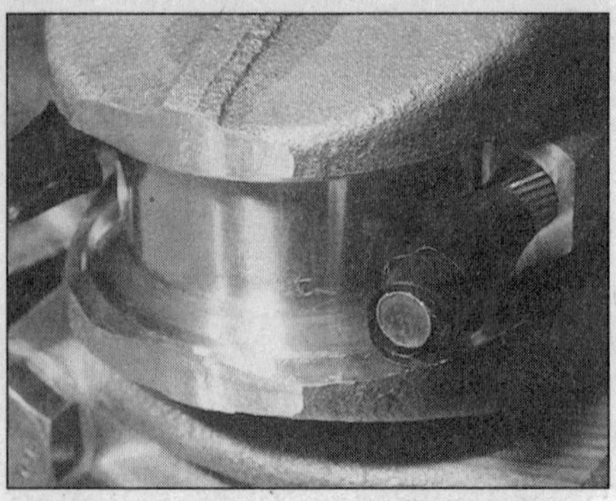

9.6 To protect the crankshaft journals, tape over the connecting rod stud threads prior to removal

10.9 On cast-iron block engines, remove the oil seal housing from the front of the cylinder block

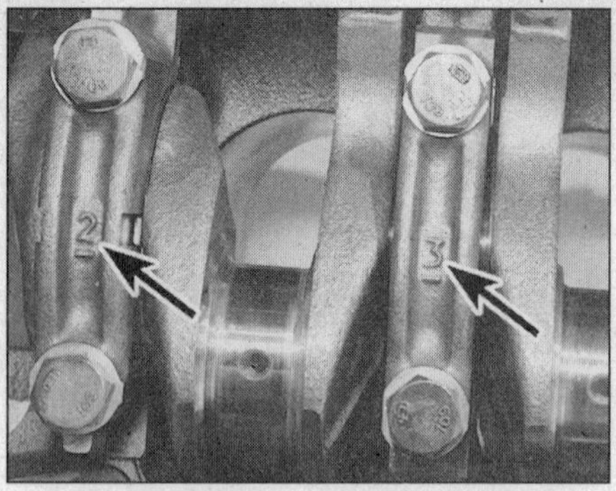

10.10 Main bearing cap identification markings (arrowed)

4 Turn the crankshaft to bring pistons 1 and 4 to BDC (bottom dead centre).

5 Unscrew the nuts from No 1 piston big-end bearing cap. Take off the cap, and recover the bottom half bearing shell **(see illustration)**. If the bearing shells are to be re-used, tape the cap and the shell together.

6 To prevent the possibility of damage to the crankshaft bearing journals, tape over the connecting rod stud threads **(see illustration)**.

7 Using a hammer handle, push the piston up through the bore, and remove it from the top of the cylinder block. Recover the bearing shell, and tape it to the connecting rod for safe-keeping.

8 Loosely refit the big-end cap to the connecting rod, and secure with the nuts - this will help to keep the components in their correct order.

9 Remove No 4 piston assembly in the same way.

10 Turn the crankshaft through 180° to bring pistons 2 and 3 to BDC (bottom dead centre), and remove them in the same way.

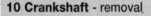

10 Crankshaft - removal

1 Remove the crankshaft timing sprocket, the oil pump and the flywheel as described in Part A or B of this Chapter (as applicable).

2 Remove the pistons and connecting rods, as described in Section 9. **Note:** *If no work is to be done on the pistons and connecting rods, there is no need to remove the cylinder head, or to push the pistons out of the cylinder bores. The pistons should just be pushed far enough up the bores that they are positioned clear of the crankshaft journals.*

3 Check the crankshaft endfloat as described in Section 13, then proceed as follows.

Aluminium block engines (petrol and Diesel)

4 Work around the outside of the cylinder block, and unscrew all the small (6 mm) bolts securing the main bearing ladder to the base of the cylinder block. Note the correct fitted depth of both the front and rear crankshaft oil seals in the cylinder block/main bearing ladder.

5 Working in a diagonal sequence, evenly and progressively slacken the ten large (11 mm) main bearing ladder retaining bolts by a turn at a time. Once all the bolts are loose, remove them from the ladder.

6 With all the retaining bolts removed, carefully lift the main bearing ladder casting away from the base of the cylinder block. Recover the lower main bearing shells, and tape them to their respective locations in the casting. If the two locating dowels are a loose fit, remove them and store them with the casting for safe-keeping.

7 Lift out the crankshaft, and discard both the oil seals. If not already removed, remove the oil pump drive chain from the end of the crankshaft, and slide off the drive sprocket. Recover the Woodruff key.

8 Recover the upper main bearing shells, and store them along with the relevant lower bearing shells. Also recover the two thrustwashers (one fitted either side of No 2 main bearing) from the cylinder block.

Cast-iron block engines (petrol)

9 Unbolt and remove the crankshaft front and rear oil seal housings from each end of the cylinder block, noting the correct fitted locations of the locating dowels **(see illustration)**. If the locating dowels are a loose fit, remove them and store them with the housings for safe-keeping.

10 Identification numbers should already be cast onto the base of each main bearing cap **(see illustration)**. If not, number the cap and crankcase using a centre-punch, as was done for the connecting rods and caps.

11 Unscrew and remove the main bearing cap retaining bolts, and withdraw the caps, complete with bearing shells. Tap the caps with a wooden or copper mallet if they are stuck.

12 Remove the bearing shells from the caps, but keep them with their relevant caps and identified for position to ensure correct refitting.

13 If not already removed, remove the oil pump drive chain from the end of the crankshaft, and slide off the drive sprocket. Recover the Woodruff key **(see illustrations)**.

10.13a Remove the oil pump drive chain . . .

10.13b . . . and drive sprocket . . .

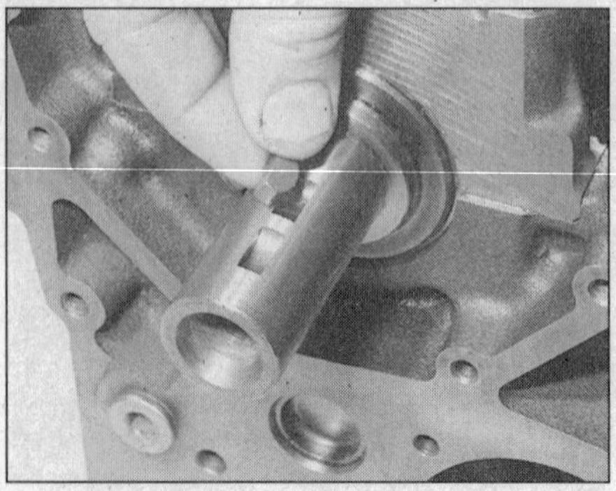

10.13c . . . then remove the Woodruff key from the crankshaft

10.14 Lifting out the crankshaft

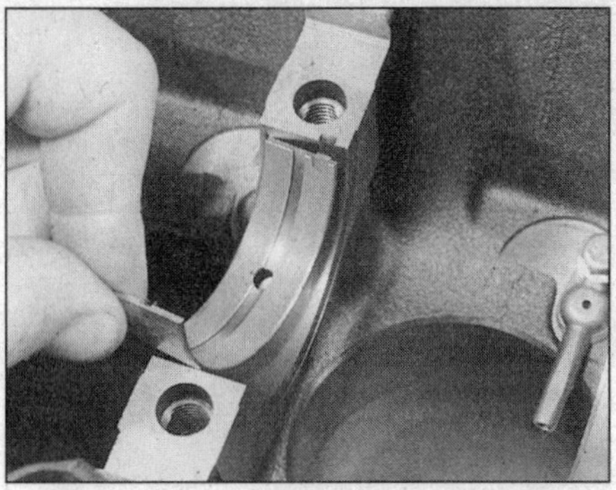

10.15 Remove the upper main bearing shells from the cylinder block/crankcase, and store them with their lower shells

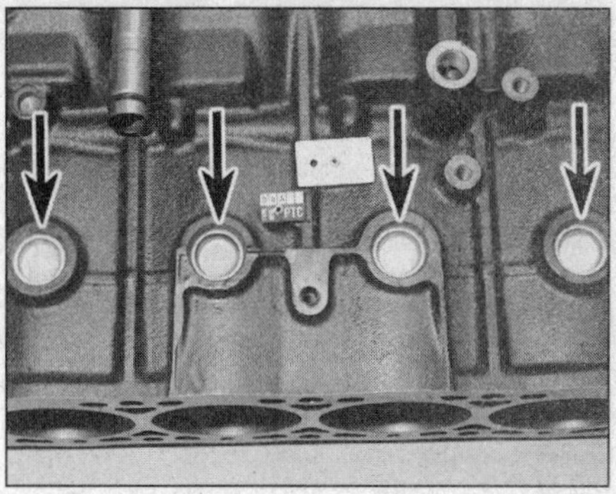

11.1 Cylinder block core plugs (arrowed)

14 Carefully lift the crankshaft from the crankcase **(see illustration)**.

15 Remove the upper bearing shells from the crankcase, keeping them identified for position. Also remove the thrustwashers at each side of the No 2 main bearing, and store them with the bearing cap **(see illustration)**.

11 Cylinder block/crankcase - cleaning and inspection

Cleaning

1 Remove all external components and electrical switches/sensors from the block. For complete cleaning, the core plugs should ideally be removed **(see illustration)**. Drill a small hole in the plugs, then insert a self-tapping screw into the hole. Pull out the plugs by pulling on the screw with a pair of grips, or by using a slide hammer.

2 On aluminium block engines with wet liners, remove the liners as described in paragraph 14.

3 Scrape all traces of sealant from the cylinder block/crankcase, and from the main bearing ladder (where fitted), taking care not to damage the gasket/sealing surfaces.

4 Remove all oil gallery plugs (where fitted). The plugs are usually very tight - they may have to be drilled out, and the holes re-tapped. Use new plugs when the engine is reassembled.

5 If any of the castings are extremely dirty, all should be steam-cleaned.

6 After the castings are returned, clean all oil holes and oil galleries one more time. Flush all internal passages with warm water until the water runs clear. Dry thoroughly, and apply a light film of oil to all mating surfaces, to prevent rusting. On cast-iron block engines, also oil the cylinder bores. If you have access to compressed air, use it to speed up the drying process, and to blow out all the oil holes and galleries.

Warning: Wear eye protection when using compressed air!

7 If the castings are not very dirty, you can do an adequate cleaning job with hot (as hot as you can stand!), soapy water and a stiff brush. Take plenty of time, and do a thorough job. Regardless of the cleaning method used, be sure to clean all oil holes and galleries very thoroughly, and to dry all components well. On cast-iron block engines, protect the cylinder bores as described above, to prevent rusting.

8 All threaded holes must be clean, to ensure accurate torque readings during reassembly. To clean the threads, run the correct-size tap into each of the holes to remove rust, corrosion, thread sealant or sludge, and to restore damaged threads **(see illustration)**. If possible, use compressed air to clear the holes of debris produced by this operation.

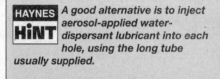

HAYNES HiNT ***A good alternative is to inject aerosol-applied water-dispersant lubricant into each hole, using the long tube usually supplied.***

Warning: Wear eye protection when cleaning out these holes in this way!

9 Apply suitable sealant to the new oil gallery plugs, and insert them into the holes in the block. Tighten them securely.

10 If the engine is not going to be reassembled right away, cover it with a large plastic bag to keep it clean; protect all mating surfaces and the cylinder bores as described above, to prevent rusting.

Inspection

Cast-iron cylinder block

11 Visually check the casting for cracks and corrosion. Look for stripped threads in the threaded holes. If there has been any history of internal water leakage, it may be worthwhile having an engine overhaul specialist check the cylinder block/crankcase with special equipment. If defects are found, have them repaired if possible, or renew the assembly.

12 Check each cylinder bore for scuffing and scoring. Check for signs of a wear ridge at the

11.8 Cleaning a cylinder block threaded hole using a suitable tap

11.14a On aluminium block engines, remove each liner . . .

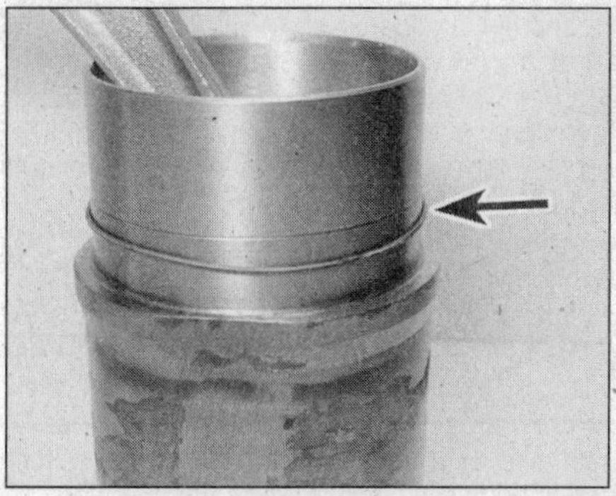

11.14b . . . and recover the bottom O-ring seal (arrowed)

top of the cylinder, indicating that the bore is excessively worn.

13 Since Citroën do not state any specific wear limits for the cylinder bores or pistons, it is not possible to assess the amount of wear by direct measurement. If there is any doubt about the condition of the cylinder bores, seek the advice of a Citroën dealer or engine reconditioning specialist. At the time of writing, oversize pistons were not available from Citroën, so therefore it is not advisable to rebore the cylinders. Consult your Citroën dealer for piston availability; if oversize pistons are not available, and the bores are worn, renewal of the block seems to be the only option.

Aluminium cylinder block with wet liners

14 Remove the liner clamps (where used), then use a hardwood drift to tap out each liner from inside the cylinder block. When all the liners are released, tip the cylinder block/crankcase on its side and remove each liner from the top of the block. As each liner is removed, stick masking tape on its left-hand (transmission side) face, and write the cylinder number on the tape. No 1 cylinder is at the transmission (flywheel) end of the engine. Remove the O-ring from the base of each liner, and discard **(see illustrations)**.

15 Check each cylinder liner for scuffing and scoring. Check for signs of a wear ridge at the top of the liner, indicating that the bore is excessively worn.

16 If the necessary measuring equipment is available, measure the bore diameter of each cylinder liner at the top (just under the wear ridge), centre, and bottom of the cylinder bore, parallel to the crankshaft axis.

17 Next, measure the bore diameter at the same three locations, at right-angles to the crankshaft axis. Compare the results with the figures given in the Specifications.

18 Repeat the procedure for the remaining cylinder liners.

19 If the liner wear exceeds the permitted tolerances at any point, or if the cylinder liner walls are badly scored or scuffed, then renewal of the relevant liner assembly will be necessary. If there is any doubt about the condition of the cylinder bores, seek the advice of a Citroën dealer or engine reconditioning specialist.

20 If renewal is necessary, new liners, complete with pistons and piston rings, can be purchased from a Citroën dealer. Note that it is not possible to buy liners individually - they are supplied only as a matched assembly complete with piston and rings.

21 To allow for manufacturing tolerances, pistons and liners are separated into three size groups. The size group of each piston is indicated by a letter (A, B or C) stamped onto its crown, and the size group of each liner is indicated by a series of 1 to 3 notches on the upper lip of the liner; a single notch for group A, two notches for group B, and three notches for group C. Ensure that each piston and its respective liner are both of the same size group. It is permissible to have different size group piston and liner assemblies fitted to the same engine, but never fit a piston of one size group to a liner in a different group.

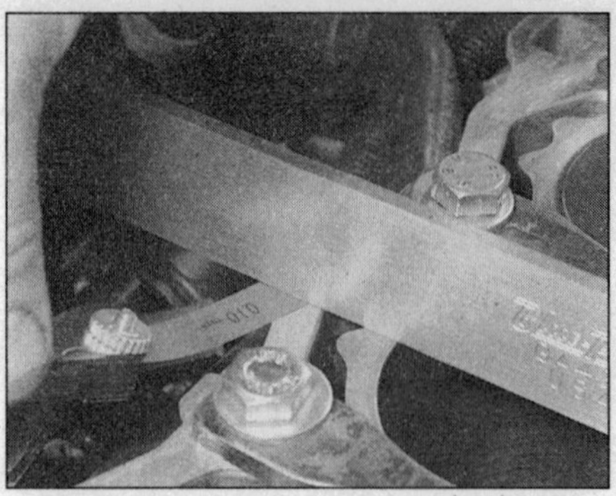

11.24 Checking cylinder liner protrusion - aluminium block engine

22 Prior to installing the liners, thoroughly clean the liner mating surfaces in the cylinder block, and use fine abrasive paper to polish away any burrs or sharp edges which might damage the liner O-rings. Clean the liners and wipe dry, then fit a new O-ring to the base of each liner. To aid installation, apply a smear of oil to each O-ring and to the base of the liner.

23 If the original liners are being refitted, use the marks made on removal to ensure that each is refitted the correct way round, and is inserted into its original position. Insert each liner into the cylinder block, taking care not to damage the O-ring, and press it home as far as possible by hand. Using a hammer and a block of wood, tap each liner lightly but fully onto its locating shoulder. Wipe clean, then lightly oil, all exposed liner surfaces, to prevent rusting.

24 With all four liners correctly installed, use a dial gauge (or a straight-edge and feeler blade) to check that the protrusion of each liner above the upper surface of the cylinder block is within the limits given in the Specifications **(see illustration)**. The maximum difference between any two liners must not be exceeded.

25 If new liners are being fitted, it is permissible to interchange them to bring the difference in protrusion within limits. Remember to keep each piston with its respective liner.

26 If liner protrusion cannot be brought within limits, seek the advice of a Citroën dealer or engine reconditioning specialist before proceeding with the engine rebuild.

12 Piston/connecting rod assembly - inspection

1 Before the inspection process can begin, the piston/connecting rod assemblies must be cleaned, and the original piston rings removed from the pistons.

2 Carefully expand the old rings over the top of the pistons. The use of two or three old feeler blades will be helpful in preventing the rings dropping into empty grooves **(see illustration)**. Be careful not to scratch the piston with the ends of the ring. The rings are brittle, and will snap if they are spread too far. They're also very sharp - protect your hands and fingers. Note that the third ring incorporates an expander. Always remove the rings from the top of the piston. Keep each set of rings with its piston if the old rings are to be re-used.

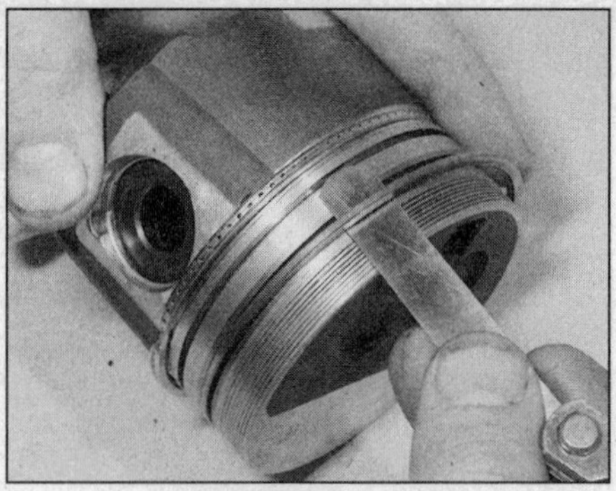

12.2 Removing a piston ring with the aid of a feeler gauge

3 Scrape away all traces of carbon from the top of the piston. A hand-held wire brush (or a piece of fine emery cloth) can be used, once the majority of the deposits have been scraped away.

4 Remove the carbon from the ring grooves in the piston, using an old ring. Break the ring in half to do this (be careful not to cut your fingers - piston rings are sharp). Be careful to remove only the carbon deposits - do not remove any metal, and do not nick or scratch the sides of the ring grooves.

5 Once the deposits have been removed, clean the piston/connecting rod assembly with paraffin or a suitable solvent, and dry thoroughly. Make sure that the oil return holes in the ring grooves are clear.

6 If the pistons and cylinder bores are not damaged or worn excessively, and if the cylinder block does not need to be rebored on cast-iron block engines, the original pistons can be refitted. Normal piston wear shows up as even vertical wear on the piston thrust surfaces, and slight looseness of the top ring in its groove. New piston rings should always be used when the engine is reassembled.

7 Carefully inspect each piston for cracks around the skirt, around the gudgeon pin holes, and at the piston ring "lands" (between the ring grooves).

8 Look for scoring and scuffing on the piston skirt, holes in the piston crown, and burned areas at the edge of the crown. If the skirt is scored or scuffed, the engine may have been suffering from overheating, and/or abnormal combustion which caused excessively high operating temperatures. The cooling and lubrication systems should be checked thoroughly. Scorch marks on the sides of the pistons show that blow-by has occurred. A hole in the piston crown, or burned areas at the edge of the piston crown, indicates that

12.14a On the Diesel engine, prise out the circlip . . .

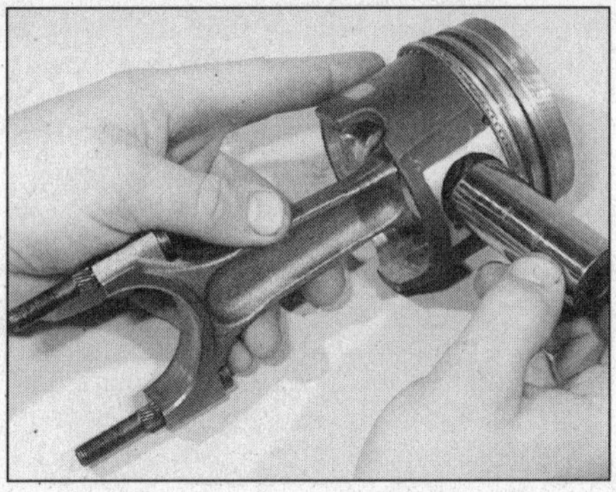

12.14b . . . withdraw the gudgeon pin . . .

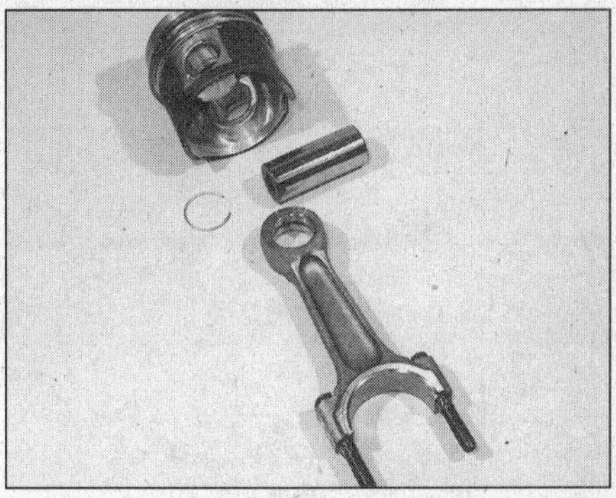

12.14c . . . and separate the piston from the connecting rod

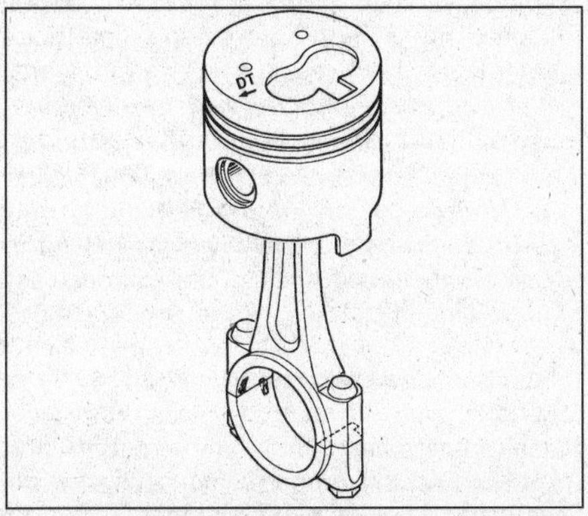

12.18 The cloverleaf recess in the crown must face the opposite way to the bearing shell cut-outs in the connecting rod

DT arrow points to the timing belt end of the engine

abnormal combustion (pre-ignition, knocking, or detonation) has been occurring. If any of the above problems exist, the causes must be investigated and corrected, or the damage will occur again. The causes may include incorrect ignition/injection timing, or a faulty injector (as applicable).

9 Corrosion of the piston, in the form of pitting, indicates that coolant has been leaking into the combustion chamber and/or the crankcase. Again, the cause must be corrected, or the problem may persist in the rebuilt engine.

10 On aluminium-block engines with wet liners, it is not possible to renew the pistons separately; pistons are only supplied with piston rings and a liner, as a part of a matched assembly (see Section 11). On cast-iron block engines, pistons can be purchased from a Citroën dealer.

11 Examine each connecting rod carefully for signs of damage, such as cracks around the big-end and small-end bearings. Check that the rod is not bent or distorted. Damage is highly unlikely, unless the engine has been seized or badly overheated. Detailed checking of the connecting rod assembly can only be carried out by a Citroën dealer or engine repair specialist with the necessary equipment.

12 On all petrol engines (aluminium and cast-iron block), the gudgeon pins are an interference fit in the connecting rod small-end bearing. Therefore, piston and/or connecting rod renewal should be entrusted to a Citroën dealer or engine repair specialist, who will have the necessary tooling to remove and install the gudgeon pins.

13 On the aluminium block Diesel engine, the gudgeon pins are of the floating type, secured in position by two circlips. On these engines, the pistons and connecting rods can be separated and reassembled as follows.

14 Using a small flat-bladed screwdriver, prise out the circlips, and push out the gudgeon pin **(see illustrations)**. Hand pressure should be sufficient to remove the pin. Identify the piston, gudgeon pin and rod to ensure correct reassembly. Discard the circlips - new ones *must* be used on refitting.

15 Examine the gudgeon pin and connecting rod small-end bearing for signs of wear or damage. Wear can be cured by renewing both the pin and bush. Bush renewal, however, is a specialist job - press facilities are required, and the new bush must be reamed accurately.

16 The connecting rods themselves should not be in need of renewal, unless seizure or some other major mechanical failure has occurred. Check the alignment of the connecting rods visually, and if the rods are not straight, take them to an engine overhaul specialist for a more detailed check.

17 Examine all components, and obtain any new parts from your Citroën dealer. If new pistons are purchased, they will be supplied complete with gudgeon pins and circlips. Circlips can also be purchased individually.

18 Position the piston so that the cloverleaf recess on the piston crown is positioned correctly in relation to the connecting rod big-end bearing shell cut-outs **(see illustration)**. Apply a smear of clean engine oil to the gudgeon pin. Slide it into the piston and through the connecting rod small-end. Check that the piston pivots freely on the rod, then secure the gudgeon pin in position with two new circlips. Ensure that each circlip is correctly located in its groove in the piston.

13 Crankshaft - inspection

2C

Checking crankshaft endfloat

1 If the crankshaft endfloat is to be checked, this must be done when the crankshaft is still installed in the cylinder block/crankcase, but is free to move (see Section 10).

2 Check the endfloat using a dial gauge in contact with the end of the crankshaft. Push the crankshaft fully one way, and then zero the gauge. Push the crankshaft fully the other way, and check the endfloat. The result can be compared with the specified amount, and will give an indication as to whether new thrustwashers are required **(see illustration)**.

3 If a dial gauge is not available, feeler gauges can be used. First push the crankshaft fully towards the flywheel end of the engine, then use feeler gauges to measure the gap between the No 1 crankpin web and No 2 main bearing thrustwasher **(see illustration)**.

13.2 Checking crankshaft endfloat using a dial gauge

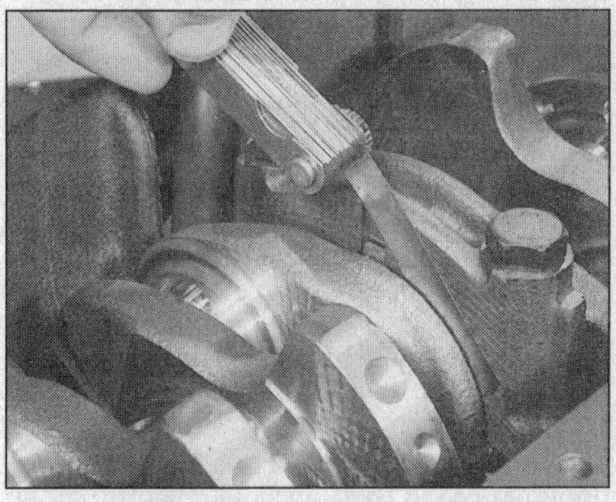

13.3 Checking crankshaft endfloat using feeler gauges

13.10 Measuring a crankshaft big-end journal diameter

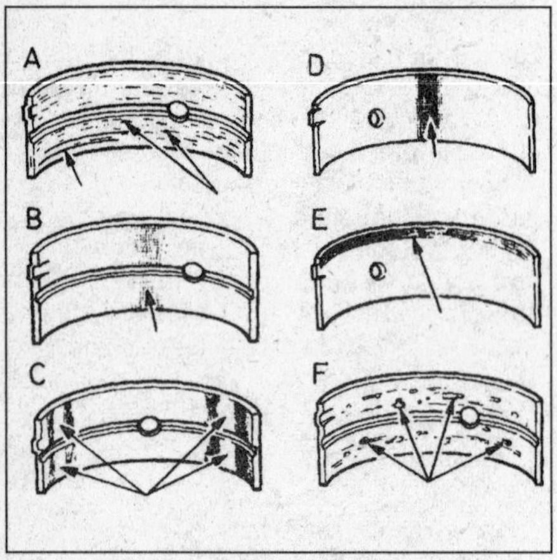

14.2 Typical bearing failures

A Scratched by dirt; dirt embedded in bearing material
B Lack of oil; overlay wiped out
C Improper seating; bright (polished) sections
D Tapered journal; overlay gone from entire surface
E Radius ride
F Fatigue failure; craters or pockets

Inspection

4 Clean the crankshaft using paraffin or a suitable solvent, and dry it, preferably with compressed air if available.

Warning: Wear eye protection when using compressed air! Be sure to clean the oil holes with a pipe cleaner or similar probe, to ensure that they are not obstructed.

5 Check the main and big-end bearing journals for uneven wear, scoring, pitting and cracking.

6 Big-end bearing wear is accompanied by distinct metallic knocking when the engine is running (particularly noticeable when the engine is pulling from low speed) and some loss of oil pressure.

7 Main bearing wear is accompanied by severe engine vibration and rumble - getting progressively worse as engine speed increases - and again by loss of oil pressure.

8 Check the bearing journal for roughness by running a finger lightly over the bearing surface. Any roughness (which will be accompanied by obvious bearing wear) indicates that the crankshaft requires regrinding (where possible) or renewal.

9 If the crankshaft has been reground, check for burrs around the crankshaft oil holes (the holes are usually chamfered, so burrs should not be a problem unless regrinding has been carried out carelessly). Remove any burrs with a fine file or scraper, and thoroughly clean the oil holes as described previously.

10 Using a micrometer, measure the diameter of the main and big-end bearing journals, and compare the results with the Specifications **(see illustration)**. By measuring the diameter at a number of points around each journal's circumference, you will be able to determine whether or not the journal is out-of-round. Take the measurement at each end of the journal, near the webs, to determine if the journal is tapered. Compare the results obtained with those given in the Specifications. Where no specified journal diameters are quoted, seek the advice of a Citroën dealer.

11 Check the oil seal contact surfaces at each end of the crankshaft for wear and damage. If the seal has worn a deep groove in the surface of the crankshaft, consult an engine overhaul specialist; repair may be possible, but otherwise a new crankshaft will be required.

12 Note that Citroën produce a set of undersize bearing shells for both the main bearings and big-end bearings. If the crankshaft has worn beyond the specified limits, and the crankshaft journals have not already been reground, it may be possible to have the crankshaft reconditioned, and to fit the undersize shells. Seek the advice of your Citroën dealer or engine specialist on the best course of action.

14 Main and big-end bearings - inspection

1 Even though the main and big-end bearings should be renewed during the engine overhaul, the old bearings should be retained for close examination, as they may reveal valuable information about the condition of the engine. The bearing shells are graded by thickness, the grade of each shell being indicated by the colour code marked on it.

2 Bearing failure can occur due to lack of lubrication, the presence of dirt or other foreign particles, overloading the engine, or corrosion **(see illustration)**. Regardless of the cause of bearing failure, the cause must be corrected (where applicable) before the engine is reassembled, to prevent it from happening again.

3 When examining the bearing shells, remove them from the cylinder block/crankcase, the main bearing ladder/caps (as appropriate), the connecting rods and the connecting rod big-end bearing caps. Lay them out on a clean surface in the same general position as their location in the engine. This will enable you to match any bearing problems with the corresponding crankshaft journal. *Do not* touch any shell's bearing surface with your fingers while checking it, or the delicate surface may be scratched.

4 Dirt and other foreign matter gets into the engine in a variety of ways. It may be left in the engine during assembly, or it may pass through filters or the crankcase ventilation system. It may get into the oil, and from there into the bearings. Metal chips from machining operations and normal engine wear are often present. Abrasives are sometimes left in engine components after reconditioning, especially when parts are not thoroughly cleaned using the proper cleaning methods. Whatever the source, these foreign objects often end up embedded in the soft bearing material, and are easily recognised. Large particles will not embed in the bearing, and will score or gouge the bearing and journal. The best prevention for this cause of bearing failure is to clean all parts thoroughly, and keep everything spotlessly-clean during engine assembly. Frequent and regular engine oil and filter changes are also recommended.

5 Lack of lubrication (or lubrication breakdown) has a number of interrelated causes. Excessive heat (which thins the oil), overloading (which squeezes the oil from the bearing face) and oil leakage (from excessive bearing clearances, worn oil pump or high engine speeds) all contribute to lubrication breakdown. Blocked oil passages, which usually are the result of misaligned oil holes in a bearing shell, will also oil-starve a bearing, and destroy it. When lack of lubrication is the cause of bearing failure, the bearing material is wiped or extruded from the steel backing of the bearing. Temperatures may increase to the point where the steel backing turns blue from overheating.

6 Driving habits can have a definite effect on bearing life. Full-throttle, low-speed operation (labouring the engine) puts very high loads on bearings, tending to squeeze out the oil film. These loads cause the bearings to flex, which produces fine cracks in the bearing face (fatigue failure). Eventually, the bearing material will loosen in pieces, and tear away from the steel backing.

7 Short-distance driving leads to corrosion of bearings, because insufficient engine heat is produced to drive off the condensed water and corrosive gases. These products collect in the engine oil, forming acid and sludge. As the oil is carried to the engine bearings, the acid attacks and corrodes the bearing material.

8 Incorrect bearing installation during engine assembly will lead to bearing failure as well. Tight-fitting bearings leave insufficient bearing running clearance, and will result in oil starvation. Dirt or foreign particles trapped behind a bearing shell result in high spots on the bearing, which lead to failure.

9 *Do not* touch any shell's bearing surface with your fingers during reassembly; there is a risk of scratching the delicate surface, or of depositing particles of dirt on it.

10 As mentioned at the beginning of this Section, the bearing shells should be renewed as a matter of course during engine overhaul; to do otherwise is false economy. Refer to Section 17 for details of bearing shell selection.

15 Engine overhaul - reassembly sequence

1 Before reassembly begins, ensure that all new parts have been obtained, and that all necessary tools are available. Read through the entire procedure to familiarise yourself with the work involved, and to ensure that all items necessary for reassembly of the engine are at hand. In addition to all normal tools and materials, thread-locking compound will be needed. A suitable tube of liquid sealant will also be required for the joint faces that are fitted without gaskets. It is recommended that Citroën's own product(s) are used, which are specially formulated for this purpose; the relevant product names are quoted in the text of each Section where they are required.

2 In order to save time and avoid problems, engine reassembly can be carried out in the following order:

a) Crankshaft (Section 17).
b) Piston/connecting rod assemblies (Section 18).
c) Oil pump.
d) Sump (See Part A or B - as applicable).
e) Flywheel (See Part A or B - as applicable).
f) Cylinder head (See Part A or B - as applicable).
g) Timing belt tensioner and sprockets, and timing belt (See Part A or B - as applicable).
h) Engine external components.

3 At this stage, all engine components should be absolutely clean and dry, with all faults repaired. The components should be laid out (or in individual containers) on a completely clean work surface.

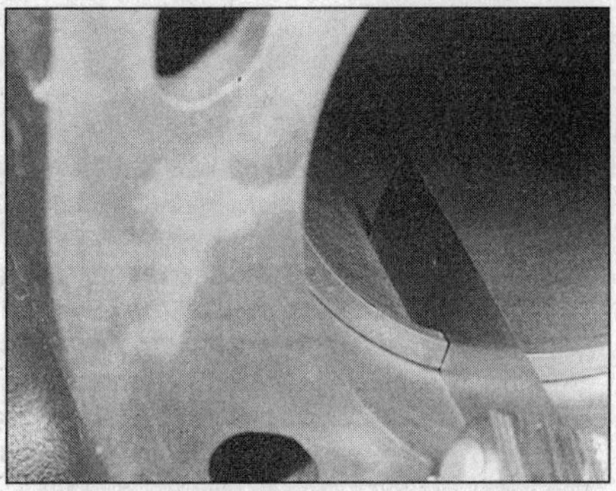

16.5 Measuring a piston ring end gap

16 Piston rings - refitting

1 Before fitting new piston rings, the ring end gaps must be checked as follows.

2 Lay out the piston/connecting rod assemblies and the new piston ring sets, so that the ring sets will be matched with the same piston and cylinder/liner during the end gap measurement and subsequent engine reassembly.

3 Insert the top ring into the first cylinder/liner, and push it down the bore using the top of the piston. This will ensure that the ring remains square with the cylinder walls. Position the ring near the bottom of the cylinder bore, at the lower limit of ring travel. Note that the top and second compression rings are different.

4 Measure the end gap using feeler gauges.

5 Repeat the procedure with the ring at the top of the cylinder bore, at the upper limit of its travel, and compare the measurements with the figures given in the Specifications **(see illustration)**.

6 If the gap is too small (unlikely if genuine Citroën parts are used), it must be enlarged, or the ring ends may contact each other during engine operation, causing serious damage. Ideally, new piston rings providing the correct end gap should be fitted. As a last resort, the end gap can be increased by filing the ring ends very carefully with a fine file. Mount the file in a vice equipped with soft jaws, slip the ring over the file with the ends contacting the file face, and slowly move the ring to remove material from the ends. Take care, as piston rings are sharp, and are easily broken.

7 With new piston rings, it is unlikely that the end gap will be too large. If the gaps are too large, check that you have the correct rings for your engine and for the particular cylinder bore size.

8 Repeat the checking procedure for each ring in the first cylinder, and then for the rings in the remaining cylinders. Remember to keep rings, pistons and cylinders matched up.

9 Once the ring end gaps have been checked and if necessary corrected, the rings can be fitted to the pistons.

10 Fit the piston rings using the same technique as for removal. Fit the bottom (oil control) ring first, and work up. When fitting the oil control ring, where applicable first insert the expander, then fit the ring with its gap positioned 180° from the expander gap. Ensure that the second compression ring is fitted the correct way up **(see illustrations)**. Arrange the gaps of the top and second compression rings 120° either side of the oil control ring gap. **Note:** *Always follow any instructions supplied with the new piston ring sets - different manufacturers may specify different procedures. Do not mix up the top and second compression rings, as they have different cross-sections.*

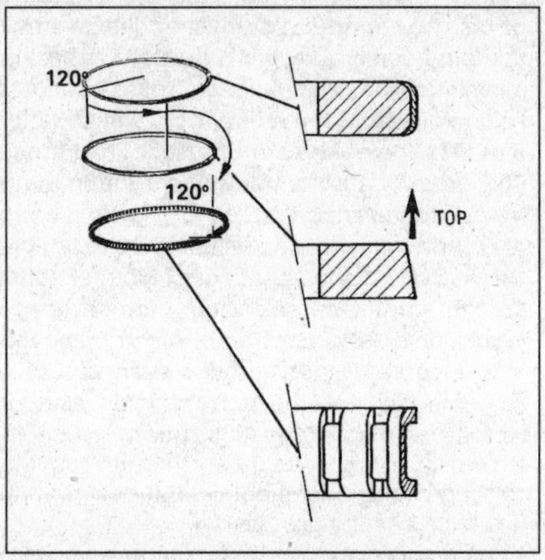

16.10a Piston ring fitting diagram - petrol engines

17 Crankshaft - refitting and main bearing running clearance check

Selection of new bearing shells

Petrol engines

1 On early engines, both upper and lower main bearing shells were of the same thickness, with only two sizes of bearing shells being available: a standard size for use with the standard crankshaft, and a set of undersize bearing shells for use once the crankshaft bearing journals have been reground.

2 However, since February 1992, the specified main bearing running clearance tolerance has been significantly reduced. This has been achieved by the introduction of three different grades of bearing shell, in both standard sizes and undersizes. The grades are

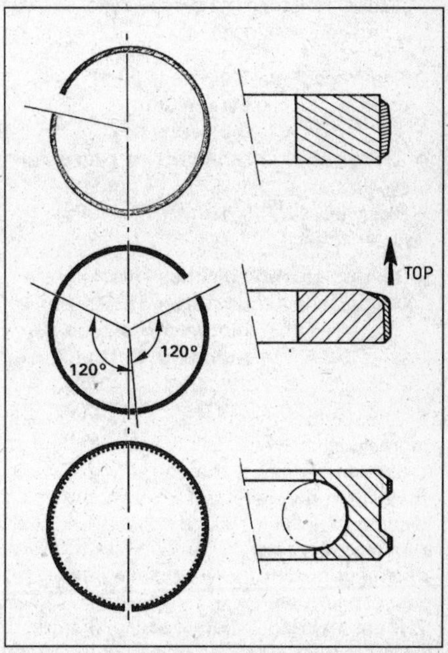

16.10b Piston ring fitting diagram - Diesel engines

2C

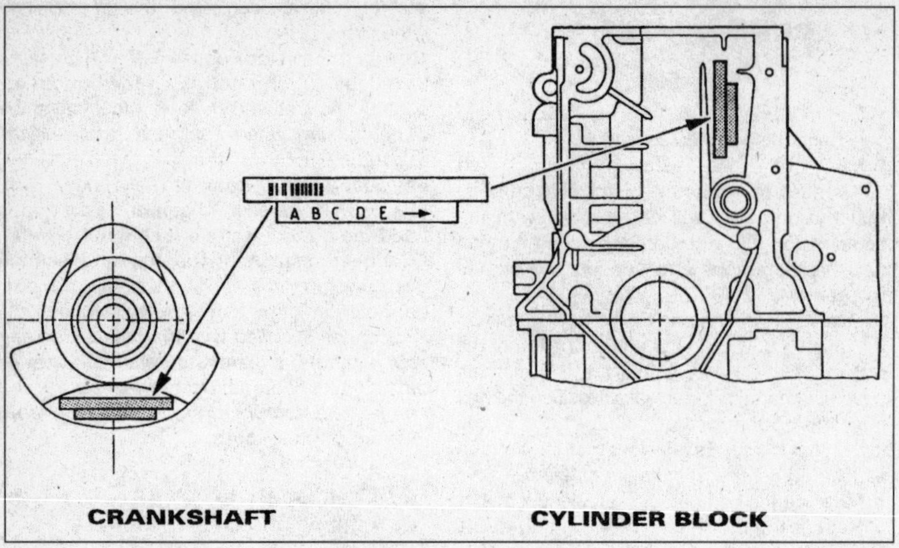

17.5 Cylinder block and crankshaft main bearing reference marking locations - February 1992-on petrol engines

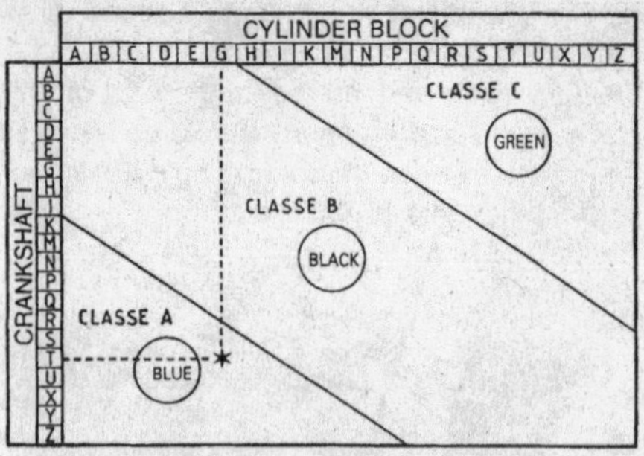

17.7 Main bearing shell selection chart, for use with later petrol engines - see text for further information

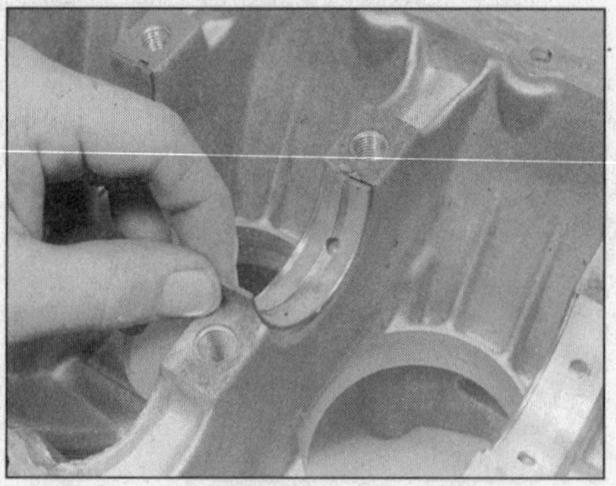

17.12 On aluminium block engines, note that the grooved bearing shells are fitted to Nos 2 and 4 main bearing journals

indicated by a colour-coding marked on the edge of each shell, which denotes the shell's thickness, as listed in the following table. The upper shell on all bearings is of the same size (class B, colour code black), and the running clearance is controlled by fitting a lower bearing shell of the required thickness. Note, however, that although the upper bearings on both aluminium and cast-iron block engines have the same colour code, they are in fact of different thickness for each engine, and have different part numbers. This arrangement has been fitted to all engines produced since February 1992 and, if possible, should also be fitted to earlier engines during overhaul. Seek the advice of your Citroën dealer on parts availability and the best course of action when ordering new bearing shells.

Bearing colour code	Thickness (mm) - aluminium block engine	
	Standard	**Undersize**
Blue (class A)	*1.823*	*1.973*
Black (class B)	*1.835*	*1.985*
Green (class C)	*1.848*	*1.998*

Bearing colour code	Thickness (mm) - cast-iron block engine	
	Standard	**Undersize**
Blue (class A)	*1.844*	*1.994*
Black (class B)	*1.858*	*2.008*
Green (class C)	*1.869*	*2.019*

3 On early engines, the correct-size bearing shell must be selected by measuring the running clearance, as described under the sub-heading below.

4 On engines produced since February 1992, when the new bearing shell sizes were introduced, the crankshaft and cylinder block/crankcase have reference marks on them, to identify the size of the journals and bearing bores.

5 The cylinder block reference marks are on the right-hand (timing belt) end of the block, and the crankshaft reference marks are on the right-hand (timing belt) end of the crankshaft, on the right-hand web of No 4 crankpin **(see illustration)**. These marks can be used to select bearing shells of the required thickness as follows.

6 On both the crankshaft and block, there are two lines of identification: a bar code, which is used by Citroën during production, and a row of five letters. The first letter in the sequence refers to the size of No 1 bearing (at the flywheel end). The last letter in the sequence (which is followed by an arrow) refers to the size of No 5 main bearing. These marks can be used to select the required bearing shell grade, as follows.

7 Obtain the identification letter of both the relevant crankshaft journal and the cylinder block bearing bore. These letters can now be used with the accompanying chart, to select the bearing shell grade. Noting that the cylinder block letters are listed across the top of the chart, and the crankshaft letters down the side, trace a vertical line down from the relevant cylinder block letter, and a horizontal line across from the relevant crankshaft letter, and find the point at which both lines cross. This crossover point will indicate the grade of lower bearing shell required to give the correct main bearing running clearance. For example, the illustration shows cylinder block reference G, and crankshaft reference T, crossing at a point within the area of Class A, indicating that a blue-coded (Class A) lower bearing shell is required to give the correct main bearing running clearance **(see illustration)**.

8 Repeat this procedure so that the required bearing shell grade is obtained for each of the five main bearing journals.

Diesel engines

9 The procedure is the same as that described in paragraphs 1 to 8. However, when the three different grades were initially introduced in February 1992, it was only possible to get blue-coded (Class A) lower bearing shells. This has now been extended, and it is now possible to get blue and black-coded lower bearing shells (Class A and B). Green-coded (Class C) lower bearing shells are not available.

Main bearing running clearance check

Aluminium block engines

10 On early engines, if the modified bearing shells are to be fitted, obtain a set of new black (Class B) upper bearing shells and new blue (Class A) lower bearing shells. On later (February 1992-on) engines where the modified bearing shells are already fitted, the running clearance check can be carried out using the original bearing shells. However, it is preferable to use a new set, since the results obtained will be more conclusive.

11 Clean the backs of the bearing shells, and the bearing locations in both the cylinder block/crankcase and the main bearing ladder.

12 Press the bearing shells into their locations, ensuring that the tab on each shell engages in the notch in the cylinder block/crankcase or main bearing ladder location. Take care not to touch any shell's bearing surface with your fingers. Note that the grooved bearing shells, both upper and lower, are fitted to Nos 2 and 4 main bearings **(see illustration)**. If the original bearing shells are being used for the check, ensure that they are

17.16 Plastigage in place on a crankshaft main bearing journal

17.19 Measuring the width of the deformed Plastigage using the scale on the card provided

17.26 Refitting a crankshaft thrustwasher - aluminium block engines

refitted in their original locations. The clearance can be checked in either of two ways.

13 One method (which will be difficult to achieve without a range of internal micrometers or internal/external expanding calipers) is to refit the main bearing ladder casting to the cylinder block/crankcase, with the bearing shells in place. With the casting retaining bolts correctly tightened, measure the internal diameter of each assembled pair of bearing shells. If the diameter of each corresponding crankshaft journal is measured and then subtracted from the bearing internal diameter, the result will be the main bearing running clearance.

14 The second (and more accurate) method is to use an American product known as "Plastigage". This consists of a fine thread of perfectly-round plastic, which is compressed between the bearing shell and the journal. When the shell is removed, the plastic is deformed, and can be measured with a special card gauge supplied with the kit. The running clearance is determined from this gauge. Plastigage should be available from your dealer (reference number OUT 30 4133 T); otherwise, enquiries at one of the larger specialist motor factors should produce the name of a stockist in your area. The procedure for using Plastigage is as follows.

15 With the main bearing upper shells in place, carefully lay the crankshaft in position. Do not use any lubricant; the crankshaft journals and bearing shells must be perfectly clean and dry.

16 Cut several lengths of the appropriate-size Plastigage (they should be slightly shorter than the width of the main bearings), and place one length on each crankshaft journal axis **(see illustration)**.

17 With the main bearing lower shells in position, refit the main bearing ladder casting, tightening its retaining bolts as described in paragraph 37. Take care not to disturb the Plastigage, and *do not* rotate the crankshaft at any time during this operation.

18 Remove the main bearing ladder casting, again taking great care not to disturb the Plastigage or rotate the crankshaft.

19 Compare the width of the crushed Plastigage on each journal to the scale printed on the Plastigage envelope, to obtain the main bearing running clearance **(see illustration)**. Compare the clearance measured with that given in the Specifications at the start of this Chapter.

20 If the clearance is significantly different from that expected, the bearing shells may be the wrong size (or excessively worn, if the original shells are being re-used). Before deciding that different-size shells are required, make sure that no dirt or oil was trapped between the bearing shells and the main bearing ladder or block when the clearance was measured. If the Plastigage was wider at one end than at the other, the crankshaft journal may be tapered.

21 If the clearance is not as specified, use the reading obtained, along with the shell thicknesses quoted above, to calculate the necessary grade of bearing shells required. When calculating the bearing clearance required, bear in mind that it is always better to have the running clearance towards the lower end of the specified range, to allow for wear in use.

22 Where necessary, obtain the required grades of bearing shell, and repeat the running clearance checking procedure as described above.

23 On completion, carefully scrape away all traces of the Plastigage material from the crankshaft and bearing shells. Use your fingernail, or a wooden or plastic scraper which is unlikely to score the bearing surfaces.

Cast-iron block engines

24 The procedure is similar to that described in the previous paragraphs for aluminium block engines, except that each main bearing has a separate cap which must be fitted and the bolts tightened to the specified torques.

Final crankshaft refitting

Aluminium block engines

25 Carefully lift the crankshaft out of the cylinder block once more.

26 Using a little grease, stick the upper thrustwashers to each side of the No 2 main bearing upper location; ensure that the oilway grooves on each thrustwasher face outwards (away from the cylinder block) **(see illustration)**.

27 Place the bearing shells in their locations as described earlier. If new shells are being fitted, ensure that all traces of protective grease are cleaned off using paraffin. Wipe dry the shells and connecting rods with a lint-free cloth. Liberally lubricate each bearing shell in the cylinder block/crankcase with clean engine oil **(see illustration)**.

28 Refit the Woodruff key, then slide on the oil pump drive sprocket, and locate the drive chain on the sprocket **(see illustration)**. Lower the crankshaft into position so that Nos 2 and 3 cylinder crankpins are at TDC; Nos 1 and 4

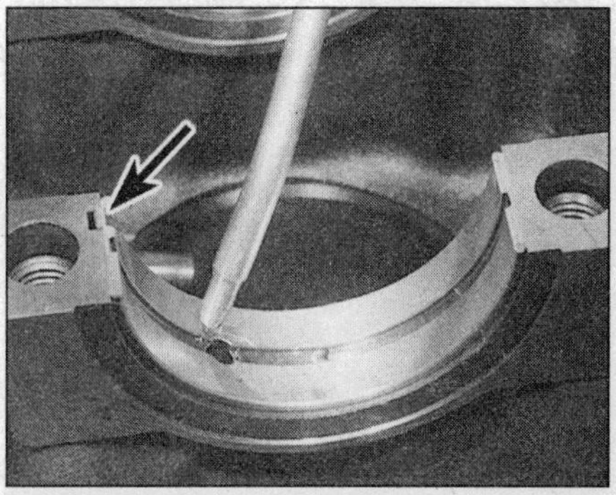

17.27 Ensure that each bearing shell tab (arrowed) is correctly located, and lubricate the shell with clean engine oil - aluminium block engines

17.28 Refitting the oil pump drive chain and sprocket - aluminium block engines

2C

17.29 Apply a thin film of suitable sealant to the cylinder block/crankcase mating surface . . .

17.30 . . . then lower the main bearing ladder into position

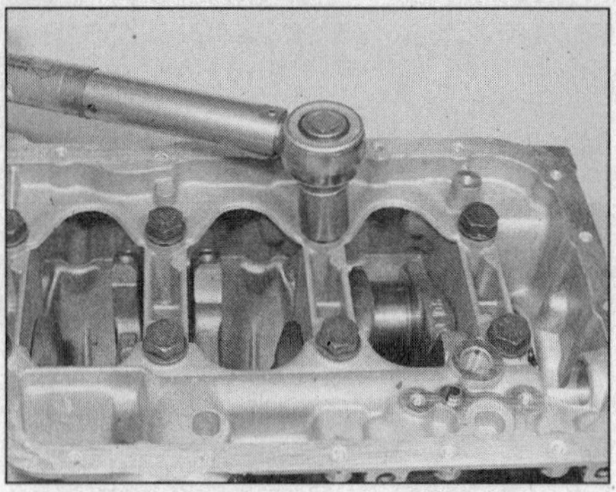

17.31a Tighten the ten 11 mm main bearing bolts to the Stage 1 torque setting . . .

cylinder crankpins will be at BDC ready for fitting No 1 piston. Check the crankshaft endfloat as described in Section 13.

29 Thoroughly degrease the mating surfaces of the cylinder block/crankcase and the main bearing ladder. Apply a thin bead of suitable sealant to the cylinder block/crankcase mating surface of the main bearing ladder casting, then spread to an even film **(see illustration)**. Citroën recommend the use of Auto Joint E10 sealant (available from your Citroën dealer); in the absence of the specified sealant, any suitable good-quality sealant may be used.

30 Lubricate the lower bearing shells with clean engine oil, then refit the main bearing ladder, ensuring that the shells are not displaced, and that the locating dowels engage correctly **(see illustration)**.

31 Install the ten 11 mm main bearing ladder retaining bolts, and tighten them all by hand only. Working progressively outwards from the centre bolts, tighten the ten bolts, by a turn at a time, to the specified Stage 1 torque wrench setting. Once all the bolts have been tightened to the Stage 1 setting, angle-tighten the bolts through the specified Stage 2 setting using a socket and extension bar. It is recommended that an angle-measuring gauge is used during this stage of the tightening, to ensure accuracy **(see illustrations)**. If a gauge is not available, use a dab of white paint to make alignment marks between the bolt head and casting prior to tightening; the marks can then be used to check that the bolt has been rotated sufficiently during tightening.

32 Refit all the 6 mm bolts securing the main bearing ladder to the base of the cylinder block, and tighten them to the specified torque. Check that the crankshaft rotates freely.

33 Refit the piston/connecting rod assemblies to the crankshaft as described in Section 18.

34 Ensuring that the drive chain is correctly located on the sprocket, refit the oil pump and sump as described in Part A or B of this Chapter.

35 Fit two new crankshaft oil seals as described in Part A or Part B (as applicable).

36 Refit the flywheel as described in Part A or B of this Chapter (as applicable).

37 Where removed, refit the cylinder head as described in Part A or Part B (as applicable). Also refit the crankshaft timing sprocket and timing belt as described in Part A or Part B (as applicable).

Cast-iron block engines (petrol)

38 Carefully lift the crankshaft out of the cylinder block once more.

39 Using a little grease, stick the upper thrustwashers to each side of No 2 main bearing upper location; ensure that the oilway grooves on each thrustwasher face outwards (away from the cylinder block).

40 Place the bearing shells in their locations as described earlier. If new shells are being fitted, ensure that all traces of protective grease are cleaned off using paraffin. Wipe dry the shells and connecting rods with a lint-free cloth. Liberally lubricate each bearing shell in the cylinder block/crankcase and cap with clean engine oil.

41 Refit the Woodruff key to the groove in the nose of the crankshaft, then slide on the drive sprocket. Locate the drive chain on the sprocket.

42 Lower the crankshaft into position so that Nos 2 and 3 cylinder crankpins are at TDC; Nos 1 and 4 cylinder crankpins will be at BDC ready for fitting No 1 piston. Check the crankshaft endfloat as described in Section 13.

43 Lubricate the lower bearing shells in the main bearing caps with clean engine oil. Make sure that the locating lugs on the shells engage with the corresponding recesses in the caps.

44 Fit the main bearing caps to their correct locations, ensuring that they are fitted the correct way round (the bearing shell lug recesses in the block and caps must be on the same side). Insert the bolts loosely.

45 Tighten the main bearing cap bolts to the specified Stage 1 torque wrench setting **(see illustration)**. Once all the bolts have been tightened to the Stage 1 setting, angle-tighten the bolts through the specified Stage 2 setting using a socket and extension bar. It is recommended that an angle-measuring gauge is used during this stage of the tightening, to ensure accuracy. If a gauge is not available, use a dab of white paint to make alignment marks between the bolt head and cap prior to tightening; the marks can then be used to check that the bolt has been rotated sufficiently during tightening.

46 Check that the crankshaft rotates freely.

47 Refit the piston/connecting rod assemblies to the crankshaft as described in Section 18.

48 Ensuring that the drive chain is correctly located on the sprocket, refit the oil pump and sump as described in Part A of this Chapter.

49 Clean the mating faces of the front and rear crankshaft oil seal housings and block, and apply suitable sealant. Refit the housings, then fit new oil seals as described in Part A.

50 Refit the flywheel as described in Part A of this Chapter.

51 Where removed, refit the cylinder head as described in Part A. Also refit the crankshaft timing sprocket and timing belt as described in Part A or Part B (as applicable).

17.31b . . . then angle-tighten them through the specified Stage 2 angle

17.45 Tighten the main bearing cap retaining bolts to the specified torque

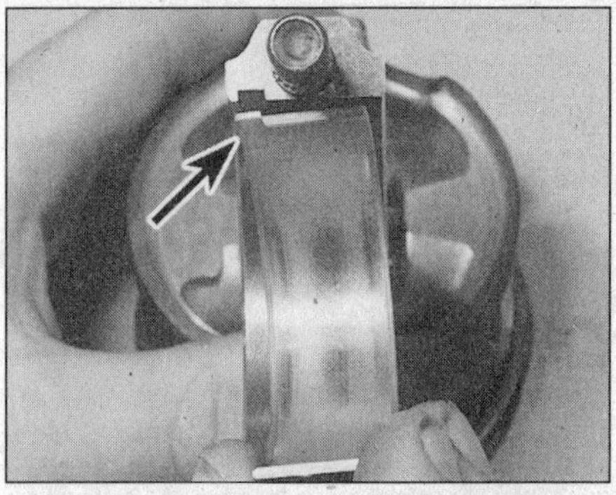

18.4 Fitting a bearing shell to a connecting rod - ensure that the tab (arrowed) engages with the recess in the connecting rod

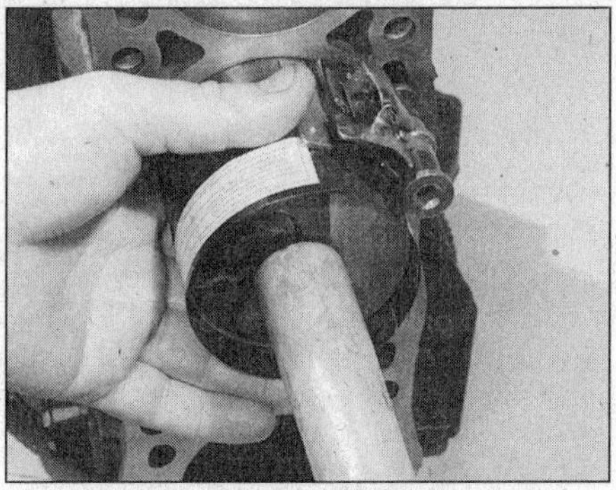

18.18 Tap the piston into the bore using a hammer handle

18.20 Tighten the big-end bearing cap nuts to the specified torque setting

18 Piston/connecting rod assembly - refitting and big-end bearing running clearance check

Selection of bearing shells

1 There are two sizes of big-end bearing shell produced by Citroën; a standard size for use with the standard crankshaft, and an undersize for use once the crankshaft journals have been reground. When ordering shells, quote the diameter of the crankshaft big-end crankpins, to ensure that the correct set of shells are purchased.

2 Prior to refitting the piston/connecting rod assemblies, it is recommended that the big-end bearing running clearance is checked as follows.

Big-end bearing running clearance check

3 Clean the backs of the bearing shells, and the bearing locations in both the connecting rod and bearing cap.

4 Press the bearing shells into their locations, ensuring that the tab on each shell engages in the notch in the connecting rod and cap **(see illustration)**. Take care not to touch any shell's bearing surface with your fingers. If the original bearing shells are being used for the check, ensure they are refitted in their original locations. The clearance can be checked in either of two ways.

5 One method is to refit the big-end bearing cap to the connecting rod, ensuring they are fitted the correct way round (see paragraph 19), with the bearing shells in place. With the cap retaining nuts correctly tightened, use an internal micrometer or vernier caliper to measure the internal diameter of each assembled pair of bearing shells. If the diameter of each corresponding crankshaft journal is measured and then subtracted from the bearing internal diameter, the result will be the big-end bearing running clearance.

6 The second, and more accurate, method is to use Plastigage (see Section 17).

7 Ensure that the bearing shells are correctly fitted. Place a strand of Plastigage on each (cleaned) crankpin journal.

8 Refit the (clean) piston/connecting rod assemblies to the crankshaft, and refit the big-end bearing caps, using the marks made or noted on removal to ensure they are fitted the correct way around.

9 Tighten the bearing cap nuts as described below in paragraph 20. Take care not to disturb the Plastigage or rotate the connecting rod during the tightening sequence.

10 Dismantle the assemblies without rotating the connecting rods. Use the scale printed on the Plastigage envelope to obtain the big-end bearing running clearance.

11 If the clearance is significantly different from that expected, the bearing shells may be the wrong size (or excessively worn, if the original shells are being re-used). Make sure that no dirt or oil was trapped between the bearing shells and the caps or connecting rods when the clearance was measured. If the Plastigage was wider at one end than at the other, the crankpins may be tapered.

12 Note that Citroën do not specify a recommended big-end bearing running clearance. The figure given in the Specifications is a guide figure, which is typical for this type of engine. Before condemning the components concerned, refer to your Citroën dealer or engine reconditioning specialist for further information on the specified running clearance. Their advice on the best course of action to be taken can then also be obtained.

13 On completion, carefully scrape away all traces of the Plastigage material from the crankshaft and bearing shells. Use your fingernail, or some other object which is unlikely to score the bearing surfaces.

Final piston/connecting rod refitting

14 Note that the following procedure assumes that the cylinder liners (where fitted) are in position in the cylinder block/crankcase as described in Section 11, and that the crankshaft and main bearing ladder/caps are in place (see Section 17). It is possible to fit the pistons to the liners before fitting the liners to the cylinder block; the advantage of using this method is that the pistons enter the liner from the bottom end, which is tapered to allow easy entry of the piston rings (a piston ring compressor will still be required).

15 Ensure that the bearing shells are correctly fitted as described in paragraphs 3 and 4. If new shells are being fitted, ensure that all traces of the protective grease are cleaned off using paraffin. Wipe dry the shells and connecting rods with a lint-free cloth.

16 Lubricate the cylinder bores/liners, the pistons, and piston rings, then lay out each piston/connecting rod assembly in its respective position.

17 Start with assembly No 1. Make sure that the piston rings are still spaced as described in Section 16, then clamp them in position with a piston ring compressor.

18 Insert the piston/connecting rod assembly into the top of cylinder/liner No 1. Ensure that the arrow on the piston crown is pointing towards the timing belt end of the engine. Using a block of wood or hammer handle against the piston crown, tap the assembly into the cylinder/liner until the piston crown is flush with the top of the cylinder/liner **(see illustration)**.

19 Ensure that the bearing shell is still correctly installed. Liberally lubricate the crankpin and both bearing shells. Taking care not to mark the cylinder/liner bores, tap the piston/connecting rod assembly down the bore/liner and onto the crankpin. Refit the big-end bearing cap, tightening its retaining nuts finger-tight at first. Note that the faces with the identification marks must match (which means that the bearing shell locating tabs abut each other).

20 Tighten the bearing cap retaining nuts evenly and progressively to the specified torque setting **(see illustration)**.

21 Rotate the crankshaft. Check that it turns freely; some stiffness is to be expected if new components have been fitted, but there should be no signs of binding or tight spots.

22 Refit the remaining three piston/connecting rod assemblies in the same way.

23 Refit the cylinder head, oil pump and sump as described in Part A or B of this Chapter (as applicable).

19 Engine - initial start-up after overhaul

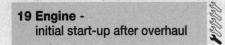

1 With the engine refitted in the vehicle, double-check the engine oil and coolant levels. Make a final check that everything has been reconnected, and that there are no tools or rags left in the engine compartment.

Petrol engine models

2 Remove the spark plugs. On models with a distributor, disable the ignition system by disconnecting the ignition HT coil lead from the distributor cap, and earthing it on the cylinder block. Use a jumper lead or similar wire to make a good connection. On models with a static (distributorless) ignition system, disable the ignition system by disconnecting the LT wiring connector from the ignition HT coil(s), referring to Chapter 5 for further information.

3 Turn the engine on the starter until the oil pressure warning light goes out. Refit the spark plugs, and reconnect the spark plug (HT) leads, referring to Chapter 1 for further information. Reconnect any HT leads or wiring which was disconnected in paragraph 2.

Diesel engine models

4 Disconnect the wiring from the stop solenoid on the injection pump (see Chapter 4D), then turn the engine on the starter motor until the oil pressure warning light goes out. Reconnect the wire to the stop solenoid.

5 Prime the fuel system as described in Chapter 4D.

6 Fully depress the accelerator pedal, turn the ignition key to position "M', and wait for the preheating warning light to go out.

All models

7 Start the engine, noting that this may take a little longer than usual, due to the fuel system components having been disturbed.

8 While the engine is idling, check for fuel, water and oil leaks. Don't be alarmed if there are some odd smells and smoke from parts getting hot and burning off oil deposits.

9 Assuming all is well, keep the engine idling until hot water is felt circulating through the top hose, then switch off the engine.

10 Check the ignition timing (petrol engines) or injection pump timing (Diesel engines), and the idle speed settings (as appropriate), then switch the engine off.

11 After a few minutes, recheck the oil and coolant levels as described in Chapter 1, and top-up as necessary.

12 If they were tightened as described, there is no need to re-tighten the cylinder head bolts once the engine has first run after reassembly.

13 If new pistons, rings or crankshaft bearings have been fitted, the engine must be treated as new, and run-in for the first 500 miles (800 km). *Do not* operate the engine at full-throttle, or allow it to labour at low engine speeds in any gear. It is recommended that the oil and filter be changed at the end of this period.

Chapter 3
Cooling, heating and ventilation systems

Contents

Degrees of difficulty

Easy, suitable for novice with little experience	**Fairly easy,** suitable for beginner with some experience	**Fairly difficult,** suitable for competent DIY mechanic	**Difficult,** suitable for experienced DIY mechanic	**Very difficult,** suitable for expert DIY or professional

Specifications

General

Expansion tank cap opening pressure:	
Petrol engine models	1.0 bar (14.5 psi) or 1.4 bars (20.3 psi)
Diesel engine models	1.5 bars (21.8 psi)

Thermostat

Opening temperatures:	
Starts to open:	
Except K6B and KFZ engines	88°C
K6B and KFZ engines	93°C
Fully-open:	
Except K6B and KFZ engines	100°C
K6B and KFZ engines	95°C

Electric cooling fan

Cut-in temperature:	
Petrol engine models:	
Except K6B and KFZ engines	95°C
K6B and KFZ engines	97°C
Diesel engine models	97°C
Cut-out temperature:	
Petrol engine models:	
Except K6B and KFZ engines	90°C
K6B and KFZ engines	92°C
Diesel engine models	92°C

Torque wrench settings

Torque wrench settings	Nm	lbf ft
Water pump housing-to-cylinder block (aluminium block engines):		
Smaller coolant pump housing securing bolts	30	22
Larger coolant pump housing securing bolts	50	37
Water pump-to-housing (aluminium block engines):		
Upper bolt	16	12
Lower bolt	7	5
Water pump rear cover-to-housing (aluminium block engines)	7	5
Water pump-to-cylinder block (cast-iron block engines)	16	12
Cooling fan thermostatic switch	45	33
Temperature gauge/temperature warning light sender	18	13

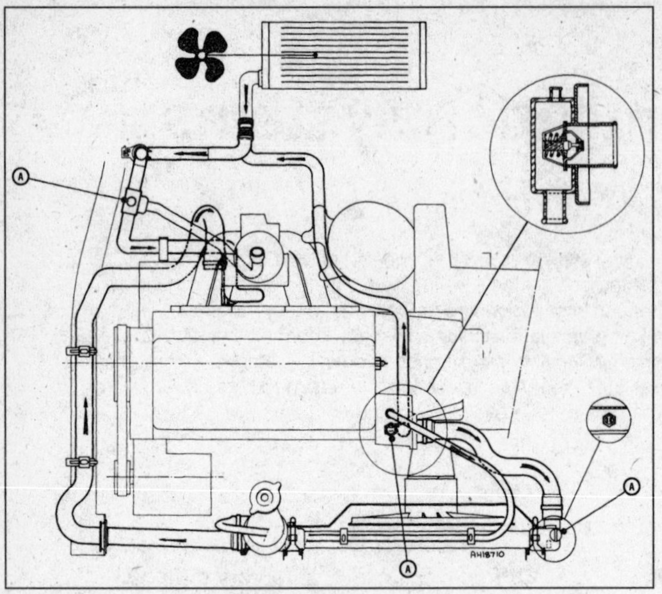

1.1a Cooling system circuit for petrol models - up to September 1987

A System bleed points

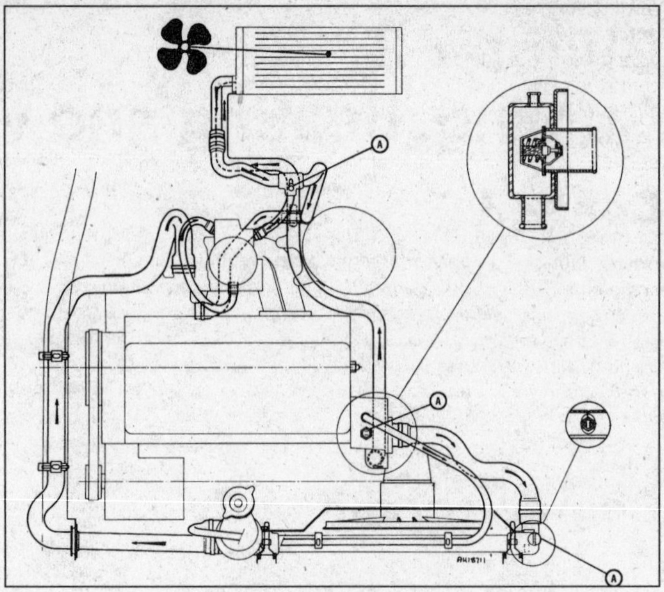

1.1b Cooling system circuit for petrol models - September 1987 to November 1988

A System bleed points

***Note:** Later petrol models similar*

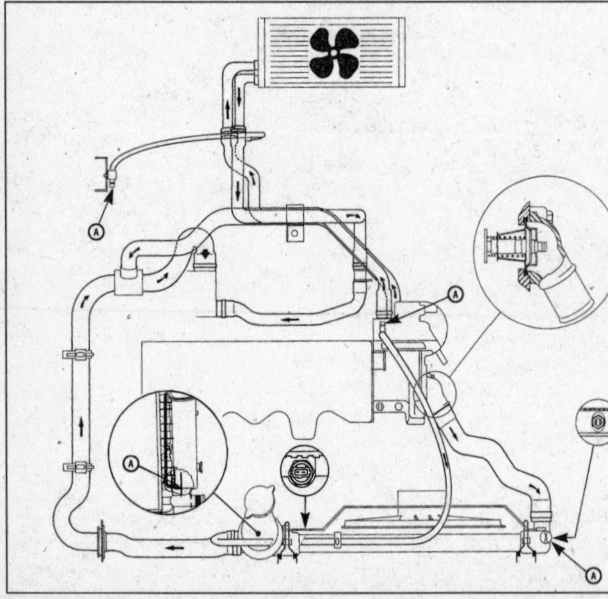

1.1c Cooling system circuit for Diesel models

A System bleed points

1 General information and precautions

General information

1 The cooling system is of pressurised type, comprising a coolant pump driven by the timing belt, an aluminium crossflow radiator, electric cooling fan, a thermostat, heater matrix, and all associated hoses and switches. The expansion tank is integral with the radiator, except on later Diesel models (VIN number from 5806 onwards) which have a remotely-mounted coolant expansion tank. On some models, a coolant level detector switch is fitted in the vertical right-hand radiator tank **(see illustrations)**.

2 The system functions as follows. Cold coolant in the bottom of the radiator passes through the bottom hose to the coolant pump, where it is pumped around the cylinder block, head passages and (on petrol models only) the inlet manifold. After cooling the cylinder bores, combustion surfaces and valve seats, the coolant reaches the underside of the thermostat, which is initially closed. The coolant passes through the heater, and is returned via the cylinder block to the coolant pump.

3 When the engine is cold, the coolant circulates only through the cylinder block, cylinder head, and heater. When the coolant reaches a predetermined temperature, the thermostat opens, and the coolant passes through the top hose to the radiator. As the coolant circulates through the radiator, it is cooled by the inrush of air when the car is in forward motion, and also by the action of the electric cooling fan when necessary. Upon reaching the bottom of the radiator, the coolant has now cooled, and the cycle is repeated.

4 When the engine is at normal operating temperature, the coolant expands, and some of it is displaced into the expansion tank. Coolant collects in the tank, and is returned to the radiator when the system cools.

5 The electric cooling fan mounted on the rear of the radiator is controlled by a thermostatic switch. At a predetermined coolant temperature, the switch/sensor actuates the fan.

Precautions

Warning: *Do not attempt to remove the expansion tank filler cap, or to disturb any part of the cooling system, while the engine is hot, as there is a high risk of scalding. If the expansion tank filler cap must be removed before the engine and radiator have fully cooled (even though this is not recommended), the pressure in the cooling system must first be relieved. Cover the cap with a thick layer of cloth, to avoid scalding, and slowly unscrew the filler cap until a hissing sound is heard. When the hissing has stopped, indicating that the pressure has reduced, slowly unscrew the filler cap until it can be removed; if more hissing sounds are heard, wait until they have stopped before unscrewing the cap completely. At all times, keep well away from the filler cap opening, and protect your hands.*

Warning: *Do not allow antifreeze to come into contact with your skin, or with the painted surfaces of the vehicle. Rinse off spills immediately, with plenty of water. Never leave antifreeze lying around in an open container, or in a puddle in the driveway or on the garage floor. Children and pets are attracted by its sweet smell, but antifreeze can be fatal if ingested.*

Warning: *If the engine is hot, the electric cooling fan may start rotating even if the engine is not running. Be careful to keep your hands, hair, and any loose clothing well clear when working in the engine compartment.*

Warning: *Refer to Section 10 for precautions to be observed when working on models equipped with air conditioning.*

2 Cooling system hoses - disconnection and renewal

1 The number, routing and pattern of hoses will vary according to model, but the same basic procedure applies. Before commencing work, make sure that the new hoses are to hand, along with new hose clips if needed. It is good practice to renew the hose clips at the same time as the hoses.

2 Drain the cooling system, as described in Chapter 1, saving the coolant if it is fit for re-use. Squirt a little penetrating oil onto the hose clips if they are corroded.

3 Release the hose clips from the hose concerned. Three types of clip are used; worm-drive, spring and "sardine-can". The worm-drive clip is released by turning its screw anti-clockwise. The spring clip is released by squeezing its tags together with pliers, at the same time working the clip away from the hose stub **(see illustration)**. The "sardine-can" clip is not re-usable, and is best cut off with snips or side cutters.

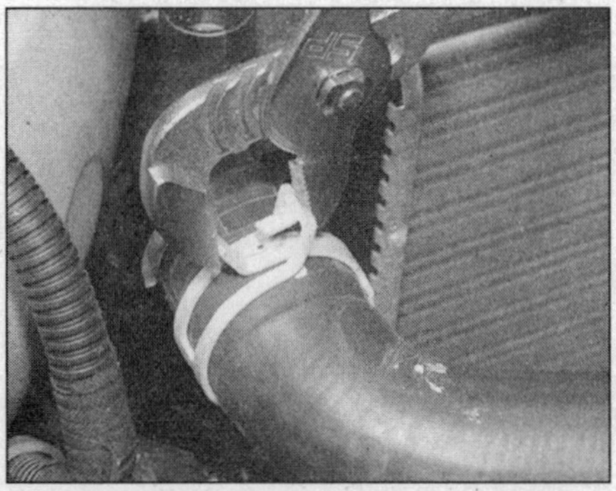

2.3 Releasing a radiator top hose spring clip

4 Unclip any wires, cables or other hoses which may be attached to the hose being removed. Make notes for reference when reassembling if necessary.

5 Release the hose from its stubs with a twisting motion. Be careful not to damage the stubs on delicate components such as the radiator. If the hose is stuck fast, try carefully prising the end of the hose with a screwdriver or similar, taking care not to use excessive force. The best course is often to cut off a stubborn hose using a sharp knife, but again be careful not to damage the stubs.

6 Before fitting the new hose, smear the stubs with washing-up liquid or a suitable rubber lubricant to aid fitting. Do not use oil or grease, which may attack the rubber.

7 Fit the hose clips over the ends of the hose, then fit the hose over its stubs. Work the hose into position. When satisfied, locate and tighten the hose clips.

8 Refill the cooling system as described in Chapter 1. Run the engine, and check that there are no leaks.

9 Recheck the tightness of the hose clips on any new hoses after a few hundred miles.

10 Top-up the coolant level if necessary.

3 Radiator - removal, inspection and refitting

Note: *If the reason for removing the radiator is to cure a leak, it is worth trying the effect of a radiator sealing compound such as Holts Radweld first - this is added to the coolant, and will often cure minor leaks with the radiator in situ.*

Removal

1 The radiator is best removed downwards from the engine compartment. First raise the front of the car and support on axle stands.

2 Disconnect the battery negative lead.

3 Drain the cooling system as described in Chapter 1.

4 Remove the air cleaner air intake ducting as described in the relevant Part of Chapter 4. If necessary for improved access, drill out the pop-rivets, and remove the air intake tube from the front body panel. On some models it is bolted in position **(see illustration)**.

5 Where applicable, remove the heat shield from the exhaust manifold.

6 Disconnect the wiring plugs from the cooling fan and the cooling fan switch mounted on the left-hand side of the radiator **(see illustrations)**. Also as applicable disconnect the wiring from the coolant level detector switch on the right-hand side of the radiator, and release the wiring harness from the clips on the fan shroud.

7 Remove the cooling fan shroud/bracket securing bolt, and disengage the bracket from the lugs on the radiator. Lift the cooling fan and shroud/bracket assembly from the radiator **(see illustrations)**.

8 Disconnect the coolant hoses from the radiator, with reference to Section 2 if necessary **(see illustration)**.

9 Unscrew the two retaining bolts and detach the bonnet lock. Remove it together with its inner cable, and place out of the way.

10 Using a suitable screwdriver, release the upper radiator securing spring clips **(see illustration)**, then tilt the radiator towards the engine at the top and lift it clear of the bottom mountings. Lower the radiator downwards and remove it from underneath the car, taking care not to damage the core.

11 Recover the radiator lower mounting rubbers.

Inspection

12 If the radiator has been removed due to suspected blockage, reverse-flush it as described in Chapter 1. Clean dirt and debris from the radiator fins, using an air line (in which case, wear eye protection) or a soft brush. Be careful, as the fins are sharp, and easily damaged.

13 If necessary, a radiator specialist can perform a "flow test" on the radiator, to establish whether an internal blockage exists.

14 A leaking radiator must be referred to a specialist for permanent repair. Do not attempt

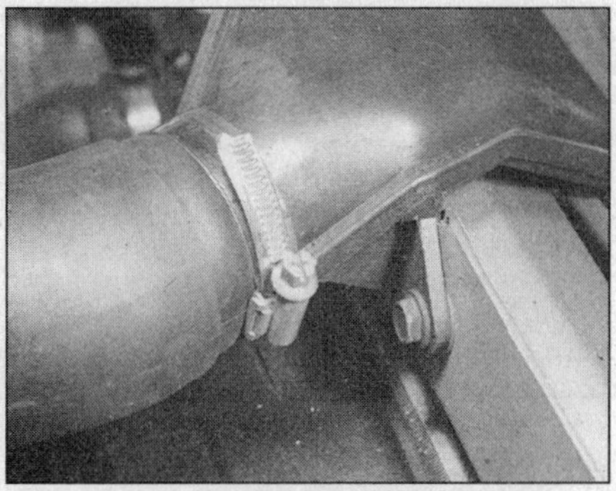

3.4 Air intake ducting bolted to crossmember (certain models only)

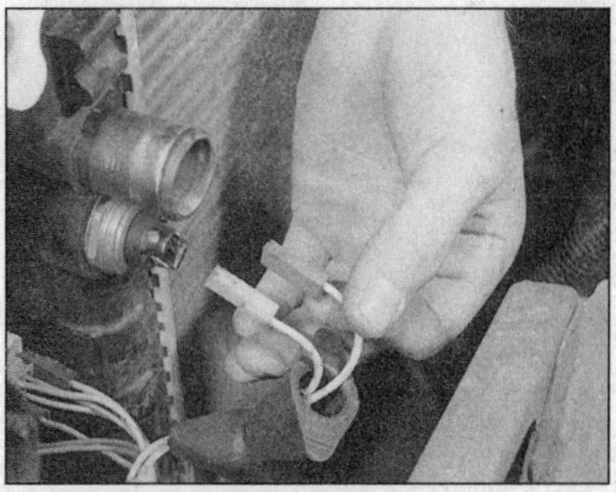

3.6a Disconnecting the wiring from the cooling fan switch

3.6b Cooling fan switch wire connector

3

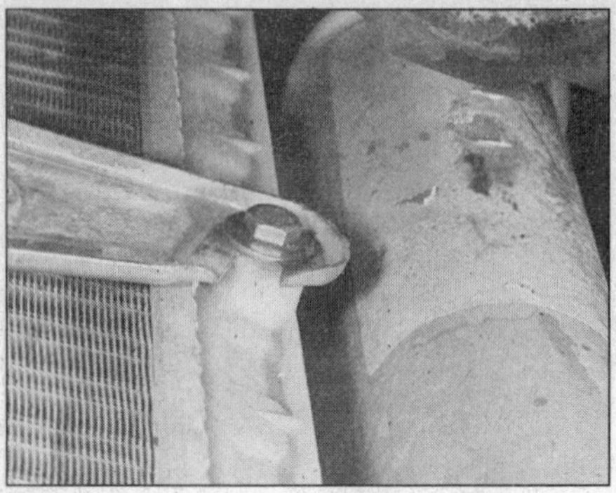

3.7a Loosen the retaining bolt . . .

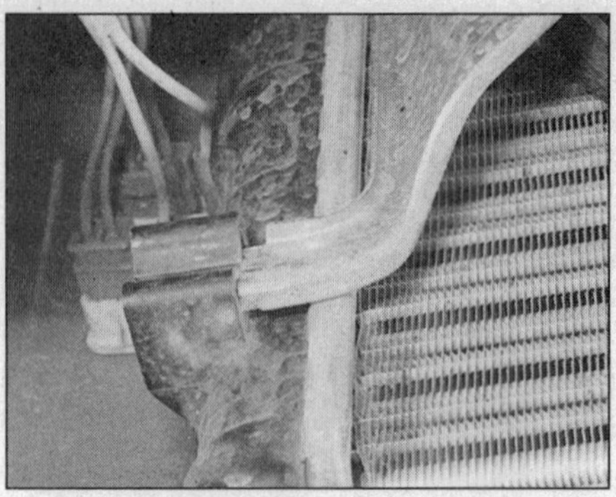

3.7b . . . and lift the cooling fan unit out of its location lugs (early petrol model shown)

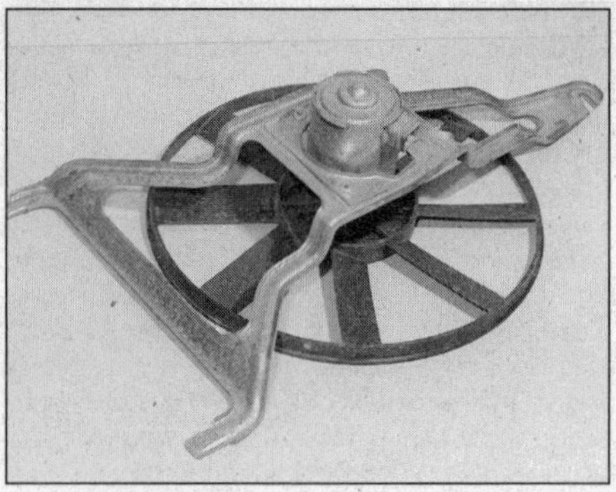

3.7c Cooling fan unit removed from the car (early petrol model shown)

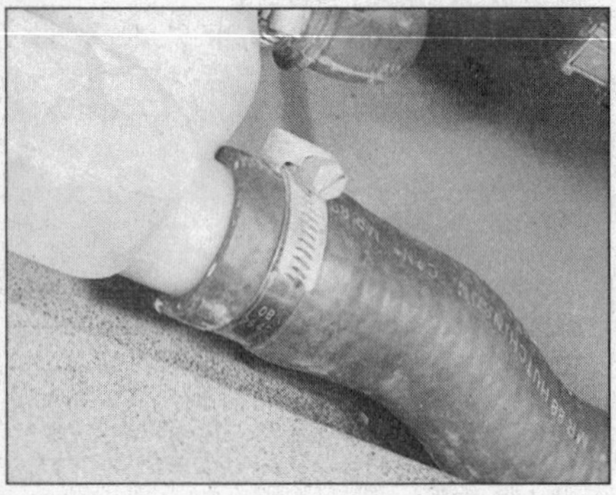

3.8 Radiator bottom hose connection

3.10 Spring retaining clips (arrowed) on the top of the radiator

to weld or solder a leaking radiator, as damage to the plastic components may result.

15 If the radiator is to be sent for repair, or is to be renewed, remove all hoses, together with the cooling fan switch and coolant level detector switch (where fitted).

16 Inspect the condition of the radiator mounting rubbers, and renew them if necessary.

Refitting

17 Refitting is a reversal of removal, bearing in mind the following points.

a) *Ensure that the lower lugs on the radiator are correctly engaged with the mounting rubbers in the body panel.*
b) *Ensure that the upper radiator securing spring clips are correctly engaged*
c) *Reconnect the hoses with reference to Section 2.*
d) *Where applicable, refit the air intake tube using new pop-rivets, and refit the air cleaner with reference to the relevant Part of Chapter 4.*
e) *On completion, refill the cooling system as described in Chapter 1.*

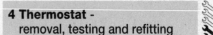

4 Thermostat - removal, testing and refitting

Removal

1 The thermostat is located on the left-hand end of the cylinder head. On petrol models, it is located in a separate housing bolted to the cylinder head **(see illustration)**; on Diesel models, it is integral with the fuel filter housing.

2 Drain the cooling system as described in Chapter 1.

3 If desired for improved access, remove the air cleaner and/or the air intake ducting as described in the relevant part of Chapter 4. Similarly, remove the battery as described in Chapter 5A.

4 According to model, release any relevant wiring and hoses from the retaining clips, and position clear of the thermostat housing to improve access.

5 Unscrew the retaining bolts, and carefully withdraw the thermostat housing cover to expose the thermostat **(see illustrations)**. There is no need to disconnect the hose from the cover.

6 Lift the thermostat from the housing, noting which way round the thermostat is fitted, and recover the sealing ring(s) **(see illustration)**.

4.1 Thermostat location on petrol models (arrowed)

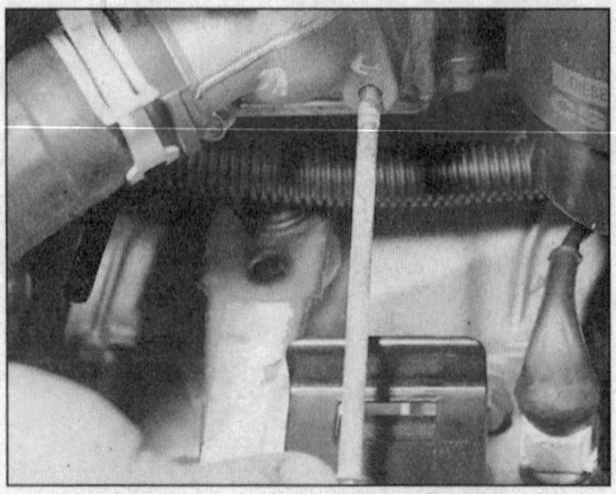

4.5a Unscrew the retaining bolts . . .

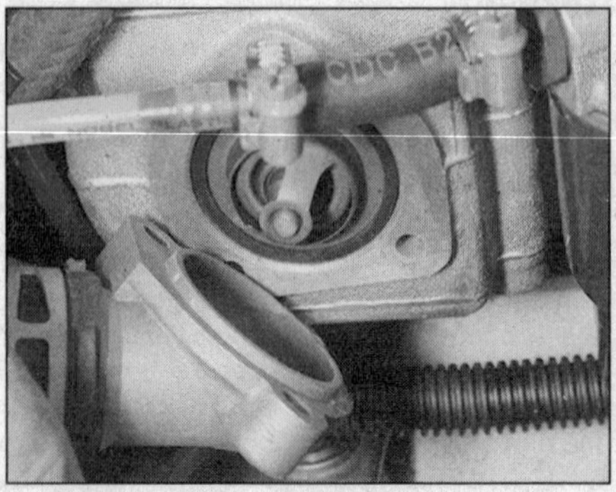

4.5b . . . and withdraw the thermostat housing cover (Diesel model shown)

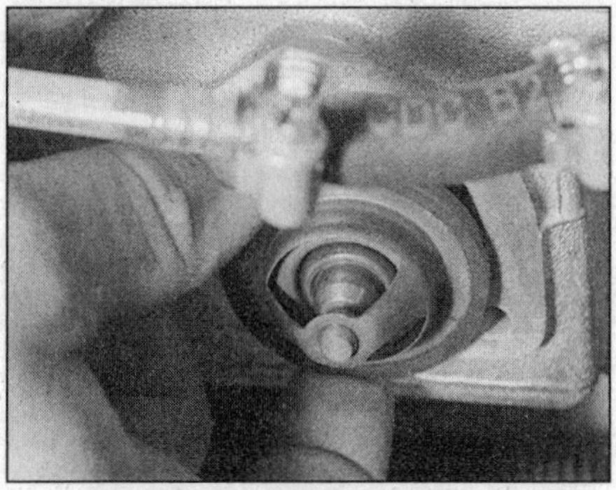

4.6 Lift the thermostat from the housing (Diesel model shown)

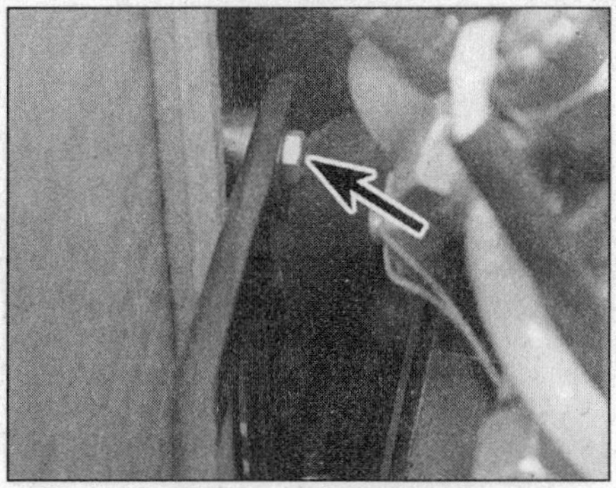

5.9a Remove the securing bolt (arrowed) . . .

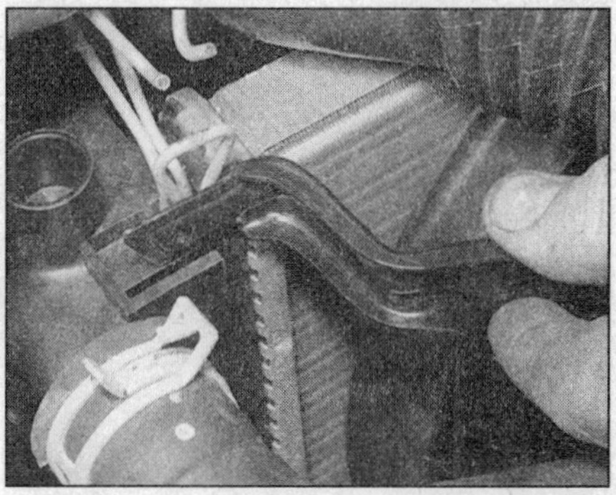

5.9b . . . and disengage the cooling fan shroud legs from the radiator brackets

Testing

7 A rough test of the thermostat may be made by suspending it with a piece of string in a container full of water. Heat the water to bring it to the boil - the thermostat must open by the time the water boils. If not, renew it.

8 If a thermometer is available, the precise opening temperature of the thermostat may be determined; compare with the figures given in the Specifications. The opening temperature is also marked on the thermostat.

9 A thermostat which fails to close as the water cools must also be renewed.

Refitting

10 Refitting is a reversal of removal, bearing in mind the following points.

a) *Examine the sealing ring(s) for signs of damage or deterioration, and if necessary, renew.*

b) *Ensure that the thermostat is fitted the correct way round, as noted before removal.*

c) *Where applicable, refit the air cleaner and/or the air intake ducting, with reference to the relevant Part of Chapter 4.*

d) *On completion, refill the cooling system as described in Chapter 1.*

5 Electric cooling fan - testing, removal and refitting

Testing

1 Current supply to the cooling fan is via the ignition switch (see Chapter 5), a fuse (see Chapter 12) and a cooling fan relay unit located behind the battery on the left-hand side of the engine compartment. The circuit is completed by the cooling fan thermostatic switch, which is mounted in the left-hand radiator tank. On models with air conditioning, the cooling fan is also controlled by the air conditioning control unit - see Section 6.

2 If the fan does not appear to work, run the engine until normal operating temperature is reached, then allow it to idle. The fan should cut in within a few minutes (before the temperature gauge needle enters the red section, or before the coolant temperature warning light comes on). If not, switch off the ignition and disconnect the wiring plug from the cooling fan switch. Bridge the two contacts in the wiring plug using a length of spare wire, and switch on the ignition. If the fan now operates, the switch is probably faulty, and should be renewed.

3 If the fan still fails to operate, check that battery voltage is available at the feed wire to the switch; if not, then there is a fault in the feed wire (possibly due to a blown fuse). If there is no problem with the feed, check that there is continuity between the switch earth terminal and a good earth point on the body; if not, then the earth connection is faulty, and must be re-made.

4 If the switch and the wiring are in good condition, the fault must lie in the motor itself. The motor can be checked by disconnecting it from the wiring loom, and connecting a 12-volt supply directly to it.

Removal

5 Disconnect the battery negative lead.

6 Remove the air cleaner air intake ducting as described in the relevant Part of Chapter 4. If necessary for improved access, drill out the pop-rivets, and remove the air intake tube from the front body panel.

7 Where applicable, remove the heat shield from the exhaust manifold.

8 Disconnect the wiring plug from the cooling fan.

9 Remove the cooling fan shroud/bracket securing bolt, and disengage the bracket from the lugs on the radiator. Lift the cooling fan and shroud/bracket assembly from the radiator **(see illustration)**.

10 If desired, the fan blades can be removed from the end of the motor shaft, after removing the securing clip **(see illustration)**. The motor can be removed from the shroud assembly after drilling out the securing rivets.

Refitting

11 Refitting is a reversal of removal, but where applicable, use new rivets to secure the fan motor and/or the air intake tube.

5.10 Removing the cooling fan blades securing clip

3

6 Cooling system electrical switches - testing, removal and refitting

Electric cooling fan thermostatic switch

Testing

1 Testing of the switch is described in Section 5 as part of the electric cooling fan test procedure.

Removal

Note: *Suitable sealing compound or a new sealing ring (as applicable) will be required on refitting.*

2 The switch is located in the left-hand tank of the radiator. The engine and radiator should be cold before removing the switch.

3 Disconnect the battery negative lead.

4 Partially drain the cooling system to just below the level of the switch (as described in Chapter 1). Alternatively, have ready a suitable bung to plug the switch aperture in the radiator when the switch is removed. If this method is used, take great care not to damage the radiator, and do not use anything which will allow foreign matter to enter the radiator.

5 Disconnect the wiring plug from the switch **(see illustration)**.

6 Carefully unscrew the switch from the radiator, and recover the sealing ring (where applicable). If the system has not been

6.5 Disconnecting the cooling fan switch wiring plug (radiator top hose disconnected for clarity)

6.11 Coolant temperature gauge/temperature warning light sender (arrowed) - Diesel model

7.4a Withdraw the coolant pump (1360 cc Diesel engine shown) . . .

drained, plug the switch aperture to prevent further coolant loss.

Refitting

7 If the switch was originally fitted using sealing compound, clean the switch threads thoroughly, and coat them with fresh sealing compound.

8 If the switch was originally fitted using a sealing ring, use a new sealing ring on refitting.

9 Refitting is a reversal of removal. Tighten the switch to the specified torque, and refill (or top-up) the cooling system as described in Chapter 1.

10 On completion, start the engine and run it until it reaches normal operating temperature. Continue to run the engine, and check that the cooling fan cuts in and out correctly.

Coolant temperature gauge/temperature warning light sender

Testing

11 On petrol engine models without air conditioning, the sender is located in the left-hand end of the cylinder head; on very early models, it is located on the thermostat housing. On Diesel engine models, and petrol engine models with air conditioning, the sender is located in the thermostat housing **(see illustration)**.

12 The temperature gauge (where fitted) is fed with a stabilised voltage from the instrument panel feed (via the ignition switch and a fuse). The gauge earth is controlled by the sender. The sender contains a thermistor - an electronic component whose electrical resistance decreases at a predetermined rate as its temperature rises. When the coolant is cold, the sender resistance is high, current flow through the gauge is reduced, and the gauge needle points towards the blue (cold) end of the scale. As the coolant temperature rises and the sender resistance falls, current flow increases, and the gauge needle moves towards the upper end of the scale. If the sender is faulty, it must be renewed.

13 On models with a temperature warning light, the light is fed with a voltage from the instrument panel. The warning light earth is controlled by the sender. The sender is effectively a switch, which operates at a predetermined temperature to earth the light and complete the circuit. If the light is fitted in addition to a gauge, on certain models, the senders for the gauge and light are incorporated in a single unit, with two wires, one each for the light and gauge earths.

14 If the gauge develops a fault, first check the other instruments; if they do not work at all, check the instrument panel electrical feed. If the readings are erratic, there may be a fault in the voltage stabiliser, which will necessitate renewal of the stabiliser (the stabiliser is integral with the instrument panel printed circuit board - see Chapter 12). If the fault lies in the temperature gauge alone, check it as follows.

15 If the gauge needle remains at the "cold" end of the scale when the engine is hot, disconnect the sender wiring plug, and earth the relevant wire to the cylinder head. If the needle then deflects when the ignition is switched on, the sender unit is proved faulty, and should be renewed. If the needle still does not move, remove the instrument panel (Chapter 12) and check the continuity of the wire between the sender unit and the gauge, and the feed to the gauge unit. If continuity is shown, and the fault still exists, then the gauge is faulty, and the gauge unit should be renewed.

16 If the gauge needle remains at the "hot" end of the scale when the engine is cold, disconnect the sender wire. If the needle then returns to the "cold" end of the scale when the ignition is switched on, the sender unit is proved faulty, and should be renewed. If the needle still does not move, check the remainder of the circuit as described previously.

17 The same basic principles apply to testing the warning light. The light should illuminate when the relevant sender wire is earthed.

Removal and refitting

18 The procedure is similar to that described previously in this Section for the electric cooling fan thermostatic switch. On some models, access to the switch is poor, and other components may need to be removed (or hoses, wiring, etc moved to one side) before the sender unit can be reached.

Fuel injection system coolant temperature sensor

Testing

19 The coolant temperature sensor is located in the thermostat housing.

20 The sensor is a thermistor (see paragraph 12). The fuel injection/engine management ECU supplies the sensor with a set voltage, and by measuring the current flowing in the sensor circuit, it determines the engine temperature. This information is then used, in conjunction with other inputs, to control the injector opening time (pulse width). On some models, the idle speed and/or ignition timing settings are also temperature-dependent.

21 If the sensor circuit should fail to provide adequate information, the ECU back-up facility will override the sensor signal. In this event, the ECU assumes a predetermined setting which will allow the fuel injection/engine management system to run, albeit at reduced efficiency. When this occurs, the engine warning light on the instrument panel will come on, and the advice of a Citroën dealer should be sought. The sensor itself can only be tested using special Citroën diagnostic equipment. *Do not* attempt to test the circuit using any other equipment, as there is a high risk of damaging the ECU.

Removal and refitting

22 The procedure is similar to that described previously in this Section for the electric cooling fan thermostatic switch. On some models, access to the switch is poor, and other components may need to be removed (or hoses, wiring, etc moved to one side) before the sensor can be reached.

Air conditioning system coolant temperature sensor

Testing

23 The sensor is located in the left-hand end of the cylinder head in the position normally occupied by the coolant temperature gauge/temperature warning light sender. The sensor provides information to the air conditioning system electronic control unit.

7.4b . . . and recover the O-ring (arrowed)

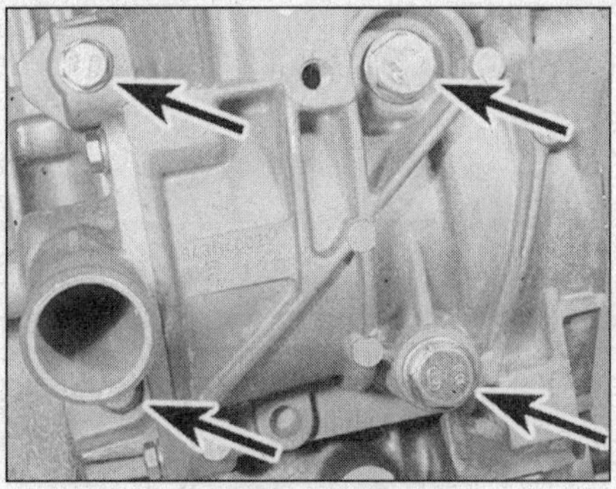

7.6a Coolant pump main housing and retaining bolts (arrowed)

7.6b Coolant pump housing O-ring seal on the cylinder block

24 The operation of the sensor is similar to the operation of the engine coolant temperature sensor described previously in this Section.

25 The sensor itself can only be tested using special Citroën diagnostic equipment. *Do not attempt to test the circuit using any other equipment, as there is a high risk of damaging the air conditioning ECU.*

Removal and refitting

26 The procedure is similar to that described previously in this Section for the electric cooling fan thermostatic switch. On some models, access to the switch is poor, and other components may need to be removed (or hoses, wiring, etc moved to one side) before the sensor can be reached.

7 Coolant pump - removal and refitting

Aluminium block engines

Note: *A new impeller assembly O-ring, and where applicable, a new impeller housing O-ring, will be required on refitting.*

Removal

1 The coolant pump is driven by the timing belt, and is located in a housing bolted to the rear of the cylinder block at the timing belt end of the engine.

2 Drain the cooling system as described in Chapter 1. Make sure that the cylinder block is drained at the same time.

3 Remove the timing belt as described in Chapter 2A or B, as applicable.

4 Remove the securing bolts, and withdraw the coolant pump from the pump housing. Manipulate the pump past the engine mounting, and withdraw it from the engine compartment. Recover the O-ring **(see illustrations)**.

5 If desired, the rear housing can be removed from the opposite end of the coolant pump housing. Access is most easily obtained from underneath the vehicle (it may be necessary to remove the exhaust heat shield). Disconnect the coolant hoses from the impeller housing (be prepared for coolant spillage), then remove the securing bolts and withdraw the impeller housing. Again, recover the O-ring.

6 If it is required to remove the coolant pump main housing from the rear of the cylinder block, it will be necessary to support the engine on a jack and piece of wood, and remove the right-hand engine mounting bracket (see Chapter 2A or B). Unbolt the housing from the cylinder block and recover the O-ring **(see illustrations)**. The housing is located on the cylinder block by two dowels - make sure these are not displaced.

Refitting

7 Ensure that all mating faces are clean. Where applicable, refit the coolant pump main housing to the cylinder block, together with a new O-ring, and tighten the bolts to the specified torque. Make sure that the location dowels are in place.

8 Where applicable, refit the rear housing to the coolant pump housing, using a new O-ring, and tighten the bolts. Reconnect the coolant hoses.

9 Refit the coolant pump to the pump housing, using a new O-ring, and tighten the bolts.

10 Refit the timing belt as described in Chapter 2A or B.

11 Refill the cooling system as described in Chapter 1.

Cast-iron block engines

Note: *A new pump O-ring must be used on refitting.*

Removal

12 The coolant pump is driven by the timing belt, and is located directly in the cylinder block, at the timing belt end.

13 Drain the cooling system as described in Chapter 1. Make sure the cylinder block is drained at the same time.

14 Remove the timing belt as described in Chapter 2A or B, as applicable.

15 Unscrew the two mounting bolts, and withdraw the coolant pump from the cylinder block **(see illustration)**. Recover the O-ring.

Refitting

16 Ensure that all mating faces are clean.

17 Refit the coolant pump to the cylinder block, using a new O-ring, and tighten the bolts to the specified torque.

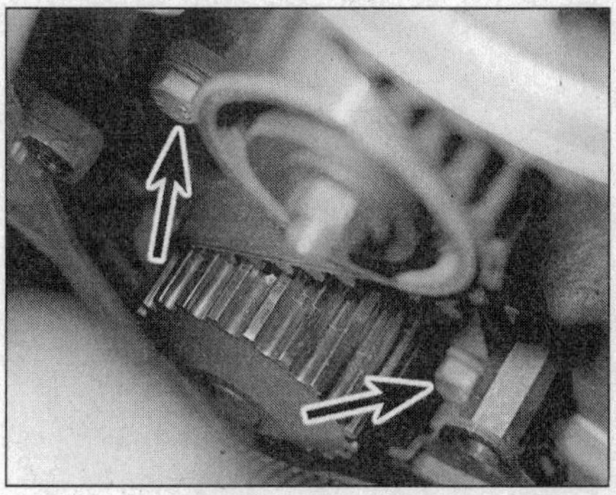

7.15 Coolant pump mounting bolts on the cylinder block

18 Refit the timing belt as described in Chapter 2A or B.

19 Refill the cooling system as described in Chapter 1.

8 Heating/ventilation system - general information

1 The heating/ventilation system consists of a two- or three-speed blower motor (housed behind the facia), face level vents in the centre and at each end of the facia, and air ducts to the front footwells.

2 The control unit is located in the facia, and the controls operate flap valves to deflect and mix the air flowing through the various parts of the heating/ventilation system. The flap valves are contained in the air distribution housing, which acts as a central distribution unit, passing air to the various ducts and vents.

3 Cold air enters the system through the grille at the rear of the engine compartment. If required, the airflow is boosted by the blower, and then flows through the various ducts, according to the settings of the controls. Stale air is expelled through ducts at the rear of the

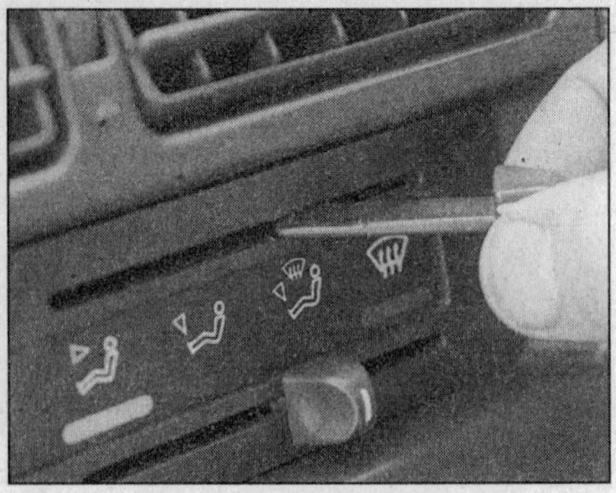

9.1a Pull free the ventilation control knobs . . .

9.1b . . . and heater blower motor control knob . . .

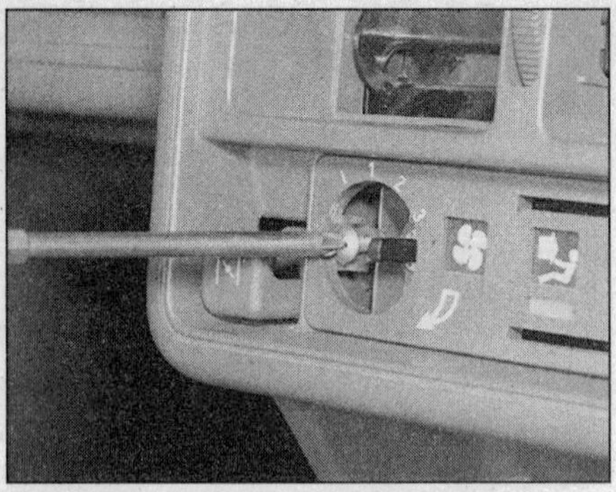

9.2a . . . undo the retaining screw . . .

9.2b . . . and remove the panel

9.9 Heater hose connections at the bulkhead

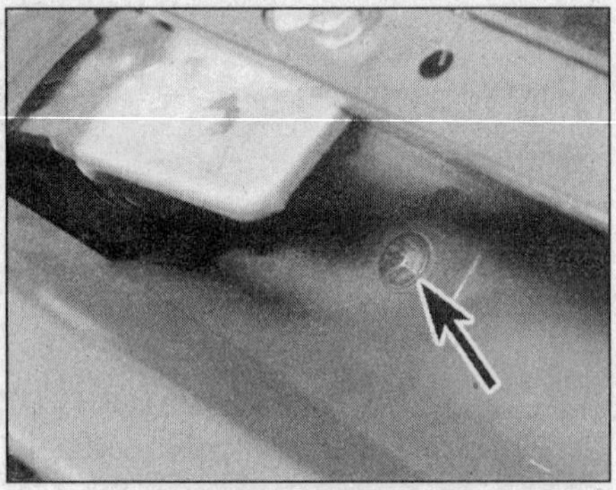

9.15 Heater unit retaining bolt (arrowed) on the engine side of the bulkhead

vehicle. If warm air is required, the cold air is passed over the heater matrix, which is heated by the engine coolant.

4 On models fitted with air conditioning, a recirculation switch enables the outside air supply to be closed off, while the air inside the vehicle is recirculated. This can be useful to prevent unpleasant odours entering from outside the vehicle, but should only be used briefly, as the recirculated air inside the vehicle will soon become stale. With the recirculation switch off, cold air enters the passenger compartment through three vents located below the heater/ventilation control panel, and the air entering the car is cooled while passing over the air conditioning evaporator.

9 Heating/ventilation system components - removal and refitting

Heating/ventilation control unit

Removal

1 Pull free the knobs from the heater/ventilation controls **(see illustrations)**.

2 Undo the retaining screw, and remove the control panel from the facia **(see illustrations)**. As it is withdrawn, detach the illumination bulb wiring.

3 Withdraw the control plate unit, and detach the control rod and cable.

Refitting

4 Refitting is a reversal of removal. Check for satisfactory operation on completion.

Heater/ventilation control cable

Removal

5 Remove the heater/ventilation control unit as described in paragraphs 1 to 3.

6 Remove the trim panels for access to the side of the heater unit, then disconnect the cable and remove it.

Refitting

7 Refitting is a reversal of the removal procedure.

Complete heater assembly

Removal

8 Drain the cooling system as described in Chapter 1.

9 Detach the heater feed and return hoses at the bulkhead, access to them being easiest from underneath **(see illustration)**.

10 Remove the centre console (and, on pre-1991 models, the right- and left-hand parcel shelves) with reference to Chapter 11.

11 Remove the heater control panel as described earlier. Also remove the centre vents and the radio (or coin box if applicable).

12 Remove the steering column with reference to Chapter 10, then disconnect the facia unit from its fixings, and carefully pivot it upwards to allow access to the heater unit retaining nut from the underside. Support the panel in this position with a prop.

13 Remove the windscreen wiper motor arm and blade with reference to Chapter 12. If necessary, completely remove the wiper motor.

14 Unscrew the retaining nut each side and the central screw, then remove the grille panel at the base of the windscreen.

15 Undo the single retaining bolt securing the heater unit to the engine side of the bulkhead, and the nut from the underside within the car **(see illustration)**.

16 Detach the ducts, and carefully withdraw the heater from the car **(see illustration)**.

Refitting

17 Refitting is a reversal of removal. Ensure that all connections are securely made, and refill the cooling system as described in Chapter 1.

Heater matrix

Removal

18 Drain the cooling system as described in Chapter 1.

19 Detach the heater feed and return hoses at the bulkhead in the engine compartment, access to them being easiest from underneath.

20 To improve access on right-hand drive models, remove the clutch pedal (Chapter 6) and brake pedal (Chapter 9).

21 To improve access on left-hand drive models, remove the side shelf from the passenger's (right-hand) side of the facia panel. Where necessary, disconnect the air duct.

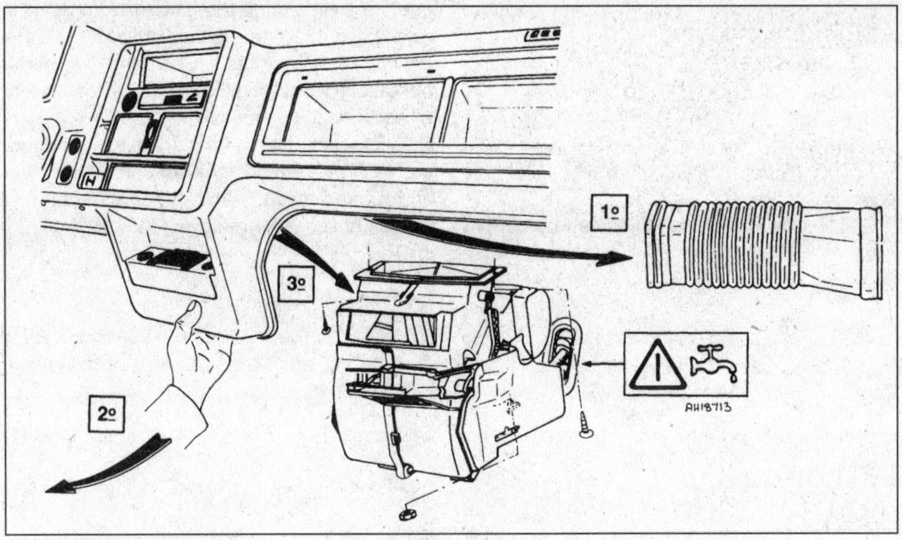

9.16 Heater unit removal

Left-hand-drive model shown - right-hand-drive models similar

22 Remove the trim panel from the right-hand side of the heater.

23 Remove the screws securing the inlet and outlet tube assembly to the matrix; remove the assembly, at the same time pulling it out of the rubber grommet. Recover the two O-ring seals.

24 Unscrew the mounting screws, and withdraw the matrix carefully from the heater unit.

Refitting

25 Refitting is a reversal of removal, but fit new O-ring seals. On completion, refill the cooling system as described in Chapter 1.

Heater blower motor

Removal

26 Disconnect the battery negative lead.

27 On left-hand drive models, detach and remove the parcel shelf or trim panel from the right-hand side of the facia panel. On right-hand drive models, remove the trim panel from under the steering column.

28 Unscrew the two motor retaining nuts, withdraw the motor, and detach the wiring and ducting **(see illustration)**. Note the location of any washers and spacers.

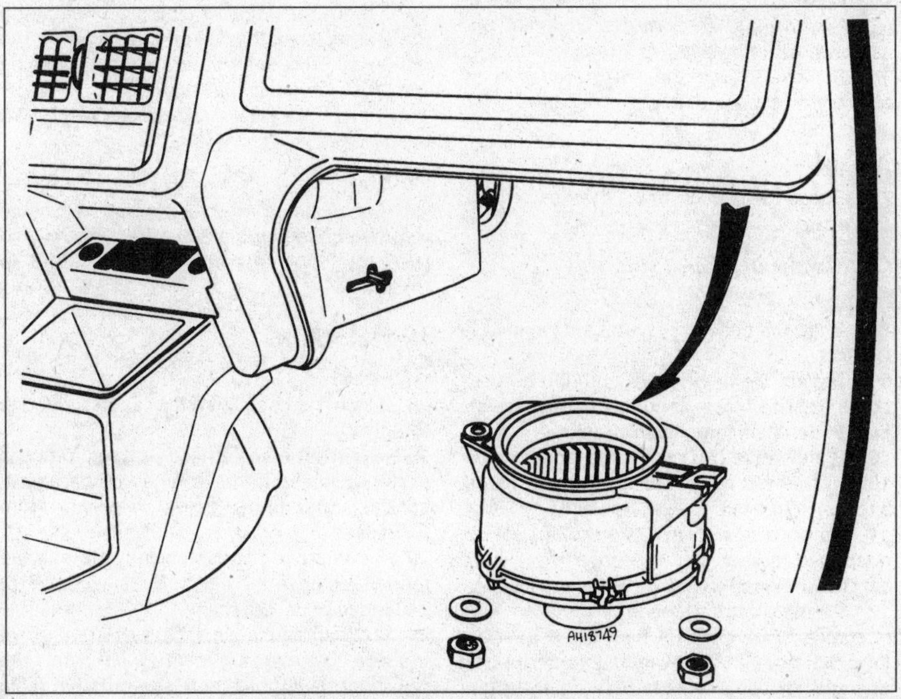

9.28 Removing the heater blower motor

Refitting

29 Refitting is a reversal of removal.

Heater blower motor resistor

30 On all models without air conditioning (and on left-hand drive models with air conditioning), the heater blower motor resistor is incorporated in the blower motor assembly itself, and is not available separately. On right-hand drive models with air conditioning, the resistor is located under the facia, and is accessed by removing the blower motor control panel.

10 Air conditioning system - general information and precautions

General information

1 An air conditioning system is available on certain models. It enables the temperature of incoming air to be lowered, and also dehumidifies the air, which makes for rapid demisting and increased comfort.

2 The cooling side of the system works in the same way as a domestic refrigerator. Refrigerant gas is drawn into a belt-driven compressor, and passes into a condenser mounted in front of the radiator, where it loses heat and becomes liquid. The liquid passes through an expansion valve to an evaporator, where it changes from liquid under high pressure to gas under low pressure. This change is accompanied by a drop in temperature, which cools the evaporator. The refrigerant returns to the compressor, and the cycle begins again.

3 Air blown through the evaporator passes to the air distribution unit. The amount of cooling is set by adjusting the knob on the control panel.

4 The heating side of the system works in the same way as on models without air conditioning (see Section 8).

5 The operation of the system is controlled by an electronic control unit, which controls the electric cooling fan, the compressor, and the facia-mounted warning light. Any problems with the system should be referred to a Citroën dealer.

Precautions

6 When working on the air conditioning system, it is necessary to observe special precautions. If for any reason the system must be disconnected, entrust this task to your Citroën dealer or a refrigeration engineer.

Warning: The refrigeration circuit contains a liquid refrigerant, and it is dangerous to disconnect any part of the system without specialised knowledge and equipment. The refrigerant is potentially dangerous, and should only be handled by qualified persons. If it is splashed onto the

3

skin, it can cause frostbite. It is not itself poisonous, but in the presence of a naked flame (including a cigarette) it forms a poisonous gas. Uncontrolled discharging of the refrigerant is dangerous, and potentially damaging to the environment. Do not operate the air conditioning system if it is known to be short of refrigerant, as this may damage the compressor.

11 Air conditioning components - removal and refitting

Warning: *Do not attempt to open the refrigerant circuit. Refer to the precautions given in Section 10.*

1 The only operation which can be carried out easily without discharging the refrigerant is renewal of the compressor drivebelt. This is described in Chapter 1, Section 21. All other operations must be referred to a Citroën dealer or an air conditioning specialist.

2 If necessary for access to other components, the compressor can be unbolted and moved aside, without disconnecting its flexible hoses, after removing the drivebelt.

Chapter 4 Part A: Fuel/exhaust systems - carburettor petrol models

Contents

Degrees of difficulty

Easy, suitable for novice with little experience	**Fairly easy,** suitable for beginner with some experience	**Fairly difficult,** suitable for competent DIY mechanic	**Difficult,** suitable for experienced DIY mechanic	**Very difficult,** suitable for expert DIY or professional

Specifications

Fuel pump

Type	Mechanical, driven by eccentric on camshaft

Carburettor

Type:	
954 models	Weber 32 IBSH or Solex 32 PBISA
1124 cc models	Solex 32 PBISA
1360 cc models	Weber 34 TLP, Solex 34 PBISA or Solex 32-34 Z2
Designation:	
954 cc models	Weber 32 IBSH 16/100, Solex 32 PBISA 16 412
1124 cc models	Solex 32 PBISA 16 PSA 411
1360 cc models	Weber 34 TLP 3/100, Solex 34 PBISA 481, or Solex 32-34 Z2 PSA 409
Choke type	Manual, cable-controlled

Weber 32 IBSH carburettor data - 954 cc models

Venturi diameter	25 mm
Main jet	122
Air correction jet	135
Emulsion tube	F112
Enrichening device	30
Econostat (fuel)	50
Econostat (air)	120
Idle jet	45
Idle air jet	150
Accelerator pump jet	40 (leak hole: 20)
Needle valve	1.5
Float weight	11 g
Float level	8.0 mm
Choke pull-down setting	4.0 to 4.5 mm
Fast idle setting (throttle valve opening)	0.8 mm
Idle speed	750 ± 100 rpm
Idle mixture CO content	0.8 to 1.2 %

Weber 34 TLP carburettor data - 1360 cc models

Venturi diameter	26 mm
Main jet	132
Air correction jet	145
Emulsion tube	F80
Enrichening device	40
Econostat (fuel)	50
Econostat (air)	90
Idle jet	43
Idle air jet	130
Accelerator pump jet	40 (leak hole: 20)
Needle valve	1.5
Float level	28.0 ± 0.25 mm
Choke pull-down setting	4.75 mm
Fast idle setting	0.8 mm
Idle speed	750 ± 100 rpm
Idle mixture CO content	0.5 to 2.0 %

Solex 32 PBISA carburettor data - 954 cc models

Venturi diameter	25 mm
Main jet	127
Idle jet	47
Idle air jet	135
Air correction jet	155
Emulsion tube	31
Accelerator pump	40
Needle valve	1.6
Float height setting	38 0 mm
Throttle valve fast idle setting	0.8 mm
Choke pull-down setting	3.0 mm
Idle speed	750 ± 100 rpm
Idle mixture CO content	0.8 to 1.2 %

Solex 32 PBISA carburettor data - 1124 cc (H1A) models

Venturi diameter	25 mm
Main jet	127.5
Air correction jet	175
Emulsion tube	EM
Enrichening device	35
Idle jet	46
Idle air jet	165
Accelerator pump	40
Econostat (fuel)	40
Econostat (air)	150
Needle valve	1.6
Float weight	5.7 g
Throttle valve fast idle setting	0.5 mm
Choke pull-down setting	2.8 mm
Idle speed	750 ± 100 rpm
Idle mixture CO content	0.8 to 1.2 %

Solex 32 PBISA carburettor data - 1360 cc (K1G) models

Venturi diameter	26 mm
Main jet	132
Air correction jet	155
Emulsion tube	EC
Enrichening device	55
Idle jet	42 to 46
Idle air jet	150
Accelerator pump	40
Needle valve	1.6
Float weight	5.7 g
Throttle valve fast idle setting	0.6 mm
Choke pull-down setting	3.5 mm
Idle speed	750 ± 100 rpm
Idle mixture CO content	1.3 ± 0.5 %

Solex 32-34 Z2 carburettor data - 1360 cc models	Primary	Secondary
Venturi diameter	24 mm	27 mm
Main jet	155	175
Idle jet	45	-
Idle air jet	150	-
Air correction jet	117	130
Emulsion tube	27	AZ
Accelerator pump	-	35
Needle valve	1.8	
Float height setting	35.0 mm	
Throttle valve fast idle setting	0.8 mm	
Choke pull-down setting	3.0 mm	
Idle speed	750 ± 100 rpm	
Idle mixture CO content	0.8 to 1.2 %	

Recommended fuel

Minimum octane rating:	
C1A and K1G engines	98 RON leaded (UK "4-star" leaded) or 98 RON unleaded (Super unleaded)
H1A, H1B, K1A*, K2A and K2D engines	95 RON unleaded (Premium unleaded) or 98 RON unleaded (Super unleaded) or 98 RON leaded (UK "4-star" leaded)

* **Note:** *For use of 95 RON unleaded fuel, ignition timing must be set to 4° BTDC at 750 rpm - see Chapter 5B.*

Torque wrench settings	Nm	lbf ft
Fuel pump retaining bolts	15	11
Inlet manifold retaining nuts	8	6
Exhaust manifold retaining nuts	15	11
Exhaust system fasteners:		
Front pipe-to-manifold nut	35	26
Front pipe-to-intermediate pipe nuts - 1360 cc models	10	7
Clamping ring nut/bolts	15	11

1 General information and precautions

1 The fuel system consists of a fuel tank mounted under the rear of the car, a mechanical fuel pump, and a carburettor. The fuel pump is operated by an eccentric on the camshaft, and is mounted on the rear of the cylinder head. The air cleaner contains a disposable paper filter element. It incorporates a flap valve air temperature control system, which allows cold air from the outside of the car and warm air from the exhaust manifold to enter the air cleaner in the correct proportions. On 954 cc C1A engines, the temperature control is manually operated, but on all other engines it is controlled automatically by vacuum from the inlet manifold.

2 The fuel pump lifts fuel from the fuel tank, via a filter which is mounted on the engine compartment bulkhead. On all post-July 1991 models, an anti-percolation chamber is located on the line between the fuel pump and carburettor **(see illustration)**. The anti-percolation chamber ensures that the supply of fuel to the carburettor is kept at a constant pressure and is free of air bubbles. Excess fuel is returned from the anti-percolation chamber to the fuel tank. Pre-July 1991 1360 cc models also have a similar return system which returns the fuel to the fuel tank, but without the anti-percolation chamber.

1.2 Anti-percolation chamber (arrowed)

3 954 cc models are fitted with a Weber 32 IBSH or Solex 32 PBISA single-choke carburettor. 1124 cc models are fitted with a Solex 32 PBISA single-choke carburettor. 1360 cc models other than the performance-orientated GT are fitted with a Weber 34 TLP or Solex 34 PBISA single-choke carburettor. On GT models, a Solex 32-34 Z2 twin-choke carburettor is fitted. On all carburettors, mixture enrichment for cold starting is by a cable-operated choke control.

4 Throughout this Part of Chapter 4, it is also occasionally necessary to identify vehicles by their engine codes rather than engine capacity. Refer to Chapter 2A for further information on engine code identification. Refer to Section 18 for information on the exhaust system.

Warning: Many of the procedures in this Chapter require the removal of fuel lines and connections, which may result in some fuel spillage. Before carrying out any operation on the fuel system, refer to the precautions given in "Safety first!" at the beginning of this manual, and follow them implicitly. Petrol is a highly-dangerous and volatile liquid, and the precautions necessary when handling it cannot be overstressed.

4A

2 Air cleaner assembly - removal and refitting

Removal

1 Slacken the retaining clips (where fitted) and disconnect the vacuum and breather hoses from the front of the air cleaner housing-to-carburettor duct **(see illustration)**. Where crimped-type hose clips or ties are fitted, cut and discard them; replace them with standard worm-drive hose clips or new cable ties on refitting.

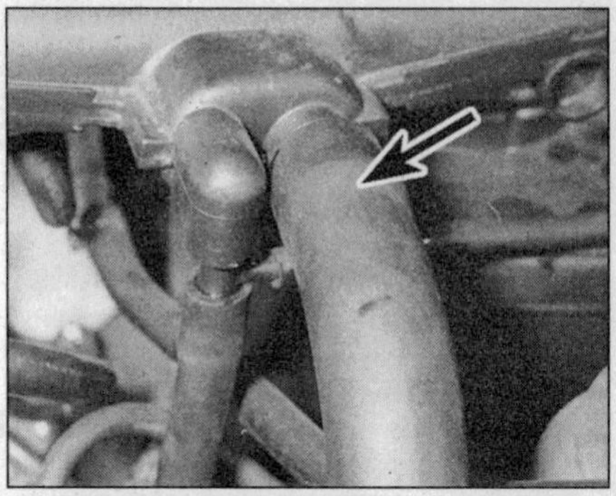

2.1 Disconnect the vacuum and breather hoses (arrowed) from the front of the duct . . .

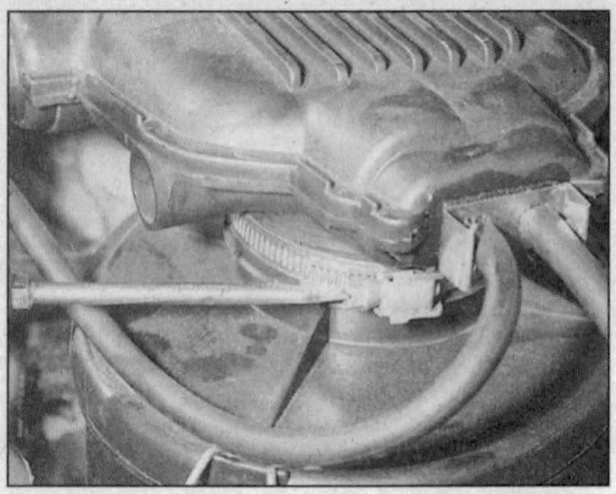

2.2a . . . slacken the retaining clips . . .

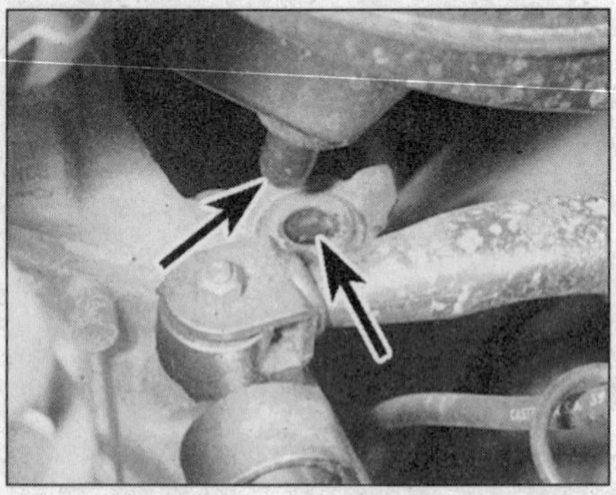

2.5 On refitting, ensure that the air cleaner housing peg is correctly located in its mounting rubber (arrowed)

2 Slacken the retaining clips, then lift the duct off the top of the carburettor and air cleaner housing. Where fitted, disconnect the air temperature control valve hose from the end of the duct, then remove the duct from the engine compartment **(see illustrations)**. Recover the rubber sealing ring(s) from the top of the carburettor and/or air cleaner housing (as applicable).

3 Disconnect the intake duct from the front of the air cleaner housing, and remove the air cleaner housing from the engine compartment.

4 To remove the intake duct assembly, drill out the rivets securing the duct to the crossmember, then release the fastener securing the rear of the duct to the cylinder head. Disconnect the hot-air intake hose from the exhaust manifold shroud, and remove the duct and hose assembly from the engine compartment **(see illustration)**.

Refitting

5 Refitting is a reversal of the removal procedure, noting the following points:

a) Examine the rubber sealing ring(s) for signs of damage or deterioration, and if necessary renew. Note that on some models the carburettor seal is fitted with an O-ring - this should also be renewed if it is damaged.

b) Ensure that the air cleaner housing locating peg is correctly engaged with its mounting on the top of the transmission **(see illustration)**.

c) Prior to tightening the air cleaner-to-carburettor duct retaining clips, ensure that the duct is correctly seated on both the air cleaner housing and carburettor flanges.

d) Secure the duct to the crossmember (where removed) with new pop-rivets.

2.2b . . . and remove the duct, disconnecting the air temperature control valve hose (arrowed)

3 Air cleaner automatic air temperature control system - general information and component renewal

General information

1 The system is controlled by a heat-sensitive bi-metal vacuum switch mounted in the end of the air cleaner housing-to-carburettor duct. When the engine is started from cold, the switch is open, and allows inlet manifold depression to act on the air temperature control valve diaphragm in the intake duct. This vacuum causes the diaphragm to move a flap valve across the cold-air intake, thus allowing only (warmed) air from the exhaust manifold to enter the air cleaner.

2 As the temperature of the exhaust-warmed air in the air cleaner-to-carburettor duct rises, the bi-metal strip in the vacuum switch deforms and closes the vacuum supply to the air temperature control valve assembly. As the vacuum supply is cut, the flap is gradually lowered across the hot-air intake until, when the engine is fully warmed up to normal operating temperature, only cold air from the front of the car is entering the air cleaner.

3 To check the system, allow the engine to cool down completely, then disconnect the intake duct from the front of the control valve assembly; the flap valve in the duct should be securely seated across the hot-air intake. Start the engine; the flap should immediately rise to close off the cold-air intake, and should then lower steadily as the engine warms up, until it is eventually seated across the hot-air intake again.

4 To check the vacuum switch, disconnect the vacuum pipe from the control valve when the engine is running and place a finger over the pipe end. When the engine is cold, full inlet manifold vacuum should be present in the pipe, and when the engine is at normal operating temperature there should be no vacuum in the pipe.

5 To check the air temperature control valve assembly, disconnect the intake duct from the front of the valve assembly; the flap valve should be securely seated across the hot-air intake. Disconnect the vacuum pipe, and suck hard at the control valve stub; the flap should rise to shut off the cold-air intake.

6 If either component is faulty, it must be renewed.

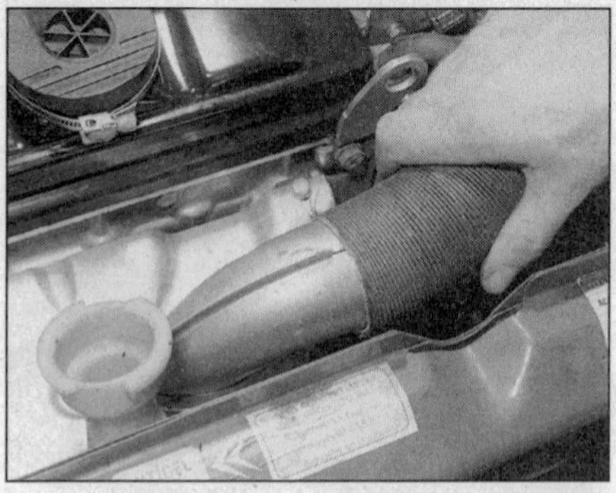

2.4 Detach the hot-air intake duct from the exhaust manifold

Vacuum switch - renewal

7 Remove the air cleaner housing-to-carburettor duct as described in paragraphs 1 and 2 of Section 2.

8 Bend up the tangs on the switch retaining clip, then remove the clip, along with its seal, and withdraw the switch from inside the duct **(see illustrations)**. Examine the seal for signs of damage or deterioration, and renew if necessary.

9 When refitting, ensure that the switch and duct mating surfaces are clean and dry, and position the switch inside of the duct.

10 Fit the seal over the switch unions, and refit the retaining clip. Ensure that the switch is pressed firmly against the duct, and secure it in position by bending down the retaining clip tangs.

11 Refit the duct as described in Section 2.

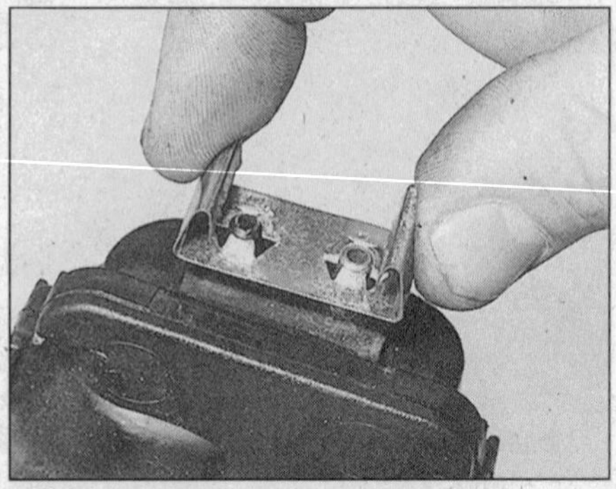

3.8a Remove the retaining clip . . .

3.8b . . . and seal . . .

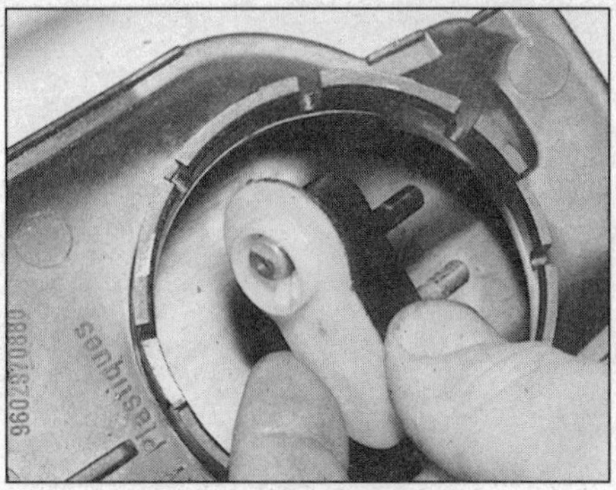

3.8c . . . then withdraw the vacuum switch from inside the duct

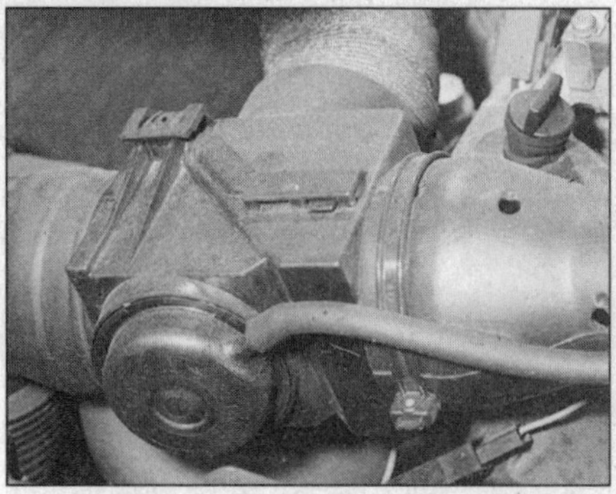

3.12 Air temperature control valve assembly

Air temperature control valve - renewal

12 Disconnect the vacuum pipe from the air temperature control valve, then slacken the retaining clips securing the intake ducts to the valve **(see illustration)**.

13 Disconnect both intake ducts and the hot-air intake hose from the control valve assembly, and remove the assembly from the vehicle.

14 The air temperature control valve assembly can only be renewed as a complete unit. Refitting is the reverse of the removal procedure.

4 Fuel pump - testing, removal and refitting

Note: *Refer to the warning note at the end of Section 1 before proceeding.*

Testing

1 To test the fuel pump without removing it, first disable the ignition system, then disconnect the outlet pipe which leads to the carburettor, and hold a wad of rag over the pump outlet while an assistant spins the engine on the starter. *Keep your hands away from the electric cooling fan.* Regular spurts of fuel should be ejected as the engine turns.

2 The pump can also be tested by removing it. With the pump outlet pipe disconnected but the inlet pipe still connected, hold the wad of rag by the outlet. Operate the pump lever by hand; if the pump is in a satisfactory condition, the lever should move and return smoothly, and a strong jet of fuel should be ejected.

Removal

3 Identify the pump inlet and outlet hoses, and slacken both retaining clips **(see illustration)**. Where crimped-type hose clips are fitted, cut the clips and discard them; replace them with standard worm-drive hose clips on refitting. Place wads of rag beneath the hose unions to catch any spilled fuel. Disconnect both hoses from the pump, and plug the hose ends to minimise fuel loss.

4 Slacken and remove the bolts securing the pump to the rear of the cylinder head. Remove the pump **(see illustration)**, and recover its gasket. Discard the gasket - a new one must be used on refitting.

Refitting

5 Ensure that the pump and cylinder head mating surfaces are clean and dry, then offer up the new gasket and refit the pump to the cylinder head. Tighten the pump retaining bolts to the specified torque setting.

6 Reconnect the inlet and outlet hoses to the relevant pump unions, and securely tighten their retaining clips.

5 Fuel gauge sender unit - removal and refitting

Note: *Refer to the warning note at the end of Section 1 before proceeding.*

Removal

1 Disconnect the battery negative lead.

2 For access to the sender unit, fold the rear seat cushion forwards.

3 Using a screwdriver, carefully prise the plastic access cover from the floor to expose the sender unit (the sender unit is located under the left-hand cover, viewed facing towards the front of the vehicle) **(see illustrations)**.

4.3 Arrows on fuel pump unions indicate the direction of fuel flow

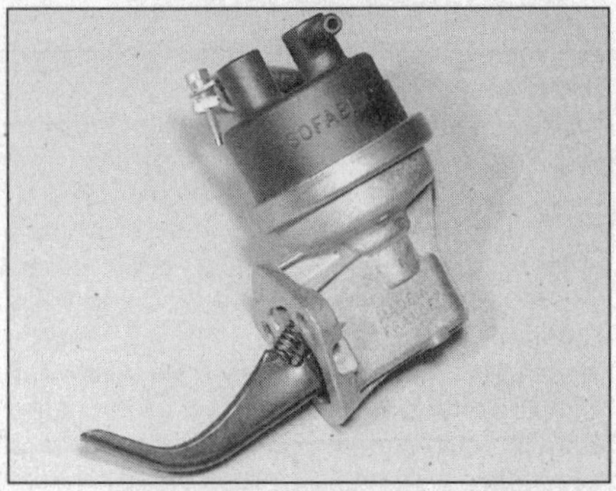

4.4 Fuel pump removed from engine

5.3a Remove the plastic cover . . .

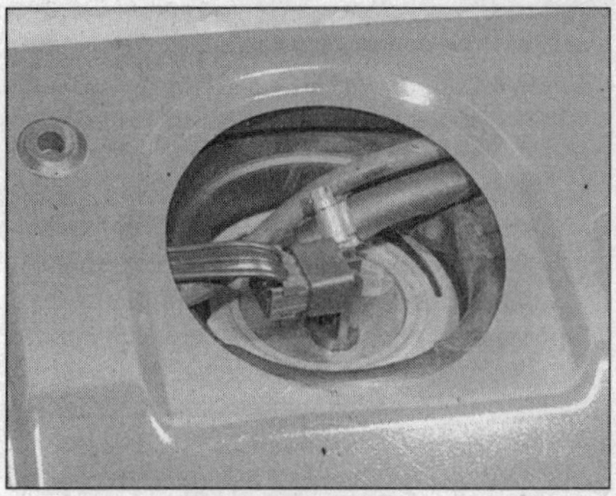

5.3b . . . for access to the fuel gauge sender unit . . .

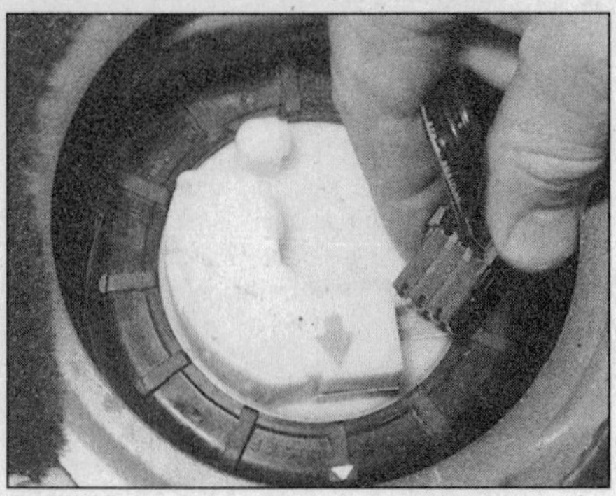

5.4 . . . then disconnect the wiring connector from the fuel gauge sender unit (fuel-injected model shown)

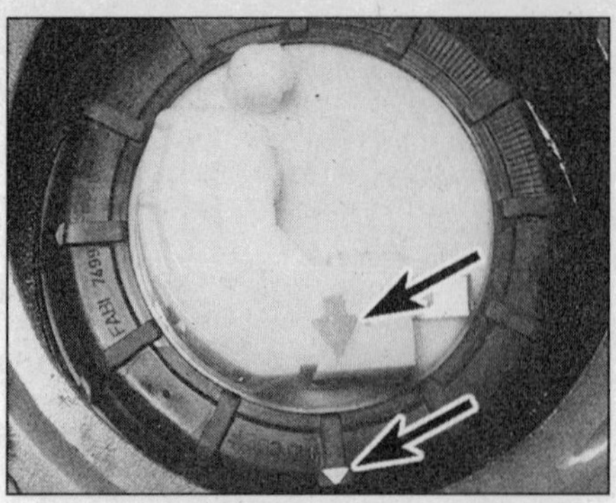

5.6a Note the position of the alignment marks (arrowed) on the sender unit and locking ring . . .

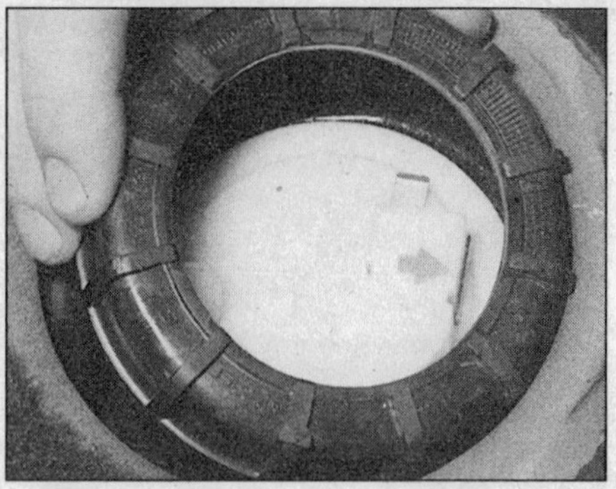

5.6b . . . then unscrew the locking ring

4 Disconnect the wiring connector from the sender unit, and tape the connector to the vehicle body to prevent it disappearing behind the tank **(see illustration)**.

5 Mark the hoses for identification purposes, then slacken the feed and return hose retaining clips. Where the crimped-type hose clips are fitted, cut the clips and discard them; replace them with standard worm-drive hose clips on refitting. Disconnect both hoses from the top of the sender unit, and plug the hose ends. Tape the hoses to the vehicle body, to prevent them disappearing behind the tank.

6 Noting the alignment marks on the tank, sender unit and the locking ring (where applicable), unscrew the ring and remove it from the tank **(see illustrations)**.

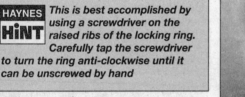

> **HAYNES HiNT** ***This is best accomplished by using a screwdriver on the raised ribs of the locking ring. Carefully tap the screwdriver to turn the ring anti-clockwise until it can be unscrewed by hand***

7 Carefully lift the sender unit from the top of the fuel tank, taking great care not to bend the sender unit float arm or to spill fuel onto the interior of the vehicle. Recover the rubber sealing ring and discard it - a new one must be used on refitting **(see illustrations)**.

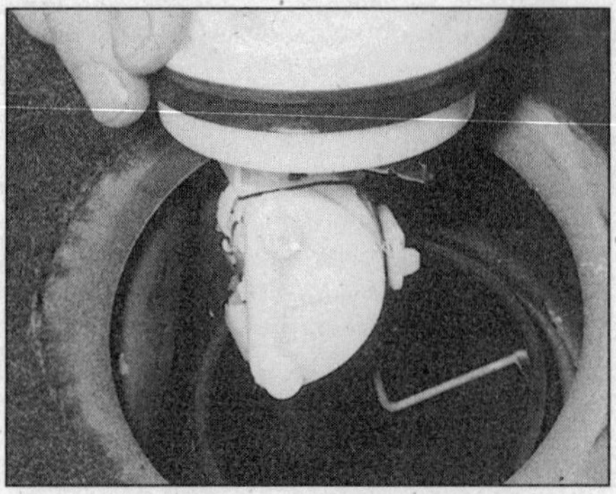

5.7a Withdraw the sender unit from the tank . . .

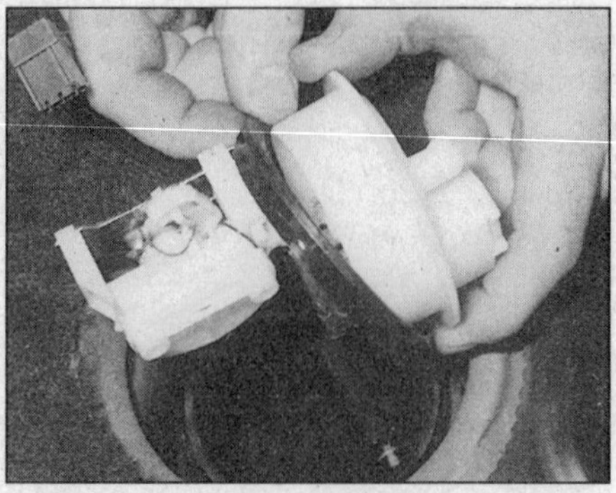

5.7b . . . and remove the rubber sealing ring

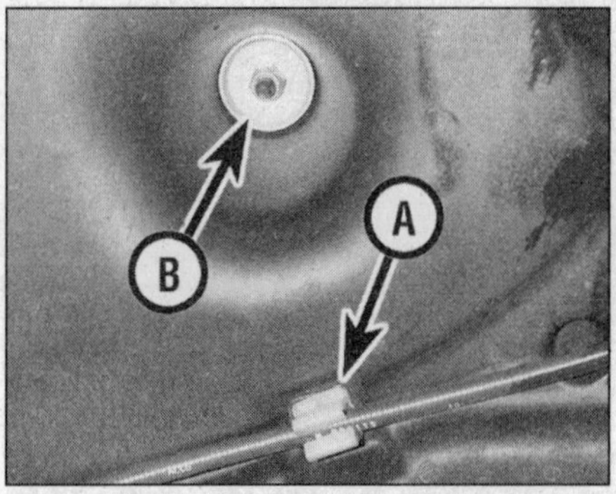

6.3 Handbrake cable retaining clip (A) on fuel tank, and tank retaining nut (B)

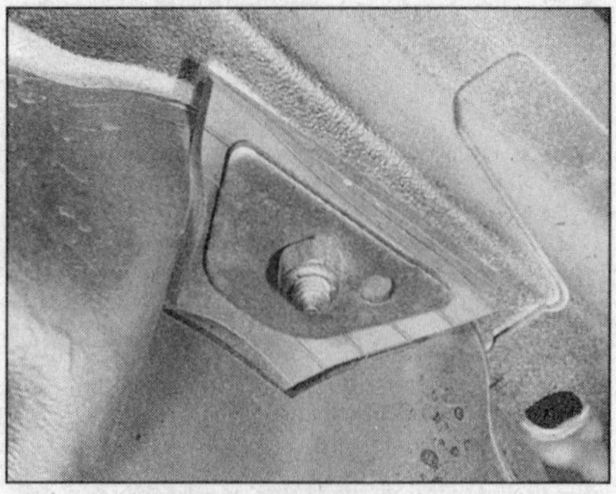

6.7 Fuel tank retaining nut, washer and insulator

Refitting

8 Refitting is a reversal of the removal procedure, noting the following points:

a) Prior to refitting, fit a new rubber sealing ring to the fuel tank.
b) Refit the sender unit to the tank, aligning its arrow with the centre of the three alignment marks on the fuel tank. Hold the sender in position, then refit the locking ring and tighten it until its mark is correctly aligned with the centre of the three fuel tank marks. All three marks should now be in alignment, as noted prior to removal.
c) Ensure that the feed and return hoses are correctly reconnected, and are securely retained by their clips.

6 Fuel tank - removal and refitting

Note: *Refer to the warning note at the end of Section 1 before proceeding.*

Removal

1 Before removing the fuel tank, all the fuel must be drained from the tank. Since a fuel tank drain plug is not provided, it is therefore preferable to carry out the removal operation when the tank is nearly empty. Before proceeding, disconnect the battery negative lead, and syphon or hand-pump the remaining fuel from the tank.

2 Remove the exhaust system and relevant heat shield(s) as described in Section 18.

3 Free both handbrake cables from their retaining clips on the base of the fuel tank **(see illustration)**.

4 Disconnect the wiring connector and fuel hoses from the fuel gauge sender unit, as described in paragraphs 2 to 5 of Section 5.

5 Working at the right-hand side of the fuel tank, release the retaining clips, then disconnect the filler neck vent pipe and main filler neck hose from the fuel tank. Where necessary, also disconnect the breather hose(s). Some breather hoses are joined to the tank with quick-release fittings; to disconnect these fittings, slide the cover along the hose, then depress the centre ring and pull the hose out of its fitting.

6 Place a trolley jack with an interposed block of wood beneath the tank, then raise the jack until it is supporting the weight of the tank.
7 Slacken and remove the two retaining nuts and washers **(see illustration)**, then slowly lower the fuel tank. Disconnect any other relevant vent pipes as they become accessible (where necessary), and remove the tank from underneath the vehicle. Recover the tank mounting rubbers, noting their correct fitted positions.
8 If the tank is contaminated with sediment or water, remove the sender unit (Section 5) and swill the tank out with clean fuel. The tank is injection-moulded from a synthetic material and if damaged, it should be renewed. However, in certain cases, it may be possible to have small leaks or minor damage repaired. Seek the advice of a suitable specialist before attempting to repair the fuel tank.

Refitting

9 Refitting is the reverse of the removal procedure, noting the following points:

a) When lifting the tank back into position, make sure that the mounting rubbers are correctly positioned, and take great care to ensure that none of the hoses become trapped between the tank and vehicle body.
b) Ensure that all pipes and hoses are correctly routed, and securely held in position with their retaining clips.
c) On completion, refill the tank with fuel, and check for signs of leakage prior to taking the vehicle out on the road.

7 Accelerator cable - removal, refitting and adjustment

Removal

1 Where necessary, prise out the retaining clip and remove the plastic cover to gain access to the carburettor.
2 On all models, free the accelerator inner cable from the carburettor throttle cam, then pull the outer cable out from its mounting bracket rubber grommet **(see illustration)**. Slide the flat washer off the end of the cable, and remove the spring clip.
3 Working back along the length of the cable, free it from any relevant retaining clips or ties, noting its correct routing.
4 Working inside the vehicle, undo the retaining nuts and remove the undercover panel from the driver's side of the facia.
5 Reach up behind the facia, then release the retaining clip and detach the inner cable from the top of the accelerator pedal **(see illustration)**.
6 Displace the rubber grommet from the end of the outer cable retainer, and tie a length of string to the end of the inner cable **(see illustration)**.
7 Return to the engine compartment, and release the outer cable retainer from the engine compartment bulkhead. Withdraw the cable from the bulkhead until the end of the cable appears, then untie the string and leave it in position. The string can then be used to draw the cable back into position on refitting.

Refitting

8 Tie the string to the end of the cable, then use the string to draw the cable into position through the bulkhead. Once the cable end is visible, untie the string.
9 Align the outer cable retainer lug with the cut-out in the bulkhead, then securely clip the retainer into position. Check that the retainer is securely fitted, then slide the rubber grommet over the retainer end, and clip the inner cable into position in the pedal.
10 Make sure that the cable is securely retained, then refit the undercover panel to the facia.
11 From within the engine compartment, ensure that the outer cable is correctly seated in the bulkhead grommet. Work along the cable, securing it in position with all the relevant retaining clips and ties, ensuring that the cable is correctly routed.
12 Slide the flat washer onto the cable end, and refit the spring clip.
13 Pass the outer cable through its carburettor mounting bracket grommet, and reconnect the inner cable to the throttle cam. Adjust the cable as described below.

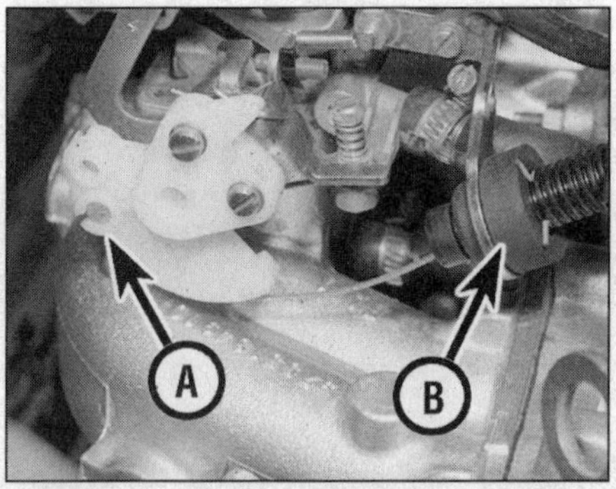

7.2 Accelerator cable removal from carburettor

A Inner cable nipple
B Rubber grommet

Adjustment

14 If not already done, prise out the retaining clip and remove the plastic cover (where fitted) from the carburettor.
15 Remove the spring clip from the accelerator outer cable then, ensuring that the throttle cam is fully against its stop, gently pull the cable out of its grommet until all free play is removed from the inner cable **(see illustration)**.
16 With the cable held in this position, ensure that the flat washer is pressed securely against the grommet. Fit the spring clip to the last exposed outer cable groove in front of the rubber grommet and washer, ie. so that when the clip is refitted and the outer cable is released, there is only a small amount of free play in the inner cable.
17 Have an assistant depress the accelerator pedal, and check that the throttle cam opens fully and returns smoothly to its stop.
18 Where necessary, clip the plastic cover back into position, and refit its retaining clip.

8 Accelerator pedal - removal and refitting

Removal

1 Undo the retaining nuts, and remove the undercover panel from the driver's side of the facia.
2 Depress the retaining clips, and detach the

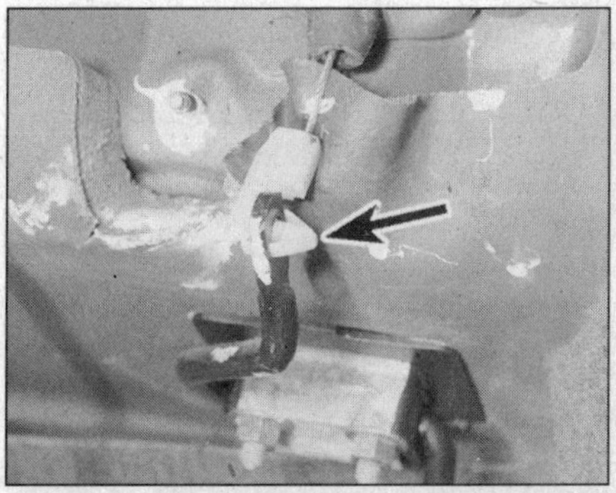

7.5 Accelerator cable-to-pedal clip (arrowed)

4A

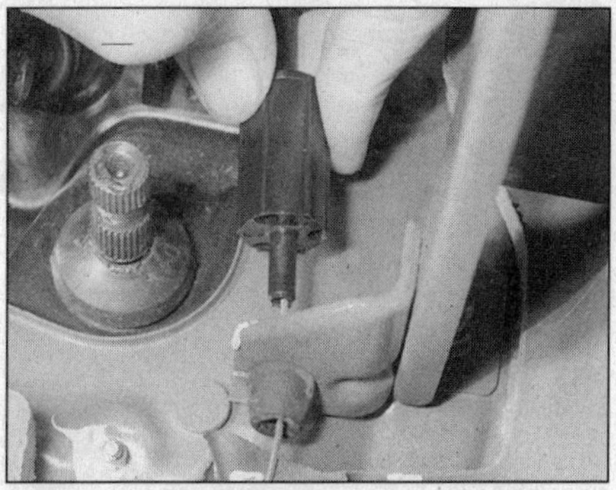

7.6 Disconnecting the accelerator cable at the pedal end

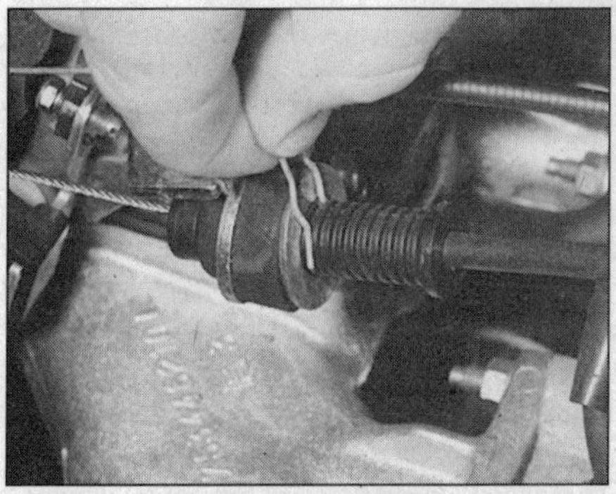

7.15 Adjusting the accelerator cable

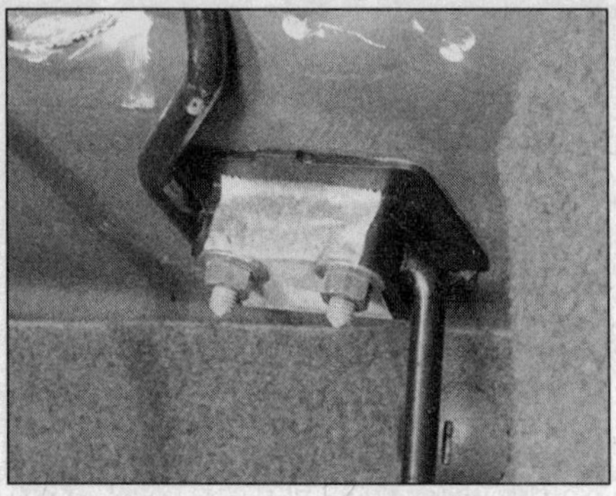

8.3 Accelerator pedal pivot and retaining nuts

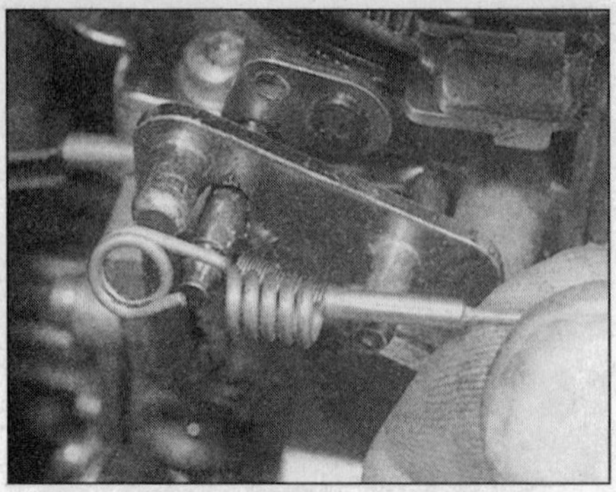

9.2a Release the choke cable from its linkage . . .

9.2b . . . then undo the retaining bolt and remove the choke cable retaining clip

inner cable from the top of the accelerator pedal.

3 Slacken and remove the two nuts securing the pedal mounting bracket to the bulkhead **(see illustration)**. Slide off the outer part of the mounting clamp, then withdraw the pedal from behind the facia, and slide off the inner part of the clamp.

4 Examine the mounting bracket and pedal pivot points for signs of wear, and renew as necessary.

Refitting

5 Refitting is a reversal of the removal procedure, applying a little multi-purpose grease to the pedal pivot point. On completion, adjust the accelerator cable as described in Section 7.

9 Choke cable - removal, refitting and adjustment

Removal

1 Where necessary, prise out the retaining clip and remove the plastic cover to gain access to the carburettor.

2 Free the choke inner cable from the carburettor linkage, then undo the retaining bolt and remove the outer cable retaining clamp **(see illustrations)**.

3 Slacken the retaining clip securing the rubber collar to the outer cable, and slide the collar off of the cable. Where the original crimped-type hose clip is still fitted, cut the clip and discard it; replace it with a standard worm-drive hose clip on refitting.

4 Working back along the length of the cable, free it from any relevant retaining clips or ties, noting its correct routing. Tie a suitable length of string to the end of the choke inner cable.

5 Working from inside the vehicle, pull the choke lever fully out, and unclip the lever from the facia (it may be necessary to twist the lever as is being removed). Withdraw the lever and cable assembly from the facia, disconnecting the wiring from the lever switch (where fitted) as it becomes accessible **(see illustrations)**. Once the end of the cable appears through the lever aperture, untie the string and leave it in position in the vehicle; it can then be used to draw the cable back into position on refitting.

Refitting

6 Tie the string to the end of the choke cable, then use the string to draw the cable into position through into the engine compartment. Once the cable end is fully in position, untie the string.

7 Reconnect the wiring connector (where fitted), and clip the choke lever in its facia panel aperture.

8 From within the engine compartment, ensure that the outer cable is correctly seated in the bulkhead grommet. Work along the cable, securing it in position with all the relevant retaining clips and ties, ensuring that the cable is correctly routed.

9 Slide the rubber collar and retaining clip onto the end of the cable, then engage the inner end of the cable with the carburettor linkage. Align the rubber collar with the carburettor bracket, then refit the retaining clip and securely tighten its retaining bolt. Adjust the cable as described below.

Adjustment

10 If not already done, prise out the retaining clip and remove the plastic cover (where fitted) from the carburettor.

11 Slacken the retaining clip securing the rubber collar to the outer cable. Where the crimped-type hose clip is still fitted, cut the clip and discard it; replace it with a standard worm-drive hose clip **(see illustration)**.

12 Ensuring that the choke lever is flush with the facia panel and the carburettor linkage is fully against its stop, move the outer cable in the rubber collar until the position is found where there is only a small amount of free play present in the inner cable. Hold the outer cable in this position, and securely tighten the clip securing the rubber collar to the outer cable.

13 Have an assistant operate the choke lever, and check that the choke linkage closes fully and returns smoothly to its stop. If necessary, repeat the adjustment procedure.

14 Where necessary, clip the plastic cover back into position, and refit its retaining clip.

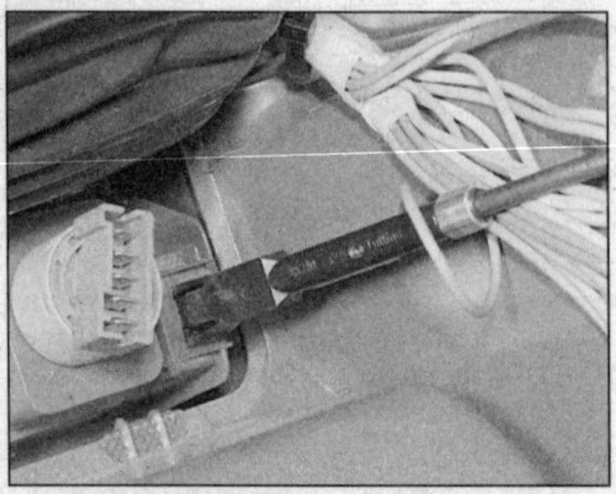

9.5a Choke cable attachment to facia panel, viewed from inside

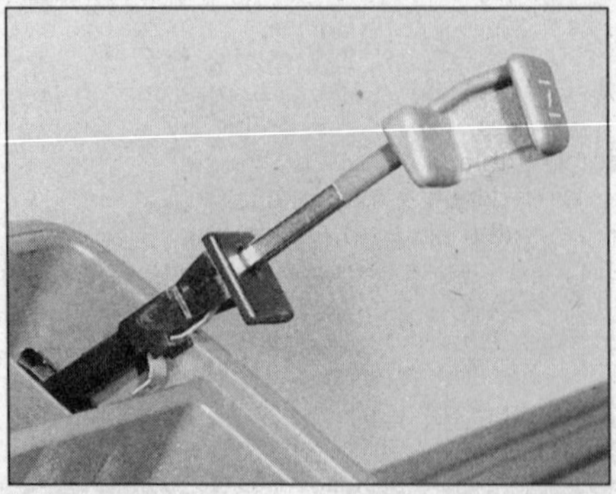

9.5b Choke cable withdrawal from facia

9.11 Cutting the original crimped-type hose clip from the choke cable rubber collar

10 Unleaded petrol - general information and usage

Note: *The information given in this Chapter is correct at the time of writing, and applies only to petrols currently available in the UK. If updated information is thought to be required, check with a Citroën dealer. If travelling abroad, consult one of the motoring organisations (or a similar authority) for advice on the petrols available and their suitability for your vehicle.*

1 The fuel recommended by Citroën is given in the Specifications at the start of this Chapter.

2 RON and MON are different testing standards; RON stands for Research Octane Number (also written as RM), whilst MON stands for Motor Octane Number (also written as MM).

11 Carburettor - general information

Weber 32 and 34 IBSH (954 cc models) and Weber 34 TLP (1360 cc models)

1 The Weber 32 and 34 IBSH and the Weber 34 TLP carburettors are of single-barrel downdraught type. The choke is manually-operated, but a vacuum-controlled choke opening (pull-down) device is fitted **(see illustrations)**.

2 The carburettor comprises three main assemblies, namely the throttle block, the main body and the top cover. The throttle block embodies the throttle plate and control linkages, and incorporates a water-heated jacket connected to the engine cooling system to provide pre-heating of the carburettor.

3 The main body incorporates the choke tube (sometimes known as the venturi or throttle barrel), the float chamber, accelerator pump and the fuel and air jets. The distributor vacuum and crankcase breather connections are made at the main body.

4 The top cover carries the choke plate, fuel inlet connection and the needle valve.

5 The cold start enrichment device comprises a strangler-type choke, which is operated manually by the driver. The choke plate is held open by a linkage when the control is pushed in; when the control is pulled out, the linkage is released, and the choke plate is closed by a spring. When the engine starts, the vacuum in the carburettor overcomes the spring tension and automatically opens the choke plate slightly (choke pull-down). Thus, once the engine is running, the mixture will be weakened by the additional air past the choke plate.

6 The accelerator pedal is connected via a cable to the carburettor linkage, and operates the throttle plate. The vacuum created in the carburettor choke tube causes fuel to be drawn from the jets, and out through the various drillings in the carburettor body. The fuel mixes with the incoming air to form a combustible mixture, the strength of which is controlled by the jet diameter.

7 When the accelerator is depressed quickly, a spring-loaded rod attached to the throttle spindle operates an accelerator pump, which provides a jet of neat fuel into the choke tube. This creates the slightly richer mixture demanded by the engine during initial acceleration, and eliminates flat spots.

8 Engine speed at tickover is adjustable by an idle speed control screw acting directly on the throttle control linkage.

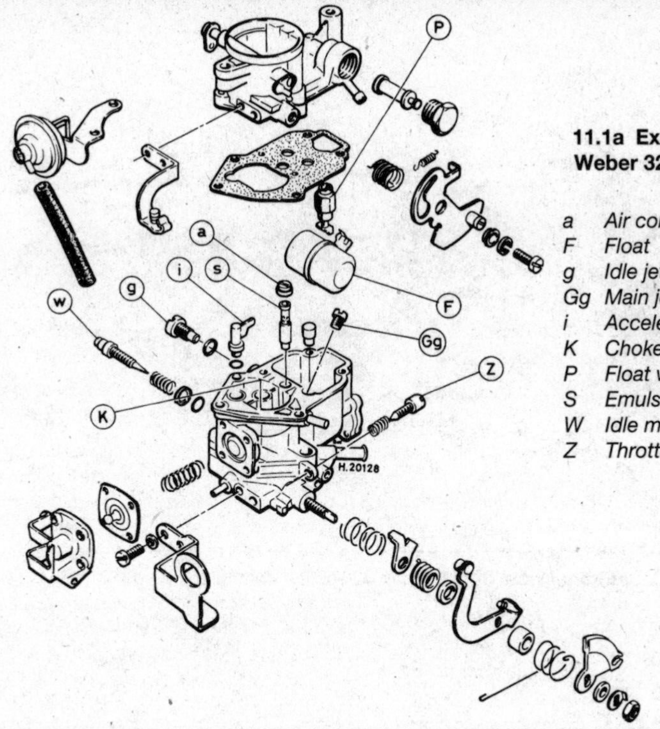

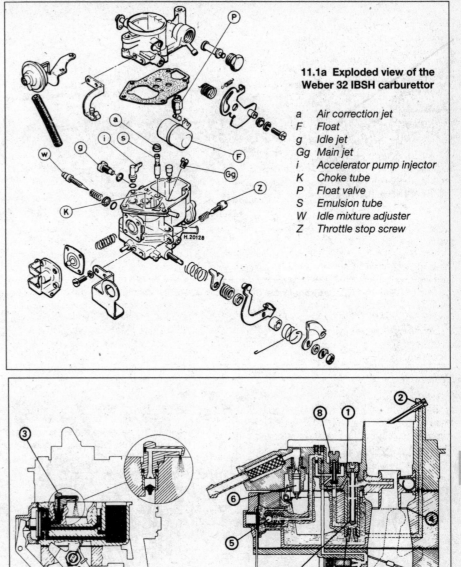

11.1a Exploded view of the Weber 32 IBSH carburettor

a Air correction jet
F Float
g Idle jet
Gg Main jet
i Accelerator pump injector
K Choke tube
P Float valve
S Emulsion tube
W Idle mixture adjuster
Z Throttle stop screw

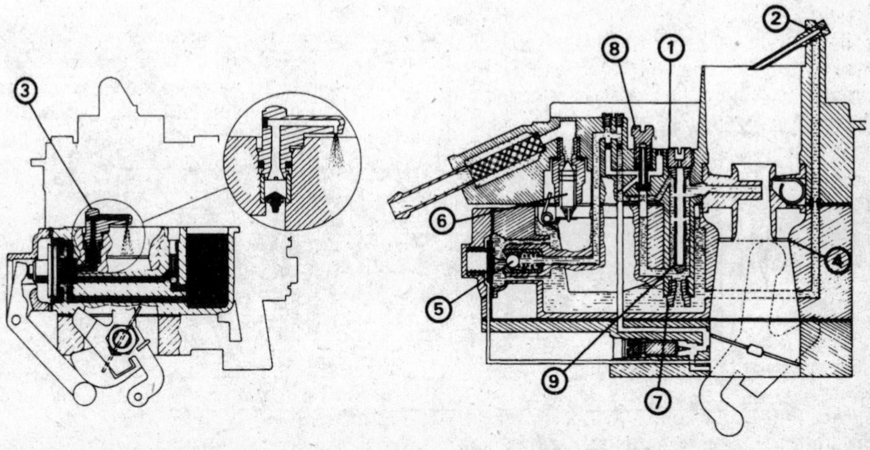

11.1b Sectional view of the Weber 34 TLP 3/100 carburettor

1 Air compensator jet
2 Fuel econostat
3 Accelerator pump injector
4 Venturi
5 Enrichener
6 Needle valve
7 Main jet
8 Idle jet
9 Emulsion tube

Solex 32 PBISA and 34 PBISA carburettors - 954, 1124 and 1360 cc models

9 The Solex PBISA carburettor is a downdraught single-venturi instrument, with a manually-controlled choke. The carburettor consists of three main components **(see illustration)**. These are the upper body, the main body and the throttle body (which contains the throttle valve assembly). An insulating block placed between the carburettor body and throttle body prevents excess heat transfer from the manifold to the main body.

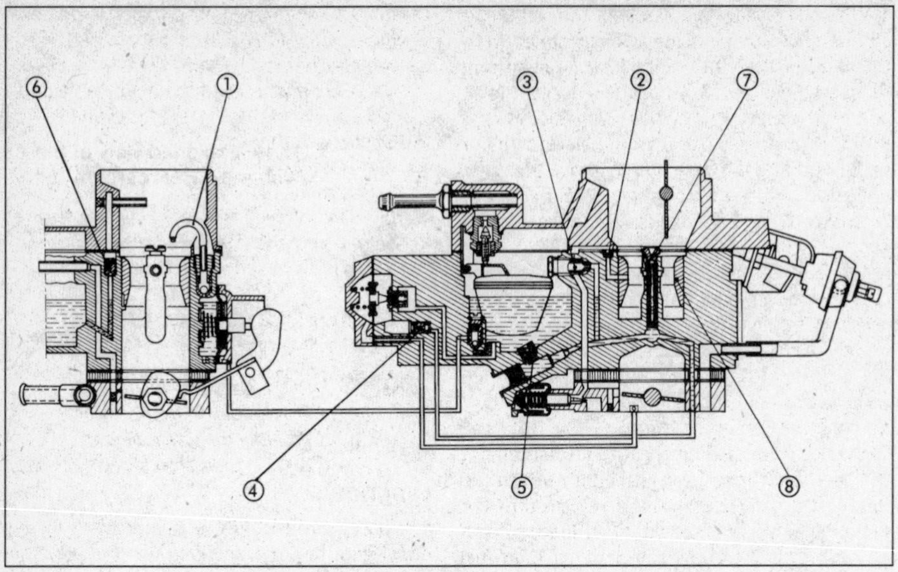

11.9 Sectional view of the Solex 32 PBISA carburettor

1 Accelerator pump tube
2 Idle air bleed
3 Idle jet
4 Enrichment jet
5 Main jet
6 Fuel econostat
7 Air correction jet
8 Venturi

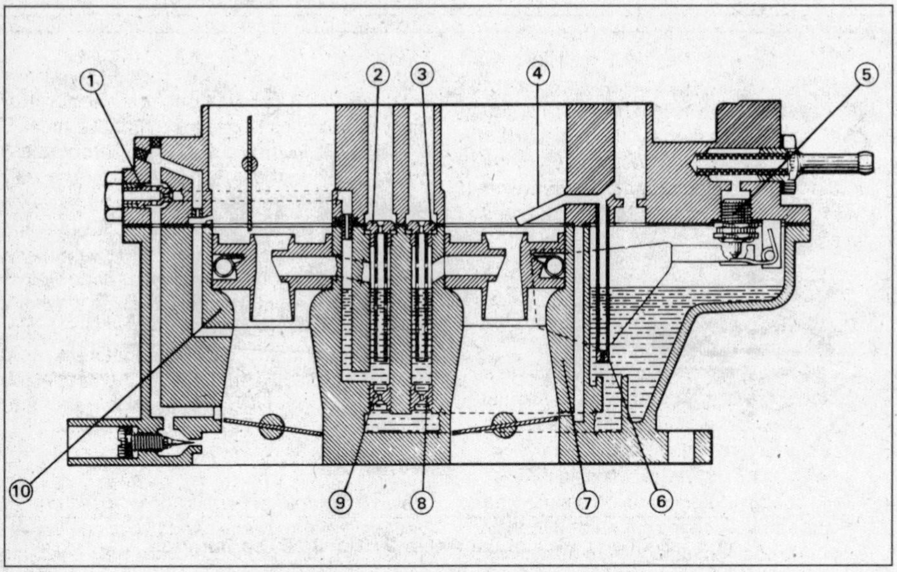

11.16 Sectional view of the Solex 32-34 Z2 carburettor

1 Idle jet
2 Primary air correction jet/emulsion tube
3 Secondary air correction jet/emulsion tube
4 Secondary fuel jet
5 Needle valve
6 Bypass jet
7 Secondary venturi
8 Secondary main jet
9 Primary main jet
10 Primary venturi

10 The throttle body contains a drilling through which the engine coolant runs. The engine coolant warms the carburettor body quickly on cold starts, improving atomisation of the fuel/air mixture, and preventing carburettor icing during warm-up.

11 During slow running and at idle, fuel sourced from the float chamber passes into the idle channel through a metered idle jet. Here it is mixed with a small amount of air from a calibrated air bleed. The resulting mixture is drawn through a channel, to be discharged from the idle orifice under the throttle valve. A tapered mixture screw is used to vary the outlet, and this ensures fine control of the idle mixture.

12 A progression slot provides extra enrichment as it is uncovered by the opening of the throttle valve during initial acceleration.

13 Under normal operating conditions, fuel is drawn through a calibrated main jet, into the base of the auxiliary venturi. An emulsion tube is placed in the auxiliary venturi, capped with an air correction jet. The fuel is mixed with air, drawn in through the holes in the emulsion tube. The resulting mixture is discharged into the main airstream via four orifices, spaced at 90° apart, in the upper part of the auxiliary venturi.

14 The carburettor is also equipped with an accelerator pump, to provide an initial spurt of extra fuel during sudden acceleration. The accelerator pump is controlled by a diaphragm, and is mechanically operated by a lever and rod which is connected to the throttle linkage.

15 The idle speed is set by an adjustable screw. The adjustable mixture screw is sealed during production with a tamperproof plug, to prevent unnecessary adjustment.

Solex 32-34 Z2 carburettor - 1360 cc models

16 The Solex 32-34 Z2 carburettor is downdraught progressive twin-venturi instrument **(see illustration)**. The throttle linkage is arranged so that the secondary throttle valve will not start to open until the primary valve is about two-thirds open; at full throttle, both valves are fully open. The choke is manually-operated.

17 An electrical heating element is fitted to the base of the carburettor. The heater warms the carburettor body quickly on cold starts, improving atomisation of the fuel/air mixture, and preventing carburettor icing during warm-up. The heater is fed directly from the ignition switch, and functions on the PTC (Positive Temperature Coefficient) principle; ie. as the heater temperature rises, so does its resistance.

18 During slow running and at idle, fuel sourced from the float chamber passes into the idle channel through a metered idle jet. Here it is mixed with a small amount of air from a calibrated air bleed. The resulting mixture is drawn through a channel, to be discharged from the idle orifice under the primary throttle plate. A tapered mixture screw is used to vary the outlet, and this ensures fine control of the idle mixture.

19 On some models, an idle cut-off valve is used to prevent run-on when the engine is switched off. The valve uses a 12-volt solenoid plunger to block the idle jet when the ignition is switched off.

20 A progression slot provides extra enrichment as it is uncovered by the opening of the throttle valve during initial acceleration.

21 Under normal operating conditions, the amount of fuel discharged into the airstream is controlled by a calibrated main jet. Fuel is drawn through the main jet, into the base of a vertical well which dips down into the fuel in the float chamber; an emulsion tube is placed in the well. The fuel is then mixed with air, drawn in through the air correction jet and through the holes in the emulsion tube. The resulting mixture is discharged from the main orifice through an auxiliary venturi.

22 The carburettor is also equipped with an accelerator pump, to provide an initial spurt of extra fuel during sudden acceleration. The accelerator pump is mechanically-operated by a lever and cam which is attached to the primary throttle linkage. During acceleration, fuel is pumped through a ball valve located in the pump injector, and is discharged into both the primary and secondary venturis. The inlet ball valve is located in a channel from the float chamber; excess fuel/air mixture is returned to the float chamber through a separate channel.

23 The idle speed is set by an adjustable screw. The adjustable mixture screw is sealed during production with a tamperproof plug to prevent unnecessary adjustment.

12 Carburettor - removal and refitting

Note: *Refer to the warning note at the end of Section 1 before proceeding.*

Removal

1 Disconnect the battery negative terminal.

2 Remove the air cleaner-to-carburettor duct as described in paragraphs 1 and 2 of Section 2.

3 Where necessary, prise out the retaining clip and remove the plastic cover to gain access to the carburettor.

12.4 Where applicable, slacken the retaining clips and disconnect the coolant hoses (arrowed) from the carburettor

4 Where applicable, slacken the retaining clips and disconnect the coolant hoses from the base of the carburettor **(see illustration)**. Plug the hose ends to minimise coolant loss, and mop up any spilt coolant immediately

5 On all models, free the accelerator inner cable from the throttle cam, then pull the outer cable out from its mounting bracket rubber grommet, along with its flat washer and spring clip.

6 Disconnect the choke inner cable from the carburettor linkage, then undo the retaining bolt and remove the retaining clamp. Position the cable clear of the carburettor.

7 Disconnect the wiring connectors from the carburettor heating element and the idle cut-off solenoid **(see illustration)**.

8 Slacken the retaining clip and disconnect the fuel feed hose from the carburettor **(see illustration)**. Place wads of rag around the union to catch any spilled fuel. Plug the hose as soon as it is disconnected, to minimise fuel loss and prevent dirt entry into the system.

9 Make a note of the correct fitted positions of all the relevant vacuum pipes and breather hoses, to ensure that they are correctly positioned on refitting, then release the retaining clips (where fitted) and disconnect them from the carburettor.

10 Unscrew the nuts and washers securing the carburettor to the inlet manifold, and remove the carburettor assembly from the car **(see illustration)**. Remove the insulating spacer and/or gasket(s), then discard the gasket(s); new ones must be used on refitting. Plug the inlet manifold aperture with a wad of clean cloth, to prevent the possible entry of foreign matter.

Refitting

11 Refitting is the reverse of the removal procedure, noting the following points:

a) Ensure that the carburettor and inlet manifold sealing faces are clean and flat. Fit a new gasket/gaskets and insulating spacer (as applicable) and securely tighten the carburettor retaining nuts.

b) Use the notes made on dismantling to ensure that all hoses are refitted to their original positions and, where necessary, are securely held by their retaining clips.

c) Where the original crimped-type hose clips where fitted, discard them and replace them with worm-drive hose clips.

d) Refit and adjust the choke cable and accelerator cables as described in Sections 7 and 9.

e) Refit the air cleaner duct as described in Section 2.

f) On completion check and, if necessary, adjust the idle speed and mixture settings as described in Chapter 1.

13 Weber 32 IBSH and Weber 34 TLP carburettors (954 cc and 1360 cc engines) - fault diagnosis, overhaul and adjustments

Diagnosis

1 If a carburettor fault is suspected, always check first that the ignition timing is accurate and the spark plugs are in good condition and correctly gapped, that the accelerator and choke cables are correctly adjusted, and that the air cleaner filter element is clean; see the relevant Sections of Chapter 1 or of this Chapter. If the engine is running very roughly, check the valve clearances and the compression pressures as described in Chapter 2A.

2 If careful checking of all of the above produces no improvement, the carburettor must be removed for cleaning and overhaul.

3 Note that in the rare event of a complete carburettor overhaul being necessary, it may prove more economical to renew the carburettor as a complete unit. Check the price and availability of a replacement carburettor and of its component parts before starting work; note that most sealing washers, screws and gaskets are available in kits, as are some of the major sub-assemblies. In most cases, it will be sufficient to dismantle the carburettor and to clean the jets and passages.

Overhaul

Note: *Refer to the warning note at the end of Section 1 before proceeding.*

4 Remove the carburettor from the vehicle as described in Section 12.

4A

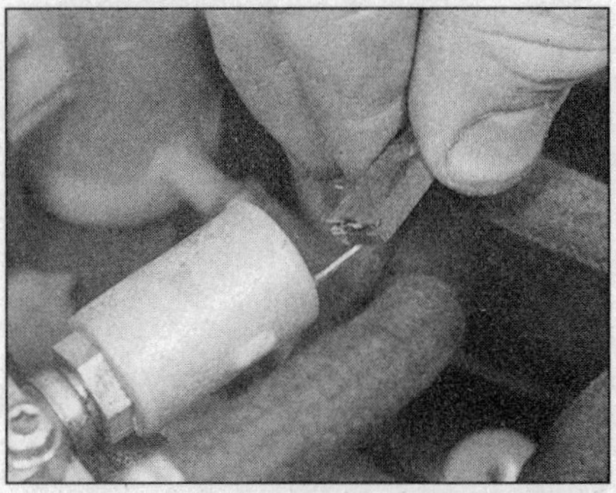

12.7 Disconnect the idle cut-off solenoid wiring connector

12.8 Carburettor fuel feed hose union

12.10 Carburettor retaining nuts (two of four arrowed on this carburettor)

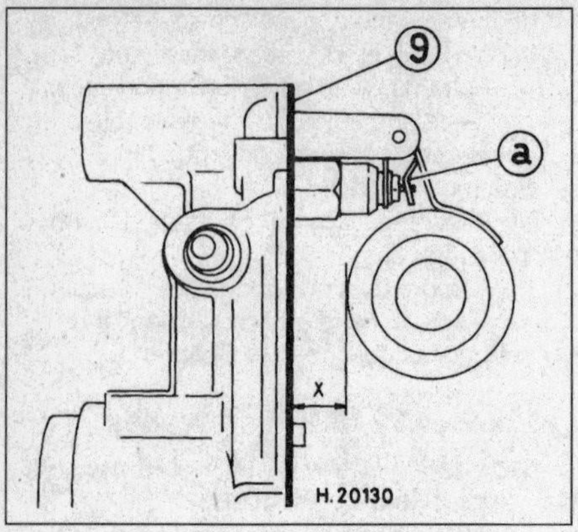

13.15a Float level adjustment check - Weber 32 IBSH carburettor

a Float arm tongue (in contact with ball)
9 Gasket (must be fitted when checking)
X 8. mm

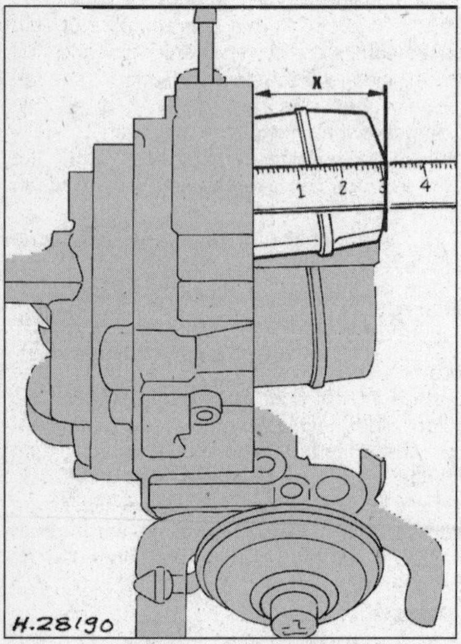

13.15b Float level adjustment check Weber 34 TLP carburettor

X Float level - refer to Specifications

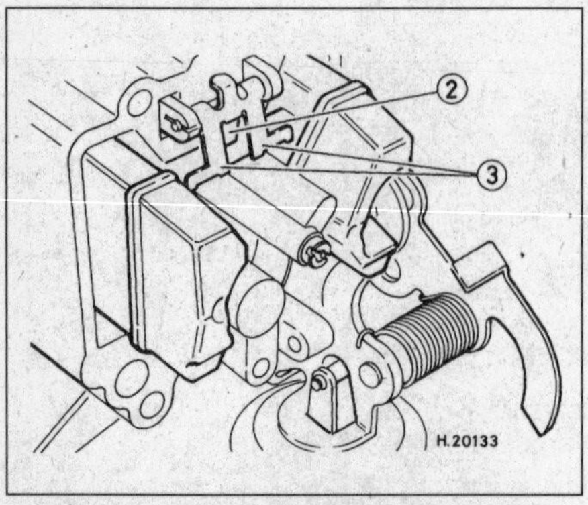

13.16 Float level adjustment is made at tongue (2) or bars (3) - Weber 34 TLP carburettor

5 Undo the retaining screws, and lift the carburettor top cover away from the main body, and the main body from the throttle body (if required).

6 The float can be removed by pushing out the hinge pin; the needle valve assembly can then be unscrewed from the cover. Unscrew the end bolt near the fuel inlet connection, and remove the gauze filter. Examine the filter for contamination and blockage. Soak the filter in petrol to clean it.

7 Carefully remove the accelerator pump valve, the main jet and the mixture adjustment screw; noting their respective fitting positions. When removing the idle jet and mixture setting adjusters, count the number of turns required to remove them, so that they can be refitted in approximately the same position, to give a provisional adjustment setting.

8 Do not disturb the choke flap and throttle butterfly valve or spindles. Their actuating mechanisms are external, and normally require no attention unless excessively worn. If the spindles in the carburettor body are worn, serious consideration should be given to renewing the complete carburettor. Such wear is an indication that the carburettor is due for renewal, and it would be false economy to refit it, even after other overhaul work is carried out. Air leaks around worn spindles make it impossible to tune the carburettor correctly, and poor performance and impaired economy will inevitably result.

9 Unscrew and remove the jets, making a note of their locations to facilitate correct refitting.

10 Clean the jets, carburettor body assemblies, float chamber and internal drillings. An air line may be used to clear the internal passages once the carburettor is fully dismantled.

Warning: If high pressure air is directed into drillings and passages where a diaphragm is fitted, the diaphragm is likely to be damaged.

HAYNES HiNT ***Aerosol cans of carburettor cleaner are widely available, and can prove very useful in helping to clear internal passages of stubborn obstructions.***

11 Use a straight edge to check all carburettor body assembly mating surfaces for distortion.

12 On reassembly, renew any worn components, and fit a complete set of new gaskets and seals. A jet kit and a gasket and seal kit are available from your Citroën dealer.

13 Reassembly is a reversal of the dismantling procedure. Ensure that all jets are securely locked in position, but take great care not to overtighten them. Ensure that all mating surfaces are clean and dry, and that all body sections are correctly assembled with their fuel and air passages correctly aligned. Prior to refitting the carburettor to the vehicle, adjust the float height setting described below. After refitting the carburettor, adjust the idle speed and mixture.

Adjustments

Idle speed and mixture

14 Refer to Chapter 1.

Float height setting

15 Check the float level with the top cover removed and held vertically on its side with the float hanging down **(see illustrations)**. The cover gasket must be fitted on the flange face of the cover. With the tongue of the float arm in light contact with the ball of the needle valve, the dimension from the bottom face of the gasket to the lower part of the float (Weber 32 IBSH) or upper part of the float (Weber 34 TLP) is the float level. The correct dimension for the various carburettor types is given in the Specifications at the start of this Chapter.

16 To adjust the float level setting, carefully bend the float arm or tongue (as applicable) as required **(see illustration)**.

14 Solex 32 PBISA carburettor (954 cc, 1124 cc and 1360 cc engines) - fault diagnosis, overhaul and adjustments

Diagnosis

1 Refer to Section 13.

Overhaul

Note: *Refer to the warning note at the end of Section 1 before proceeding.*

2 Remove the carburettor from the vehicle as described in Section 12.

3 Disconnect the vacuum hose from the choke pull-down diaphragm.

4 Disconnect the choke spring (where necessary), then undo the six screws and lift off the carburettor upper body.

5 Tap out the float pivot pin and remove the float assembly, needle valve and float chamber gasket. Check that the needle valve anti-vibration ball is free in the valve end, then examine the needle valve tip and seat for wear or damage. Examine the float assembly and pivot pin for signs of wear and damage. The float assembly must be renewed if it appears to be leaking.

6 Unscrew the fuel inlet union, and inspect the fuel filter. Clean the filter housing of debris and dirt, and renew the filter if it is blocked.

7 Undo the screws, then detach the accelerator pump cover and remove the pump diaphragm and spring, noting which way around they are fitted. Examine the diaphragm for signs of damage and deterioration, and renew if necessary.

8 Unscrew the idle jet from the main body.

9 Unscrew the main jet from the float chamber. Note that it may be necessary to remove a plug in the float chamber body to expose an opening through which the main jet can be withdrawn.

10 Remove the combined air correction jet and emulsion tube from the auxiliary venturi.

11 Remove the two screws, then separate the carburettor main body and throttle body assemblies, and recover the insulating spacer. Examine the throttle valve spindle and throttle bore for signs of wear or damage and, if necessary, renew the throttle body assembly.

12 Remove the idle mixture adjustment screw tamperproof cap. Screw the screw in until it seats lightly, counting the **exact** number of turns required to do this, then unscrew and remove it. When refitting, turn the screw in until it seats lightly, then back the screw off by the number of turns noted on removal, to return the screw to its original location.

13 Clean the jets, carburettor body assemblies, float chamber and internal drillings. An air line may be used to clear the internal passages once the carburettor is fully dismantled.

HAYNES HiNT *Aerosol cans of carburettor cleaner are widely available, and can prove very useful in helping to clear internal passages of stubborn obstructions.*

Warning: If high pressure air is directed into drillings and passages were a diaphragm is fitted, the diaphragm is likely to be damaged.

14 Use a straight edge to check all carburettor body assembly mating surfaces for distortion.

15 On reassembly, renew any worn components, and fit a complete set of new gaskets and seals. A jet kit and a gasket and seal kit are available from your Citroën dealer.

16 Reassembly is a reversal of the dismantling procedure. Ensure that all jets are securely locked in position, but take great care not to overtighten them. Ensure that all mating surfaces are clean and dry, and that all body sections are correctly assembled with their fuel and air passages correctly aligned. Prior to refitting the carburettor to the vehicle, set the throttle valve fast idle and choke pull-down settings as described below.

Adjustments

Idle speed and mixture

17 Refer to Chapter 1.

Float height setting

18 To accurately check the float height setting, a special float height checking gauge is required. Therefore, this task must be entrusted to a Citroën dealer. As a guide, with the carburettor body inverted, so that the float is at the top and the needle valve is depressed, the distance between the upper edge of the float and the sealing face of the upper body (with its gasket fitted) should be approximately 38 mm. To adjust the float height setting, **carefully** bend the pivot arm.

Throttle valve fast idle setting

19 Invert the carburettor, and operate the carburettor choke linkage to fully close the choke valve. The fast idle screw will butt against the fast idle cam, and force the open the throttle valve slightly.

20 Using the shank of a suitable twist drill, measure the clearance between the edge of the throttle valve and bore, and compare this to the clearance given in the Specifications. If necessary, adjust by turning the fast idle adjustment screw in the appropriate direction until the specified clearance is obtained **(see illustration)**.

Choke pull-down setting

21 Operate the carburettor choke linkage to fully close the choke valve; hold the linkage in this position.

22 Attach a hand-held vacuum pump to the choke pull-down diaphragm, and apply a vacuum to the diaphragm so that the diaphragm rod is pulled fully into the diaphragm body. In the absence of a vacuum pump, the rod can be pushed into the diaphragm using a small screwdriver.

23 With the rod fully retracted, use the shank of a suitable twist drill to measure the clearance between the edge of the choke valve and bore, and compare this to the clearance given in the Specifications **(see illustration)**. If necessary, remove the plug from the diaphragm cover, and adjust by turning the adjustment screw. Once the pull-down setting is correctly adjusted, refit the plug to the diaphragm cover, and remove the vacuum pump (where fitted).

15 Solex 32-34 Z2 carburettor (1360 cc engines) - fault diagnosis, overhaul and adjustments

Diagnosis

1 Refer to Section 13.

Overhaul

Note: *Refer to the warning note at the end of Section 1 before proceeding.*

2 Remove the carburettor from the vehicle as described in Section 12.

3 Unscrew the idle cut-off solenoid from the carburettor body, and remove it along with its plunger and spring. To test the solenoid, connect a 12-volt battery to it (positive terminal to the solenoid terminal, negative terminal to the solenoid body) and check that the plunger is retracted fully into the body. Disconnect the battery, and check that the plunger is pushed out by spring pressure. If the valve does not perform as expected, and cleaning does not improve the situation, the solenoid valve must be renewed.

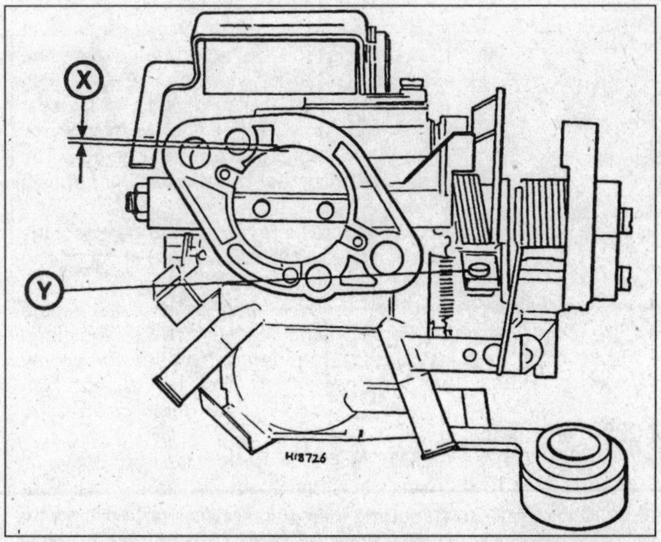

14.20 Throttle valve fast idle setting - Solex 32 PBISA carburettor

Adjust screw Y until clearance X is as given in the Specifications

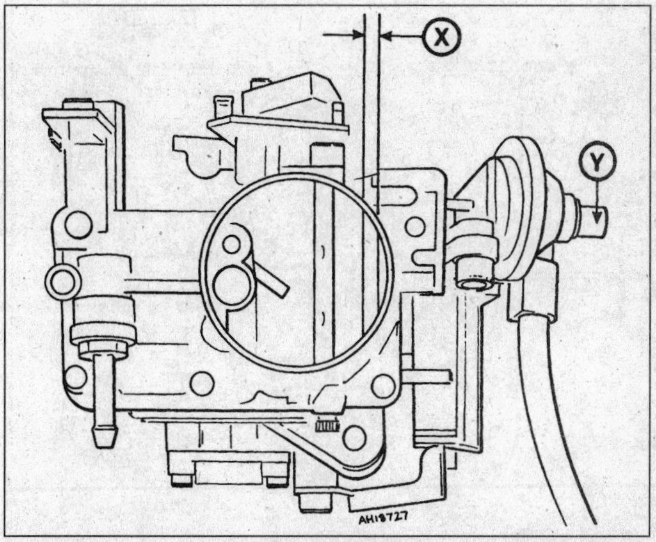

14.23 Choke pull-down setting - Solex 32 PBISA carburettor

Adjust screw Y until clearance X is as given in the Specifications

4 Remove the five screws, and lift off the carburettor upper body.
5 Tap out the float pivot pin, and remove the float assembly, needle valve and float chamber gasket. Check that the needle valve anti-vibration ball is free in the valve end, then examine the needle valve tip and seat for wear or damage. Examine the float assembly and pivot pin for signs of wear and damage. The float assembly must be renewed if it appears to be leaking.
6 Unscrew the fuel inlet union, and inspect the fuel filter. Clean the filter housing of debris and dirt, and renew the filter if it is blocked.
7 Undo the four screws, then detach the accelerator pump cover and remove the pump diaphragm and spring, noting which way round they are fitted. Examine the diaphragm for signs of damage and deterioration, and renew if necessary. Remove the choke pull-down diaphragm and part-load enrichment diaphragms, and examine them in the same way.
8 Unscrew the idle jet from the upper body.
9 Unscrew both the primary and secondary combined air correction jets and emulsion tubes.
10 Using a long thin screwdriver, unscrew the main jets from the bottom of the emulsion tube drillings. Invert the carburettor, and catch the jets as they fall out of the drillings.
11 Remove the idle mixture adjustment screw tamperproof cap. Screw the screw in until it seats lightly, counting the **exact** number of turns required to do this, then unscrew it. On refitting, screw the screw in until it seats lightly, then back the screw off by the number of turns noted on removal, to return the screw to its original location.
12 Examine the carburettor components as described in paragraphs 10 to 13 of Section 13.
13 To test the carburettor heating element, connect a multimeter, set to the resistance function, between the heater wiring terminal and the carburettor body. A resistance reading of approximately 0.25 to 0.5 ohms should be obtained. If an open-circuit is present, or an extremely high resistance reading is obtained, it is likely that the heating element is faulty. To remove the element, undo the retaining screw and plate, then slide out the element, noting the correct locations of the insulators positioned on each side of the element.
14 Reassembly is a reversal of the dismantling procedure. Ensure that all jets are securely locked in position, but take great care not to overtighten them. Ensure that all mating surfaces are clean and dry, and that all body sections are correctly assembled with their fuel and air passages correctly aligned. If the heating element has been disturbed, ensure that the insulators are correctly fitted so that the element is in no danger of contacting the carburettor body. Prior to refitting the carburettor to the vehicle, adjust the float height, throttle valve fast idle and choke pull-down settings as described below.

Adjustments

Idle speed and mixture

15 Refer to Chapter 1.

Float height setting

16 To accurately check the float height setting, a special float height checking gauge is required. Therefore, this task must be entrusted to a Citroën dealer. As a guide, with the carburettor body inverted, so that the float is at the top and the needle valve is depressed, the distance between the upper edge of the float and the sealing face of the upper body (with its gasket fitted) should be approximately 35 mm.
17 If necessary, the float height can be adjusted by **carefully** bending the small tang on the float arm which contacts the needle valve.

Throttle valve fast idle setting

18 Invert the carburettor, and pull the carburettor choke linkage to fully close the choke valve. The fast idle screw will butt against the fast idle cam, and force open the throttle valve slightly.
19 Using the shank of a suitable twist drill, measure the clearance between the edge of the throttle valve and bore, and compare this to the clearance given in the Specifications at the start of this Chapter. If necessary, adjust by turning the fast idle adjustment screw in the appropriate direction until the specified clearance is obtained **(see illustration)**.

Choke pull-down setting

20 Pull the carburettor choke linkage to fully close the choke valve; hold the linkage in this position.
21 Attach a hand-held vacuum pump to the choke pull-down diaphragm, and apply a vacuum to the diaphragm so that the diaphragm rod is pulled fully into the diaphragm body. In the absence of a vacuum pump, the rod can be pushed into the diaphragm with a small screwdriver.
22 With the rod fully retracted, use the shank of a suitable twist drill to measure the clearance between the edge of the choke valve and bore, and compare this to the clearance given in the Specifications **(see illustration)**. If necessary, remove the plug from the diaphragm cover, and adjust by turning the adjustment screw. Once the pull-down setting is correctly adjusted, refit the plug to the diaphragm cover, and remove the vacuum pump (where fitted).

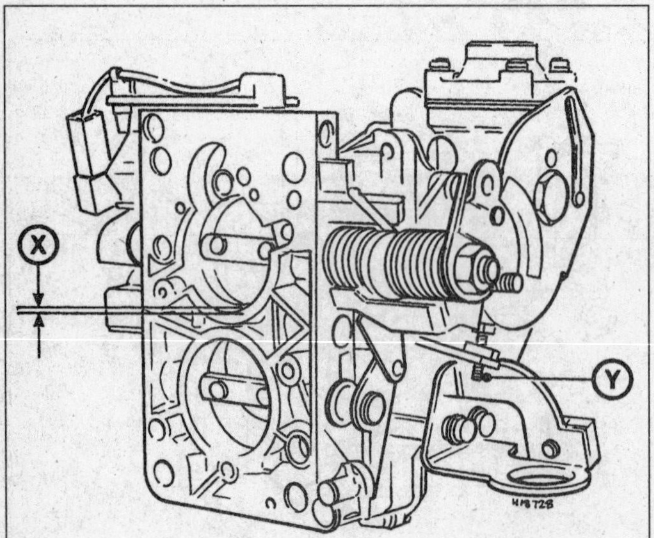

15.19 Throttle valve fast idle setting - Solex 32-34 Z2 carburettor
Adjust screw Y until clearance X is as given in the Specifications

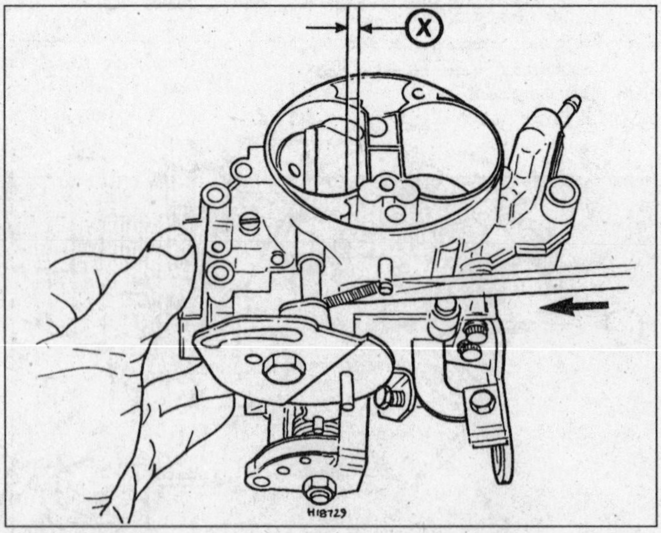

15.22 Choke pull-down setting (using a screwdriver to retract the diaphragm rod) - Solex 32-34 Z2 carburettor
Adjust as described in text until clearance X is as given in the Specifications

16 Inlet manifold - removal and refitting

Note: *Refer to the warning note at the end of Section 1 before proceeding.*

Removal

1 Remove the carburettor as described in Section 12.

2 Drain the cooling system as described in Chapter 1.

3 Where necessary, undo the bolt(s) securing the anti-percolation chamber mounting bracket to the manifold **(see illustration)**. Position the chamber clear of the manifold, so that it does not hinder removal.

4 Slacken the retaining clips, and disconnect the vacuum servo unit hose from the left-hand side of the manifold, and the coolant hose from the base of the manifold.

5 Make a final check that all the necessary vacuum/breather hoses have been disconnected from the manifold.

6 Unscrew the six retaining nuts **(see illustration)**, then manoeuvre the manifold away from the head and out of the engine compartment. Note that there is no manifold gasket.

Refitting

7 Refitting is the reverse of the removal procedure, noting the following points:

a) Ensure that the manifold and cylinder head mating surfaces are clean and dry, and apply a thin coating of suitable sealing compound to the manifold mating surface. Install the manifold, and tighten its retaining nuts to the specified torque setting.

b) Ensure that all relevant hoses are reconnected to their original positions, and are securely held (where necessary) by their retaining clips.

c) Refit the carburettor as described in Section 12.

d) On completion, refill the cooling system as described in Chapter 1.

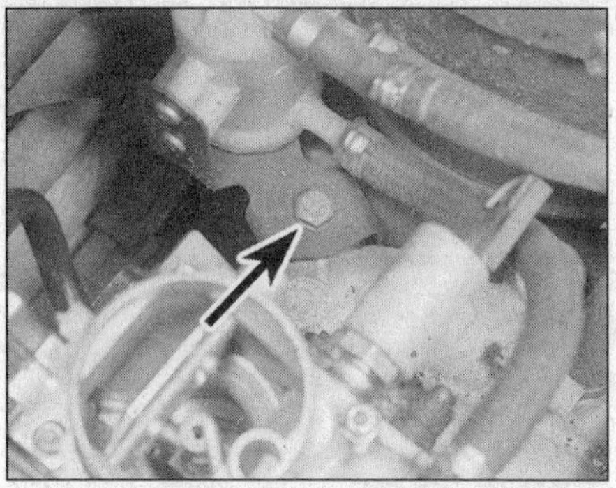

16.3 Anti-percolation chamber retaining bolt (arrowed)

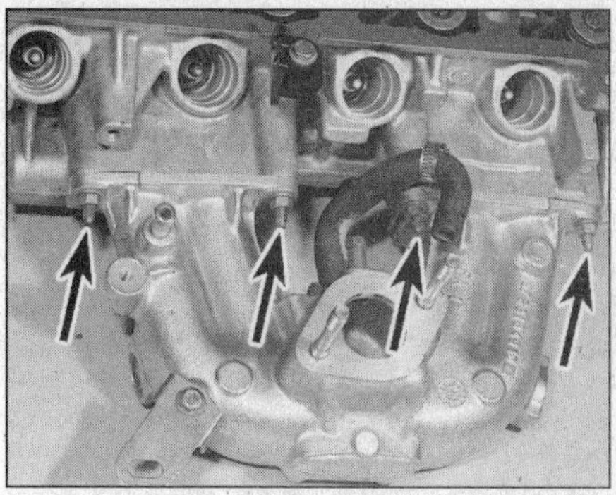

16.6 Inlet manifold and upper retaining nuts (arrowed)

17 Exhaust manifold - removal and refitting

Removal

1 Disconnect the hot-air intake hose from the manifold shroud, and remove it from the vehicle **(see illustration)**.

2 Slacken and remove the retaining screws, and remove the shroud from the top of the exhaust manifold **(see illustration)**.

3 Firmly apply the handbrake, then jack up the front of the vehicle and support it on axle stands.

4 Undo the nuts securing the exhaust front pipe to the manifold, then free the front pipe and recover the gasket. Note that on some models it may be necessary to remove the bolt securing the front pipe to its mounting bracket in order to disconnect the exhaust.

5 Undo the eight retaining nuts securing the manifold to the head **(see illustration)**. Manoeuvre the manifold out of the engine compartment, and discard the manifold gaskets.

Refitting

6 Refitting is the reverse of the removal procedure, noting the following points:

a) Examine all the exhaust manifold studs for signs of damage and corrosion; remove all traces of corrosion, and repair or renew any damaged studs.

b) Ensure that the manifold and cylinder head sealing faces are clean and flat, and fit the new manifold gaskets. Tighten the manifold retaining nuts to the specified torque.

c) Reconnect the front pipe to the manifold using the information given in Section 18.

18 Exhaust system - general information and component renewal

General information

1 On 954 cc models, the exhaust system consists of two sections; the front pipe and a tailpipe. The front pipe is secured to the manifold flange by nuts, and to the silencer by a split clamping ring.

2 On 1124 cc models manufactured before July 1990, the exhaust system consists of two sections as for the 954 cc models. After this date, a three-piece exhaust system is fitted. With this system, the front pipe is divided into two sections, connected with a split clamping ring.

3 On early 1360 cc models, the exhaust system consists of three sections as described

4A

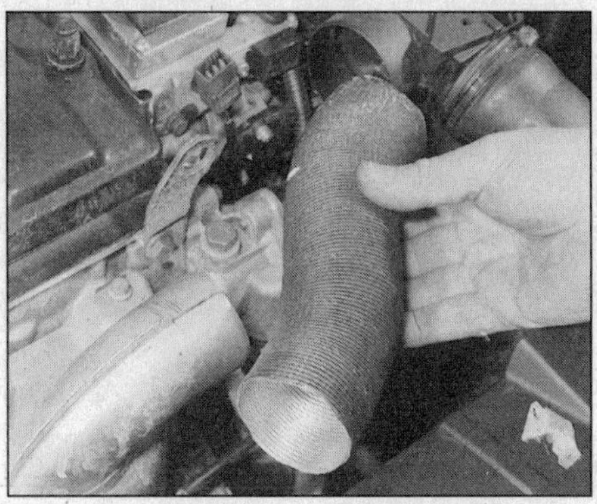

17.1 Remove the hot-air intake hose . . .

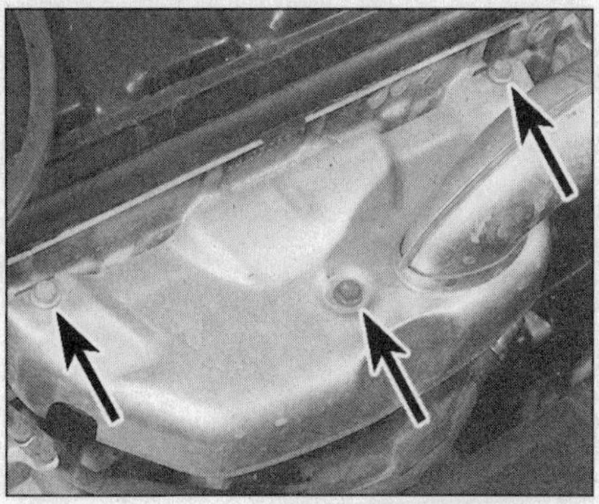

17.2 . . . then undo the three retaining bolts (arrowed) and remove the exhaust manifold shroud

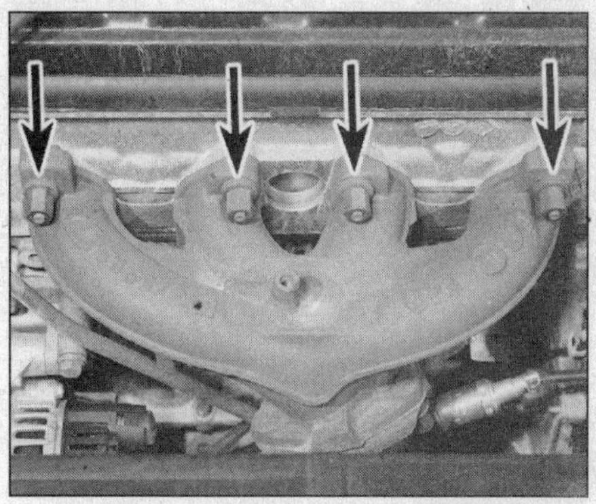

17.5 The exhaust manifold is retained by eight nuts (upper four arrowed)

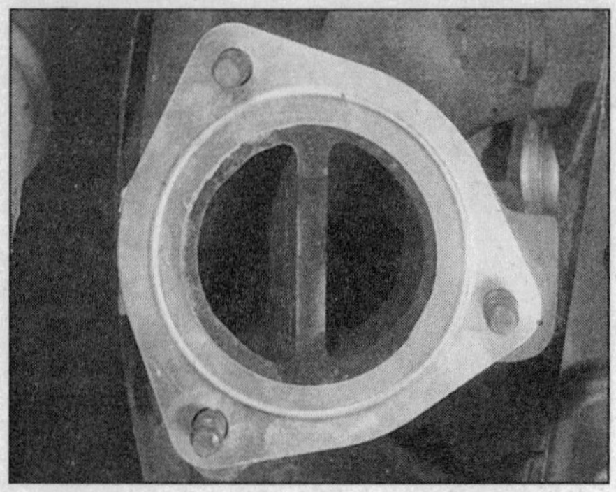

18.7 Exhaust manifold downpipe flange and gasket

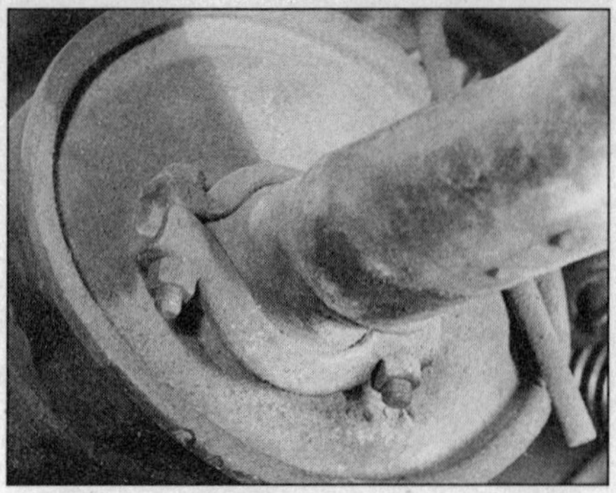

18.10 The intermediate pipe-to-tailpipe clamping ring

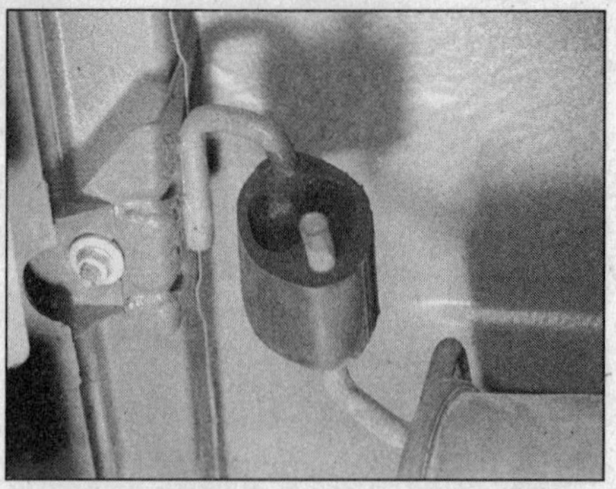

18.13 Exhaust system mounting rubber

for the later 1124 cc model. On later models, the intermediate section is replaced with an additional silencer (damper). The front end of this silencer is connected to the front pipe by a flanged joint, incorporating a metal ring and spring-tensioned bolts.

4 The system is suspended throughout its entire length by rubber mountings.

Removal

5 Each exhaust section can be removed individually or, alternatively, the complete system can be removed as a unit.

6 To remove the system or part of the system, first jack up the front or rear of the car, and support it on axle stands. Alternatively, position the car over an inspection pit, or on car ramps.

Front pipe

7 Undo the nuts securing the front pipe flange joint to the manifold, then separate the flange joint and collect the gasket **(see illustration)**. Where necessary, also unscrew the bolt securing the front pipe to its mounting bracket.

8 Disconnect the front pipe from the tailpipe or intermediate section by unscrewing the clamp bolts. Recover the tension springs (and, where necessary, the sealing ring). Manoeuvre the front pipe out from underneath the vehicle.

Intermediate pipe

9 Undo the bolts securing the front pipe flange joint to the intermediate pipe. Recover the tension springs and sealing ring.

10 Slacken the intermediate pipe-to-tailpipe clamping ring bolts, and disengage the clamp from the flange joint **(see illustration)**.

11 Free the intermediate pipe from its mounting rubbers, then withdraw it from underneath the vehicle.

Tailpipe

12 Slacken the intermediate pipe-to-tailpipe clamping ring bolt(s), and disengage the clamp from the flange joint.

13 Unhook the tailpipe from its mounting rubbers, and remove it from the vehicle **(see illustration)**.

Complete system

14 Disconnect the front pipe from the manifold as described previously.

15 On all models, with the aid of an assistant, free the system from all its mounting rubbers and manoeuvre it out from underneath the vehicle.

Heat shield(s)

16 The heat shields (where fitted) are secured to the underside of the body by a mixture of nuts and bolts. Each shield can be removed once the relevant exhaust section has been removed.

Refitting

17 Each section is refitted by a reverse of the removal sequence, noting the following points:

HAYNES HiNT ***If the heat shield is being removed to gain access to a component located behind it, it may prove sufficient to simply remove the fasteners and lower the shield, without disturbing the exhaust system.***

a) Ensure that all traces of corrosion have been removed from the flanges, and renew all necessary gaskets.
b) Inspect the rubber mountings for signs of damage or deterioration, and renew as necessary.
c) Prior to assembling the front pipe-to-intermediate pipe flanged joint, a smear of high-temperature grease should be applied to the joint mating surfaces.
d) In the case of the front pipe/intermediate pipe-to-tailpipe joint, apply a smear of exhaust system jointing paste to the flange joint, to ensure a gastight seal. Tighten the clamping ring nuts evenly and progressively to the specified torque, so that the clearance between the clamp halves remains equal on either side.
e) Prior to tightening the exhaust system fasteners, ensure that all rubber mountings are correctly located, and that there is adequate clearance between the exhaust system and vehicle underbody.

Chapter 4 Part B: Fuel/exhaust systems - single-point petrol injection models

Contents

Degrees of difficulty

Easy, suitable for novice with little experience	**Fairly easy,** suitable for beginner with some experience	**Fairly difficult,** suitable for competent DIY mechanic	**Difficult,** suitable for experienced DIY mechanic	**Very difficult,** suitable for expert DIY or professional

Specifications

System type

954 cc (CDY and CDZ engine) models	Bosch Monopoint MA3.0
1124 cc (HDY and HDZ engine) models:	
Pre-July 1992	Bosch Monopoint A2.2
July 1992 to July 1994	Magneti Marelli G6
July 1994 onwards	Bosch Monopoint A2.2 or MA3.0
1360 cc models:	
KDY and KDZ engines	Bosch Monopoint A2.2
KDX engine	Bosch Monopoint MA3.0

Note: *Refer to Chapter 2A for further information on engine code identification.*

Fuel system data

Fuel pump type	Electric, immersed in tank
Fuel pump regulated constant pressure (approximate):	
Bosch system	1.0 bar (approx)
Magneti Marelli system	0.8 ± 0.1 bars
Specified idle speed (not adjustable)	850 ± 50 rpm (controlled by ECU)
Idle mixture CO content (not adjustable*)	Less than 1.0 % (controlled by ECU)

**On the Magneti Marelli system, idle mixture adjustment is possible, but only using special electronic equipment - see Chapter 1.*

Recommended fuel

Minimum octane rating	95 RON unleaded (Premium unleaded) **only**

Torque wrench settings

Torque wrench settings	Nm	lbf ft
Inlet manifold retaining nuts	8	6
Exhaust manifold retaining nuts	15	11
Exhaust system fasteners:		
Front pipe-to-manifold nut	35	26
Front pipe-to-intermediate pipe/catalytic converter nuts	10	7
Clamping ring nuts	15	11

1 General information and precautions

1 The fuel system consists of a fuel tank mounted under the rear of the car with an electric fuel pump immersed in it, a fuel filter, fuel feed and return lines, the throttle body assembly (which incorporates the single fuel injector and the fuel pressure regulator), as well as the Electronic Control Unit (ECU) and the various sensors, electrical components and related wiring.
2 The air cleaner contains a disposable paper filter element. It incorporates a flap valve air temperature control system, which allows cold air from the outside of the car and warm air from the exhaust manifold to enter the air cleaner in the correct proportions.
3 Refer to Section 7 for further information on the operation of each relevant fuel injection system, and to Section 18 for information on the exhaust system. Throughout this Part of Chapter 4, it is also occasionally necessary to identify vehicles by their engine codes rather than engine capacity. Refer to Part A of Chapter 2 for further information on engine code identification.

Warning: Many of the procedures in this Chapter require the removal of fuel lines and connections, which may result in some fuel spillage. Before carrying out any operation on the fuel system, refer to the precautions given in "Safety first!" at the beginning of this manual, and follow them implicitly. Petrol is a highly-dangerous and volatile liquid, and the precautions necessary when handling it cannot be overstressed.

Note: *Residual pressure will remain in the fuel lines long after the vehicle was last used. Before disconnecting any fuel line, depressurise the fuel system as described in Section 8.*

2 Air cleaner assembly - removal and refitting

1 Refer to Chapter 4A, Section 2, substituting "throttle body" for all references to the carburettor. The accompanying photos show the air cleaner-to-throttle body duct attachment at the throttle body end **(see illustrations)**.

3 Air cleaner air temperature control system - general information and component renewal

1 Refer to Chapter 4A, Section 3, substituting "throttle body" for all references to the carburettor.

2.1a Undo the retaining nuts . . .

2.1b . . . then detach the duct from the throttle body, and recover the sealing ring

4 Accelerator cable - removal, refitting and adjustment

Removal and refitting

1 Refer to Chapter 4A; Section 7, substituting "throttle body" for all references to the carburettor. Adjust the cable as described below.

Adjustment

2 Remove the spring clip from the accelerator outer cable then, ensuring that the throttle cam is fully against its stop, gently pull the cable out of its grommet until all free play is removed from the inner cable.
3 With the cable held in this position, ensure the flat washer is pressed securely against the grommet, then fit the spring clip to the third outer cable groove visible in front of the rubber grommet and washer **(see illustration)**. This will leave a fair amount of free play in the inner cable, which is necessary to ensure correct operation of the idle control stepper motor (see Section 7).
4 Have an assistant depress the accelerator pedal, and check that the throttle cam opens fully and returns smoothly to its stop.

4.3 Adjust the accelerator cable as described in text

5 Accelerator pedal - removal and refitting

Refer to Chapter 4A, Section 8.

6 Unleaded petrol - general information and usage

Note: *The information given in this Chapter is correct at the time of writing, and applies only to petrols currently available in the UK. If updated information is thought to be required, check with a Citroën dealer. If travelling abroad, consult one of the motoring organisations (or a similar authority) for advice on the petrols available and their suitability for your vehicle.*
1 The fuel recommended by Citroën is given in the Specifications at the start of this Chapter, followed by the equivalent petrol currently on sale in the UK.
2 RON and MON are different testing standards; RON stands for Research Octane Number (also written as RM), while MON stands for Motor Octane Number (also written as MM).
3 All Citroën AX single-point injection models are designed to run on fuel with a minimum octane rating of 95 (RON). All models are equipped with catalytic converters, and therefore must be run on unleaded fuel **only**. **Under no circumstances** should leaded fuel be used, or the catalytic converter may be damaged.

7 Fuel injection systems - general information

Bosch Monopoint A2.2 system - early 1124 and 1360 cc models

1 The Bosch Monopoint A2.2 fuel injection system is fitted to all early (pre-July 1992) 1124 cc fuel-injected models, and to early fuel-injected 1360 cc (KDY and KDZ engines) models. The system incorporates a closed-loop catalytic converter and an evaporative emission control system, and complies to the very latest emission control standards. Note that the ignition is not controlled by this system. The system operates as follows.
2 The fuel pump, immersed in the fuel tank, pumps fuel from the fuel tank to the fuel injector, via a filter mounted underneath the rear of the vehicle. Fuel supply pressure is

controlled by the pressure regulator in the throttle body assembly, which lifts to allow excess fuel to return to the tank when the optimum operating pressure of the fuel system is exceeded.

3 The electrical control system consists of the ECU, along with the following sensors and idle control regulator:

a) Throttle potentiometer - informs the ECU of the throttle valve position.
b) Coolant temperature sensor - informs the ECU of engine temperature.
c) Intake air temperature sensor - informs the ECU of the temperature of the air passing through the throttle body.
d) Lambda sensor - informs the ECU of the oxygen content of the exhaust gases (explained in Chapter 4E).
e) Idle control regulator - when the throttle is at the idle position, the ECU compares the engine idle speed with the idle speed stored in its memory. The idle control regulator is then activated by the ECU until the engine idle speed is correct.
f) Ignition coil - ECU monitors the pulses in the coil low tension (LT) circuit to determine the engine speed.

4 All the above signals are compared by the ECU and, based on this information, the ECU selects the response appropriate to those values, and controls the fuel injector (varying its pulse width - the length of time the injector is held open - to provide a richer or weaker mixture, as appropriate). The mixture and idle speed are constantly varied by the ECU, to provide the best settings for cranking, starting (with either a hot or cold engine) and engine warm-up, idle, cruising and acceleration.

5 The ECU also has full control over the engine idle speed, via a stepper motor which is fitted to the throttle body. The motor pushrod rests against a cam on the throttle valve spindle. When the throttle valve is closed (accelerator pedal released), the ECU uses the motor to vary the opening of the throttle valve, and so control the idle speed.

6 The ECU also controls the exhaust and evaporative emission control systems, which are described in detail in Part E of this Chapter.

7 If there is an abnormality in any of the readings obtained from either the coolant temperature sensor, the intake air temperature sensor or the lambda sensor, the ECU enters its back-up mode. If this happens, it ignores the sensor signal, and assumes a pre-programmed value which will allow the engine to continue running, albeit at reduced efficiency. If the ECU enters this back-up mode, the warning light on the instrument panel will come on, and the relevant fault code will be stored in the ECU memory.

8 If the warning light comes on, the vehicle should be taken to a Citroën dealer at the earliest opportunity. Once there, a complete test of the engine management system can be carried out, using a special electronic diagnostic test unit which is simply plugged into the system's diagnostic connector.

Bosch Monopoint MA3.0 system - 954 cc and later 1360 cc models

9 The Bosch Monopoint MA3.0 engine management (fuel injection/ignition) system is fitted to all 954 cc (CDY and CDZ engine) models, and also to later 1360 cc (KDX engine) models. The system differs from the earlier A2.2 system in that it is an engine management system, controlling both the fuel injection system and ignition system, rather than purely a fuel injection system. Refer to Chapter 5B for information on the ignition side of the system.

10 The fuel injection side of the system is very similar to the A2.2 system described above, with the following differences.

11 On 954 cc models, a crankshaft sensor is also fitted to the engine, to inform the ECU of engine speed and crankshaft position. The crankshaft sensor is needed since the ECU also controls the ignition side of the system, and cannot use the ignition low tension (LT) circuit to calculate engine speed. The sensor works in conjunction with a segmented ring fixed to the flywheel. The ring has a total of 60 teeth, which are equally spaced at intervals of 6°. Of these 60 teeth, 2 adjacent teeth are removed to leave a gap of 18°. The ECU uses the gap to establish where TDC is, and calculates engine speed from the frequency of teeth passing the crankshaft sensor.

12 On 1360 cc models, a crankshaft sensor and a vehicle speed sensor are incorporated into the system. The vehicle speed sensor is fitted to the transmission, and informs the ECU of the actual speed of the vehicle. The crankshaft sensor functions as described above in paragraph 11.

Magneti Marelli G6 system - later 1124 cc models

13 On later (July 1992-on) 1124 cc models, a Magneti Marelli G6 engine management (fuel injection/ignition) system is fitted.

14 The fuel injection side of the system operates as follows. Refer to Chapter 5B for information on the ignition side of the system.

15 The fuel pump, immersed in the fuel tank, pumps fuel from the fuel tank to the fuel injector via a filter. Fuel supply pressure is controlled by the pressure regulator in the throttle body assembly, which lifts to allow excess fuel to return to the tank when the optimum operating pressure of the fuel system is exceeded. To reduce emissions and to improve driveability when the engine is cold, an electrical heating element is fitted to the throttle body, to quickly warm it up on cold starts.

16 The electrical control system consists of the ECU, along with the following sensors:

a) Manifold absolute pressure (MAP) sensor - informs the ECU of load on engine.
b) Crankshaft sensor - informs the ECU of crankshaft position and engine speed.
c) Throttle potentiometer - informs the ECU of the throttle valve position.
d) Coolant temperature sensor - informs the ECU of engine temperature.
e) Intake air temperature sensor - informs the ECU of the temperature of the air passing through the throttle body.
f) Lambda (oxygen) sensor - informs the ECU of the oxygen content of the exhaust gases (explained in greater detail in Part E of this Chapter).

17 In addition, the ECU senses battery voltage (adjusting the injector pulse width to suit, and using the stepper motor to increase the idle speed and, therefore, the alternator output if it is too low). The ECU has short-circuit protection and diagnostic capabilities, and can both receive and transmit information via the engine management circuit diagnostic connector, thus permitting engine diagnosis and tuning by special diagnostic equipment.

18 All the above signals are compared by the ECU, using digital techniques, with set values pre-programmed (mapped) into its memory. Based on this information, the ECU selects the response appropriate to those values, and controls the ignition system (see Chapter 5B) and the fuel injector (varying its pulse width - the length of time the injector is held open - to provide a richer or weaker mixture, as appropriate). The mixture, idle speed and ignition timing are constantly varied by the ECU, to provide the best settings for cranking, starting (with either a hot or cold engine), warm-up, idle, cruising and acceleration.

19 The ECU regulates the engine idle speed via a stepper motor which is fitted to the throttle body. The motor has a pushrod which controls the opening of an air passage which bypasses the throttle valve. When the throttle valve is closed, the ECU controls the movement of the motor pushrod, which regulates the amount of air which flows through the throttle body passage, and so controls the idle speed. The bypass passage is also used as an additional air supply during cold starting.

20 The ECU also controls the exhaust and evaporative emission control systems which are described in detail later in Part E of this Chapter.

21 If there is an abnormality in any of the readings obtained from any of engine management circuit sensors, the ECU enters its back-up mode. If this happens, it ignores the sensor signal, and assumes a pre-programmed value which will allow the engine to continue running, albeit at reduced efficiency. If the ECU enters its back-up mode, the engine management warning light will come on, and the relevant fault code will be stored in the ECU memory.

22 If the warning light comes on, the vehicle should be taken to a Citroën dealer at the earliest opportunity. A complete test of the engine management system can then be carried out, using a special electronic diagnostic test unit which is simply plugged into the system's diagnostic connector.

8 Fuel system - depressurisation

Note: *Refer to the warning note at the end of Section 1 before proceeding.*

Warning: The following procedure will merely relieve the pressure in the fuel system - remember that fuel will still be present in the system components, and to take precautions accordingly before disconnecting any of them.

1 The fuel system referred to in this Section is defined as the tank-mounted fuel pump, the fuel filter, the fuel injector and the pressure regulator in the injector housing, and the metal pipes and flexible hoses of the fuel lines between these components. All these contain fuel, which will be under pressure while the engine is running and/or while the ignition is switched on. The pressure will remain for some time after the ignition has been switched off, and must be relieved before any of these components are disturbed for servicing work.
2 Disconnect the battery negative terminal.
3 Place a suitable container beneath the relevant connection/union to be disconnected, and have a large rag ready to soak up any escaping fuel not being caught by the container.
4 Slowly loosen the connection or union nut (as applicable) to avoid a sudden release of pressure, and position the rag around the connection to catch any fuel spray which may be expelled. Once the pressure is released, disconnect the fuel line and insert plugs to minimise fuel loss and prevent the entry of dirt into the fuel system.

9 Fuel pump - removal and refitting

Note: *Refer to the warning notes at the end of Section 1 before proceeding.*

Removal

1 Disconnect the battery negative lead.
2 For access to the fuel pump, fold the rear seat cushion forwards.
3 Using a screwdriver, carefully prise the plastic access cover from the floor to expose the fuel pump (the pump is located under the right-hand cover, viewed facing towards the front of the vehicle).
4 Disconnect the wiring connector from the fuel pump **(see illustration)** and tape the connector to the vehicle body to prevent it disappearing behind the tank.
5 Mark the hoses for identification purposes, then slacken the feed and return hose retaining clips. Where crimped-type hose clips are fitted, cut the clips and discard them; replace them with worm-drive hose clips on refitting. Disconnect both hoses from the top of the pump, and plug the hose ends.
6 Noting the alignment marks on the tank, pump cover and the locking ring, unscrew the ring and remove it from the tank **(see illustration)**.

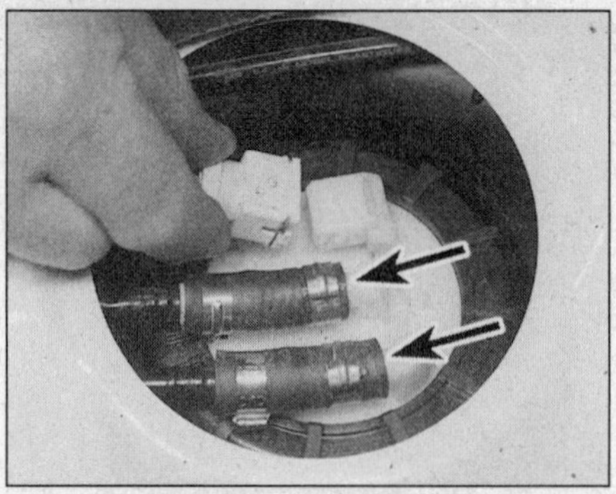

9.4 Disconnect the wiring connector, then release the fuel feed and return hoses (arrowed) from the fuel pump

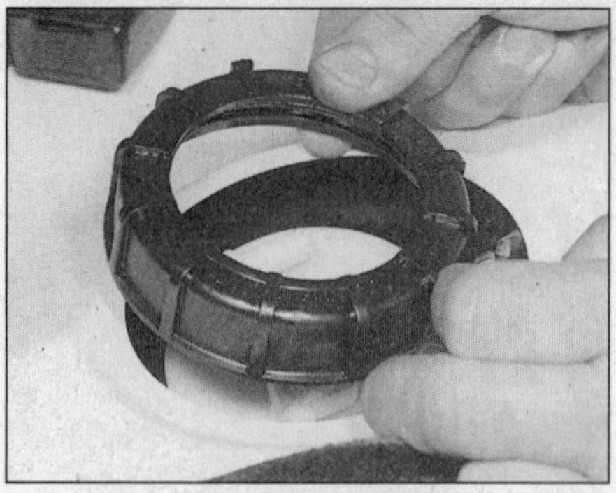

9.6 Unscrew the locking ring . . .

> **HAYNES HiNT** ***This is best accomplished using a screwdriver on the raised ribs of the locking ring. Carefully tap the screwdriver to turn the ring anti-clockwise until it can be unscrewed by hand***

7 Carefully lift the fuel pump assembly out of the fuel tank, taking great care not to damage the filter or to spill fuel onto the interior of the vehicle. Recover the rubber sealing ring and discard it - a new one must be used on refitting **(see illustrations)**.
8 On early models, the fuel pump can be disconnected from the bottom of the unit and renewed separately; on later models, it is only available as a complete assembly.

Refitting

9 Ensure the fuel pump pick-up filter is clean and free of debris. Fit the new sealing ring to the top of the fuel tank.
10 Carefully manoeuvre the pump assembly into the fuel tank, aligning the marks noted on removal.
11 Refit the locking ring, tightening it so that its mark is correctly aligned with the line on the fuel tank, as noted prior to removal **(see illustration)**.
12 Reconnect the feed and return hoses to the top of the fuel pump, using the marks made on removal to ensure they correctly reconnected, and securely tighten their retaining clips.
13 Reconnect the pump wiring connector.
14 Reconnect the battery negative terminal and start the engine. Check the fuel pump feed and return hose unions for signs of leakage.
15 If all is well, refit the plastic access cover and fold down the rear seat cushion.

10 Fuel gauge sender unit - removal and refitting

1 Refer to Chapter 4A, Section 5, noting that there are no fuel pipe connections to the sender unit **(see illustration)**.

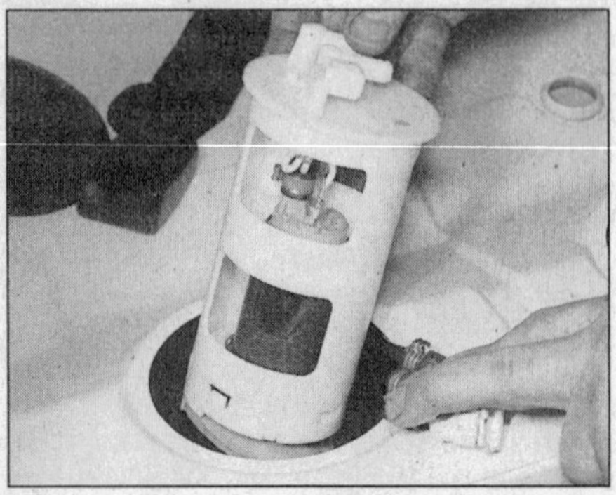

9.7a . . . then lift out the fuel pump . . .

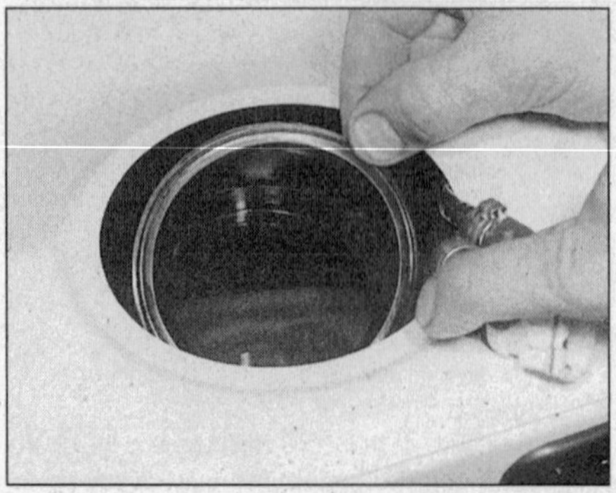

9.7b . . . and recover the rubber sealing ring

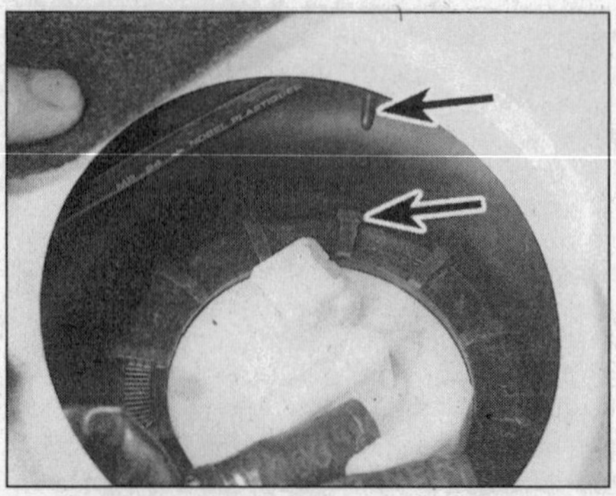

9.11 When refitting, tighten the locking ring until it is correctly aligned with the fuel tank mark (arrowed)

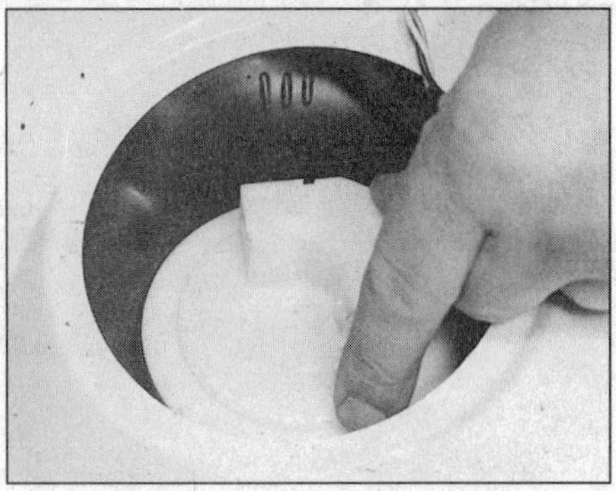

10.1 Removing the fuel gauge sender unit

12.3a Disconnect the wiring connectors from the throttle potentiometer . . .

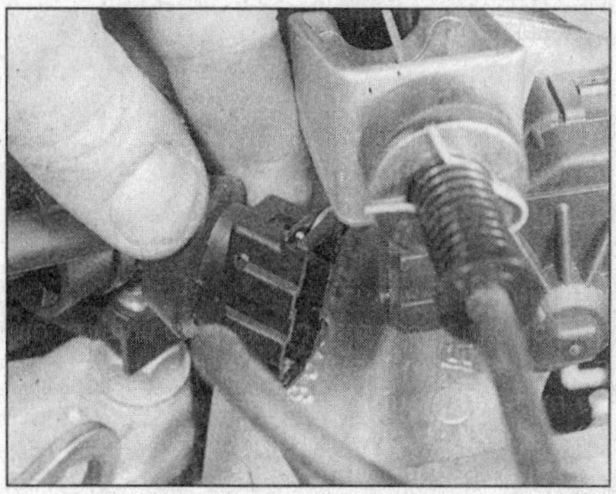

12.3b . . . the injector cap, and the stepper motor

11 Fuel tank - removal and refitting

1 Refer to Chapter 4A, Section 6, noting that it will be necessary to depressurise the fuel system before the feed and return hoses are disconnected from the fuel pump (see Section 8). It will also be necessary to disconnect the wiring connector from the fuel pump prior to lowering the tank out of position. Where applicable, unclip the fuel filter retaining strap, and free the filter from the left-hand side of the fuel tank.

12 Throttle body - removal and refitting

Note: *Refer to the warning notes at the end of Section 1 before proceeding.*

Removal

1 Disconnect the battery negative terminal.

2 Remove the air cleaner housing-to-throttle body duct using the information given in Section 2.

3 Depress the retaining clips and disconnect the wiring connectors from the throttle potentiometer, the idle control stepper motor, and the injector wiring loom connector which

12.4 Fuel feed and return hose connections (arrowed) - later model shown

is situated on the side of the throttle body **(see illustrations).** On later 1124 cc models (with the Magneti Marelli system) the injector, heating element and intake air temperature sensor wiring are all joined to one large connector.

4 Bearing in mind the information given in Section 8 about depressurising the fuel system, release the retaining clips and disconnect the fuel feed and return hoses from the throttle body assembly **(see illustration).** If the original crimped-type clips are still fitted, cut the clips and discard them; replace them with worm-drive hose clips on refitting.

5 Disconnect the accelerator inner cable from

12.5a Disconnect the accelerator inner cable from the throttle cam . . .

the throttle cam, then withdraw the outer cable from the mounting bracket along with its flat washer and spring clip **(see illustrations).**

6 Where necessary, disconnect the distributor vacuum hose, and the idle control auxiliary air valve and/or purge valve hose from the throttle body (as applicable) **(see illustration).**

7 Slacken and remove the bolts securing the throttle body assembly to the inlet manifold **(see illustration)**, then remove the assembly along with its gasket.

8 If necessary, the upper and lower sections of the throttle body can be separated after removing the retaining screws; note the gasket which is fitted between the two.

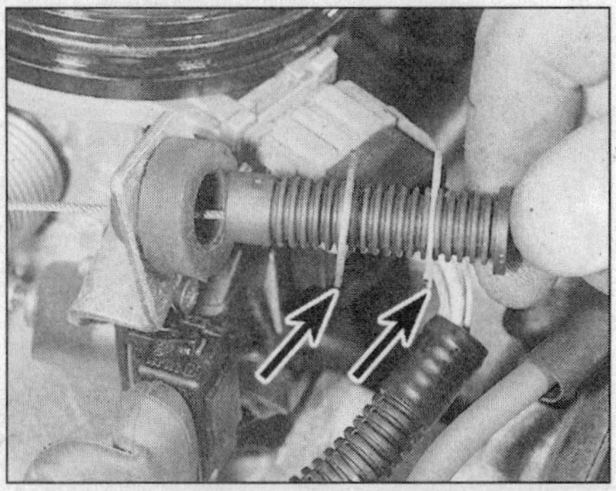

12.5b . . . then free the outer cable from its bracket, and recover the flat washer and spring clip (arrowed) - 1360 cc model

12.6 Disconnecting the purge valve hose from the throttle body - 1360 cc model

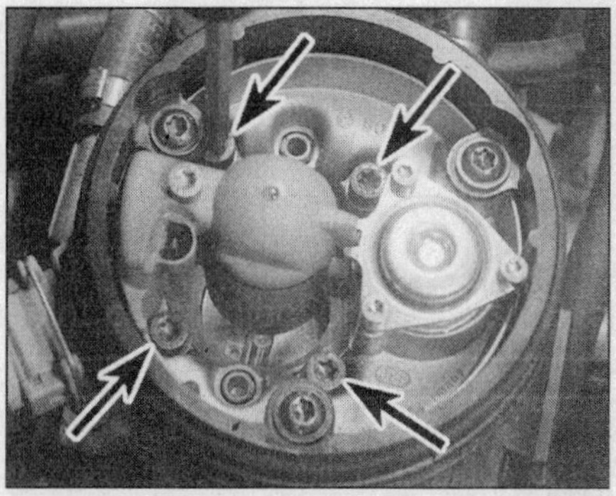

12.7 Throttle body retaining bolts (arrowed)

Refitting

9 Refitting is a reverse of the removal procedure, bearing in mind the following points:

a) Where applicable, ensure that the mating surfaces of the upper and lower throttle body sections are clean and dry, then fit the insulating spacer and new gaskets, or a new gasket (as applicable) and reassemble the two, tightening the retaining screws securely.
b) Ensure that the mating surfaces of the manifold and throttle body are clean and dry, then fit a new gasket. Securely tighten the throttle body retaining bolts.
c) Ensure that all hoses are correctly reconnected and, where necessary, that their retaining clips are securely tightened.
d) On completion, adjust the accelerator cable using the information given in Section 3.

13 Fuel injection system - testing and adjustment

Testing

1 If a fault appears in the fuel injection system, first ensure that all the system wiring connectors are securely connected and free of corrosion. Then ensure that the fault is not due to poor maintenance - ie, check that the air cleaner filter element is clean, the spark plugs are in good condition and correctly gapped, the valve clearances are correctly adjusted, the cylinder compression pressures are correct, the ignition timing is correct, and that the engine breather hoses are clear and undamaged, referring to Chapters 1, 2 and 5 for further information.

2 If these checks fail to reveal the cause of the problem, the vehicle should be taken to a suitably-equipped Citroën dealer for testing. A wiring block connector is incorporated in the engine management circuit, into which a special electronic diagnostic tester can be plugged; the connector is clipped onto the side of the ECU mounting bracket **(see illustration)**. The tester will locate the fault quickly and simply, alleviating the need to test all the system components individually, which is a time-consuming operation that carries a high risk of damaging the ECU.

Adjustment

3 Experienced home mechanics with a considerable amount of skill and equipment (including a good-quality tachometer and a good-quality, carefully-calibrated exhaust gas analyser) may be able to *check* the exhaust CO level and the idle speed. However, if these are found to be in need of *adjustment*, the car **must** be taken to a suitably-equipped Citroën dealer.

4 With the Bosch Monopoint system, no adjustment is possible. Should the idle speed or exhaust gas CO level be incorrect, then a fault must be present in the fuel injection system.

5 With the Magneti Marelli system, it is possible to adjust the mixture setting (exhaust gas CO level) and ignition timing. However, adjustments can be made only by re-programming the ECU, using special diagnostic equipment connected to the system via the diagnostic connector.

14 Bosch Monopoint system components - removal and refitting

Fuel injector

Note: *Refer to the warning notes at the end of Section 1 before proceeding. If a faulty injector is suspected, before condemning the injector, it is worth trying the effect of one of the proprietary injector-cleaning treatments.*

Note: *On some later models, at the time of writing, neither the fuel injector or its seals are available separately. If the injector is faulty, the complete throttle body assembly must be renewed. Refer to your Citroën dealer for the latest information on parts availability. Although the unit can be dismantled for cleaning, if required, it should not be disturbed unless absolutely necessary.*

1 Disconnect the battery negative terminal.

2 Remove the air cleaner-to-throttle body duct using the information given in Section 2,

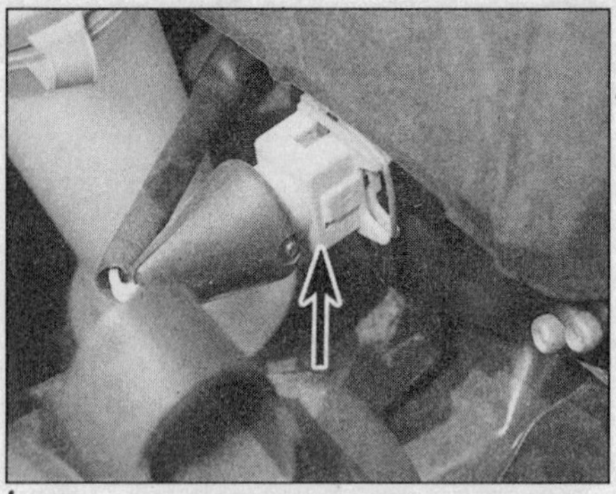

13.2 The diagnostic wiring connector (arrowed) is clipped onto the front of the ECU mounting bracket

then proceed as described under the relevant sub-heading.

A2.2 system (early 1124 and 1360 cc models)

3 Undo the injector cap retaining screw, then lift off the cap and withdraw the injector from the housing, noting the sealing ring locations. As the cap screw is slackened and the injector is withdrawn, place a rag over the injector to catch any fuel spray which may be released **(see illustrations)**.

4 Refitting is a reversal of the removal procedure, ensuring that the injector sealing ring(s) and injector cap O-ring are in good condition. When refitting the injector cap, ensure that the injector pins are correctly aligned with the cap terminals; the terminals are marked "+" and "-" for identification **(see illustration)**.

MA3.0 system (954 cc and later 1360 cc models)

5 Remove the intake air temperature sensor as described later in this Section.

6 Lift out the injector, and recover its lower sealing ring.

7 Refitting is a reversal of the removal procedure, ensuring that the injector sealing ring(s) and injector cap O-ring are in good condition. When refitting the injector cap, ensure that the injector pins are correctly aligned with the cap terminals; the terminals are marked "+" and "-" for identification.

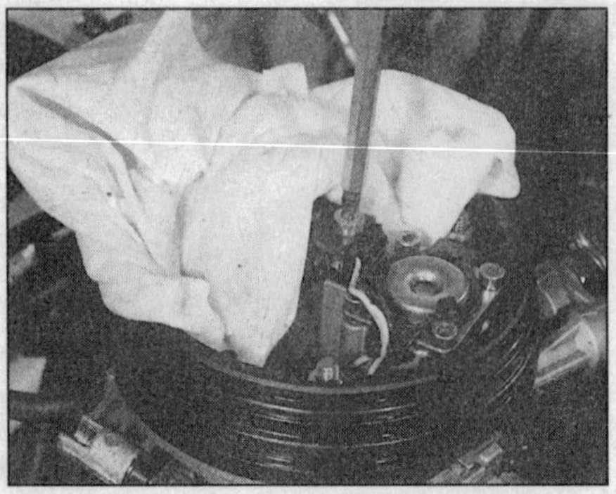

14.3a Undo the injector cap retaining screw, noting the use of a rag to catch any fuel spray . . .

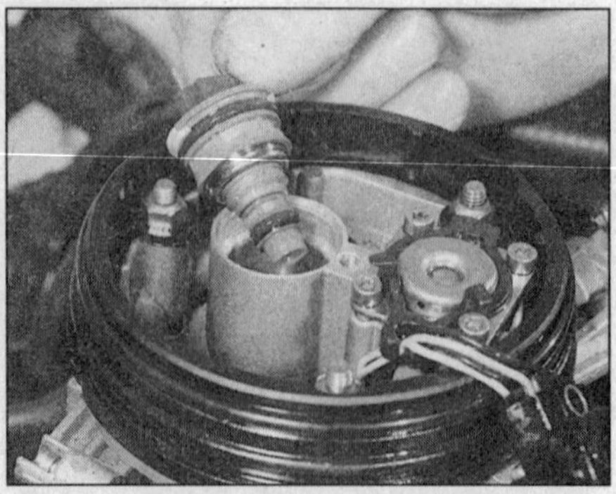

14.3b . . . then lift off the cap and withdraw the injector

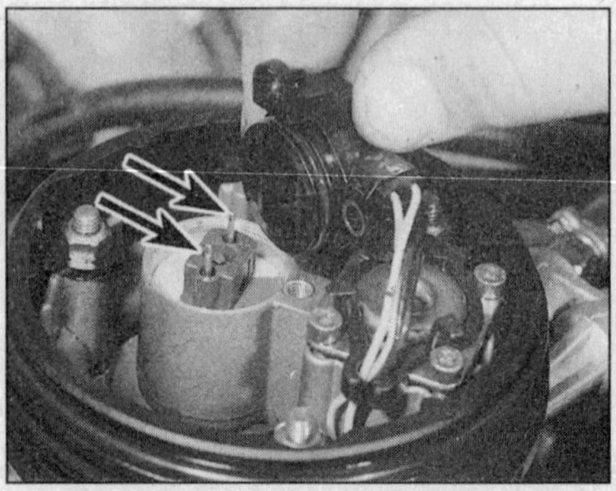

14.4 On refitting, ensure that the cap terminals are correctly aligned with the injector pins (arrowed)

14.10 Fuel pressure regulator retaining screws (arrowed)

14.15 Idle control stepper motor retaining screws (arrowed)

14.18 Intake air temperature sensor (arrowed) is an integral part of the injector cap

Fuel pressure regulator

Note: *Refer to the warning notes at the end of Section 1 before proceeding.*

Note: *At the time of writing, the fuel pressure regulator assembly is not available separately. If the fuel pressure regulator assembly is faulty, the complete throttle body assembly must be renewed. Refer to a Citroën dealer for the latest information on parts availability. Although the unit can be dismantled for cleaning, if required, it should not be disturbed unless absolutely necessary.*

8 Disconnect the battery negative terminal.

9 Remove the air cleaner-to-throttle body duct using the information given in Section 2.

10 Using a suitable marker pen, make alignment marks between the regulator cover and throttle body, then slacken and remove the cover retaining screws **(see illustration)**. As the screws are slackened, place a rag over the cover to catch any fuel spray which may be released.

11 Lift off the cover, then remove the spring and withdraw the diaphragm, noting its correct fitted orientation. Remove all traces of dirt, and examine the diaphragm for signs of splitting. If damage is found, renewal will be necessary.

12 Refitting is a reverse of the removal procedure, ensuring that the diaphragm and cover are fitted the correct way round, and that the retaining screws are securely tightened.

Idle control stepper motor

Note: *On some later models, at the time of writing, the idle control stepper motor is not available separately. If the motor is faulty, the complete throttle body assembly must be renewed. Refer to your Citroën dealer for the latest information on parts availability.*

13 Disconnect the battery negative terminal.

14 Depress the retaining clip, and disconnect the wiring connector from the idle control stepper motor.

15 Undo the retaining screws, and remove the motor from the throttle body **(see illustration)**.

16 Refitting is a reverse of the removal procedure, ensuring that the motor retaining screws are securely tightened.

Throttle potentiometer

17 The throttle potentiometer is a sealed unit, and under **no** circumstances should it be disturbed. For this reason, on some models it is secured to the throttle body assembly by tamperproof screws. If the throttle potentiometer is faulty, the complete throttle body assembly must be renewed. Refer to your Citroën dealer for further information.

Intake air temperature sensor

Note: *Refer to the warning notes at the end of Section 1 before proceeding.*

Note: *On some later models, at the time of writing, the intake air temperature sensor is not available separately. If the sensor is faulty, the complete throttle body assembly must be renewed. Refer to your Citroën dealer for the latest information on parts availability.*

18 The intake air temperature sensor is an integral part of the throttle body injector cap **(see illustration)**. To remove the cap, first disconnect the battery negative terminal, then remove the air cleaner-to-throttle body duct using the information given in Section 2.

19 Undo the three retaining screws, and remove the circular plastic ring from the top of the throttle body. Recover its sealing ring **(see illustrations)**.

20 Depress the retaining clip, and disconnect the wiring connector from the injector wiring connector **(see illustration)**.

21 Undo the injector cap retaining screw, then lift off the cap and recover the gasket and/or sealing ring (as applicable). As the cap screw is slackened, place a rag over the injector to catch any fuel spray which may be released. On models fitted with the A2.2 system, it will be necessary to release the injector cap connector from the throttle body as the cap is removed **(see illustration)**.

22 Refitting is a reversal of the removal procedure, ensuring that the injector cap gasket and/or O-ring is in good condition. Take care to ensure that the cap terminals are correctly aligned with the injector pin, and securely tighten the cap retaining screw.

14.19a Undo the three retaining screws (arrowed) . . .

14.19b . . . then lift off the plastic ring. Recover the sealing ring

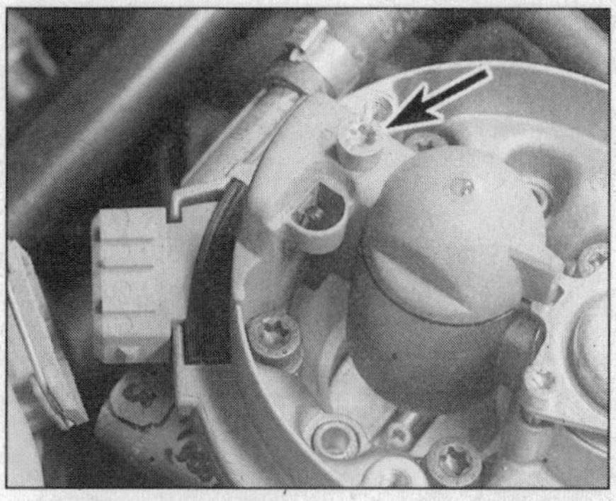

14.20 Disconnecting the injector wiring connector. Injector retaining screw is arrowed

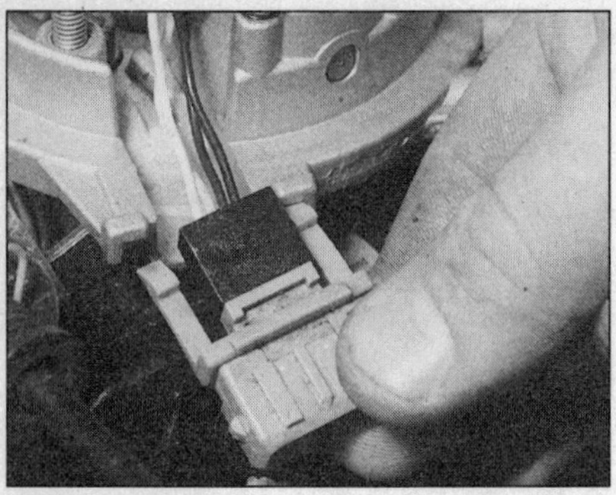

14.21 Injector cap wiring connector is a push fit in the throttle body (A2.2 system)

14.26a Unclip the plastic cover to gain access to the ECU . . .

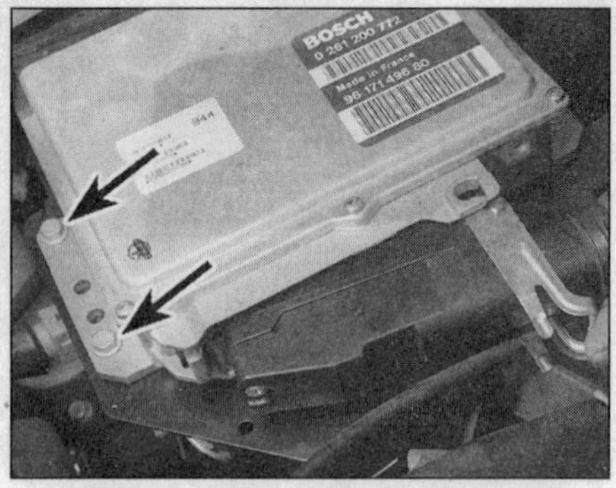

14.26b . . . then disconnect its wiring connector, and undo the two retaining bolts (arrowed)

Coolant temperature sensor

23 Refer to Chapter 3.

Electronic control unit (ECU)

24 The ECU is located on the right-hand side of the engine compartment, underneath a large plastic cover

25 To remove the ECU, first disconnect the battery negative terminal.

26 Unclip the cover from the mounting plate, then lift the retaining clip and disconnect the wiring connector from the ECU. Slacken and remove the ECU retaining bolts, and remove it from the vehicle **(see illustrations)**.

27 Refitting is a reverse of the removal procedure, ensuring that the wiring connector is securely reconnected.

Fuel injection system relay unit

28 The relay unit is clipped onto the underside of the ECU mounting plate, on the right-hand side of the engine compartment.

29 To remove the relay unit, first disconnect the battery negative terminal.

30 Unclip the relay unit from the mounting plate, disconnect the wiring connector, and remove it from the vehicle **(see illustration)**.

31 Refitting is the reverse of removal, ensuring that the relay unit is securely held in position by its retaining clip.

Injector resistor

32 The injector resistor is fixed to the underside of the ECU mounting plate, on the right-hand side of the engine compartment.

33 To remove the resistor, first disconnect the battery negative terminal.

34 Unscrew the resistor retaining nut, then disconnect the wiring connector and remove the resistor from the vehicle **(see illustration)**. On some models, the resistor maybe riveted in position - if this is the case, drill out or cut the rivets to release it from the mounting plate.

35 Refitting is a reversal of the removal procedure. Where the resistor was riveted in position, secure it with either a suitable nut and bolt or new pop-rivets.

Crankshaft sensor (MA3.0 system) - 954 cc and later 1360 cc models

36 The crankshaft sensor is situated on the front face of the clutch bellhousing on the transmission.

37 To remove the sensor, first disconnect the battery negative terminal.

38 Trace the wiring back from the sensor to the wiring connector, and disconnect it from the main harness.

39 Prise out the rubber grommet, then undo the retaining bolt and withdraw the sensor from the transmission.

40 Refitting is a reverse of the removal procedure, ensuring that the sensor retaining bolt is securely tightened and the grommet is correctly seated in the bellhousing.

Vehicle speed sensor (MA3.0 system) - later 1360 cc models

41 The vehicle speed sensor is an integral part of the speedometer drive housing. Refer to Chapter 7 for removal and refitting details.

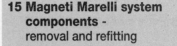

15 Magneti Marelli system components - removal and refitting

Fuel injector

Note: *Refer to the warning notes at the end of Section 1 before proceeding.*

Note: *If a faulty injector is suspected, before condemning the injector, it is worth trying the effect of one of the proprietary injector-cleaning treatments. If this fails, the vehicle should be taken to a Citroën dealer for testing using the appropriate specialist equipment. At the time of writing, it appears that neither the fuel injector or its seals are available separately and, if faulty, the complete upper throttle body assembly must be renewed. Refer to your Citroën dealer for the latest information on parts availability.*

1 Disconnect the battery negative terminal.

2 Remove the air cleaner-to-throttle body duct using the information given in Section 2.

3 Release the retaining tangs and disconnect the injector wiring connector **(see illustration)**.

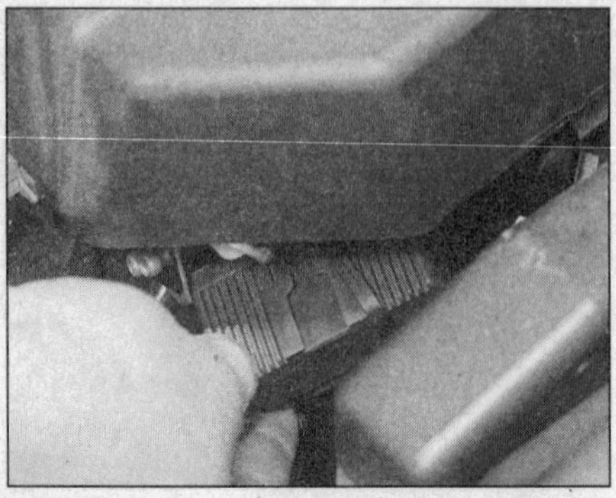

14.30 Removing the fuel injection system relay unit from the ECU mounting plate

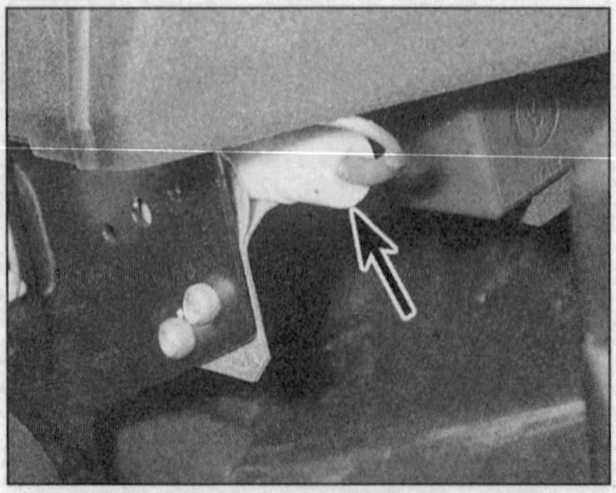

14.34 The injector resistor (arrowed) is mounted onto the ECU mounting plate

15.3 Disconnecting the injector wiring connector - injector retaining clip screw arrowed

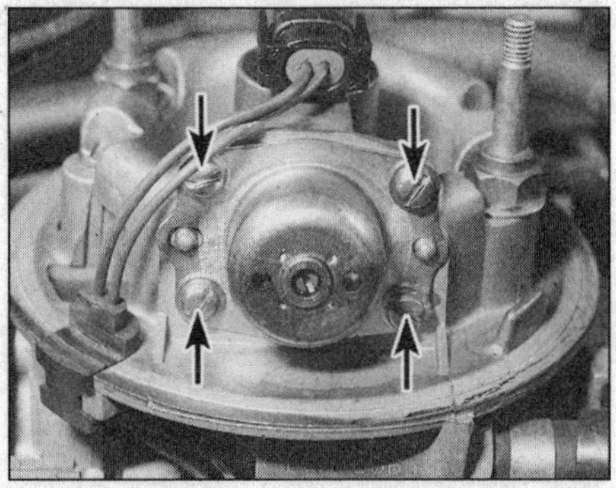

15.8 Fuel pressure regulator is retained by four screws (arrowed)

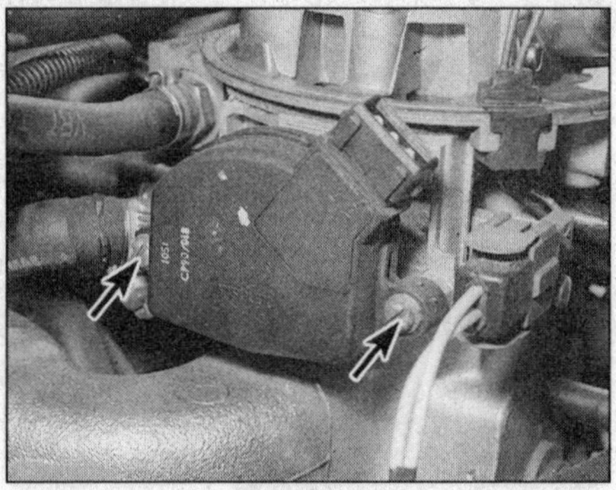

15.15 Throttle potentiometer is secured to the throttle body by two screws (arrowed)

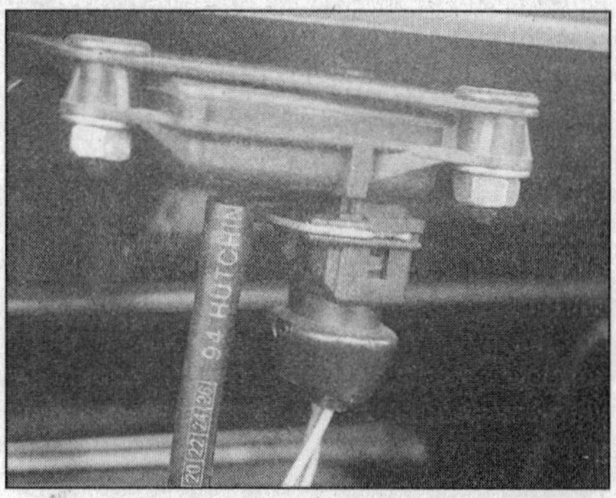

15.21 Manifold absolute pressure (MAP) sensor

4 Undo the retaining screw then remove the retaining clip and lift the injector out of the housing, noting its sealing ring. As the screw is slackened, place a rag over the injector to catch any fuel spray which may be released.

5 Refitting is a reverse of the removal procedure, ensuring that the injector sealing ring is in good condition.

Fuel pressure regulator

Note: *Refer to the warning notes at the end of Section 1 before proceeding.*

Note: *At the time of writing, it appears that the fuel pressure regulator is not available separately. If the fuel pressure regulator assembly is faulty, the complete upper throttle body assembly must be renewed. Refer to a Citroën dealer for the latest information on parts availability. Although the unit can be dismantled for cleaning, if required, it should not be disturbed unless absolutely necessary.*

6 Disconnect the battery negative terminal.

7 Remove the air cleaner-to-throttle body duct using the information given in Section 2.

8 Using a suitable marker pen, make alignment marks between the regulator cover and throttle body, then undo the four retaining screws **(see illustration)**. As the screws are slackened, place a rag over the cover to catch any fuel spray which may be released.

9 Lift off the cover, then remove the spring and withdraw the diaphragm, noting its correct fitted orientation. Remove all traces of dirt, and examine the diaphragm for signs of splitting. If damage is found, it will be necessary to renew the complete upper throttle body assembly as described earlier in this Section.

10 Refitting is a reverse of the removal procedure, ensuring that the diaphragm and cover are fitted the correct way round, and that the retaining screws are securely tightened.

Idle control stepper motor

11 Disconnect the battery negative terminal.

12 To remove the stepper motor, depress the retaining tabs and disconnect the wiring connector. Undo the two retaining screws, and withdraw the motor from the rear of the throttle body assembly.

13 Refitting is a reverse of removal.

Throttle potentiometer

14 Disconnect the battery negative terminal, then depress the retaining tabs and disconnect the wiring connector from the throttle potentiometer.

15 Undo the two retaining screws, and remove the throttle potentiometer from the right-hand side of the throttle body assembly **(see illustration)**.

16 Refitting is a reversal of the removal procedure, ensuring that the throttle potentiometer tang is correctly engaged with the throttle spindle.

Intake air temperature sensor

17 The intake air temperature sensor is screwed into the underside of the upper throttle body, on the left-hand side of the fuel injector.

18 To remove the sensor, first disconnect the battery negative terminal.

19 Disconnect the wiring connector, then unscrew the fuel/air mixture temperature sensor from the throttle body. **Note:** *The sensor retaining screw is very difficult to reach. If it proves impossible to unscrew, the throttle body will have to be removed to permit sensor removal.*

20 Refitting is a reverse of the removal procedure, ensuring that the switch is securely tightened.

Manifold absolute pressure (MAP) sensor

21 The MAP sensor is mounted on a bracket on the engine compartment bulkhead, behind the throttle body **(see illustration)**.

22 To remove the sensor, first disconnect the battery negative terminal.

23 Slacken and remove the three retaining bolts, then free the MAP sensor from the bulkhead. Disconnect the wiring connector and vacuum hose, and remove the sensor from the engine compartment.

24 Refitting is a reverse of the removal procedure.

Coolant temperature sensor

25 Refer to Chapter 3.

Crankshaft sensor

26 Refer to paragraphs 36 to 40 of Section 14.

15.27 Magneti Marelli electronic control unit (ECU)

Electronic control unit (ECU)

27 Refer to paragraphs 24 to 27 of Section 14 **(see illustration)**.

Fuel injection system relay unit

28 Refer to paragraphs 28 to 31 of Section 14.

Throttle body heating element

29 The throttle body heating element is situated in the front of the throttle body.

30 To remove the element, first disconnect the battery negative terminal.

31 Remove the air cleaner housing-to-throttle body duct, using the information given in Section 2.

32 Disconnect the wiring connectors from the intake air temperature sensor and the injector. Also disconnect the main wiring connector from the throttle body, and free the connector from its mounting bracket.

33 Undo the retaining screws, and free the accelerator cable mounting bracket from the throttle body. As the bracket is released, recover the spring from the front of the heating element.

34 Ease the heating element out from the throttle housing, and remove it along with the wiring connector and wiring harness. Examine the O-ring for signs of damage or deterioration, and renew if necessary.

35 Refitting is a reversal of the removal procedure, using a new O-ring where necessary.

16 Inlet manifold - removal and refitting

Removal

1 Remove the throttle body as described in Section 12.
2 Drain the cooling system as described in Chapter 1.
3 Slacken the retaining clip and disconnect the coolant hose(s) from the manifold.
4 Similarly, disconnect the vacuum servo unit hose from the left-hand side of the manifold.
5 Make a final check that all the necessary vacuum/breather hoses have been disconnected from the manifold.
6 Unscrew the six retaining nuts, then manoeuvre the manifold away from the head and out of the engine compartment. Note that there is no manifold gasket.

Refitting

7 Refitting is the reverse of the removal procedure, noting the following points:

a) Ensure that the manifold and cylinder head mating surfaces are clean and dry, and apply a thin coating of suitable sealing compound to the manifold mating surface. Install the manifold, and tighten its retaining nuts to the specified torque setting.
b) Ensure that all relevant hoses are reconnected to their original positions, and are securely held (where necessary) by their retaining clips.
c) Refit the throttle body as described in Section 12.
d) On completion, refill the cooling system as described in Chapter 1.

17 Exhaust manifold - removal and refitting

1 Refer to Chapter 4A, Section 17, noting that the lambda (oxygen) sensor wiring connectors must either be disconnected, or care must be taken to support the front pipe to avoid any strain being placed on the sensor wiring.

18 Exhaust system - general information and component removal

General information

1 On 954 and 1124 cc models, the exhaust system consists of three sections; the front pipe, the intermediate pipe and catalytic converter, and the tailpipe and main silencer box. The front pipe-to-manifold flanged joint is sealed with a gasket, and is secured with three nuts. The front pipe-to-intermediate pipe is secured by two nuts and bolts, and is of the spring-loaded ball type to allow for movement in the exhaust system. The intermediate pipe-to-tailpipe joint is secured by a clamping ring.
2 On 1360 cc models, the exhaust system consists of four sections; the front pipe, the catalytic converter, the intermediate pipe, and the tailpipe and main silencer box. The front pipe joints are secured by nuts and bolts, the catalytic converter joint being of the spring-loaded ball type to allow for movement in the exhaust system. The catalytic converter-to-intermediate pipe joint and the intermediate pipe-to-silencer joint are secured by a clamping ring.

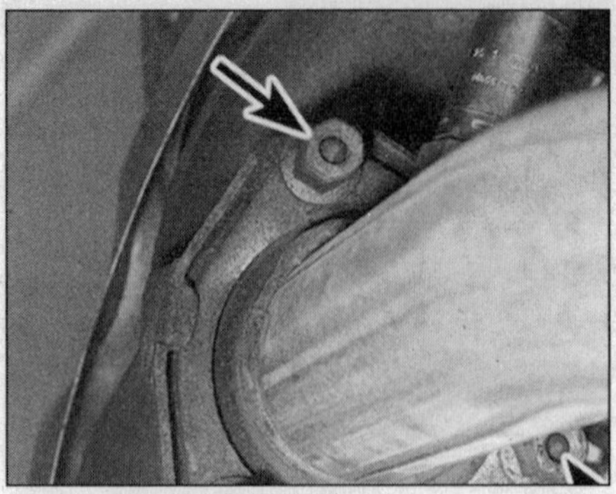
18.7a Remove the front pipe-to-manifold retaining nuts (arrowed) . . .

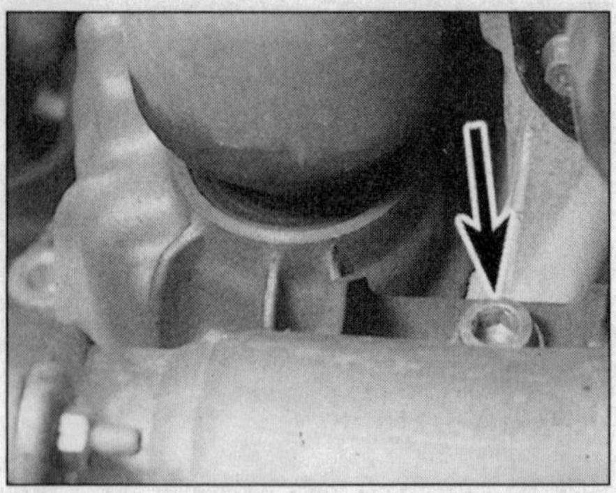
18.7b . . . and the front pipe mounting bolt where necessary (arrowed)

18.8 Front pipe-to-intermediate pipe/catalytic converter joint

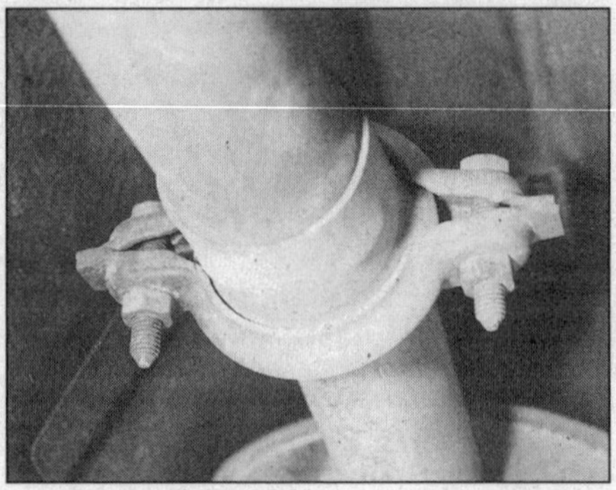
18.10 Typical exhaust system clamp

3 The system is suspended throughout its entire length by rubber mountings.

Removal

4 Each exhaust section can be removed individually or, alternatively, the complete system can be removed as a unit.
5 To remove the system or part of the system, first jack up the front or rear of the car, and support it on axle stands. Alternatively, position the car over an inspection pit, or on car ramps.

Front pipe

6 Trace the wiring back from the lambda (oxygen) sensor to its wiring connectors, which are clipped onto the top of the transmission, and disconnect them from the main wiring harness.
7 Undo the nuts securing the front pipe flange joint to the manifold and, where necessary, the single bolt securing the front pipe to its mounting bracket **(see illustrations)**. Separate the flange joint, and collect the gasket.
8 Slacken and remove the two nuts securing the front pipe to the intermediate pipe/catalytic converter (as applicable), and recover the spring cups and springs **(see illustration)**. Remove the bolts, then withdraw the front pipe from underneath the vehicle, taking great care not to damage the lambda sensor, and recover the sealing ring from the joint.

Catalytic converter (separate) - 1360 cc models

9 Undo the two nuts securing the front pipe flange joint to the catalytic converter. Recover the springs and spring cups, and withdraw the bolts.
10 Slacken the catalytic converter-to-intermediate pipe clamp bolts, and disengage the clamp **(see illustration)**.
11 Free the catalytic converter from the intermediate pipe, then withdraw it from underneath the vehicle and recover the sealing ring from the front pipe joint. Do not drop the catalytic converter, as it contains a fragile ceramic element.

Intermediate pipe and catalytic converter - 954 and 1124 cc models

12 Undo the two nuts securing the front pipe flange joint to the intermediate pipe. Recover the springs and spring cups, and withdraw the bolts.
13 Slacken the clamping ring bolts, and disengage the clamp from the intermediate pipe-to-tailpipe joint **(see illustration)**.
14 Free the intermediate pipe from its

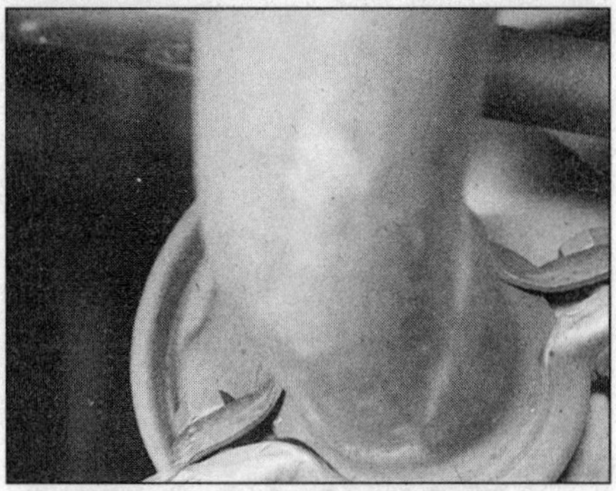

18.13 Intermediate pipe-to-tailpipe clamping ring

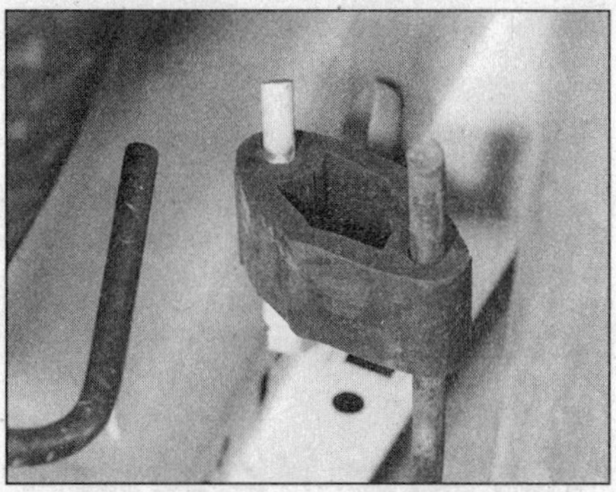

18.22 When refitting, ensure that the exhaust system is correctly located on its rubber mountings before tightening its fasteners securely

mounting rubbers, then disengage it from the tailpipe and the front pipe and remove it from underneath the vehicle. Recover the sealing ring from the front pipe joint.

Intermediate pipe - 1360 cc models

15 Slacken the clamping ring bolts, and disengage the clamps from both the intermediate pipe flange joints.

16 Free the intermediate pipe from its mounting rubbers. Disengage it first from the tailpipe, then the catalytic converter, and remove it from underneath the vehicle.

Tailpipe

17 Slacken the intermediate pipe-to-tailpipe clamping ring bolts, and disengage the clamp from the joint.

18 Unhook the tailpipe from its mounting rubbers, and remove it from the vehicle.

Complete system

19 Disconnect the front pipe from the manifold as described in paragraphs 6 and 7.

20 With the aid of an assistant, free the system from all its mounting rubbers, and manoeuvre it out from underneath the vehicle.

Heat shield(s)

21 The heat shields are secured to the underside of the body by a mixture of nuts and bolts. Each shield can be removed once the relevant exhaust section has been removed.

> HAYNES HiNT *If the heat shield is being removed to gain access to a component located behind it, it may prove sufficient to remove the fasteners and simply lower the shield, without disturbing the exhaust system.*

Refitting

22 Each section is refitted by a reversal of the removal sequence, noting the following points:

a) Ensure that all traces of corrosion have been removed from the flanges, and renew all necessary gaskets/sealing rings.

b) Inspect the rubber mountings for signs of damage or deterioration, and renew as necessary.

c) Prior to assembling the spring-loaded ball type joint, a smear of high-temperature grease should be applied to the joint mating surfaces.

d) On joints which are secured by clamping rings, apply a smear of exhaust system jointing paste to the joint mating surfaces, to ensure a gastight seal. Tighten the clamping ring nuts evenly and progressively to the specified torque, so that the clearance between the clamp halves is equal on either side.

e) Prior to tightening the exhaust system fasteners, ensure that all rubber mountings are correctly located, and that there is adequate clearance between the exhaust system and vehicle underbody **(see illustration)**.

Chapter 4 Part C: Fuel/exhaust systems - multi-point petrol injection models

Contents

Degrees of difficulty

Easy, suitable for novice with little experience	**Fairly easy,** suitable for beginner with some experience	**Fairly difficult,** suitable for competent DIY mechanic	**Difficult,** suitable for experienced DIY mechanic	**Very difficult,** suitable for expert DIY or professional

Specifications

System type

1360 cc GTi models	Bosch Motronic MP3.1

Fuel system data

Fuel pump type	Electric, immersed in tank
Fuel pump regulated constant pressure (approximate)	2.5 to 3.0 bars
Idle speed	880 rpm (not adjustable - controlled by ECU)
Idle mixture CO content:	
K6B engine	1.0 ± 0.5 % (adjustable via mixture potentiometer)
KFZ engine	Less than 1.0 % (not adjustable - controlled by ECU)

Recommended fuel

Minimum octane rating:	
K6B engine	95 RON unleaded (Premium unleaded), 98 RON unleaded (Super unleaded) or 98 RON leaded (UK "4-star" leaded)
KFZ engine	95 RON unleaded (Premium unleaded) or 98 RON unleaded (Super unleaded) **only**

Torque wrench settings

Torque wrench settings	Nm	lbf ft
Inlet manifold retaining nuts	8	6
Exhaust manifold retaining nuts	15	11
Exhaust system fasteners:		
Front pipe-to-manifold nut	35	26
Front pipe-to-intermediate pipe/catalytic converter nuts	10	7
Clamping ring nuts	15	11

1 General information and precautions

1 The fuel system consists of a fuel tank mounted under the rear of the car with an electric fuel pump immersed in it, a fuel filter, and the fuel feed and return lines. The fuel pump supplies fuel to the fuel rail, which acts as a reservoir for the four fuel injectors which inject fuel into the inlet tracts. A fuel filter is incorporated in the feed line from the pump to the fuel rail, to ensure that the fuel supplied to the injectors is clean.

2 Refer to Section 6 for further information on the operation of the fuel injection system, and to Section 16 for information on the exhaust system. Throughout this Part of Chapter 4, it is also occasionally necessary to identify vehicles by their engine codes rather than engine capacity. Refer to Chapter 2A for further information on engine code identification.

Warning: Many of the procedures in this Chapter require the removal of fuel lines and connections, which may result in some fuel spillage. Before carrying out any operation on the fuel system, refer to the precautions given in "Safety first!" at the beginning of this manual, and follow them implicitly. Petrol is a highly-dangerous and volatile liquid, and the precautions necessary when handling it cannot be overstressed.

Note: *Residual pressure will remain in the fuel lines long after the vehicle was last used. Before disconnecting any fuel line, depressurise the fuel system as described in Section 7.*

2 Air cleaner assembly - removal and refitting

Removal

1 Slacken the retaining clips (where fitted) and disconnect the supplementary air supply hose and breather hose from the top of the air cleaner housing. Where crimped-type hose clips or ties are fitted, cut and discard them; replace them with worm-drive hose clips or new cable ties on refitting.

2 Slacken the retaining clips or ties, and free the throttle housing duct from the air cleaner upper housing, and the intake duct from the side of the lower housing. If necessary, free the duct from the throttle housing and remove it along with its sealing ring.

3 Disconnect the wiring from the air temperature sensor on the upper air cleaner housing.

4 Lift the air cleaner housing assembly out of the engine compartment.

5 To remove the intake duct assembly, first drill out the rivets securing the duct to the crossmember. Release the fastener securing the rear of the duct to the cylinder head, and remove the duct and hose assembly from the engine compartment.

Refitting

6 Refitting is a reversal of the removal procedure, noting the following points:

a) Ensure that the air cleaner housing locating peg is correctly engaged with its mounting on the top of the transmission.
b) Ensure that all hoses are properly reconnected.
c) Make sure that all the ducts are correctly seated and securely held in position.
d) Secure the intake duct to the crossmember (where removed) with new pop-rivets.

3 Accelerator cable - removal, refitting and adjustment

1 Refer to Chapter 4A, Section 7, substituting "throttle housing" for all references to the carburettor.

4 Accelerator pedal - removal and refitting

Refer to Chapter 4A, Section 8.

5 Unleaded petrol - general information and usage

Note: *The information given in this Chapter is correct at the time of writing, and applies only to petrols currently available in the UK. If updated information is thought to be required, check with a Citroën dealer. If travelling abroad, consult one of the motoring organisations (or a similar authority) for advice on the petrols available and their suitability for your vehicle.*

1 The fuel recommended by Citroën is given in the Specifications at the start of this Chapter, followed by the equivalent petrol currently on sale in the UK.

2 RON and MON are different testing standards; RON stands for Research Octane Number (also written as RM), while MON stands for Motor Octane Number (also written as MM).

3 All Citroën AX multi-point injection models are designed to run on fuel with a minimum octane rating of 95 (RON). With the exception of the 1360 cc (K6B engine) model (which does not have a catalytic converter), all models are equipped with a catalytic converter, and must be run on unleaded fuel **only. Under no circumstances** should leaded fuel be used, as this may damage the catalytic converter. On models without a catalytic converter, either unleaded or leaded fuel can be used without modification.

6 Fuel injection system - general information

Bosch Motronic MP3.1 system

1 The Bosch Motronic MP3.1 engine management (fuel injection/ignition) system is fitted to the performance-orientated 1360 cc GTi models. There are, however, two different versions of the system available **(see illustrations)**. On later models (fitted with the KFZ engine), the system incorporates a closed-loop catalytic converter and an evaporative emission control system, and complies to the very latest emission control standards. Earlier models (fitted with the K6B engine) have neither a catalytic converter nor the evaporative emission control system.

2 Refer to Chapter 5B for information on the ignition side of the system. The fuel side of the system operates as follows.

3 The fuel pump, immersed in the fuel tank, pumps fuel from the fuel tank to the fuel rail, via a filter mounted underneath the rear of the vehicle. Fuel supply pressure is controlled by the pressure regulator in the fuel rail, which lifts to allow excess fuel to return to the tank when the optimum operating pressure of the fuel system is exceeded.

4 The electrical control system consists of the ECU, along with the following sensors:

a) Throttle potentiometer - informs the ECU of the throttle valve position.
b) Coolant temperature sensor - informs the ECU of engine temperature.
c) Intake air temperature sensor - informs the ECU of the temperature of the air passing through the air cleaner housing.
d) Crankshaft sensor - informs the ECU of the crankshaft position and speed of rotation.
e) Manifold Absolute Pressure (MAP) sensor - informs the ECU of the load on the engine.
f) Lambda (oxygen) sensor (KFZ engine only) - informs ECU of oxygen content of the exhaust gases (explained in greater detail in Part E of this Chapter).

5 All the above signals are compared by the ECU with values pre-programmed (mapped) into its memory. Based on this information, the ECU selects the response appropriate to those values, and controls the fuel injectors (varying their pulse width - the length of time the injectors are held open - to provide a richer or weaker mixture, as appropriate). The mixture and idle speed are constantly varied by the ECU to provide the best settings for cranking, starting (with either a hot or cold engine), warm-up, idle, cruising and acceleration.

6 The ECU also has full control over the engine idle speed, via an auxiliary air valve which bypasses the throttle valve. When the throttle valve is closed, the ECU controls the opening of the valve, which in turn regulates the amount of air entering the manifold and so controls the idle speed.

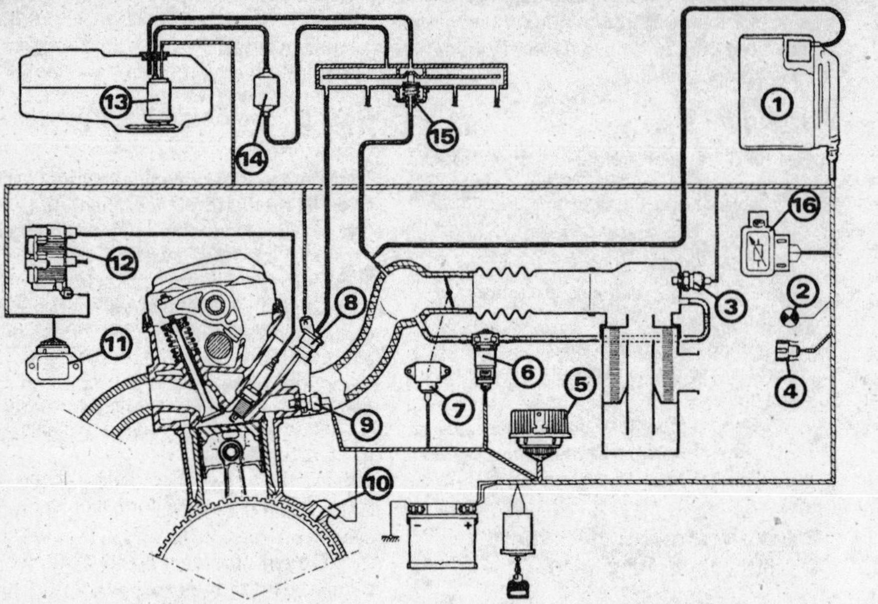

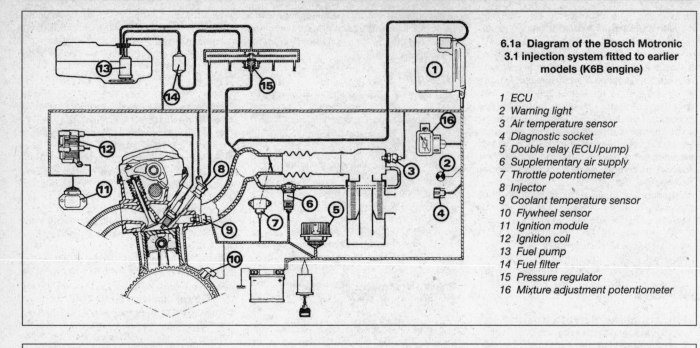

6.1a Diagram of the Bosch Motronic 3.1 injection system fitted to earlier models (K6B engine)

1 ECU
2 Warning light
3 Air temperature sensor
4 Diagnostic socket
5 Double relay (ECU/pump)
6 Supplementary air supply
7 Throttle potentiometer
8 Injector
9 Coolant temperature sensor
10 Flywheel sensor
11 Ignition module
12 Ignition coil
13 Fuel pump
14 Fuel filter
15 Pressure regulator
16 Mixture adjustment potentiometer

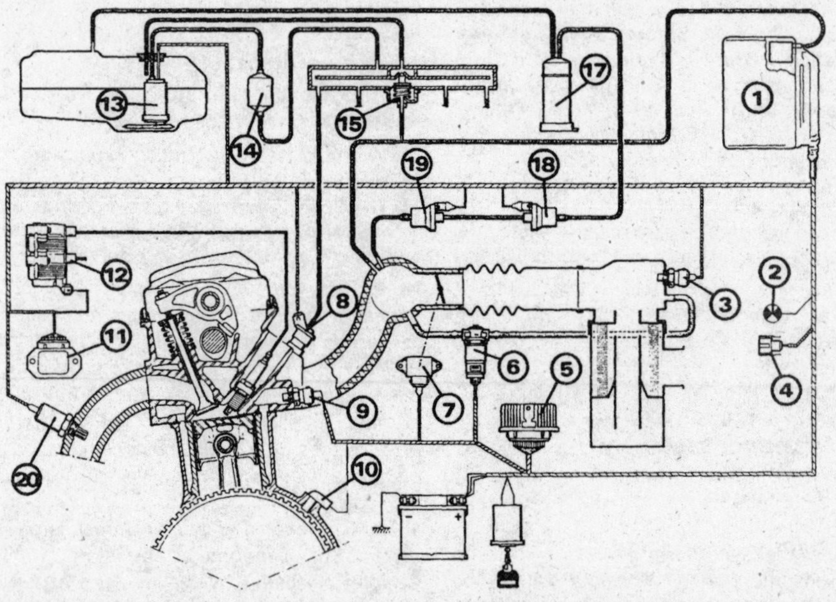

6.1b Diagram of the Bosch Motronic 3.1 injection system fitted to later models (KFZ engine)

1 ECU
2 Warning light
3 Air temperature sensor
4 Diagnostic socket
5 Double relay (ECU/pump)
6 Supplementary air supply
7 Throttle potentiometer
8 Injector
9 Coolant temperature sensor
10 Flywheel sensor
11 Ignition module
12 Ignition coil
13 Fuel pump
14 Fuel filter
15 Pressure regulator
17 Charcoal canister
18 Purge electrovalve
19 Isolating electrovalve
20 Lambda (oxygen) sensor

7 The throttle housing is fitted with an electric heating element. The heater is supplied with current by the ECU, and warms the throttle housing on cold starts to prevent possible icing of the throttle valve.

8 On KFZ engine models, the ECU also controls the exhaust and evaporative emission control systems, which are described in detail in Part E of this Chapter.

9 If there is an abnormality in any of the readings obtained from the system sensors, the ECU enters its back-up mode. If this happens, it ignores the sensor signal and assumes a pre-programmed value which will allow the engine to continue running, albeit at reduced efficiency. If the ECU enters this back-up mode, the warning light on the instrument panel will come on, and the relevant fault code will be stored in the ECU memory.

10 If the warning light comes on, the vehicle should be taken to a Citroën dealer at the earliest opportunity. A complete test of the engine management system can then be carried out, using a special electronic diagnostic test unit which is simply plugged into the system's diagnostic connector.

7 Fuel system - depressurisation

Note: *Refer to the warning notes at the end of Section 1 before proceeding.*

Warning: The following procedure will merely relieve the pressure in the fuel system - remember that fuel will still be present in the system components, and to take precautions accordingly before disconnecting any of them.

1 The fuel system referred to in this Section is defined as the tank-mounted fuel pump, the fuel filter, the fuel injectors, the fuel rail and the pressure regulator, and the metal pipes and flexible hoses of the fuel lines between these components. All these contain fuel, which will be under pressure while the engine is running and/or while the ignition is switched on. The pressure will remain for some time after the ignition has been switched off, and must be relieved before any of these components are disturbed for servicing work.

2 Disconnect the battery negative terminal.

3 Place a suitable container beneath the relevant connection/union to be disconnected, and have a large rag ready to soak up any escaping fuel not being caught by the container.

4 Slowly loosen the connection or union nut (as applicable) to avoid a sudden release of pressure, and position the rag around the connection to catch any fuel spray which may be expelled. Once the pressure is released, disconnect the fuel line. Plug or cap the fuel line/union, to minimise fuel loss and to prevent the entry of dirt into the fuel system.

8 Fuel pump - removal and refitting

Refer to Chapter 4B, Section 9.

9 Fuel gauge sender unit - removal and refitting

1 Refer to Chapter 4A, Section 5, noting that there are no fuel pipe connections to the sender unit.

10 Fuel tank - removal and refitting

1 Refer to Chapter 4A, Section 6, noting that it will be necessary to depressurise the fuel system before the feed and return hoses are disconnected (see Section 7). It will also be necessary to disconnect the wiring connector from the fuel pump, prior to lowering the tank out of position.

11 Fuel injection system - testing and adjustment

Testing

1 If a fault appears in the fuel injection system, first ensure that all the system wiring connectors are securely connected and free of corrosion. Then ensure that the fault is not due to poor maintenance - ie, check that the air cleaner filter element is clean, the spark plugs are in good condition and correctly gapped, the valve clearances and cylinder compression pressures are correct, the ignition timing is correct, and that the engine breather hoses are clear and undamaged, referring to Chapters 1, 2 and 5 for further information.

2 If these checks fail to reveal the cause of the problem, the vehicle should be taken to a suitably-equipped Citroën dealer for testing. A wiring block connector is incorporated in the engine management circuit, into which a special electronic diagnostic tester can be plugged; the connector is clipped onto the side of the ECU mounting bracket. The tester will locate the fault quickly and simply, alleviating the need to test all the system components individually, which is a time-consuming operation that carries a high risk of damaging the ECU.

Adjustment

3 On 1360 cc (K6B engine) models without a catalytic converter, the idle mixture (exhaust gas CO level) is adjustable. Refer to Chapter 1 for information on the adjustment procedure. The engine idle speed is not adjustable, however, and is fully under the control of the ECU.

4 On 1360 cc (KFZ engine) models, experienced home mechanics with a considerable amount of skill and equipment (including a good-quality tachometer and a good-quality, carefully-calibrated exhaust gas analyser) may be able to *check* the exhaust CO level and the idle speed. However, if these are found to be in need of *adjustment,* the car **must** be taken to a suitably-equipped Citroën dealer for testing. Neither the mixture (exhaust gas CO level) or idle speed are adjustable, and should either be incorrect, a fault must be present in the fuel injection system.

12 Throttle housing - removal and refitting

Removal

1 Disconnect the battery negative terminal.

2 Slacken the retaining clip, then disconnect the intake duct from the throttle housing, and recover the sealing ring. Where a crimped-type hose clip or tie fitted, cut and discard it; replace it with a worm-drive hose clip or new cable tie on refitting.

3 Disconnect the accelerator inner cable from the throttle cam. Withdraw the outer cable from the mounting bracket, along with its flat washer and spring clip.

4 Depress the retaining clip and disconnect the wiring connector(s) from the throttle potentiometer. Where necessary, disconnect the wiring from the electric heating element, the air temperature sensor, and/or the stepper motor (as applicable).

5 Disconnect the auxiliary idle air hose from the throttle housing.

6 Slacken and remove the three retaining screws, and remove the throttle housing from the inlet manifold. Recover the O-ring from the manifold and discard it; a new one must be used on refitting.

Refitting

7 Refitting is a reversal of the relevant removal procedure, noting the following points:

a) Fit a new O-ring to the manifold, then refit the throttle housing and securely tighten its screws.
b) Ensure that all hoses are correctly reconnected and, where necessary, are securely held in position by the retaining clips.
c) Ensure that all wiring is correctly routed and that the connectors are securely reconnected.
d) On completion, adjust the accelerator cable using the information in Section 3.

13 Bosch Motronic MP 3.1 system components - removal and refitting

Fuel rail and injectors

Note: *Refer to the warning notes at the end of Section 1 before proceeding.*

Note: *If a faulty injector is suspected, before condemning the injector, it is worth trying the effect of one of the proprietary injector-cleaning treatments.*

1 Disconnect the battery negative terminal.

2 Disconnect the vacuum pipe from the fuel pressure regulator.

3 Bearing in mind the information given in Section 7, slacken the retaining clips and disconnect the fuel feed and return hoses from the either end of the fuel rail. Where the original crimped-type Citroën hose clips are still fitted, cut and discard them; replace them with worm-drive hose clips on refitting **(see illustration)**.

4 Depress the retaining tangs, and disconnect the wiring connectors from the four injectors **(see illustration)**.

5 Slacken and remove the fuel rail retaining bolts and the two retaining nuts, then carefully ease the fuel rail and injector assembly out

13.3 Where original crimped-type Citroën hose clips are fitted, cut and discard them

13.4 Disconnecting the injector wiring connectors

4C

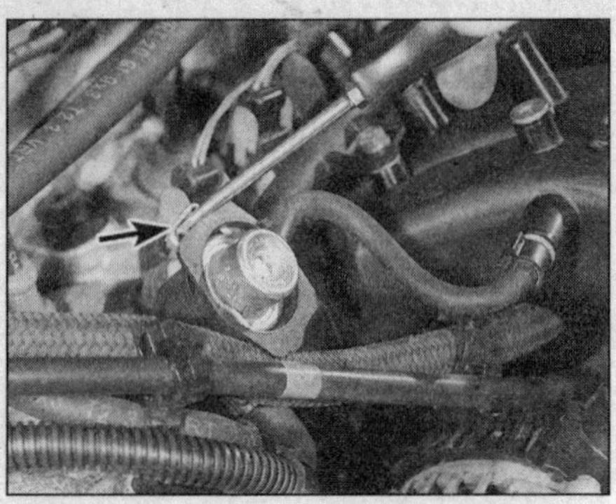

13.9 Fuel pressure regulator retaining clip (arrowed) can be prised out of position using a flat-bladed screwdriver

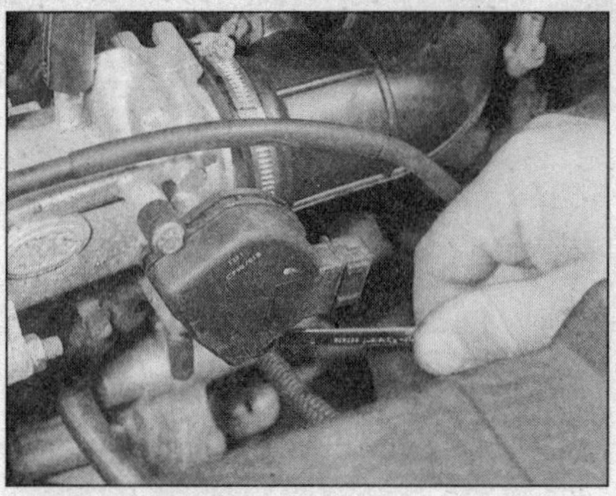

13.13 Throttle potentiometer is secured to the throttle housing by two screws

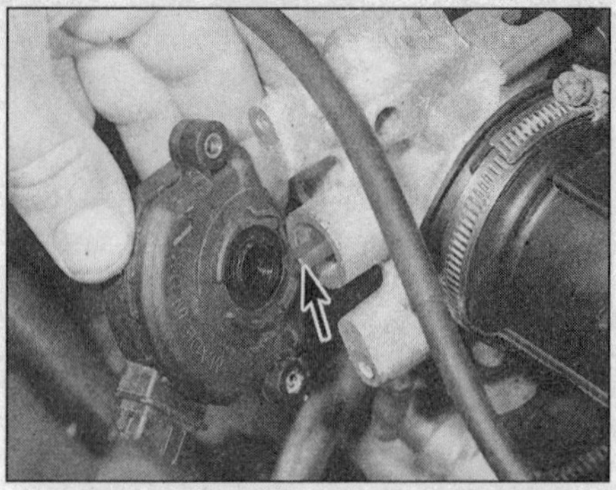

13.14 On refitting, ensure that the potentiometer is correctly engaged with the throttle valve spindle (arrowed)

from the inlet manifold and remove it from the vehicle. Remove the O-rings from the end of each injector and discard them; they must be renewed whenever they are disturbed.

6 Slide out the retaining clip(s) and remove the relevant injector(s) from the fuel rail. Remove the upper O-ring from each disturbed injector and discard; all disturbed O-rings must be renewed.

7 Refitting is a reversal of the removal procedure, noting the following points:

a) Fit new O-rings to all disturbed injector unions.

b) Apply a smear of engine oil to the O-rings, to aid installation. Ease the injectors and fuel rail into position, ensuring that none of the O-rings are displaced.

c) On completion, start the engine and check for fuel leaks.

Fuel pressure regulator

Note: *Refer to the warning notes at the end of Section 1 before proceeding.*

8 Disconnect the vacuum pipe from the regulator.

9 Place a wad of rag over the regulator, to catch any fuel spray which may be released. Remove the retaining clip, and ease the regulator out from the fuel rail **(see illustration)**.

10 Refitting is a reversal of the removal procedure. Examine the regulator seal for signs of damage or deterioration, and renew if necessary.

Throttle potentiometer

11 Disconnect the battery negative terminal.

12 Depress the retaining clip, and disconnect the wiring connector from the throttle potentiometer.

13 Slacken and remove the two retaining screws, then disengage the potentiometer from the throttle valve spindle and remove it from the vehicle **(see illustration)**.

14 Refitting is a reverse of the removal procedure, ensuring that the potentiometer is correctly engaged with the throttle valve spindle **(see illustration)**.

Electronic control unit (ECU)

15 The ECU is located on the right-hand side of the engine compartment, underneath a large plastic cover

16 To remove the ECU, first disconnect the battery negative lead.

17 Unclip the cover from the mounting plate, then lift the retaining clip and disconnect the wiring connector from the ECU. Slacken and remove the ECU retaining bolts, disconnect the vacuum hose, and remove the unit from the vehicle **(see illustrations)**.

18 Refitting is a reverse of the removal procedure, ensuring the wiring connector and vacuum hose are securely reconnected.

Idle mixture adjustment potentiometer - K6B engine models

19 The idle mixture adjustment potentiometer is situated on the right-hand side of the engine compartment, on the underside of the ECU bracket. To remove it, first disconnect the battery negative terminal.

20 Depress the retaining tangs and disconnect the wiring connector, then undo the retaining screw and remove the potentiometer from the vehicle **(see illustrations)**.

21 Refitting is the reverse of removal. On completion check and, if necessary, adjust the idle mixture setting (exhaust gas CO level) as described in Chapter 1.

Idle speed auxiliary air valve

22 The auxiliary air valve is mounted on the underside of the inlet manifold.

23 To remove it, first disconnect the battery negative terminal.

24 Depress the retaining clip, and disconnect the wiring connector from the air valve.

25 Slacken the retaining clips, and disconnect both vacuum hoses from the end of the auxiliary air valve.

26 Slide the valve out from its mounting rubber, and remove it from the engine compartment.

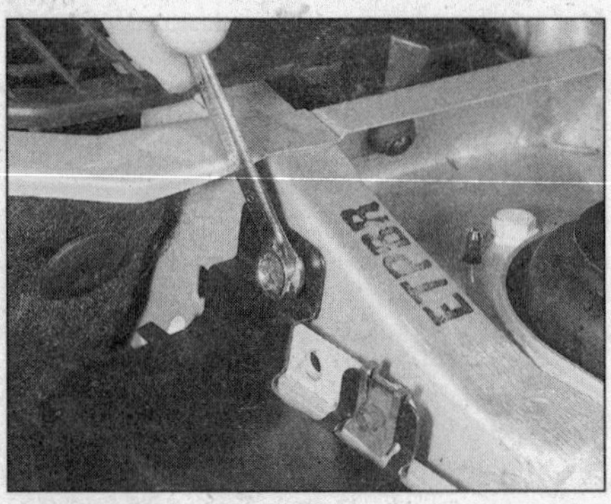

13.17a Undo the ECU upper retaining bolt . . .

13.17b . . . and loosen its lower mounting nut. The lower mounting is slotted, to ease removal

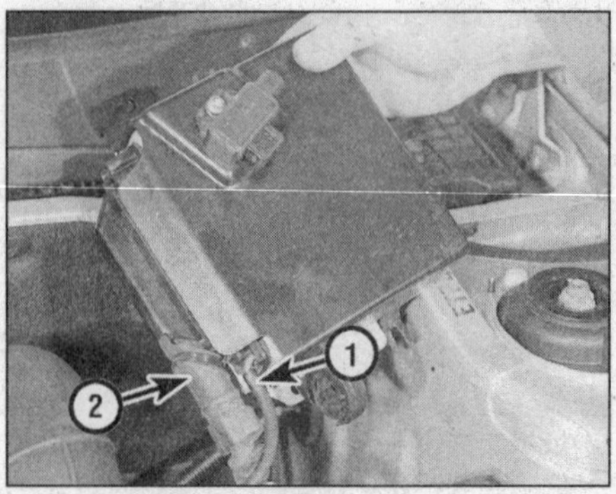

13.17c Remove the ECU, disconnecting its vacuum hose (1) and wiring connector (2) as they become accessible

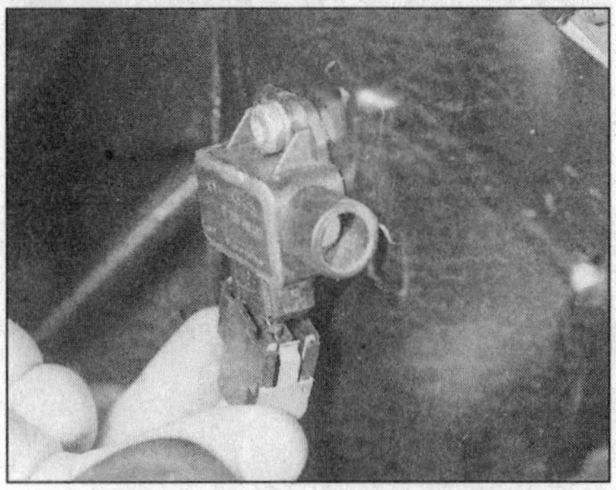

13.20a Disconnect the wiring connector . . .

13.20b . . . then undo the retaining screw and remove the idle mixture potentiometer

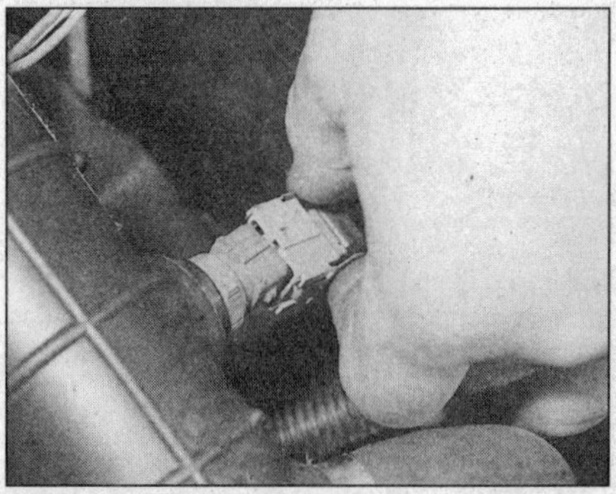

13.31 Disconnecting the wiring connector from the intake air temperature sensor

27 Refitting is a reversal of the removal procedure. Examine the mounting rubber for signs of deterioration, and renew it if necessary.

Manifold absolute pressure (MAP) sensor

28 The MAP sensor is an integral part of the electronic control unit (ECU). Refer to paragraphs 15 to 18 for removal and refitting details.

Coolant temperature sensor

29 Refer to Chapter 3.

Intake air temperature sensor

30 The intake air temperature sensor is screwed into the top of the air cleaner housing. To remove the sensor, first disconnect the battery negative terminal.

31 Disconnect the wiring connector, then unscrew the sensor and remove it from the vehicle **(see illustration)**.

32 Refitting is the reverse of removal.

Crankshaft sensor

33 The crankshaft sensor is situated on the front face of the clutch bellhousing, on the transmission.

34 To remove the sensor, first disconnect the battery negative terminal.

35 Trace the wiring back from the sensor to the wiring connector, and disconnect it from the main harness.

36 Prise out the rubber grommet, then undo the retaining bolt and withdraw the sensor from the transmission.

37 Refitting is a reverse of the removal procedure, ensuring that the sensor retaining bolt is securely tightened and that the grommet is correctly seated in the transmission housing.

Fuel injection system relay unit

38 The relay unit is clipped onto the underside of the ECU mounting plate, on the right-hand side of the engine compartment.

39 To remove the relay unit, first disconnect the battery negative lead.

40 Unclip the relay unit from the mounting plate, disconnect the wiring connector and remove it from the vehicle **(see illustrations)**.

41 Refitting is the reverse of removal, ensuring that the relay unit is securely held in position by its retaining clip.

13.40a Disconnect the wiring connector . . .

13.40b . . . then undo the retaining bolt, and remove the fuel injection relay unit

4C

14 Inlet manifold - removal and refitting

Removal

1 Remove the throttle housing as described in Section 12.

2 Depress the retaining clip and disconnect the wiring connector from the idle speed auxiliary air valve, which is mounted on the underside of the manifold. Slacken the retaining clip and disconnect the vacuum hose from the valve, leaving it free to be removed with the manifold.

3 Release the retaining clips (where fitted) and disconnect all the relevant vacuum and breather hoses from the manifold. Make identification marks on the hoses to ensure that they are connected correctly on refitting.

4 Bearing in mind the information given in Section 7, slacken the retaining clips and disconnect the fuel feed and return hoses from the fuel rail. Where the original crimped-type Citroën hose clips are still fitted, cut and discard them; replace them with worm-drive hose clips on refitting. If preferred at this stage, the complete fuel rail may be removed with reference to Section 13. If this course of action is taken, go to paragraph 6.

5 Depress the retaining tangs and disconnect the wiring connectors from the four injectors. Free the wiring from any relevant retaining clips, and position it clear of the manifold.

6 Where necessary, undo the retaining bolts and remove the support bracket from the underside of the manifold.

7 Undo the manifold retaining nuts, and withdraw the manifold from the engine compartment. Recover the four manifold seals and discard them; new ones must be used on refitting.

Refitting

8 Refitting is a reverse of the relevant removal procedure, noting the following points:

a) Ensure that the manifold and cylinder head mating surfaces are clean and dry.
b) Locate the new seals in their recesses in the manifold. Refit the manifold, and tighten its retaining nuts to the specified torque.
c) Ensure that all relevant hoses are reconnected to their original positions, and are securely held (where necessary) by the retaining clips.

15 Exhaust manifold - removal and refitting

Removal

1 Slacken and remove the retaining screws, and remove the shroud from the top of the exhaust manifold.
2 Firmly apply the handbrake, then jack up the front of the vehicle and support it on axle stands.
3 Unscrew the nut securing the front pipe to its mounting stud, and recover the spring cup and spring.
4 Undo the nuts securing the exhaust front pipe to the manifold, then free the front pipe and recover the gasket.
5 Undo the eight retaining nuts securing the manifold to the head. Manoeuvre the manifold out of the engine compartment, and discard the manifold gaskets.

Refitting

6 Refitting is the reverse of the removal procedure, noting the following points:

a) Examine all the exhaust manifold studs for signs of damage and corrosion. Remove all traces of corrosion, and repair or renew any damaged studs.
b) Ensure that the manifold and cylinder head sealing faces are clean and flat, and fit new manifold gaskets. Tighten the manifold retaining nuts to the specified torque.
c) Reconnect the front pipe to the manifold using the information given in Section 16.

16 Exhaust system - general information and component removal

General information

1 On models without a catalytic converter, the exhaust system consists of three sections; the front pipe, the intermediate pipe and silencer box, and the tailpipe and main silencer box. The exhaust system sections are joined by either a flange and ring or a clamp-type joint. The front pipe-to-manifold joint is of gasket type, and is secured by nuts and bolts. The front pipe-to-intermediate pipe joint is of the spring-loaded ball/ring type, to allow for movement in the exhaust system. The intermediate pipe-to-tailpipe joint is secured by a clamping ring.
2 On models with a catalytic converter, the exhaust system consists of four sections; the front pipe, the catalytic converter, the intermediate pipe and silencer box, and the tailpipe and main silencer box. The exhaust system sections are joined by either a flange and ring or a clamp-type joint. The front pipe-to-manifold joint is of gasket type, and is secured by nuts and bolts. The front pipe-to-catalytic converter joint is of the spring-loaded ball/ring type, to allow for movement in the exhaust system. The catalytic converter-to-intermediate pipe joint and the intermediate pipe-to-silencer joint are secured by a clamping ring.
3 On all models, the system is suspended throughout its entire length by rubber mountings.

Removal

4 Each exhaust section can be removed individually or, alternatively, the complete system can be removed as a unit.
5 To remove the system or part of the system, first jack up the front or rear of the car and support it on axle stands. Alternatively, position the car over an inspection pit, or on car ramps.

Front pipe

6 On models with a catalytic converter, trace the wiring back from the lambda (oxygen) sensor to its wiring connectors, which are clipped onto the top of the transmission unit, and disconnect them from the main wiring harness.
7 Unscrew the nut securing the front pipe to its mounting stud, and recover the spring cup and spring.
8 Undo the nuts securing the exhaust front pipe to the manifold, then free the front pipe and recover the gasket.
9 Slacken and remove the two nuts securing the front pipe to the catalytic converter/intermediate pipe (as applicable), and recover the spring cups and springs. Remove the bolts, then withdraw the front pipe from underneath the vehicle, taking great care not to damage the lambda sensor (where fitted). Recover the sealing ring from the joint.

Catalytic converter

10 Undo the two nuts securing the front pipe flange joint to the catalytic converter. Recover the springs and spring cups, and withdraw the bolts.
11 Slacken the catalytic converter-to-intermediate pipe clamping ring bolts, and disengage the clamp from the flange joint.
12 Free the catalytic converter from the intermediate pipe, then withdraw it from underneath the vehicle and recover the sealing ring from the front pipe joint. Do not drop the catalytic converter, as it contains a fragile ceramic element.

Intermediate pipe - models without a catalytic converter

13 Undo the two nuts securing the front pipe flange joint to the intermediate pipe. Recover the springs and spring cups, and withdraw the bolts.
14 Slacken the clamping ring bolts, and disengage the clamp from the intermediate pipe-to-tailpipe joint.
15 Free the intermediate pipe from its mounting rubbers, then disengage it from the tailpipe and the front pipe and remove it from underneath the vehicle. Recover the wire-mesh gasket from the front pipe joint.

Intermediate pipe - models with a catalytic converter

16 Slacken the clamping ring bolts and disengage the clamps from both the intermediate pipe joints.
17 Free the intermediate pipe from its mounting rubbers. Disengage it first from the tailpipe, then the catalytic converter, and remove it from underneath the vehicle.

Tailpipe

18 Slacken the intermediate pipe-to-tailpipe clamping ring bolts, and disengage the clamp from the joint.
19 Unhook the tailpipe from its mounting rubbers, and remove it from the vehicle.

Complete system

20 Disconnect the front pipe from the manifold as described in paragraphs 6 to 9.
21 With the aid of an assistant, free the system from all its mounting rubbers, and manoeuvre it out from underneath the vehicle.

Heat shield(s)

22 The heat shields are secured to the underside of the body by a mixture of nuts and bolts. Each shield can be removed once the relevant exhaust section has been removed.

> **HAYNES HiNT** *If the heat shield is being removed to gain access to a component located behind it, it may prove sufficient to remove the fasteners and simply lower the shield, without disturbing the exhaust system.*

Refitting

23 Each section is refitted by a reversal of the removal sequence, noting the following points:

a) Ensure that all traces of corrosion have been removed from the flanges, and renew all necessary gaskets/sealing rings.
b) Inspect the rubber mountings for signs of damage or deterioration, and renew as necessary.
c) Prior to assembling the spring-loaded ball type joint, a smear of high-temperature grease should be applied to the joint mating surfaces.
d) On joints which are secured by clamping rings, apply a smear of exhaust system jointing paste to the joint mating surfaces, to ensure a gastight seal. Tighten the clamping ring nuts evenly and progressively to the specified torque, so that the clearance between the clamp halves is equal on either side.
e) Prior to tightening the exhaust system fasteners, ensure that all rubber mountings are correctly located, and that there is adequate clearance between the exhaust system and vehicle underbody.

Chapter 4 Part D: Fuel/exhaust systems - Diesel models

Contents

Degrees of difficulty

Easy, suitable for novice with little experience	**Fairly easy,** suitable for beginner with some experience	**Fairly difficult,** suitable for competent DIY mechanic	**Difficult,** suitable for experienced DIY mechanic	**Very difficult,** suitable for expert DIY or professional

Specifications

General

System type	Rear-mounted fuel tank, distributor fuel injection pump with integral transfer pump, indirect injection
Firing order	1-3-4-2 (No 1 at transmission/flywheel end)

Recommended fuel

Type	Commercial diesel fuel for road vehicles (DERV)

Injection pump

Type:	
1360 cc engine	Roto-Diesel or Bosch
1527 cc engine	Roto-Diesel/Lucas
Direction of rotation	Clockwise, viewed from sprocket end
Static timing:	
Setting:	
Engine position	No 4 piston at TDC
Pump position:	
Roto-Diesel	Value shown on pump (see text)
Bosch	0.80 mm (ABDC on the pump)
Equivalent static advance:	
1360 cc engine	11° 30' BTDC
1527 cc engine	14° BTDC
Dynamic timing (at normal operating temperature):	
1360 cc engine	12° BTDC
1527 cc engine	Not available
Idle speed and anti-stall speed	See Chapter 1
Fast idle speed:	
Roto-Diesel	950 ± 50 rpm
Bosch	850 to 900 rpm
Maximum no-load speed:	
1360 cc engine	5500 rpm
1527 cc engine	5450 rpm

Injectors

Type	Pintle	
Opening pressure:		
Roto-Diesel	115 ± 5 bars	
Bosch	130 bars	

Torque wrench settings

	Nm	lbf ft
Injector pipe union nuts	20	15
Injection pump:		
Feed and return hose union bolts	25	18
Front mounting nuts	18	12
Rear mounting bolt	23	17
Injectors	70	52
Inlet manifold nuts and bolts	16	11
Exhaust manifold nuts	18	12
Exhaust system fasteners:		
Front pipe-to-manifold nut	35	26
Front pipe-to-intermediate pipe/catalytic converter nuts	10	7
Clamping ring nuts	15	11

1 General information and precautions

1 The fuel system consists of a rear-mounted fuel tank, a fuel filter with integral water separator, a fuel injection pump, injectors and associated components. As the fuel passes through the filter, the fuel is heated by coolant flowing through the filter housing - this reduces the chance of wax crystals forming in the fuel ("waxing"), in cold weather, which would otherwise cause fuel starvation.

2 The exhaust system is conventional, but on certain models, an unregulated catalytic converter may be fitted to reduce exhaust gas emissions. On the 1527 cc cast-iron block engine (code VJY), an exhaust gas recirculation system (EGR) is fitted. This system circulates a proportion of the exhaust gas back into the combustion chambers during certain operating conditions, in order to reduce harmful exhaust gas emissions. This is achieved by reducing the peak temperatures in the combustion chambers.

3 Fuel is drawn from the fuel tank to the fuel injection pump by a vane-type transfer pump incorporated in the fuel injection pump. Before reaching the pump, the fuel passes through a fuel filter, where foreign matter and water are removed. Any excess fuel lubricates the moving components of the pump, and is then returned to the tank.

4 The fuel injection pump is driven at half crankshaft speed by the timing belt. The high pressure required to inject the fuel into the compressed air in the swirl chambers is achieved by a cam plate acting on a single piston on the Bosch pump, or by two opposed pistons forced together by rollers running in a cam ring on the Lucas/CAV pump. The fuel passes through a central rotor with a single outlet drilling which aligns with ports leading to the injector pipes.

5 Fuel metering is controlled by a centrifugal governor which reacts to accelerator pedal position and engine speed. The governor is linked to a metering valve, which increases or decreases the amount of fuel delivered at each pumping stroke.

6 Basic injection timing is determined when the pump is fitted. When the engine is running, it is varied automatically to suit the prevailing engine speed, by a mechanism which turns the cam plate or ring.

7 The four fuel injectors produce a homogeneous spray of fuel into the swirl chambers located in the cylinder head. The injectors are calibrated to open and close at critical pressures to provide efficient and even combustion. Each injector needle is lubricated by fuel, which accumulates in the spring chamber and is channelled to the injection pump return hose by leak-off pipes.

8 Bosch or Lucas CAV/Roto-Diesel fuel system components may be fitted, depending on model. Components from the latter manufacturer are marked either "CAV", "Roto-Diesel", or "Con-Diesel", depending on their date and place of manufacture. With the exception of the fuel filter assembly, replacement components must be of the same make as those originally fitted.

9 Cold starting is assisted by preheater or "glow" plugs fitted to each swirl chamber (see Chapter 5C for further details).

10 On Lucas pumps, the fast idle system is operated by a thermostatic valve which is screwed into the fuel filter/thermostat housing. The valve operates a fast idle lever on the injection pump, via a cable, to increase the idle speed when the engine is cold. Bosch pumps have the same system, but additionally, the fast idle system incorporates an electrically-heated device which advances the pump timing when the engine is cold.

11 A stop solenoid cuts the fuel supply to the injection pump rotor when the ignition is switched off. On some pumps, there is also a hand-operated stop lever for use in an emergency.

12 Provided that the specified maintenance is carried out, the fuel injection equipment will give long and trouble-free service. The injection pump itself may well outlast the engine. The main potential cause of damage to the injection pump and injectors is dirt or water in the fuel.

13 Servicing of the injection pump and injectors is very limited for the home mechanic, and any dismantling or adjustment other than that described in this Chapter must be entrusted to a Citroën dealer or fuel injection specialist.

Warning: It is necessary to take certain precautions when working on the fuel system components, particularly the fuel injectors. Before carrying out any operations on the fuel system, refer to the precautions given in "Safety first!" at the beginning of this manual, and to any additional warning notes at the start of the relevant Sections.

2 Air cleaner housing - removal and refitting

1 The air cleaner housing is built into the inlet manifold. Cover and element removal are described in Chapter 1.

2 If necessary, the intake duct can be removed, once its retaining clip has been slackened, the nut securing it to the cylinder head has been removed, and the two pop-rivets securing it to the crossmember have been drilled out. When refitting, tighten the retaining clip, and secure the duct in position with new pop-rivets.

3 Accelerator cable - removal, refitting and adjustment

Removal and refitting

1 Refer to Chapter 4A, Section 7, substituting "injection pump" for all references to the carburettor. Adjust the cable as described below.

Adjustment

2 Remove the spring clip from the accelerator outer cable ferrule then, ensuring that the pump accelerator lever is fully against the anti-stall screw, gently pull the cable out of its grommet until all free play is removed from the inner cable.

3 With the cable held in this position, ensure that the flat washer is pressed securely against the grommet, then fit the spring clip to the first outer cable groove visible in front of the rubber grommet and washer **(see illustration)**.

4 Have an assistant depress the accelerator pedal, and check that the accelerator lever opens fully, so that it contacts the maximum speed screw. Check also that it returns smoothly to its stop against the anti-stall screw.

4 Accelerator pedal - removal and refitting

Refer to Chapter 4A, Section 8.

5 Fuel level sender - removal and refitting

Refer to Chapter 4A, Section 5.

6 Fuel pick-up unit - removal and refitting

1 Disconnect the battery negative lead.

2 For access to the fuel pick-up unit, fold the rear seat cushion forwards.

3 Using a screwdriver, carefully prise the plastic access cover from the floor to expose the fuel pick-up (the pick-up is located under the right-hand cover, viewed facing towards the front of the vehicle) **(see illustration)**.

4 Mark the hoses for identification purposes, then slacken the feed and return hose retaining clips. Where crimped-type hose clips are fitted, cut the clips and discard them; replace them with worm-drive hose clips on refitting. On later models, quick-release fittings may be fitted to the fuel hoses; these are released by depressing their metal collars with a small, flat-bladed screwdriver **(see illustrations)**.

3.3 Adjusting the accelerator cable

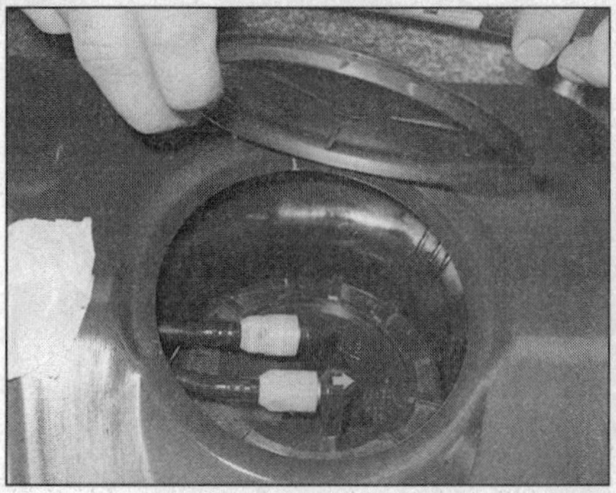

6.3 Remove the right-hand access cover to reveal the fuel pick-up unit

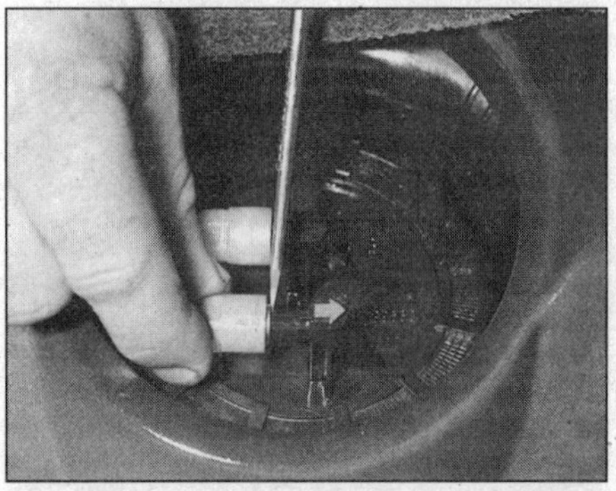

6.4a Where quick-release type fittings are used, depress their metal centre collars to release them . . .

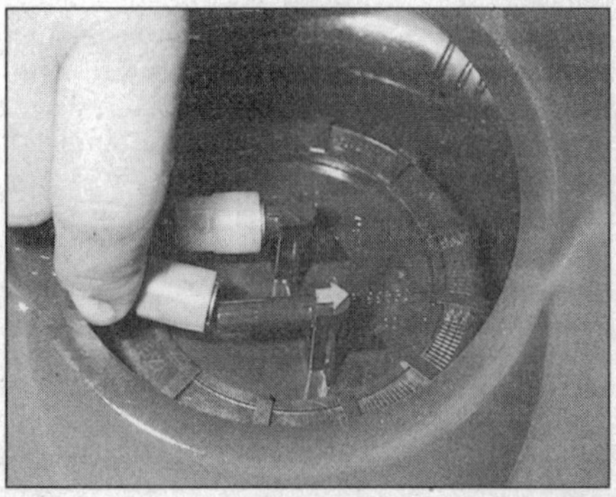

6.4b . . . then pull the hoses away from the pick-up unit

5 Disconnect both hoses from the top of the pick-up, and plug the hose ends.

6 Make alignment marks between the tank and pick-up unit, then unscrew the locking ring and remove it from the tank **(see illustration)**. This is best accomplished by using a screwdriver on the raised ribs of the locking ring. Carefully tap the screwdriver to turn the ring anti-clockwise until it can be unscrewed by hand.

7 Carefully lift the fuel pick-up assembly out of the fuel tank, taking great care not to damage the filter or to spill fuel onto the interior of the vehicle. Recover the rubber sealing ring and discard it - a new one must be used on refitting **(see illustration)**.

8 Note that the fuel pick-up assembly is only available as a complete assembly - no individual components are available separately.

4D

Refitting

9 Ensure that the fuel pick-up filter is clean and free of debris. Fit the new sealing ring to the top of the fuel tank.

10 Carefully manoeuvre the assembly into the fuel tank, aligning the marks made prior to removal.

11 Refit the locking ring, tightening it until its mark is correctly aligned with the centre of the three lines on the fuel tank, as noted prior to removal **(see illustration)**.

6.6 Unscrew the locking ring . . .

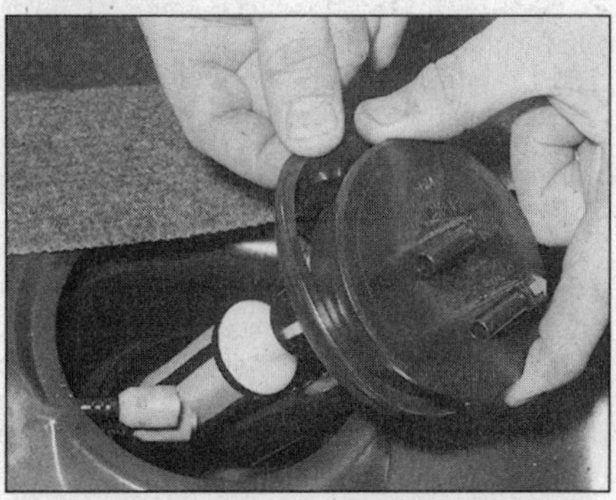

6.7 . . . then lift out the pick-up unit, and recover the rubber sealing ring

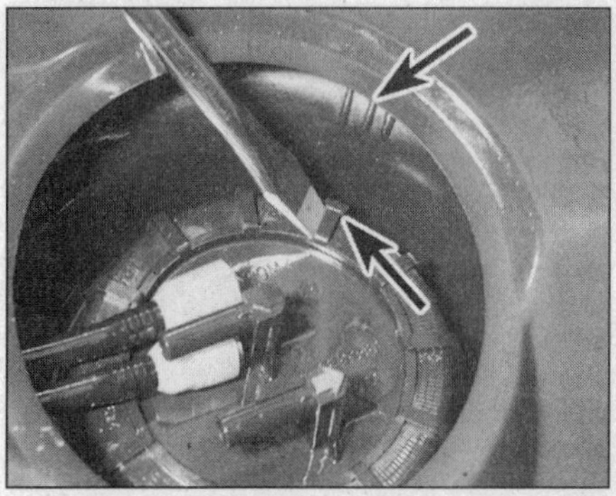

6.11 On refitting, tighten the sealing ring until its mark is aligned with the centre of the three ribs on the fuel tank (arrowed)

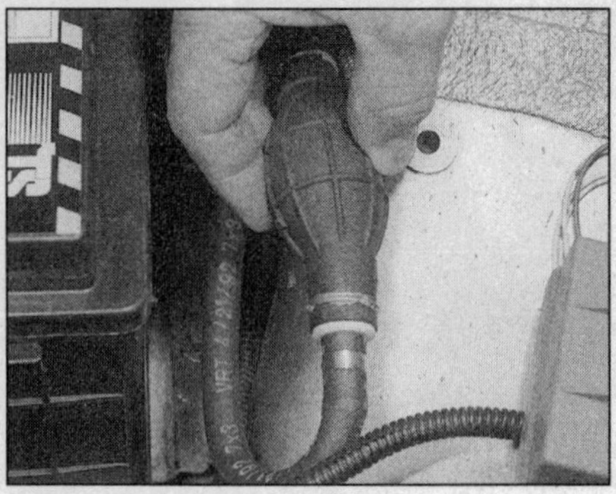

8.2 Priming the fuel system

8.3 Fuel system bleed screw (arrowed) is located on the top of the fuel filter/thermostat housing

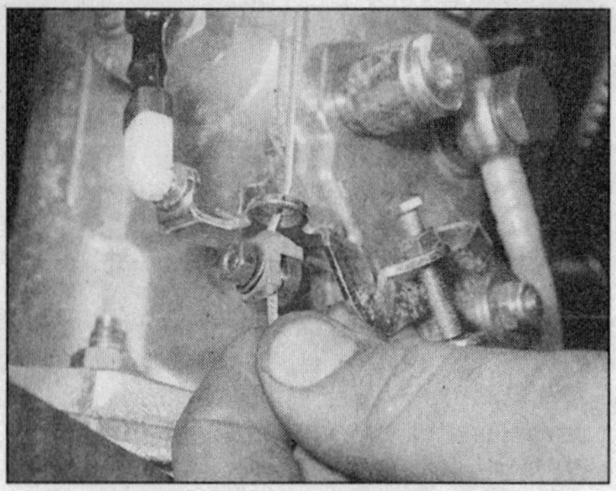

10.3 Slacken the clamp nut, and slide the end fitting off the fast idle cable

12 Reconnect the feed and return hoses, using the marks made on removal to ensure that they are correctly reconnected, and securely tighten their retaining clips.

13 Reconnect the battery negative terminal, and start the engine. Check the fuel feed and return hoses unions for signs of leakage.

14 If all is well, refit the plastic access cover, and fold down the rear seat cushion.

7 Fuel tank - removal and refitting

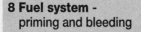

1 Refer to Chapter 4A, Section 6, ignoring the remark about the fuel filter, and disconnecting the fuel hoses from the pick-up unit.

8 Fuel system - priming and bleeding

Warning: Diesel injection pumps supply fuel at very high pressure. Extreme care must be taken when working on the fuel injectors and fuel pipes. It is advisable to place an absorbent cloth around the union before slackening a fuel pipe. Never expose the hands, face or any other part of the body to injector spray; the high working pressure can penetrate the skin, with potentially-fatal results. Refer also to "Safety first!" at the start of this manual.

1 After disconnecting part of the fuel supply system or running out of fuel, it is necessary to prime the system and bleed off any air which may have entered the system components.

2 All models are fitted with a hand-operated priming pump, consisting of a rubber bulb, which is clipped onto the side of the left-hand suspension strut turret, or located near the battery **(see illustration).**

3 To prime the system, loosen the bleed screw located on the top of the fuel filter/thermostat housing, mounted on the left-hand end of the cylinder head **(see illustration)**. If no bleed screw is fitted, loosen the outlet union itself (either at the filter/thermostat housing or at the injection pump); place an absorbent cloth around the union.

4 Pump the priming plunger until fuel free from air bubbles emerges from the outlet union or bleed screw (as applicable). Retighten the bleed screw or outlet union.

5 If air has entered the injector pipes, place wads of rag around the injector pipe unions at the injectors (to absorb spilt fuel), then slacken the unions. Refer to the warning at the start of this Section. Crank the engine on the starter motor until fuel emerges from the unions, then stop cranking the engine and retighten the unions. Mop up spilt fuel.

6 Start the engine with the accelerator pedal fully depressed. Additional cranking may be necessary to finally bleed the system before the engine starts.

9 Maximum engine speed - checking and adjustment

Caution: The maximum speed adjustment screw is sealed by the manufacturers at the factory using locking wire and a lead seal, and should not be disturbed.

1 Run the engine to normal operating temperature. If the vehicle does not have a tachometer (rev counter), connect a suitable instrument in accordance with its manufacturer's instructions.

2 Have an assistant fully depress the accelerator pedal, and check that the maximum engine speed is as given in the Specifications. Do not keep the engine at maximum speed for more than two or three seconds.

3 If adjustment is necessary, the vehicle should taken to Citroën dealer or suitable Diesel specialist. Adjustment should not be attempted by the home mechanic.

10 Fast idle thermostatic valve - removal, refitting and adjustment

Removal

1 Disconnect the battery negative terminal.

2 Partially drain the cooling system as described in Chapter 2.

3 Loosen the clamp nut, and slide the fast idle cable end fitting off the injection pump end of the inner cable **(see illustration)**.

4 Free the fast idle cable from the bracket or lever (as applicable) on the fuel injection pump.

5 Using a suitable spanner, unscrew the thermostatic valve from the cylinder head outlet housing, and remove the valve and cable assembly. Recover the sealing ring **(see illustrations)**.

Refitting

6 Fit a new sealing ring to the valve, and

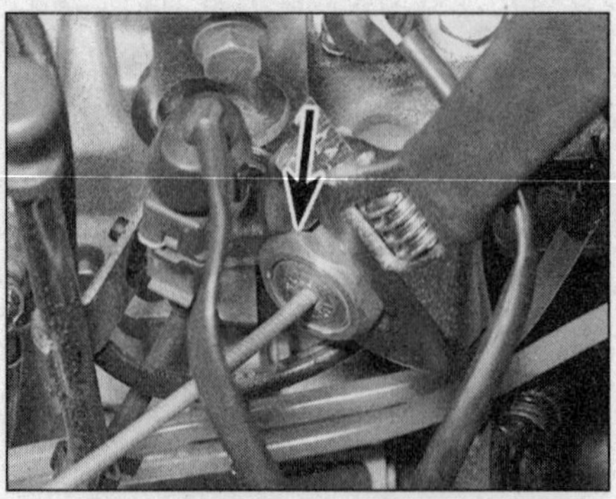

10.5a Unscrew the fast idle valve (arrowed) from the cylinder head . . .

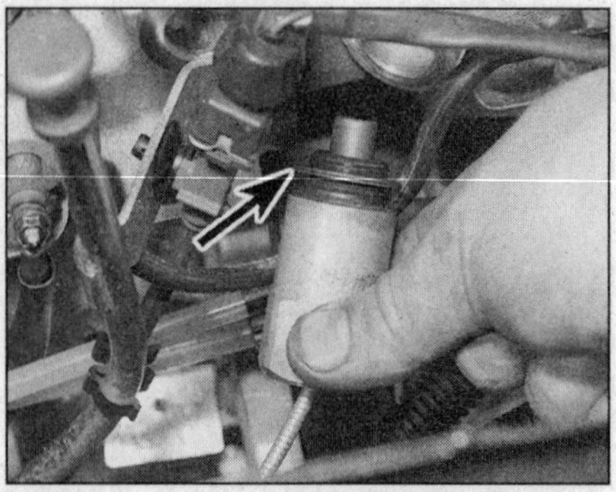

10.5b . . . and remove it along with its sealing washer (arrowed)

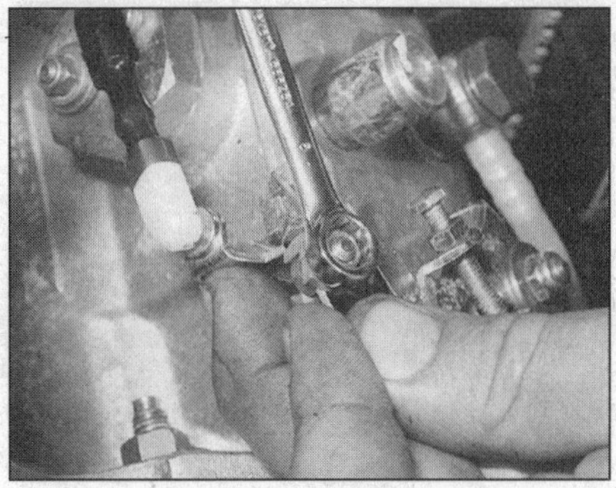

10.10 Adjust the fast idle cable as described in text

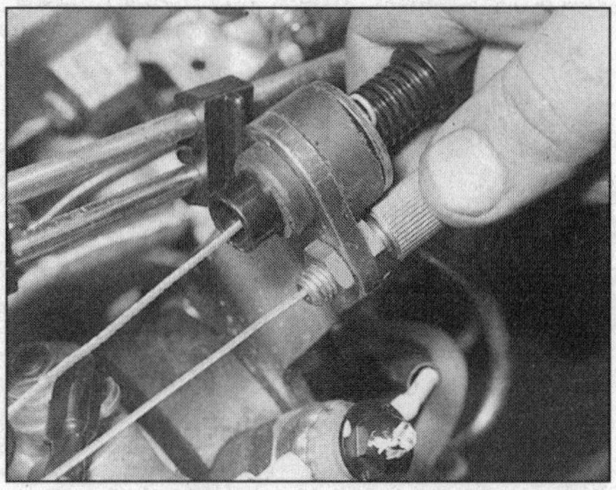

10.12 Fine adjustment of the fast idle cable can be made using the adjuster on the cable mounting bracket

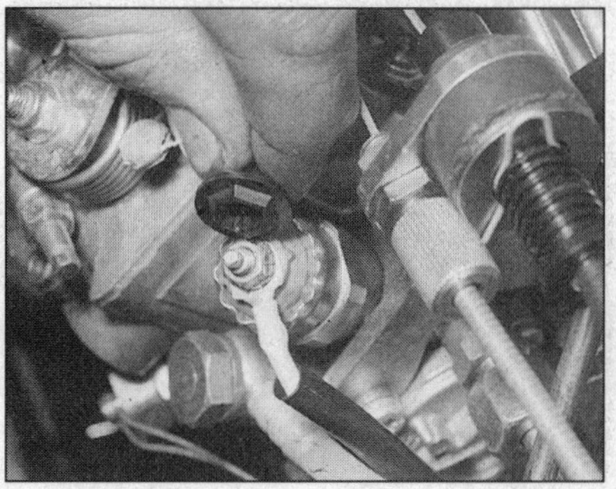

11.4a Remove the rubber cover . . .

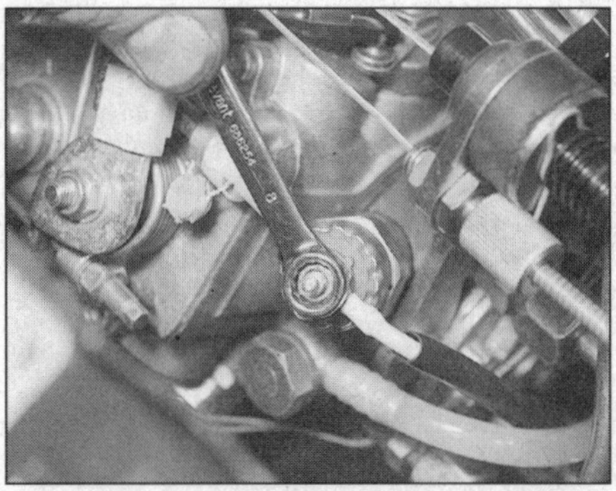

11.4b . . . then unscrew the retaining nut, and disconnect the stop solenoid wiring connector

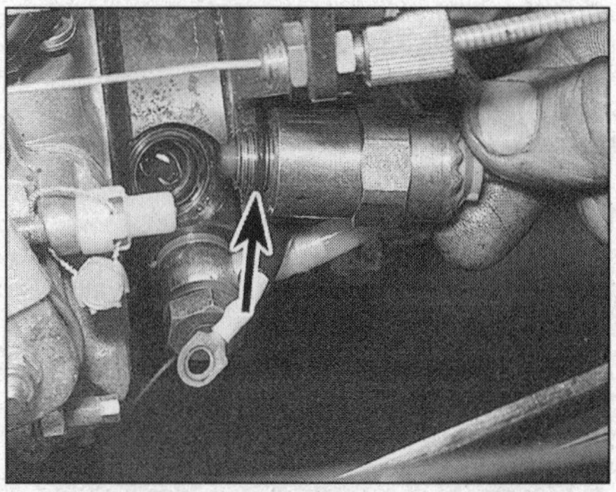

11.5a Unscrew the stop solenoid from the pump, and recover the O-ring (arrowed)

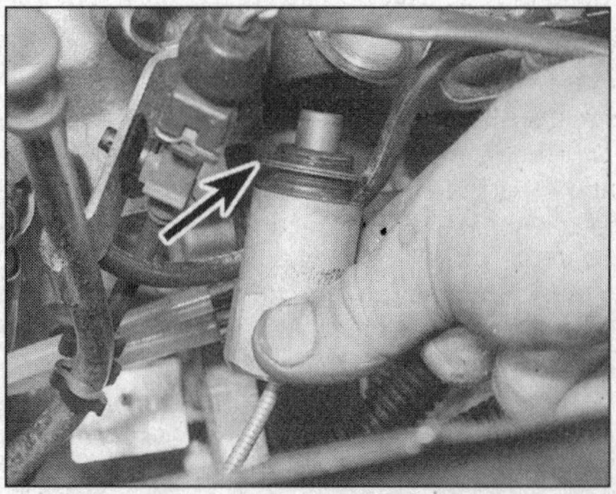

11.5b Remove the solenoid, and withdraw the plunger and spring

screw the valve into position in the cylinder head outlet housing, tightening it securely.

7 Insert the cable through the pump bracket, and pass the inner cable through the fast idle lever. Slide the end fitting onto the inner, and lightly tighten its clamp nut.

8 Refill the cooling system as described in Chapter 1.

9 Adjust the cable as follows.

Testing and adjustment

10 With the engine cold, push the fast idle lever fully to the end of its travel (towards the rear of the pump). Hold it in this position, and slide the cable end fitting on the cable until its abuts the fast idle lever or bracket (as applicable) then securely tighten its clamp nut **(see illustration)**.

11 Start the engine, and warm it up to its normal operating temperature. As the engine warms up, the fast idle cable should extend so that the fast idle lever returns to is stop.

12 Once the cooling fan has cut in, switch off the engine and measure the clearance between the fast idle lever and the cable end fitting. There should be a gap of approximately 0.5 to 1 mm. If not, slacken the clamp nut, move the end fitting to the correct position, then securely retighten the screw or nut. Note that fine adjustment of the cable can be made using the adjuster ferrule on the mounting bracket **(see illustration)**..

13 With the cable correctly adjusted, allow the engine to cool. As it cools, the fast idle cable should be drawn back into the valve, moving the fast idle lever back against its stop.

11 Stop solenoid - description, removal and refitting

Description

1 The stop solenoid is located on top of the fuel injection pump. Its purpose is to cut the fuel supply when the ignition is switched off. If an open-circuit occurs in the solenoid or its electrical supply, it will be impossible to start the engine, as the fuel will not be allowed to pass through the injection pump. The same applies if the solenoid jams shut. If the solenoid jams open, the engine will not stop when the ignition is switched off.

2 If the solenoid has failed and the engine will not run, a temporary repair may be made be removing the solenoid as described in the following paragraphs. Refit the solenoid body without the plunger and spring, and tape up its feed wire so that it cannot touch earth. The engine can then be started as usual, but it will be necessary to use the manual stop lever on the injection pump, or to stall the engine in gear, to stop it.

Removal

3 Disconnect the battery negative lead.

4 Remove the rubber cover (where fitted) then slacken and remove the retaining nut and washer, and disconnect the solenoid wiring connector **(see illustrations)**.

5 Unscrew the solenoid valve from the pump, and recover the plunger, spring and sealing ring. Take great care not to allow dirt to enter the pump **(see illustrations)**.

Refitting

6 Refitting is a reversal of removal, using a new sealing ring.

12 Fuel injection pump - removal and refitting

Removal

1 Disconnect the battery negative terminal.

2 Remove the right-hand headlight unit as described in Chapter 12. This will provide additional working room.

3 Remove the timing belt covers as described in Chapter 2B.

4 Align the engine TDC timing holes as described in Chapter 2B, Section 3, and lock the crankshaft, camshaft sprocket and injection pump sprocket in position. *Do not attempt to rotate the engine whilst the locking tools are in position.*

5 Remove the injection pump sprocket as described in Chapter 2B, Section 7.

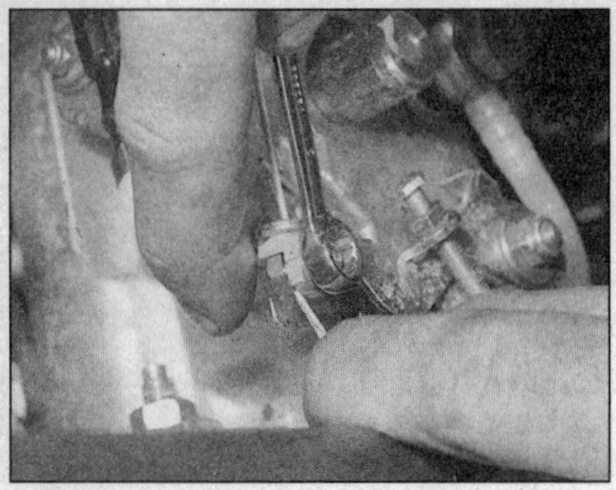

12.6 Loosen the clamp nut, and remove the end fitting from the fast idle cable

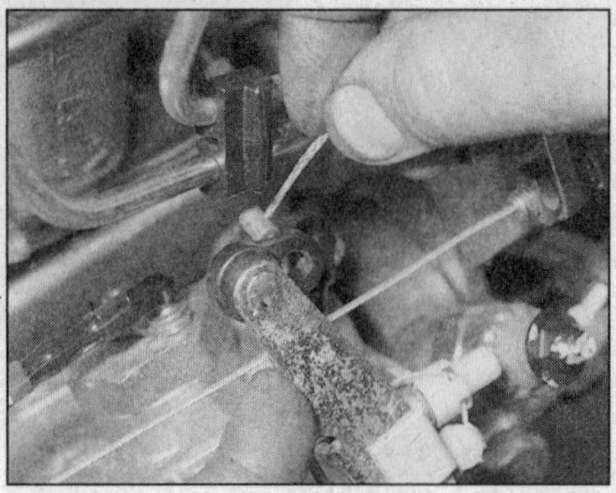

12.7a Free the accelerator inner cable from the pump lever . . .

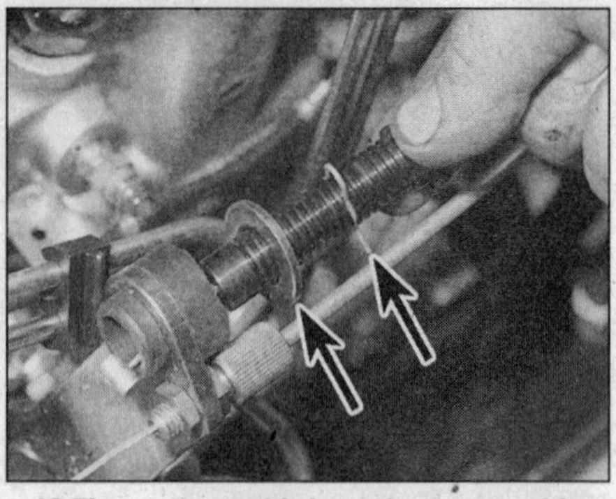

12.7b . . . then withdraw the outer cable from the mounting bracket, and recover the washer and spring clip (arrowed)

6 Loosen the clamp nut, and disconnect the fast idle cable end fitting from the injection pump end of the inner cable **(see illustration)**. Free the fast idle cable from the bracket or lever (as applicable) on the fuel injection pump.

7 Free the accelerator inner cable from the pump lever, then pull the outer cable out from its mounting bracket rubber grommet. Slide the flat washer off the end of the cable, and remove the spring clip **(see illustrations)**.

8 Wipe clean the fuel feed and return unions on the injection pump. Cover the alternator with a clean cloth or plastic bag, to protect it from any fuel being spilt onto it during the following operations.

9 Slacken and remove the fuel feed hose union bolt from the pump. Recover the sealing washer from each side of the hose union, and position the hose clear of the pump. Screw the union bolt back into position on the pump for safe-keeping, and cover both the hose end and union bolt to prevent the ingress of dirt into the fuel system.

10 Detach the fuel return hose from the pump as described in the previous paragraph **(see illustration)**. **Note:** *The injection pump feed and return hose union bolts are not interchangeable.*

11 Wipe clean the pipe unions, then slacken the union nut securing the injector pipes to the top of each injector, and the four union nuts securing the pipes to the rear of the injection pump. As each pump union nut is slackened, retain the adapter with a suitable open-ended spanner, to prevent it being unscrewed from the pump. With all the union nuts undone, remove the injector pipes from the engine (the pipes are removed in pairs) **(see illustrations)**.

12 Remove the rubber cover (where fitted) then undo the retaining nut and disconnect the wiring from the injection pump stop solenoid **(see illustration)**.

13 Using a scriber or suitable marker pen, make alignment marks between the injection pump front flange and the front mounting bracket. These marks can then be used to ensure that the pump is correctly positioned on refitting. To improve access to the pump, undo the two screws and remove the cover panel (where fitted) from the right-hand side of the radiator.

14 Unscrew the bolt securing the rear of the injection pump to its mounting bracket on the cylinder block **(see illustration)**.

15 Slacken and remove the three nuts and washers securing the pump to its front mounting bracket, then manoeuvre the pump away from the bracket and out of the engine compartment **(see illustrations)**.

Refitting

16 If a new pump is being fitted, transfer the alignment mark from the original pump onto the mounting flange of the new pump.

17 Manoeuvre the pump into position, and refit its three front washers and mounting nuts, and the rear mounting bolt. Align the marks made prior to removal, then securely tighten the retaining nuts and bolt.

18 Refit the injection pump sprocket as described in Chapter 2B, Section 7. Align the sprocket timing holes with those in the mounting plate, and lock the sprocket in position with the two locking tools.

19 Check the crankshaft, camshaft and injection pump sprockets are all correctly positioned, then engage the timing belt and tension it as described in Chapter 2B, Section 6. With the timing belt correctly fitted, remove the locking tools from the sprockets.

20 Set the injection pump timing as described in Section 14.

21 With the pump timing correctly set, reconnect the wiring to the stop solenoid, and securely tighten its retaining nut. Refit the rubber boot.

22 Reconnect the fuel feed and return hose unions to the pump, not forgetting to fit the filter to the feed hose union. Position a new sealing washer on each side of both unions, and tighten the union bolts to the specified torque setting.

23 Refit the injector pipes, and tighten their union nuts to the specified torque setting.

24 Mop up any spilt fuel, then remove any materials used to cover the alternator (paragraph 8).

25 Reconnect the accelerator cable, and adjust as described in Section 3.

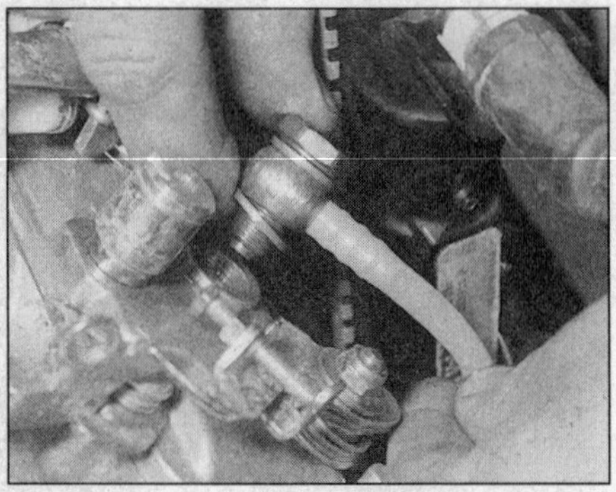

12.10 Unscrew the fuel return hose union bolt, and recover the sealing washer from each side of the hose union

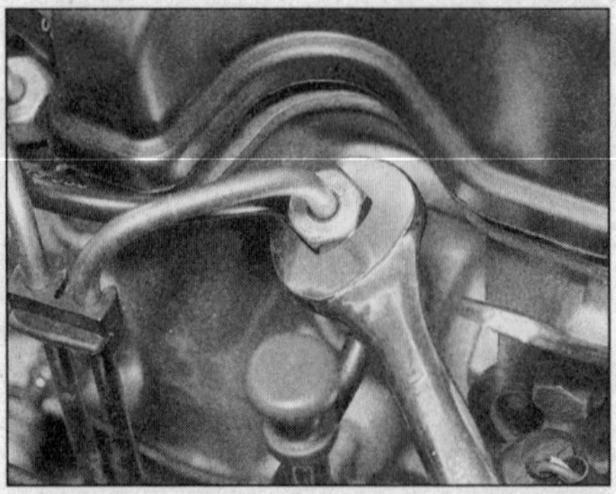

12.11a Unscrew the union nuts securing the injector pipes to the injectors . . .

12.11b . . . and to the pump. Whilst slackening the pump nuts, retain the pump adapters with an open-ended spanner

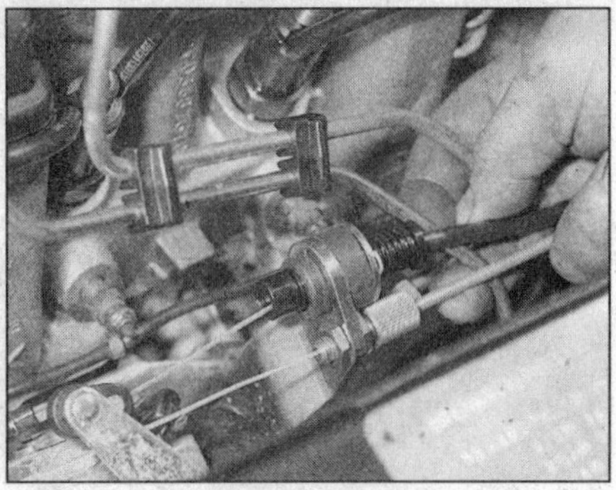
12.11c Remove the injector pipes in pairs

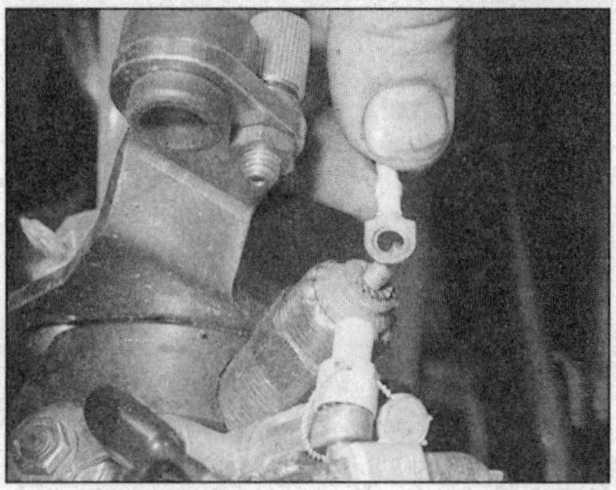
12.12 Disconnecting the wiring from the injection pump stop solenoid

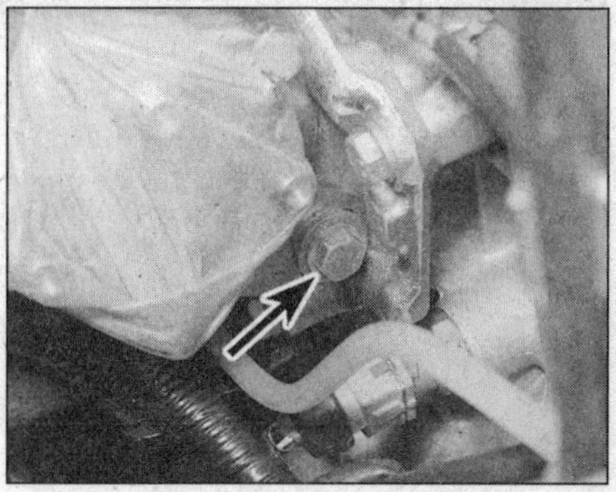
12.14 Unscrew the rear mounting bracket bolt (arrowed) . . .

26 Reconnect the fast idle valve cable, and adjust as described in Section 10.

27 Refit the right-hand headlight unit as described in Chapter 12.

28 Reconnect the battery negative lead.

29 Bleed the fuel system as described in Section 8.

30 On completion, start the engine, and adjust the idle speed and anti-stall speed as described in Chapter 1.

13 Injection timing - checking methods

1 Checking the injection timing is not a routine operation. It should only be necessary after the injection pump has been disturbed.

2 Dynamic timing equipment does exist, but it is unlikely to be available to the home mechanic. The equipment works by converting pressure pulses in an injector pipe into electrical signals. If such equipment is available, use it in accordance with its maker's instructions. The engine should be at normal operating temperature, to ensure that it is running at the correct idle speed. On the Bosch injection pump, running at normal operating temperature will also ensure that the cold advance system is not functioning.

3 Static timing as described in this Chapter gives good results if carried out carefully. A dial test indicator will be needed, with probes and adapters appropriate to the type of injection pump. Read through the procedures before starting work, to find out what is involved.

14 Injection timing - checking and adjustment

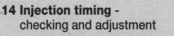

Caution: The maximum engine speed and transfer pressure settings, together with timing access plugs, are sealed by the manufacturers at the factory, using locking wire and lead seals. Do not disturb the wire if the vehicle is still within the warranty period, otherwise the warranty will be invalidated. Also do not attempt the timing procedure unless accurate instrumentation is available. Suitable special tools for carrying out pump timing are available from motor factors, and a dial test indicator will be required regardless of the method used. Refer to the precautions given in Section 1 of this Chapter before proceeding.

Note: *The following procedure describes checking the injection timing using the special Citroën tools and mounting brackets (Citroën tool number 4093-T for Lucas/CAV pumps, and tool number 7010-T and 2438-T for Bosch pumps). Without access to this equipment (or similar accurate tooling designed specifically for the injection pump being worked on), injection pump timing should be entrusted to a Citroën dealer.*

1 If the injection timing is being checked with the pump in position on the engine, rather than as part of the pump refitting procedure, disconnect the battery negative lead, and cover the alternator with a clean cloth or plastic bag to protect it from any fuel being spilt onto it. Remove the injector pipes as described in paragraph 11 of Section 12.

2 Referring to Chapter 2B, Section 3, align the engine TDC timing holes, then lock the crankshaft by inserting the locking tool into the flywheel (do not insert the camshaft and injection pump locking tools). Remove the locking tool, then turn the crankshaft **backwards** (anti-clockwise) approximately a quarter of a turn. Turning the engine will be much easier if the glow plugs are removed first - see Chapter 5C.

3 On Lucas/CAV pumps, unscrew the access plug from the guide on the top of the pump body, and recover the sealing washer **(see illustration)**. On Bosch pumps, unscrew the blanking plug from the end of the pump (between the injector pipe connections) and recover the sealing washer.

4 Clean the tool guide and the contact surface on the pump, then locate the dial gauge and bracket on the pump. On the Lucas/CAV pump, make sure that the probe is correctly

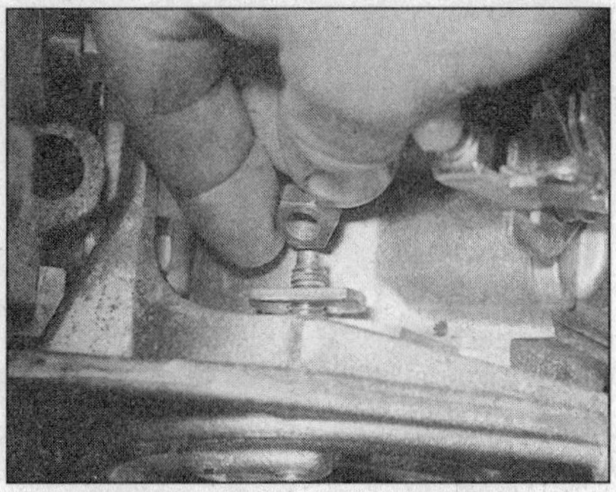
12.15a . . . then unscrew the front mounting nuts and washer . . .

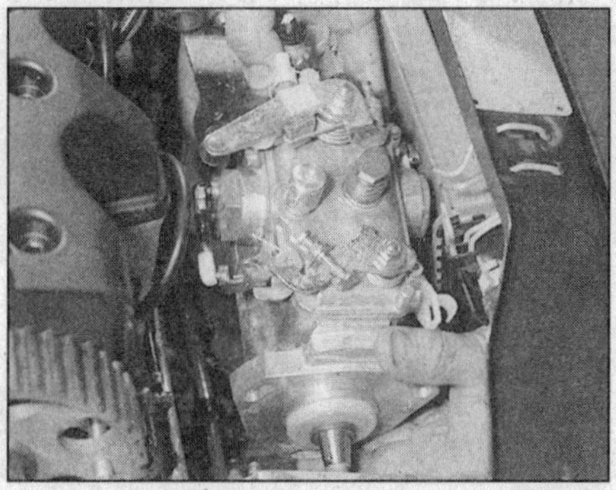
12.15b . . . and remove the injection pump from the engine

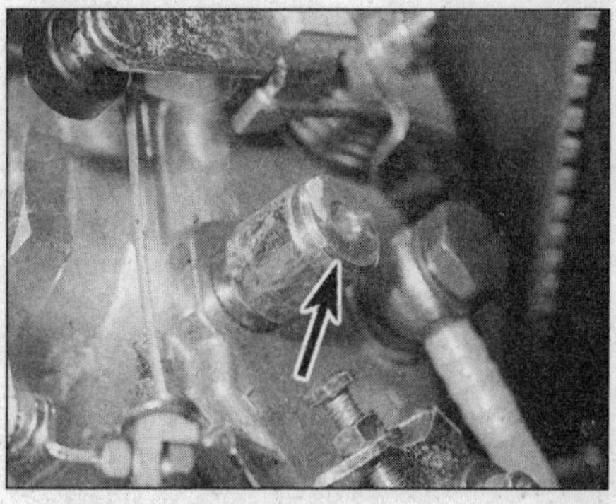
14.3 Injection pump timing access plug (arrowed)

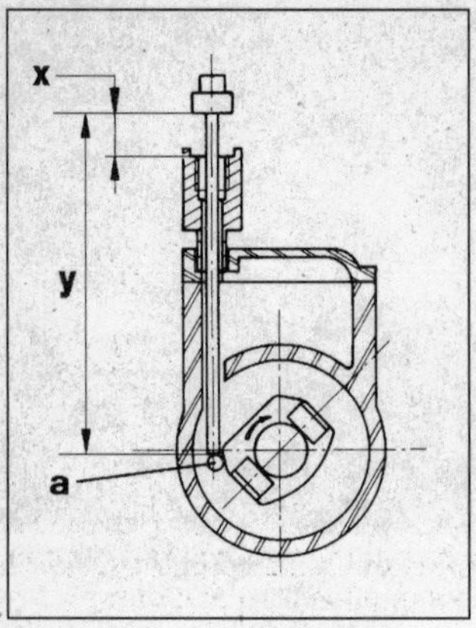

14.4a Using the Lucas/CAV injection pump timing tool

a Timing piece
x Timing value (engraved on disc or label)
y 95.5 ± 0.1 mm
Probe diameter = 7. mm

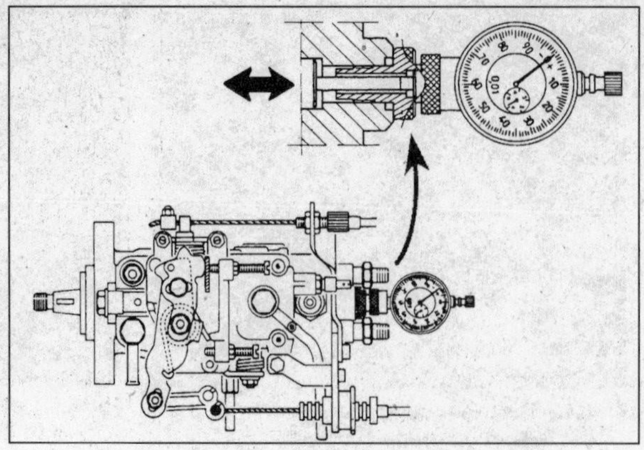

14.4b Using the Bosch injection pump timing tool

14.7 Injection pump timing value is usually on a tag attached to the pump accelerator lever

seated against the guide sealing washer surface **(see illustrations)**. **Note:** *The timing probe must be seated against the guide sealing washer surface, and not the upper lip of the guide, for the measurement to be accurate.*

5 Position the dial gauge so that its plunger is at the mid-point of its travel, and zero the gauge.

6 Rotate the crankshaft slowly in the correct direction of rotation (clockwise) until the crankshaft locking tool can be re-inserted.

7 With the crankshaft locked in position, read the dial gauge; the reading should correspond to the value marked on the pump (there is a tolerance of ± 0.04 mm) or with the information given in the Specifications. The timing value may be marked on a plastic disc attached to the front of the pump, or alternatively on a tag attached to the accelerator pump lever **(see illustration)**.

8 If adjustment is necessary, slacken the pump front mounting nuts and the rear mounting bolt, then slowly rotate the pump body until the point is found where the specified reading is obtained on the dial gauge. When the pump is correctly positioned, tighten both its front mounting nuts and rear bolt to their specified torque settings. To improve access to the pump nuts, undo the two screws and remove the cover panel (where fitted) from the side of the radiator, if not already done.

9 Remove the crankshaft locking tool. On the Lucas/CAV pump, withdraw the timing probe, so that it is positioned clear of the pump rotor dowel. Rotate the crankshaft through one and three-quarter rotations in the normal direction of rotation.

10 Slide the timing probe back into position (ensuring that it is correctly seated against the guide sealing washer surface, not the upper lip on the Lucas/CAV pump), then zero the dial gauge.

11 Rotate the crankshaft slowly in the correct direction of rotation until the crankshaft locking tool can be re-inserted. Recheck the timing measurement.

12 If adjustment is necessary, slacken the pump mounting nuts and bolt, and repeat the timing operations.

13 When the pump timing is correctly set, remove the dial gauge and mounting bracket, and withdraw the timing probe.

14 Refit the access plug and sealing washer, and tighten it securely.

15 If the procedure is being carried out as part of the pump refitting sequence, proceed as described in Section 12.

16 If the procedure is being carried out with the pump fitted to the engine, refit the injector pipes, tightening their union nuts to the specified torque setting. Reconnect the battery, then bleed the fuel system as described in Section 8. Start the engine, and adjust the idle speed and anti-stall speeds as described in Chapter 1.

15 Fuel injectors - testing, removal and refitting

Warning: Exercise extreme caution when working on the fuel injectors. Never expose the hands or any part of the body to injector spray, as the high working pressure can cause the fuel to penetrate the skin, with possibly fatal results. You are strongly advised to have any work which involves testing the injectors under pressure carried out by a Citroën dealer or fuel injection specialist. Refer to the precautions given in Section 1 of this Chapter before proceeding.

Testing

1 Injectors do deteriorate with prolonged use, and it is reasonable to expect them to need reconditioning or renewal after 60 000 miles (100 000 km) or so. Accurate testing, overhaul and calibration of the injectors must be left to a specialist. A defective injector which is causing knocking or smoking can be located without dismantling as follows.

2 Run the engine at a fast idle. Slacken each injector union in turn, placing rag around the union to catch spilt fuel, and being careful not to expose the skin to any spray. When the union on the defective injector is slackened, the knocking or smoking will stop.

Removal

Note: *Take great care not to allow dirt into the injectors or fuel pipes during this procedure. Do not drop the injectors or allow the needles at their tips to become damaged. The injectors are precision-made to fine limits, and must not be handled roughly. In particular, do not mount them in a bench vice.*

3 Disconnect the battery negative lead, and cover the alternator with a clean cloth or plastic bag to protect it from any fuel being spilt onto it.

4 Carefully clean around the injectors and return pipes, and disconnect the return pipe from each injector. Note the location of any clips attached to the pipes.

5 Wipe clean the pipe unions, then slacken the union nut securing the injector pipes to each injector, and the four union nuts securing the pipes to the injection pump. As each pump union nut is slackened, retain the adapter with a suitable open-ended spanner, to prevent it being unscrewed from the pump. With all the

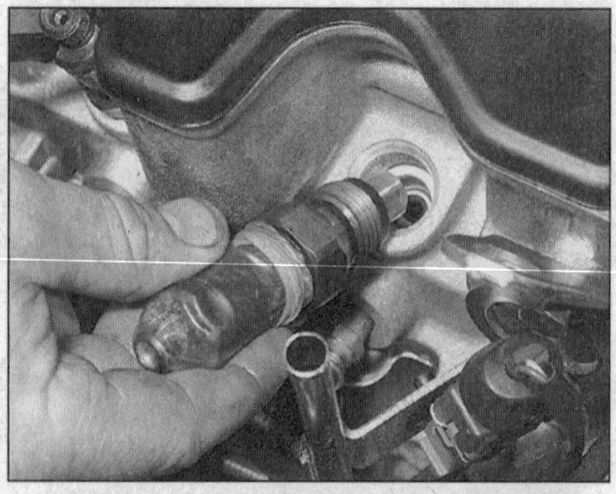

15.6 Unscrew the injector, and remove it from the cylinder head - note cover over the pipe opening, secured with an elastic band

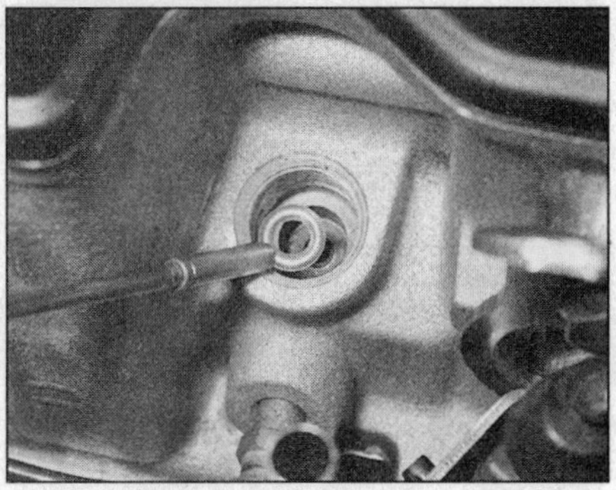

15.10a Fit the new flame shield washer to the cylinder head . . .

union nuts undone, remove the injector pipes from the engine. Cover the injector and pipe unions, to prevent the entry of dirt into the system.

6 Unscrew the injector, using a deep socket or box spanner, and remove it from the cylinder head **(see illustration).**

7 Recover the sealing and flame shield washers. Also remove the injector sleeve if it is a loose fit in the cylinder head.

Refitting

8 Obtain a new sealing washer and flame shield washer. Where removed, also renew the injector sleeve if it is damaged.

9 Where necessary, refit the injector sleeve to the cylinder head.

10 Fit the new flame shield washer to the sleeve, noting that it must be fitted with its convex side facing upwards (towards the injector) **(see illustrations).**

11 Fit the new sealing washer to the top of the sleeve **(see illustration).**

12 Screw the injector into position, and tighten it to the specified torque **(see illustration).**

13 Refit the injector pipes, and tighten the union nuts to the specified torque setting. Position any clips attached to the pipes as noted before removal.

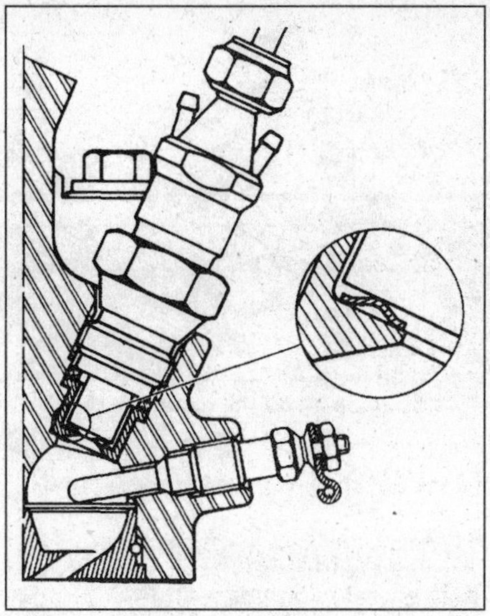

15.10b . . . making sure that its convex side is facing towards the injector (see inset)

15.11 Fit a new sealing washer . . .

14 Reconnect the return pipes securely to the injectors.

15 Start the engine. If difficulty is experienced, bleed the fuel system as described in Section 8.

16 Inlet manifold - removal and refitting

Removal

1 Disconnect the battery negative terminal.

2 Remove the air cleaner element as described in Chapter 1.

3 Slacken the retaining clip, and disconnect the intake duct from the left-hand side of the manifold **(see illustration).**

4 Unscrew the three manifold retaining bolts and the two retaining nuts, then manoeuvre the manifold away from the head and out of the engine compartment. Note that there is no manifold gasket.

15.12 . . . then refit the injector and tighten it to the specified torque setting

Refitting

5 Ensure that the manifold and cylinder head mating surfaces are clean and dry, and apply a thin coating of suitable sealing compound to the manifold mating surface.

6 Manoeuvre the manifold into position, and refit its retaining nuts and bolts, tightening them evenly and progressively to the specified torque setting **(see illustration).**

7 Refit the air cleaner element as described in Chapter 1.

8 Connect the intake duct to the manifold, tighten its retaining clip securely, and reconnect the battery.

17 Exhaust manifold - removal and refitting

Removal

1 Firmly apply the handbrake, then jack up the front of the vehicle and support it on axle stands.

2 Remove the inlet manifold as described in Section 16.

3 Place a jack beneath the engine, with a block of wood on the jack head. Raise the jack until it is supporting the weight of the engine.

4 Slacken and remove the four nuts securing

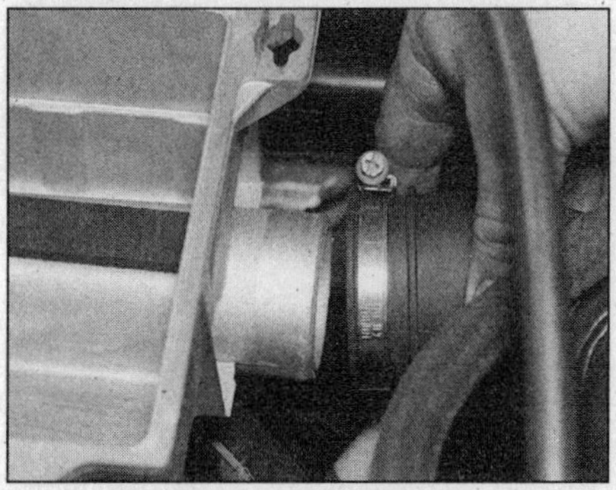

16.3 Slacken the retaining clip, and disconnect the air intake duct from the left side of the inlet manifold

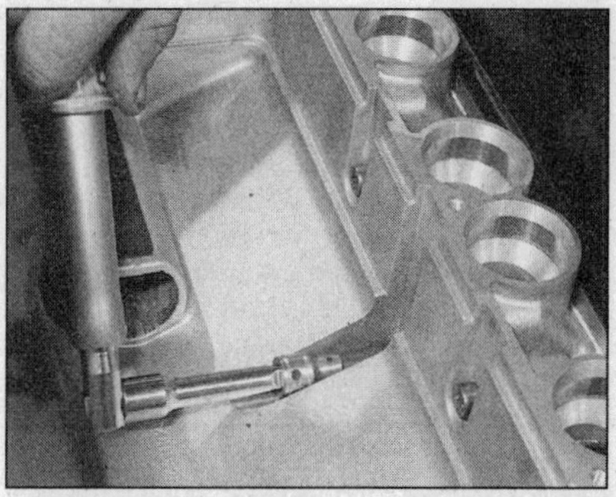

16.6 When refitting, tighten the manifold fasteners to the specified torque setting

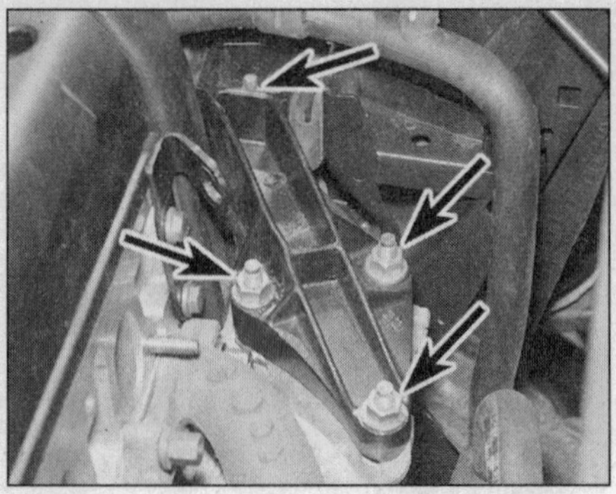

17.4a Unscrew the four retaining nuts (arrowed) . . .

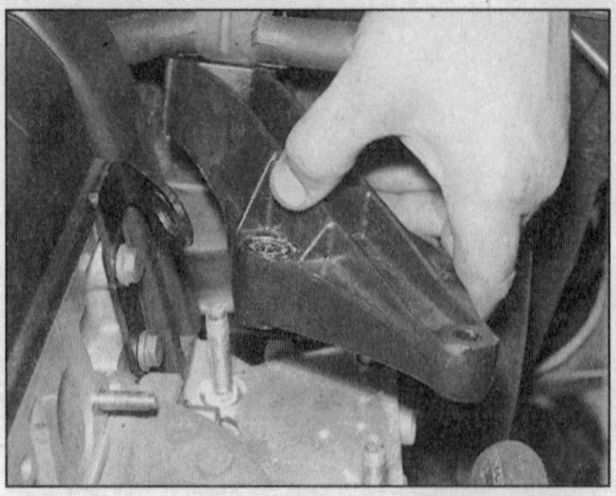

17.4b . . . then lift off the mounting bracket . . .

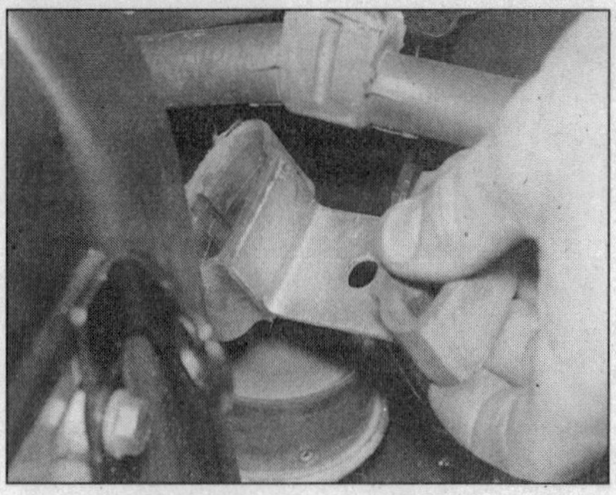

17.4c . . . and recover the buffer plate from the mounting stud

the right-hand engine mounting upper bracket to the cylinder block and body, and lift off the bracket. Lift the buffer plate off the mounting stud **(see illustrations)**

5 Unscrew the bolt securing the front pipe to its mounting, then undo the nuts securing the exhaust front pipe to the manifold. Free the front pipe from the manifold, and recover the gasket.

6 Undo the eight retaining nuts securing the manifold to the head. Manoeuvre the manifold out of the engine compartment, and discard the manifold gasket(s) **(see illustration)**.

Refitting

7 Refitting is the reverse of the removal procedure, noting the following points:

a) Examine all the exhaust manifold studs for signs of damage and corrosion. Remove all traces of corrosion, and repair or renew any damaged studs.
b) Ensure that the manifold and cylinder head sealing faces are clean and flat, and fit the new manifold gaskets. Tighten the manifold retaining nuts to the specified torque **(see illustration)**.
c) Refit the right-hand engine mounting bracket, and tighten its retaining nuts to the specified torque (see Chapter 2B).
d) Reconnect the front pipe to the manifold using the information given in Section 18.

18 Exhaust system - general information and component removal

General information

1 On models without a catalytic converter, the exhaust system consists of three sections; the front pipe, the intermediate pipe and silencer box, and the tailpipe and main silencer box. The exhaust system sections are joined by either a flange and ring or a clamp-type joint. The front pipe-to-manifold joint is of gasket type, and is secured by nuts and bolts. The front pipe-to-intermediate pipe joint is of the spring-loaded ball/ring type, to allow for movement in the exhaust system. The intermediate pipe-to-tailpipe joint is secured by a clamping ring.

2 On models fitted with a catalytic converter, the exhaust system consists of four sections; the front pipe, the catalytic converter, the intermediate pipe and silencer box, and the tailpipe and main silencer box. The exhaust system sections are joined by either a flange and ring or a clamp-type joint. The front pipe-to-manifold joint is of gasket type, and is secured by nuts and bolts. The front pipe-to-catalytic converter joint is of the spring-loaded ball/ring type, to allow for movement in the exhaust system. The catalytic converter-to-intermediate pipe joint and the intermediate pipe-to-silencer joint are secured by a clamping ring.

3 On all models, the system is suspended throughout its entire length by rubber mountings.

Removal

4 Each exhaust section can be removed individually or, alternatively, the complete system can be removed as a unit.

5 To remove the system or part of the system, first jack up the front or rear of the car, and support it on axle stands. Alternatively, position the car over an inspection pit, or on car ramps.

Front pipe

6 Slacken and remove the bolt securing the front pipe to its support mounting **(see illustration)**.

7 Undo the nuts securing the exhaust front pipe to the manifold, then free the front pipe from the manifold and recover the gasket. If necessary, undo the two bolts and remove the heat shield to improve access to the nuts.

8 Slacken and remove the two nuts securing the front pipe to the catalytic converter/intermediate pipe (as applicable), and recover the spring cups and springs. Remove the bolts, then withdraw the front pipe from

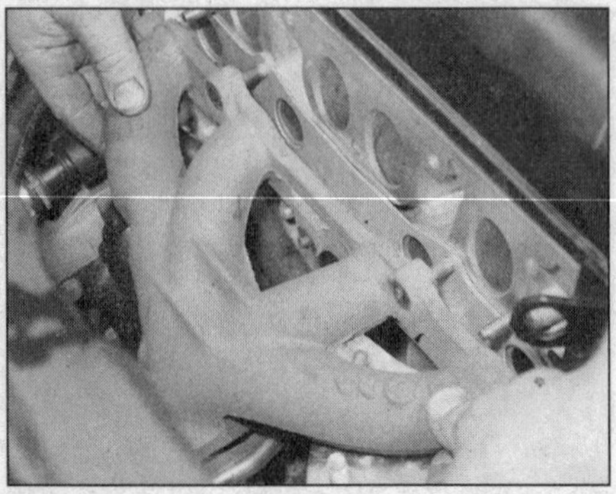

17.6 Remove the manifold along with its gasket

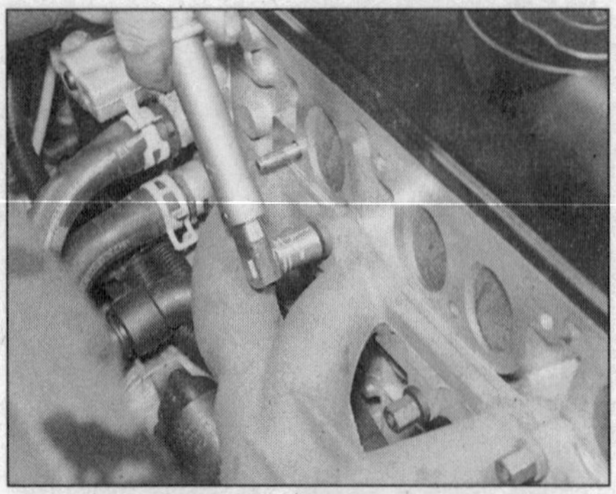

17.7 When refitting, tighten the manifold retaining nuts to the specified torque

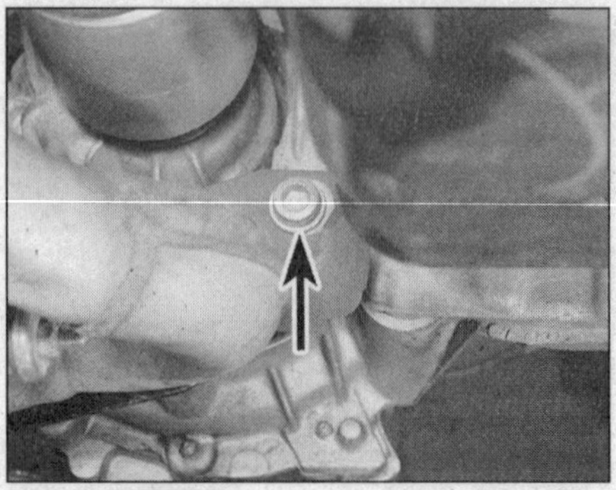

18.6 Exhaust front pipe-to-transmission bolt (arrowed)

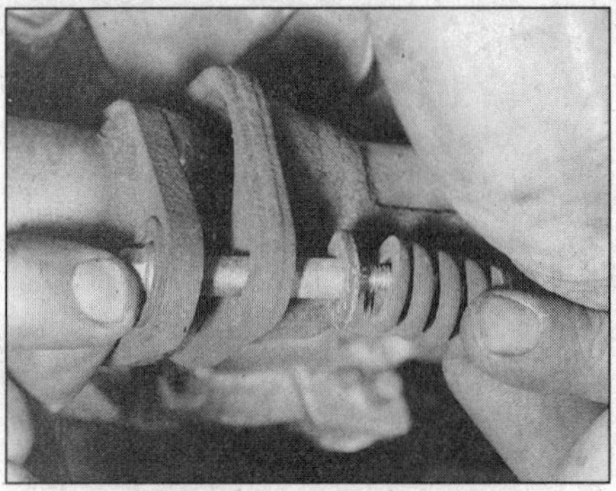

18.8a Remove the front pipe-to-intermediate pipe/catalytic converter fasteners, noting the correct fitted location of each component . . .

18.8b . . . then remove the front pipe and recover the gasket

18.17 Intermediate pipe-to-tailpipe clamp

underneath the vehicle, and recover the sealing ring from the joint **(see illustrations)**.

Catalytic converter

9 Undo the two nuts securing the front pipe flange joint to the catalytic converter. Recover the springs and spring cups, and withdraw the bolts.

10 Slacken the catalytic converter-to-intermediate pipe clamping ring bolts, and disengage the clamp from the flange joint.

11 Free the catalytic converter from the intermediate pipe, then withdraw it from underneath the vehicle and recover the sealing ring from the front pipe joint. Do not drop the catalytic converter, as it contains a fragile ceramic element.

Intermediate pipe - models without a catalytic converter

12 Undo the two nuts securing the front pipe flange joint to the intermediate pipe. Recover the springs and spring cups, and withdraw the bolts.

13 Slacken the clamping ring bolts, and disengage the clamp from the intermediate pipe-to-tailpipe joint.

14 Free the intermediate pipe from its mounting rubbers, then disengage it from the tailpipe and the front pipe, and remove it from underneath the vehicle. Recover the wire-mesh gasket from the front pipe joint.

Intermediate pipe - models with a catalytic converter

15 Slacken the clamping ring bolts, and disengage the clamps from both the intermediate pipe joints.

16 Free the intermediate pipe from its mounting rubbers. Disengage it first from the tailpipe, then the catalytic converter, and remove it from underneath the vehicle.

Tailpipe

17 Slacken the intermediate pipe-to-tailpipe clamping ring bolts, and disengage the clamp from the joint **(see illustration)**.

18 Unhook the tailpipe from its mounting rubbers, and remove it from the vehicle.

Complete system

19 Disconnect the front pipe from the manifold as described in paragraphs 6 and 7.

20 With the aid of an assistant, free the system from all its mounting rubbers and manoeuvre it out from underneath the vehicle.

Heat shield(s)

21 The heat shields are secured to the underside of the body by a mixture of nuts and bolts. Each shield can be removed once the relevant exhaust section has been removed. If the shield is being removed to gain access to a component located behind it, it may prove sufficient to remove the fasteners and simply lower the shield, without disturbing the exhaust system.

Refitting

22 Each section is refitted by a reversal of the removal sequence, noting the following points:

a) Ensure that all traces of corrosion have been removed from the flanges, and renew all necessary gaskets/sealing rings.

b) Inspect the rubber mountings for signs of damage or deterioration, and renew as necessary.

c) Prior to assembling the spring-loaded ball type joint, a smear of high-temperature grease should be applied to the joint mating surfaces.

d) On joints which are secured by clamping rings, apply a smear of exhaust system jointing paste to the joint mating surfaces, to ensure a gastight seal. Tighten the clamping ring nuts evenly and progressively to the specified torque, so that the clearance between the clamp halves is equal on either side.

e) Prior to tightening the exhaust system fasteners, ensure that all rubber mountings are correctly located, and that there is adequate clearance between the exhaust system and vehicle underbody.

Chapter 4 Part E: Emissions control systems

Contents

Degrees of difficulty

Easy, suitable for novice with little experience	**Fairly easy,** suitable for beginner with some experience	**Fairly difficult,** suitable for competent DIY mechanic	**Difficult,** suitable for experienced DIY mechanic	**Very difficult,** suitable for expert DIY or professional

1 General information

1 All petrol engine models have the ability to use unleaded petrol, and also have various other features built into the fuel system to help minimise harmful emissions. All models have the crankcase emissions control system described below. All later petrol models are equipped with a catalytic converter. Some later models are also fitted with exhaust gas recirculation and evaporative emissions control systems.
2 Diesel engine models are also designed to meet the strict emissions requirements, and all have a crankcase emissions control system. Some models may also be fitted with a catalytic converter to reduce exhaust emissions. An exhaust gas recirculation system (EGR) is fitted on the 1527 cc cast-iron block engine (code VJY); however, details of the system were not available at the time of writing.
3 The emissions control systems function as follows.

Crankcase emissions control

4 To reduce emissions of unburned hydrocarbons from the crankcase into the atmosphere, the engine is sealed. The blow-by gases and oil vapour are drawn from inside the crankcase, through a wire-mesh oil separator, into the inlet tract, to be burned by the engine during normal combustion **(see illustration)**.
5 On petrol engines, under conditions of high manifold depression (idling, deceleration) the gases will be sucked positively out of the crankcase. Under conditions of low manifold depression (acceleration, full-throttle running) the gases are forced out of the crankcase by the (relatively) higher crankcase pressure; if the engine is worn, the raised crankcase pressure (due to increased blow-by) will cause some of the flow to return under all manifold conditions. The system operates similarly on Diesel engines, except that the manifold depression will remain relatively constant, since the engine is not throttled.

Exhaust emissions control - petrol models

6 To minimise the amount of pollutants which escape into the atmosphere, some models are fitted with a catalytic converter in the exhaust system. On all models, the catalytic converter system is of the closed-loop type, in which a lambda sensor in the exhaust system provides the fuel-injection/ignition system ECU with constant feedback on the oxygen content of the exhaust gases. This enables the ECU to adjust the mixture to provide the best possible conditions for the converter to operate.
7 The lambda sensor has a built-in heating element, controlled by the ECU through the lambda sensor relay, to quickly bring the sensor's tip to an efficient operating temperature. The sensor's tip is sensitive to oxygen, and sends the ECU a varying voltage depending on the amount of oxygen in the exhaust gases; if the intake air/fuel mixture is too rich, the sensor sends a high-voltage signal. The voltage falls as the mixture weakens. Peak conversion efficiency of all major pollutants occurs if the intake air/fuel mixture is maintained at the chemically-correct ratio for the complete combustion of petrol - 14.7 parts (by weight) of air to 1 part of fuel (the `stoichiometric' ratio). The sensor output voltage alters in a large step at this point, the ECU using the signal change as a reference point, and correcting the intake air/fuel mixture accordingly by altering the fuel injector pulse width (injector opening time).

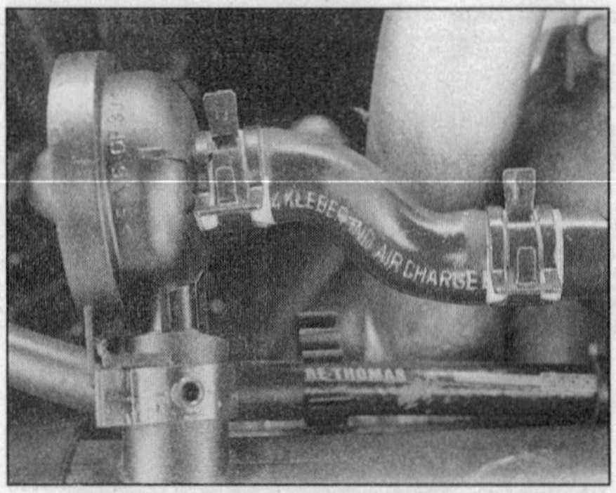

1.4 Crankcase emissions oil separator (1527 cc Diesel engine)

Exhaust emissions control - Diesel models

8 To minimise the level of exhaust pollutants released into the atmosphere, an unregulated catalytic converter is fitted in the exhaust system of some models.
9 The catalytic converter consists of a canister containing a fine mesh impregnated with a catalyst material, over which the hot exhaust gases pass. The catalyst speeds up the oxidation of harmful carbon monoxide, unburnt hydrocarbons and soot, effectively reducing the quantity of harmful products released into the atmosphere via the exhaust gases.

Exhaust gas recirculation system

10 This system circulates a proportion of the exhaust gas back into the combustion chambers during certain operating conditions, in order to reduce harmful exhaust gas emissions. This is achieved by effectively reducing the peak temperatures reached in the combustion chambers by the introduction of the inert exhaust gas.

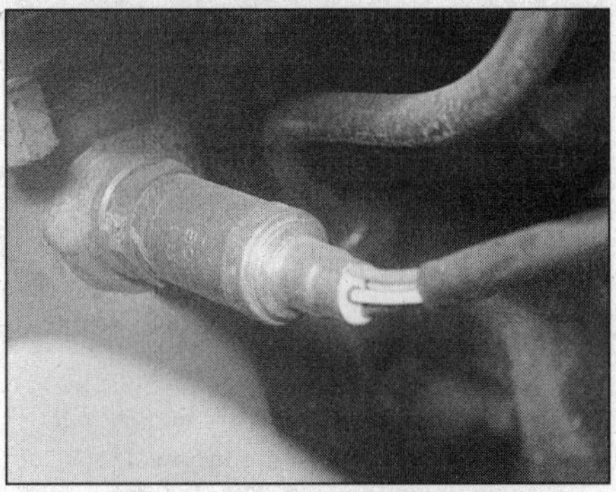

2.6a The lambda sensor is screwed into the top of the exhaust front pipe

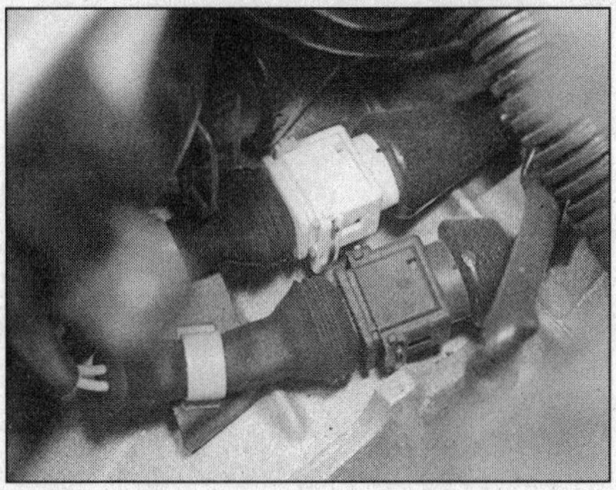

2.6b Trace the lambda sensor wiring back to the top of the transmission, then disconnect the connectors

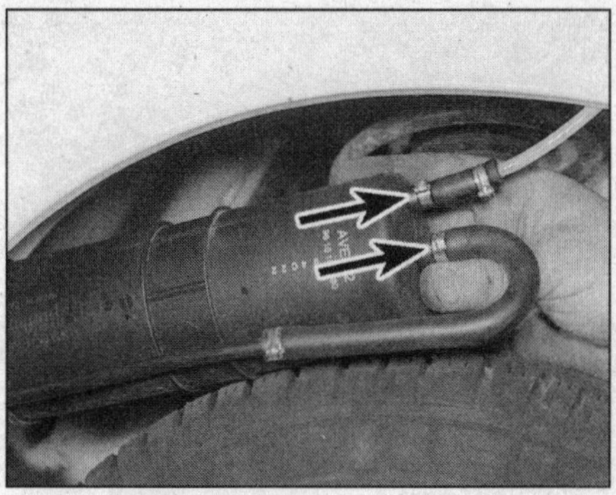

2.14 Lower the canister out of position, and disconnect its hoses (arrowed)

Evaporative emissions control - petrol models

11 To minimise the escape into the atmosphere of unburned hydrocarbons, an evaporative emissions control system is fitted to petrol models equipped with a catalytic converter. The fuel tank filler cap is sealed, and a charcoal canister is mounted underneath the right-hand wing, to collect the petrol vapours generated in the tank when the car is parked. The vapours are stored until they can be cleared from the canister (under the control of the fuel/ignition system ECU) via the purge valve(s), into the inlet tract, to be burned by the engine during normal combustion.

12 To ensure that the engine runs correctly when it is cold and/or idling, and to protect the catalytic converter from the effects of an over-rich mixture, the purge control valve(s) is/are not opened by the ECU until the engine has warmed up, and the engine is under load; the valve solenoid is then modulated on and off to allow the stored vapour to pass into the inlet tract.

2 Emissions control systems - testing and component renewal

Crankcase emissions control

1 The components of this system require no attention, other than to check at regular intervals that the hose(s) are clear and undamaged.

Exhaust emissions control

Testing

2 The performance of the catalytic converter can be checked only by measuring the exhaust gases using a good-quality, carefully-calibrated exhaust gas analyser as described in Chapter 1.

3 On fuel-injected petrol models, if the CO level at the tailpipe is too high, the vehicle should be taken to a Citroën dealer so that the fuel injection and ignition systems, including the lambda sensor, can be thoroughly checked using the special diagnostic equipment. Once these have been checked and are known to be free from faults, the fault must be in the catalytic converter, which must be renewed as described in the Part B or C of this Chapter (as applicable).

4 On Diesel engine models, if the CO level is too high, it is worth checking that the problem is not due to a faulty injector(s), particularly before condemning the catalytic converter (if fitted). Refer to your Citroën dealer for further information.

Catalytic converter - renewal

5 Refer to Part B, C or D of this Chapter (as applicable).

Lambda sensor (petrol models with catalytic converter) - renewal

Note: *The lambda sensor is DELICATE. It will not work if it is dropped or knocked, if its power supply is disrupted, or if any cleaning materials are used on it.*

6 Trace the wiring back from the lambda sensor (which is screwed into the top of the exhaust front pipe) to the top of the transmission. Disconnect both wiring connectors, and free the wiring from any relevant retaining clips or ties **(see illustrations)**.

7 Unscrew the sensor from the exhaust system front pipe, and remove it along with its sealing washer.

8 Refitting is a reverse of the removal procedure, using a new sealing washer. Prior to installing the sensor, apply a smear of high-temperature grease to the sensor threads. Ensure that the sensor is securely tightened. Also, the wiring must be correctly routed, and in no danger of contacting either the exhaust system or the engine.

Exhaust gas recirculation (EGR) system

Testing

9 Testing of the system should be entrusted to a Citroën dealer.

Component renewal

10 At the time of writing, no specific information was available regarding removal and refitting of the system components.

Evaporative emissions control - petrol models

Testing

11 If the system is thought to be faulty, disconnect the hoses from the charcoal canister and purge control valve, and check that they are clear by blowing through them. If the purge control valve(s) or charcoal canister are thought to be faulty, they must be renewed.

Charcoal canister - renewal

12 The charcoal canister is located behind the right-hand front wing. To gain access to the canister, undo the retaining screw from the base of the wheelarch liner, then prise out the retaining clips and remove the liner from underneath the wing.

13 Slacken and remove the clamp bolt, then free the canister from its mounting clamp, and lower it out from underneath the wing. Mark the hoses for identification purposes.

14 Slacken the retaining clips, then disconnect both hoses and remove the canister from the vehicle **(see illustration)**. Where crimped-type hose clips are fitted, cut the clips and discard them; replace them with worm-drive hose clips on refitting.

15 Refitting is a reverse of the removal procedure, ensuring that the hoses are correctly reconnected.

Purge valve(s) - renewal

16 Either a single purge valve is used, or a twin purge valve arrangement is fitted, depending on model. The purge valve(s) is/are located in the right-hand rear corner of the engine compartment **(see illustration)**.

17 To renew a purge valve, first disconnect the battery negative terminal. Depress the retaining clip, and disconnect the wiring connector from the valve.

18 Disconnect the hoses from either end of the valve. Release the valve from its retaining clip, and remove it from the engine compartment, noting which way around it is fitted.

19 Refitting is a reversal of the removal procedure, ensuring that the valve is fitted the correct way around and that the hoses are securely connected.

2.16 The purge valve(s) can be found in the right-hand rear corner of the engine compartment

3 Catalytic converter - general information and precautions

1 The catalytic converter is a reliable and simple device which needs no maintenance in itself, but there are some facts of which an owner should be aware if the converter is to function properly for its full service life.

Petrol models

a) DO NOT use leaded petrol in a car equipped with a catalytic converter - the lead will coat the precious metals, reducing their converting efficiency, and will eventually destroy the converter.
b) Always keep the ignition and fuel systems well-maintained in accordance with the manufacturer's schedule (see Chapter 1).
c) If the engine develops a misfire, do not drive the car at all (or at least as little as possible) until the fault is cured.
d) DO NOT push- or tow-start the car - this will soak the catalytic converter in unburned fuel, causing it to overheat when the engine does start.
e) DO NOT switch off the ignition at high engine speeds - ie, do not "blip" the throttle immediately before switching off.
f) DO NOT use fuel or engine oil additives - these may contain substances harmful to the catalytic converter.
g) DO NOT continue to use the car if the engine burns oil to the extent of leaving a visible trail of blue smoke.
h) Remember that the catalytic converter operates at very high temperatures. DO NOT, therefore, park the car in dry undergrowth, over long grass, or over piles of dead leaves, after a long run.
i) Remember that the catalytic converter is FRAGILE - do not strike it with tools during servicing work.
j) In some cases, a sulphurous smell (like that of rotten eggs) may be noticed from the exhaust. This is common to many catalytic converter-equipped cars. Once the car has covered a few thousand miles, the problem should disappear. In the meantime, try changing the brand of petrol used.
k) The catalytic converter, used on a well-maintained and well-driven car, should last for between 50 000 and 100 000 miles - if the converter is no longer effective, it must be renewed.

Diesel models

The advice given in paragraphs d), f), g), h), i) and k) above applies equally to the converter fitted to Diesel models.

Chapter 5 Part A: Starting and charging systems

Contents

Degrees of difficulty

Easy, suitable for novice with little experience	**Fairly easy,** suitable for beginner with some experience	**Fairly difficult,** suitable for competent DIY mechanic	**Difficult,** suitable for experienced DIY mechanic	**Very difficult,** suitable for expert DIY or professional

Specifications

System type	12-volt, negative earth
Battery	
Type	Lead-acid, low-maintenance or "maintenance-free" (sealed for life). Fulmen, Delco or Steco
Battery capacity:	
Petrol models	33, 35 and 38 amp hr
Diesel models	45 and 50 amp hr
Charge condition:	
Poor	12.5 volts
Normal	12.6 volts
Good	12.7 volts
Alternator	
Type	Paris-Rhone, Valeo, Mitsubishi or Bosch (depending on model)
Starter motor	
Type	Ducellier, Bosch or Valeo (depending on model)

1 General information and precautions

General information

1 Because of their engine-related functions, the components of the starting and charging systems are covered separately from the body electrical devices such as the lights, instruments, etc (which are covered in Chapter 12). On petrol models, refer to Part B of this Chapter for information on the ignition system. On Diesel models, refer to Part C for information on the preheating system.

2 The electrical system is of the 12-volt negative earth type.

3 The battery is of the low-maintenance or "maintenance-free" (sealed for life) type and is charged by the alternator, which is belt-driven from the crankshaft pulley.

4 The starter motor is of the pre-engaged type, incorporating an integral solenoid. On starting, the solenoid moves the drive pinion into engagement with the flywheel ring gear before the starter motor is energised. Once the engine has started, a one-way clutch prevents the motor armature being driven by the engine until the pinion disengages from the flywheel.

Precautions

5 Further details of the various systems are given in the relevant Sections of this Chapter. While some repair procedures are given, the usual course of action is to renew the component concerned. The owner whose interest extends beyond mere component renewal should obtain a copy of the *"Automobile Electrical & Electronic Systems Manual"*, available from the publishers of this manual.

6 It is necessary to take extra care when working on the electrical system, to avoid damage to semi-conductor devices (diodes and transistors), and to avoid the risk of personal injury. In addition to the precautions given in *"Safety first!"* at the beginning of this manual, observe the following when working on the system:

7 *Always remove rings, watches, etc before working on the electrical system.* Even with the battery disconnected, capacitive discharge could occur if a component's live terminal is earthed through a metal object. This could cause a shock or nasty burn.

8 *Do not reverse the battery connections.* Components such as the alternator, electronic control units, or any other components having semi-conductor circuitry could be irreparably damaged.

9 If the engine is being started using jump leads and a slave battery, connect the batteries *positive-to-positive* and *negative-to-negative* (see *"Booster battery (jump) starting"*). This also applies when connecting a battery charger.

10 Never disconnect the battery terminals, the alternator, any electrical wiring or any test instruments when the engine is running.

11 Do not allow the engine to turn the alternator when the alternator is not connected.

12 Never "test" for alternator output by "flashing" the output lead to earth.

13 Never use an ohmmeter of the type incorporating a hand-cranked generator for circuit or continuity testing.

14 Always ensure that the battery negative lead is disconnected when working on the electrical system.

15 Before using electric-arc welding equipment on the car, disconnect the battery, alternator and components such as the fuel injection/ignition electronic control unit, to protect them from the risk of damage.

16 The radio/cassette unit fitted as standard equipment by Citroën has a built-in security code, to deter thieves. If the power source to the unit is cut, the anti-theft system will activate. Even if the power source is immediately reconnected, the radio/cassette unit will not function until the correct security code has been entered. Therefore, if you do not know the correct security code for the radio/cassette unit, **do not** disconnect the battery negative terminal of the battery, or remove the radio/cassette unit from the vehicle. Refer to *"Radio/cassette unit anti-theft system - precaution"'* at the beginning of this manual for further information.

2 Electrical fault-finding - general information

Refer to Chapter 12.

3 Battery - testing and charging

Standard and low-maintenance battery - testing

1 If the vehicle covers a small annual mileage, it is worthwhile checking the specific gravity of the electrolyte every three months, to determine the state of charge of the battery. Use a hydrometer to make the check, and compare the results with the following table. Note that the specific gravity readings assume an electrolyte temperature of 15°C (60°F); for every 10°C (18°F) below 15°C (60°F), subtract 0.007. For every 10°C (18°F) above 15°C (60°F), add 0.007. However, for convenience, the temperatures quoted in the table are **ambient** (outdoor air) temperatures, above or below 25°C (77°F):

	Above 25°C (77°F)	**Below 25°C (77°F)**
Fully-charged	*1.210 to 1.230*	*1.270 to 1.290*
70% charged	*1.170 to 1.190*	*1.230 to 1.250*
Fully-discharged	*1.050 to 1.070*	*1.110 to 1.130*

2 If the battery condition is suspect, first check the specific gravity of electrolyte in each cell. A variation of 0.040 or more between any cells indicates loss of electrolyte or deterioration of the internal plates.

3 If the specific gravity variation is 0.040 or more, the battery should be renewed. If the cell variation is satisfactory but the battery is discharged, it should be charged as described later in this Section.

Maintenance-free battery - testing

4 In cases where a "sealed for life" maintenance-free battery is fitted, topping-up and testing of the electrolyte in each cell is not possible. The condition of the battery can therefore only be tested using a battery condition indicator or a voltmeter.

5 Certain models may be fitted with a battery with a built-in charge condition indicator. The indicator is located in the top of the battery casing, and indicates the condition of the battery from its colour. If the indicator shows green, then the battery is in a good state of charge. If the indicator turns darker, eventually to black, then the battery requires charging, as described later in this Section. If the indicator shows clear/yellow, then the electrolyte level in the battery is too low to allow further use, and the battery should be renewed. **Do not** attempt to charge, load or jump-start a battery when the indicator shows clear/yellow.

6 If testing the battery using a voltmeter, connect the voltmeter across the battery, and compare the result with those given in the Specifications under "charge condition". The test is only accurate if the battery has not been subjected to any kind of charge for the previous six hours, including charging by the alternator. If this is not the case, switch on the headlights for 30 seconds, then wait four to five minutes after switching off the headlights before testing the battery. All other electrical circuits must be switched off, so check (for instance) that the doors and tailgate are fully shut when making the test.

7 If the voltage reading is less than 12.2 volts, then the battery is discharged. A reading of 12.2 to 12.4 volts indicates a partially-discharged condition.

8 If the battery is to be charged, remove it from the vehicle (Section 4) and charge it as described later in this Section.

Standard and low-maintenance battery - charging

Note: *The following is intended as a guide only. Always refer to the manufacturer's recommendations (often printed on a label attached to the battery) before charging a battery.*

9 Charge the battery at a rate of 3.5 to 4 amps, and continue to charge the battery at this rate until no further rise in specific gravity is noted over a four-hour period.

10 Alternatively, a trickle charger charging at the rate of 1.5 amps can safely be used overnight.

11 Specially rapid "boost" charges which are claimed to restore the power of the battery in 1 to 2 hours are not recommended, as they can cause serious damage to the battery plates through overheating.

12 While charging the battery, note that the temperature of the electrolyte should never exceed 37.8°C (100°F).

Maintenance-free battery - charging

Note: *The following is intended as a guide only. Always refer to the manufacturer's recommendations (often printed on a label attached to the battery) before charging a battery.*

13 This battery type takes longer to fully recharge than the standard type, the time taken being dependent on the extent of discharge, but it can take anything up to three days.

14 A constant-voltage type charger is required, to be set, where possible, to 13.9 to 14.9 volts with a charger current below 25 amps. Using this method, the battery should be usable within three hours, giving a voltage reading of 12.5 volts, but this is for a partially-discharged battery and, as mentioned, full charging can take considerably longer.

4 Battery - removal and refitting

Note: *On models equipped with a Citroën anti-theft alarm system, disable the alarm before disconnecting the battery (see Chapter 12).*

Removal

1 The battery is located on the left-hand side of the engine compartment.

2 Remove the insulation cover (where fitted), then loosen the clamp nut and disconnect the lead at the negative (earth) terminal **(see illustrations)**.

3 Remove the insulation cover (where fitted), then loosen the clamp nut and disconnect the lead to the positive terminal in the same way.

4 Unscrew the nut/bolt (as applicable) and remove the battery retaining clamp.

5 Lift the battery out of the engine compartment (take care not to tilt it excessively) and, where necessary, remove the insulation plate(s).

Refitting

6 Refitting is a reversal of removal. Smear petroleum jelly on the terminals when reconnecting the leads, and always reconnect the positive lead first, and the negative lead last.

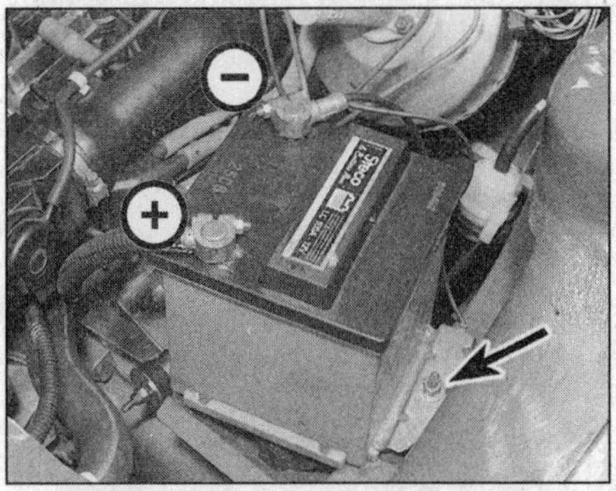

4.2a Battery showing earth (-) and positive (+) lead connections and the retaining clamp (arrowed)

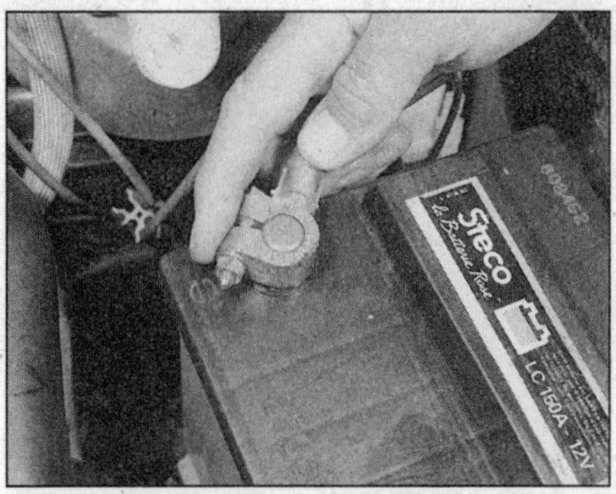

4.2b Always detach the negative lead first (reconnect last)

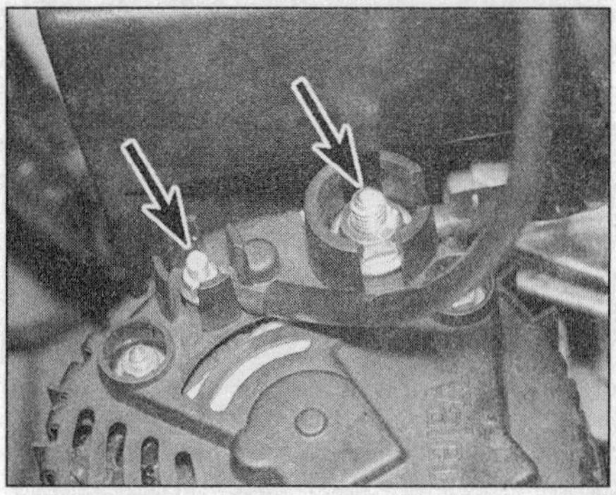

7.3 Undo the retaining nuts (arrowed) and disconnect the wiring from the rear of the alternator

5 Charging system - testing

Note: *Refer to the warnings given in "Safety first!" and in Section 1 of this Chapter before starting work.*

1 If the ignition/no-charge warning light does not come on when the ignition is switched on, first check the alternator wiring connections for security. If satisfactory, check that the warning light bulb has not blown, and that the bulbholder is secure in its location in the instrument panel. If the light still fails to illuminate, check the continuity of the warning light feed wire from the alternator to the bulbholder. If all is satisfactory, the alternator is at fault, and should be renewed or taken to an auto-electrician for testing and repair.

2 If the ignition warning light comes on when the engine is running, stop the engine and check that the drivebelt is correctly tensioned (see Chapter 1) and that the alternator connections are secure. If all is so far satisfactory, check the alternator brushes and slip rings as described in Section 8. If the fault persists, the alternator should be renewed, or taken to an auto-electrician for testing and repair.

3 If the alternator output is suspect even though the warning light functions correctly, the regulated voltage may be checked as follows.

4 Connect a voltmeter across the battery terminals, and start the engine.

5 Increase the engine speed until the voltmeter reading remains steady; the reading should be approximately 12 to 13 volts, and no more than 14 volts.

6 Switch on as many electrical accessories (eg, the headlights, heated rear window and heater blower) as possible, and check that the alternator maintains the regulated voltage at around 13 to 14 volts.

7 If the regulated voltage is not as stated, the fault may be due to worn brushes, weak brush springs, a faulty voltage regulator, a faulty diode, a severed phase winding, or worn or damaged slip rings. The brushes and slip rings may be checked (see Section 8), but if the fault persists, the alternator should be renewed or taken to an auto-electrician for testing and repair.

6 Alternator drivebelt - removal, refitting and tensioning

1 Refer to the procedure given for the auxiliary drivebelt in Chapter 1.

7 Alternator - removal and refitting

Removal

1 Disconnect the battery negative lead.

2 Slacken the auxiliary drivebelt as described in Chapter 1, and disengage it from the alternator pulley.

3 Remove the rubber covers (where fitted) from the alternator terminals, then unscrew the retaining nuts and disconnect the wiring from the rear of the alternator **(see illustration)**.

4 Unscrew the alternator upper and lower mounting bolts, then manoeuvre the alternator away from its mounting brackets and out of position. On Diesel models, prise out the cover shield fastener, to allow the cover to be lifted slightly in order to improve access to the upper bolt **(see illustrations)**.

Refitting

5 Refitting is a reversal of removal. Ensure that the alternator mountings are securely tightened, and tension the auxiliary drivebelt as described in Chapter 1.

8 Alternator brushes and regulator - inspection and renewal

1 Remove the alternator as described in Section 7. Proceed as described below the relevant sub-heading.

Valeo alternator

2 Where applicable, scrape the sealing compound from the rear plastic cover to expose the three rear cover retaining nuts.

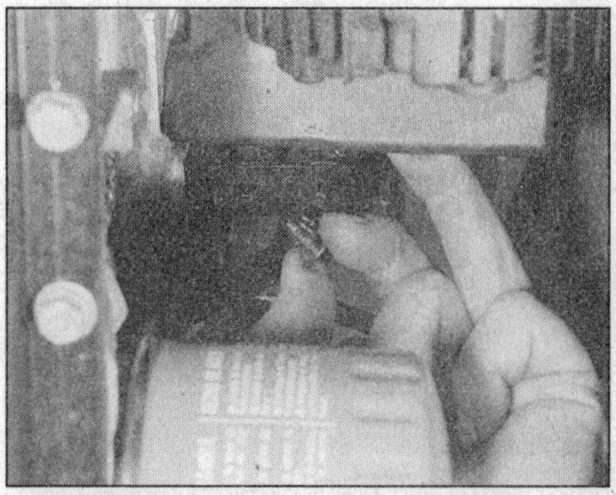

7.4a On Diesel models, to improve access to the upper bolt, remove the fastener and lift the alternator cover slightly

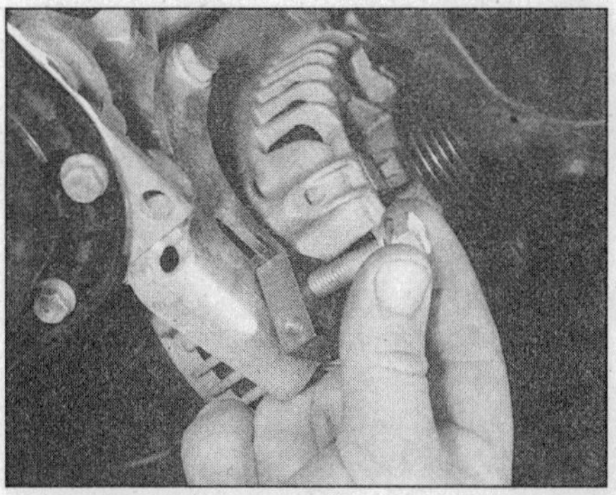

7.4b Unscrew the upper and lower mounting bolts . . .

7.4c . . . then manoeuvre the alternator out of position (Diesel model shown)

5A

8.3a On the Valeo alternator, undo the retaining nuts (arrowed) . . .

8.3b . . . and lift off the rear cover

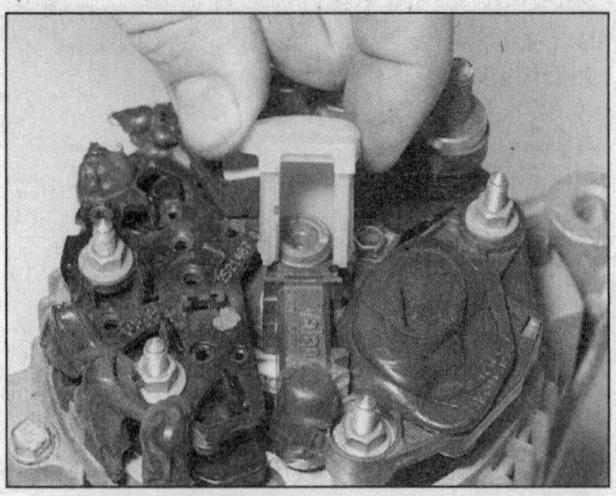

8.5 Pull the plastic cover to reveal the armature shaft

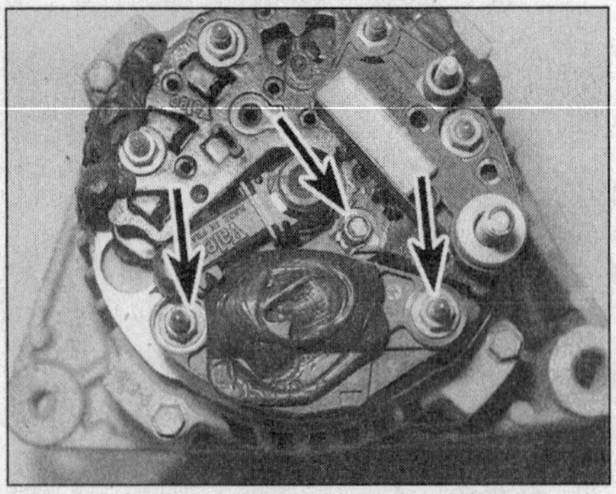

8.6 Regulator/brush holder retaining nuts and screw (arrowed)

8.7 Check the protrusion of the brushes (arrowed) from the holder

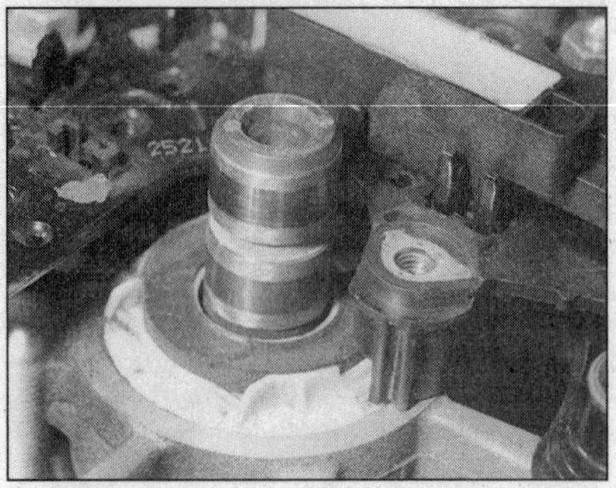

8.9 Clean the armature slip rings, and examine them for signs of damage

3 Undo the retaining nuts and remove the rear cover **(see illustrations)**.
4 If necessary, scrape the sealing compound from the rear of the alternator to expose the regulator/brush holder assembly fixings. The assembly is retained by two nuts and a single screw.
5 Pull the plastic cover from the rear of the armature shaft **(see illustration)**.
6 Undo the retaining nuts and screw, and withdraw the regulator/brush holder assembly from the rear of the alternator **(see illustration)**.
7 Measure the protrusion of each brush from the its holder. No minimum dimension is specified by the manufacturers, but excessive wear should be self-evident **(see illustration)**. If either brush requires renewal, the complete regulator/brush holder assembly must be renewed. It is not possible to renew the brushes separately.
8 If the brushes are still serviceable, clean them with a petrol-moistened cloth. Check that the brush spring tension is equal for both brushes and provides a reasonable pressure. The brushes must move freely in their holders.
9 Clean the alternator slip-rings with a petrol-moistened cloth. Check for signs of scoring, burning or severe pitting on the surface of the slip-rings. It may be possible to have the slip rings renovated by an electrical specialist **(see illustration)**.
10 Refit the regulator/brush holder assembly using a reverse of the removal procedure.
11 Refit the alternator as described in Section 7.

Bosch alternator

12 Unclip the cover from the rear of the alternator.
13 If necessary, scrape the sealing compound from the rear of the alternator to expose the regulator/brush holder assembly retaining screws. Slacken and remove the two retaining screws, and remove the regulator/brush holder from the rear of the alternator.
14 Examine the alternator components as described above in paragraphs 7 to 9.
15 Refit the regulator/brush holder assembly, and securely tighten its retaining screws.
16 Clip the rear cover onto the alternator, and refit the alternator as described in Section 7.

Paris-Rhone alternator

17 Unclip the cover from the rear of the alternator **(see illustration)**.
18 Disconnect the brush holder/regulator wire, then unscrew and remove the two retaining screws and remove the unit from the rear of the alternator.

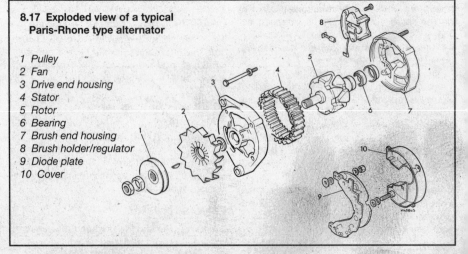

8.17 Exploded view of a typical Paris-Rhone type alternator

1 Pulley
2 Fan
3 Drive end housing
4 Stator
5 Rotor
6 Bearing
7 Brush end housing
8 Brush holder/regulator
9 Diode plate
10 Cover

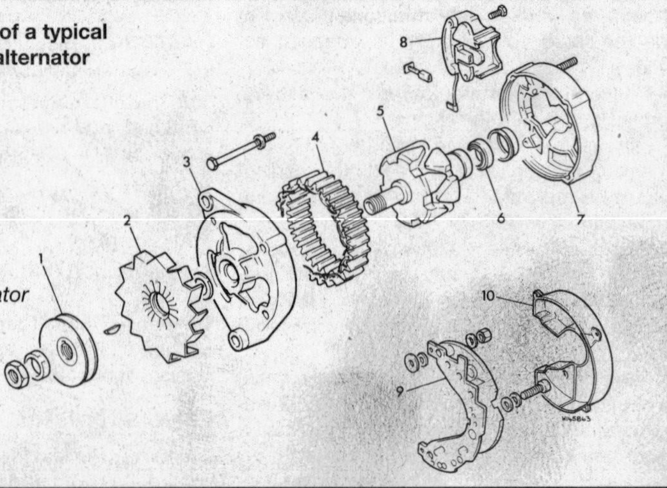

19 Examine the alternator components as described above in paragraphs 7 to 9.
20 Refit the regulator/brush holder assembly, and securely tighten its retaining screws.
21 Refit the cover to the rear of the alternator.

Mitsubishi alternator

22 At the time of writing, no information on the Mitsubishi alternator was available. Although the components differ in detail, the same basic principles outlined previously for the Valeo alternator are applicable.

9 Starting system - testing

Note: *Refer to the precautions given in "Safety first!" and in Section 1 of this Chapter before starting work.*

1 If the starter motor fails to operate when the ignition key is turned to the appropriate position, the following possible causes may be to blame:

a) The battery is faulty.
b) The electrical connections between the switch, solenoid, battery and starter motor are somewhere failing to pass the necessary current from the battery through the starter to earth.
c) The solenoid is faulty.
d) The starter motor is mechanically or electrically defective.

2 To check the battery, switch on the headlights. If they dim after a few seconds, this indicates that the battery is discharged - recharge (see Section 3) or renew the battery. If the headlights glow brightly, operate the ignition switch and observe the lights. If they dim, this indicates that current is reaching the starter motor - therefore, the fault must lie in the starter motor. If the lights continue to glow brightly (and no clicking sound can be heard from the starter motor solenoid), this indicates that there is a fault in the circuit or solenoid - see the following paragraphs. If the starter motor turns slowly when operated, but the battery is in good condition, then this indicates that either the starter motor is faulty, or there is considerable resistance somewhere in the circuit.
3 If a fault in the circuit is suspected, disconnect the battery leads (including the earth connection to the body), the starter/solenoid wiring and the engine/transmission earth strap. Thoroughly clean the connections, and reconnect the leads and wiring, then use a voltmeter or test lamp to check that full battery voltage is available at the battery positive lead connection to the solenoid, and that the earth is sound. Smear petroleum jelly around the battery terminals to prevent corrosion - corroded connections are amongst the most frequent causes of electrical system faults.
4 If the battery and all connections are in good condition, check the circuit by disconnecting the wire from the solenoid blade terminal. Connect a voltmeter or test light between the wire end and a good earth (such as the battery negative terminal), and check that the wire is live when the ignition switch is turned to the "start" position. If it is, then the circuit is sound - if not, the circuit wiring can be checked as described in Chapter 12.
5 The solenoid contacts can be checked by connecting a voltmeter or test light between the battery positive feed connection on the starter side of the solenoid, and earth. When the ignition switch is turned to the "start" position, there should be a reading or lighted bulb, as applicable. If there is no reading or lighted bulb, the solenoid is faulty and should be renewed.
6 If the circuit and solenoid are proved sound, the fault must lie in the starter motor. Begin checking the starter motor by removing it (see Section 10), and checking the brushes (see Section 11). If the fault does not lie in the brushes, the motor windings must be faulty. In this event, it may be possible to have the starter motor overhauled by a specialist, but check on the availability and cost of spares before proceeding, as it may prove more economical to obtain a new or exchange motor.

10 Starter motor - removal and refitting

Removal

1 Disconnect the battery negative lead.
2 So that access to the motor can be gained both from above and below, firmly apply the handbrake then jack up the front of the vehicle and support it on axle stands.
3 On Diesel models, although not strictly necessary, access to the starter motor is considerably improved if the exhaust system front pipe is first removed as described in Chapter 4D. Remove the heat shield from the rear starter motor, then slacken and remove the retaining bolts and remove the rear mounting bracket **(see illustrations).**
4 On all models, slacken and remove the two retaining nuts, and disconnect the wiring from the starter motor solenoid. Recover the washers under the nuts **(see illustration).**
5 Undo the three mounting bolts (two at the rear of the motor, and one which comes through from the top of the transmission

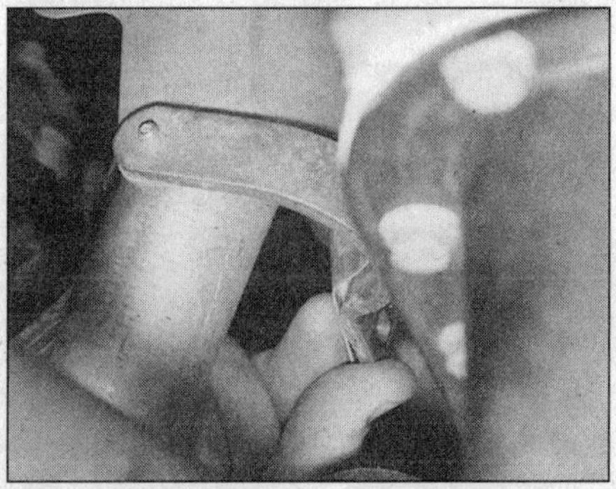

10.3a On Diesel models, remove the exhaust system heat shield . . .

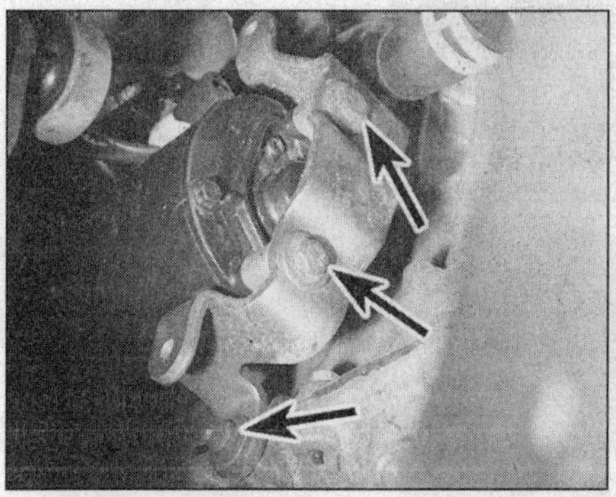

10.3b . . . then undo the retaining bolts (three arrowed) and remove the rear mounting bracket from the starter

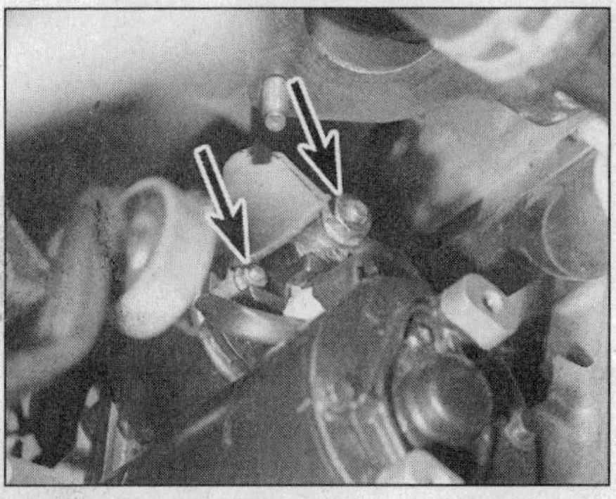

10.4 Unscrew the retaining nuts (arrowed) and disconnect the wiring from the starter motor solenoid

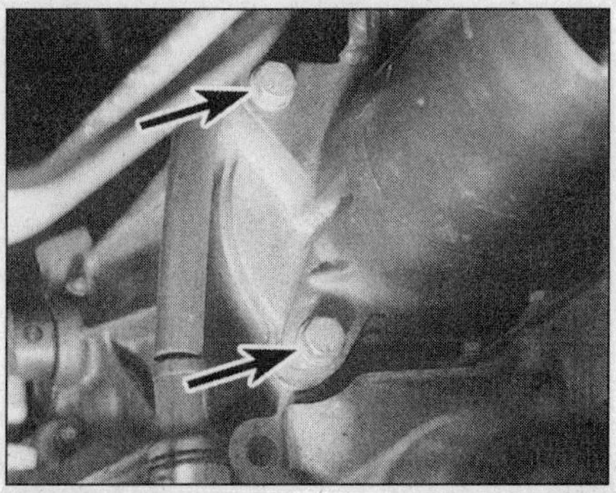

10.5a Undo the starter motor retaining bolts (rear two arrowed) . . .

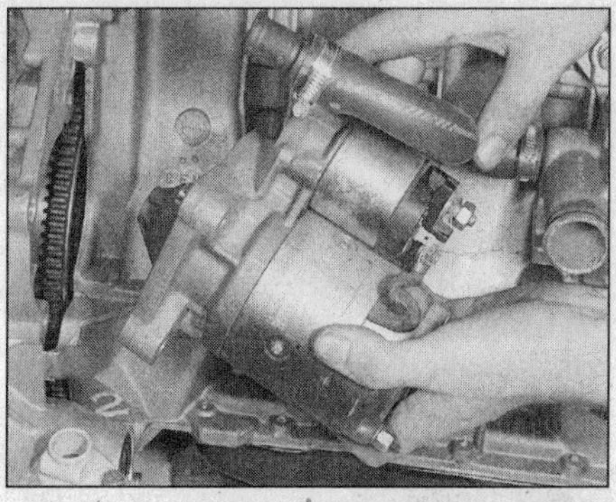

10.5b . . . and remove the starter motor

5A

housing), supporting the motor as the bolts are withdrawn. Recover the washers from under the bolt heads, and note the locations of any wiring or hose brackets secured by the bolts. Note that two of the bolts also secure the air filter support bracket **(see illustrations)**.

6 Manoeuvre the starter motor out from underneath the engine, and recover the locating dowel(s) from the motor/transmission (as applicable).

Refitting

7 Refitting is a reversal of removal, ensuring that the locating dowel(s) are correctly positioned. Also make sure that any wiring or hose brackets are in place under the bolt heads, as noted prior to removal.

11.2 Starter motor cable from solenoid (arrowed)

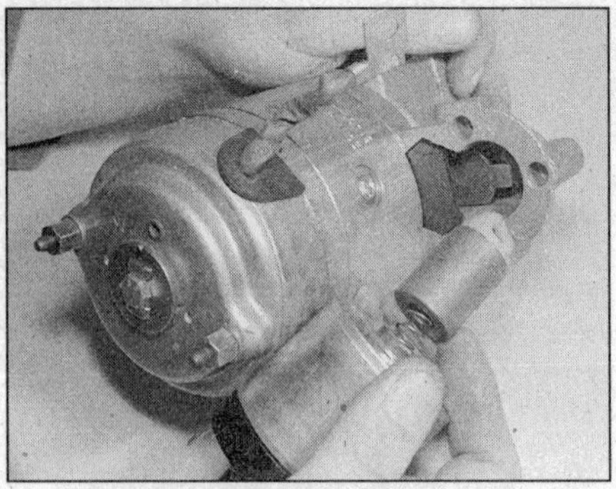

11.3 Removing the solenoid from the drive end bracket

11.4a Unscrew the bolt . . .

11.4b . . . and remove the washers

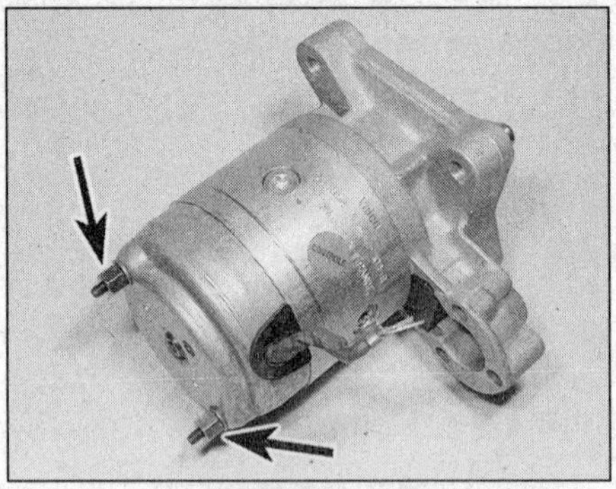

11.5a Unscrew the through-bolt nuts (arrowed) . . .

11.5b . . . and withdraw the end cover

11.6 Removing the armature thrustwashers

11.7 Removing the yoke

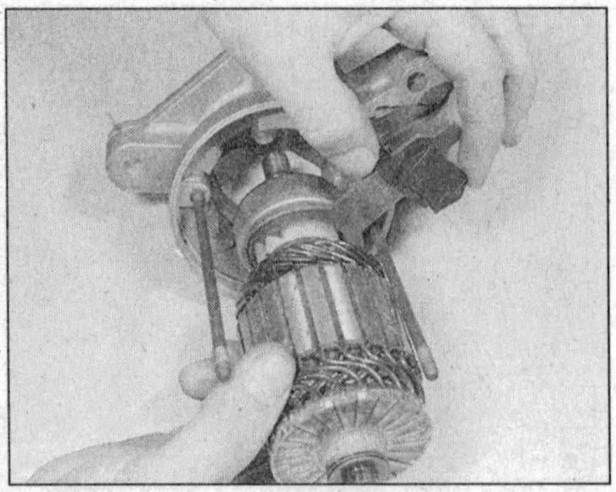

11.8 Withdrawing the armature from the drive end bracket

11.9 Armature and lever (rubber bearing removed)

11.10 Solenoid with core and spring

11 Starter motor - brush renewal

Note: *Consult your Citroën dealer on the cost and availability of spare parts before stripping the starter motor, as spare parts for certain starter motors may not be available.*

1 Note that no minimum brush length is specified by the manufacturers, but it should be self-evident if the brushes are worn to the extent where renewal is required. With the motor removed as described in Section 10, proceed as described under the relevant sub-heading.

Ducellier starter motor

2 Unscrew the nut and disconnect the starter motor cable from the solenoid **(see illustration)**

3 Unscrew the through-bolts and remove the solenoid from the drive end bracket, at the same time unhooking the solenoid core from the lever **(see illustration)**

4 Unscrew the bolt and remove the washers from the commutator end **(see illustrations)**.

5 Unscrew the nuts from the through-bolts and withdraw the end cover, at the same time extracting the field brush **(see illustrations)**.

6 If further dismantling is necessary, remove the thrustwashers from the armature **(see illustration)**.

7 Mark the yoke and end bracket in relation to each other, then remove the yoke **(see illustration)**.

8 Prise out the rubber bearing, and withdraw the armature from the drive end bracket **(see illustration)**.

9 Remove the rubber bearing from the lever **(see illustration)**.

10 Remove the core and spring from the solenoid **(see illustration)**.

11 Check all of the components for wear and damage, and renew as necessary. Clean all the components before reassembly.

12 Reassembly is a reversal of dismantling.

Valeo starter motor

Diesel models

13 Carefully prise the plastic cap from the end of the armature shaft, using a screwdriver or similar tool **(see illustration)**.

14 Prise the C-clip from the end of the

11.13 On the Valeo starter motor, remove the plastic cap from the end of the starter motor armature shaft . . .

11.14a . . . then prise off the C-clip . . .

11.14b . . . and recover the shim

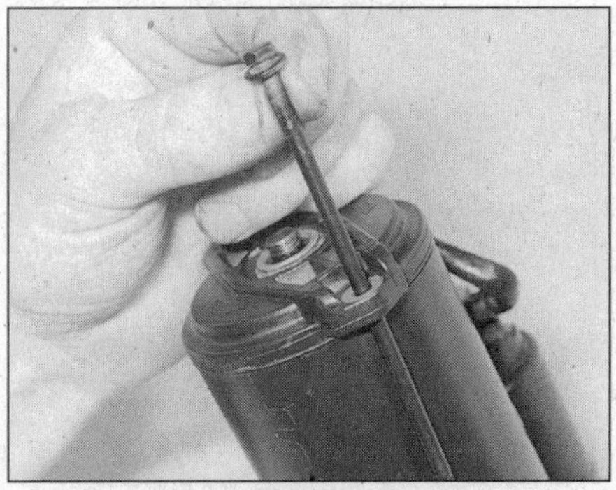

11.15a Remove the through-bolts . . .

11.15b . . . then withdraw the end cover, and recover the shim (arrowed)

11.16 Carefully pull the brush plate from the end of the armature . . .

11.17a . . . then, using a screwdriver . . .

11.17b . . . release the brush retainers . . .

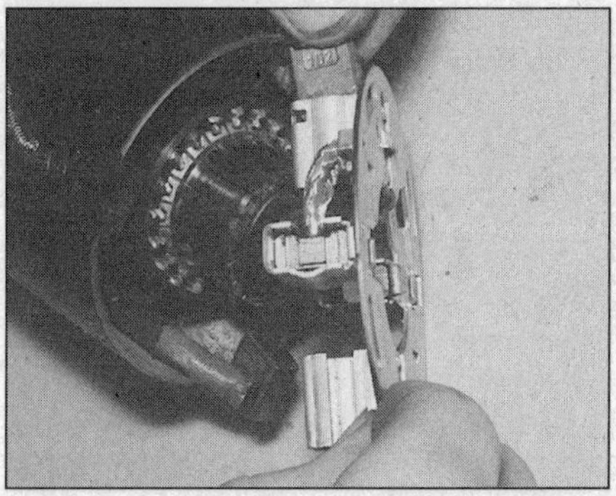

11.17c . . . and withdraw the brushes from the brush holders

armature shaft, and recover the shim **(see illustrations)**.

15 Unscrew the two through-bolts, then withdraw the end cover from the motor casing, and recover the shim from the armature shaft. Do not mix up the shim with the one removed in the previous paragraph **(see illustrations)**.

16 Carefully pull the brush plate from the end of the armature **(see illustration)**.

17 Using a suitable screwdriver, release the brush retainers, and withdraw the brushes from the brush holders **(see illustrations)**.

18 Unsolder the brush leads, or release them from the clips on the brush plate, as applicable.

19 Fit the new brushes. Solder the leads into position, or secure them to the brush plate by bending the securing clips into position, as applicable. Where the brush plate is supplied as a complete assembly, undo the terminal nut and remove the old brush plate. Install the new assembly, and securely tighten the terminal nut.

20 Fit the brush plate over the end of the armature shaft, leaving enough clearance to fit the brushes. Note that when finally fitted, the lug on the brush plate must locate in the corresponding hole in the motor casing. Push the brushes into their holders, so that they rest against the commutator on the armature shaft.

21 Carefully fit the brush retainers, complete with springs, and secure them to retain the brushes.

22 Check that the brushes are seated on the commutator, then slide the brush plate down the armature shaft until the lug on the brush plate engages with the hole in the motor casing.

23 Further refitting is a reversal of removal, ensuring that the shims are fitted to the armature shaft as noted before removal.

Petrol models

24 Undo the retaining nuts, then withdraw the end cover from the armature, and recover any shims which maybe fitted to the armature end, noting their correct fitted positions.

25 Carefully pull the brush plate from the end of the armature.

26 Using a suitable screwdriver, lift the brush springs and withdraw the brushes from the brush holders.

27 Fit the new brushes. Solder the leads into position, or secure them to the brush plate by bending the securing clips into position, as applicable. Lift the springs, and slide the brushes into position. Fit the springs on the side of each brush so that the brushes are jammed in the holders. Where the brush plate is supplied as a complete assembly, undo the terminal nut and remove the old brush plate. Install the new assembly, and securely tighten the terminal nut.

28 Locate the brush plate over the end of the armature shaft, then push the brushes fully into their holders. Ensure that the springs are correctly located against the end of each brush, then check that each brush is seated against the commutator and is free to move easily in its holder.

29 Refit the shim(s) to the end of the armature shaft.

30 Slide the rear cover fully into position, and securely tighten its retaining nuts.

Bosch starter motor

31 Undo the two retaining screws, and remove the centre cap from the starter motor rear cover **(see illustrations)**.

32 Prise the C-clip from the end of the armature shaft, and recover the shims, noting their correct fitted positions **(see illustrations)**.

33 Unscrew the two through-bolts, then withdraw the end cover from the motor casing, and recover any relevant shims from the armature shaft **(see illustrations)**. Do not mix up the shim with the ones removed in the previous paragraph.

34 Carefully pull the brush plate from the end of the armature.

35 Replace the brushes as described above.

36 Refit any relevant shims to the armature end, then install the rear cover and secure it in position with the through-bolts.

37 Refit the outer shims in their correct order, and secure them in position with the C-clip. Install the centre cap, and securely tighten its screw.

11.31a On the Bosch starter motor, undo the two screws . . .

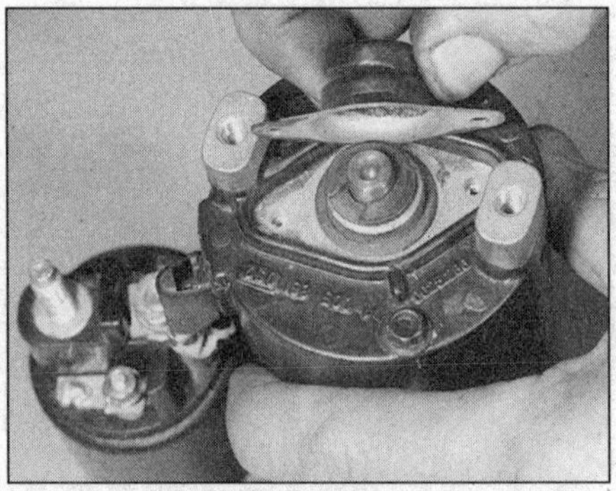

11.31b . . . and remove the centre cap from the end cover

11.32a Slide out the C-clip . . .

11.32b . . . and recover the shim(s) from the armature

11.33a Undo the two through-bolts . . .

11.33b . . . and remove the end cover from the motor

12 Ignition switch - removal and refitting

1 The ignition switch is integral with the steering column lock, and can be removed as described in Chapter 10.

13 Oil pressure warning light switch - removal and refitting

Removal

1 The switch is located at the front of the cylinder block, above the oil filter mounting. On some models, access to the switch may be improved if the vehicle is jacked up and supported on axle stands, so that the switch can be reached from underneath.

2 Disconnect the battery negative lead.

3 Remove the protective sleeve from the wiring plug (where applicable), then disconnect the wiring from the switch.

4 Unscrew the switch from the cylinder block, and recover the sealing washer. Be prepared for oil spillage; if the switch is to be left removed from the engine for any length of time, plug the hole in the cylinder block.

Refitting

5 Examine the sealing washer for signs of damage or deterioration, and if necessary renew it.

6 Refit the switch, complete with washer, and tighten it securely. Reconnect the wiring connector.

7 Lower the vehicle to the ground. Check and, if necessary, top-up the engine oil as described in Chapter 1.

14 Oil level sensor - removal and refitting

1 The sensor is located on the front side of the cylinder block, just to the right of the oil filter.

2 The removal and refitting procedure is as described for the oil pressure switch in Section 13. Access is most easily obtained from underneath the vehicle.

15 Oil temperature sensor - removal and refitting

Removal

1 The oil temperature sensor is screwed into the rear of the sump.

2 To gain access to the sensor, firmly apply the handbrake then jack up the front of the vehicle and support it on axle stands.

3 Drain the engine oil into a clean container, then refit the drain plug and tighten it to the specified torque (see Chapter 1).

4 Disconnect the wiring connector, then unscrew the sensor from the sump, and remove it from underneath the vehicle along with its sealing washer.

Refitting

5 Examine the sealing washer for signs of damage or deterioration, and if necessary renew.

6 Refit the sensor, tightening it securely, and reconnect the wiring connector.

7 Lower the vehicle to the ground, and refill the engine with oil as described in Chapter 1.

Notes

the stator. When the reluctor teeth are in alignment with the stator projections, a small AC voltage is created. The amplifier unit uses this voltage to switch the transistors in the unit and complete the ignition system primary (LT) circuit.

5 As the reluctor teeth move out of alignment with the stator projections, the AC voltage changes and the transistors in the amplifier unit are switched again to interrupt the primary (LT) circuit. This causes a high voltage to be induced in the coil secondary (HT) windings, which then travels down the HT lead to the distributor and onto the relevant spark plug.

6 A TDC sensor is fitted to the rear of the flywheel, but the sensor is not part of the ignition system. It is there to be used for diagnostic purposes only.

Early 1124 cc and 1360 cc fuel-injected models

7 On early (pre-July 1992) 1124 cc models and 1360 cc (KDZ/KDY engine) fuel-injected models, equipped with the Bosch Monopoint A2.2 fuel injection system (see Chapter 4B), a breakerless electronic ignition system is fitted. This operates in the same way as that described above for the carburettor models.

8 In addition to the components described above, the system is equipped with an ignition timing retard system. This reduces the nitrous oxide (NOx) content of the exhaust gases. This is achieved by reducing the temperature at the end of the combustion by reducing the ignition advance at certain engine temperatures. This system is controlled by the fuel injection ECU. The ECU has control over an electrically-operated solenoid valve, mounted in the engine compartment, which is fitted in the vacuum pipe linking the distributor vacuum diaphragm unit to the inlet manifold. At certain engine temperatures, the ECU switches off the solenoid valve, which cuts off the vacuum supply to the distributor vacuum diaphragm, reducing the ignition advance.

9 A TDC sensor is fitted to the rear of the flywheel, but the sensor is not part of the ignition system. It is there to be used for diagnostic purposes only.

All other fuel-injected models

10 On all other models, the ignition system is integrated with the fuel injection system, to form a combined engine management system under the control of one ECU (See the relevant Part of Chapter 4 for further information).

11 The ignition side of the system is of the static (distributorless) type, consisting only of a four-output ignition coil. The ignition coil actually consists of two separate HT coils, which supply two cylinders each (one coil supplies cylinders 1 and 4, and the other cylinders 2 and 3). Under the control of the ECU, the ignition coil operates on the "wasted spark" principle. The spark plugs are fired in two pairs, twice for each complete cycle of the engine. One plug of each pair will fire on a compression stroke, and one on an exhaust stroke; the spark on the exhaust stroke has no effect on the running of the engine, and is therefore "wasted". The ECU uses inputs from various sensors to calculate the required ignition advance setting and coil charging time.

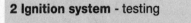

2 Ignition system - testing

Warning: Voltages produced by an electronic ignition system are considerably higher than those produced by conventional ignition systems. Extreme care must be taken when working on the system with the ignition switched on. Persons with surgically-implanted cardiac pacemaker devices should keep well clear of the ignition circuits, components and test equipment

Models with a distributor

Note: *Refer to the precautions in Chapter 5A, Section 1 before starting work. Always switch off the ignition before disconnecting or connecting any component, and when using a multi-meter to check resistances.*

General

1 The components of electronic ignition systems are normally very reliable; most faults are far more likely to be due to loose or dirty connections or to "tracking" of HT voltage due to dirt, dampness or damaged insulation than to the failure of any of the system's components. **Always** check all wiring thoroughly before condemning an electrical component, and work methodically to eliminate all other possibilities before deciding that a particular component is faulty.

2 The old practice of checking for a spark by holding the live end of an HT lead a short distance away from the engine is **not** recommended; not only is there a high risk of a powerful electric shock, but the HT coil or amplifier unit will be damaged. Similarly, **never** try to "diagnose" misfires by pulling off one HT lead at a time.

Engine will not start

3 If the engine either will not turn over at all, or only turns very slowly, check the battery and starter motor. Connect a voltmeter across the battery terminals (meter positive probe to battery positive terminal). Disconnect the ignition coil HT lead from the distributor cap, and earth it. Note the voltage reading obtained while turning over the engine on the starter for (no more than) ten seconds. If the reading obtained is less than approximately 9.5 volts, first check the battery, starter motor and charging system as described in the relevant Sections of this Chapter.

4 If the engine turns over at normal speed but will not start, check the HT circuit by connecting a timing light (following its manufacturer's instructions) and turning the engine over on the starter motor; if the light flashes, voltage is reaching the spark plugs, so these should be checked first. If the light does not flash, check the HT leads themselves, followed by the distributor cap, carbon brush and rotor arm, using the information given in Chapter 1.

5 If there is a spark, check the fuel system for faults, referring to the relevant Part of Chapter 4 for further information.

6 If there is still no spark, check the voltage at the ignition HT coil "+" terminal; it should be the same as the battery voltage (ie, at least 11.7 volts). If the voltage at the coil is more than 1 volt less than that at the battery, check the feed back through the fusebox and ignition switch to the battery and its earth until the fault is found.

7 If the feed to the HT coil is sound, check the coil's primary and secondary winding resistance as described later in this Section; renew the coil if faulty, but be careful to check carefully the condition of the LT connections themselves before doing so, to ensure that the fault is not due to dirty or poorly-fastened connectors.

8 If the HT coil is in good condition, the fault is probably within the amplifier unit or distributor stator assembly. Testing of these components should be entrusted to a Citroën dealer.

Engine misfires

9 An irregular misfire suggests either a loose connection or intermittent fault on the primary circuit, or an HT fault on the coil side of the rotor arm.

10 With the ignition switched off, check carefully through the system, ensuring that all connections are clean and securely fastened. If the equipment is available, check the LT circuit as described above.

11 Check that the HT coil, the distributor cap and the HT leads are clean and dry. Check the leads themselves and the spark plugs (by substitution, if necessary), then check the distributor cap, carbon brush and rotor arm as described in Chapter 1.

12 Regular misfiring is almost certainly due to a fault in the distributor cap, HT leads or spark plugs. Use a timing light (paragraph 4 above) to check whether HT voltage is present at all leads.

13 If HT voltage is not present on any particular lead, the fault will be in that lead or in the distributor cap. If HT is present on all leads, the fault will be in the spark plugs; check and renew them if there is any doubt about their condition.

14 If no HT is present, check the HT coil; its secondary windings may be breaking down under load.

Models with a static (distributorless) ignition system

15 If a fault appears in the engine management (fuel injection/ignition) system, first ensure that the fault is not due to a poor electrical connection or poor maintenance; ie, check that the air cleaner filter element is clean, the spark plugs are in good condition

Chapter 5 Part B: Ignition system (petrol models)

Contents

Degrees of difficulty

Easy, suitable for novice with little experience	**Fairly easy,** suitable for beginner with some experience	**Fairly difficult,** suitable for competent DIY mechanic	**Difficult,** suitable for experienced DIY mechanic	**Very difficult,** suitable for expert DIY or professional

Specifications

System type

Carburettor models	Breakerless electronic ignition system
Fuel-injected models:	
954 cc models	Static (distributorless) ignition system controlled by engine management ECU
1124 cc models:	
Early (pre-July 1992) models	Breakerless electronic ignition system
Later (July 1992-on) models	Static (distributorless) ignition system controlled by engine management ECU
1360 cc single-point injection models*:	
KDZ/KDY engine models	Breakerless electronic ignition system
KDX engine models	Static (distributorless) ignition system controlled by engine management ECU
1360 cc multi-point injection (GTi) models (K6B/KFZ engine)*	Static (distributorless) ignition system controlled by engine management ECU

**Refer to Chapter 2A for further information on engine codes.*

Firing order	1-3-4-2 (No 1 cylinder at transmission end)

Ignition timing

Models with a distributor	8° BTDC @ 750 rpm
Models with static (distributorless) ignition	Controlled by the ECU - see text

Ignition HT coil

Ignition HT coil resistances:*	
Models with a distributor:	
Primary windings	0.8 ohms
Secondary windings	6.5 k ohms
Models with static (distributorless) ignition:	
Primary windings	0.5 to 0.8 ohms
Secondary windings - Bosch coil	14.6 k ohms
Secondary windings - Valeo coil	8.6 k ohms

**The above results are approximate values, and are accurate only when the coil is at 20°C. See text for further information.*

Torque wrench setting	**Nm**	**lbf ft**
Distributor mounting nuts	8	5

1 General information

Carburettor models

1 On all carburettor models, a breakerless electronic ignition system is used. The system comprises solely of the HT ignition coil and the distributor, both of which are mounted on the left-hand end of the cylinder head, the distributor being driven off the end of the camshaft.

2 The distributor contains a reluctor mounted onto its shaft and a magnet and stator fixed to its body. The ignition amplifier unit is also mounted onto the side of the distributor body. The system operates as follows.

3 When the ignition is switched on but the engine is stationary, the transistors in the amplifier unit prevent current flowing through the ignition system primary (LT) circuit.

4 As the crankshaft rotates, the reluctor moves through the magnetic field created by and correctly gapped, that the engine breather hoses are clear and undamaged, referring to Chapter 1 for further information. Also check that the accelerator cable is correctly adjusted, as described in the relevant Part of Chapter 4. If the engine is running very roughly, check the compression pressures and the valve clearances as described in Chapter 2A.

16 If these checks fail to reveal the cause of the problem, the vehicle should be taken to a suitably-equipped Citroën dealer for testing. A wiring block connector is incorporated in the engine management circuit, into which a special electronic diagnostic tester can be plugged. The tester will locate the fault quickly and simply, alleviating the need to test all the system components individually, which is a time-consuming operation that carries a high risk of damaging the ECU.

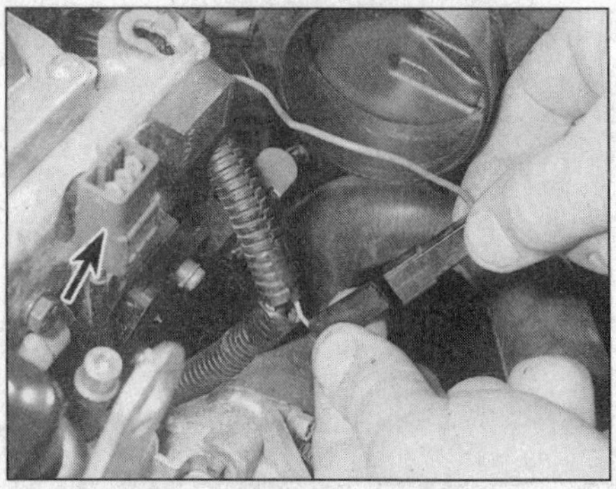

3.3 On models with a distributor, disconnect the capacitor wiring connector, and release the TDC sensor connector (arrowed) . . .

17 The only ignition system checks which can be carried out by the home mechanic are those described in Chapter 1, relating to the spark plugs, and the ignition coil test described in this Chapter. If necessary, the system wiring and wiring connectors can be checked as described in Chapter 12, ensuring that the ECU wiring connector(s) have first been disconnected.

3 Ignition HT coil - removal, testing and refitting

Removal

Models with a distributor

1 Disconnect the battery negative terminal.

2 Disconnect the hot-air intake hose from the exhaust manifold shroud and air temperature control valve, and remove it from the engine. Release the intake duct fastener, and position the duct clear of the coil.

3 Disconnect the wiring connector from the capacitor mounted on the coil mounting bracket, and release the TDC sensor wiring connector from the front of the bracket **(see illustration)**.

4 Disconnect the HT lead from the coil, then depress the retaining clip and disconnect the coil wiring connector **(see illustrations)**.

5 Slacken and remove the two retaining bolts, and remove the coil and mounting bracket from the cylinder head. Where necessary, slacken and remove the four screws and nuts, and separate the HT coil and mounting bracket **(see illustrations)**.

Models with a static (distributorless) ignition system

6 Disconnect the battery negative terminal. The ignition HT coil is mounted on the left-hand end of the cylinder head.

7 Depress the retaining clip, and disconnect the wiring connector from the HT coil **(see illustration)**.

8 Make a note of the correct fitted positions of the HT leads, then disconnect them from the coil terminals.

9 Undo the four retaining screws securing the coil to its mounting bracket, and remove it from the engine compartment **(see illustration)**.

Testing

10 Testing of the coil is carried out using a multi-meter set to its resistance function, to check the primary (LT "+" to "-" terminals) and secondary (LT "+" to HT lead terminal) windings for continuity. Bear in mind that on the four-output, static type HT coil, there are two sets of each windings. Compare the results obtained to those given in the Specifications at the start of this Chapter. The resistance of the coil windings will vary slightly according to the coil temperature - the results in the Specifications are approximate values for when the coil is at 20°C.

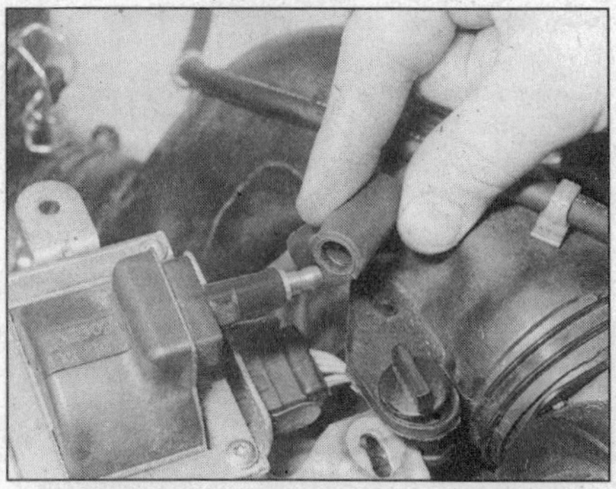

3.4a . . . then disconnect the HT lead . . .

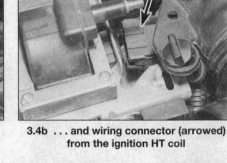

3.4b . . . and wiring connector (arrowed) from the ignition HT coil

3.5a Undo the two retaining bolts (arrowed) . . .

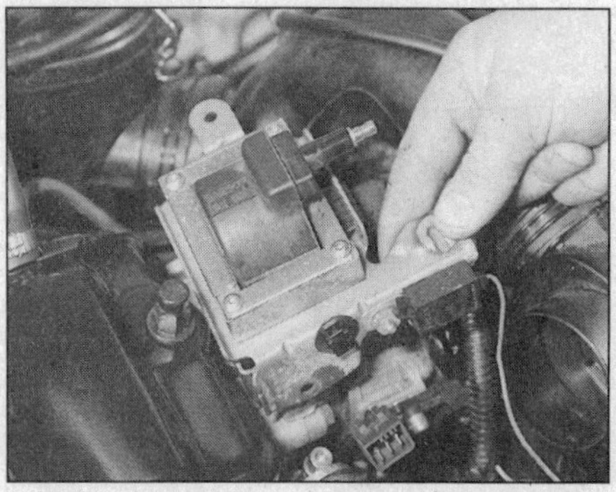

3.5b . . . and remove the coil and mounting bracket from the engine

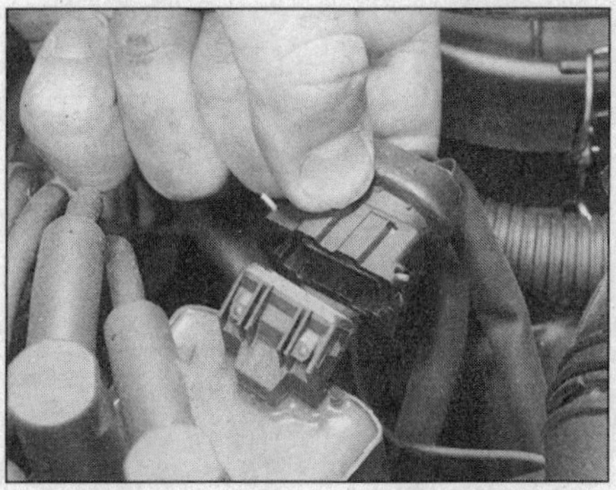

3.7 On models with a static (distributorless) ignition system, disconnect the wiring connector from the HT coil . . .

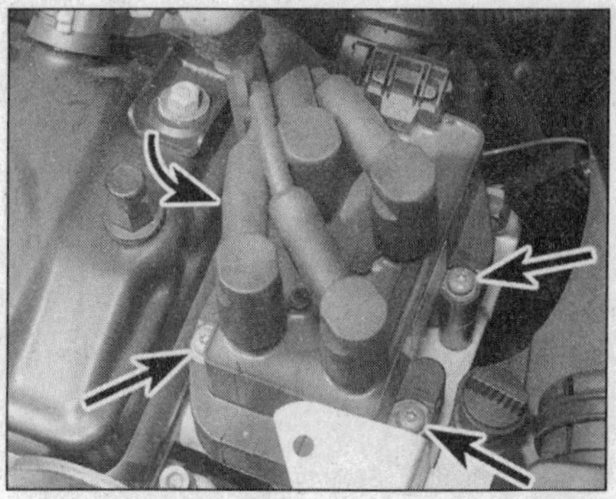

3.9 . . . then disconnect the HT leads from the coil. Undo the four retaining screws (arrowed) and remove the coil

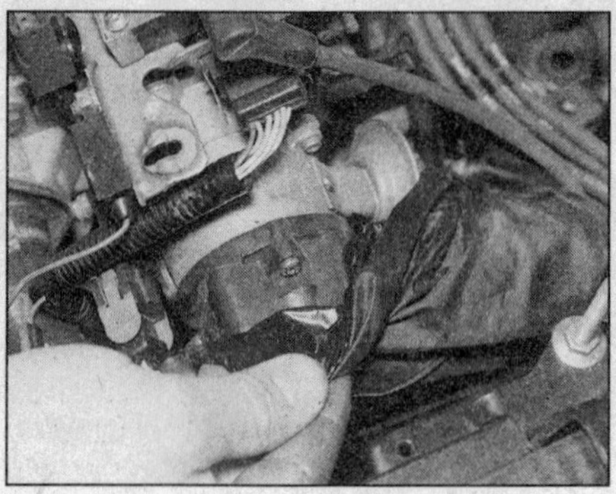
4.2a Peel back the waterproof cover . . .

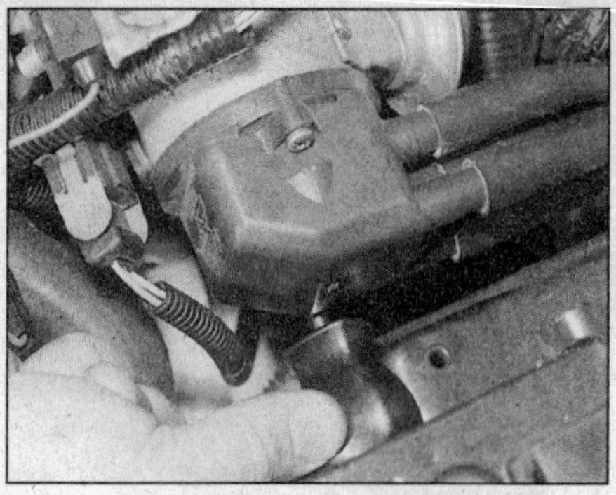
4.2b . . . then undo the retaining screws . . .

4.2c . . . and remove the cap from the end of the distributor

11 Check that there is no continuity between the HT lead terminal and the coil body/mounting bracket.

12 If the coil is thought to be faulty, have your findings confirmed by a Citroën dealer before renewing the coil.

Refitting

13 Refitting is a reversal of the relevant removal procedure. Ensure that the wiring connectors and the HT lead(s) are securely reconnected.

4 Distributor - removal and refitting

Removal

1 Disconnect the battery negative terminal. If necessary, to improve access to the distributor, remove the ignition HT coil as described in Section 3, and the intake duct as described in Chapter 4A.

2 Peel back the waterproof cover, then slacken and remove the distributor cap retaining screws. Remove the cap, and place it clear of the distributor body **(see illustrations)**. Recover the seal from the cap.

3 Depress the retaining clip, and disconnect the wiring connector from the distributor. Disconnect the hose from the vacuum diaphragm unit **(see illustrations)**.

4 Check the cylinder head and distributor flange for signs of alignment marks. If no marks are visible, using a scriber or suitable marker pen, mark the relationship of the distributor body to the cylinder head. Slacken and remove the two mounting nuts **(see illustration)**, and withdraw the distributor from the cylinder head. Remove the O-ring from the end of the distributor body, and discard it; a new one must be used on refitting.

Refitting

5 Lubricate the new O-ring with a smear of engine oil, and fit it to the groove in the distributor body. Examine the distributor cap seal for wear or damage, and renew if necessary.

6 Align the distributor rotor shaft drive coupling key with the slots in the camshaft end, noting that the slots are offset to ensure that the distributor can only be fitted in one position. Carefully insert the distributor into the cylinder head, rotating the rotor arm slightly to ensure that the coupling is correctly engaged.

7 Align the marks noted or made (as applicable) on removal. Install the distributor retaining nuts, tightening them only lightly at this stage.

8 Ensure that the seal is correctly located in its groove, then refit the cap assembly to the distributor, and tighten its retaining screws securely. Fold the waterproof cover back over the distributor cap, ensuring that it is correctly located.

4.3a Disconnect the distributor wiring connector . . .

9 Reconnect the vacuum hose to the diaphragm unit, and the distributor wiring connector. Where necessary, refit the ignition HT coil as described in Section 3, and the intake duct as described in Chapter 4A.

10 Check and, if necessary, adjust the ignition timing as described in Section 6, then tighten the distributor mounting nuts to the specified torque.

5 Ignition system amplifier unit - removal and refitting

Removal

1 Disconnect the battery negative terminal.

2 The amplifier unit is mounted onto the side

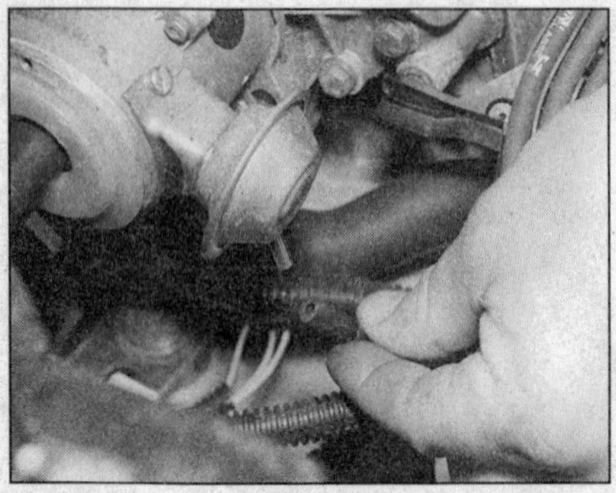
4.3b . . . and the vacuum diaphragm hose . . .

4.4 . . . then undo the retaining nuts and remove the distributor

5.2 On models with a distributor, the ignition amplifier unit is secured to the side of the distributor by two screws of the distributor body **(see illustration)**. To improve access to the unit, disengage the hot-air intake hose from the control valve and the exhaust manifold shroud, and remove it from the vehicle.

3 Disconnect the wiring connector, then undo the two retaining screws and remove the amplifier unit.

Refitting

4 Refitting is a reverse of the removal procedure.

6 Ignition timing - checking and adjustment

Models with a distributor

1 To check the ignition timing, a stroboscopic timing light will be required. It is also recommended that the flywheel timing mark is highlighted as follows.

2 Remove the plug from the aperture on the front of the clutch bellhousing on the transmission. Using a socket and suitable extension bar on the crankshaft pulley bolt, slowly turn the engine over until the timing mark (a straight line) scribed on the edge of the flywheel appears in the aperture. (Turning the engine will be much easier if the spark plugs are removed first - see Chapter 1.) **(see illustrations)**.

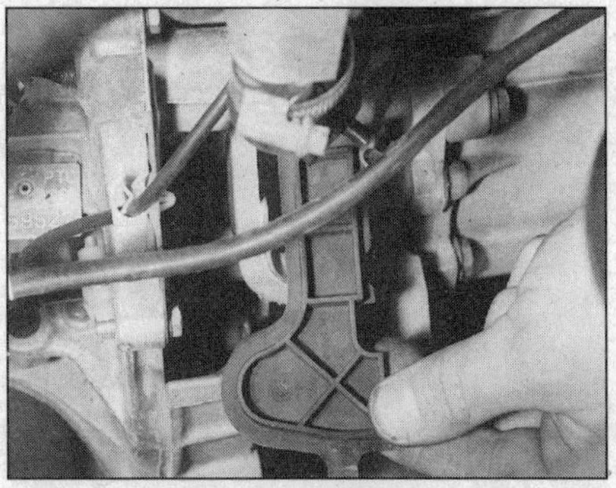

6.2a On models with a distributor, remove the plug from the transmission bellhousing . . .

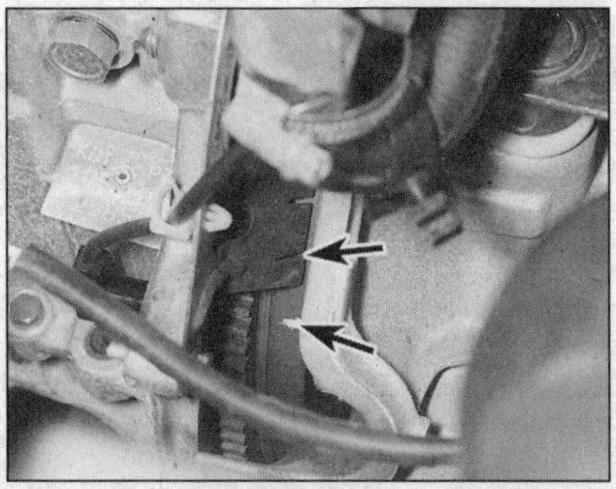

6.2b . . . to reveal the timing plate and flywheel timing mark (arrowed)

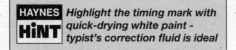

HAYNES HiNT ***Highlight the timing mark with quick-drying white paint - typist's correction fluid is ideal***

3 Start the engine, allow it to warm up to normal operating temperature, then switch off.

4 Disconnect the vacuum hose from the distributor diaphragm, and plug the hose end.

5 Connect the timing light to No 1 cylinder (nearest the transmission) plug lead as described in the timing light manufacturer's instructions.

6 Start the engine, allowing it to idle at the specified speed, and point the timing light at the transmission housing aperture. The flywheel timing mark should be aligned with the relevant notch on the timing plate (refer to the Specifications for the correct timing setting); the numbers on the plate indicate degrees Before Top Dead Centre (BTDC).

7 If adjustment is necessary, slacken the two distributor mounting nuts, then slowly rotate the distributor body as required until the flywheel mark and relevant timing plate notch are brought into alignment. Once the marks are correctly aligned, hold the distributor stationary, and tighten its mounting nuts to the specified torque. Recheck the timing marks are still correctly aligned and, if necessary, repeat the adjustment procedure.

8 When the timing is correctly set, increase the engine speed and check that the pulley mark advances to beyond the beginning of the timing plate reference marks, returning to close to the specified mark when the engine is allowed to idle. This check shows that the centrifugal advance mechanism is at least functioning - a detailed check must be left to a Citroën dealer. Reconnect the vacuum hose to the distributor, and repeat the check. The rate of advance should significantly increase if the vacuum diaphragm is functioning correctly, but again, a detailed check must be left to a Citroën dealer.

9 When the ignition timing is correct, stop the engine and disconnect the timing light.

Models with a static (distributorless) ignition system

10 On models with static (distributorless) ignition systems, Citroën do not quote any specified timing settings. Therefore, it is not possible for the home mechanic to even check the ignition timing.

11 The timing setting is constantly being monitored and adjusted by the engine management ECU and, therefore, nominal values cannot be given. The only way to check the ignition timing is using special electronic test equipment which is connected to the engine management system diagnostic connector (see the relevant Part of Chapter 4 for further information).

12 On later (July 1992-on) 1124 cc models with a Magneti Marelli engine management system (see relevant Part of Chapter 4), adjustment of the ignition timing is possible. However, adjustments can be made only by re-programming the ECU using the special electronic test equipment.

13 On all other models with Bosch engine management systems, no adjustment of the ignition timing is possible. Should the ignition timing be incorrect, a fault must be present in the engine management system, and the vehicle should be taken to a Citroën dealer for testing.

Notes

Chapter 5 Part C: Preheating system (Diesel models)

Contents

Degrees of difficulty

Easy, suitable for novice with little experience	**Fairly easy,** suitable for beginner with some experience	**Fairly difficult,** suitable for competent DIY mechanic	**Difficult,** suitable for experienced DIY mechanic	**Very difficult,** suitable for expert DIY or professional

Specifications

Torque wrench setting	Nm	lbf ft
Glow plugs	22	16

1 Preheating system - description and testing

Description

1 Each swirl chamber has a heater plug (commonly called a glow plug) screwed into it. The plugs are electrically operated before start-up by the preheating control unit.

2 A warning light in the instrument panel tells the driver that preheating is taking place. When the light goes out, the engine is ready to be started. If no attempt is made to start, the timer then cuts off the supply, in order to avoid draining the battery and overheating the glow plugs.

Testing

3 If the system malfunctions, testing is ultimately by substitution of known good units, but some preliminary checks may be made as follows.

4 Connect a voltmeter or 12-volt test light between the glow plug supply cable and earth (engine or vehicle metal). Make sure that the live connection is kept clear of the engine and bodywork.

5 Have an assistant switch on the ignition, and check that voltage is supplied to the glow plugs. Note the time for which the warning light is lit, and the total time for which voltage is supplied before the system cuts out. Switch off the ignition.

6 If all is well, voltage will be supplied and the warning light will illuminate for approximately 5 to 6 seconds.

7 If there is no supply at all, the control unit or associated wiring is at fault.

8 To locate a defective glow plug, disconnect the main supply cable and interconnecting wire from the top of the glow plugs. Be careful not to drop the nuts and washers.

9 Use a continuity tester, or a 12-volt test light connected to the battery positive terminal, to check for continuity between each glow plug terminal and earth. The resistance of a glow plug in good condition is very low (less than 1 ohm), so if the test light does not come on or the continuity tester shows a high resistance, the glow plug is certainly defective.

10 If an ammeter is available, the current draw of each glow plug can be checked. After an initial surge of around 15 to 20 amps, each plug should draw around 10 amps. Any plug which draws much more or less than this is probably defective.

11 As a final check, the glow plugs can be removed and inspected as described in Section 2.

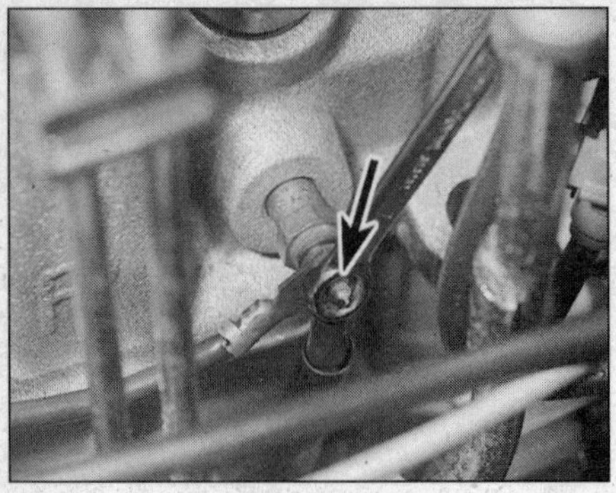

2.2a Unscrew the nut . . .

2.2b . . . and disconnect the wiring from the glow plug

2.2c Glow plug position (arrowed) on the 1527 cc engine

2 Glow plugs - removal, inspection and refitting

Removal

Caution: If the preheating system has just been energised, or if the engine has been running, the glow plugs will be very hot.

1 Disconnect the battery negative lead.

2 Unscrew the nut from the relevant glow plug terminal(s), and recover the washer(s). Note that the main supply cable is connected to No 1 cylinder glow plug, and an interconnecting wire is fitted between the four plugs **(see illustrations)**.

3 Where applicable, carefully move any obstructing pipes or wires to one side, to gain access to the relevant glow plug(s).

4 Unscrew the glow plug(s) and remove them from the cylinder head **(see illustration)**.

Inspection

5 Inspect each glow plug for physical damage. Burnt or eroded glow plug tips can be caused by a bad injector spray pattern. Have the injectors checked if this sort of damage is found.

6 If the glow plugs are in good physical condition, check them electrically using a 12-volt test light or continuity tester, as described in the previous Section.

7 The glow plugs can be energised by applying 12 volts to them, to verify that they heat up evenly and in the required time. Observe the following precautions:

a) Support the glow plug by clamping it carefully in a vice or in self-locking pliers. **Remember - it will become red-hot.**

b) Make sure that the power supply or test lead incorporates a fuse or overload trip, to protect against damage from a short-circuit.

c) After testing, allow the glow plug to cool for several minutes before attempting to handle it.

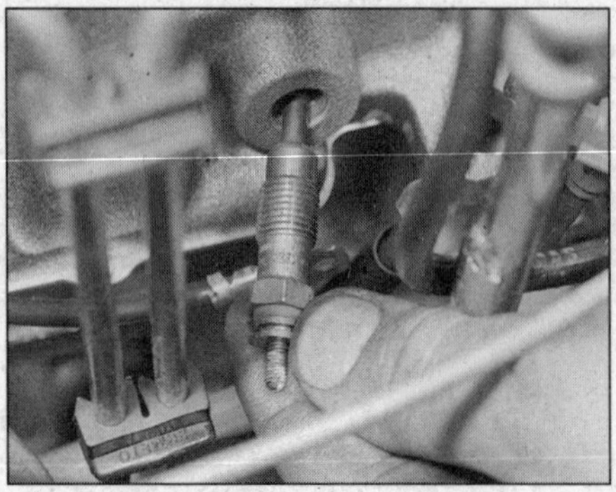

2.4 Unscrew the glow plugs, and remove them from the cylinder head

8 A glow plug in good condition will start to glow red at the tip after drawing current for 5 seconds or so. Any plug which takes much longer to start glowing, or which starts glowing in the middle instead of at the tip, is defective.

Refitting

9 Refit by reversing the removal operations. Apply a smear of copper-based anti-seize compound to the plug threads, and tighten the glow plugs to the specified torque. Do not overtighten, as this can damage the glow plug element.

3.1 Preheating system control unit

3 Preheating system control unit - removal and refitting

Removal

1 The unit is located on the left-hand side of the engine compartment, on the inner wing panel **(see illustration)**.

2 Disconnect the battery negative lead.

3 Unscrew the retaining bolt securing the unit to the inner wing panel.

4 Note the location of the wiring, then disconnect it from the base of the unit. Remove the unit from the engine compartment.

Refitting

5 Refitting is a reversal of removal, ensuring that all wiring is securely connected to its original location, as noted on removal.

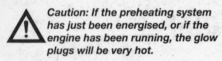

Chapter 6 Clutch

Contents

Degrees of difficulty

Easy, suitable for novice with little experience	**Fairly easy,** suitable for beginner with some experience	**Fairly difficult,** suitable for competent DIY mechanic	**Difficult,** suitable for experienced DIY mechanic	**Very difficult,** suitable for expert DIY or professional

Specifications

Type	Single dry plate with diaphragm spring. Cable-operated release mechanism	
Clutch pedal travel (minimum)	130 mm	
Clutch pedal-to-bulkhead clearance (maximum)	71 mm	
Friction plate diameter		
954 cc models:		
Pre-March 1993 models	160 mm	
March 1993-on models	180 mm	
1124 cc carburettor models:		
Pre-March 1993 models	160 mm	
March 1993-on models	180 mm	
1124 cc fuel-injected models	180 mm	
1360 cc (petrol and Diesel) and 1527 cc (Diesel) models	180 mm	
Torque wrench setting	**Nm**	**lbf ft**
Pressure plate retaining bolts	15	11

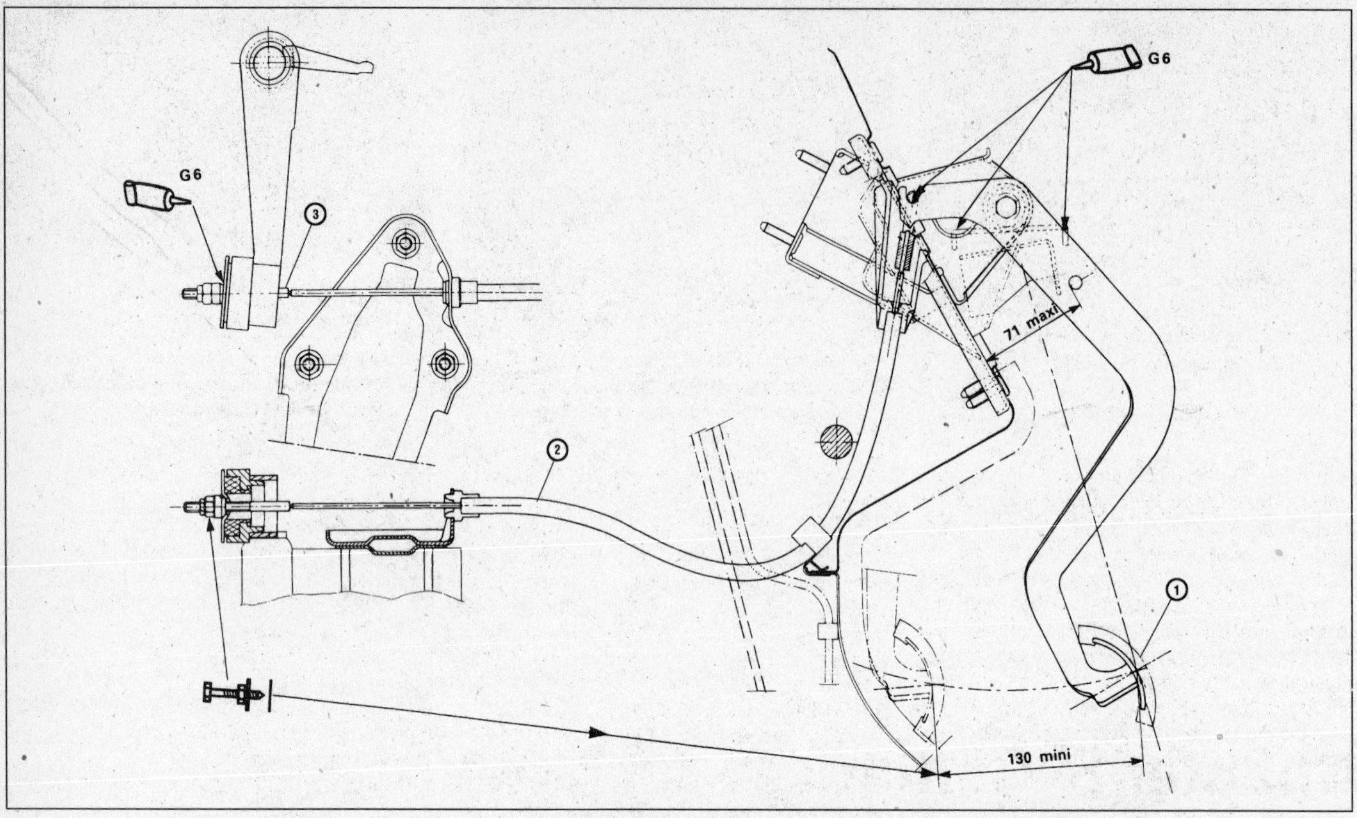

2.1 Cross-section view of the clutch pedal (1) cable (2) and cable connection at the release lever (3)

Clearances shown in mm. Use G6 grease or multi-purpose grease at the lubrication points.

1 General information

1 The clutch consists of a friction plate, a pressure plate assembly, a release bearing, and the release mechanism; all of these components are contained in the large cast aluminium alloy bellhousing, sandwiched between the engine and the transmission. The release mechanism is mechanical, being operated by a cable.

2 The friction plate is fitted between the engine flywheel and the clutch pressure plate, and is allowed to slide on the transmission input shaft splines. It consists of two circular facings of friction material riveted in position to provide the clutch bearing surface, and a spring-cushioned hub to damp out transmission shocks.

3 The pressure plate assembly is bolted to the flywheel, and is located by three dowel pins. When the engine is running, drive is transmitted from the crankshaft via the flywheel to the friction plate (these components being clamped securely together by the pressure plate assembly) and from the friction plate to the transmission input shaft.

4 The clutch is disengaged by a sealed release bearing fitted concentrically around the transmission input shaft; when the driver depresses the clutch pedal, the release bearing is pressed against the fingers at the centre of the diaphragm spring. Since the spring is held by rivets between two annular fulcrum rings, the pressure at its centre causes it to deform, so that it releases the clamping force from the pressure plate.

5 Depressing the clutch pedal pulls the control cable, and this in turn pulls the lever which rotates the release fork. The release fork forces the release bearing against the diaphragm spring.

6 As the friction plate facings wear, the pressure plate moves towards the flywheel; this causes the diaphragm spring fingers to push against the release bearing, thus changing the position of the clutch pedal. To ensure correct operation, the clutch cable must be regularly adjusted.

2 Clutch - adjustment

1 The clutch adjustment is checked by measuring the clutch pedal travel **(see illustration)**.

2 Ensure that there are no obstructions beneath the clutch pedal. Depress the clutch pedal fully to the floor, measuring the distance that the centre of the clutch pedal pad travels through from the at-rest position to the floor **(see illustration)**. If this is not as given in the Specifications at the start of this Chapter, adjust the clutch as follows.

HAYNES HiNT ***Using a ruler for this check might prove awkward - as an alternative, mark the at-rest and fully-depressed positions on a strip of wood, and measure the distance (the pedal travel) between them.***

3 The clutch cable is adjusted by means of the adjuster nut on the transmission end of the cable. Access to the locknut is limited and, if required, the air inlet ducts can be removed to improve access. Refer to Chapter 4 for further information.

2.2 To check clutch cable adjustment, measure the clutch pedal travel as described in text

2.4 Adjusting the clutch cable

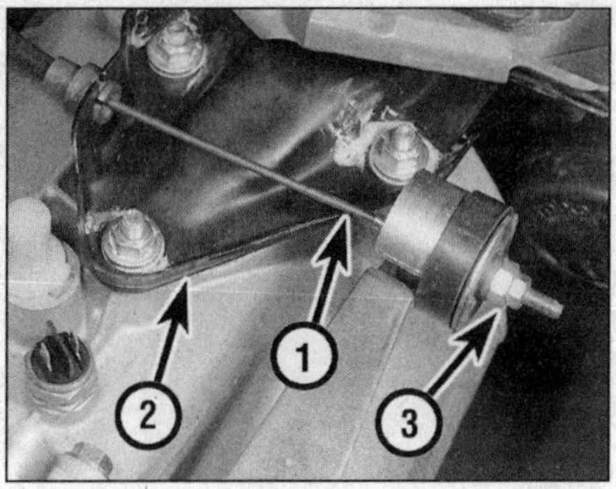

3.2 Clutch cable attachment to operating lever (1) and mounting/support bracket (2). Also shown are the adjuster nut and its locknut (3)

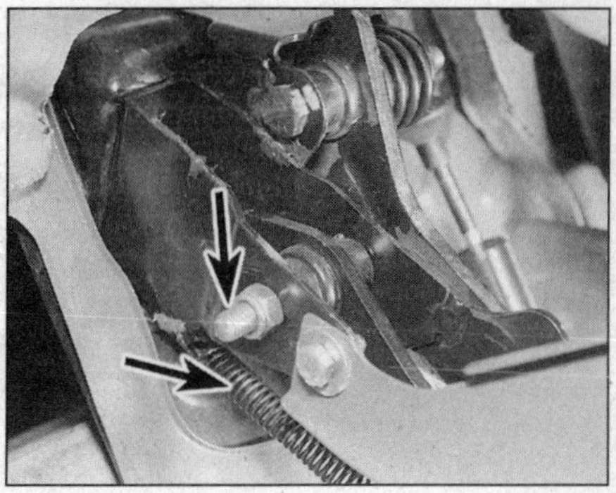

4.3 Pedal mounting assembly on right-hand drive models, showing pivot bolt and clutch pedal return spring (arrowed)

4 Slacken the locknut on the end of the clutch cable. Adjust the position of the adjuster nut **(see illustration)**, then re-measure the clutch pedal travel. Repeat this procedure until the clutch pedal travel is as specified. Note that the clutch pedal travel dimension is a minimum amount, so after making the adjustment check that the maximum dimension shown in illustration 2.1 is not exceeded.
5 Once the adjuster nut is correctly positioned and the pedal travel is correctly set, securely tighten the cable locknut. Refit the air inlet ducts, if removed.

3 Clutch cable - removal and refitting

Removal

1 Working in the engine compartment, fully slacken the locknut and adjuster nut from the end of the clutch cable. To improve access, remove the air inlet duct with reference to Chapter 4.
2 Release the inner cable and outer cable fittings from the clutch release lever and mounting bracket, and free the cable from the transmission bellhousing **(see illustration)**.
3 Working inside the vehicle, undo the retaining nuts and remove the shelf or trim panel (as applicable) from the driver's side of the facia.
4 Unhook the clutch inner cable from the top of the clutch pedal. Access to the top of the pedal is very poor.
5 Return to the engine compartment, and release the outer cable from the engine compartment bulkhead.
6 Withdraw the cable forwards through the bulkhead, noting its correct routing, and remove it from the vehicle.
7 Examine the cable, looking for worn end fittings or a damaged outer casing, and for signs of fraying of the inner wire. Check the cable's operation - the inner wire should move smoothly and easily through the outer casing. Remember, however, that a cable that appears serviceable when tested off the car may well be much heavier in operation, when compressed into its working position. Renew the cable if it shows any signs of excessive wear or damage.

Refitting

8 Apply a thin smear of multi-purpose grease to the cable end fittings, then pass the cable through the engine compartment bulkhead. Clip the cable into position, making sure that it is routed correctly.
9 From inside the vehicle, hook the inner cable over the clutch pedal end, and check that it is securely retained. Refit the under-facia trim panel or shelf (as applicable).
10 Refit the plastic locating collar to the release lever, and ensure that the rubber spacer is correctly located on the transmission end of the outer cable.
11 Ensuring that the cable is correctly routed and retained by all the relevant retaining clips and guides, pass the lower end through the release lever/mounting bracket, and engage the inner cable with the clutch release lever/mounting bracket (as applicable). Refit the rubber spacer and flat washer to the end of the inner cable, and screw on the adjuster nut and locknut.
12 Adjust the clutch cable as described in Section 2.

4 Clutch pedal - removal and refitting

Note: *Access to the pedal pivot bolt is very poor, and can only be significantly improved by removing the facia as described in Chapter 11.*

Removal

1 Remove the brake pedal as described in Chapter 9.
2 Working as described in Section 2, slacken the clutch cable locknut and adjuster nut to obtain maximum freeplay in the cable. Unhook the cable from the upper end of the clutch pedal.
3 On right-hand drive models, slacken and remove the nut and pivot bolt, then withdraw the clutch pedal from the vehicle, and disconnect the return spring **(see illustration)**.
4 On left-hand drive models, note the correct fitted position of the clutch pedal return spring, then withdraw the pivot bolt and remove the pedal, spring and spacer.
5 Carefully clean all components, renewing any that are worn or damaged. Check the bearing surfaces of the pivot bushes and bolt with particular care; the bushes can be renewed separately if worn.

Refitting

6 Press the pivot bushes into the pedal bore, then apply a smear of multi-purpose grease to their bearing surfaces.
7 Refit the pedal using a reversal of the removal procedure, referring to Chapter 9 when refitting the brake pedal. On completion, check that the clutch pedal pivots smoothly, and adjust it as described in Section 2.

5 Clutch assembly - removal, inspection and refitting

Warning: Dust created by clutch wear and deposited on the clutch components may contain asbestos, which is a health hazard. DO NOT blow it out with compressed air, and don't inhale any of it. DO NOT use petrol or petroleum-based solvents to clean off the dust. Brake system cleaner or methylated spirit should be used to flush the dust into a suitable receptacle. After the clutch components are wiped clean with rags, dispose of the contaminated rags and cleaner in a sealed, marked container. Although some friction materials may no longer contain asbestos, it is safest to assume that they DO, and to take precautions accordingly.

Removal

1 Unless the engine/transmission is to be removed from the car and separated for major overhaul (Chapter 2C), the clutch can be reached by removing the transmission alone, as described in Chapter 7.
2 Before disturbing the clutch, use chalk or a marker pen to mark the relationship of the pressure plate assembly to the flywheel.
3 Working in a diagonal sequence, slacken

5.4 Remove the pressure plate and friction plate, noting which way around the friction plate is fitted

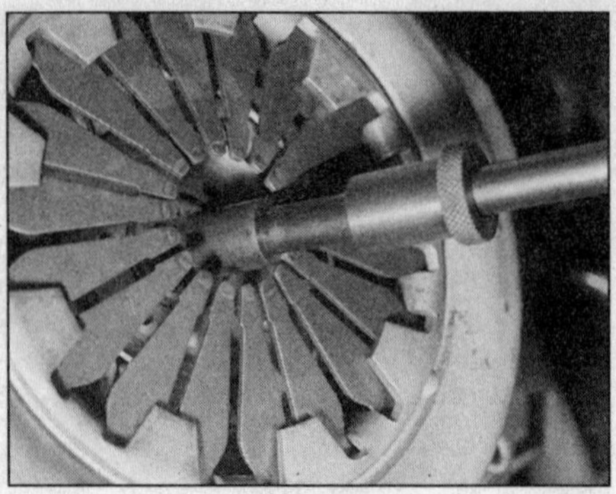

5.16a Insert the aligning tool into the end of the crankshaft . . .

5.16b . . . and engage it with the friction plate hub

the pressure plate bolts by half a turn at a time, until the spring pressure is released and the bolts can be unscrewed by hand.

4 Prise the pressure plate assembly off its locating dowels, and collect the friction plate, noting which way round the friction plate is fitted **(see illustration)**.

Inspection

Note: *Due to the amount of work necessary to gain access to the clutch components, it is usually considered good practice to renew the clutch friction plate, pressure plate assembly and release bearing as a matched set, even if only one of these is actually worn enough to require renewal.*

5 When cleaning clutch components, first read the warning at the beginning of this Section; remove any dust using a clean, dry cloth, and working in a well-ventilated atmosphere.

6 Check the friction plate facings for signs of wear, damage or oil contamination. If the friction material is cracked, burnt, scored or damaged, or if it is contaminated with oil or grease (shown by shiny black patches), the friction plate must be renewed.

7 If the friction material is still serviceable, check that the centre boss splines are unworn, that the torsion springs are in good condition and securely fastened, and that all the rivets are tightly fastened. If any wear or damage is found, the friction plate must be renewed.

8 If the friction material is fouled with oil, this must be due to an oil leak from the crankshaft left-hand oil seal, from the sump-to-cylinder block joint, or from the transmission input shaft. If a leak is evident, renew the seal or repair the joint (as appropriate) as described in Chapter 2 or 7, before installing the new friction plate.

9 Check the pressure plate assembly for obvious signs of wear or damage. Shake it to check for loose rivets or damaged fulcrum rings; check that the drive straps securing the pressure plate to the cover do not show signs (such as a deep yellow or blue discoloration) of overheating. If the diaphragm spring is worn or damaged, or if its pressure is in any way suspect, the pressure plate assembly should be renewed.

5.16c Home-made centralising tool - dimensions in mm

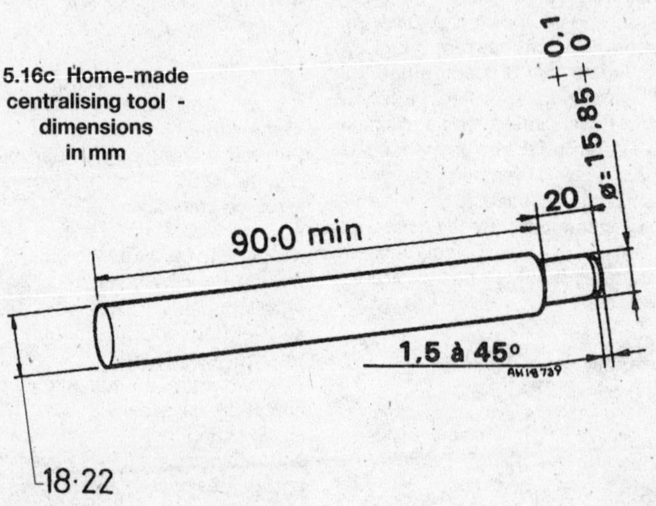

10 Examine the machined bearing surfaces of the pressure plate and of the flywheel; they should be clean, completely flat and free from scratches or scoring (minor damage of this nature can sometimes be polished away using emery paper). If either is discoloured from excessive heat, or shows signs of cracking, it should be renewed.

11 Check that the release bearing contact surface rotates smoothly and easily, with no sign of noise or roughness, and that the surface itself is smooth and unworn, with no signs of cracks, pitting or scoring. If there is any doubt about its condition, the bearing must be renewed. It is generally considered good practice to renew the bearing regardless of its apparent condition, whenever a new clutch plate is fitted (see note above).

Refitting

12 On reassembly, ensure that the bearing surfaces of the flywheel and pressure plate are completely clean, smooth, and free from oil or grease. Use solvent to remove any protective grease from new components.

13 Fit the friction plate so that its spring hub assembly faces away from the flywheel; there may also be a marking showing which way round the plate is to be refitted.

14 Refit the pressure plate assembly, aligning the marks made on dismantling (if the original pressure plate is re-used) and locating the pressure plate on its three locating dowels. Fit the pressure plate bolts, but tighten them only finger-tight, so that the friction plate can still be moved.

15 The friction plate must now be centralised, so that when the transmission is refitted, its input shaft will pass through the splines at the centre of the friction plate.

16 Centralisation can be achieved by passing a screwdriver or other long bar through the friction plate and into the hole in the crankshaft; the friction plate can then be moved around until it is centred on the crankshaft hole.

HAYNES HiNT ***A clutch-aligning tool can be used to eliminate the guesswork. These can be obtained from most accessory shops, or can be made up from a length of metal rod or wooden dowel which fits closely inside the crankshaft hole, and has insulating tape wound around it to match the diameter of the friction plate splined hole (see illustrations).***

5.17 Once the friction plate is centralised, tighten the pressure plate retaining bolts to the specified torque

6.2a Clutch release bearing location

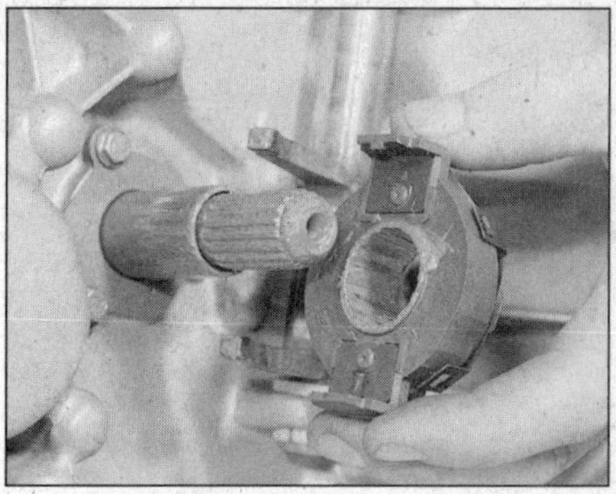

6.2b Clutch release bearing removal

6.3a Using a hammer and suitable punch . . .

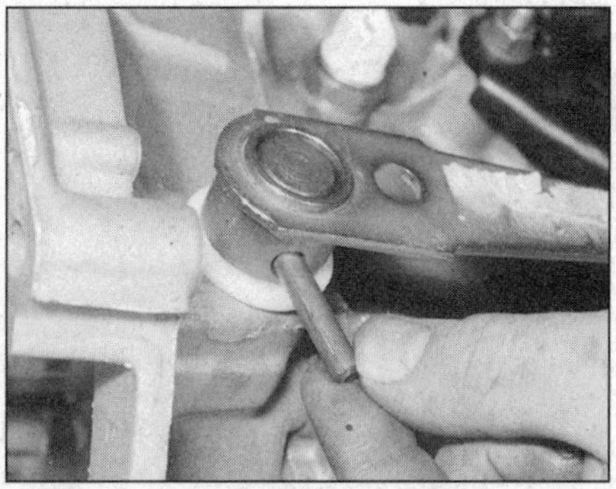

6.3b . . . tap out the retaining pin . . .

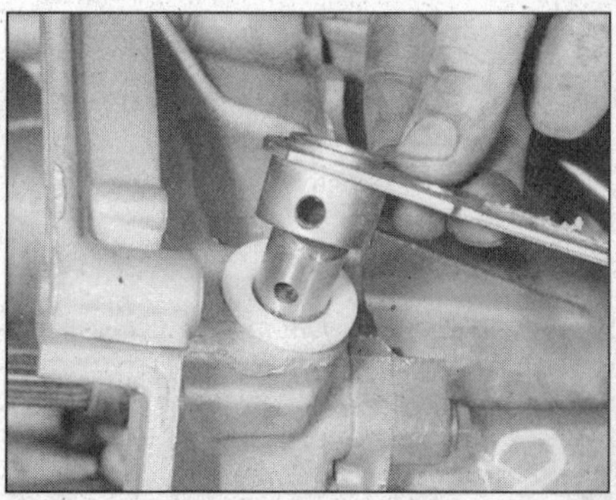

6.3c . . . then remove the release lever from the top of the release fork shaft

17 When the friction plate is centralised, tighten the pressure plate bolts evenly and in a diagonal sequence to the specified torque setting **(see illustration)**.

18 Apply a thin smear of high-melting point grease to the splines of the friction plate and the transmission input shaft, and also to the release bearing bore and release fork shaft. Do not apply too much grease, or it may find its way onto the friction surfaces of the new clutch plate.

19 Refit the transmission as described in Chapter 7.

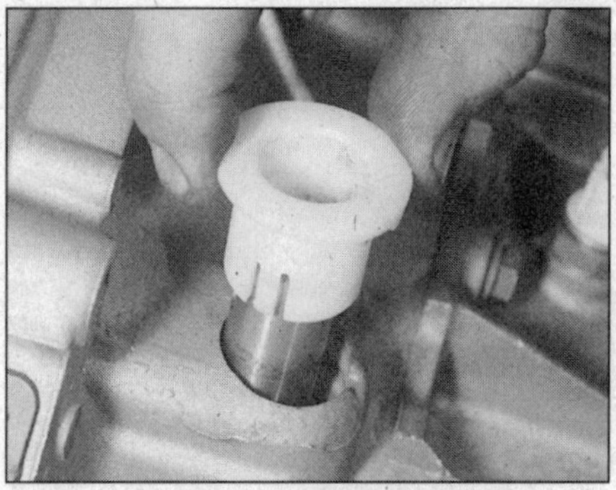

6.4a Release the upper pivot bush, and slide it off the shaft . . .

6.4b . . . then withdraw the release fork shaft and remove the lower bush (arrowed)

6

6 Clutch release mechanism - removal, inspection and refitting

Note: *Refer to the warning concerning the dangers of asbestos dust at the beginning of Section 5.*

Removal

1 Unless the engine/transmission is to be removed from the car and separated for major overhaul (Chapter 2C), the clutch release mechanism can be reached by removing the transmission alone, as described in Chapter 7.

2 Unhook the release bearing from the fork, and slide it off the input shaft **(see illustrations)**.

3 If required, the release lever and shaft can be removed as follows. Drive out the retaining pin or unscrew the retaining bolt (as applicable), then remove the release lever from the top of the release fork shaft **(see illustrations)**.

4 Depress the retaining tabs, then slide the upper bush off the end of the release fork shaft. Disengage the shaft from its lower bush, and manoeuvre it out from the transmission **(see illustrations)**. Depress the retaining tabs, and remove the lower pivot bush from the transmission housing.

Inspection

5 Check the release mechanism, renewing any components which are worn or damaged. Carefully check all bearing surfaces and points of contact.

6 Check the release bearing itself, noting that it is generally considered worthwhile to renew it as a matter of course, having got this far. Check that the contact surface rotates smoothly and easily, with no sign of noise or roughness, and that the surface itself is smooth and unworn, with no signs of cracks, pitting or scoring. If there is any doubt about its condition, the bearing must be renewed.

Refitting

7 Apply a smear of high-melting point grease to the shaft pivot bushes and the contact surfaces of the release fork.

8 Locate the lower pivot bush in the transmission, ensuring that it is securely retained by its locating tangs, and refit the release fork **(see illustration)**. Slide the upper bush down the shaft, and clip it into position in the transmission housing.

9 Refit the release lever to the shaft. Align the lever with the shaft hole, and secure it in position by tapping in the retaining pin or securely tightening its retaining bolt (as applicable). Slide the release bearing onto the input shaft, and engage it with the release fork **(see illustration)**.

10 Refit the transmission as described in Chapter 7.

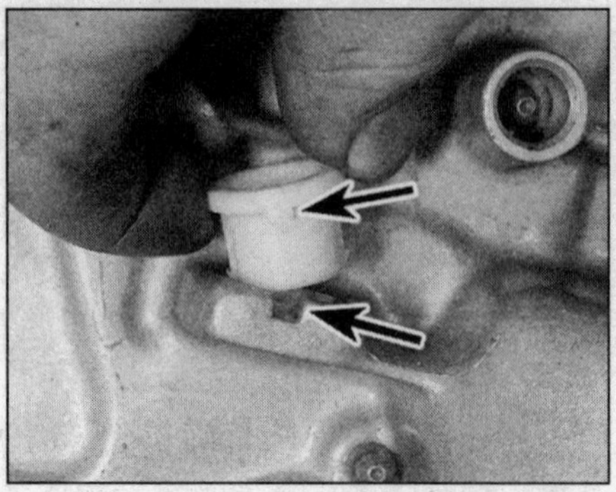

6.8 On refitting, ensure that the bush lug and housing recess (arrowed) are correctly aligned

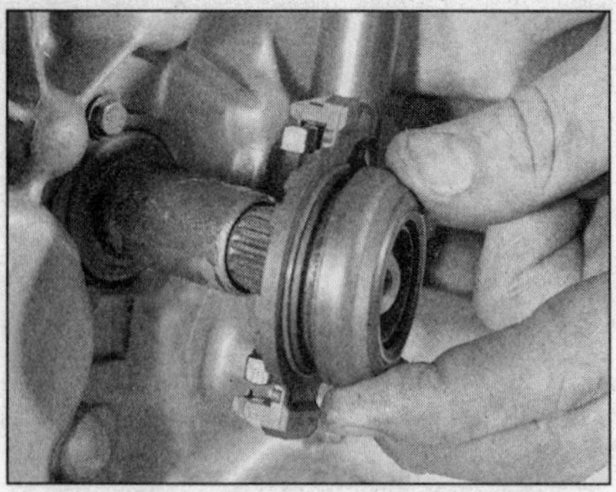

6.9 Install the release bearing, ensuring that its hooks are correctly engaged with the release fork

Chapter 7 Manual transmission

Contents

Degrees of difficulty

Easy, suitable for novice with little experience	**Fairly easy,** suitable for beginner with some experience	**Fairly difficult,** suitable for competent DIY mechanic	**Difficult,** suitable for experienced DIY mechanic	**Very difficult,** suitable for expert DIY or professional

Specifications

General

Type	Manual, four or five forward speeds and reverse. Synchromesh on all forward speeds
Designation:	
Four-speed transmission	MA4
Five-speed transmission	MA5

Gear ratios

MA4 transmission:	
1st	3.417 : 1 (12/41 teeth)
2nd	1.810 : 1 (21/38 teeth)
3rd	1.130 : 1 (31/35 teeth)
4th	0.810 : 1 (43/35 teeth)
Reverse	3.583 : 1 (12/43 teeth)
Final drive (typical)	3.588 : 1 (17/61 teeth)
MA5 transmission (petrol models):	
1st	3.417 : 1 (12/41 teeth)
2nd	1.950 : 1 (20/39 teeth)
3rd	1.360 : 1 (28/38 teeth)
4th	1.054 : 1 (37/39 teeth)
5th	0.850 : 1 (41/35 teeth)
Reverse	3.583 : 1 (12/43 teeth)
Final drive (typical)	3.444 : 1 (18/62 teeth)
MA5 transmission (Diesel models):	
1st	3.417 : 1 (12/41 teeth)
2nd	1.810 : 1 (21/38 teeth)
3rd	1.276 : 1 (29/37 teeth)
4th	0.975 : 1 (40/39 teeth)
5th	0.767 : 1 (43/33 teeth)
Reverse	3.583 : 1 (12/43 teeth)
Final drive (typical)	3.938 : 1 (16/63 teeth)

Lubrication

Recommended oil	See Chapter 1
Capacity	2.0 litres

Torque wrench settings

	Nm	lbf ft
Oil filler/level plug	25	18
Oil drain plug	25	18
Clutch release bearing guide sleeve bolts	6	4
Reversing light switch	25	18
Engine/transmission left-hand mounting:		
Mounting bracket-to-transmission nuts	18	13
Mounting bracket-to-body bolts	17	13
Centre bolt	50	37
Engine/transmission rear mounting:		
Mounting assembly-to-block bolts	40	30
Mounting bracket-to-mounting centre bolt	60	44
Mounting bracket-to-subframe bolt	90	66

1 General information

1 The transmission is contained in a cast aluminium alloy casing bolted to the engine's left-hand end, and consists of the gearbox and final drive differential.

2 Drive is transmitted from the crankshaft via the clutch to the input shaft, which rotates in sealed ball-bearings, and has a splined extension to accept the clutch friction plate. From the input shaft, drive is transmitted to the output shaft, which rotates in a roller bearing at its right-hand end, and a sealed ball-bearing at its left-hand end. From the output shaft, the drive is transmitted to the differential crownwheel, which rotates with the differential and planetary gears, thus driving the sun gears and driveshafts. The rotation of the planetary gears on their shaft allows the inner roadwheel to rotate at a slower speed than the outer roadwheel when the car is cornering.

3 The input and output shafts are arranged side by side, parallel to the crankshaft and driveshafts, so that their gear pinion teeth are in constant mesh.

4 Gear selection is via a floor-mounted lever and selector rod mechanism. The selector rod causes the appropriate selector fork to move its respective synchro-sleeve along the shaft, to lock the gear pinion to the synchro-hub. Since the synchro-hubs are splined to the output shaft, this locks the pinion to the shaft so that drive is transmitted. To ensure that gear-changing can be made quickly and quietly, a synchromesh system is fitted to all forward gears, consisting of baulk rings and spring-loaded fingers; the synchromesh cones are formed on the mating faces of the baulk rings and gear pinions.

2 Manual transmission - draining and refilling

Note: *A suitable square-section wrench may be required to undo the transmission filler/level and drain plugs on some models. These wrenches can be obtained from most motor factors, or from your Citroën dealer.*

1 This operation is much quicker and more effective if the car is first taken on a journey of sufficient length to warm the engine/transmission up to normal operating temperature.

2 Park the car on level ground, switch off the engine, and apply the handbrake firmly. For improved access, jack up the front of the car and support it securely on axle stands. Note that the car must be lowered to the ground, and level, to ensure accuracy, when refilling and checking the oil level.

3 Wipe clean the area around the filler/level plug, which is situated on the left-hand end of the transmission, next to the end cover. Unscrew the filler/level plug from the transmission, and recover the sealing washer **(see illustration)**.

4 Position a suitable container under the drain plug, situated on the left-hand side of the differential housing, and unscrew the plug from the transmission **(see illustration)**.

5 Allow the oil to drain completely into the container. If the oil is hot, take precautions against scalding. Clean both the filler/level and the drain plugs, being especially careful to wipe any metallic particles off the magnetic inserts. Discard the original sealing washers; they should be renewed whenever they are disturbed.

6 When the oil has finished draining, clean the drain plug threads in the transmission casing. Fit a new sealing washer and refit the drain plug, tightening it to the specified torque wrench setting. It the car was raised for the draining operation, now lower it to the ground.

7 Refilling the transmission is an extremely awkward operation. Above all, allow plenty of time for the oil level to settle properly before checking the level. Note that the car must be parked on flat level ground when checking the oil level.

8 Refill the transmission with the exact amount of the specified type of oil, then check the oil level as described in Chapter 1. If the correct amount was poured into the transmission, and a large amount flows out on checking the level, refit the filler/level plug and take the car on a short journey. When the new oil is distributed fully around the transmission components, check the level again on your return, and top-up if necessary.

3 Gearchange linkage - general information and adjustment

General information

1 If a stiff, sloppy or imprecise gearchange leads you to suspect that a fault exists within the linkage, dismantle it completely and check it for wear or damage as described in Section 4. Reassemble the linkage, applying a smear of multi-purpose grease to all bearing surfaces.

2 If this does not cure the fault, the car should be examined by an expert, as the fault must lie within the transmission itself. There is no adjustment as such in the linkage.

3 While the length of the link rods can be altered as described below, this is for initial setting-up only, and is not intended to provide a form of compensation for wear. If the link rods have been renewed, or if the length of the originals is incorrect, adjust them as follows.

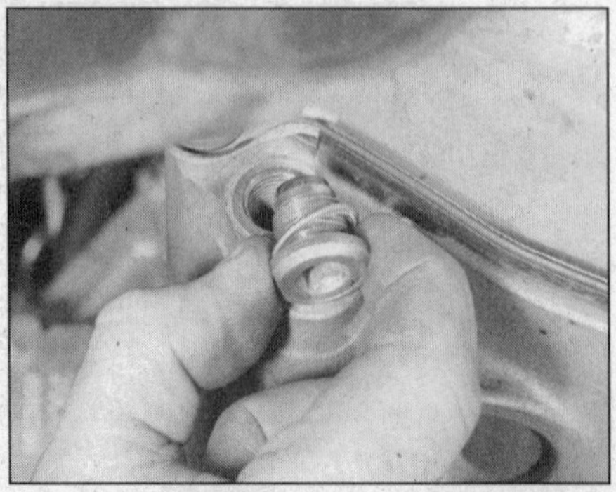

2.3 Unscrew the filler/level plug from the transmission, and recover the sealing washer

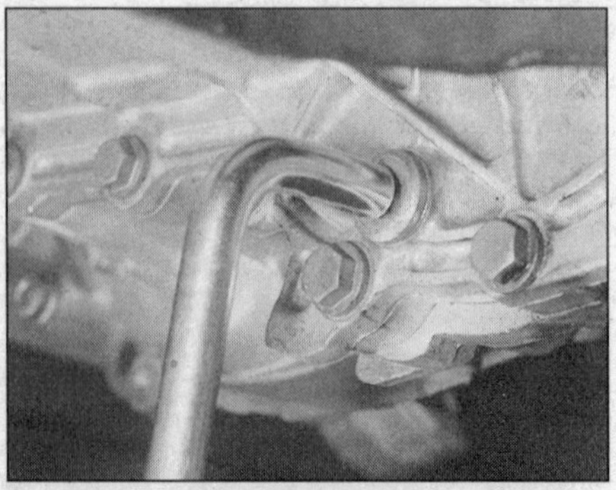

2.4 Using the special square-section wrench to unscrew the transmission drain plug

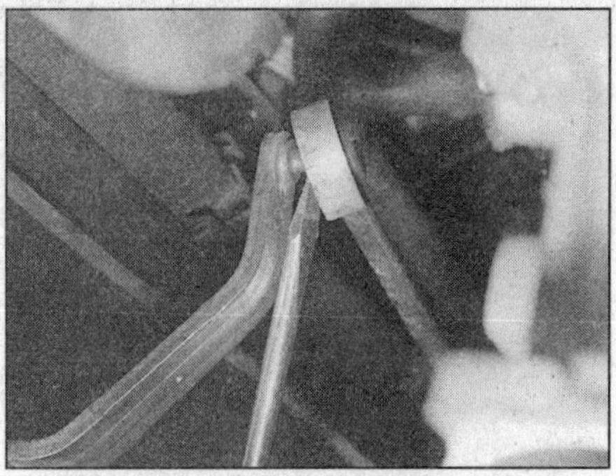

3.5 Carefully lever the link rods off their balljoints, using a large flat-bladed screwdriver

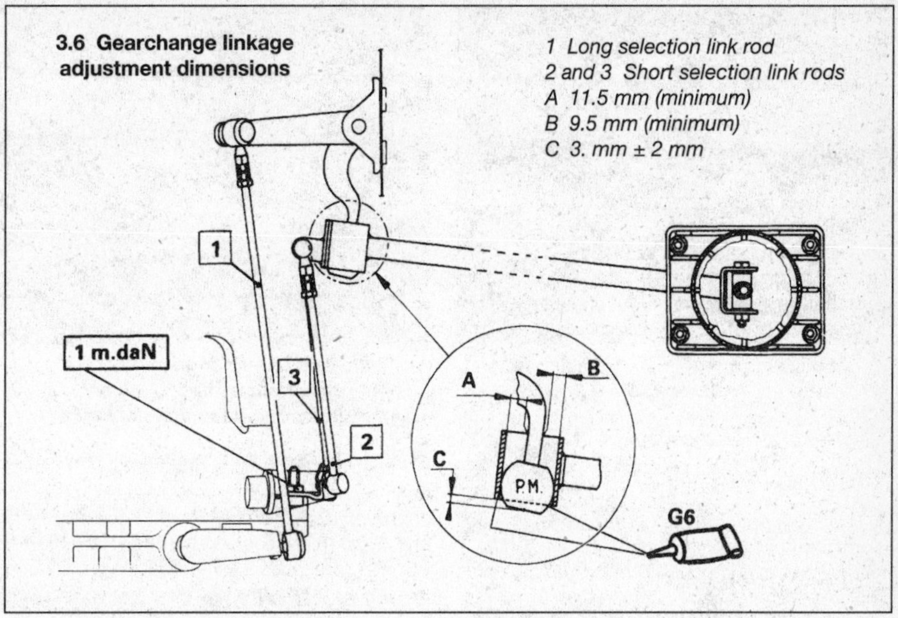

3.6 Gearchange linkage adjustment dimensions

1 Long selection link rod
2 and 3 Short selection link rods
A 11.5 mm (minimum)
B 9.5 mm (minimum)
C 3. mm ± 2 mm

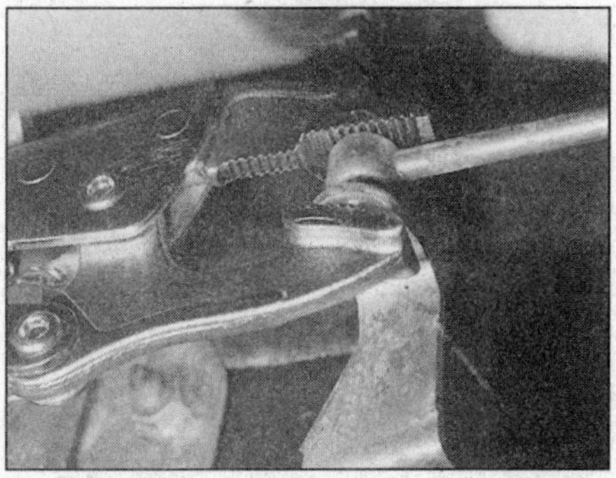

3.7 Securely press the socket back onto its balljoint

Adjustment

4 Firmly apply the handbrake and select neutral, then jack up the front of the vehicle and support it on axle stands. Access to the link rods is poor, but they can be reached both from above and below the vehicle.

5 The length of each selection link rod is adjustable by loosening the locknut then rotating the end fitting, after disconnecting it from the balljoint. First disconnect the two short selection link rods from the front of the main gearchange rod, leaving the long selection link rod connected to the lever arm on the right-hand side of the bulkhead. Use a screwdriver to carefully lever the link rods from their balljoints **(see illustration)**.

6 Measure dimensions A and B (see illustration 3.5). If they are not as given on the illustration, loosen the locknut and disconnect the long selection link rod and adjust its length until the dimensions are correct.

7 Make sure the socket is located fully on the balljoint - early models incorporate a spring clip, while later models are simply pressed onto the balljoint **(see illustration)**. Tighten the locknut when the adjustment is correct.

8 Connect the two short selection link rods to the end of the main gearchange rod then measure dimension C. If the dimension is not as given on the illustration, both rods must be adjusted until the dimension is correct making sure that the transmission is still in neutral.

9 Once the adjustments have been made check that all gears can be selected, and that the gearchange lever returns properly to its correct at-rest position.

4 Gearchange linkage - removal and refitting

Removal

1 Firmly apply the handbrake, then jack up the front of the vehicle and support it on axle stands.

2 Slacken and remove the nut, and withdraw the pivot bolt securing the selector rod to the base of the gearchange lever **(see illustration)**.

3 Using a flat-bladed screwdriver, carefully lever the two selector rod link rods off their balljoints on the transmission. Disengage the selector rod from the bellcrank arm and remove it, complete with link rods, from underneath the vehicle.

4 Carefully lever the long selector link rod balljoint off the transmission lever, then undo the two retaining nuts and remove the bellcrank assembly from the bulkhead **(see illustration)**.

5 Inspect all the linkage components for signs of wear or damage, paying particular attention to the bellcrank pivot bushes and link rod balljoints, and renew worn components as necessary. If necessary, the gearchange lever can also be removed as follows.

6 Remove the centre console as described in Chapter 11, then undo the four retaining nuts and remove the gearchange lever, complete with rubber mounting plate, from the vehicle. The lever can be separated from its baseplate after the retaining ring has been unclipped **(see illustrations)**.

7 Examine the lever components for signs of wear or damage, paying particular attention to the rubber gaiters, and renew components as necessary.

Refitting

8 Refitting is a reversal of the removal procedure, noting the following points:

a) Apply a smear of multi-purpose grease to the gearchange lever pivot ball, the link rod balljoints, and the bellcrank ball and pivot bushes.
b) Ensure that all link rods are securely pressed onto their balljoints.
c) Adjust the link rods as described in Section 3.

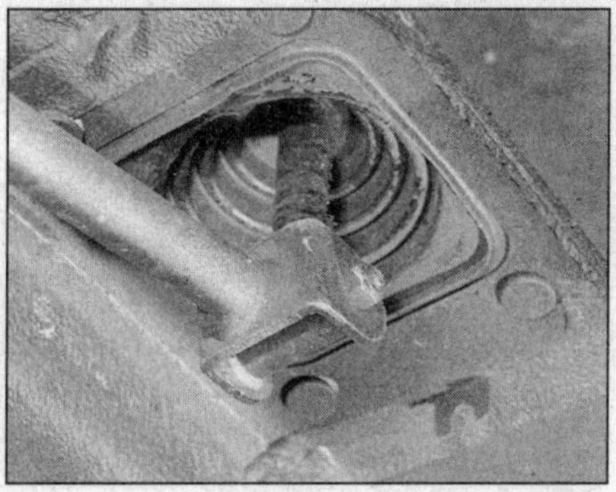

4.2 Gearchange lever-to-selector rod connection

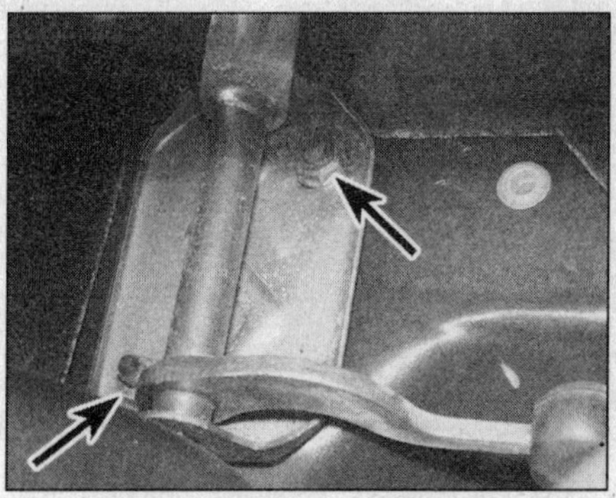

4.4 Gearchange linkage bellcrank is secured to the bulkhead by two nuts (arrowed)

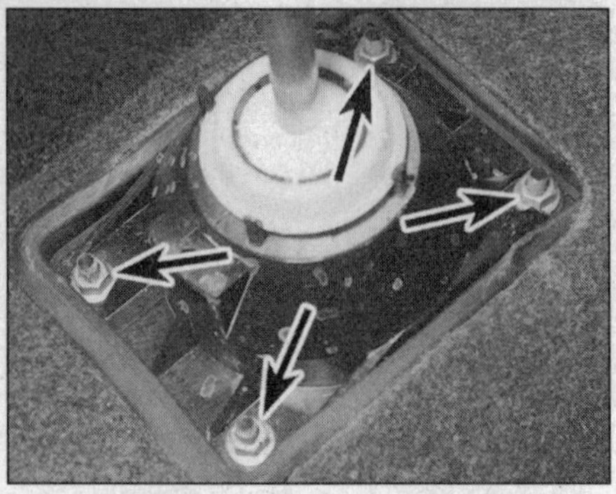

4.6a Gearchange lever retaining nuts (arrowed)

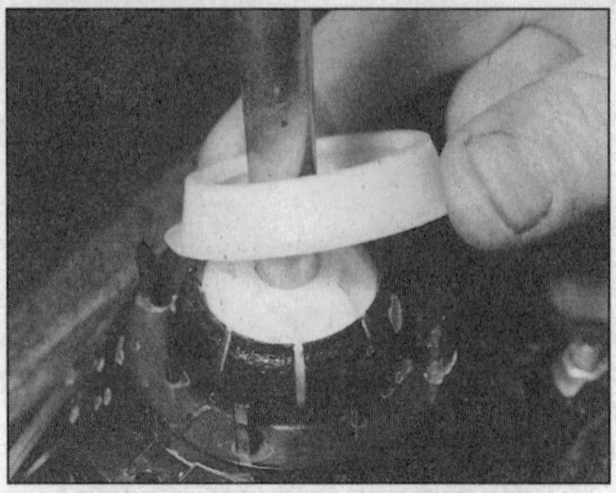

4.6b The gearchange lever can be separated from its baseplate once its retaining ring has been unclipped

5.4 Use a large flat-bladed screwdriver to prise the driveshaft oil seal out of position

5 Oil seals - renewal

Driveshaft oil seal

1 Chock the rear wheels of the car, firmly apply the handbrake, then jack up the front of the car and support it on axle stands. Remove the appropriate front roadwheel.

2 Drain the transmission oil as described in Section 2.

3 Working as described in Chapter 8, free the inner end of the driveshaft from the transmission, and place it clear of the seal. There is no need to unscrew the driveshaft retaining nut; the driveshaft can be left secured to the hub. Support the driveshaft, to avoid placing any strain on the driveshaft joints or gaiters.

4 Carefully prise the oil seal out of the transmission, using a large flat-bladed screwdriver **(see illustration)**.

5 Remove all traces of dirt from the area around the oil seal aperture, then apply a smear of grease to the outer lip of the new oil seal. Fit the new seal into its aperture, and drive it squarely into position until it abuts its locating shoulder. If the seal was supplied with a plastic protector sleeve, leave this in position until the driveshaft has been refitted.

TOOL TiP

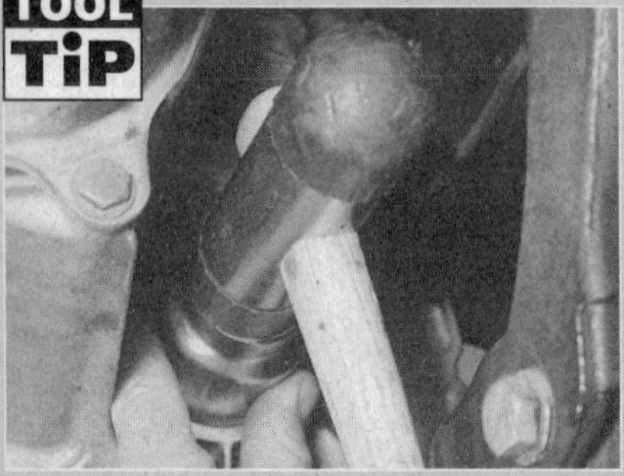

Use a suitable tubular drift (such as a socket) which bears only on the hard outer edge of the seal

6 Refit the driveshaft as described in Chapter 8.

7 Refill the transmission with the specified type and amount of oil as described in Section 2.

Input shaft oil seal

8 Remove the transmission from the car as described in Section 8.

9 Undo the three bolts securing the clutch release bearing guide sleeve in position, and slide the guide off the input shaft along with its O-ring or gasket, as applicable **(see illustration)**. Recover any relevant thrustwashers which have stuck to the rear of the guide sleeve, and refit them to the input shaft.

10 Before fitting a new seal, check the input shaft's seal rubbing surface for signs of burrs, scratches or other damage which may have caused the seal to fail in the first place. It may be possible to polish away minor defects of this sort using fine abrasive paper; however, more serious defects will require the renewal of the input shaft. Ensure that the input shaft is clean and greased, to protect the seal lips on refitting.

11 Fit a new O-ring or gasket (as applicable) to the rear of the guide sleeve, then carefully slide the sleeve into position over the input shaft. Refit the retaining bolts, and tighten them to the specified torque setting.

12 Refit the transmission to the car as described in Section 8.

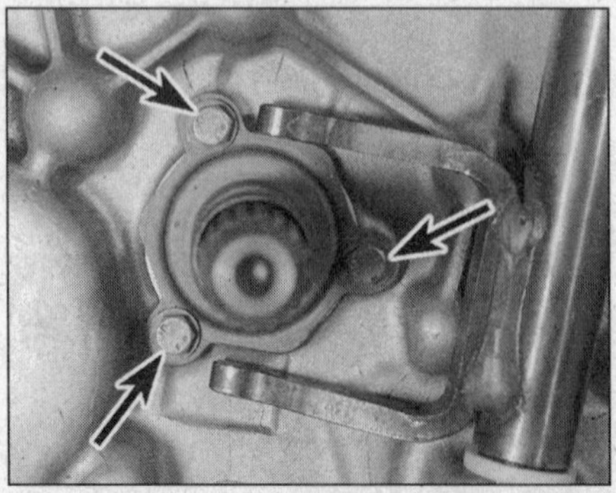

5.9 Clutch release bearing guide sleeve is retained by three bolts (arrowed)

Selector shaft oil seal

13 To renew the selector shaft seal, the transmission must be dismantled. This task should therefore be entrusted to a Citroën dealer.

6 Reversing light switch - testing, removal and refitting

Testing

1 The reversing light circuit is controlled by a plunger-type switch screwed into the top of the transmission casing. If a fault develops in the circuit, first ensure that the circuit fuse has not blown.

2 To test the switch, disconnect the wiring connector, and use a multi-meter (set to the resistance function) or a battery-and-bulb test circuit to check that there is continuity between the switch terminals only when reverse gear is selected. If this is not the case, the switch is faulty, and must be renewed. If the switch functions correctly, check the associated wiring for possible open- or short-circuits.

Removal

3 Remove the air inlet ducting from the engine compartment, with reference to Chapter 4.

4 Disconnect the wiring connector from the switch **(see illustration)**. Unscrew it from the transmission casing, and remove it along with its sealing washer.

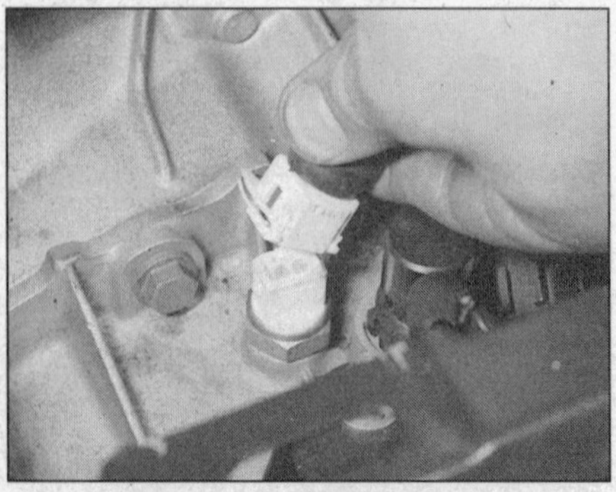

6.4 Disconnecting the wiring connector from the reversing light switch

7.2a Withdraw the rubber retaining pin (arrowed) . . .

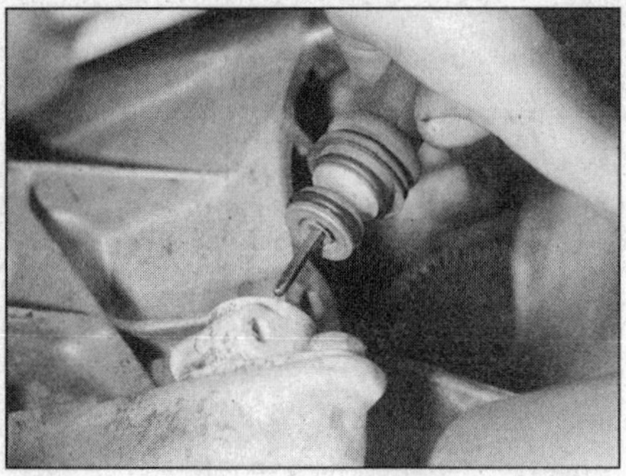

7.2b . . . then disconnect the speedometer cable from its drive

7.3a Unscrew the retaining bolt . . .

Refitting

5 Fit a new sealing washer to the switch, then screw it back into position in the top of the transmission housing, tightening it to the specified torque setting. Reconnect the wiring connector, then refit the air inlet ducting and test the operation of the circuit.

7 Speedometer drive - removal and refitting

Removal

1 Chock the rear wheels of the car, and firmly apply the handbrake. Jack up the front of the car, and support it securely on axle stands. The speedometer drive is situated on the rear of the transmission housing, next to the inner end of the right-hand driveshaft.

2 Pull out the speedometer cable rubber retaining pin, and disconnect the cable from the speedometer drive **(see illustrations)**. Where necessary, disconnect the wiring connector from the speedometer drive (models with a speed sensor).

3 Unscrew and remove the retaining bolt, and withdraw the speedometer drive and driven pinion assembly from the transmission housing, along with its O-ring **(see illustrations)**.

4 Examine the pinion for signs of damage, and renew if necessary. Renew the housing O-ring as a matter of course. On models where the speedometer drive is also the fuel injection system vehicle speed sensor (these are easily identified by the wiring connector on the housing), the drive assembly is a sealed unit. However, on all other models, the speedometer drive can be dismantled, and the driven pinion and oil seal renewed individually.

5 If the driven pinion is worn or damaged, also examine the drive ring in the transmission housing for signs of wear or damage **(see illustration)**. To renew the drive ring, the transmission must be dismantled and the differential gear removed. This task should therefore be entrusted to a Citroën dealer.

Refitting

6 Fit a new O-ring to the speedometer drive. Refit the drive to the transmission, ensuring that the drive ring and driven pinion are correctly engaged.

7 Refit the retaining bolt and tighten it securely. Where necessary, reconnect the wiring connector to the speedometer drive.

8 Apply a smear of oil to the speedometer cable O-rings, then reconnect the cable to the drive, securing it in position with the rubber retaining pin. Lower the vehicle to the ground.

8 Manual transmission - removal and refitting

Note: *The transmission can be removed on its own, or together with the engine. If the latter method is to be employed, refer to Chapter 2C for details for the removal and separation procedure. This Section describes the removal of the transmission on its own, leaving the engine in the vehicle.*

Removal

1 Chock the rear wheels, then firmly apply the handbrake. Jack up the front of the vehicle, and support it securely on axle stands. Remove both front roadwheels.

2 Drain the transmission oil as described in Section 2, then refit the drain and filler/level plugs, and tighten them to their specified torque settings.

3 Remove the battery as described in Chapter 5A.

4 Remove the air cleaner housing and/or intake duct (as applicable), as described in the relevant Part of Chapter 4.

5 Remove the starter motor as described in Chapter 5A.

6 Disconnect the clutch cable from the release lever and bracket on the transmission, with reference to Chapter 6 **(see illustration)**. Release the cable from any relevant retaining clips, and place it clear of the transmission.

7 Disconnect the wiring connectors from the reversing light switch, TDC sensor and speedometer drive housing (as applicable). Undo the retaining nut, and disconnect the earth straps from the top of the transmission housing **(see illustration)**. Free the wiring from any relevant retaining clips, and place it clear of the transmission.

8 Using a flat-bladed screwdriver, carefully lever the three gearchange mechanism link rods off their respective balljoints on the transmission. Position the rods clear of the transmission.

9 Withdraw the rubber retaining pin, and disconnect the speedometer cable from the

7

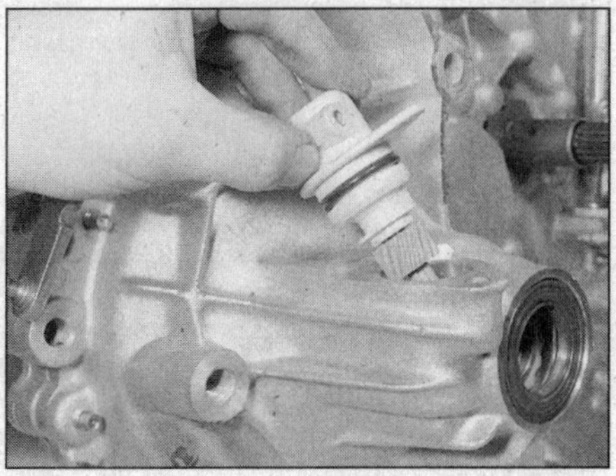

7.3b . . . and remove the speedometer drive pinion

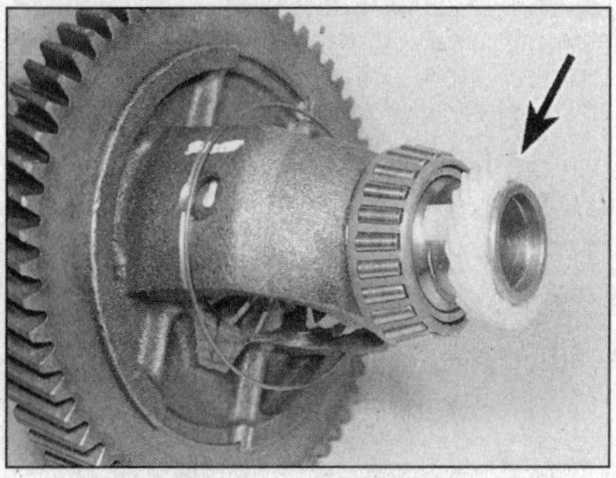

7.5 Speedometer drive ring (arrowed)

8.6 Free the clutch cable from the release lever, and place it clear of the transmission

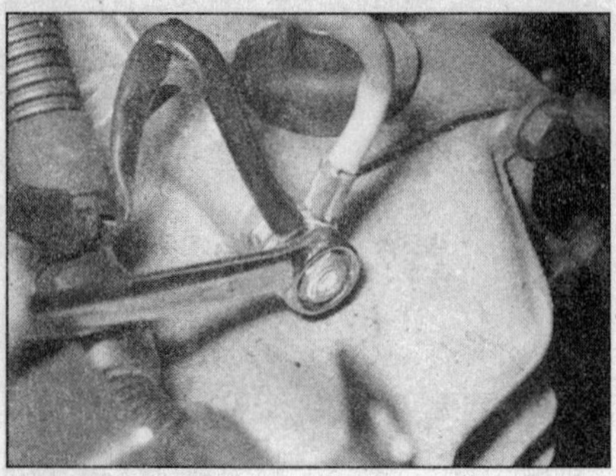

8.7 Undo the retaining nut, and release the earth straps from the top of the transmission housing

8.11 Disconnect the driveshafts from the transmission, noting that it is not necessary to disconnect them from the hubs

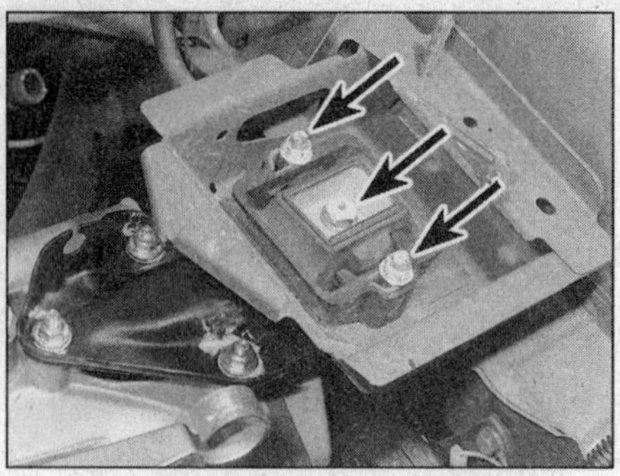

8.14 Transmission left-hand mounting retaining nuts and bolts (arrowed)

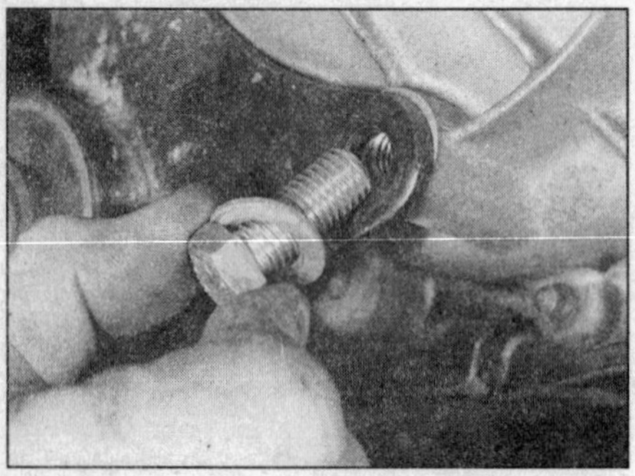

8.15a Unscrew the two bolts securing the rear mounting to the transmission . . .

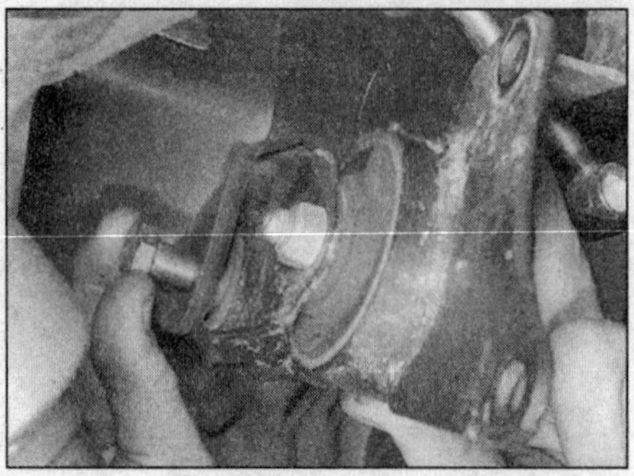

8.15b . . . then undo the bolt securing the mounting link to the body, and remove the mounting assembly from the vehicle

drive housing, freeing it from any relevant retaining clips.

10 On cast-iron block engines, unbolt the flywheel cover plate from the base of the transmission, and remove it from the vehicle.

11 Working as described in Chapter 8, free the inner end of each driveshaft from the transmission, and position them clear of the transmission **(see illustration)**. Note that there is no need to unscrew the driveshaft retaining nuts; each driveshaft can be left secured to the hub. Support the driveshafts, however, to avoid placing any strain on the driveshaft joints or gaiters.

12 Place a jack with interposed block of wood beneath the engine, to take the weight of the engine. Alternatively, attach a hoist or support bar to the engine lifting eyes, and take the weight of the engine.

13 Place a trolley jack and block of wood beneath the transmission, and raise the jack to take the weight of the transmission **(see illustration)**.

14 Slacken and remove the centre nut and washer from the left-hand engine/transmission mounting. Undo the two bolts securing the mounting bracket assembly to the vehicle body, then remove the mounting bracket assembly **(see illustration)**. Recover the spacer from the stud.

15 Slacken and remove the two bolts securing the rear engine mounting to the transmission. Unscrew the nut and bolt securing the mounting link to the vehicle body, and remove the mounting assembly from the vehicle **(see illustrations)**.

16 With the jack beneath the transmission taking its weight, slacken and remove the remaining bolts securing the transmission housing to the engine. Note the correct fitted positions of each bolt, and the necessary brackets, as they are removed, to use as a reference on refitting. On Diesel models, it may be necessary to remove the fuel filter to gain access to the upper transmission-to-engine unit bolts (see Chapter 1); if the filter is damaged on removal, a new one must be used on refitting.

17 Make a final check that all necessary components have been disconnected, and are positioned clear of the transmission so that they will not hinder the removal procedure.

18 With the bolts removed, move the trolley jack and transmission to the left, to free it from its locating dowels.

19 Once the transmission is free, lower the jack and manoeuvre the unit out from under the car **(see illustration)**. If they are loose, remove the locating dowels from the transmission or engine, and keep them in a safe place.

Refitting

20 The transmission is refitted using a reversal of the removal procedure, bearing in mind the following points:

a) Apply a little high-melting point grease to the splines of the transmission input shaft. Do not apply too much, otherwise there is a possibility of the grease contaminating the clutch friction plate.
b) Ensure that the locating dowels are correctly positioned prior to installation.
c) Tighten all nuts and bolts to the specified torque (where given).
d) Renew the driveshaft oil seals using the information given in Section 5.
e) On completion, refill the transmission with the specified type and quantity of oil, as described in Section 2.
f) Check and if necessary adjust the clutch cable with reference to Chapter 6.

9 Manual transmission overhaul - general information

1 Overhauling a manual transmission unit is a difficult and involved job for the DIY home mechanic. In addition to dismantling and reassembling many small parts, clearances must be precisely measured and, if necessary, changed by selecting shims and spacers. Internal transmission components are also often difficult to obtain and, in many instances, extremely expensive. Because of this, if the transmission develops a fault or becomes noisy, the best course of action is to have the unit overhauled by a specialist repairer, or to obtain an exchange reconditioned unit.

2 Nevertheless, it is not impossible for the more experienced mechanic to overhaul the transmission, provided the special tools are available, and the job is done in a deliberate step-by-step manner, so that nothing is overlooked.

3 The tools necessary for an overhaul include internal and external circlip pliers, bearing pullers, a slide hammer, a set of pin punches, a dial test indicator, and (possibly) a hydraulic press. In addition, a large, sturdy workbench and a vice will be required.

4 During dismantling of the transmission, make careful notes of how each component is fitted, to make reassembly easier and more accurate.

5 Before dismantling the transmission, it will help if you have some idea of which area is malfunctioning. Certain problems can be closely related to specific areas in the transmission, which can reduce the amount of dismantling and component examination required. Refer to the *"Fault diagnosis"* Section at the beginning of this manual for more information.

Chapter 8 Driveshafts

Contents

Degrees of difficulty

Easy, suitable for novice with little experience	**Fairly easy,** suitable for beginner with some experience	**Fairly difficult,** suitable for competent DIY mechanic	**Difficult,** suitable for experienced DIY mechanic	**Very difficult,** suitable for expert DIY or professional

Specifications

General

Lubrication (overhaul only)	Use only special grease supplied in sachets with gaiter kits - joints are otherwise pre-packed with grease and sealed
Grease quantity:	
Inner joint	160 g
Outer joint	160 g

Torque wrench settings	Nm	lbf ft
Driveshaft nut*:		
All except right-hand driveshaft with intermediate bearing	250	185
Right-hand driveshaft with intermediate bearing	260	192
Driveshaft intermediate bearing bracket securing bolts	45	33
Driveshaft intermediate bearing securing nuts	10	7
Lower arm balljoint-to-hub carrier nut and clamp bolt*	28	21
Front anti-roll bar end clamp-to-lower arm bolts	25	18
Front anti-roll bar drop link securing nuts*	30	22

**Use a new nut.*

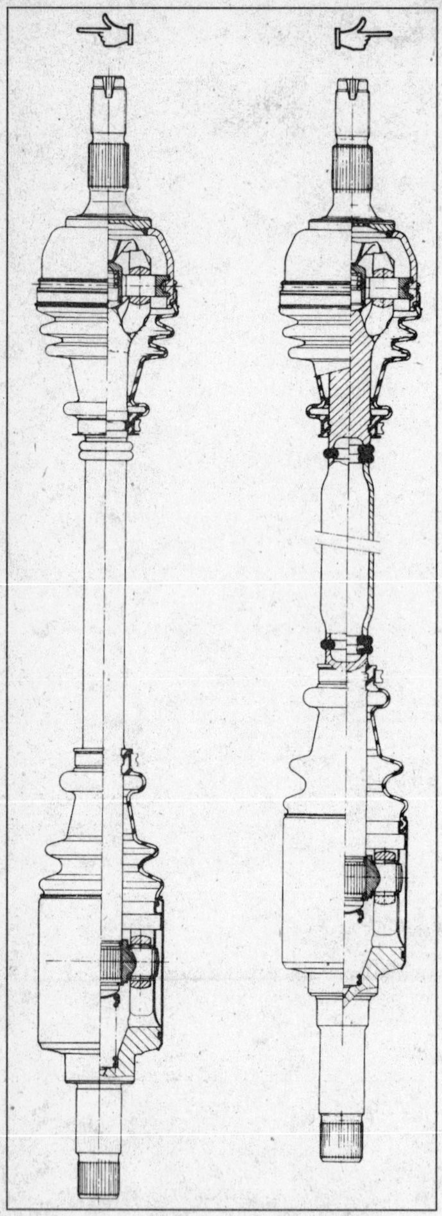

1.1 Left- and right-hand driveshafts (except K6B engine models)

1 General information

1 Drive is transmitted from the differential to the front wheels by means of two solid-steel driveshafts of unequal length **(see illustration)**.

2 Both driveshafts are splined at their outer ends, to accept the wheel hubs, and are threaded so that each hub can be fastened to the driveshaft by a large nut. The inner end of each driveshaft is splined, to engage with the differential sun gear.

3 Constant velocity (CV) joints are fitted to each end of the driveshafts, to ensure the smooth and efficient transmission of power at all suspension and steering angles. The inner and outer constant velocity joints are of the spider-and-yoke type.

4 On GTi models fitted with the 1360 cc multi-point injection engine (code K6B), the inner constant velocity joint is situated approximately halfway along the length of the shaft, and an intermediate bearing is mounted in a bracket bolted to the rear of the cylinder block. The inner section of the driveshaft passes through the bearing.

2 Driveshafts - removal and refitting

Note: *A balljoint separator tool will be required for this operation. A new driveshaft nut, a new track-rod end-to-steering arm nut, and a new hub carrier-to-lower arm balljoint clamp nut must be used on refitting.*

Removal

1 Chock the rear wheels, apply the handbrake, then jack up the front of the vehicle and support on axle stands (see *"Jacking, towing and wheel changing"*). Remove the appropriate roadwheel.

2 Drain the transmission oil as described in Chapter 7.

3 To avoid any possibility of damage during the following procedure, remove the ABS wheel sensor (where applicable) from the hub carrier as described in Chapter 9.

4 Using a hammer and a suitable cold chisel or punch, relieve the staking on the driveshaft nut **(see illustration)**.

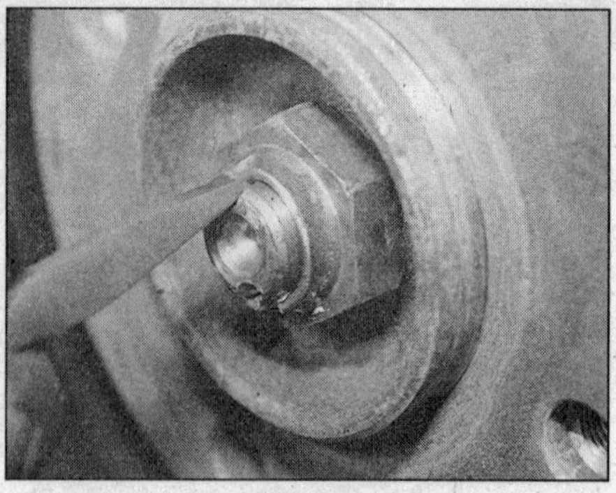

2.4 Relieve the retaining nut staking with a suitable cold chisel

5 The front hub must now be held stationary in order to loosen the driveshaft nut. Ideally, the hub should be held by a suitable tool bolted into place using two of the wheel bolts **(see illustration)**. Using a socket and extension bar, slacken and remove the driveshaft nut.

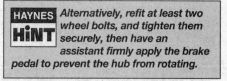

HAYNES HiNT *Alternatively, refit at least two wheel bolts, and tighten them securely, then have an assistant firmly apply the brake pedal to prevent the hub from rotating.*

Warning: Take care, the nut is very tight! Discard the nut - a new one must be used on refitting.

6 On models where the anti-roll bar is connected to the suspension strut body, undo the nut and washer securing the drop link to the strut, and position the link clear of the strut.

7 On models where the anti-roll bar is connected directly to the lower arm, remove the two screws and washers securing the anti-roll bar end clamp to the lower arm. Remove the clamp and the rubber bush.

8 Partially unscrew (do not completely remove) the nut securing the track-rod end to the steering arm on the suspension strut. Using a balljoint separator tool, separate the track-rod end from the steering arm. Remove the nut and washer **(see illustrations)**.

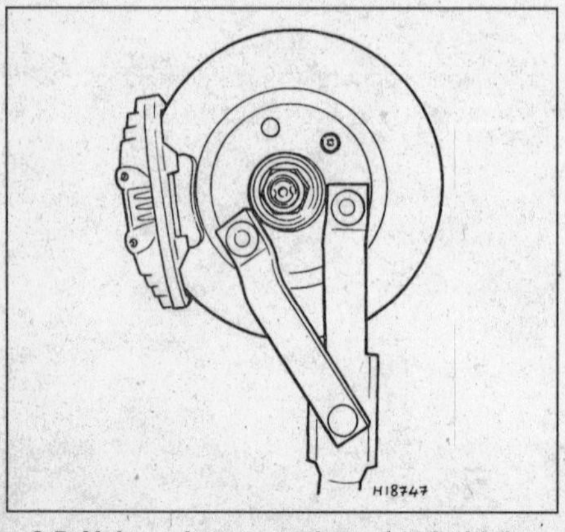

2.5 Using a home-made tool to hold the front hub stationary

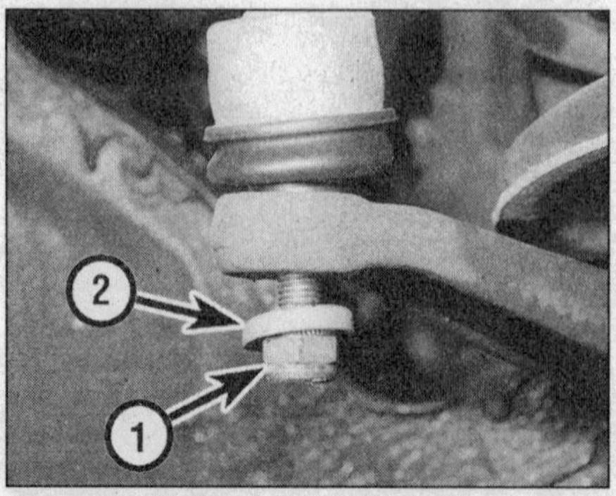

2.8a Unscrew (but do not yet remove) the nut (1). Note the washer (2)

2.8b Using a balljoint separator tool to separate the track-rod end from the steering arm

2.9a Undo the nut, while counterholding the bolt . . .

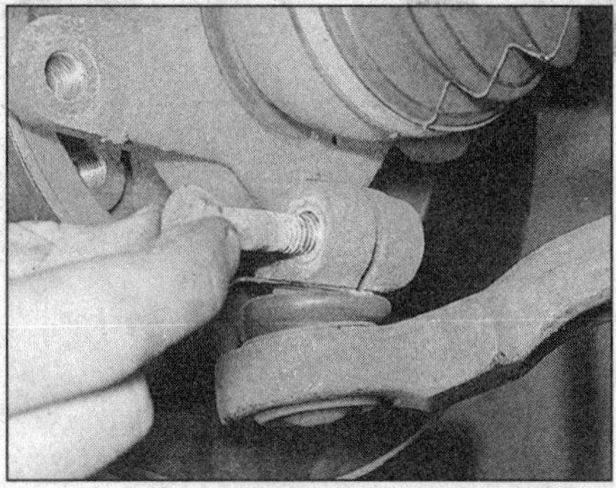
2.9b . . . and withdraw the bolt. Note that the bolt fits from the front of the strut

2.11 Pulling the strut/hub carrier outwards to release the driveshaft from the hub

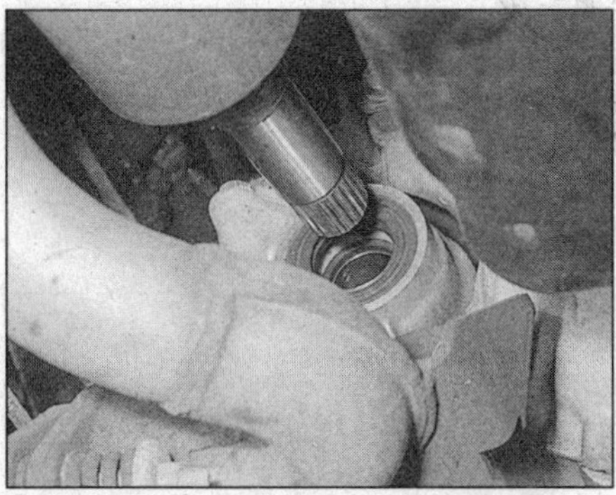
2.12 Withdrawing the driveshaft from the transmission

9 Undo the nut (while counterholding the bolt) and withdraw the hub carrier-to-lower arm clamp bolt, noting which way round it is fitted **(see illustrations)**.

10 Using a suitable metal bar, lever the lower arm downwards just enough to release the balljoint taper from the lower arm. If the taper is a tight fit in the hub carrier, use a large flat-bladed screwdriver to carefully open up the clamp a little. Recover the balljoint rubber gaiter protector if it is loose.

11 Release the hub from the driveshaft splines by pulling the strut/hub carrier assembly outwards **(see illustration)**. If necessary, the shaft can be tapped out of the hub using a soft-faced mallet. Support the driveshaft - do not allow the end of the driveshaft to hang down.

All except right-hand driveshaft with intermediate bearing

12 Support the driveshaft, then withdraw the inner constant velocity joint from the transmission, taking care not to damage the driveshaft oil seal **(see illustration)**. Remove the driveshaft from the vehicle.

Right-hand driveshaft with intermediate bearing

13 Loosen the two intermediate bearing retaining bolt nuts, then rotate the bolts through 90°, so that their offset heads are clear of the bearing outer race **(see illustrations)**.

14 Support the outer end of the driveshaft, then pull on the inner end of the shaft to free the intermediate bearing from its mounting bracket.

15 Once the driveshaft end is free from the transmission, slide the dust seal off the inner end of the shaft, noting which way around it is fitted, and remove the driveshaft from the vehicle.

Refitting

16 Before installing the driveshaft, examine the driveshaft oil seal in the transmission for signs of damage or deterioration and, if necessary, renew it, referring to Chapter 7 for further information (it is advisable to renew the seal as a matter of course).

17 Thoroughly clean the driveshaft splines, and the apertures in the transmission and hub assembly. Apply a thin film of grease to the oil seal lips, and to the driveshaft splines and shoulders. Check that all driveshaft gaiter clips are securely fastened.

All except right-hand driveshaft with intermediate bearing

18 Offer up the driveshaft, and engage the joint splines with those of the differential sun gear, taking great care not to damage the oil seal. Push the joint fully into position.

19 Ensure that the driveshaft splines and the corresponding splines in the hub are clean, then engage the driveshaft with the hub, and fit a new driveshaft nut. Do not tighten the nut at this stage.

20 Ensure that the protector plate is in place over the lower arm balljoint, then engage the balljoint taper with the hub carrier **(see illustration)**. If necessary, lever the arm downwards just enough to engage the balljoint, as during removal. Similarly, use a screwdriver to open up the clamp a little if necessary.

21 Fit the hub carrier-to-lower arm clamp bolt (from the front of the strut) and a new nut, and tighten to the specified torque.

22 Reconnect the track-rod end to the steering arm, and refit the washer and a new nut. Tighten the nut to the specified torque.

23 Reconnect the anti-roll bar to the lower arm, or the anti-roll bar drop link to the strut,

2.13a On the right-hand driveshaft, slacken the two intermediate bearing retaining bolt nuts . . .

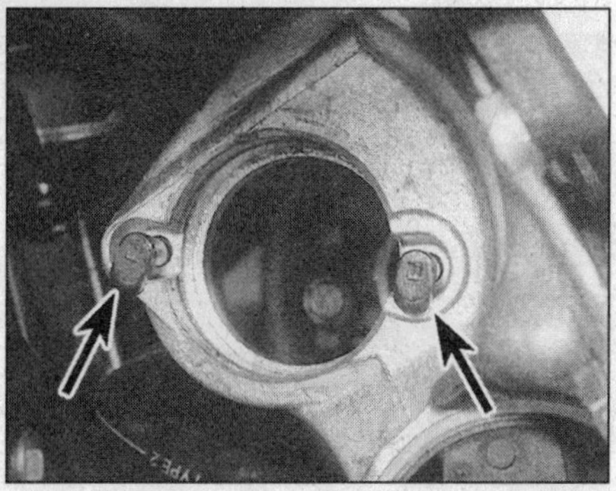
2.13b . . . then rotate the bolts through 90° to disengage their offset heads (arrowed) from the bearing (shown with driveshaft removed)

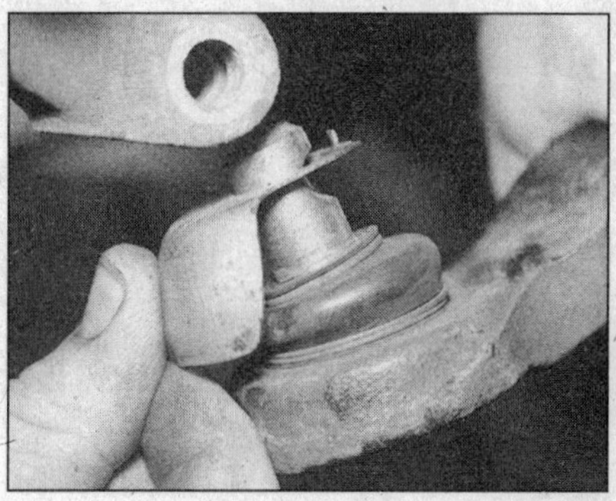
2.20 Ensure that the lower arm balljoint protector plate is in place

2.24a Tighten the nut to the specified torque . . .

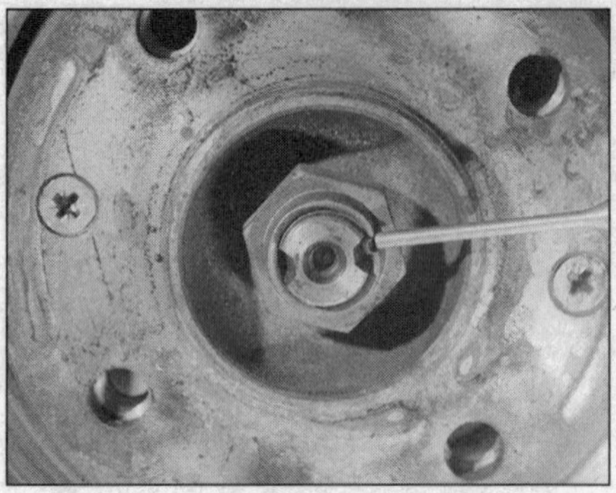

2.24b . . . then stake it firmly into the driveshaft groove

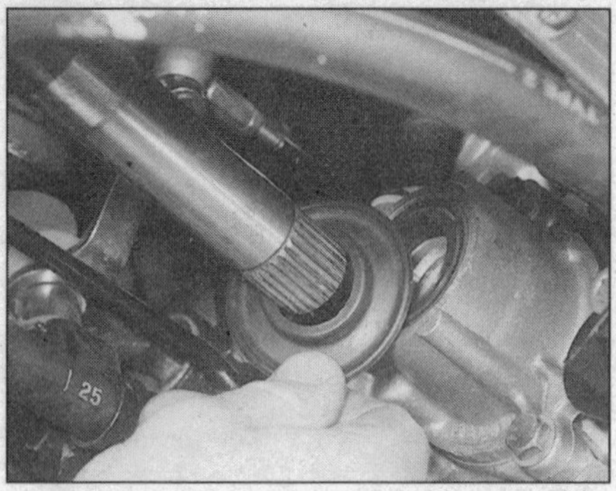

2.30 Locate the dust seal on the driveshaft, ensuring that it is fitted the correct way round

as applicable. Ensure that the washers are in place, then tighten the fixings to the specified torque.

24 Grease the driveshaft nut contact face of the hub bearing, and the threads of the driveshaft nut, then hold the hub stationary as during removal, and tighten the new driveshaft nut to the specified torque. Stake the nut in position **(see illustrations)**.

25 Where applicable, refit the ABS wheel sensor.

26 Refit the roadwheel, and lower the vehicle to the ground.

27 Refill the transmission with oil as described in Chapter 7.

Right-hand driveshaft with intermediate bearing

28 Check that the intermediate bearing rotates smoothly, without any sign of roughness, or of undue free play between its inner and outer races. If necessary, renew the bearing as described in Section 5. Examine the dust seal for signs of damage or deterioration, and renew if necessary.

29 Apply a smear of grease to the outer race of the intermediate bearing, and to the inner lip of the dust seal.

30 Pass the inner end of the shaft through the bearing mounting bracket, then carefully slide the dust seal into position on the driveshaft, ensuring that its flat surface is facing the transmission **(see illustration)**.

31 Carefully engage the inner driveshaft splines with those of the differential sun gear, taking care not to damage the oil seal. Align the intermediate bearing with its mounting bracket, and push the driveshaft fully into position. If necessary, use a soft-faced mallet to tap the outer race of the bearing into position in the mounting bracket.

32 Ensure that the driveshaft splines and the corresponding splines in the hub are clean, then engage the driveshaft with the hub, and fit a new driveshaft nut. Do not tighten the nut at this stage.

33 Ensure that the intermediate bearing is correctly seated, then rotate its retaining bolts back through 90°, so that their offset heads are resting against the bearing outer race. Tighten the retaining nuts to the specified torque. Ensure that the dust seal is tight against the driveshaft oil seal **(see illustration)**.

34 Carry out the operations described previously in paragraphs 20 to 27.

3 Driveshaft rubber gaiters - renewal

Outer joint

1 Remove the driveshaft as described in Section 2.

2 Remove the inner constant velocity joint and gaiter as described in paragraphs 13 to 20. It is recommended that the inner gaiter is also renewed, regardless of its apparent condition.

3 Release the two outer gaiter retaining clips, then slide the gaiter off the inner end of the driveshaft.

4 Thoroughly clean the outer constant velocity joint using paraffin, or a suitable solvent, and dry it thoroughly. Carry out a visual inspection of the joint.

5 Check the driveshaft spider and outer member yoke for signs of wear, pitting or scuffing on their bearing surfaces. Also check that the outer member pivots smoothly and easily, with no traces of roughness.

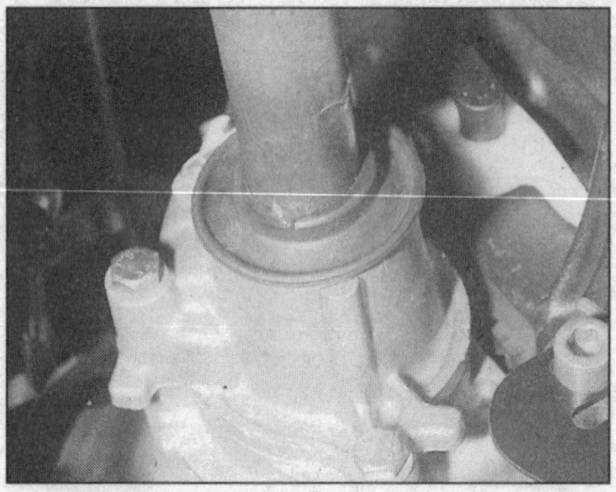

2.33 Secure the intermediate bearing in position, then slide the dust seal up tight against the driveshaft oil seal

6 If on inspection, the spider or outer member reveal signs of wear or damage, it will be necessary to renew the complete driveshaft as an assembly, since no components are available separately. If the joint components are in satisfactory condition, obtain a repair kit from your Citroën dealer, consisting of a new gaiter, retaining clips, and the correct type and quantity of grease **(see illustration)**.

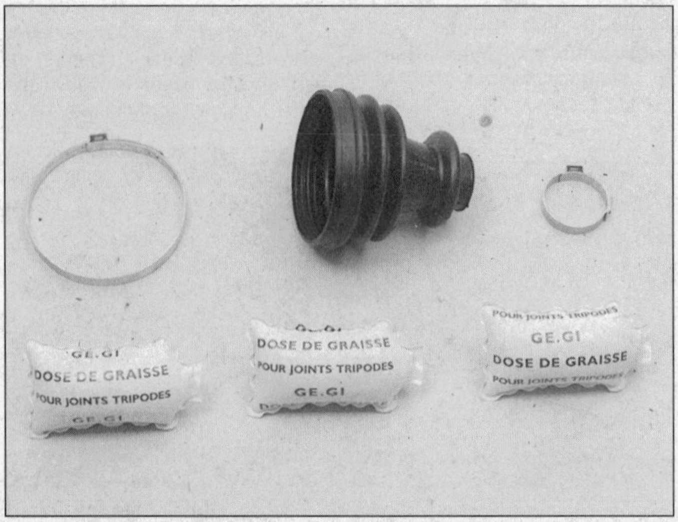

3.6 Driveshaft outer joint gaiter repair kit components

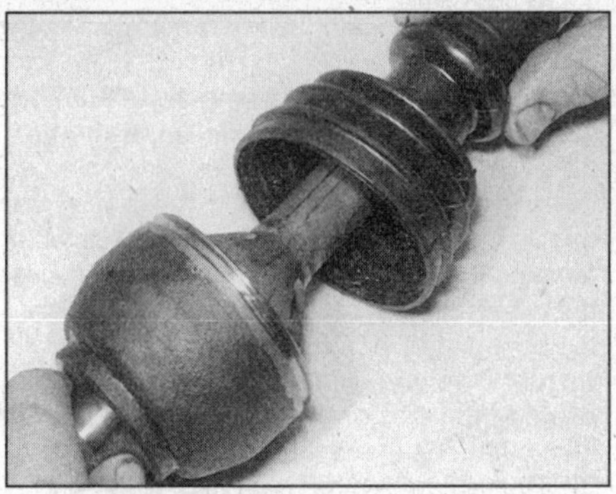

3.7 Sliding the outer joint gaiter onto the driveshaft

3.8 Pack the joint with the grease supplied in the repair kit

3.10 Securing a gaiter securing clip using side cutters

7 Tape over the splines on the inner end of the driveshaft, then carefully slide the outer gaiter onto the shaft **(see illustration)**.

8 Pack the joint with the grease supplied in the repair kit **(see illustration)**. Work the grease well into the bearing tracks whilst twisting the joint, and fill the rubber gaiter with any excess.

9 Ease the gaiter over the joint, and ensure that the gaiter lips are correctly located in the grooves on both the driveshaft and constant velocity joint. Lift the outer sealing lip of the gaiter, to equalise air pressure within the gaiter.

10 Fit the large metal retaining clip to the gaiter. Remove any slack in the gaiter retaining clip by carefully compressing the raised section of the clip. In the absence of the special tool, a pair of side cutters or pincers may be used. Secure the small retaining clip using the same procedure **(see illustration)**. Check that the constant velocity joint moves freely in all directions before proceeding further.

3.13 Peeling back the lip of the joint outer member cover

11 Refit the inner constant velocity joint as described in paragraphs 21 to 28.

Inner joint

12 Remove the driveshaft as described in Section 2.

13 Secure the driveshaft in a vice equipped with soft jaws. Using a suitable pair of pliers, carefully peel back the lip of the constant velocity joint outer member cover **(see illustration)**. Mark the cover in relation to the joint outer member.

14 Once the lip of the cover is fully released, pull the joint outer member out from the cover, and recover the spring and thrust cap from the end of the shaft. Remove the O-ring from the outside of the outer member, and discard it.

15 Fold the gaiter back, and wipe away the excess grease from the tripod joint. If the rollers are not secured to the joint with circlips, wrap adhesive tape around the joint to hold them in position.

16 Using a dab of paint, or a hammer and punch, mark the relative position of the tripod joint in relation to the driveshaft. Using circlip pliers, extract the circlip securing the joint to the driveshaft **(see illustration)**.

17 The tripod joint can now be removed. If it is tight, draw the joint off the driveshaft end, using a two- or three-legged bearing puller. Ensure that the legs of the puller are located behind the joint inner member, and do not contact the joint rollers **(see illustrations)**. Alternatively, support the inner member of the tripod joint, and press the shaft out of the joint using a hydraulic press, ensuring that no load is applied to the joint rollers.

18 With the tripod joint removed, remove the small retaining clip, and slide the gaiter and inner retaining collar off the end of the driveshaft.

19 Thoroughly clean the constant velocity joint components using paraffin, or a suitable solvent, and dry them thoroughly - take great care not to remove the alignment marks made on dismantling, especially if paint was used. Carry out a visual inspection of the joint.

20 Examine the tripod joint, rollers and outer member for any signs of scoring or wear, and for smoothness of movement of the rollers on the tripod stems. If any component is worn, the complete driveshaft assembly must be renewed; no joint components are available separately. If the joint components are in good condition, obtain a repair kit from your Citroën

3.16 Removing the inner tripod joint securing circlip

3.17a Using a three-legged puller to remove the inner tripod joint

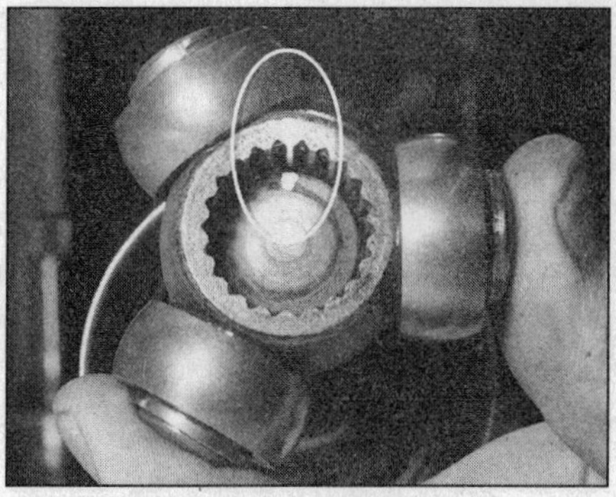

3.17b Withdrawing the inner tripod joint. Note the alignment marks

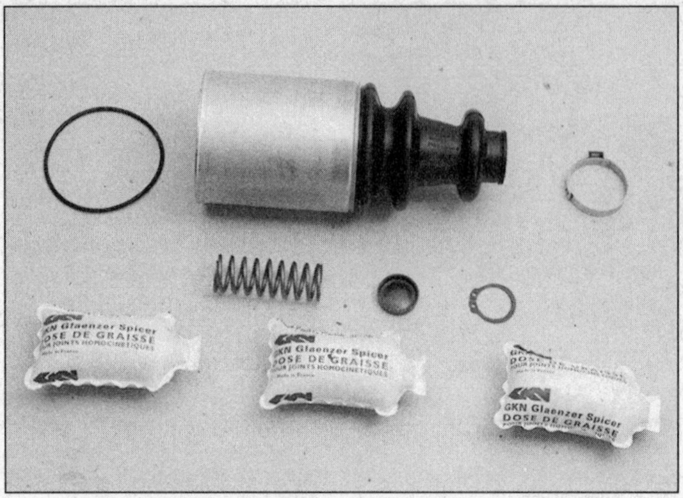

3.20 Driveshaft inner joint gaiter repair kit components

dealer, consisting of a new rubber gaiter and outer cover, circlip, thrust cap, spring, O-ring, and the correct quantity of the special grease **(see illustration)**.

21 Slide the gaiter into position inside the metal outer cover. Tape over the splines on the end of the driveshaft, and carefully slide the inner retaining collar and gaiter/cover assembly onto the shaft. Make sure that the small retaining clip is located loosely on the gaiter **(see illustrations)**.

22 Remove the tape then, aligning the marks made on dismantling, engage the tripod joint with the driveshaft splines. Use a hammer and soft metal drift to tap the joint onto the shaft, taking great care not to damage the driveshaft splines or joint rollers **(see illustration)**.

23 Secure the tripod joint in position with the new circlip, ensuring that it is correctly located in the driveshaft groove.

24 Remove the tape (where fitted), and evenly distribute the special grease contained in the repair kit around the tripod joint and outer member **(see illustration)**. Pack the gaiter/cover with the remainder, then draw the cover over the tripod joint. Leave one sachet of grease to lubricate the outer member as the joint is fitted.

25 Fit the new O-ring, spring and thrust cap to the joint outer member **(see illustrations)**.

26 Position the outer member assembly over the tripod joint, and locate the thrust cap against the end of the driveshaft. Apply the remainder of the grease to the joint, then push the outer member onto the shaft, compressing the spring, and locate it inside the outer cover. Secure the outer member in position by peening the end of the cover evenly over the joint outer edge **(see illustrations)**.

27 Briefly lift the inner gaiter lip, using a blunt instrument such as a knitting needle, to equalise the air pressure within the gaiter. Secure the inner clip in position **(see illustration)**.

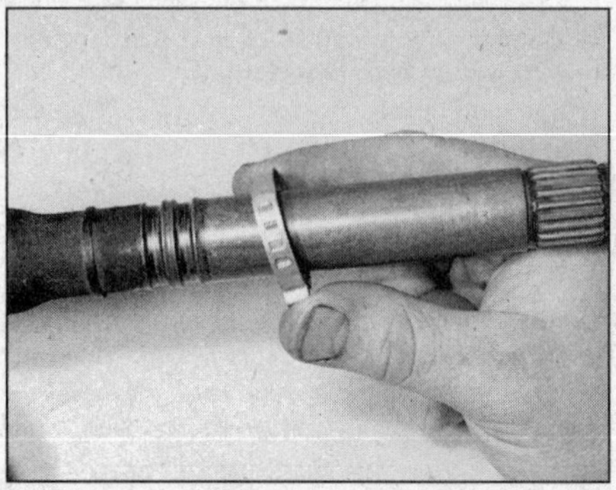

3.21a Slide on the inner retaining collar . . .

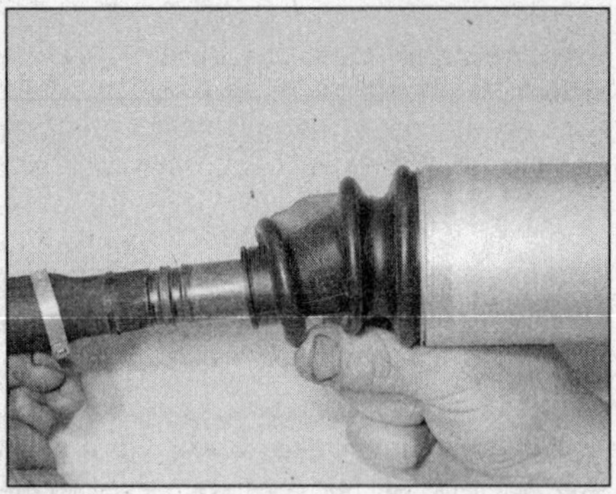

3.21b . . . and the gaiter/cover assembly

3.22 Using a hammer and a socket to tap the joint onto the driveshaft

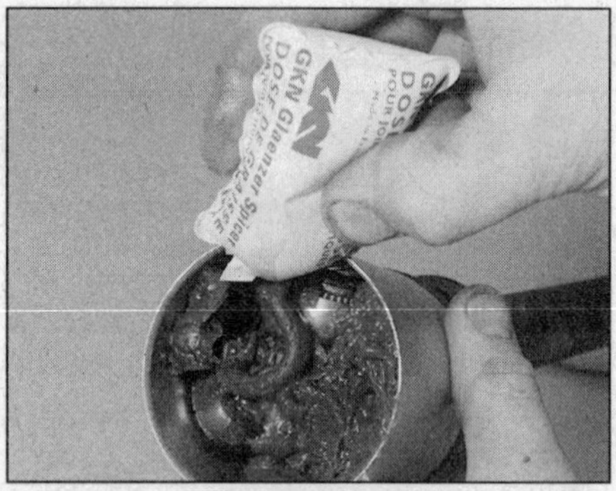

3.24 Pack the joint and gaiter/cover with grease

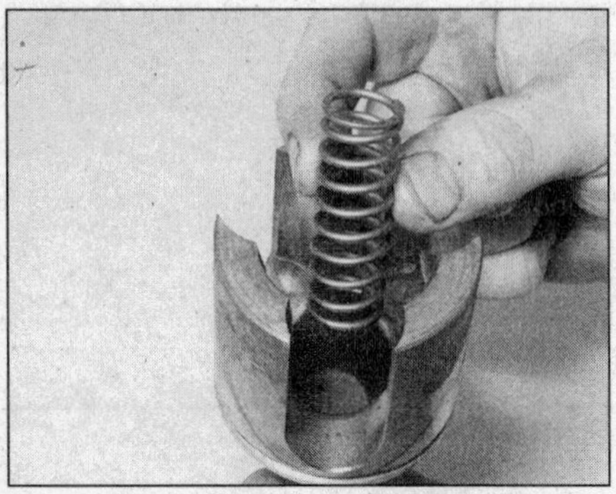

3.25a Fit the new spring . . .

3.25b . . . thrust cap . . .

3.25c . . . and O-ring

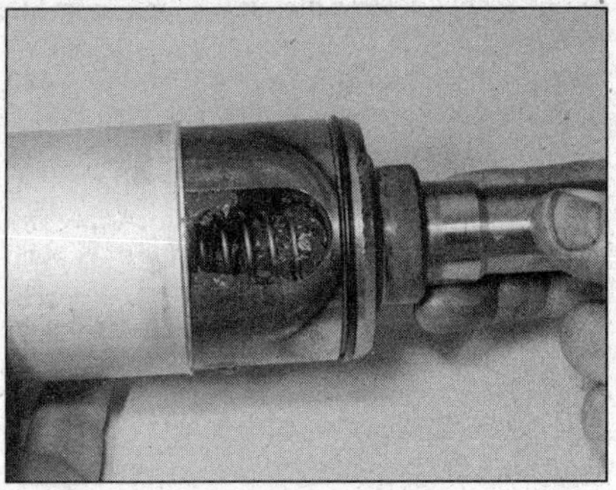

3.26a Position the outer member over the tripod joint . . .

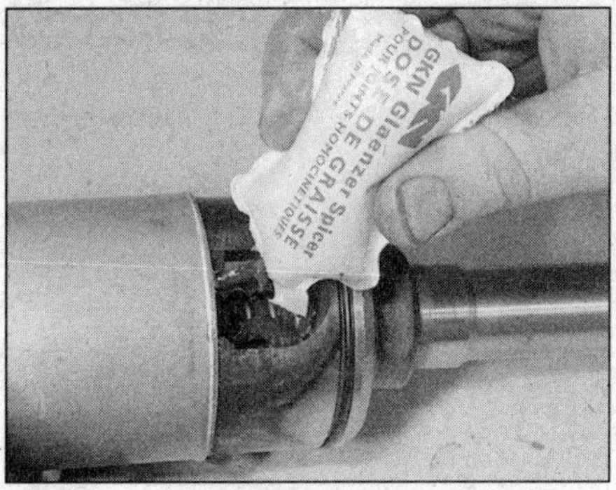

3.26b . . . then apply the remainder of the grease . . .

3.26c . . . and peen over the end of the cover

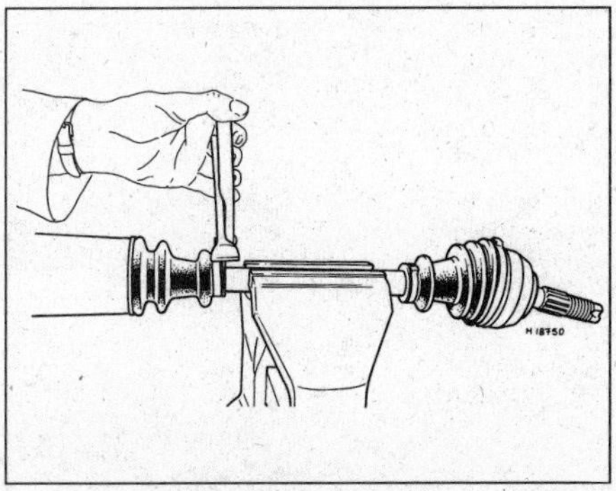

3.27 Using pincers to tighten the small retaining clip onto the rubber gaiter

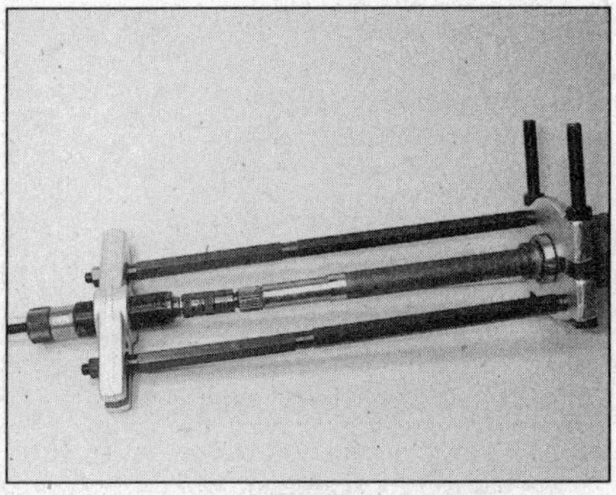

5.3 Using a long-reach bearing puller to remove the intermediate bearing from the right-hand driveshaft

28 Check that the constant velocity joint moves freely in all directions, then refit the driveshaft to the vehicle as described in Section 2.

4 Driveshaft overhaul - general information

1 If any of the checks described in Chapter 1 reveal wear in any driveshaft joint, first remove the roadwheel trim or centre cap (as appropriate).

2 If the staking is still firmly in the driveshaft groove, the driveshaft nut should still be correctly tightened; if in doubt, relieve the staking, then tighten the nut to the specified torque and restake it into the driveshaft groove. Refit the roadwheel trim or centre cap (as applicable), and repeat the check on the remaining driveshaft nut.

3 Road-test the vehicle, and listen for a metallic clicking from the front as the vehicle is driven slowly in a circle on full-lock. If a clicking noise is heard, this indicates wear in the outer constant velocity joint.

4 If vibration, consistent with road speed, is felt through the car when accelerating, there is a possibility of wear in the inner constant velocity joints.

5 To check the joints comprehensively for wear, remove the driveshafts, then dismantle them as described in Section 3. If any wear or free play is found, the complete driveshaft assembly must be renewed, as the joints are not available separately. Refer to a Citroën dealer for information on the availability of driveshaft components.

5 Right-hand driveshaft intermediate bearing - renewal

Note: *A suitable bearing puller will be required, to draw the bearing and collar off the driveshaft end.*

1 Remove the right-hand driveshaft as described in Section 2.

2 Check that the bearing outer race rotates smoothly and easily, without any signs of roughness or undue free play between the inner and outer races. If necessary, renew the bearing as follows.

3 Using a long-reach universal bearing puller, carefully draw the collar and intermediate bearing off the driveshaft inner end **(see illustration)**. Apply a smear of grease to the inner race of the new bearing, then fit the bearing over the end of the driveshaft. Using a hammer and a suitable long piece of tubing which bears only on the bearing inner race, tap the new bearing into position on the driveshaft, until it abuts the constant velocity joint outer member. Once the bearing is correctly positioned, tap the bearing collar onto the shaft until it contacts the bearing inner race.

4 Check that the bearing rotates freely, then refit the driveshaft as described in Section 2.

Notes

Chapter 9 Braking system

Contents

Degrees of difficulty

Easy, suitable for novice with little experience	**Fairly easy,** suitable for beginner with some experience	**Fairly difficult,** suitable for competent DIY mechanic	**Difficult,** suitable for experienced DIY mechanic	**Very difficult,** suitable for expert DIY or professional

Specifications

General

System type	Dual hydraulic circuit, split diagonally. Anti-lock braking system (ABS) available as an option on GTi models. Front disc brakes (ventilated on certain models), and rear drum brakes fitted on all models. Vacuum servo-assistance on most models, vacuum provided by camshaft-driven pump on Diesel models. Cable-operated handbrake acting on rear wheels.

Front brakes

Type	Disc, with single-piston sliding caliper
Disc diameter:	
954 cc and 1124 cc engine models	238.0 mm
1360 cc engine models (except GT) to July 1991	238.0 mm
1360 cc engine models (GT) to January 1989	238.0 mm
1360 cc engine models (GT) January 1989 to July 1991	258.0 mm
1360/1527 cc engine models from July 1991	247.0 mm
Disc thickness:	
New:	
954 cc and 1124 cc engine models	8.0 mm
1360 cc engine models (except GT/GTi) to July 1991	8.0 mm
1360/1527 cc engine models (except GT/GTi) from July 1991	10.0 mm
1360 cc engine models (GT)	10.0 mm
1360 cc engine models (GTi)	20.4 mm (ventilated)
Minimum thickness (1.0 mm maximum variation between sides):	
954 cc and 1124 cc engine models	6.0 mm
1360 cc engine models (except GT/GTi) to July 1991	6.0 mm
1360/1527 cc engine models (except GT/GTi) from July 1991	8.0 mm
1360 cc engine models (GT)	8.0 mm
1360 cc engine models (GTi)	18.2 mm (ventilated)
Maximum disc run-out (disc mounted on hub):	
Except GTi models	0.1 mm
GTi models	0.05 mm
Maximum thickness difference (measured with micrometer)	0.025 mm
Minimum pad friction material thickness	2.0 mm

Rear brakes

Type	Drum with leading and trailing shoes
Drum diameter:	
New:	
Except GTi models	165.0 mm
GTi models	180.0 mm
Maximum diameter after machining:	
Except GTi models	166.0 mm
GTi models	181.0 mm
Minimum shoe lining thickness	1.0 mm

Torque wrench settings

Torque wrench settings	Nm	lbf ft
Stop-light switch locknut	10	7
Master cylinder-to-servo unit	14	10
Master cylinder-to-bulkhead bracket	8	6
Vacuum servo unit-to-bracket	14	10
Rear hub nut*	140	103
Handbrake lever mounting bolts	14	10
Handbrake cable adjustment locknuts	25	18
Hydraulic system bleed screws	3	2
Brake fluid pipe union nuts	15	11
Front brake caliper-to-hub carrier bolts:		
M8 bolts	30	22
M12 bolts	120	89
ABS wheel sensor securing stud**	10	7
Roadwheel bolts	90	66

**Use a new nut.*
***Use suitable thread-locking compound.*

1 General information

1 The braking system is of dual-circuit hydraulic type, and all except certain very early models are fitted with a vacuum servo. The arrangement of the hydraulic system is such that each circuit operates one front and one rear brake from a tandem master cylinder. Under normal circumstances, both circuits operate in unison. However, in the event of hydraulic failure in one circuit, full braking force will still be available at two diagonally-opposite wheels **(see illustrations)**.

2 All models are fitted with front disc brakes and rear drum brakes. An anti-lock braking system (ABS) is available as an option on GTi models (refer to Section 20 for further information on ABS operation).

3 The front disc brakes are actuated by single-piston sliding type calipers, which ensure that equal pressure is applied to each disc pad **(see illustration)**.

4 The rear drum brakes incorporate leading and trailing shoes, which are actuated by twin-piston wheel cylinders. A self-adjust mechanism is incorporated, to automatically compensate for rear brake shoe wear. As the brake shoe linings wear, the footbrake operation automatically operates the adjuster mechanism, which effectively lengthens the shoe strut and repositions the brake shoes, to adjust the lining-to-drum clearance **(see illustration)**.

5 On 3-door models manufactured up to April 1989, a suspension-mounted pressure limiter is fitted in the hydraulic lines to the rear wheels. On 3-door models after this date, the rear wheel cylinders incorporate integral

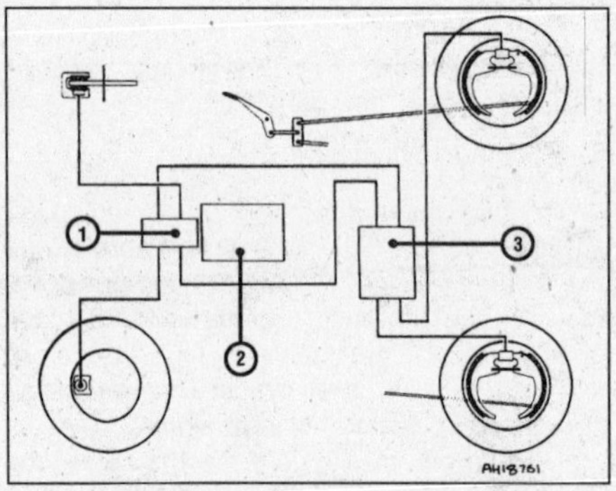

1.1a Braking system layout with suspension-mounted pressure limiter
1 Master cylinder 2 Vacuum servo 3 Pressure limiter

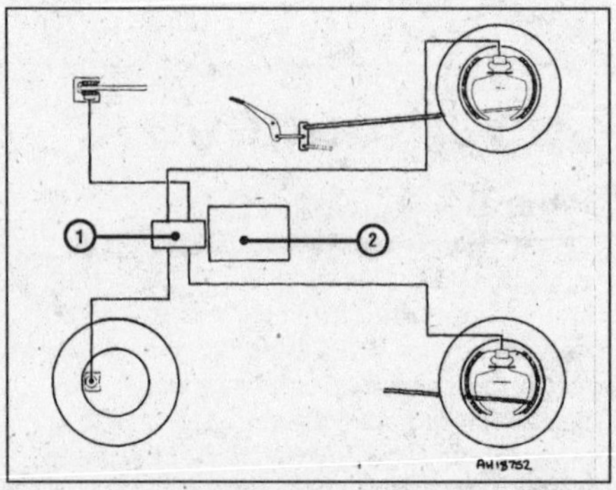

1.1b Braking system layout with pressure-regulating valves integral with the rear wheel cylinders
1 Master cylinder 2 Vacuum servo

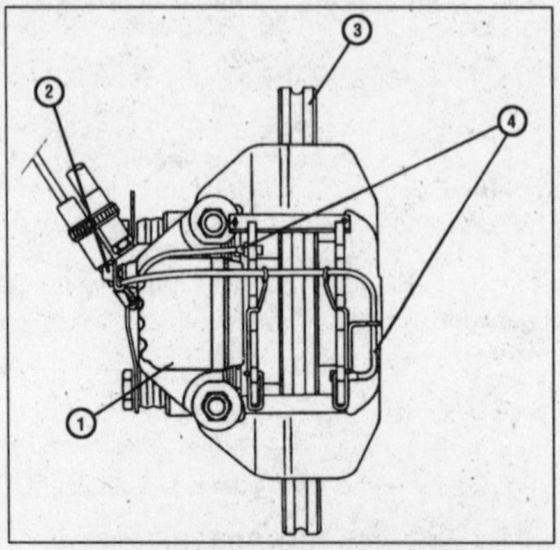

1.3 Typical front brake caliper/disc assembly
1 Caliper piston 2 Bleed screw 3 Brake disc 4 Pad wear indicator/wiring

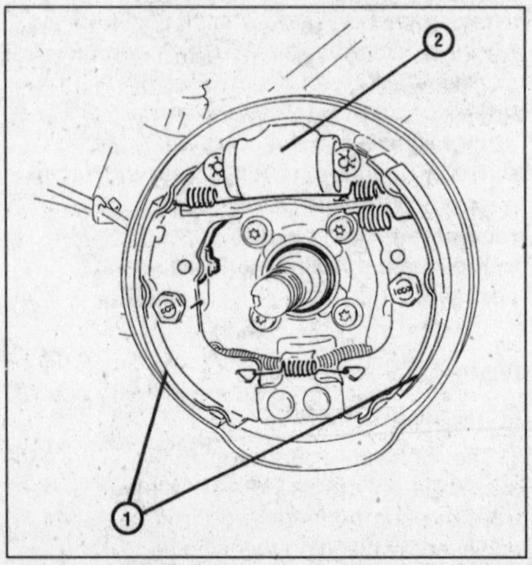

1.4 Typical rear drum brake assembly
1 Brake shoes 2 Wheel cylinder

pressure-regulating valves instead of the suspension-mounted pressure limiter. On 5-door models, this modification was introduced in June 1992. The regulating valves help to prevent rear wheel lock-up during emergency braking. On models with ABS, a load-sensitive rear pressure-regulating valve is fitted.

6 On all models, the handbrake provides an independent mechanical means of rear brake application.

7 On Diesel models, there is insufficient vacuum in the inlet manifold to operate the braking system servo. To overcome this problem, a vacuum pump is fitted to the engine, to provide vacuum to the servo unit. The vacuum pump is mounted on the left-hand end of the cylinder head, and is driven directly from the camshaft.

Note: *When servicing any part of the system, work carefully and methodically; also observe scrupulous cleanliness when overhauling any part of the hydraulic system. Always renew components in axle sets where applicable if in doubt about their condition, and use only genuine Citroën replacement parts, or at least those of known good quality. Note the warnings given in "Safety first!" at the start of this manual, and at relevant points in this Chapter, concerning the dangers of asbestos dust and hydraulic fluid.*

2 Hydraulic system - bleeding

Warning: Hydraulic fluid is poisonous; wash off immediately and thoroughly in the case of skin contact, and seek immediate medical advice if any fluid is swallowed or gets into the eyes. Certain types of hydraulic fluid are inflammable, and may ignite when allowed into contact with hot components; when servicing the hydraulic system, it is safest to assume that the fluid is inflammable, and to take precautions against the risk of fire as though it is petrol that is being handled. Hydraulic fluid is also an effective paint stripper, and will attack plastics; if any is spilt, it should be washed off immediately, using copious quantities of fresh water. Finally, it is hygroscopic (it absorbs moisture from the air) - old fluid may be contaminated and unfit for further use. When topping-up or renewing the fluid, always use the recommended type, and ensure that it comes from a freshly-opened sealed container.

Non-ABS models

General

1 The correct operation of any hydraulic system is only possible after removing all air from the components and circuit; and this is achieved by bleeding the system.

2 During the bleeding procedure, add only clean, unused hydraulic fluid of the recommended type; never re-use fluid that has already been bled from the system. Ensure that sufficient fluid is available before starting work.

3 If there is any possibility of incorrect fluid being already in the system, the brake components and circuit must be flushed completely with uncontaminated, correct fluid, and new seals should be fitted throughout the system.

4 If hydraulic fluid has been lost from the system, or air has entered because of a leak, ensure that the fault is cured before proceeding further.

5 Park the vehicle on level ground and apply the handbrake. Switch off the engine, then (where applicable) depress the brake pedal several times to dissipate the vacuum from the servo unit.

6 Check that all pipes and hoses are secure, unions tight and bleed screws closed. Remove the dust caps (where applicable), and clean any dirt from around the bleed screws.

7 Unscrew the master cylinder reservoir cap, and top-up the master cylinder reservoir to the "MAX" level line **(see illustration)**. *Remember to maintain the fluid level at least above the "MIN" level line throughout the procedure, otherwise there is a risk of further air entering the system.*

8 There are a number of one-man, do-it-yourself brake bleeding kits currently available from motor accessory shops. It is recommended that one of these kits is used whenever possible, as they greatly simplify the bleeding operation, and also reduce the risk of expelled air and fluid being drawn back into the system. If such a kit is not available, the basic (two-man) method must be used, which is described in detail below.

9 If a kit is to be used, prepare the vehicle as described previously, and follow the kit manufacturer's instructions, as the procedure may vary slightly according to the type being used; generally, they are as outlined below in the relevant sub-section.

10 Whichever method is used, the same sequence must be followed (paragraphs 11 and 12) to ensure the removal of all air from the system.

Bleeding sequence

11 If the system has been only partially disconnected, and suitable precautions were taken to minimise fluid loss, it should be necessary to bleed only that part of the system (ie the primary or secondary circuit).

12 If the complete system is to be bled, then it should be done working in the following sequence:

a) Left-hand rear wheel.
b) Right-hand front wheel.
c) Right-hand rear wheel.
d) Left-hand front wheel.

Bleeding - basic (two-man) method

13 Collect a clean glass jar, a suitable length of plastic or rubber tubing which is a tight fit over the bleed screw, and a ring spanner to fit

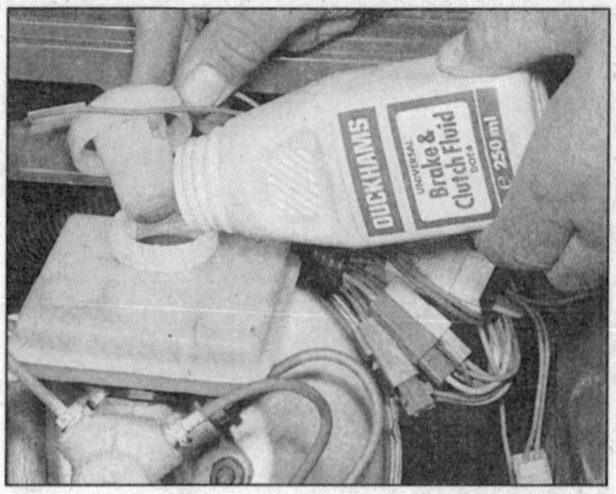

2.7 Topping-up the hydraulic fluid level in the reservoir

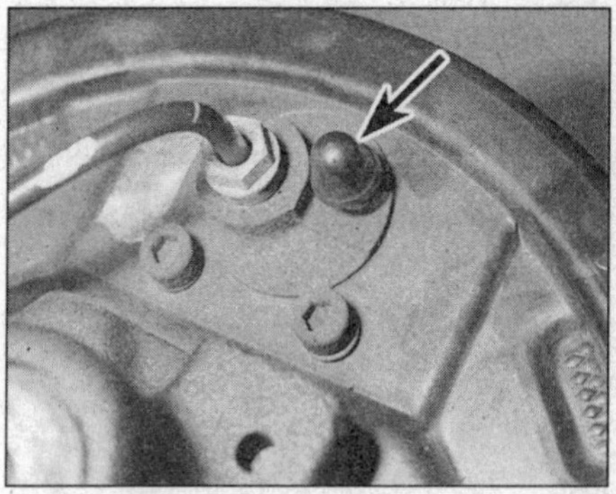

2.14 Rear brake bleed screw dust cap (arrowed)

the screw. The help of an assistant will also be required.

14 Remove the dust cap from the first screw in the sequence (if not already done) **(see illustration)**. Fit a suitable spanner and tube to the screw, place the other end of the tube in the jar, and pour in sufficient fluid to cover the end of the tube.

15 Ensure that the master cylinder reservoir fluid level is maintained at least above the "MIN" level line throughout the procedure.

16 Have the assistant fully depress the brake pedal several times to build up pressure, then maintain it down on the final downstroke.

17 While pedal pressure is maintained, unscrew the bleed screw (approximately one turn) and allow the compressed fluid and air to flow into the jar. The assistant should maintain pedal pressure, following the pedal down to the floor if necessary, and should not release the pedal until instructed to do so. When the flow stops, tighten the bleed screw again. Have the assistant release the pedal slowly, and recheck the reservoir fluid level.

18 Repeat the steps given in paragraphs 16 and 17 until the fluid emerging from the bleed screw is free from air bubbles. If the master cylinder has been drained and refilled, and air is being bled from the first screw in the sequence, allow at least five seconds between cycles for the master cylinder passages to refill.

19 When no more air bubbles appear, tighten the bleed screw securely, remove the tube and spanner, and refit the dust cap (where applicable). Do not overtighten the bleed screw.

20 Repeat the procedure on the remaining screws in the sequence, until all air is removed from the system and the brake pedal feels firm again.

Bleeding - using a one-way valve kit

21 As their name implies, these kits consist of a length of tubing with a one-way valve fitted, to prevent expelled air and fluid being drawn back into the system; some kits include a translucent container, which can be positioned so that the air bubbles can be more easily seen flowing from the end of the tube.

22 The kit is connected to the bleed screw, which is then opened **(see illustration)**. The user returns to the driver's seat, depresses the brake pedal with a smooth, steady stroke, and slowly releases it; this is repeated until the expelled fluid is clear of air bubbles.

23 Note that these kits simplify work so much that it is easy to forget the master cylinder reservoir fluid level; ensure that this is maintained at least above the "MIN" level line at all times.

Bleeding - using a pressure-bleeding kit

24 These kits are usually operated by the reservoir of pressurised air contained in the spare tyre. However, note that it will probably be necessary to reduce the pressure to a lower level than normal; refer to the instructions supplied with the kit.

25 By connecting a pressurised, fluid-filled container to the master cylinder reservoir, bleeding can be carried out simply by opening each screw in turn (in the specified sequence), and allowing the fluid to flow out until no more air bubbles can be seen in the expelled fluid.

26 This method has the advantage that the large reservoir of fluid provides an additional safeguard against air being drawn into the system during bleeding.

27 Pressure-bleeding is particularly effective when bleeding "difficult" systems, or when bleeding the complete system at the time of routine fluid renewal.

All methods

28 When bleeding is complete, and firm pedal feel is restored, wash off any spilt fluid, tighten the bleed screws securely, and refit their dust caps.

29 Check the hydraulic fluid level in the master cylinder reservoir, and top-up if necessary (Chapter 1).

30 Discard any hydraulic fluid that has been bled from the system; it will not be fit for re-use.

31 Check the feel of the brake pedal. If it feels at all spongy, air must still be present in the system, and further bleeding is required. Failure to bleed satisfactorily after a reasonable repetition of the bleeding procedure may be due to worn master cylinder seals.

Anti-lock braking system (ABS)

Warning: On ABS models, ensure that the ignition is switched off before starting the bleeding procedure, to avoid any possibility of voltage being applied to the modulator before the bleeding procedure is completed. Ideally, the battery should be disconnected. If voltage is applied to the modulator before the bleeding procedure is complete, this will effectively drain the hydraulic fluid in the modulator, rendering the unit unserviceable. Note that internal bleeding of the modulator solenoid valves, low-pressure circuit, pump and high-pressure circuit is not possible without the use of special equipment available to a Citroën dealer.

General

32 Proceed as described previously for non-ABS models, but follow the bleeding sequence shown below. After bleeding the system at the front calipers and rear wheel cylinders, the hydraulic modulator assembly must be bled in a similar manner **(see illustration)**.

Bleeding sequence

33 If the system has been only partially disconnected, and suitable precautions were taken to minimise fluid loss, it should be necessary to bleed only that part of the system.

34 If the complete system is to be bled, then it should be done working in the following sequence:

a) Left-hand rear wheel.
b) Right-hand rear wheel.
c) Left-hand front wheel.
d) Right-hand front wheel.
e) Left-hand bleed screw on the modulator.
f) Right-hand bleed screw on the modulator.

3 Hydraulic pipes and hoses - renewal

Note: *Before starting work, refer to the note at the beginning of Section 2 concerning the dangers of hydraulic fluid.*

1 If any pipe or hose is to be renewed, minimise fluid loss by first removing the master cylinder reservoir cap, then tightening it down onto a piece of polythene to obtain an airtight seal. Alternatively, flexible hoses can be sealed, if required, using a proprietary brake hose clamp; metal brake pipe unions can be plugged (if care is taken not to allow dirt into the system) or capped immediately they are disconnected. Place a wad of rag under any union that is to be disconnected, to catch any spilt fluid.

2 If a flexible hose is to be disconnected, unscrew the brake pipe union nut before removing the spring clip which secures the hose to its mounting bracket **(see illustration)**.

3 To unscrew the union nuts, it is preferable to obtain a brake pipe spanner of the correct size; these are available from most large motor accessory shops. Failing this, a close-fitting open-ended spanner will be required, though if the nuts are tight or corroded, their flats may be rounded-off if the spanner slips. In such a case, a self-locking wrench is often the only way to unscrew a stubborn union, but it follows that the pipe and the damaged nuts must be renewed on reassembly. Always clean a union and surrounding area before disconnecting it. If disconnecting a component with more than one union, make a careful note of the connections before disturbing any of them.

4 If a brake pipe is to be renewed, it can be obtained, cut to length and with the union nuts

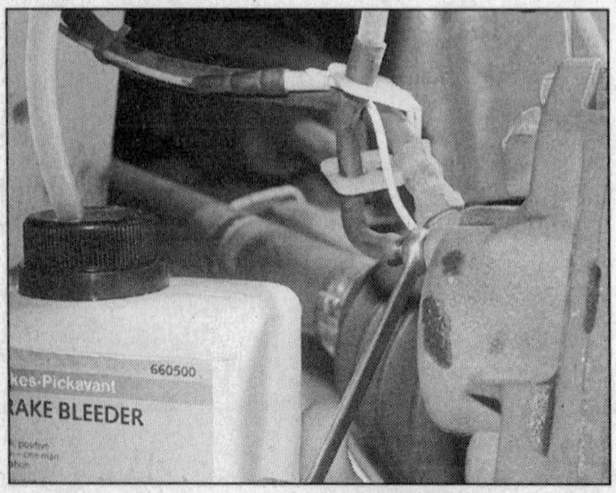

2.22 Bleeding a front brake caliper using a one-way valve kit

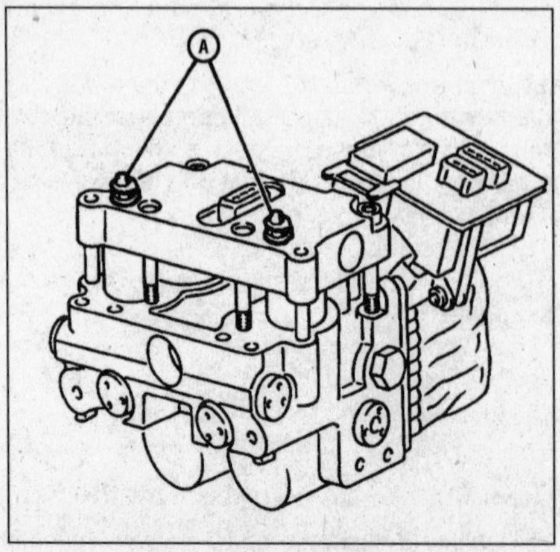

2.32 ABS hydraulic modulator bleed screws (A)

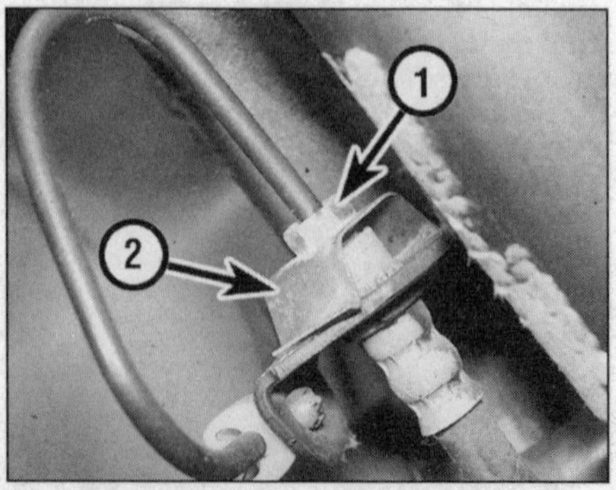

3.2 Brake pipe union nut (1) and hose spring clip (2)

and end flares in place, from Citroën dealers. All that is then necessary is to bend it to shape, following the line of the original, before fitting it to the vehicle. Alternatively, most motor accessory shops can make up brake pipes from kits, but this requires very careful measurement of the original, to ensure that the replacement is of the correct length. The safest answer is usually to take the original to the shop as a pattern.

5 On refitting, do not overtighten the union nuts. It is not necessary to exercise brute force to obtain a sound joint.

6 Ensure that the pipes and hoses are correctly routed, with no kinks, and that they are secured in the clips or brackets provided. After fitting, remove the polythene from the reservoir, and bleed the hydraulic system as described in Section 2. Wash off any spilt fluid, and check carefully for fluid leaks.

4 Front brake pads - renewal

Warning: Renew BOTH sets of front brake pads at the same time - NEVER renew the pads on only one wheel, as uneven braking may result. Note that the dust created by wear of the pads may contain asbestos, which is a health hazard. Never blow it out with compressed air, and don't inhale any of it. An approved filtering mask should be worn when working on the brakes. DO NOT use petrol or petroleum-based solvents to clean brake parts; use brake cleaner or methylated spirit only.

1 Apply the handbrake, then jack up the front of the vehicle and support it on axle stands (see *"Jacking, towing and wheel changing"*). Remove the front roadwheels.

2 Trace the brake pad wear sensor wiring back from the pads, and disconnect it from the wiring connector **(see illustration)**. Note the routing of the wiring, and free it from any relevant retaining clips.

3 Push the piston into its bore by pulling the caliper outwards.

4 There are three different types of front brake caliper fitted to the models covered in this manual - Bendix, ATE (Teves) or Girling. GTi models are only fitted with Girling brakes, 954 cc models are only fitted with Teves brakes, but other models may be fitted with either Teves or Bendix brakes. Proceed as described under the relevant sub-heading.

Bendix caliper

5 Using pliers, extract the small spring clip from the pad retaining plate, and then slide the plate out of the caliper (it will probably be necessary to tap the plate from the caliper) **(see illustrations)**.

6 Withdraw the pads from the caliper, then make a note of the correct fitted position of each anti-rattle spring, and remove the spring from each pad (where applicable unclip the pad wear sensor wiring) **(see illustrations)**. It may be necessary to push the inboard pad back against the piston to retract the piston into its bore before the pad can be removed.

7 First measure the thickness of each brake pad's friction material. If either pad is worn at any point to the specified minimum thickness or less, all four pads must be renewed **(see illustration)**. Also, the pads should be renewed if any are fouled with oil or grease; there is no satisfactory way of degreasing friction material, once contaminated. If any of the brake pads are worn unevenly, or are fouled with oil or grease, trace and rectify the cause before reassembly. New brake pads and spring kits are available from Citroën dealers.

8 If the brake pads are still serviceable, carefully clean them using a clean, fine wire brush or similar, paying particular attention to the sides and back of the metal backing. Clean out the grooves in the friction material, and pick out any large embedded particles of dirt or debris. Carefully clean the pad locations in the caliper body/mounting bracket.

9 Prior to fitting the pads, check that the guide pins are free to slide easily in the caliper body/mounting bracket, and check that the rubber guide pin gaiters are undamaged. Brush the dust and dirt from the caliper and piston, but *do not* inhale it, as it is a health

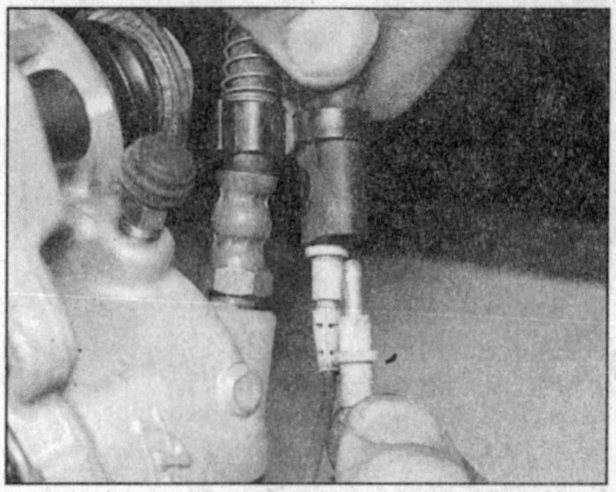

4.2 Disconnecting the brake pad wear sensor wiring - ATE caliper

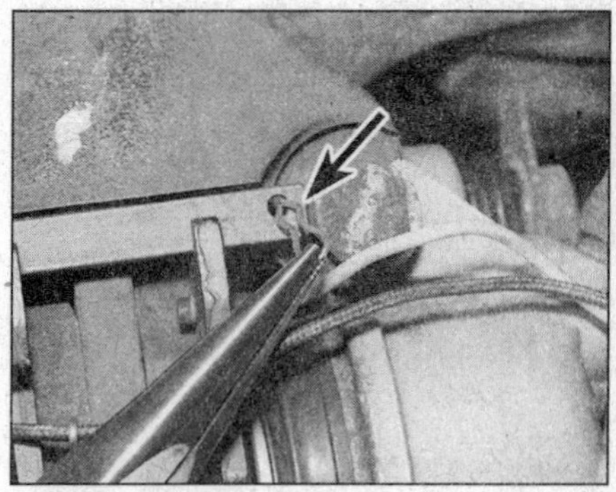

4.5a Extract the spring clip . . .

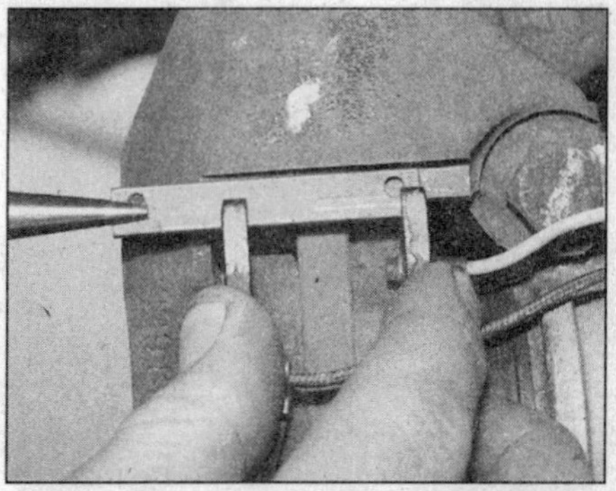

4.5b . . . and slide out the pad retaining plate - Bendix caliper

9

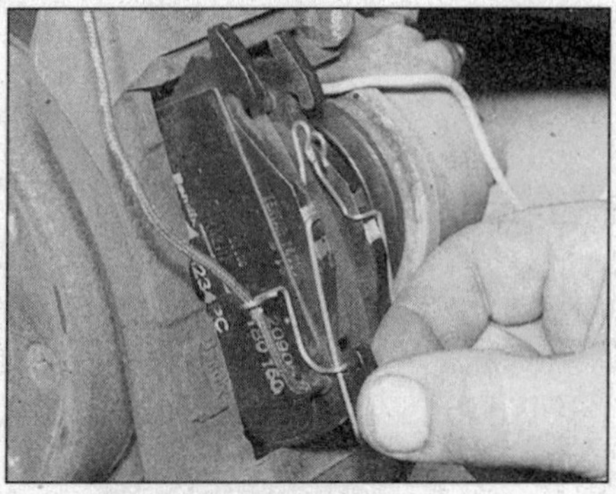

4.6a Withdraw the outer . . .

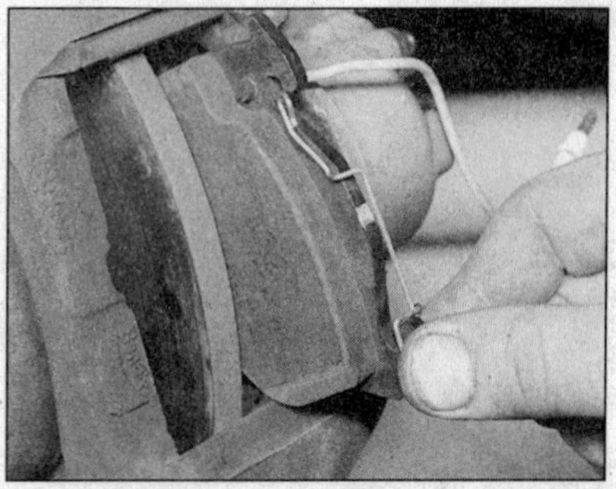

4.6b . . . and inner pads - Bendix caliper

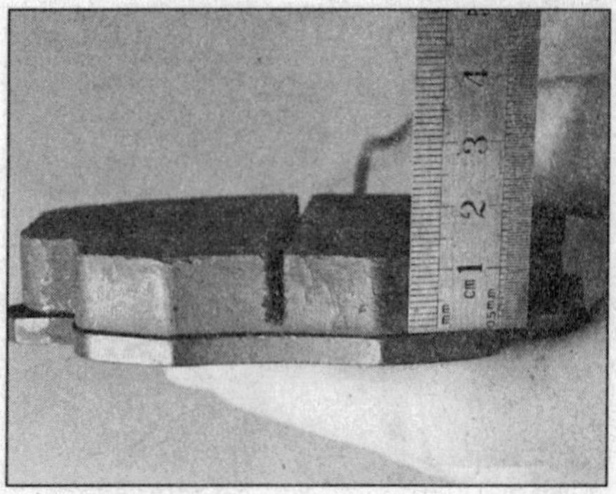

4.7 Measuring brake pad friction material thickness

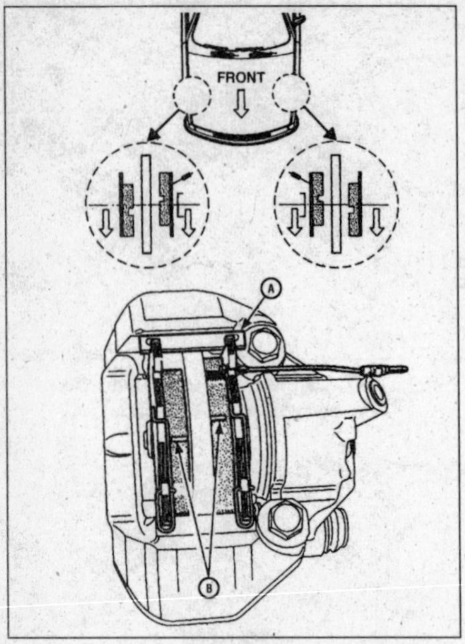

4.13 Correct fitting of brake pads - Bendix caliper

A Pad retaining plate spring clip
B Pad central grooves

hazard. Inspect the dust seal around the piston for damage, and the piston for evidence of fluid leaks, corrosion or damage. If attention to any of these components is necessary, refer to Section 8.

10 If new brake pads are to be fitted, the caliper piston must be pushed back into the cylinder to make room for them. Either use a G-clamp or similar tool, or use suitable pieces of wood as levers. Provided that the master cylinder reservoir has not been overfilled with hydraulic fluid, there should be no spillage, but keep a careful watch on the fluid level while retracting the piston. If the fluid level rises above the "MAX" level line at any time, the surplus should be siphoned off or ejected via a plastic tube connected to the bleed screw (see Section 2). **Note:** *Do not syphon the fluid by mouth, as it is poisonous; use a syringe or an old poultry baster.*

11 Apply a little anti-squeal brake grease to the pad backing plates, but take great care not to allow any grease onto the pad friction linings.

12 Fit the anti-rattle springs to the pads, so that when the pads are installed in the caliper, the spring end will be located at the opposite end of the pad, in relation to the pad retaining plate.

13 Locate the pads in the caliper, ensuring that the friction material of each pad is against the brake disc, and check that the anti-rattle spring ends are at the opposite end of the pad to which the retaining plate is to be inserted. Note that if the pads are installed correctly, looking at the pads from the front of the vehicle, the innermost pad groove must be higher than the outer pad groove. Ensure that the pads are fitted correctly before proceeding **(see illustration)**.

14 Slide the retaining plate into place, and install the new small spring clip at its inner end. It may be necessary to file an entry chamfer on the edge of the retaining plate, to enable it to be fitted without difficulty.

15 Reconnect the brake pad wear sensor wiring connectors, ensuring that the outer wire is correctly routed through the anti-rattle spring loops, and that both wires pass through the loop of the bleed screw cap **(see illustration)**.

16 Depress the brake pedal repeatedly, until the pads are pressed into firm contact with the brake disc, and normal (non-assisted) pedal pressure is restored.

17 Repeat the above procedure on the remaining front brake caliper.

18 Refit the roadwheels, then lower the vehicle to the ground and tighten the roadwheel bolts to the specified torque.

19 Check the hydraulic fluid level as described in Chapter 1.

ATE (Teves) caliper

20 Note the location and orientation of the pad anti-rattle spring (note the routing of the brake pad wear sensor wiring through the anti-rattle spring). Remove the pad retaining pins by tapping them from the caliper using a suitable pin-punch. Note that the pad retaining spring will be released as the pins are removed **(see illustrations)**.

21 Withdraw the pad retaining spring **(see illustration)**.

22 Withdraw the pads from the caliper. It may

4.15 Brake pad wear sensor wiring routes through anti-rattle springs (1) and bleed screw cap (2)

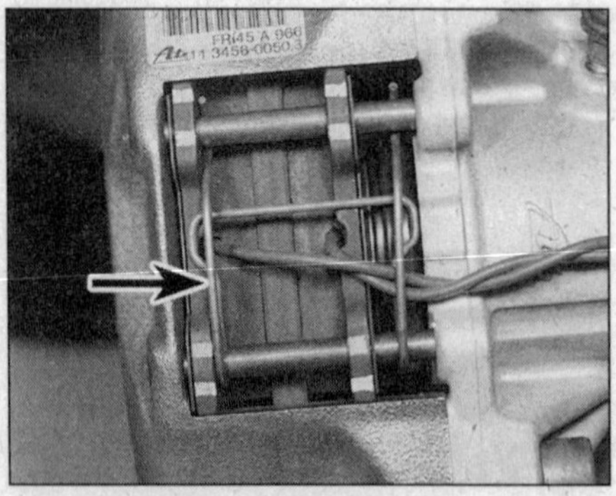

4.20a Note the orientation of the pad anti-rattle spring (arrowed) - ATE caliper

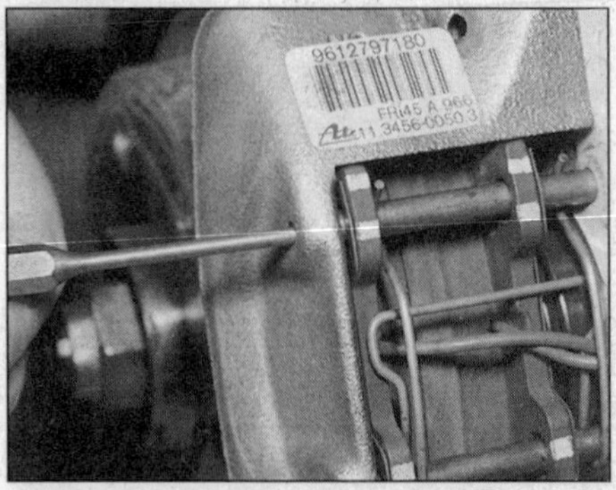

4.20b Free the pad retaining pins from the caliper using a pin-punch . . .

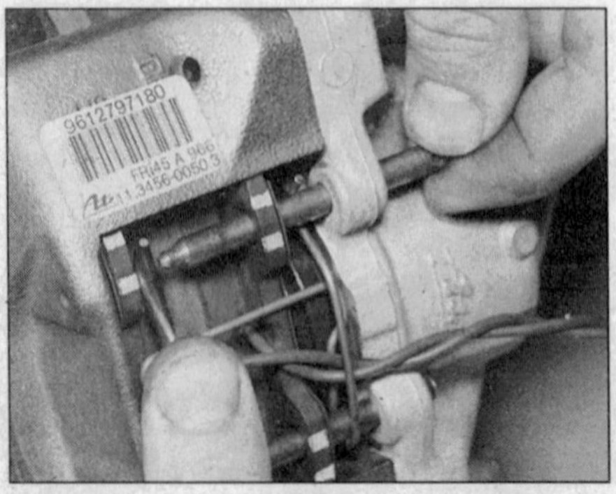

4.20c . . . then withdraw the upper . . .

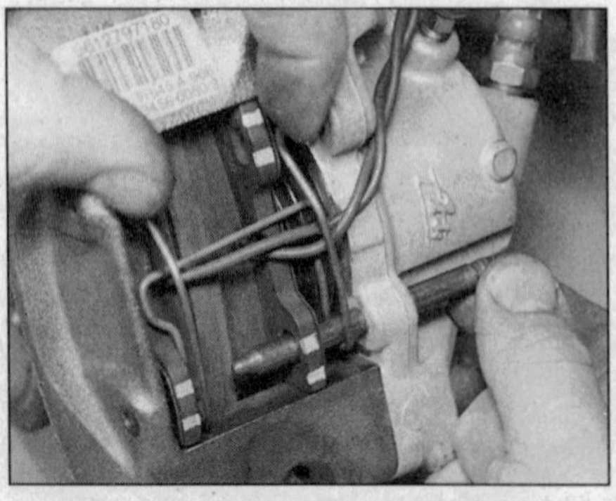

4.20d . . . and lower pins - ATE caliper

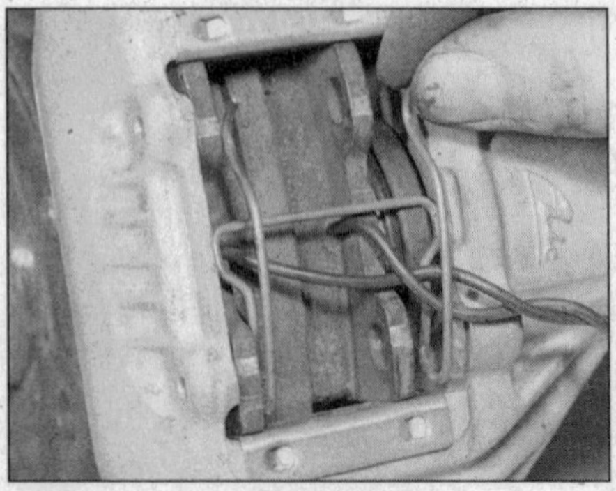

4.21 Removing the pad retaining spring

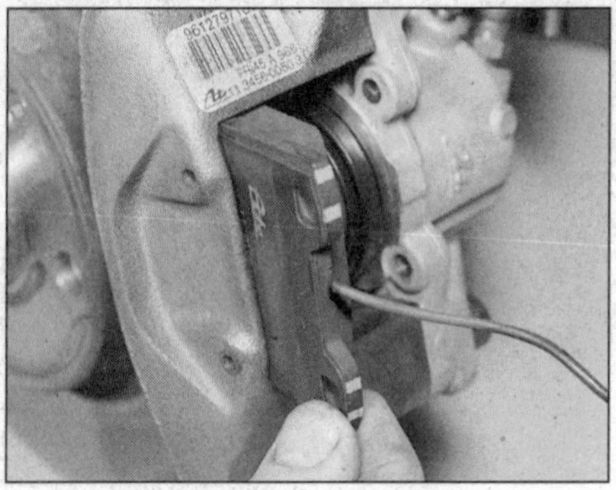

4.22a Withdraw the outer . . .

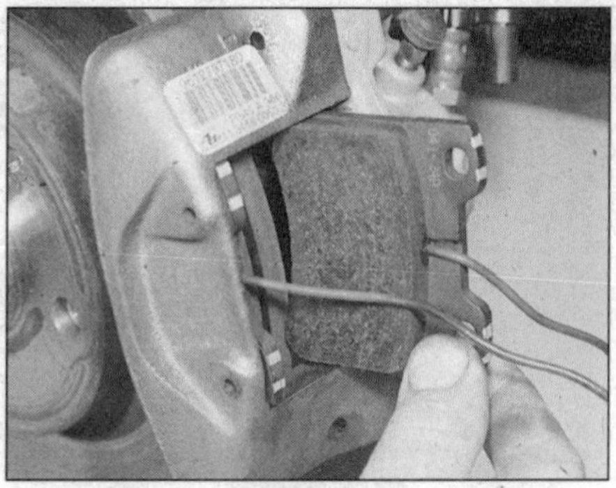

4.22b . . . and inner brake pads - ATE caliper

4.22c Inner brake pad, showing engagement clip

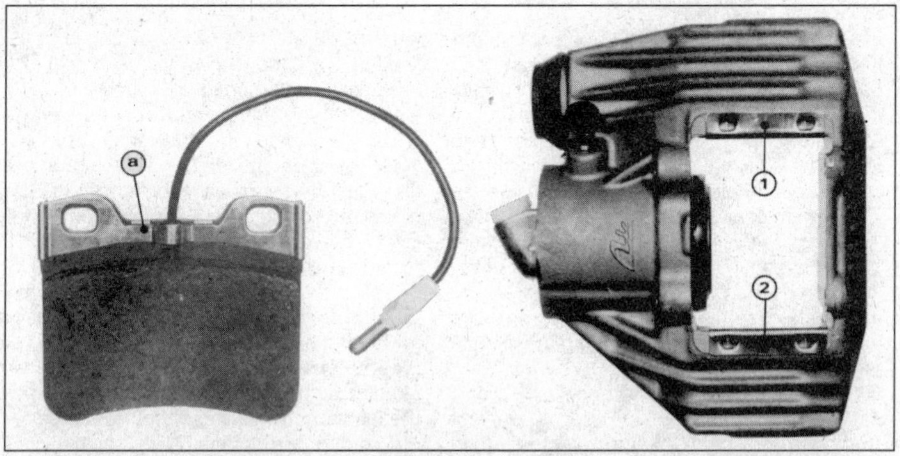

4.23 If fitting later-type pads with anti-rattle plate (a) to an earlier caliper, remove stainless plates (1) and (2)

be necessary to push the inboard pad back against the piston to retract the piston into its bore before the pad can be removed, because it has an engagement clip attached to its backing plate **(see illustrations)**.

23 Proceed as described in paragraphs 7 to 11 inclusive. Note the anti-rattle plate modification shown **(see illustration)**.

24 Slide the pads into position in the caliper, ensuring that the friction material of each pad is against the brake disc.

25 Locate the anti-rattle spring on the pads, as noted before removal, and ensure that the pad wear sensor wiring is correctly routed through the spring **(see illustration)**.

26 Fit the upper pad retaining pin, ensuring that the top arms of the pad retaining spring locate behind the pin, then tap the pin into position in the caliper.

27 Refit the lower pad retaining pin, ensuring that it passes through the anti-rattle spring, then tap the pin into position in the caliper **(see illustration)**.

28 Reconnect the brake pad wear sensor wiring connectors, ensuring that the wiring is correctly routed.

29 Proceed as described in paragraphs 16 to 19 inclusive.

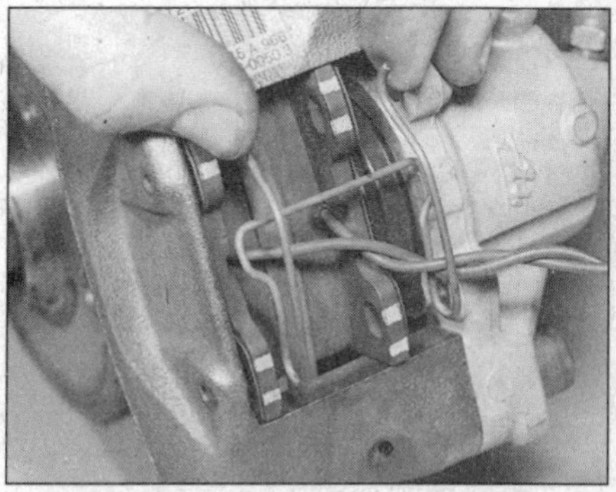

4.25 Ensure that the pad wear sensor wiring is correctly routed through the anti-rattle spring - ATE caliper

Girling caliper (GTi models)

30 Note the location and orientation of the pad anti-rattle spring, and the routing of the brake pad wear sensor wiring through the retaining pin spring clip **(see illustration)**.

31 Extract the spring retaining clip, and tap out the pad retaining pins. As the pins are removed, the pad anti-rattle springs will be released.

32 Pull the caliper outwards, and withdraw the outer pad. Push the caliper inwards to withdraw the inner pad. Note the location of the special spring on the inner pad, and the metal shim located between the inner pad and the caliper piston **(see illustration)**.

33 Proceed as described in paragraphs 7 to 11 inclusive.

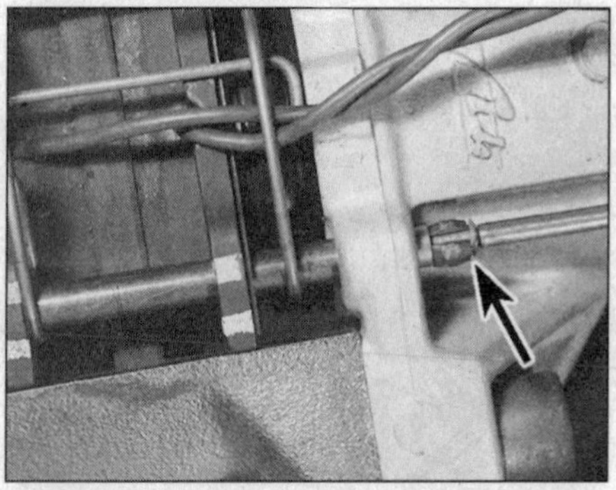

4.27 Tapping the lower pad retaining pin (arrowed) into position - ATE caliper

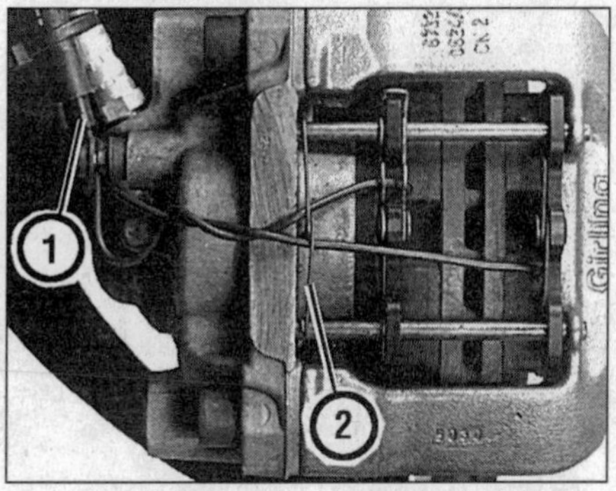

4.30 Girling disc caliper and pads

1 Wear sensor wiring
2 Retaining pin spring clip

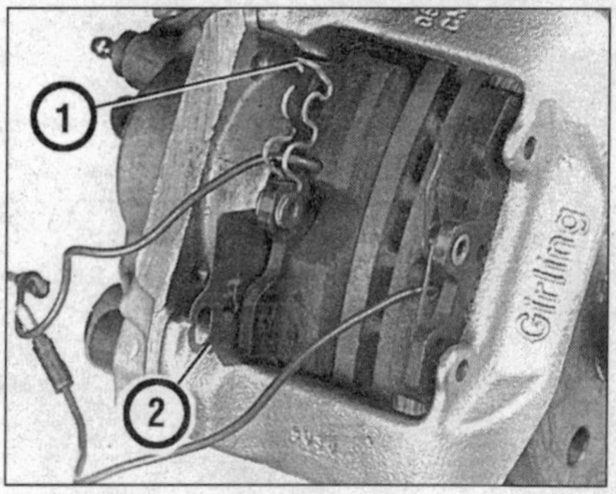

4.32 Special spring (1) and metal shim (2) on the inner pad

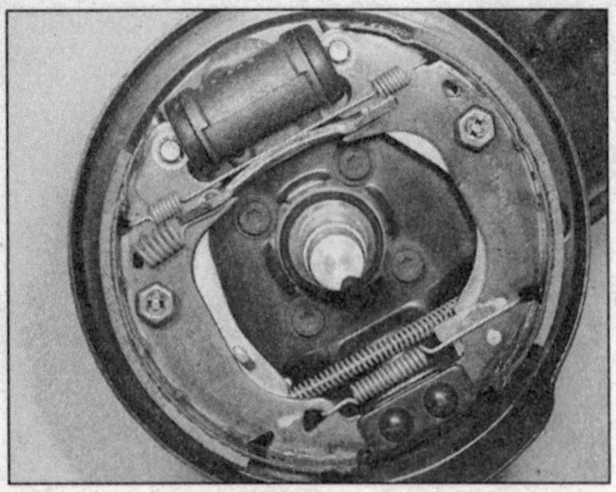
5.3 Rear brake shoes and associated components. Note the locations of the springs

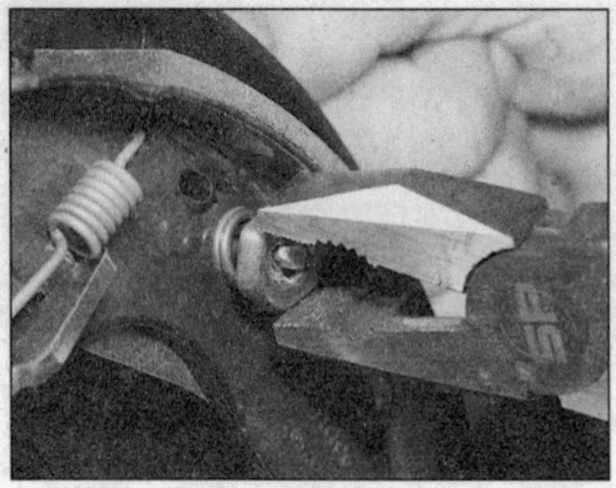
5.4a Use pliers . . .

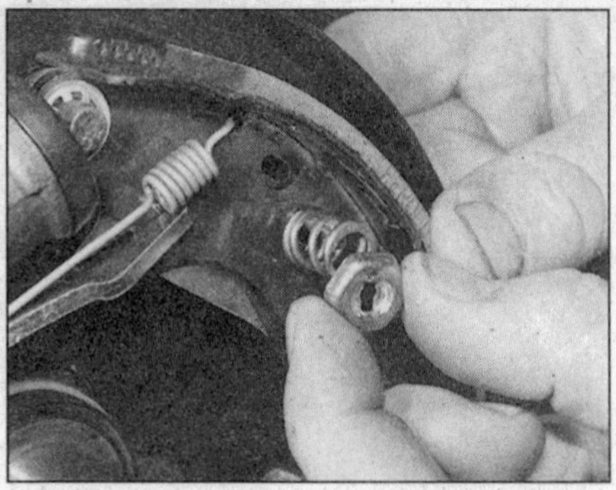
5.4b . . . to remove the outer hold-down spring cups, and remove the springs and pins

34 Slide the pads into position in the caliper, ensuring that the friction material of each pad is against the brake disc, and that the metal shim and special spring are correctly located.

35 Fit the lower retaining pin, making sure that it enters the correct hole in the metal shim, and that the anti-rattle springs are located under it. Tap the pin into position in the caliper.

36 Fit the upper retaining pin, making sure that the special spring and anti-rattle spring are located under it. Tap the pin into position in the caliper.

37 Reconnect the brake pad wear sensor wiring connectors, ensuring that the wiring is correctly routed.

38 Proceed as described in paragraphs 16 to 19 inclusive.

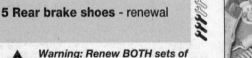

5 Rear brake shoes - renewal

Warning: Renew BOTH sets of rear brake shoes at the same time - NEVER renew the shoes on only one wheel, as uneven braking may result. Note that the dust created by wear of the shoes may contain asbestos, which is a health hazard. Never blow it out with compressed air, and don't inhale any of it. An approved filtering mask should be worn when working on the brakes. DO NOT use petrol or petroleum-based solvents to clean brake parts; use brake cleaner or methylated spirit only.

Note: *The rear brake components on GTi models differ slightly from the illustrations shown in this Section, but the procedure is the same.*

1 Remove the rear brake drums, as described in Section 7.

2 Working on one side of the vehicle, brush the dirt and dust from the brake backplate and drum. **Do not** inhale the dust, as it may be injurious to health.

3 Note the position of each shoe, and the location of the return and steady springs **(see illustration)**.

4 Remove the shoe hold-down springs. Use pliers to depress the outer spring cups, and turn them through 90° **(see illustrations)**.

5 Recover the springs and cups, and remove the spring retainer pins from the backplate.

6 Carefully pull the leading brake shoe forwards from the backplate, then using a suitable pair of pliers, unhook and remove the lower return spring **(see illustrations)**.

7 Disengage the lower ends of the shoes from the bottom anchor, pull the upper ends of the shoes from the wheel cylinder. Withdraw the shoe assembly, and unhook the handbrake cable from the lever on the trailing brake shoe **(see illustration)**.

8 If necessary, position a rubber band or a cable-tie over the wheel cylinder, to prevent the pistons from being ejected **(see illustration)**. If there is any evidence of fluid leakage from the wheel cylinder, renew it or overhaul it as described in Section 9.

9 Unhook the upper return spring from the shoes, and unhook the adjuster strut spring.

10 Working on the leading brake shoe, prise the adjuster lever retaining plate over the pivot pin on the adjuster lever, then pull the adjuster lever forwards to allow the adjuster strut to be removed **(see illustrations)**.

11 Transfer the handbrake and automatic adjuster levers to the new shoes as required (prise off the spring clips to remove the levers) **(see illustration)**. Note that the levers and strut on each rear wheel are different, and that the leading and trailing shoes are fitted with different grade linings. New shoes will be

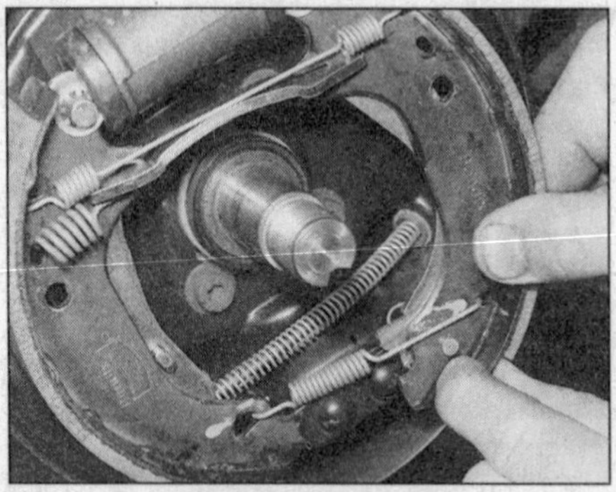
5.6a Pull the leading brake shoe forwards . . .

5.6b . . . and remove the lower return spring

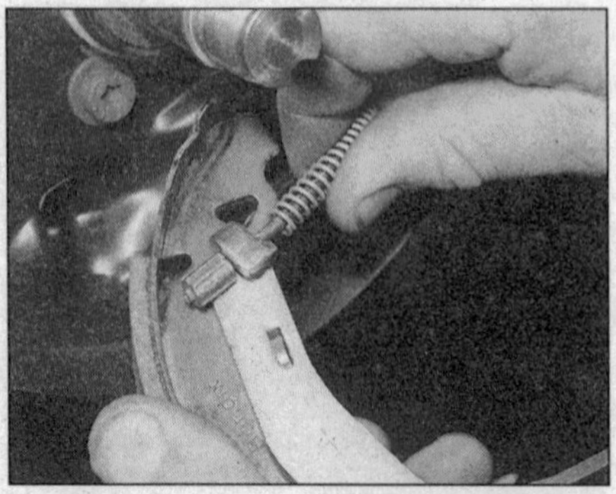
5.7 Unhooking the handbrake cable from the lever on the trailing shoe

5.8 Rubber band positioned over wheel cylinder to retain pistons

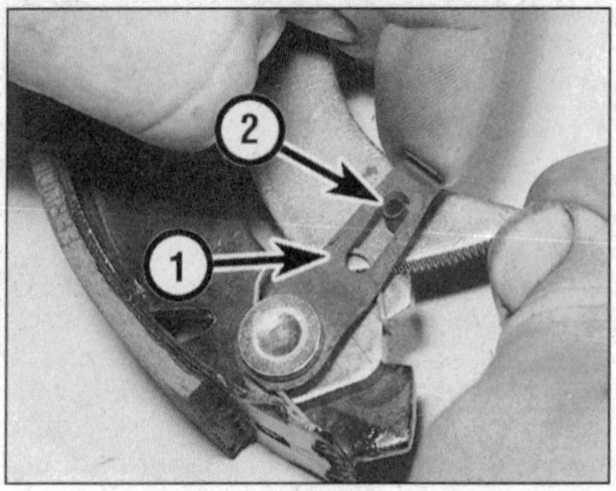

5.10a Prise the retaining plate (1) over the pivot pin (2) . . .

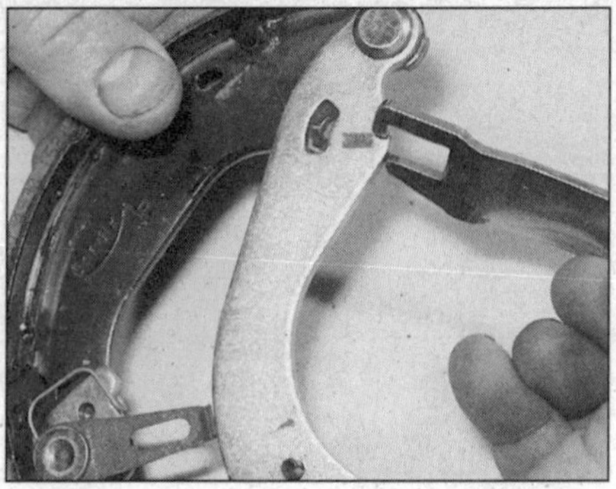

5.10b . . . and remove the adjuster strut

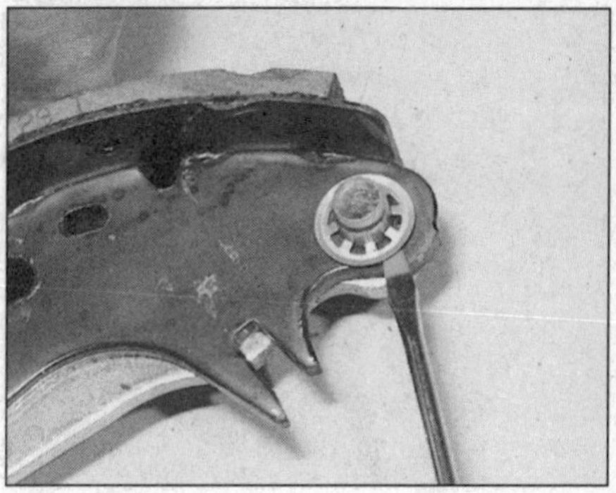

5.11 Prising off the spring clip to remove the adjuster lever from the trailing shoe

5.14 Fit the adjuster strut spring (arrowed) between the shoe and the adjuster strut

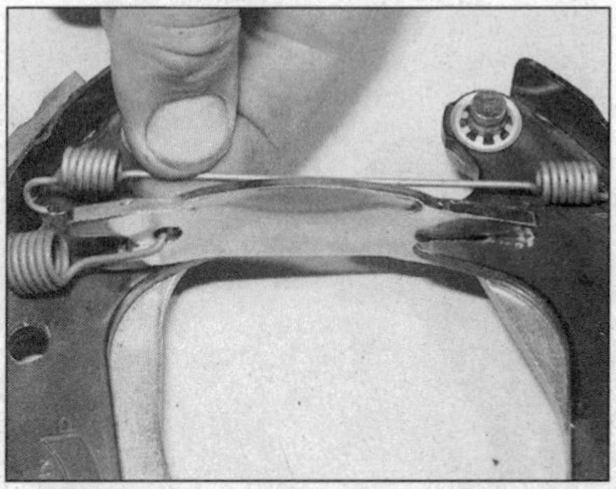

5.15a Fit the upper return spring to the shoes . . .

supplied complete with the adjuster retaining plate riveted to the leading shoe.

12 Place the shoes on the bench in their correct positions, and lay the adjuster strut in position.

13 With the adjuster strut engaged with the leading shoe, push the adjuster lever back towards the shoe, and clip the adjuster lever retaining plate over the pivot pin on the adjuster lever.

14 Fit the adjuster strut spring between the trailing shoe and the adjuster strut, but do not fully engage the adjuster strut with the trailing shoe at this stage **(see illustration)**.

15 Fit the upper return spring to the shoes, then carefully manipulate the adjuster strut into position to engage it with the slot in the trailing shoe **(see illustrations)**.

16 Apply brake grease sparingly to the shoe contact areas of the brake backplate **(see illustration)**. Where applicable, remove the rubber band or cable tie from the wheel cylinder.

17 Offer the shoes into position, and reconnect the handbrake cable to the handbrake lever on the trailing shoe.

18 Position the shoes on the backplate, and lever the upper ends of the shoes apart to engage them with the wheel cylinder pistons.

19 Carefully refit the lower return spring to the shoes **(see illustration)**, then lever the lower ends of the shoes apart to engage them with the lower anchor.

20 Insert the steady spring retainer pins in the backplate and through the holes in the shoes, then fit the hold-down springs and the cups.

21 Move the serrated automatic adjuster lever quadrant against the spring tension, to set the shoes at their minimum diameter.

22 Check that the handbrake lever on the trailing brake shoe is positioned with the lug on the edge of the shoe web, and not behind the shoe.

23 Repeat the procedure on the remaining side of the vehicle, then refit the brake drums as described in Section 7.

24 On completion, apply the brakes several times, then check the handbrake adjustment as described in Chapter 1.

6 Front brake disc - inspection, removal and refitting

Note: *Before starting work, refer to the warning at the beginning of Section 4 concerning the dangers of asbestos dust.*

Inspection

Note: *If either disc requires renewal, BOTH should be renewed at the same time, to ensure even and consistent braking. New brake pads should also be fitted.*

1 Apply the handbrake, then jack up the front of the vehicle and support it on axle stands

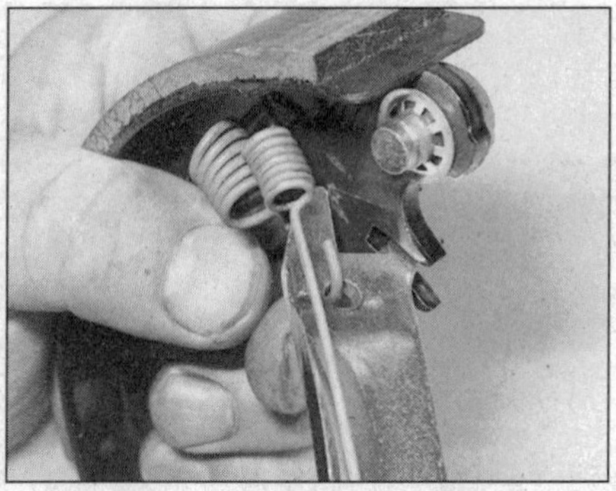

5.15b . . . then engage the adjuster strut

5.16 Apply brake grease to the shoe contact areas

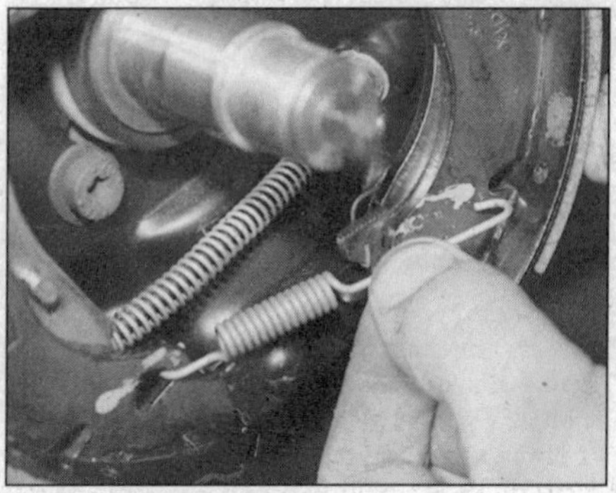

5.19 Refitting the lower return spring

6.3 Using a micrometer to measure disc thickness

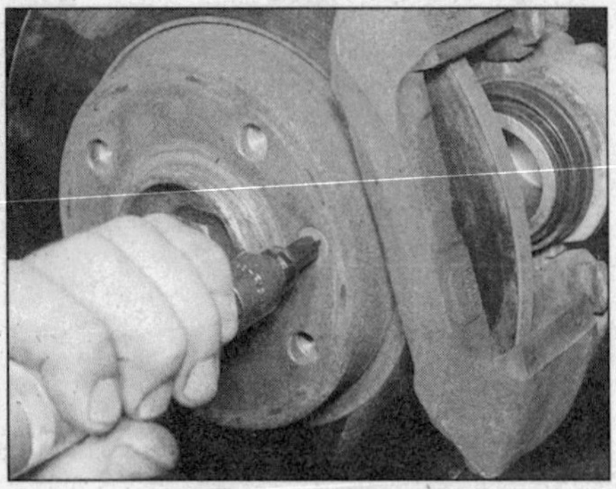

6.7a Using an impact screwdriver to free a brake disc securing screw

(see *"Jacking, towing and wheel changing"*). Remove the appropriate front roadwheel.

2 Slowly rotate the brake disc so that the full area of both sides can be checked. Remove the brake pads (see Section 4) if better access is required to the inboard surface. Light scoring is normal in the area swept by the brake pads, but if heavy scoring or cracks are found, the disc must be renewed.

3 It is normal to find a lip of rust and brake dust around the disc's perimeter; this can be scraped off if required. If, however, a lip has formed due to excessive wear of the brake pad swept area, then the disc's thickness must be measured using a micrometer **(see illustration)**. Take measurements at several places around the disc, at the inside and outside of the pad swept area; if the disc has

6.4 Checking disc run-out using a dial gauge

6.7b Removing a brake disc - model with Bendix caliper

worn at any point to the specified minimum thickness or less, the disc must be renewed.

4 If the disc is thought to be warped, it can be checked for run-out. Either use a dial gauge mounted on any convenient fixed point, while the disc is slowly rotated, or use feeler gauges to measure (at several points all around the disc) the clearance between the disc and a fixed point, such as the caliper mounting bracket **(see illustration)**. If the measurements obtained are at the specified maximum or beyond, the disc is excessively warped, and must be renewed; however, it is worth checking first that the hub bearing is in good condition (Chapters 1 and/or 10). Also try the effect of removing the disc and turning it through 180°, to reposition it on the hub; if the run-out is still excessive, the disc must be renewed.

5 Check the disc for cracks (especially around the wheel bolt holes) and for any other wear or damage, and renew if necessary.

Removal

6 Remove the brake pads as described in Section 4. It is not necessary to remove the brake caliper in order to remove the disc.

7 Use chalk or paint to mark the relationship of the disc to the hub, then remove the single screw (or two screws on GTi models) securing the brake disc to the hub, and withdraw the disc **(see illustrations)**. Note that it may be necessary to use an impact screwdriver to free the disc securing screws. If it is tight, lightly tap its rear face with a hide or plastic mallet. Tilt the disc as necessary to clear the hub and caliper.

Refitting

8 Ensure that the mating faces of the disc and the hub are clean and flat. If necessary, wipe the mating surfaces clean.

9 Refit the disc, then refit and securely tighten the disc retaining screw(s).

10 If a new disc has been fitted, use a suitable solvent to wipe any preservative coating from the disc.

11 Refit the brake pads as described in Section 4.

7 Rear brake drum - removal, inspection and refitting

Note: *Before starting work, refer to the warning at the beginning of Section 5 concerning the dangers of asbestos dust.*

Note: *A new rear hub nut and dust cap must be used when refitting.*

Removal

1 Chock the front wheels, then jack up the rear of the vehicle and support it on axle stands (see *"Jacking, towing and wheel changing"*). Remove the appropriate rear wheel.

2 Using a hammer and a large flat-bladed screwdriver, carefully tap and prise the dust cap out of the centre of the brake drum **(see illustrations)**. If the cap is damaged, it should be discarded and a new one obtained.

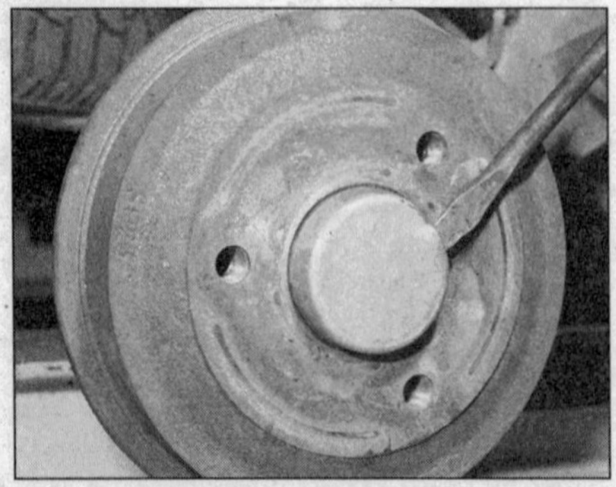

7.2a Carefully tap off the dust cap . . .

7.2b . . . and remove it

7.4a Removing the hub nut . . .

7.4b . . . and thrustwasher

7.5 Withdrawing the brake drum

7.7a Using a screwdriver to release the shoe adjuster mechanism and retract the shoes (left-hand side of the car)

3 Using a hammer and a suitable cold chisel or punch, relieve the staking on the rear hub nut.
4 Using a socket and long bar, slacken and remove the rear hub nut, and withdraw the thrustwasher **(see illustrations)**. Discard the hub nut - a new nut must used when refitting.
5 It should now be possible to withdraw the brake drum assembly from the stub axle by hand **(see illustration)**. It may be difficult to remove the drum, either due to the tightness of the hub bearing on the stub axle, or to the brake shoes binding on the inner circumference of the drum. If the brake shoes are binding, first check that the handbrake is fully released, then proceed as follows.

HAYNES HiNT ***If the bearing is tight, tap the periphery of the drum using a hide or plastic mallet, or use a universal puller, secured to the drum with the wheel bolts, to pull it off.***

6 Referring to the handbrake adjustment procedure in Chapter 1 for further information, fully slacken the handbrake cable adjuster nut, to obtain maximum free play in the cable.
7 Insert a screwdriver through one of the wheel bolt holes in the brake drum, so that it contacts the handbrake operating lever on the trailing brake shoe. Push the lever until the stop-peg slips behind the brake shoe web, allowing the brake shoes to retract fully **(see illustrations)**. The brake drum can now be withdrawn.

Inspection

Note: *If either drum requires renewal, BOTH should be renewed at the same time, to ensure even and consistent braking. New brake shoes should also be fitted.*
8 Working carefully, remove all traces of brake dust from the drum, but *avoid inhaling the dust, as it is injurious to health.*
9 Clean the outside of the drum, and check it for obvious signs of wear or damage, such as cracks around the roadwheel bolt holes; renew the drum if necessary.
10 Carefully examine the inside of the drum. Light scoring of the friction surface is normal, but if heavy scoring is found, the drum must be renewed. It is usual to find a lip on the outer edge of the drum which consists of a mixture of rust and brake dust; this should be scraped away, to leave a smooth surface which can be polished with fine (120- to 150-grade) emery paper. If, however, the lip is due to the friction surface being recessed by excessive wear, then the drum must be renewed.
11 If the drum is thought to be excessively worn, or oval, its internal diameter must be measured at several points using an internal micrometer. Take measurements in pairs, the second at right-angles to the first, and compare the two, to check for signs of ovality. Provided that it does not enlarge the drum to beyond the specified maximum diameter, it may be possible to have the drum refinished by skimming or grinding; if this is not possible, the drums on BOTH sides must be renewed. Note that if the drum is to be skimmed, BOTH drums must be refinished, to maintain a consistent internal diameter on both sides.
12 Check the condition of the oil seal on the stub axle, and renew if necessary. To renew the oil seal, simply prise the old seal from the stub axle, then push the new seal into position until it is seated on the spacer. At the same time, check the condition of the oil seal thrust cup in the rear of the drum, and if any signs of wear or damage are present, renew the cup (if the surface of the cup is damaged, this is likely to quickly result in damage to the oil seal).

Refitting

13 If a new brake drum is to be installed, use a suitable solvent to remove any preservative coating that may have been applied to its internal friction surfaces. Note that it may also be necessary to release the adjustment quadrant on the rear of the leading shoe, to allow the drum to pass over the brake shoes.
14 Ensure that the handbrake lever stop-peg is correctly repositioned against the edge of the brake shoe web **(see illustration)**, then apply a smear of clean engine oil to the stub axle, and slide on the drum assembly.
15 Fit the thrustwasher and new hub nut, and tighten the hub nut to the specified torque. Stake the nut firmly into the groove on the stub

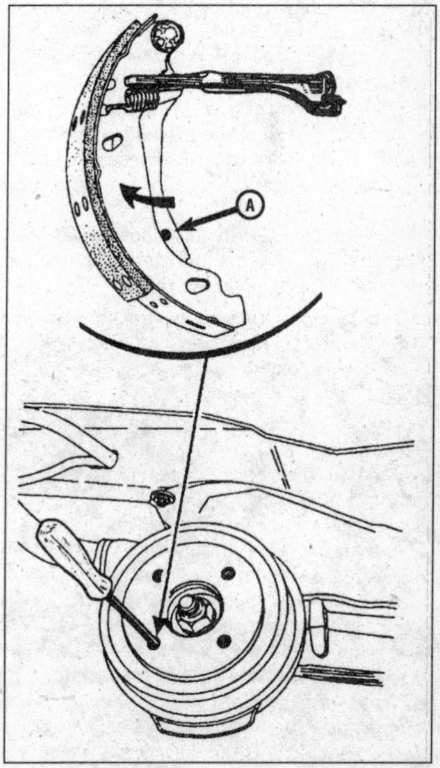

7.7b Handbrake operating lever stop-peg location (A) (right-hand side of the car)

9

7.14 Ensure that the handbrake lever stop peg (arrowed) is positioned against the edge of the shoe web

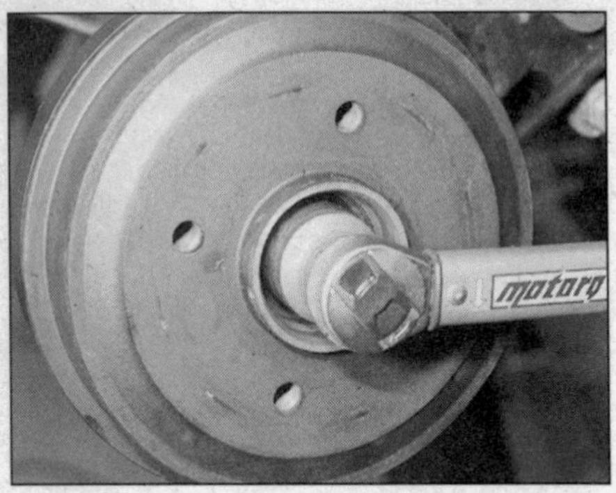

7.15a Tighten the hub nut to the specified torque . . .

7.15b . . . then stake the nut in position

axle, to secure it in position **(see illustrations)**.

16 Tap the new dust cover into place in the centre of the brake drum.

17 Depress the footbrake several times to operate the self-adjusting mechanism.

18 Repeat the above procedure on the remaining rear brake assembly (where necessary). Check and, if necessary, adjust the handbrake cable as described in Chapter 1.

19 On completion, refit the roadwheel(s), then lower the vehicle to the ground and tighten the wheel bolts to the specified torque.

8 Front brake caliper - removal, overhaul and refitting

Note: *Before starting work, refer to the note at the beginning of Section 2 concerning the dangers of hydraulic fluid, and to the warning at the beginning of Section 4 concerning the dangers of asbestos dust. From October 1990, the front brake calipers are manufactured of both aluminium and cast iron; prior to this date, they were manufactured of aluminium only, and were of monobloc construction. It is not permitted to have front brake calipers of both designs on the same vehicle.*

Removal

1 Apply the handbrake, then jack up the front of the vehicle and support it on axle stands (see *"Jacking, towing and wheel changing"*). Remove the appropriate roadwheel.

2 To minimise fluid loss, first remove the master cylinder reservoir cap, and then tighten it down onto a piece of polythene, to obtain an airtight seal. Alternatively, use a brake hose clamp, a G-clamp or a similar suitable tool to clamp the flexible hose running to the caliper.

3 Remove the brake pads as described in Section 4.

4 Clean the area around the union, then loosen the brake hose union nut on the caliper.

5 Where applicable, remove the dust cover(s) from the caliper securing bolts, then slacken the two bolts securing the caliper assembly to the hub carrier, and remove them. On models with Bendix calipers, recover the mounting plate from the bolts, noting which way around the plate is fitted **(see illustrations)**.

6 Lift the caliper assembly away from the brake disc, and unscrew it from the end of the brake hose **(see illustration)**.

Overhaul

7 With the caliper on the bench, wipe away all traces of dust and dirt, but *avoid inhaling the dust, as it is injurious to health.*

8 Where necessary, use a small flat-bladed screwdriver to carefully prise the dust seal retaining clip out of the caliper bore.

9 Withdraw the partially-ejected piston from the caliper body, and remove the dust seal. The piston can be withdrawn by hand, or if necessary pushed out by applying compressed air to the brake hose union hole. Only low pressure should be required, such as is generated by a foot pump.

Caution: The piston may be ejected with some force.

10 Using a small screwdriver, extract the piston hydraulic seal, taking great care not to damage the caliper bore.

11 Where applicable, prise off the retaining clips, then withdraw the guide sleeves/pins

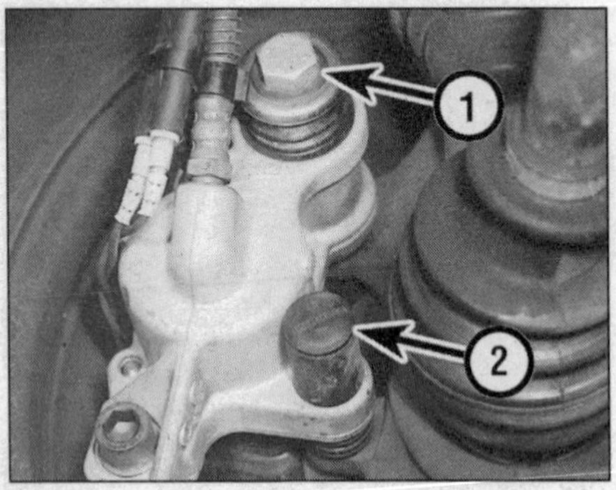

8.5a ATE brake caliper mountings
1 Upper (M12) mounting bolt
2 Lower (M8) mounting bolt dust cover

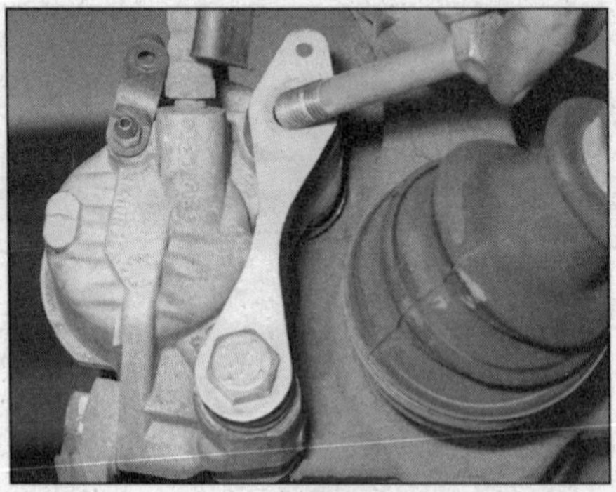

8.5b Removing a brake caliper mounting bolt - Bendix caliper

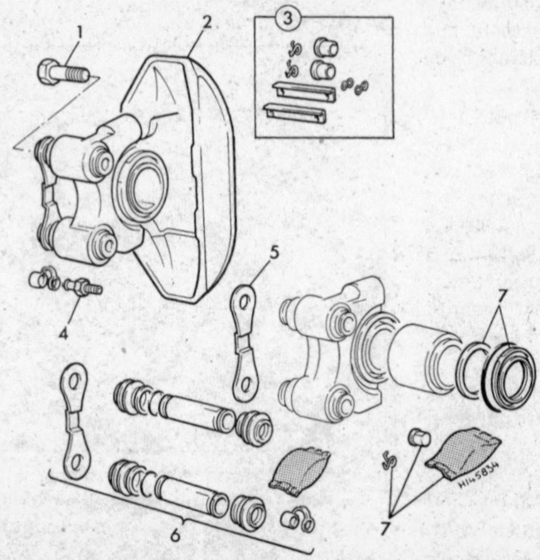

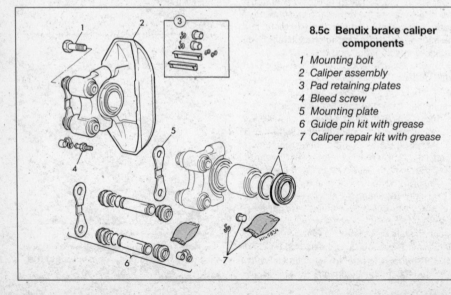

8.5c Bendix brake caliper components
1 Mounting bolt
2 Caliper assembly
3 Pad retaining plates
4 Bleed screw
5 Mounting plate
6 Guide pin kit with grease
7 Caliper repair kit with grease

8.6 Withdrawing a brake caliper

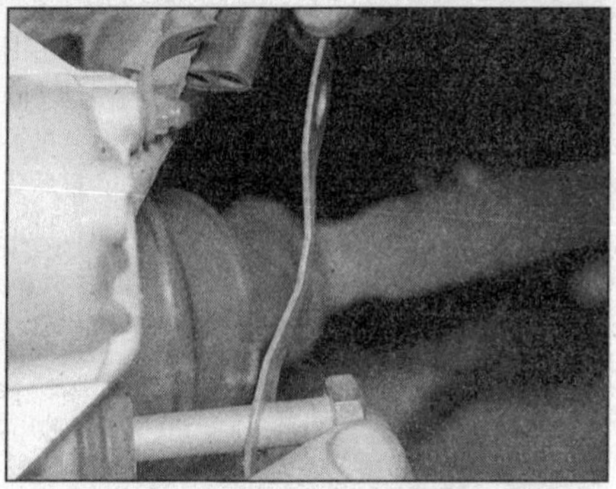

8.22 The mounting plate fits with the bend curving away from the caliper body - Bendix caliper

from the caliper body/mounting bracket (as applicable), and remove the rubber gaiters.

12 Thoroughly clean all components, using only methylated spirit or clean hydraulic fluid as a cleaning medium. Never use mineral-based solvents such as petrol or paraffin, as they will attack the hydraulic system's rubber components. Dry the components immediately, using compressed air or a clean, lint-free cloth. Use compressed air to blow clear the fluid passages.

13 Check all components, and renew any that are worn or damaged. Check particularly the cylinder bore and piston; these should be renewed (note that this means the renewal of the complete body assembly) if they are scratched, worn or corroded in any way. Similarly check the condition of the guide sleeves/pins and their bores in the caliper

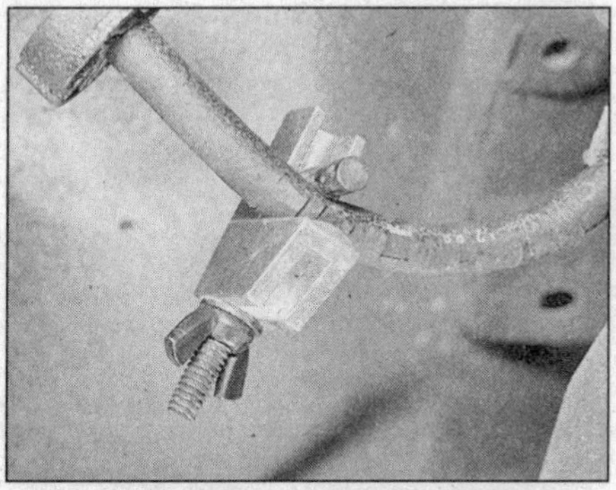

9.3 To minimise fluid loss, fit a brake hose clamp to the flexible hose

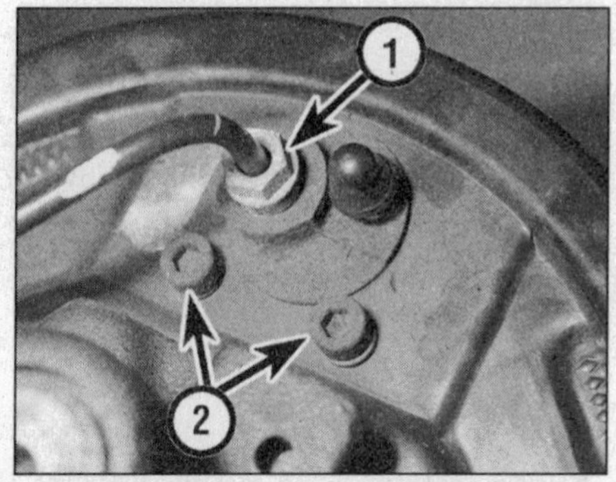

9.4 Wheel cylinder brake pipe union nut (1) and wheel cylinder retaining bolts (2)

body/mounting bracket (as applicable); both sleeves/pins should be undamaged and (when cleaned) a reasonably tight sliding fit in the body/mounting bracket bores. If there is any doubt about the condition of any component, renew it.

14 If the assembly is fit for further use, obtain the appropriate repair kit; the components are available from Citroën dealers in various combinations.

15 Renew all rubber seals, dust covers and caps disturbed on dismantling as a matter of course; these should never be re-used.

16 On reassembly, ensure that all components are absolutely clean and dry.

17 Dip the piston and the new piston (fluid) seal in clean hydraulic fluid. Smear clean fluid on the cylinder bore surface.

18 Fit the new piston (fluid) seal, using only your fingers (no tools) to manipulate it into the cylinder bore groove. Fit the new dust seal to the piston, and refit the piston to the cylinder bore using a twisting motion; ensure that the piston enters squarely into the bore. Press the piston fully into the bore, then press the dust seal into the caliper body.

19 Where fitted, install the dust seal retaining clip, ensuring that it is correctly seated in the caliper groove.

20 Apply the grease supplied in the repair kit, or a good quality high-temperature brake grease or anti-seize compound to the guide sleeves/pins. Fit the guide sleeves/pins to the caliper body/mounting bracket, and fit the new rubber gaiters, ensuring that they are correctly located in the grooves on both the sleeve/pin and body/mounting bracket (as applicable).

Refitting

21 Screw the caliper fully onto the flexible hose union, then position the caliper over the brake disc.

22 If the threads of the new caliper mounting bolts are not already pre-coated with locking compound, apply a suitable locking compound to them. Refit the bolts, along with the mounting plate on models with Bendix calipers, ensuring that the plate is fitted so that its bend curves away from the caliper body **(see illustration)**. Tighten the caliper bolts to the specified torque. Where applicable, refit the dust cover(s) to the bolt(s).

23 Securely tighten the brake hose union nut, then refit the brake pads as described in Section 4.

9.5 Remove the rear wheel cylinder from the backplate

24 Remove the brake hose clamp, or remove the polythene from the fluid reservoir (as applicable), and bleed the hydraulic system as described in Section 2. Note that, providing the precautions described were taken to minimise brake fluid loss, it should only be necessary to bleed the relevant front brake circuit.

25 Refit the roadwheel, then lower the vehicle to the ground and tighten the roadwheel bolts to the specified torque.

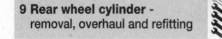

9 Rear wheel cylinder - removal, overhaul and refitting

Removal

1 Remove the brake drum as described in Section 7.

2 Using pliers, carefully unhook the upper brake shoe return spring, and remove it from both brake shoes (note the orientation of the spring, to ensure correct refitting). Pull the upper ends of the shoes away from the wheel cylinder to disengage them from the pistons.

> HAYNES HiNT ***Pull the handbrake lever on the trailing shoe fully forwards, so that the upper ends of the shoes are clear of the wheel cylinder. Wedge the lever in this position using a block of wood.***

3 To minimise fluid loss, first remove the master cylinder reservoir cap, then tighten it down onto a piece of polythene, to obtain an airtight seal. Alternatively, use a brake hose clamp, a G-clamp or a similar tool to clamp the flexible hose (connected between the metal pipe sections on the rear axle and trailing arm) at the nearest convenient point to the wheel cylinder **(see illustration)**.

4 Wipe away all traces of dirt around the brake pipe union at the rear of the wheel cylinder, and unscrew the union nut **(see illustration)**. Carefully ease the pipe out of the wheel cylinder, and plug or tape over its end,

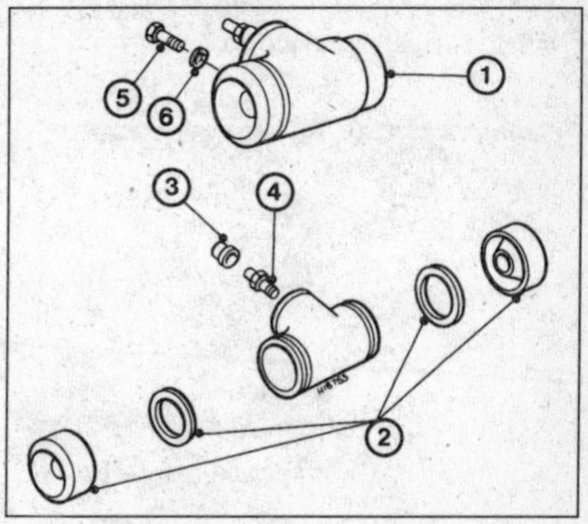

9.7 Exploded view of the rear wheel cylinder unit (non-compensated type)

1 Cylinder body 2 Seals kit 3 Dust cap 4 Bleed nipple 5 Retaining bolt 6 Washer

to prevent dirt entry. Wipe off any spilt fluid immediately.

5 Unscrew the two wheel cylinder retaining bolts from the rear of the backplate, and remove the cylinder, taking great care not to allow surplus hydraulic fluid to contaminate the brake shoe linings **(see illustration)**.

Overhaul

Note: *At the time of writing, it is not clear whether repair kits are available for both types of rear wheel cylinder (ie compensated and non-compensated) - check with your Citroën dealer. Where no kits are available, the complete rear wheel cylinder must be renewed if faulty.*

6 Clean the exterior of the cylinder to remove all traces of dirt and brake dust.

7 Pull the dust seals from the ends of the cylinder **(see illustration)**.

8 Extract the pistons and seals, and return spring, noting the locations of all components to ensure correct refitting.

9 Examine the surfaces of the cylinder bore and pistons for signs of scoring and corrosion; if evident, renew the complete wheel cylinder. If the components are in good condition, discard the seals and obtain a repair kit which will contain all the necessary renewable components.

10 Clean the pistons and the cylinder with methylated spirit or clean brake fluid, and reassemble in reverse order, making sure that the components are fitted in the correct sequence and orientated correctly, as noted before removal. Ensure that the lips of the seals face into the cylinder.

11 On completion, wipe the outer surfaces of the dust seals to remove any excess brake fluid.

Refitting

12 Clean the backplate, then place the wheel cylinder in position, and tighten the securing bolts.

13 Reconnect and tighten the brake pipe to the rear of the wheel cylinder, taking care not to allow dirt into the system.

14 Where applicable, release the handbrake lever on the trailing brake shoe, and reposition the upper ends of the shoes to engage them with the wheel cylinder pistons.

15 Refit the upper brake shoe return spring, ensuring that it is orientated as noted before removal.

16 Refit the brake drum as described in Section 7.

17 On completion, remove the brake hose clamp, or remove the polythene from the fluid reservoir (as applicable), and bleed the hydraulic system as described in Section 2. Note that, providing the precautions described were taken to minimise brake fluid loss, it should only be necessary to bleed the relevant rear brake circuit.

10 Master cylinder - removal, overhaul and refitting

Note: *Before starting work, refer to the warning at the beginning of Section 2 concerning the dangers of hydraulic fluid.*

Removal

1 Disconnect the wiring connector from the brake fluid level sender unit **(see illustration)**.

2 Remove the master cylinder fluid reservoir cap, and syphon the hydraulic fluid from the reservoir. **Note:** *Do not syphon the fluid by mouth, as it is poisonous; use a syringe or an old poultry baster.* Alternatively, open any convenient bleed screw in the system, and gently pump the brake pedal to expel the fluid through a plastic tube connected to the screw (see Section 2).

3 At this stage, the reservoir may be prised from the master cylinder and the seals extracted, if required.

4 Wipe clean the area around the brake pipe unions on the side of the master cylinder, and place absorbent rags beneath the pipe unions to catch any surplus fluid. Make a note of the correct fitted positions of the unions, then unscrew the union nuts and carefully withdraw the pipes **(see illustration)**. Plug or tape over the pipe ends and master cylinder orifices, to minimise the loss of brake fluid, and to prevent the entry of dirt into the system. Wash off any spilt fluid immediately with cold water.

5 Slacken and remove the two nuts securing the master cylinder to the vacuum servo unit (or bulkhead bracket), then withdraw the unit from the engine compartment.

6 Recover the seal from the rear of the master cylinder, and discard it.

Overhaul

7 Pull the fluid reservoir from the top of the master cylinder. Prise the reservoir seals from the reservoir or the master cylinder, as applicable **(see illustration)**.

8 Using a wooden dowel (or suitable instrument), press the piston assembly into the master cylinder body, then extract the circlip from the end of the master cylinder bore.

9 Noting the order of removal, and the direction of fitting of each component, withdraw the washer and the piston assemblies with their springs and seals, tapping the body on to a clean wooden surface to dislodge them. If necessary, clamp the master cylinder body in a vice (fitted with soft jaw covers) and use compressed air (applied through the secondary circuit fluid port) to assist the removal of the secondary piston assembly.

10 Thoroughly clean all components, using only methylated spirit or clean hydraulic fluid as a cleaning medium. Never use mineral-based solvents such as petrol or paraffin, as they will attack the hydraulic system rubber components. Dry the components immediately, using compressed air or a clean, lint-free cloth.

11 Check all components, and renew any that are worn or damaged. Check particularly the cylinder bores and pistons; the complete assembly should be renewed if these are scratched, worn or corroded. If there is any doubt about the condition of the assembly or

10.1 Disconnecting the wiring connector from the master cylinder fluid level sender

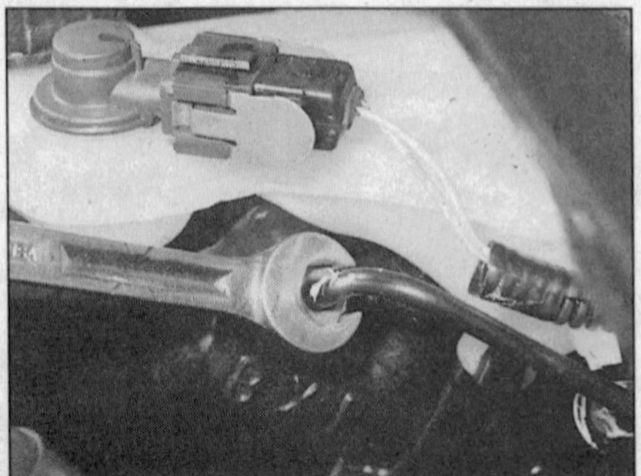

10.4 Using a brake pipe spanner to unscrew a master cylinder union nut

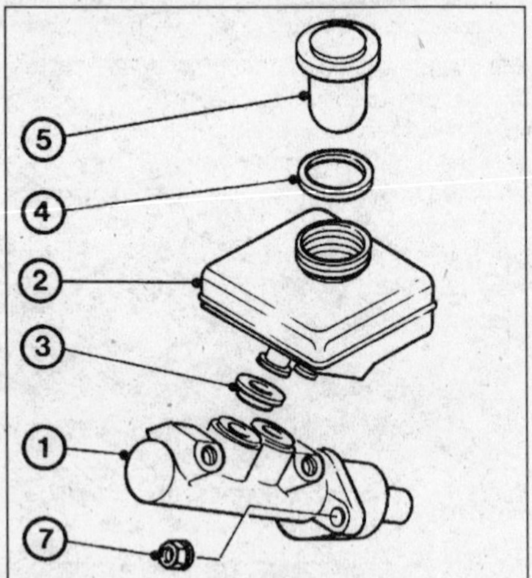

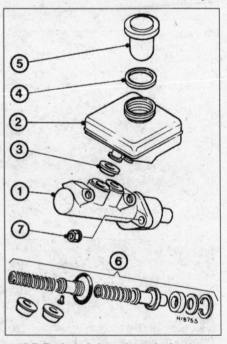

10.7 Exploded view of a typical master cylinder

Note: *Components vary according to model*

1 Master cylinder
2 Reservoir
3 Seal
4 Seal
5 Cap
6 Seal/piston kit (primary and secondary)
7 Nut

of any of its components, renew it. Check that the cylinder body fluid passages are clear.

12 If the assembly is fit for further use, obtain a repair kit from your Citroën dealer; the kit consists of both piston assemblies and springs, complete with all seals and washers. Never re-use the old components.

13 Before reassembly, dip the pistons and the new seals in clean hydraulic fluid. Smear clean fluid onto the cylinder bore.

14 Insert the piston assemblies into the cylinder bore, using a twisting motion to avoid trapping the seal lips. Ensure that all components are refitted in the correct order and the right way round, then fit the washer to the end of the primary piston. Where applicable, follow the assembly instructions supplied with the repair kit.

15 Press the piston assemblies fully into the bore using a clean wooden dowel, and secure them in position with the new circlip. Ensure that the circlip is correctly located in the groove in the cylinder bore.

16 Examine the fluid reservoir seals, and if necessary renew them. Fit the reservoir seals to the master cylinder body, then refit the reservoir.

Refitting

17 Remove all traces of dirt from the master cylinder and servo unit (or bulkhead) mating surfaces, and fit a new seal to the master cylinder.

18 Fit the master cylinder to the servo unit/bulkhead, ensuring that the pushrod enters the master cylinder bore centrally. Refit the master cylinder mounting nuts, and tighten them to the specified torque.

19 Wipe clean the brake pipe unions, then refit them to the correct master cylinder ports, as noted before removal, and tighten the union nuts securely.

20 Refill the master cylinder reservoir with new fluid, and bleed the complete hydraulic system as described in Section 2.

11 Brake pedal - removal and refitting

Removal

1 Refer to Chapter 11 and remove the shelf or trim panel (as applicable) from below the steering column. For improved access, remove the complete facia.

2 Note the position of the brake pedal return spring, then release it from the pedal bracket and pedal **(see illustration)**.

3 Remove the clevis pin and disconnect the pushrod from the brake pedal.

4 Unscrew the nut from the end of the pedal pivot bolt. Carefully withdraw the pivot bolt, and remove the pedal components one at a time. Note the position of the components to ensure correct refitting. On left-hand drive models, the clutch pedal can remain in position with the pivot bolt partially removed.

Refitting

5 Refitting is a reversal of removal. Lubricate the pivot bolt, and on completion adjust the stop-light switch as described in Section 18.

12 Brake pedal-to-servo linkage (right-hand-drive models) - removal, overhaul and refitting

Removal

1 Refer to Chapter 11 and remove the facia completely.

2 Remove the brake pedal as described in Section 11, and the clutch pedal as described in Chapter 6.

3 To give improved working room, remove the steering gear assembly as described in Chapter 10.

4 Remove the vacuum servo unit as described in Section 13.

5 Unbolt the linkage from the bulkhead, then unbolt the sections from each other **(see illustration)**. Note the location of any shims and spacers.

Overhaul

6 Before dismantling the assembly, note the adjusted length of the cross-shaft for correct reassembly.

7 Remove the pivot bolts and take out the pivots.

8 Clean all components and examine them for wear and damage. Renew them as necessary.

9 Reassemble the components using a reversal of dismantling.

Refitting

10 Refitting is a reversal of removal.

13 Vacuum servo unit - testing, removal and refitting

Testing

1 To test the operation of the servo unit, depress the footbrake several times to exhaust the vacuum, then start the engine whilst keeping the pedal firmly depressed. As the engine starts, there should be a noticeable "give" in the brake pedal as the vacuum builds up. Allow the engine to run for about one

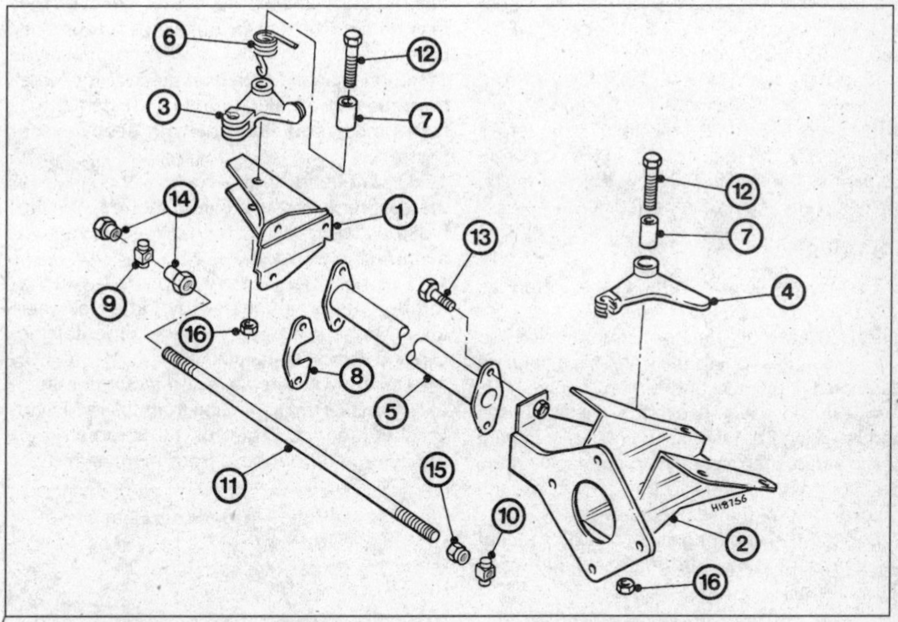

12.5 Brake pedal-to-servo linkage (right-hand-drive models)

1 *Return bracket*
2 *Support mounting*
3 *Pedal return lever*
4 *Servo/master cylinder return lever*
5 *Cross-shaft housing*
6 *Spring*
7 *Spacer*
8 *Shim*
9 *Pivot*
10 *Pivot*
11 *Cross-shaft*
12 *Bolt*
13 *Bolt*
14 *Adjuster nuts*
15 *Adjuster nut*
16 *Self-locking nut*

11.2 Brake pedal assembly

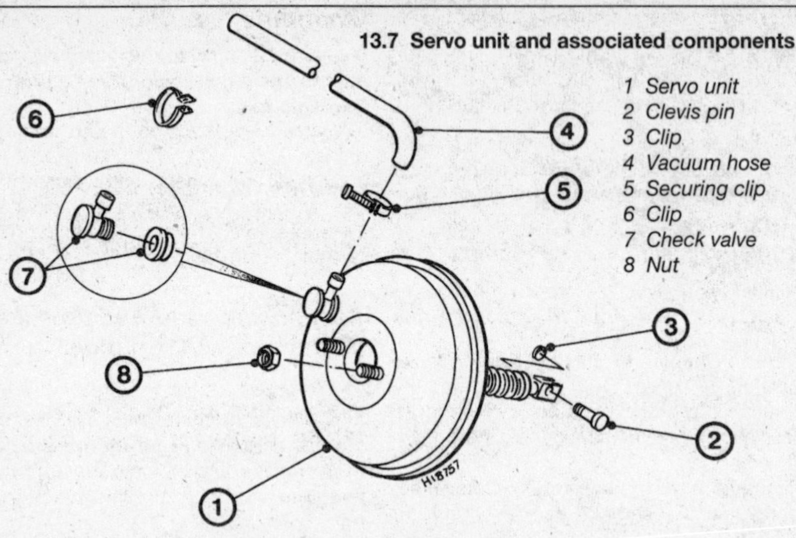

13.7 Servo unit and associated components

minute, then switch it off. If the brake pedal is now depressed it should feel normal, but further applications should result in the pedal feeling firmer, with the pedal stroke decreasing with each application.

2 If the servo does not operate as described, first inspect the servo unit check valve as described in Section 14. On Diesel engine models, also check the operation of the vacuum pump as described in Section 22.

3 If the servo unit still fails to operate satisfactorily, the fault lies within the unit itself. Repairs to the unit are not possible - if faulty, the servo unit must be renewed.

Removal

4 To improve access, remove the battery as described in Chapter 5A.

5 Remove the air cleaner assembly and (on Diesel models only) the inlet manifold as described in the relevant Part of Chapter 4.

6 Where necessary, unclip any relevant hoses and/or wiring from the fusebox bracket in front of the servo, then remove the nut securing the bracket to the wheel arch, and move the bracket clear of the working area.

7 Loosen the securing clip, and disconnect the vacuum hose from the servo **(see illustration)**.

13.14 Servo unit mounting and bracket viewed through the aperture in the left-hand wheel arch (right-hand drive models)

8 Disconnect the low fluid warning light wires from the reservoir cap.

9 Unscrew and remove the nuts securing the master cylinder to the vacuum servo **(see illustration)**.

10 Working under the servo, unclip the master cylinder brake fluid pipes from the bulkhead.

11 Carefully pull the master cylinder forwards from the servo, taking care not to strain the fluid pipes **(see illustration)**. Recover the gasket.

12 On left-hand drive models, working inside the car, remove the clevis pin attaching the brake pedal to the pushrod. Remove the trim panel first if necessary.

13 On right-hand drive models, working through the area vacated by the air cleaner unit, release the pushrod clevis pin retaining clip and withdraw the pin.

14 Unscrew and remove the mounting nuts, and withdraw the servo unit from the mounting bracket **(see illustration)**. If it is required to remove the rubber boot from the pushrod on left-hand drive models, the brake and clutch pedals must be removed first.

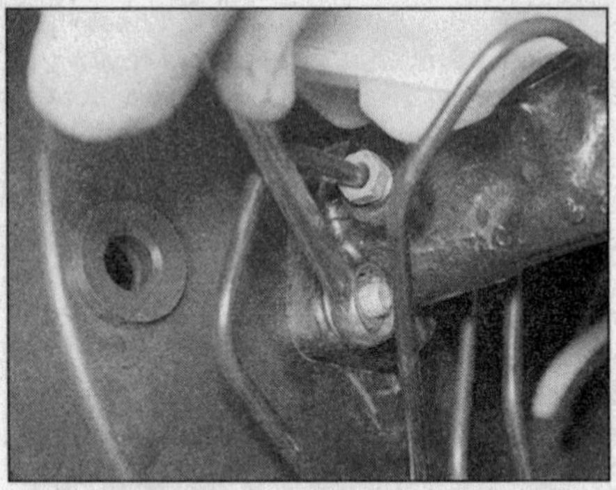

13.9 Unscrewing the nuts securing the master cylinder to the servo unit

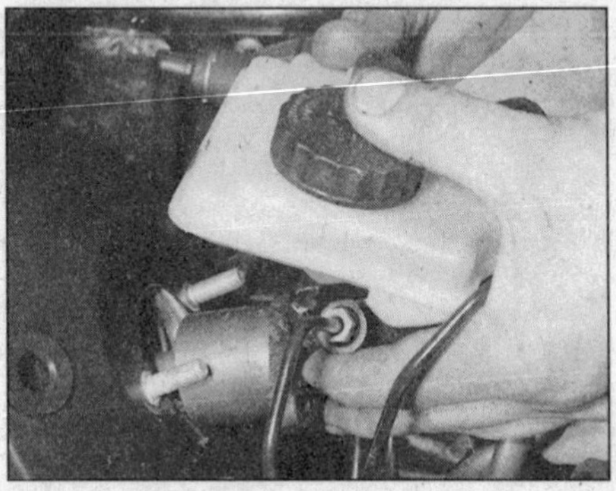

13.11 Withdrawing the master cylinder from the servo unit

Refitting

15 Refitting is a reversal of removal, but note the following points:

a) Check that the pushrod setting is as shown **(see illustration)**.
b) Tighten all nuts and bolts to the specified torque.
c) Where disconnected, adjust the clutch cable as described in Chapter 6.

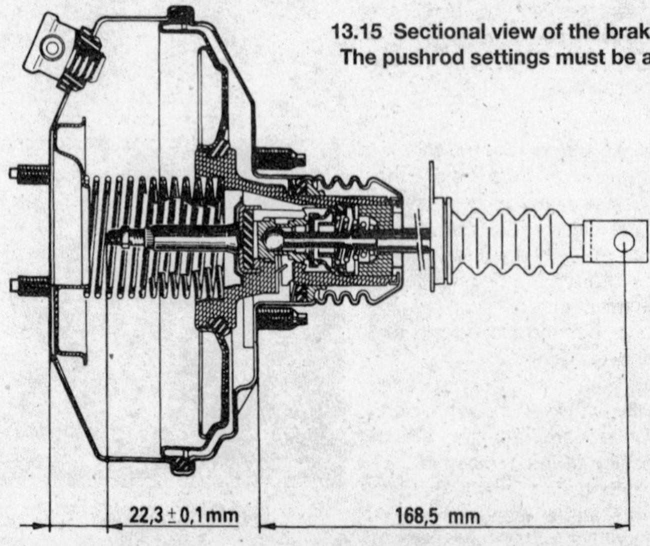

13.15 Sectional view of the brake servo unit. The pushrod settings must be as indicated

14 Vacuum servo unit check valve - removal, testing and refitting

Removal

1 Slacken the securing clip (where fitted), and disconnect the vacuum hose from the servo unit check valve.

2 Withdraw the valve from its rubber sealing grommet, using a pulling and twisting motion. Remove the grommet from the servo.

Testing

3 Examine the check valve for signs of damage, and renew if necessary. The valve may be tested by blowing through it in both directions. Air should flow through the valve in one direction only - when blown through from the servo unit end of the valve. Renew the valve if this is not the case.

4 Examine the rubber sealing grommet and flexible vacuum hose for signs of damage or deterioration, and renew as necessary.

Refitting

5 Fit the sealing grommet into position in the servo unit.

6 Carefully ease the check valve into position, taking great care not to displace or damage the grommet. Reconnect the vacuum hose to the valve and, where necessary, securely tighten its retaining clip.

7 On completion, start the engine and check the servo as described in Section 13.

15 Handbrake lever - removal and refitting

Removal

1 Jack up the rear of the car and support on axle stands (see *"Jacking, towing and wheel changing"*). Chock the front wheels.

2 Working under the vehicle, slacken the adjuster nuts on the rear of each handbrake cable until the cables can be disengaged from the equaliser plate on the rear of the handbrake lever assembly.

3 Working inside the car, move the front seats fully forwards then remove the retaining screw and lift the cover from the handbrake lever.

4 Pull the carpet back then unscrew and remove the mounting bolts.

5 Separate the handbrake warning light switch and bracket, then detach the gaiter from the floorpan and withdraw the lever from the car.

Refitting

6 Refitting is a reversal of removal, but adjust the cables as described in Chapter 1 and check for correct operation.

16 Handbrake cable(s) - removal and refitting

Removal

1 Remove the rear brake shoes as described in Section 5.

2 Disconnect the cable(s) from the rear brake backplate(s) **(see illustration)**.

3 Release the cable(s) from the retaining clips on the underside of the car, and from the equaliser plate at the front end **(see illustrations)**.

Refitting

4 Refitting is a reversal of removal, but adjust the cables as described in Chapter 1, and check for correct operation.

17 Rear brake pressure-regulating valves - testing, removal and refitting

Suspension-mounted pressure limiter (non-ABS models)

Testing

1 The limiter is located on the left-hand end of the rear axle **(see illustration)**. Its purpose is to maintain equal braking effect on the front and rear wheels, to prevent the rear brakes from locking up.

2 If you feel that, on applying the brakes, the rear wheels are not being braked sufficiently, or you find that the rear brakes are locking up under heavy braking, it is likely that the pressure limiter is defective.

3 A Citroën dealer will have to test the component if its performance is in doubt, as

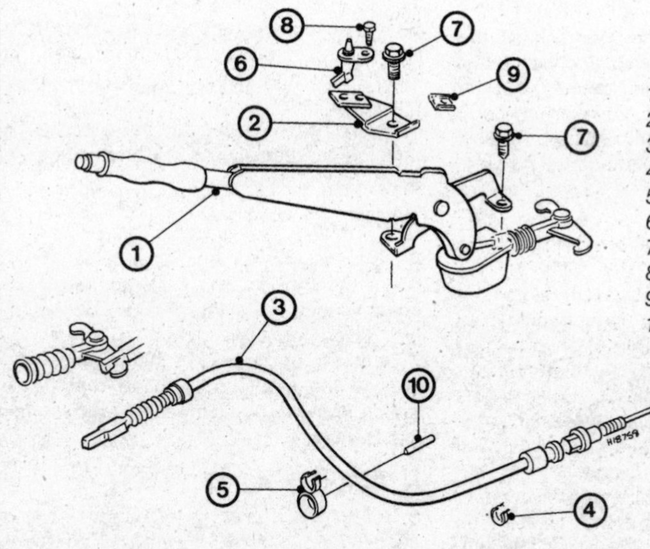

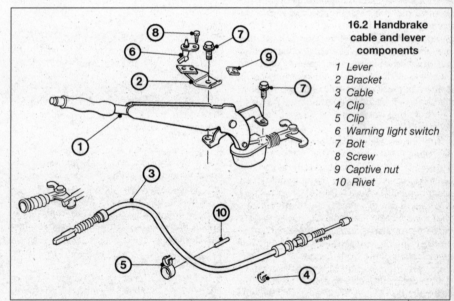

16.2 Handbrake cable and lever components

1 Lever
2 Bracket
3 Cable
4 Clip
5 Clip
6 Warning light switch
7 Bolt
8 Screw
9 Captive nut
10 Rivet

16.3a Handbrake cable connections to the rear brake and suspension arm (arrowed)

16.3b Handbrake cable-to-floor mounting clip

16.3c Handbrake cable equaliser plate (arrowed)

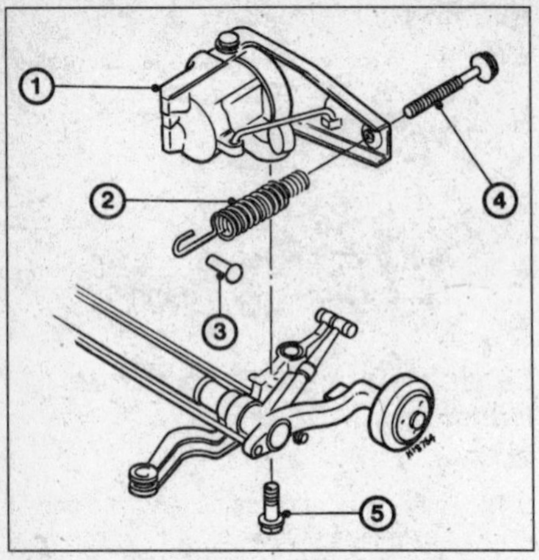

17.1 Suspension-mounted rear brake pressure limiter

1 Limiter 2 Limit spring 3 Spring rivet 4 Adjustment screw (do not alter the setting) 5 Retaining bolt

pressure-testing equipment is necessary. No attempt must be made to dismantle the unit.

Removal

4 To remove the limiter, chock the front wheels, then jack up the rear of the car and support on axle stands.

5 To minimise fluid loss, first remove the master cylinder reservoir cap, and then tighten it down onto a piece of polythene, to obtain an airtight seal.

6 Identify the location of the brake pipes on the limiter, then unscrew the union nuts and carefully pull out the pipes so that they are clear of the unit.

7 Unhook the spring from the underbody.

8 Unbolt the unit from the rear axle.

Refitting

9 Refitting is a reversal of removal. Tighten the union nuts to the specified torque, and tighten the mounting bolt securely.

Pressure-regulating valves integral with wheel cylinder (non-ABS models)

10 No adjustment is possible on this type of regulating valve. If the pressure-regulating valves are thought to be faulty, the hydraulic circuit should be tested by a Citroën dealer. Removal and refitting of the rear wheel cylinders is described in Section 9.

Load-sensitive pressure-regulating valve (ABS models)

Testing, removal and refitting

11 The load-sensitive pressure regulating valve is similar to the suspension-mounted unit fitted to non-ABS models.

12 Refer to paragraphs 1 to 9 for details of testing, removal and refitting.

18 Stop-light switch - adjustment, removal and refitting

Adjustment

1 The stop-light switch is attached to the footbrake pedal bracket. Remove the shelf and reach up behind the facia for access to the switch.

2 With the brake pedal released, the distance from the lug on the pedal to the threaded portion of the switch should be between 4.0 mm and 5.0 mm on models with a brake servo unit, or between 2.0 mm and 5.0 mm on models without a brake servo unit.

3 If adjustment is necessary, loosen the locknut and turn the switch as required until the dimension is correct. Tighten the locknut on completion.

4 Check that the stop-lights operate when the pedal is depressed, and that they extinguish when the pedal is released.

Removal

5 Disconnect the battery negative lead.

6 Remove the trim from beneath the steering column, then reach up and disconnect the wiring plug from the switch.

7 Unscrew and remove the locknut, then release the securing clip and remove the switch from the pedal bracket assembly **(see illustration)**.

Refitting

8 Refitting is a reversal of removal, but on completion check the adjustment of the switch as described previously in this Section.

19 Handbrake "on" warning light switch - removal and refitting

Removal

1 Disconnect the battery negative lead.

2 Lift the carpet panel for access to the switch.

3 Carefully prise out the switch, and disconnect the wiring plug **(see illustrations)**.

Refitting

4 Refitting is a reversal of removal.

20 Anti-lock braking system (ABS) - general information

1 The Bendix "additional" anti-lock braking system is available as an option on certain models **(see illustration)**.

2 The system is fail-safe, and is fitted in addition to the conventional braking system; this allows the vehicle to retain conventional braking in the event of an ABS failure.

3 The system prevents wheel lock-up by controlling the hydraulic pressure in the braking circuits. Sensors mounted at each front wheel monitor the rotational speeds of the wheels by toothed rings on the driveshafts, and are able to detect when there is a risk of wheel lock-up. Solenoid valves are positioned in the brake circuits in a modulator assembly, which is controlled by an electronic control unit. The electronic control unit controls the braking effort applied to each front wheel, according to the information supplied by the wheel sensors, by switching the solenoid valves on and off, as appropriate. The electronic control unit is mounted on a bracket attached to the modulator assembly.

4 Should a fault develop in the system, a self-diagnostic facility is incorporated in the electronic control unit, which can be used in conjunction with special diagnostic equipment available to a Citroën dealer to determine the nature of the fault.

5 The braking system components used on

18.7 Stop-light switch (1) and locknut (2) - right-hand-drive model viewed with facia removed

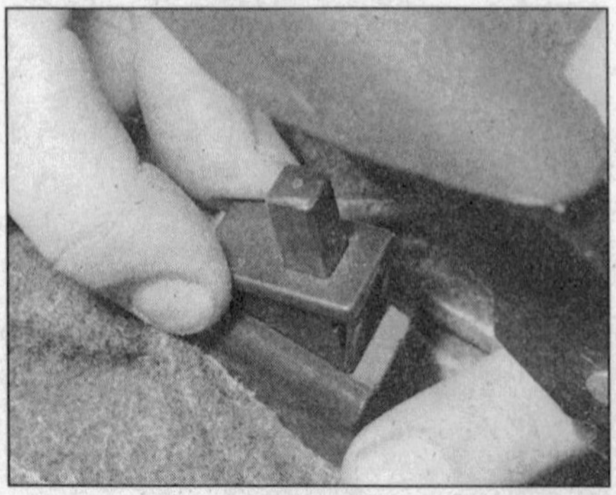

19.3a Prise out the handbrake "on" warning light switch . . .

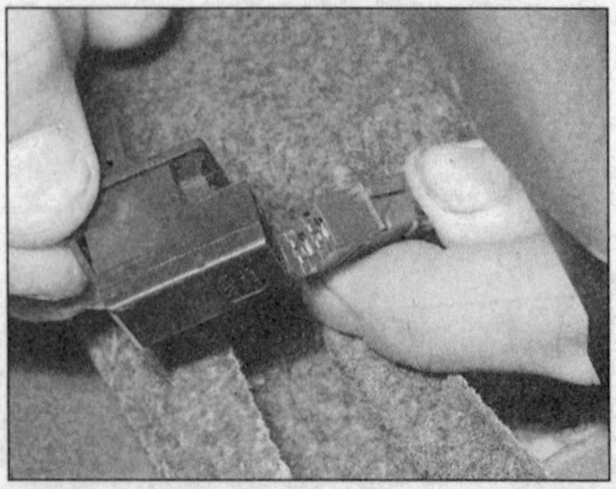

19.3b . . . and disconnect the wiring plug

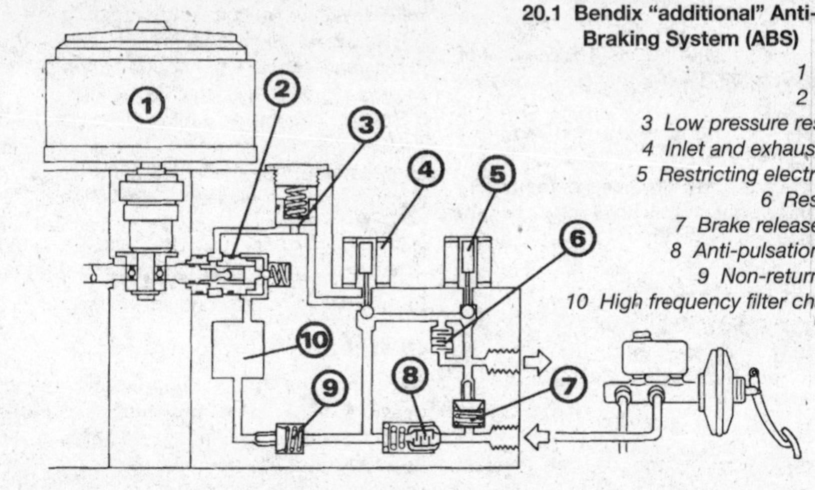

20.1 Bendix "additional" Anti-lock Braking System (ABS)

1 Motor
2 Pump
3 Low pressure reservoir
4 Inlet and exhaust valve
5 Restricting electrovalve
6 Restrictor
7 Brake release valve
8 Anti-pulsation valve
9 Non-return valve
10 High frequency filter chamber

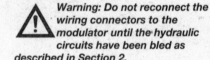

models fitted with ABS are similar to those used on models with a conventional braking system.

6 Note that when bleeding the brake hydraulic system, the modulator assembly must be bled as described in Section 2.

21 Anti-lock braking system (ABS) components - removal and refitting

Modulator assembly

Note: *Before starting work, refer to the warning at the beginning of Section 2 concerning the dangers of hydraulic fluid.*

Removal

1 Disconnect the battery negative lead.

2 Remove the master cylinder as described in Section 10.

3 Remove the brake servo as described in Section 13.

4 Mark the locations of the hydraulic fluid pipes to ensure correct refitting, then unscrew the union nuts, and disconnect the pipes from the modulator assembly. Be prepared for fluid spillage, and plug the open ends of the pipes and the modulator, to prevent dirt ingress and further fluid loss. Note the position of the clip on the brake pipes, to ensure correct refitting.

5 Disconnect the wiring connectors from the modulator assembly.

6 Remove the upper securing nut from the modulator mounting bracket.

7 Working under the modulator mounting bracket, unscrew the two lower mounting nuts, then withdraw the assembly, complete with the mounting bracket.

Refitting

Warning: Do not reconnect the wiring connectors to the modulator until the hydraulic circuits have been bled as described in Section 2.

8 Commence refitting by positioning the assembly in the engine compartment, and refitting the upper and lower securing nuts.

9 Reconnect the fluid pipes to the assembly, as noted before removal, ensuring that no dirt enters the system. Ensure that the brake pipe clip is fitted as noted before removal.

10 Refit the brake servo as described in Section 13.

11 Refit the master cylinder as described in Section 10.

12 Bleed the complete hydraulic system as described in Section 2.

13 Reconnect the modulator assembly wiring plugs.

14 Reconnect the battery negative lead.

Electronic control unit

Removal

15 Disconnect the battery negative lead.

16 Disconnect the wiring connector from the control unit, located near the battery.

17 Unscrew the mounting bolts and remove the control unit from the engine compartment.

Refitting

18 Refitting is a reversal of removal.

Wheel sensor

Note: *Suitable thread-locking compound must be applied to the sensor securing stud on refitting.*

Removal

19 Disconnect the battery negative lead.

20 Apply the handbrake, then jack up the front of the vehicle and support securely on axle stands (see *"Jacking, towing and wheel changing"*). If desired, remove the appropriate front roadwheel to improve access.

21 Follow the wiring back from the sensor, and separate the two halves of the wiring connector. Release the wiring from the securing clips, noting its routing.

22 Unscrew the securing nut, and withdraw the shield from the sensor.

23 Unscrew the securing stud, and withdraw the sensor from its mounting bracket.

Refitting

24 Refitting is a reversal of removal, bearing in mind the following points:

a) Ensure that the mating faces of the sensor and the mounting bracket are clean, and apply a little grease to the mounting bracket bore before refitting.
b) Apply thread-locking compound to the threads of the sensor securing stud.
c) Ensure that the sensor wiring is routed as noted before removal.

9

22 Vacuum pump (Diesel engine models) - removal and refitting

Removal

Note: *A new O-ring should be used on refitting.*

1 The pump is located at the transmission end of the cylinder head.

2 Release the securing clip (where applicable), and disconnect the vacuum hose from the pump **(see illustration)**.

3 Slacken and remove the securing bolts and washers, then withdraw the pump from the cylinder head. Recover the O-ring **(see illustrations)**.

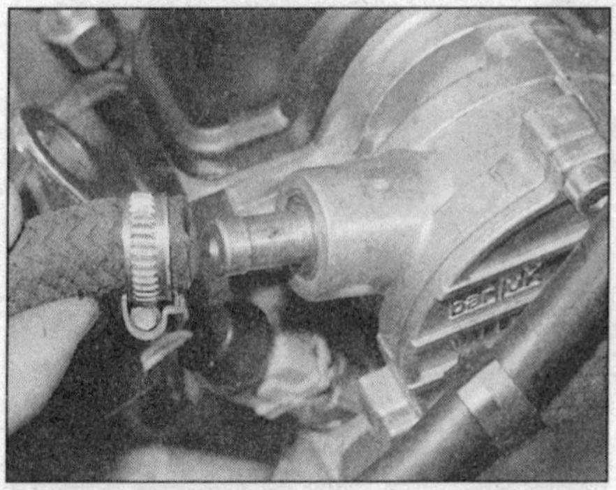

22.2 Disconnecting the vacuum hose from the brake vacuum pump - Diesel engine model

22.3a Remove the brake vacuum pump . . .

22.3b . . . and recover the O-ring

Refitting

4 Fit a new O-ring to the pump, then align the pump drive dogs with the slots in the end of the camshaft, and refit the pump to the cylinder head.

5 Refit the securing bolts and washers, and tighten them securely.

6 Reconnect the vacuum hose to the pump, and tighten the retaining clip (where applicable).

23 Vacuum pump (Diesel engine models) - testing and overhaul

Testing

1 The operation of the braking system vacuum pump can be checked using a suitable vacuum gauge.

2 Disconnect the vacuum hose from the pump, and connect the gauge to the pump union using a suitable length of hose.

3 Start the engine and allow it to idle, then measure the vacuum created by the pump. As a guide, after one minute, a minimum of approximately 500 mm Hg should be recorded. If the vacuum registered is significantly less than this, it is likely that the pump is faulty. However, seek the advice of a Citroën dealer before condemning the pump.

Overhaul

4 Overhaul of the vacuum pump is not possible, since no components are available separately for it. If faulty, the complete pump assembly must be renewed.

Chapter 10 Suspension and steering

Contents

Degrees of difficulty

Easy, suitable for novice with little experience	**Fairly easy,** suitable for beginner with some experience	**Fairly difficult,** suitable for competent DIY mechanic	**Difficult,** suitable for experienced DIY mechanic	**Very difficult,** suitable for expert DIY or professional

Specifications

Front suspension

Type	Independent by MacPherson struts, with inclined coil springs and integral shock absorbers. Certain models have an anti-roll bar linked to the lower arms or struts (depending on model)

Rear suspension

Type	Trailing arms with transverse torsion bars and telescopic shock absorbers. Certain models have a rear anti-roll bar running through the axle tube, linking both trailing arms

Steering

Type	Rack-and-pinion

Wheel alignment and steering angles

Front wheel camber angle:	
All models up to July 1991	0° ± 30'
954 cc and 1124 cc engine models, July 1991 onwards	0° ± 30'
1360 cc and 1527 cc engine models, July 1991 onwards	-0° 31' ± 30'
Front wheel castor angle	2°15' ± 30'
Front wheel toe setting:	
Except GTi models	0.5 mm to 3.5 mm toe-out
GTi models	1 mm to 3 mm toe-in
Rear wheel camber setting (all models)	-1°15' ± 20' negative
Rear wheel toe setting (all models)	1.8 mm to 5.4 mm toe-in

Roadwheels

Type	Pressed-steel or aluminium alloy (depending on model)
Size	4B x 13, 4.5B x 13, 5B x 13, 5.5B x 13, 5.5B x 14, 4.5J x 13, 5J x 13, 5J x 14 or 5.5J x 14 (depending on model)

Tyres

Tyre sizes and pressures - see Chapter 1 Specifications.

Torque wrench settings	Nm	lbf ft
Front suspension		
Driveshaft nut*		
All except right-hand driveshaft with intermediate bearing	250	185
Right-hand driveshaft with intermediate bearing	260	192
Front suspension strut upper mounting-to-body nuts	20	15
Front suspension strut damper rod nut*	45	33
Lower arm balljoint-to-hub carrier nut and clamp bolt*	28	21
Lower arm front mounting nut and through-bolt:		
Except GTi	70	52
GTi	85	63
Lower arm rear mounting through-bolt:		
Except GTi	70	52
GTi	87	64
Lower arm rear mounting bracket-to-body nuts	40	30
Front anti-roll bar mounting clamp-to-body bolts:		
Models up to July 1991 (nuts)	25	18
Models from July 1991 (bolts)	50	37
Front anti-roll bar end clamp-to-lower arm bolts (non-GTi models)	25	18
Front anti-roll bar drop link securing nuts* (GTi models)	30	22
Rear suspension		
Rear hub nut	140	103
Rear shock absorber upper mounting bolt and nut	90	66
Rear shock absorber lower mounting bolt and nut	110	81
Rear suspension assembly-to-body mounting bolts:		
Up to September 1990	55	41
September 1990 onwards	80	59
Steering		
Steering wheel nut	35	26
Track rod end-to-steering arm nut	35	26
Steering column lower clamp bolt and nut**	22	16
Steering column securing nuts/bolts	17	13
Steering gear-to-bulkhead bolts	18	13
Track rod locknuts	40	30
Track rod inner end to yoke	21	16
Track rod yoke to steering rack	24	18
Roadwheels		
Roadwheel bolts	90	66

**Use a new nut.*
***Use a new nut and bolt.*

1 General information

1 The independent front suspension is of the MacPherson strut type, incorporating coil springs and integral telescopic shock absorbers. The MacPherson struts are located by transverse lower suspension arms, which utilise rubber inner mounting bushes, and incorporate a balljoint at the outer ends. The front hub carriers, which carry the wheel bearings, brake calipers and the hub/disc assemblies, are integral with the MacPherson struts, and are connected to the lower arms via the balljoints. A front anti-roll bar is fitted to certain models. The anti-roll bar is rubber-mounted onto the subframe, and is either connected to both lower suspension arms on non-GTi models, or directly to the front suspension struts on GTi models **(see illustrations)**.

2 The rear suspension is of the independent trailing arm type, which consists of two trailing arms, linked by a tubular crossmember.

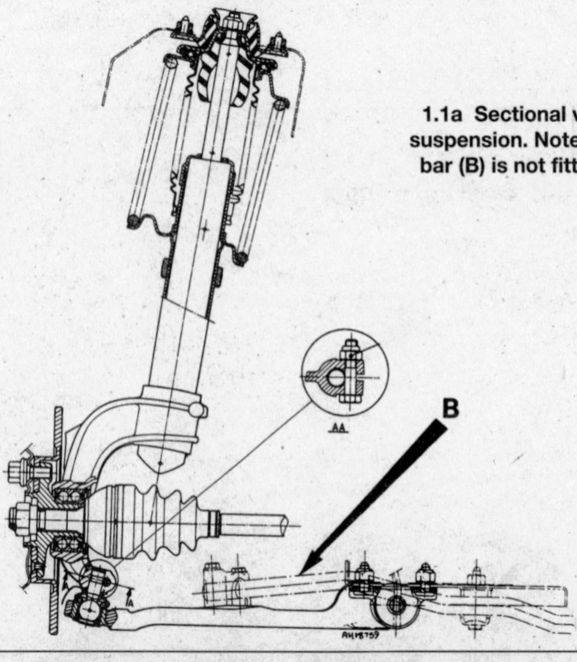

1.1a Sectional view of the front suspension. Note that the anti-roll bar (B) is not fitted to all models

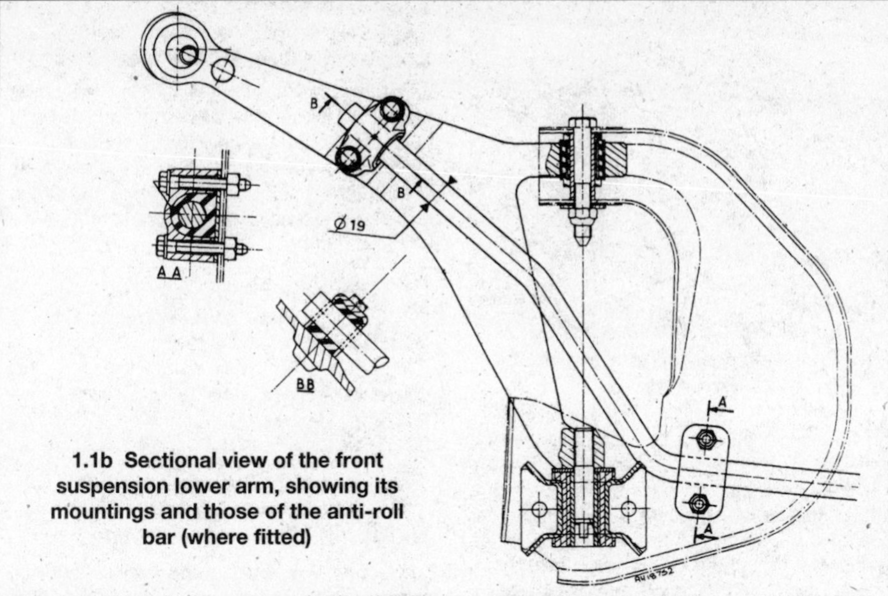

1.1b Sectional view of the front suspension lower arm, showing its mountings and those of the anti-roll bar (where fitted)

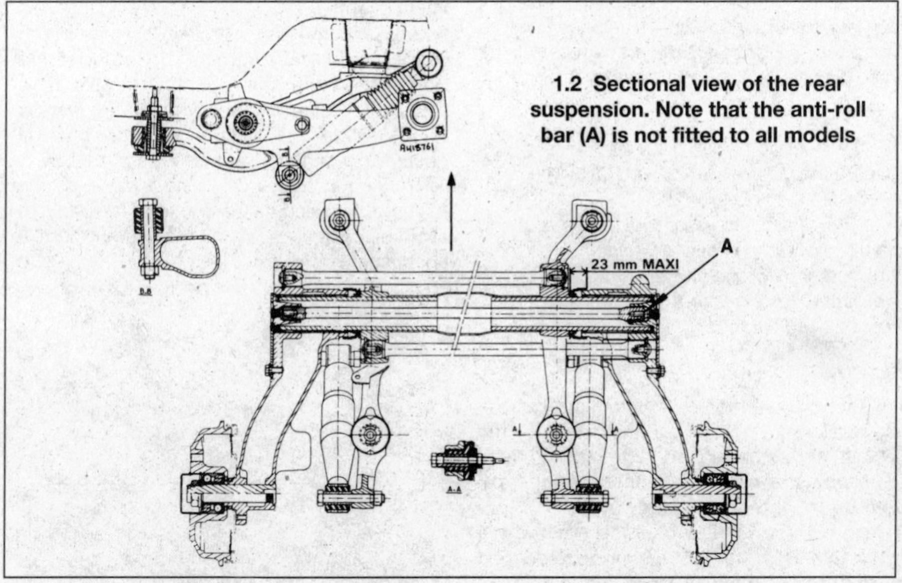

1.2 Sectional view of the rear suspension. Note that the anti-roll bar (A) is not fitted to all models

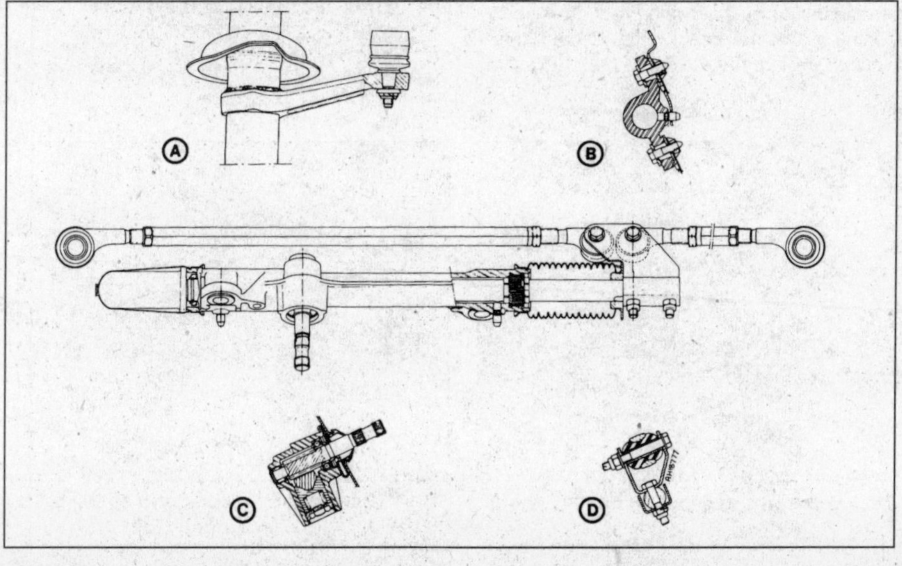

Torsion bars linking the trailing arms are situated in front of and behind the crossmember, and on certain models, an anti-roll bar linking the arms passes through the centre of the crossmember **(see illustration)**.

3 The complete rear axle assembly is mounted onto the vehicle underbody by four rubber mountings.

4 The steering column has a universal joint fitted at its lower end, which is clamped to the steering gear pinion by means of a clamp bolt and nut.

5 The steering gear is mounted on the engine compartment bulkhead. It is connected by two track rods, with balljoints at their outer ends and rubber bushes at their inner ends, to the steering arms projecting rearwards from the suspension struts **(see illustration)**. The track rod ends and inner ends are threaded, to facilitate steering angle adjustment.

2 Front hub bearings - renewal

Note: *The bearing is a sealed, pre-adjusted and pre-lubricated, double-row roller type, and is intended to last the vehicle's entire service life without maintenance or attention.*

Note: *Citroën special tools are available to carry out this operation, in which case the task can be carried out without removing the suspension strut. The procedure described in this Section assumes that the special tools are not available - in this case, the task can be accomplished using improvised tools, but only once the suspension strut assembly has been removed.*

Note: *A press will be required to dismantle and rebuild the assembly; if such a tool is not available, a large bench vice and spacers (such as large sockets) will serve as an adequate substitute. The bearing's inner races are an interference fit on the hub; if the inner race remains on the hub when it is pressed out of the hub carrier, a bearing puller will be required to remove it.*

1 Remove the relevant front suspension strut assembly as described in Section 3.

2 If not already done, remove the securing screw(s) and withdraw the brake disc from the hub (refer to Chapter 9 if necessary).

3 Support the strut assembly securely on blocks, or in a vice. Using a tubular spacer which bears only on the inner end of the hub

1.5 Steering gear unit and track rods (left-hand drive type shown - right-hand drive similar)

A Steering arm and track rod end balljoint
B Steering gear mounting
C Steering gear pinion
D Steering yoke

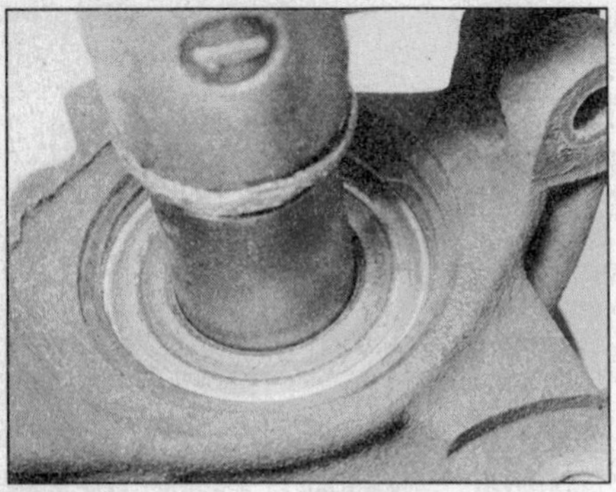

2.3 Driving the hub flange from the front hub bearing

flange, press the hub flange out of the bearing **(see illustration)**. If the bearing outboard inner race remains on the hub, remove it using a bearing puller (see note above).

4 Extract the bearing retaining circlip from the inner end of the hub carrier **(see illustration)**.

5 Where necessary, refit the bearing inner race back in position over the ball cage, and securely support the inner face of the hub carrier. Using a tubular spacer which bears only on the bearing inner race, press the complete bearing assembly out of the hub carrier.

6 Thoroughly clean the hub and hub carrier, removing all traces of dirt and grease, and polish away any burrs or raised edges which might hinder reassembly. Check the components for cracks or any other signs of wear or damage, and renew them if necessary. Renew the bearing retaining circlip, regardless of its apparent condition.

7 Commence reassembly by applying a light film of oil to the bearing outer race and the contact faces of the hub, to aid installation of the bearing.

8 Securely support the hub carrier, and locate the bearing in the hub. Press the bearing fully into position, ensuring that it enters the hub squarely, using a tubular spacer which bears only on the bearing outer race.

9 Once the bearing is correctly seated, fit a new bearing retaining circlip, ensuring that it is correctly located in the groove in the hub carrier.

10 Securely support the outer face of the hub,

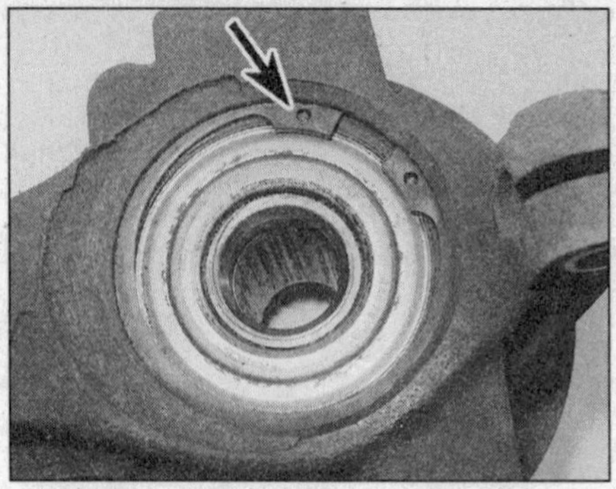

2.4 Front hub bearing retaining circlip (arrowed)

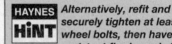

and the suspension strut, and locate the hub carrier bearing inner race over the end of the hub. Press the bearing onto the hub, using a tubular spacer which bears only on the inner race of the bearing, until the bearing seats against the hub shoulder. Check that the hub rotates freely, and wipe off any excess oil or grease.

11 Refit the suspension strut assembly as described in Section 3. If removed, refit the brake disc as described in Chapter 9.

3 Front suspension strut - removal, overhaul and refitting

Note: *A balljoint separator tool will be required for this operation. A new driveshaft nut, a new track rod end-to-steering arm nut, and a new hub carrier-to-lower arm balljoint clamp nut, must be used when refitting.*

Removal

1 Chock the rear wheels, apply the handbrake, then jack up the front of the vehicle and support on axle stands (see *"Jacking, towing and wheel changing"*). Remove the appropriate roadwheel.

2 Remove the ABS wheel sensor (where applicable) from the hub carrier as described in Chapter 9, to avoid any possibility of damage during the following procedure.

3 Using a hammer and a suitable cold chisel or punch, relieve the staking on the driveshaft nut.

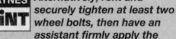

Warning: Wear suitable eye protection.

4 The front hub must now be held stationary in order to loosen the driveshaft nut. Ideally, the hub should be held by a suitable tool bolted into place using two of the wheel bolts (see illustration 2.5 in Chapter 8). Using a socket and extension bar, slacken and remove the driveshaft nut.

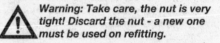

HAYNES HiNT ***Alternatively, refit and securely tighten at least two wheel bolts, then have an assistant firmly apply the brake pedal to prevent the hub from rotating.***

Warning: Take care, the nut is very tight! Discard the nut - a new one must be used on refitting.

5 Unscrew the bolt securing the brake pad wear sensor earth lead to the hub carrier **(see illustration)**.

6 Unscrew the two bolts securing the brake caliper to the hub carrier, then remove the bolts, along with the mounting plate (where applicable - note which way round the plate is fitted). Slide the caliper off the disc (if necessary, remove the brake pads first, with reference to Chapter 9). Using a piece of wire or string, suspend the caliper from the body, to avoid placing any strain on the hydraulic brake hose **(see illustration)**.

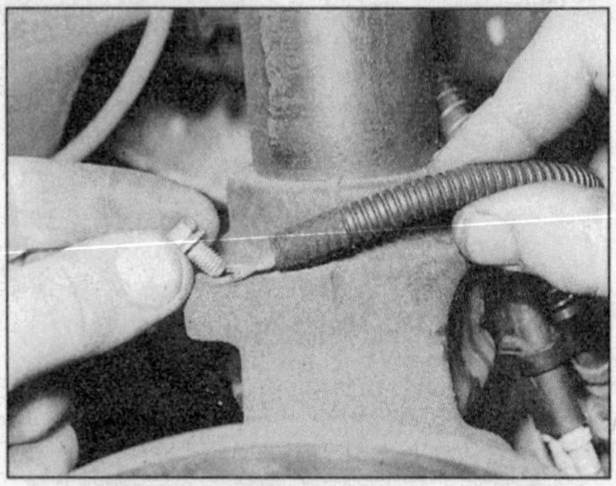

3.5 Unscrew the bolt securing the brake pad wear sensor earth lead to the hub carrier

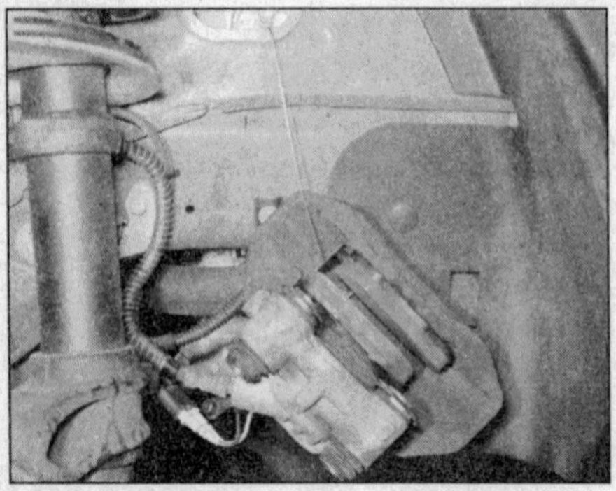

3.6 Suspend the caliper from the body

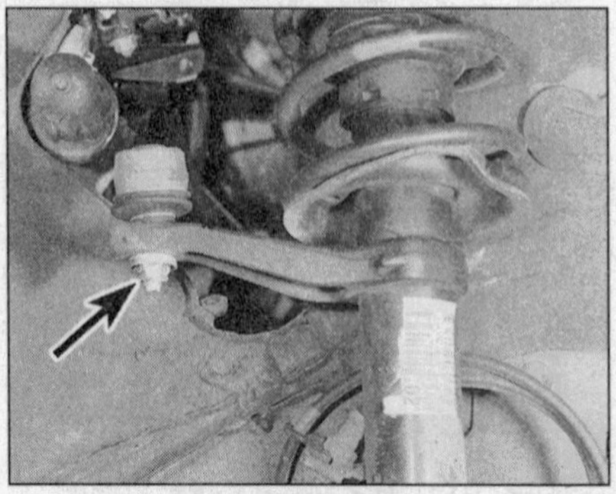

3.9 Track-rod end securing nut (arrowed)

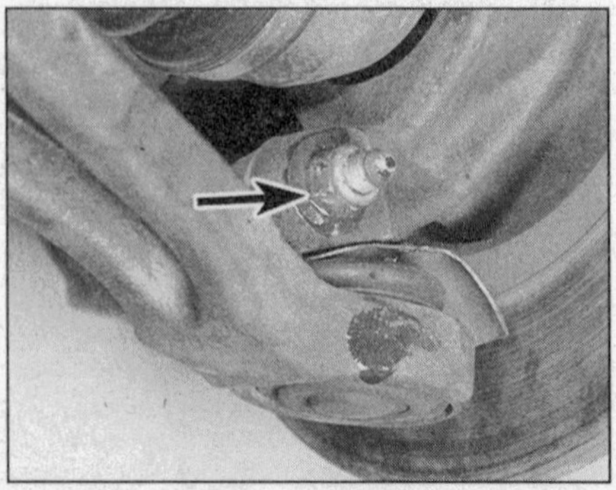

3.10 Hub carrier-to-lower arm clamp bolt (arrowed)

7 On models where the anti-roll bar is connected to the suspension strut body, undo the nut and washer securing the drop link to the strut, and position the link clear of the strut.

8 On models where the anti-roll bar is connected directly to the lower arm, remove the two bolts and washers securing the anti-roll bar end clamp to the lower arm. Remove the clamp and the rubber bush. Disconnecting the anti-roll bar will enable the lower suspension arm to be lowered more easily, but if preferred, the anti-roll bar can be left attached to the lower arm.

9 Unscrew the nut securing the track rod end to the steering arm on the suspension strut, and recover the washer **(see illustration)**. Using a balljoint separator tool, separate the track rod end from the steering arm.

10 Undo the nut and withdraw the hub carrier-to-lower arm clamp bolt, noting which way round it is fitted **(see illustration)**.

11 Using a suitable metal bar, lever the lower arm downwards just enough to release the balljoint from the lower arm. If the balljoint is a tight fit in the hub carrier, use a large flat-bladed screwdriver to carefully open up the clamp a little. Note the location of the protector shield **(see illustration)**.

12 Release the hub from the driveshaft splines by pulling the strut/hub carrier assembly outwards. If necessary, the shaft can be tapped out of the hub using a soft-faced mallet. Support the driveshaft by suspending it from the body using wire or string - do not allow the end of the driveshaft to hang down.

13 Disconnect the earth wire from the top of the strut **(see illustration)**. Ensure that any wires or hoses attached to the strut are released from the clips or brackets, and moved to one side to facilitate strut removal. Note the locations of any clips or brackets.

14 Have an assistant support the strut from under the wheel arch, then slacken and remove the suspension strut upper mounting nuts.

15 Carefully lower the suspension strut, and withdraw it from under the wheel arch **(see illustration)**.

Overhaul

Warning: Before attempting to dismantle the front suspension strut, a suitable tool to hold the coil spring in compression must be obtained. Adjustable coil spring compressors are readily-available, and are recommended for this operation. Any attempt to dismantle the strut without such a tool is likely to result in damage or personal injury.

Note: *A new damper rod nut must be used on reassembly.*

16 With the strut removed from the vehicle as described previously in this Section, clean away all external dirt, then mount the strut upright in a vice.

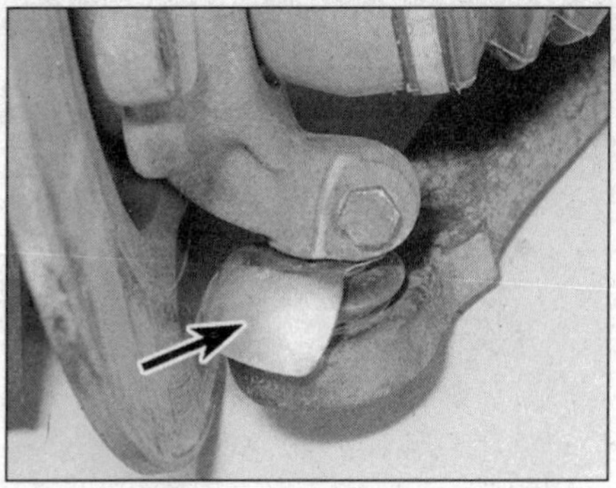

3.11 Balljoint protection shield (arrowed)

17 Fit the spring compressor(s), and compress the coil spring until all tension is relieved from the upper spring seat **(see illustration)**.

18 Hold the strut damper rod using a T40 Torx bit, and unscrew the strut top nut. Discard the nut - a new nut must be used on refitting.

19 Withdraw the upper spring seat and associated components, the spring, complete with the compressor(s), then the rubber gaiter, thrustwasher (where applicable), bump rubber and bump rubber collar. Remove the compressors from the spring.

20 With the strut assembly now dismantled, examine all the components for wear, damage or deformation, and check the upper bearing for smoothness of operation. Renew any of the components as necessary.

21 Examine the strut for signs of fluid leakage. Check the strut piston for signs of pitting along its entire length, and check the strut body for signs of damage. While holding it in an upright position, test the operation of the strut by moving the piston through a full stroke, and then through short strokes of 50 to 100 mm. In both cases, the resistance felt should be smooth and continuous. If the resistance is jerky, or uneven, or if there is any visible sign of wear or damage to the strut, renewal is necessary. The strut damper cartridge can be renewed independently of the strut, but a special tool is required to unscrew the damper nut. This nut is very tight, and it is not possible to safely improvise a suitable tool. Unless the Citroën special tool is available

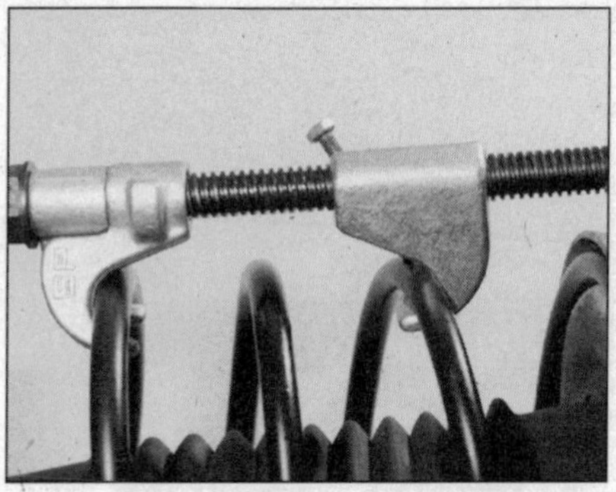

3.17 Coil spring compressors fitted to suspension strut coil spring

3.13 Earth lead connection on the special nut. Also shown are the two top mounting bracket retaining nuts

3.15 Withdrawing the suspension strut

(tool No 4501-T), the strut should be taken to a Citroën dealer for renewal of the damper cartridge.

22 If any doubt exists about the condition of the coil spring, carefully remove the spring compressor, and check the spring for distortion and signs of cracking. Renew the spring if it is damaged or distorted, or if there is any doubt as to its condition.

23 Inspect all other components for signs of damage or deterioration, and renew any that are suspect.

24 To reassemble the strut, follow the accompanying photo sequence, beginning with illustration 3.24a. Be sure to follow each step in sequence, and carefully read the caption underneath each photo **(see illustrations)**. Compress the spring sufficiently

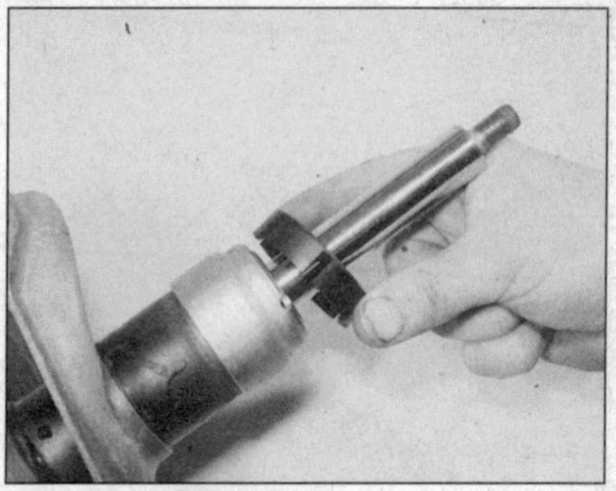

3.24a Fit the bump rubber collar . . .

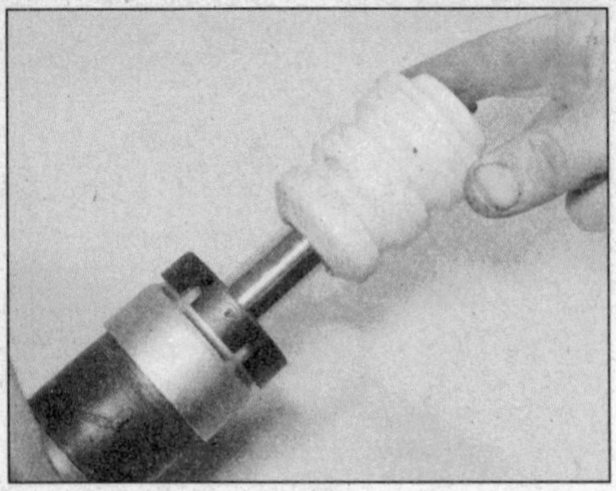

3.24b ... the bump rubber ...

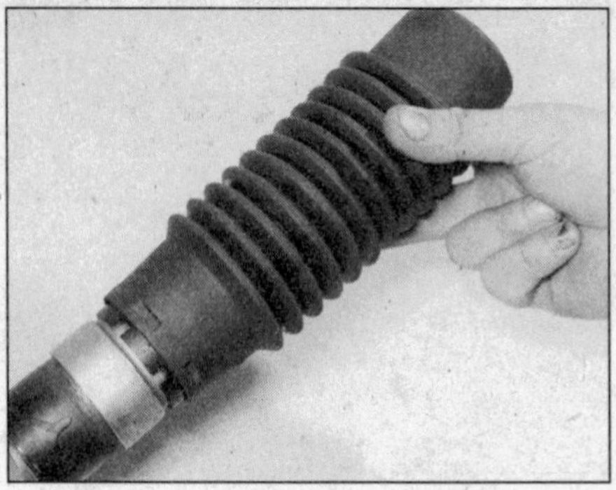

3.24c ... and the rubber gaiter

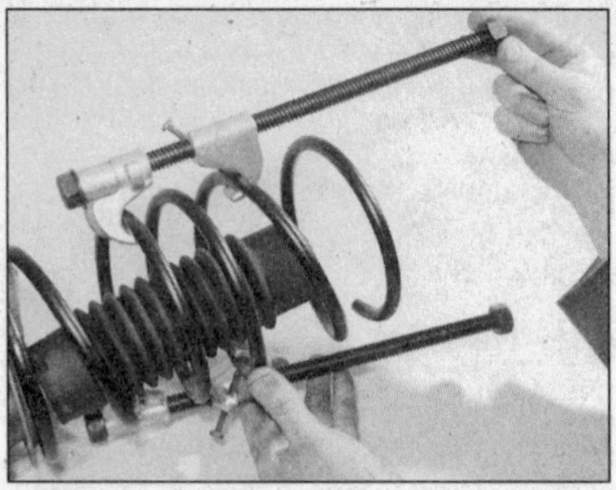

3.24d Slide the spring, complete with compressors, onto the strut ...

3.24e ... ensuring that the end of the spring locates against the stop on the lower seat

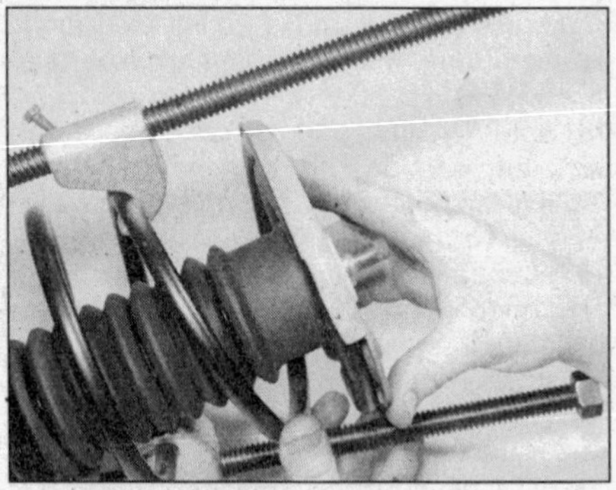

3.24f Fit the upper spring seat ...

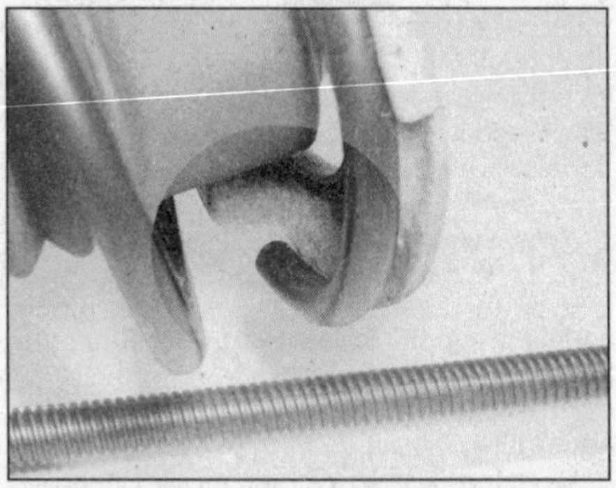

3.24g ... again ensuring that the end of the spring locates against the stop

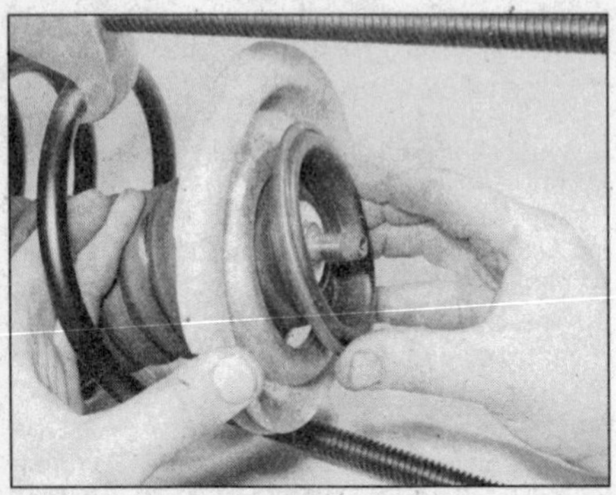

3.24h Fit the spring seat collar ...

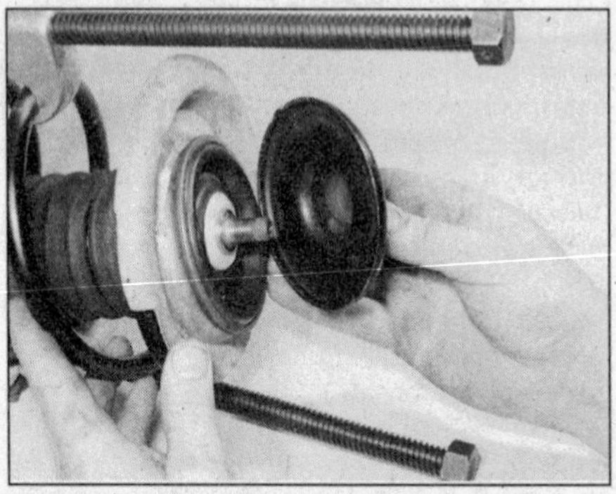

3.24i ... the top mounting lower seat ...

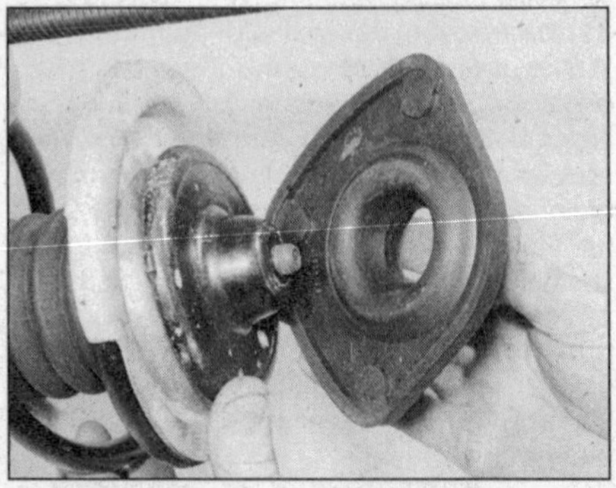

3.24j ... the top mounting plate ...

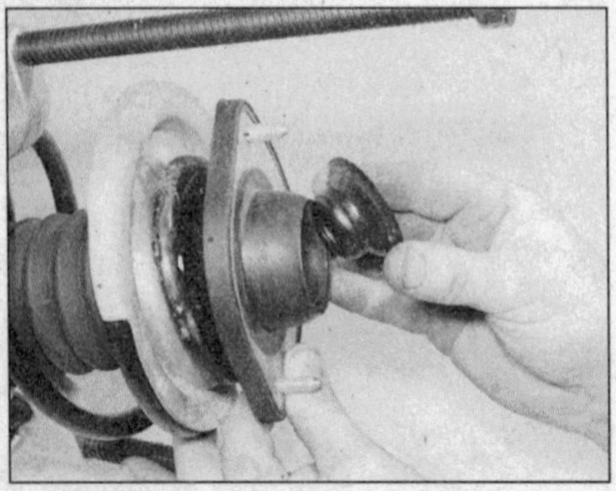

3.24k ... and the top mounting upper seat ...

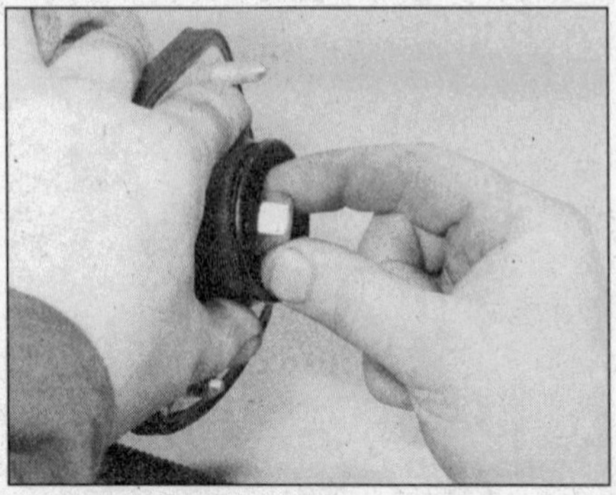

3.24l ... then refit the top nut ...

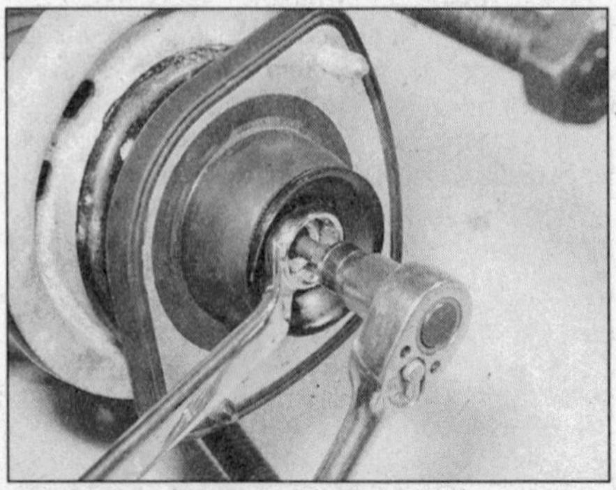

3.24m ... and tighten using a spanner, whilst counterholding the piston rod

to allow the top mounting components to be refitted, and if necessary pull on the end of the piston rod to extend the damper.

Refitting

25 Manoeuvre the strut assembly into position under the wheel arch, passing the mounting studs through the holes in the body turret, then refit the upper mounting nuts, and tighten them to the specified torque. Reconnect the earth wire to the top of the strut on early models.

26 Ensure that the driveshaft splines and the corresponding splines in the hub are clean, then engage the driveshaft with the hub, and fit a new driveshaft nut. Do not tighten the nut at this stage.

27 Ensure that the protector shield is in place over the lower arm balljoint, then engage the balljoint with the hub carrier. If necessary, lever the arm downwards just enough to engage the balljoint, as during removal. Similarly, use a screwdriver to open up the clamp a little if necessary.

28 Fit the hub carrier-to-lower arm clamp bolt, from the front of the strut, and a new nut, and tighten to the specified torque.

29 Reconnect the track rod end to the steering arm, and refit the washer and a new nut. Tighten the nut to the specified torque.

30 Reconnect the anti-roll bar to the lower arm (where disconnected), or the anti-roll bar drop link to the strut, as applicable. Ensure that the washers are in place, then tighten the fixings to the specified torque.

31 Refit the brake caliper to the hub carrier. Where applicable, ensure that the mounting plate is correctly orientated as noted before removal, and tighten the securing bolts to the specified torque. Where applicable, refit the brake pads as described in Chapter 9.

32 Refit the bolt securing the brake pad wear sensor earth lead to the hub carrier.

33 Where applicable, refit any wires and/or hoses to the clips or brackets on the strut.

34 Grease the driveshaft nut contact face of the hub bearing, and the threads of the driveshaft nut, then hold the hub stationary as during removal, and tighten the new driveshaft nut to the specified torque. Stake the nut in position.

35 Where applicable, refit the ABS wheel sensor.

36 Refit the roadwheel, and lower the vehicle to the ground.

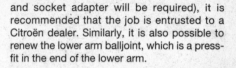

4 Front suspension lower arm - removal, overhaul and refitting

Note: *A new hub carrier-to-lower arm balljoint clamp nut must be used on refitting.*

Removal

1 Chock the rear wheels, firmly apply the handbrake, then jack up the front of the vehicle and support on axle stands (see *"Jacking, towing and wheel changing"*). Remove the appropriate front roadwheel.

2 On models where the anti-roll bar is mounted onto the suspension lower arm, remove the two bolts and washers securing the anti-roll bar end clamp to the lower arm. Remove the clamp and the rubber bush.

3 Undo the nut and withdraw the hub carrier-to-lower arm clamp bolt, noting which way round it is fitted.

4 Using a suitable metal bar, lever the lower arm downwards just enough to release the balljoint from the lower arm. If the balljoint is a tight fit in the hub carrier, use a large flat-bladed screwdriver to carefully open up the clamp a little. Note the location of the protector shield.

5 Working inside the passenger compartment, release the securing clips, and lift the carpet and sound insulation panels for access to the two lower arm rear bracket securing nuts **(see illustrations)**. Unscrew the securing nuts.

6 Working under the vehicle, unscrew the nut and remove the washer, then remove the through-bolt securing the front of the lower arm to the bracket on the body **(see illustration)**.

7 Pull the lower arm down to disengage the rear mounting studs from the holes in the body, and withdraw the lower arm from under the vehicle.

Overhaul

8 It is possible to renew the lower arm pivot bushes, but due to the requirement for Citroën special tools (a suitable press, positioning jig and socket adapter will be required), it is recommended that the job is entrusted to a Citroën dealer. Similarly, it is also possible to renew the lower arm balljoint, which is a press-fit in the end of the lower arm.

Refitting

9 Commence refitting by ensuring that the bushes, the bush contact faces on the body, and the lower arm securing bolt and studs are clean.

10 Place the lower arm in position under the vehicle, then refit the front through-bolt and nut, and tighten to the specified torque.

11 Working inside the passenger compartment, refit the rear bracket securing nuts, and tighten them to the specified torque. Fit the carpet and sound insulation panels back into position.

12 Ensure that the protector shield is in place over the lower arm balljoint, then engage the balljoint with the hub carrier. If necessary, lever the arm downwards just enough to engage the balljoint, as during removal. Similarly, use a screwdriver to open up the clamp a little if necessary.

13 Fit the hub carrier-to-lower arm clamp bolt (from the front of the strut), and a new nut, and tighten to the specified torque.

14 Where applicable, refit the anti-roll bar end clamp and bush. Position the end of the anti-roll bar on the lower arm, and refit the securing bolts and washers. Tighten the bolts to the specified torque.

15 Refit the roadwheel, and lower the vehicle to the ground.

16 If the driver' s side lower arm has been removed, ensure that the sound insulation and carpet panels have been correctly refitted so that the throttle pedal operates correctly.

5 Front suspension anti-roll bar (and drop link) - removal and refitting

Anti-roll bar

Note: *On GTi models where the anti-roll bar is connected to the suspension struts by drop links, new drop link-to-anti-roll bar nuts must be used on refitting.*

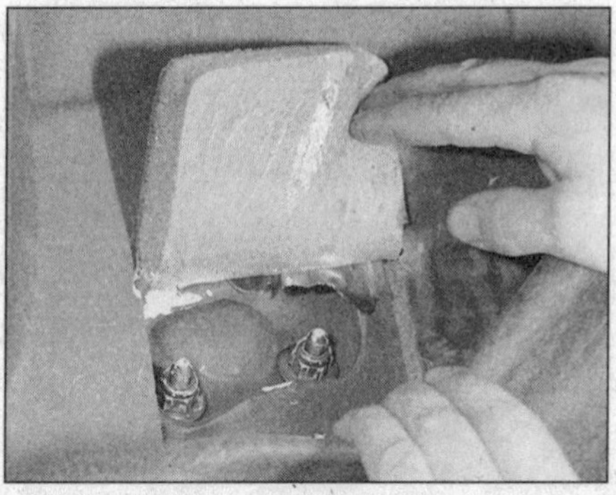

4.5a Fold back the carpet insulation for access to the nuts . . .

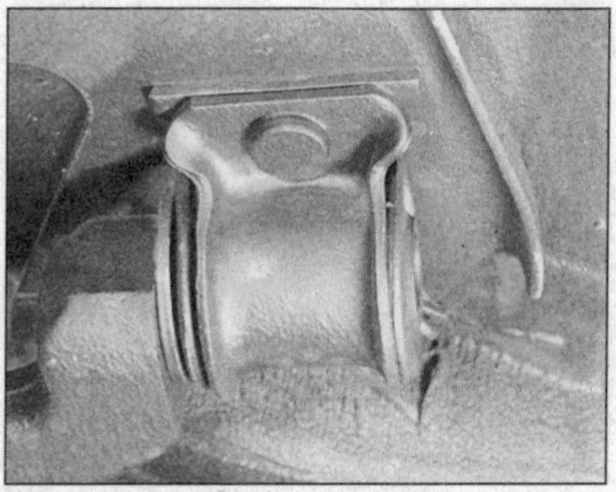

4.5b . . . that secure the suspension arm rear mounting

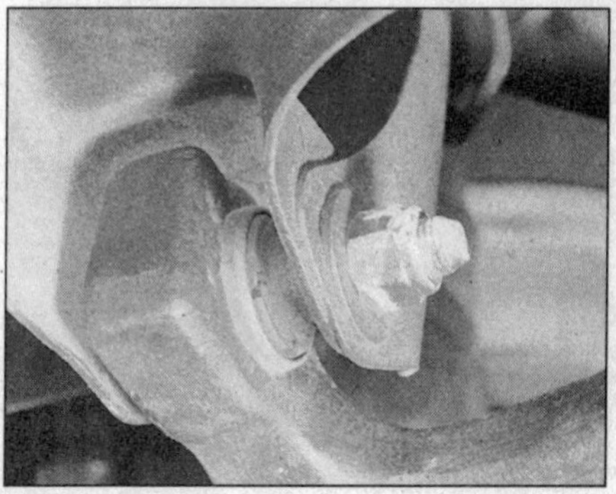

4.6 Suspension lower arm front mounting

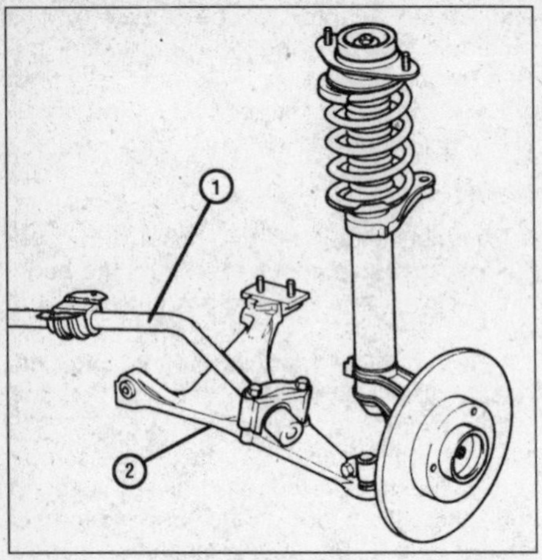

5.2 Front suspension layout for model with anti-roll bar mounted directly on lower arms

1 Anti-roll bar 2 Lower arm

Removal

1 Chock the rear wheels, firmly apply the handbrake, then jack up the front of the vehicle and support on axle stands (see *"Jacking, towing and wheel changing"*). Remove both front roadwheels.

2 On models where the anti-roll bar is mounted onto the lower arms, working at each end of the anti-roll bar, remove the bolts and washers securing the anti-roll bar end clamps to the lower arms. Remove the clamps and the rubber bushes **(see illustration)**.

3 On GTi models where the anti-roll bar has drop links connecting the ends of the bar to the suspension struts, remove the nuts securing the lower ends of the drop links to the anti-roll bar **(see illustration)**.

4 Remove the bolts securing the anti-roll bar mounting clamps to the body. Withdraw the clamps.

5 Manipulate the anti-roll bar out from under the vehicle.

Refitting

6 Examine the condition of the anti-roll bar mounting bushes, and renew if necessary. The anti-roll bar-to-body clamp bushes can be renewed by sliding the old bushes from the bar, and sliding the new bushes into position. (On GTi models, the bushes are split, and can therefore be prised directly from the anti-roll bar.) Before removing the old bushes, mark their fitted position on the bar, so that the new bushes can be fitted in the same position.

7 Manipulate the bar into position under the vehicle, then refit the mounting clamps. Fit the mounting clamp securing bolts, but do not fully tighten them at this stage.

8 On GTi models where the anti-roll bar is connected to the suspension struts by drop links, reconnect the drop links to the ends of the bar, and fit new securing nuts. Tighten the nuts to the specified torque.

9 On models where the anti-roll bar is mounted onto the lower arms, refit the rubber

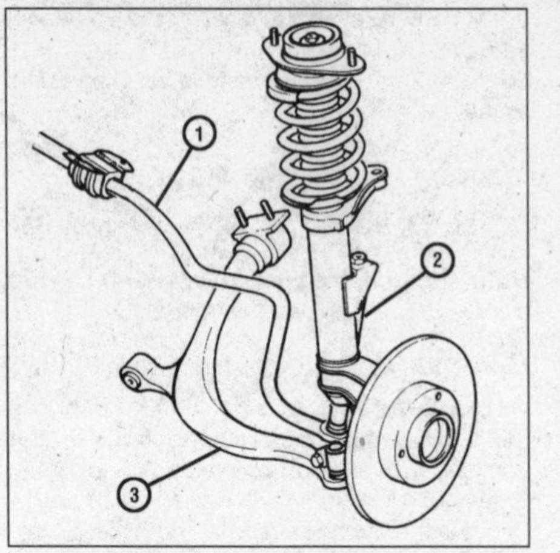

5.3 Front suspension layout for model with anti-roll bar incorporating drop links

1 Anti-roll bar
2 Drop link (to rear of suspension strut)
3 Lower arm

bushes and the clamps, then refit the washers and the bolts. Tighten the bolts to the specified torque.

10 Finally, tighten the anti-roll bar clamp-to-body bolts to the specified torque.

11 Refit the roadwheels, and lower the vehicle to the ground.

Drop link (GTi models)

Note: *New drop link securing nuts must be used on refitting.*

Removal

12 Chock the rear wheels, firmly apply the handbrake, then jack up the front of the vehicle and support on axle stands (see *"Jacking, towing and wheel changing"*). Remove the relevant front roadwheel.

13 Unscrew the nut securing the lower end of the drop link to the end of the anti-roll bar.

14 If necessary, using a suitable metal bar, carefully lever the end of the anti-roll bar down, to separate it from the end of the drop link.

15 Unscrew the nut securing the drop link to the suspension strut, and remove the drop link from the vehicle.

Refitting

16 Check the drop link balljoints for excessive wear, and check the condition of the balljoint rubber gaiters. If the balljoints or gaiters are worn or damaged, the complete drop link must be renewed, as the components cannot be renewed individually. Note that wear in the drop links is often indicated by a "clonking" noise produced when driving over bumps or cornering.

17 Refitting is a reversal of removal, but use new securing nuts.

6 Rear hub assembly - removal and refitting

The rear hub is integral with the brake drum. Refer to Chapter 9 for details of brake drum removal and refitting.

7 Rear hub bearings - renewal

1 Remove the rear brake drum as described in Chapter 9.

2 Using circlip pliers, extract the bearing retaining circlip from the centre of the brake drum **(see illustration)**.

3 Prise the oil seal thrust cup from the rear of the hub **(see illustration)**.

4 Securely support the drum hub, then press or drive the bearing out of position, using a tubular drift which bears on the bearing inner race.

TOOL TiP

Alternatively, the bearing can be removed using an improvised tool made up from a suitable socket or tube, washers, nut, and a suitable long bolt or threaded rod.

7.2 Extracting the rear wheel bearing circlip

7.3 Prising the oil seal thrust cup from the hub

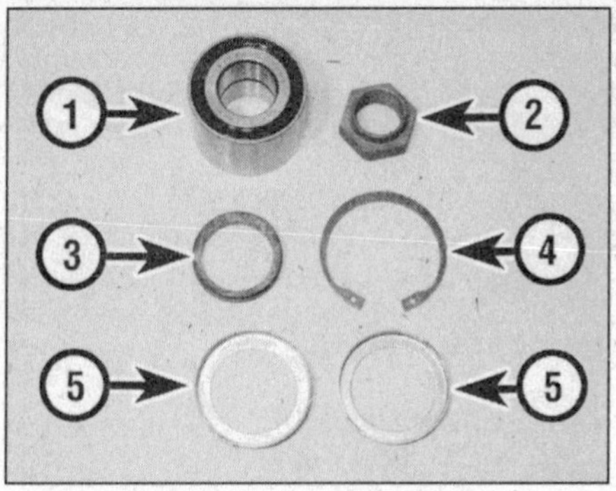

7.5 Rear hub bearing kit
1 Bearing 2 Hub nut 3 Oil seal 4 Circlip
5 Oil seal spacer and hub bearing thrust cup

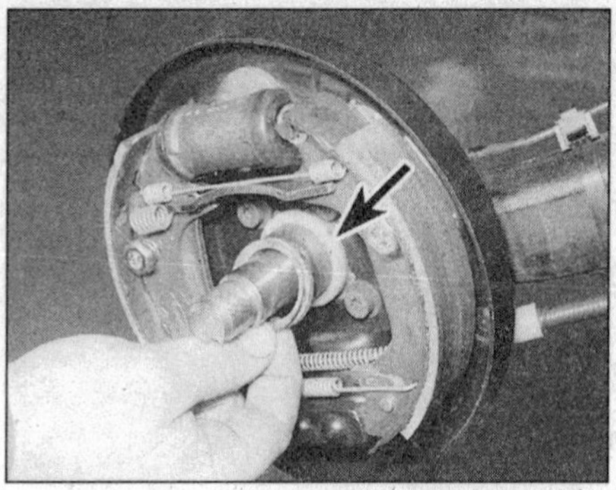

7.6 Fitting a new oil seal to the stub axle. Note spacer (arrowed)

7.9a Locate the bearing in the hub . . .

7.9b . . . then draw the bearing into position

7.11a Fit the new oil seal thrust cup . . .

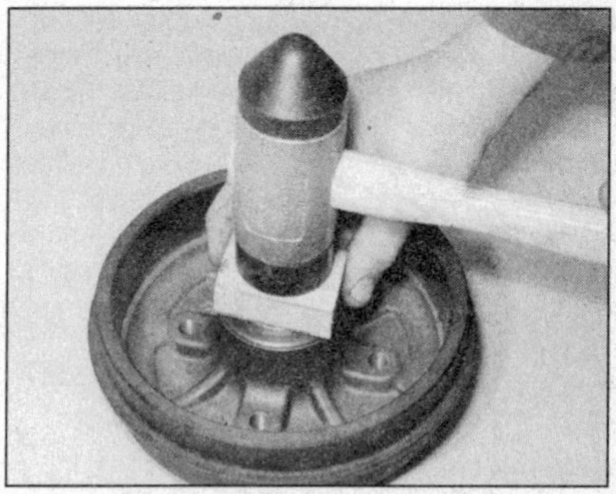

7.11b . . . and tap it into position

5 Thoroughly clean the hub, removing all traces of dirt and grease, and polish away any burrs or raised edges which might hinder reassembly. Check the hub for cracks or any other signs of wear or damage, and renew them if necessary. The bearing and its circlip must be renewed whenever they are disturbed. Obtain a new bearing kit from a Citroën dealer **(see illustration)**.

6 Carefully prise the oil seal from the stub axle, and fit the new seal supplied in the bearing kit. Note the spacer fitted behind the oil seal **(see illustration)**.

7 Examine the stub axle shaft for signs of wear or damage. The shaft is an integral part of the trailing arm, and if worn or damaged, the complete trailing arm must be renewed. Refer to Section 9 for further details.

8 On reassembly, apply a light film of clean engine oil to the bearing outer race, to aid installation of the bearing.

9 Securely support the drum, and locate the bearing in the hub. Press the bearing fully into position, ensuring that it enters the hub squarely, using a tubular spacer which bears only on the bearing outer race. Alternatively, the bearing can be drawn into position with the improvised tool used previously, but note that a different socket or tube will be required, to bear on the bearing outer race **(see illustrations)**.

10 Ensure that the bearing is correctly seated against the hub shoulder, and secure it in position with the new circlip. Ensure that the circlip is correctly seated in its hub groove.

11 Tap the new oil seal thrust cup into position in the rear of the hub, taking care not to damage the oil seal seating surface **(see illustrations)**.

12 Refit the brake drum as described in Chapter 9.

8 Rear shock absorber - removal, testing and refitting

Removal

1 Chock the front wheels, then jack up the rear of the vehicle and support it on axle stands (see *"Jacking, towing and wheel changing"*). Remove the relevant rear roadwheel.

2 Using a trolley jack, raise the trailing arm until the shock absorber is slightly compressed.

3 Slacken and remove the nuts from both the upper and lower shock absorber mounting bolts. Access to the right-hand rear shock absorber can be improved by removing the spare wheel from its cage.

4 Withdraw the mounting bolts, noting which way around they are fitted, and manoeuvre the shock absorber out from underneath the vehicle **(see illustrations)**.

Testing

5 Examine the shock absorber for signs of fluid leakage or damage. Test the operation of the shock absorber, while holding it in an

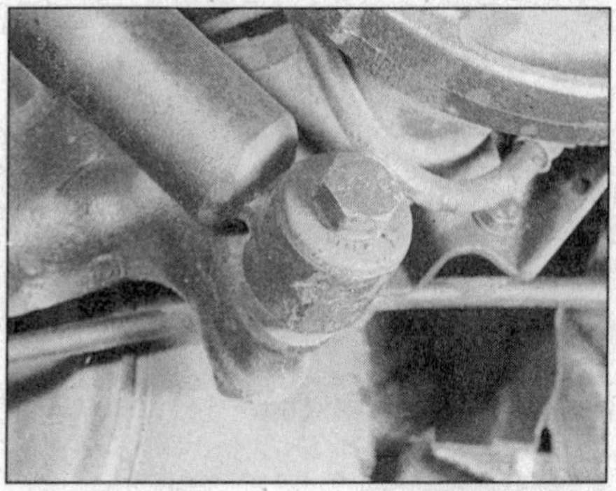

8.4a Rear shock absorber lower mounting bolt

8.4b Rear shock absorber upper mounting bolt

10.2 Steering wheel nut and washer removal

11.5 Ignition switch/steering column lock retaining screw (arrowed)

11.7 Ignition switch/steering column lock retaining lug location (arrowed)

upright position, by moving the piston through a full stroke and then through short strokes of 50 to 100 mm. In both cases, the resistance felt should be smooth and continuous. If the resistance is jerky, or uneven, or if there is any visible sign of wear or damage, renewal is necessary. Also check the rubber mounting bushes for damage and deterioration. Renew the complete unit if any damage or excessive wear is evident; the mounting bushes are not available separately. Inspect the shanks of the mounting bolts for signs of wear or damage, and renew as necessary.

Refitting

6 Prior to refitting the shock absorber, mount it upright in the vice, and operate it fully through several strokes in order to prime it. Apply a smear of multi-purpose grease to both the shock absorber mounting bolts.

7 Manoeuvre the shock absorber into position, and insert the mounting bolts. Ensure that the upper bolt is inserted from the outside of the trailing arm, and the lower bolt from the inside.

8 Refit the nuts, tightening them by hand only at this stage.

9 Refit the roadwheel, then lower the vehicle to the ground and tighten the roadwheel bolts to the specified torque.

10 With the vehicle standing on its wheels, rock the vehicle to settle the shock absorber in position, then tighten both the upper and lower mountings to the specified torque setting.

9 Rear suspension assembly - general

The operations in the following list can only be carried out using suitable special tools. Due to the difficulty in improvising such tools easily, these procedures are considered to be beyond the scope of the home mechanic, and should be referred to a Citroën dealer:

a) Removal and refitting of torsion bars.
b) Removal and refitting of rear anti-roll bar (where applicable).
c) Removal and refitting of trailing arms.
d) Renewal of suspension bushes and bearings.
e) Adjustment of rear suspension ride height.

10 Steering wheel - removal and refitting

Removal

1 Set the front wheels in the straight-ahead position, and release the steering lock by inserting the ignition key.

2 Carefully ease off the steering wheel centre pad, then slacken and remove the steering wheel retaining nut **(see illustration)**. Recover the washer.

3 Mark the steering wheel and steering column shaft in relation to each other, then lift the steering wheel off the column splines. If it is tight, twist it from side to side whilst pulling upwards to release it from the shaft splines.

Refitting

4 Refitting is a reversal of removal, but align the marks made on removal, and use a new retaining nut tightened to the specified torque. Ensure that the indicator switch is in the central, cancelled position, and make sure that the lug on the steering wheel engages with the switch lever. If necessary, the position of the steering wheel on the column shaft can be altered in order to centralise the wheel (ensure that the front roadwheels are pointing in the straight-ahead position), by moving the wheel the required number of splines on the shaft.

11 Ignition switch/steering column lock - removal and refitting

Removal

1 Disconnect the battery negative lead.

2 Remove the steering wheel as described in Section 10.

3 Remove the securing screws, then unclip and lift off the upper shroud, followed by the lower shroud. Note that the lower shroud clips over a metal bracket on the steering column, and the shroud must be slid from the bracket before it can be removed.

4 Unclip the ignition switch wiring connectors from the steering column bracket or the facia, as applicable. Note the location of the connectors, so that they can be refitted in their original positions. Separate the two halves of each connector.

5 Unscrew the lock retaining screw, and recover the washer from the side of the lock **(see illustration)**.

6 Insert the key, and turn it to the mark positioned between the "A" and "S" marks on the barrel.

7 Using a small flat-bladed screwdriver, depress the lock retaining lug **(see illustration)**, then withdraw the lock assembly from the steering column. As the wiring is being removed, the lock surround can be removed from the column.

Refitting

8 Refitting is a reversal of the removal procedure. Ensure that the lock assembly is securely held in position by its retaining lug. Before refitting the steering column shrouds, remove the ignition key, and check that the steering lock functions correctly.

12 Steering column - removal, inspection and refitting

Note: *A new steering column lower clamp bolt and nut must be used when refitting.*

Removal

1 Disconnect the battery negative lead.

2 Remove the steering wheel as described in Section 10 **(see illustration)**.

3 Unscrew the retaining screws, and remove the upper and lower steering column shrouds **(see illustration)**.

4 Where applicable, detach and remove the parcel shelf from under the facia on the driver's side.

5 Unclip and remove the insulation panel from the underside of the facia and steering column.

6 Mark the column lower universal joint in relation to the column shaft, then unscrew and remove the clamp bolt and nut **(see illustration)**. Where applicable, also remove the clip. Discard the clamp bolt and nut - new ones must be used when refitting.

7 Unscrew and remove the column upper

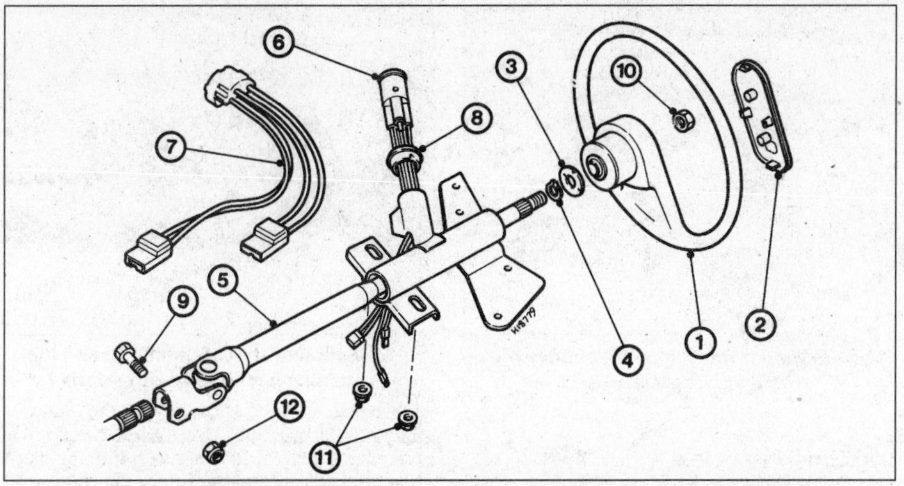

12.2 Steering column and associated fittings (early model shown)

1 *Steering wheel*
2 *Centre pad*
3 *Washer*
4 *Stop-ring*
5 *Column*
6 *Steering lock/ignition switch*
7 *Wiring harness*
8 *Gasket*
9 *Bolt*
10 *Self-locking nut*
11 *Mounting nuts (bolts on later models)*
12 *Self-locking nut*

mounting nuts (bolts on later models), then lower the column from the mounting **(see illustration)**.

8 Detach the wiring connectors from the column switches and ignition switch, then pull the column upwards and disengage the universal joint coupling from the steering gear pinion splines. Remove the column.

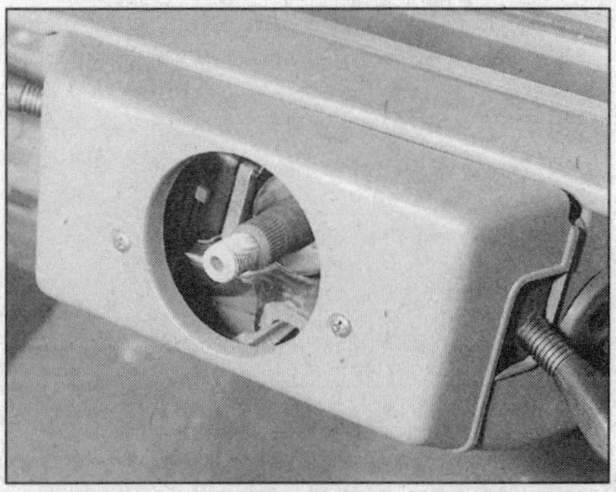

12.3 Upper steering column shroud and retaining screws

Inspection

9 Check the steering shaft for signs of free play in the column bushes, and check the universal joints for signs of damage or roughness in the joint bearings. If any damage or wear is found on the steering column universal joints or shaft bushes, the column must be renewed as an assembly.

Refitting

10 Locate the column universal joint on the steering gear pinion splines, making sure that the previously-made marks are correctly aligned. Insert the clamp bolt, but do not tighten it at this stage.

11 Refit and tighten the upper mounting nuts/bolts to the specified torque.

12 Fit the new lower clamp bolt and nut, and tighten to the specified torque. Refit the clip, where applicable.

13 Reconnect the wiring to the ignition switch and column switches.

14 Where applicable, refit the parcel shelf under the facia.

15 Refit the upper and lower steering column shrouds.

16 Refit the steering wheel as described in Section 10.

17 Reconnect the battery negative lead.

13 Steering gear assembly - removal, overhaul and refitting

Note: *A new steering column lower clamp bolt and nut must be used when refitting.*

Removal

1 Set the front wheels in the straight-ahead position, and ensure that the steering lock is engaged by removing the ignition key.

2 Chock the rear wheels, firmly apply the handbrake, then jack up the front of the vehicle and support on axle stands (see *"Jacking, towing and wheel changing"*). Remove both front roadwheels.

3 Working inside the car, remove the parcel shelf (where applicable) and the lower facia trim on the steering column side.

4 Mark the column lower universal joint in relation to the column shaft, then unscrew and remove the clamp bolt and nut. Where applicable, also remove the clip. Discard the clamp bolt and nut - new ones must be used when refitting.

5 Working on each side of the vehicle in turn, unscrew the nut securing the track rod end to the steering arm on the suspension strut. Using a balljoint separator tool, separate the track rod ends from the steering arms.

6 Remove the air cleaner assembly as described in Chapter 4.

7 Where applicable, unclip and remove the side access panels from under the front wheel arches for improved access.

8 On models manufactured from July 1991 onwards, remove the clutch cable (if necessary) as described in Chapter 6.

9 Unscrew and remove the three mounting bolts, and withdraw the steering gear from the bulkhead location dowels **(see illustration)**. Remove the unit from the side aperture under the right-hand wheel arch; the steering gear is removed complete with the track rod ends.

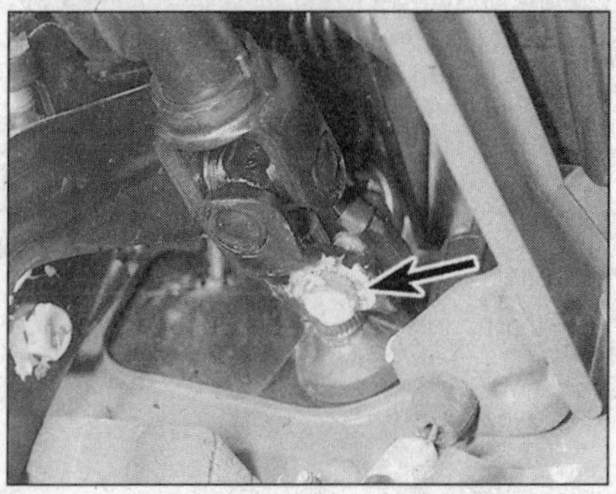

12.6 Steering column lower universal joint showing clamp bolt (arrowed)

12.7 Steering column upper mounting nuts (arrowed)

Note: *Later models have mounting bolts instead of nuts*

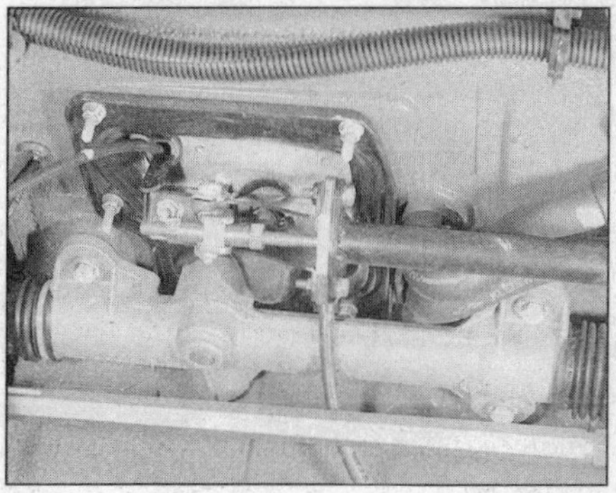

13.9 Steering gear and mounting points on the bulkhead

10

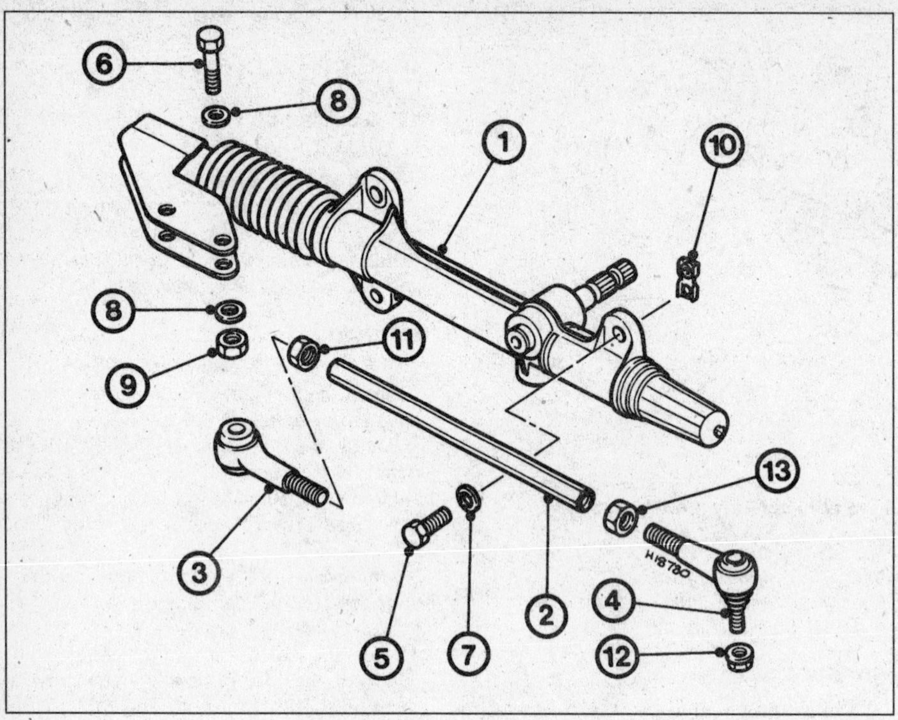

13.10 Steering gear and associated fittings

1 Steering gear unit
2 Track rod
3 End piece (inner)
4 Track-rod end balljoint
5 Mounting bolt
6 Bolt
7 Washer
8 Washer
9 Self-locking nut
10 Caged nut
11 Nut
12 Self-locking nut
13 Nut

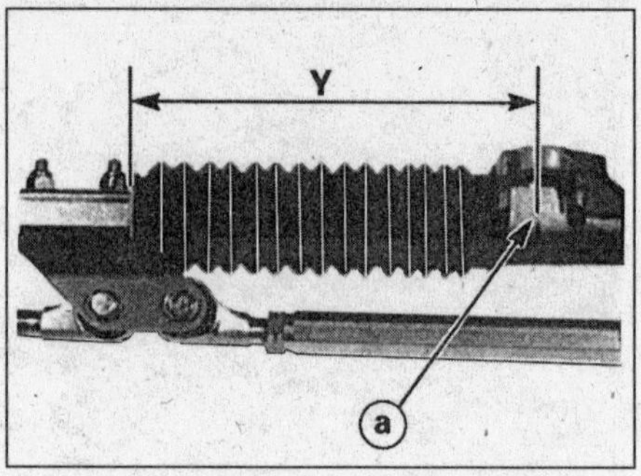

13.11 Steering gear fully-extended dimension (Y)

a Mark on the steering gear mounting

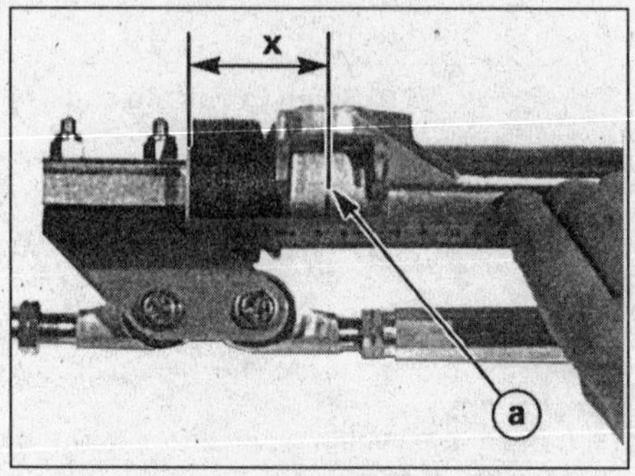

13.12 Steering gear fully-retracted dimension (X)

a Mark on the steering gear mounting

Overhaul

10 Examine the steering gear assembly for signs of wear or damage **(see illustration)**. Check that the rack moves freely throughout the full length of its travel, with no signs of roughness or excessive free play between the steering gear pinion and rack. It is possible to overhaul the steering gear assembly housing components, but this task should be entrusted to a Citroën dealer. The only components which can be renewed easily by the home mechanic are the steering gear rubber gaiters, the track rod balljoints and the track rods. These procedures are covered in Sections 14, 15 and 16 respectively.

Refitting

11 Before refitting the steering gear, the rack must be centralised as follows. Make a mark on the rack housing, corresponding with the centre-line of the steering gear securing bolt hole nearest the steering gear rubber gaiter. Move the rack to its full extent of movement, so that the steering gear rubber gaiter is fully extended. Measure the distance from the mark made on the rack housing to the end of the steering gear rubber gaiter nearest the track rod sleeve **(see illustration)**. Call this dimension "Y".

12 Move the rack fully in the opposite direction, until the rubber gaiter is fully compressed. Again, measure the distance from the mark made on the rack housing to the end of the steering gear rubber gaiter nearest the track rod sleeve **(see illustration)**. Call this dimension "X".

13 In order that the rack is centralised when fitted, now work out the mid-point between the two measurements "X" and "Y". Call this dimension "Z". Dimension "Z" can be calculated as follows:

a) Subtract "X" from "Y", and divide the result by 2.
b) Add "X" to the result of the previous calculation to give dimension "Z". ie: $Z = (Y - X)/2 + X$

14 Set the steering gear to dimension "X", then proceed with the refitting procedure as follows, ensuring that the rack position is not altered during the refitting procedure.

15 Check the condition of the pinion shaft seal located in the engine compartment bulkhead. Ensure that the seal is correctly located, and renew the seal if there are any signs of damage or wear.

16 Offer the steering gear into position through the right-hand wheel arch. Check the routing of the clutch cable, to make sure that the cable is not trapped.

17 Engage the steering gear pinion with the lower universal joint on the column, making sure that the previously-made marks are aligned. Locate the steering gear on the bulkhead, ensuring that the dowels on the bulkhead engage with the corresponding holes in the steering gear.

18 Fit the steering gear mounting bolts, and tighten them to the specified torque.

19 Reconnect the track rods to the steering arms, then tighten the nuts to the specified torque.

20 Where applicable, refit the clip, then fit a new lower column pinch-bolt and nut, and tighten to the specified torque.

21 Where necessary, refit the clutch cable with reference to Chapter 6.

22 Refit the air cleaner with reference to Chapter 4.

23 Refit the lower parcel shelf (where applicable) and the lower facia trim.

24 Refit the roadwheels, and lower the vehicle to the ground.

25 Have the front wheel alignment checked at the earliest opportunity (refer to Section 17 for details), and check that the steering wheel is centralised. If necessary, the steering wheel position can be altered by removing the wheel and moving it the required number of splines on the column shaft before refitting - see Section 10.

14 Steering gear rubber gaiter - renewal

1 On Diesel engine models, to improve access, remove the inlet manifold as described in Chapter 4D.

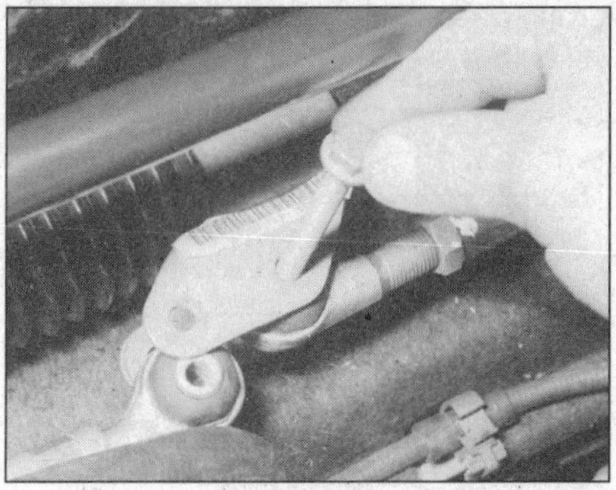

14.2 Remove the track-rod securing bolts

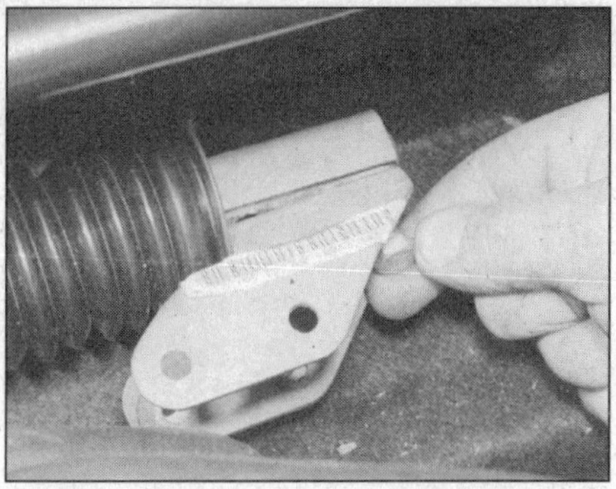

14.3a Unscrew the securing bolts . . .

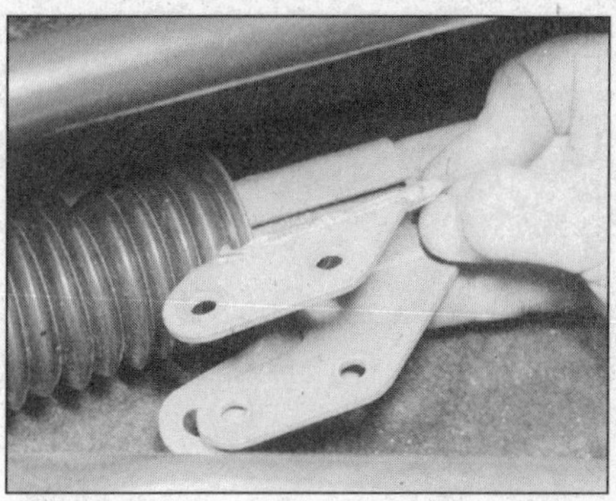

14.3b . . . and remove the upper . . .

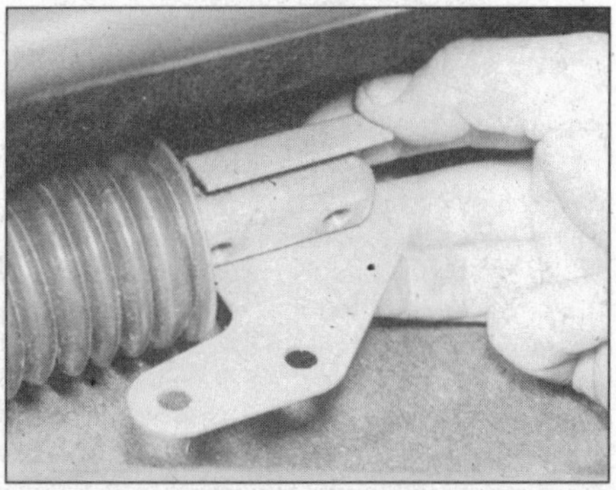

14.3c . . . and lower sections of the track-rod yoke

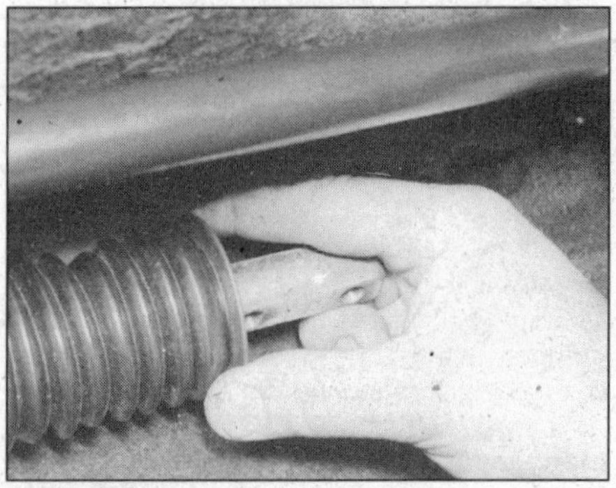

14.4 Slide the gaiter from the steering gear

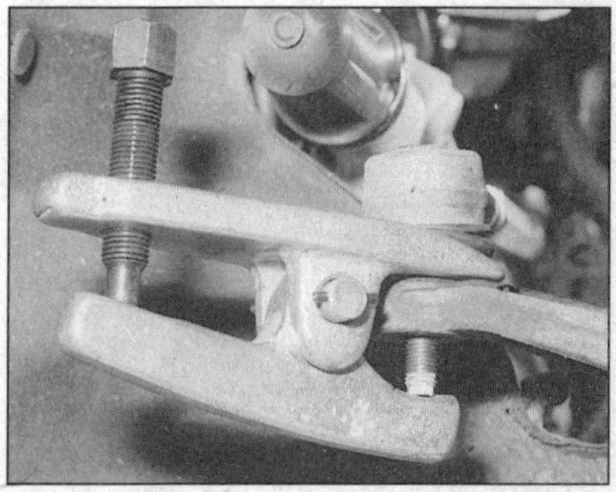

15.4 Track-rod end balljoint and separator tool

2 Unscrew the securing bolts (while counterholding the nuts), and disconnect the inner ends of the track-rods from the yoke on the steering gear **(see illustration)**.

3 Unscrew the two securing bolts, and remove the upper and lower sections of the track-rod yoke **(see illustrations)**.

4 Release the securing clip from the pinion end of the gaiter, then slide the gaiter from the steering gear **(see illustration)**.

5 Fit the new gaiter using a reversal of the removal procedure, but tighten all fixings to the specified torque, and where applicable, refit the inlet manifold as described in Chapter 4D.

15 Track rod end balljoint - removal and refitting

Removal

1 Chock the rear wheels, firmly apply the handbrake, then jack up the front of the vehicle and support on axle stands (see *"Jacking, towing and wheel changing"*). Remove the relevant front roadwheel.

2 Using a straight-edge and a scriber, or similar, mark the relationship of the track rod end balljoint to the track rod. This is not strictly necessary if the track rod end is being renewed, but the mark can be transferred to the new unit to ensure that it is fitted in the correct position.

3 Hold the track rod, and loosen the track rod end locknut by a quarter of a turn. Do not move the locknut from this position, as it will serve as a handy reference mark on refitting.

4 Unscrew the nut securing the track rod end to the steering arm on the suspension strut. Using a balljoint separator tool, separate the track rod end from the steering arm **(see illustration)**. To prevent any possible damage to the threaded shank of the balljoint, leave the nut in position until the shank is released.

5 Counting the **exact** number of turns necessary to do so, unscrew the track rod end balljoint from the track rod.

Refitting

6 If a new track rod end is being fitted, locate the locknut in the same position as noted on the old track rod end (ie with the same number of threads from the locknut to the end of the track rod end). Transfer the alignment mark from the old rod to the new one, if required.

7 Screw the track rod end into the track rod the same number of turns as noted during removal.

8 Clean the taper surfaces, then fit the track rod end to the steering arm on the suspension strut, and tighten the nut to the specified torque.

9 Hold the track rod, then tighten the locknut. Make sure that the previously-made alignment marks are lined up.

10 Refit the roadwheel, and lower the car to the ground.

11 Have the front wheel alignment checked at the earliest opportunity.

16 Track rod - removal and refitting

Removal

1 Chock the rear wheels, firmly apply the handbrake, then jack up the front of the vehicle and support on axle stands (see *"Jacking, towing and wheel changing"*). Remove the relevant front roadwheel.

2 Unscrew the nut securing the track rod end to the steering arm on the suspension strut. Using a balljoint separator tool, separate the track rod end from the steering arm.

3 If the track rod end is also being removed, follow the procedures given in Section 15 first.

4 Unscrew the nut, and withdraw the retaining bolt from the yoke on the steering gear **(see illustration)**. Recover the washers and remove the track rod.

5 If required, the inner track rod end can be removed from the rod by loosening off the locknut and unscrewing it. Note its **exact** position before unscrewing it, using the procedure described for the outer track rod end (Section 15).

Refitting

6 Refitting is a reversal of removal, bearing in mind the following points:

a) Tighten all fixings to the specified torques.

b) On completion, have the front wheel alignment checked at the earliest opportunity.

16.4 Track-rod inner end connections to the yoke on the steering gear

17 Wheel alignment and steering angles - general information

Definitions

1 A vehicle's steering and suspension geometry is defined in four basic settings - all angles are expressed in degrees (toe settings are also expressed as a measurement); the steering axis is defined as an imaginary line drawn through the axis of the suspension strut, extended where necessary to contact the ground **(see illustration)**.

2 Camber is the angle between each roadwheel and a vertical line drawn through its centre and tyre contact patch, when viewed from the front or rear of the car. "Positive" camber is when the roadwheels are tilted outwards from the vertical at the top; "negative" camber is when they are tilted inwards.

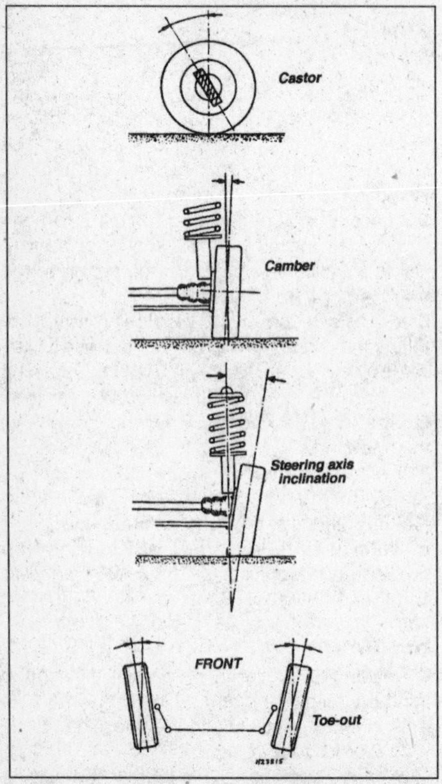

17.1 Wheel alignment and steering angle measurements

3 Camber is not adjustable, and is given for reference only; while it can be checked using a camber checking gauge, if the figure obtained is significantly different from that specified, the vehicle must be taken for careful checking by a professional, as the fault can only be caused by wear or damage to the body or suspension components.

4 Castor is the angle between the steering axis and a vertical line drawn through each roadwheel centre and tyre contact patch, when viewed from the side of the car. "Positive" castor is when the steering axis is tilted so that it contacts the ground ahead of the vertical; "negative" castor is when it contacts the ground behind the vertical.

5 Castor is not adjustable, and is given for reference only; while it can be checked using a castor checking gauge, if the figure obtained is significantly different from that specified, the vehicle must be taken for careful checking by a professional, as the fault can only be caused by wear or damage to the body or suspension components.

6 Steering axis inclination/SAI - also known as **kingpin inclination/KPI** - is the angle between the steering axis and a vertical line drawn through each roadwheel centre and tyre contact patch, when viewed from the front of the car.

7 SAI/KPI is not adjustable, and is given for reference only.

8 Toe is the difference between lines drawn through the roadwheel centres and the car's centre-line. "Toe-in" is when the roadwheels point inwards, towards each other at the front, while "toe-out" is when they splay outwards from each other at the front.

9 The front wheel toe setting is adjusted by screwing the track rods onto or away from the track rod ends, to alter the effective length of the track rod assemblies.

10 Rear wheel toe setting is not adjustable, and is given for reference only. While it can be checked, if the figure obtained is significantly different from that specified, the vehicle must be taken for careful checking by a professional, as the fault can only be caused by wear or damage to the body or suspension components.

Checking - general

11 Due to the special measuring equipment necessary to check the wheel alignment, and the skill required to use it properly, the checking and adjustment of these settings is best left to a Citroën dealer or similar expert. Note that most tyre-fitting shops now possess sophisticated checking equipment.

12 For **accurate** checking, the vehicle **must** be at kerb weight, ie unladen and with a full tank of fuel, and the ride height must be correct (see Section 9).

13 Before starting work, check first that the tyre sizes and types are as specified, then check the tyre pressures and tread wear, the roadwheel run-out, the condition of the hub bearings, and the condition of the front suspension components (Chapter 1). Correct any faults found.

14 Park the vehicle on level ground, check that the front roadwheels are in the straight-ahead position, then rock the rear and front ends to settle the suspension. Release the handbrake, and roll the vehicle backwards approximately 1 metre, then forwards again the same distance, to relieve any stresses in the steering and suspension components.

Toe setting - checking and adjusting

Front wheel toe setting

15 The front wheel toe setting is checked by measuring the distance between the front and rear inside edges of the roadwheel rims. Proprietary toe measurement gauges are available from motor accessory shops.

16 Prepare the vehicle as described in paragraphs 12 to 14 above.

17 Measure the distance between the front edges of the wheel rims and the rear edges of the rims. Subtract the rear measurement from the front measurement for toe-out, or the front measurement from the rear measurement for toe-in, and check that the result is within the specified range.

18 If adjustment is necessary, turn the steering wheel onto full-left lock, and record the number of exposed threads on the right-hand outer track rod end. Now turn the steering onto full-right lock, and record the number of threads on the left-hand side. If there are the same number of threads visible on both sides, then subsequent adjustment should be made equally on both sides. If there are more threads visible on one side than the other, it will be necessary to compensate for this during adjustment. Note this assumes that the inner track rod ends are located at identical positions on the inner ends of the track rods; any deviation will mean a corresponding allowance has to be made on the outer ends of the track rods. **Note:** *It is most important that after adjustment, the length of each track rod (including the ends) is the same of each side.*

19 Loosen the track rod end locknuts (ie the two locknuts on each track rod) and turn the track rods equally. Only turn them a quarter of a turn at a time before rechecking the alignment, and reposition the gaiters so that they are not twisted. Shortening the track rods will reduce toe-in/increase toe-out, and vice versa.

20 When the setting is correct, hold the track rods and securely tighten the locknuts.

Rear wheel toe setting

21 The procedure for checking the rear toe setting is same as described for the front, but the setting is not adjustable. If the figure obtained is significantly different from that specified, the vehicle must be taken for careful checking by a professional, as the fault can only be caused by wear or damage to the body or suspension components.

Chapter 11 Bodywork and fittings

Contents

Degrees of difficulty

Easy, suitable for novice with little experience	**Fairly easy,** suitable for beginner with some experience	**Fairly difficult,** suitable for competent DIY mechanic	**Difficult,** suitable for experienced DIY mechanic	**Very difficult,** suitable for expert DIY or professional

Specifications

Torque wrench settings	**Nm**	**lbf ft**
Seat rail-to-floor securing bolts	25	18
Seat belt mounting bolts	20	15

1 General information

The bodyshell is made of pressed-steel sections, and is available in three- or five-door Hatchback versions. At the time of writing, no specific information was available on Van versions. Most components are welded together, but some use is made of structural adhesives; the front wings are bolted on.

The bonnet, door, and some other vulnerable panels are made of zinc-coated metal, and are further protected by being coated with an anti-chip primer, prior to being sprayed. Side impact bars were introduced in early 1993.

Extensive use is made of plastic materials, mainly in the interior, but also in exterior components. The front and rear bumpers are injection-moulded from a synthetic material which is very strong and yet light. Plastic components such as wheel arch liners are fitted to the underside of the vehicle on later models, to improve the body's resistance to corrosion.

2 Maintenance - bodywork and underframe

The general condition of a vehicle's bodywork is the one thing that significantly affects its value. Maintenance is easy, but needs to be regular. Neglect, particularly after minor damage, can lead quickly to further deterioration and costly repair bills. It is important also to keep watch on those parts of the vehicle not immediately visible, for instance the underside, inside all the wheel arches, and the lower part of the engine compartment.

The basic maintenance routine for the bodywork is washing - preferably with a lot of water, from a hose. This will remove all the loose solids which may have stuck to the vehicle. It is important to flush these off in such a way as to prevent grit from scratching the finish. The wheel arches and underframe need washing in the same way, to remove any accumulated mud, which will retain moisture and tend to encourage rust. Paradoxically enough, the best time to clean the underframe and wheel arches is in wet weather, when the mud is thoroughly wet and soft. In very wet weather, the underframe is usually cleaned of large accumulations automatically, and this is a good time for inspection.

Periodically, except on vehicles with a wax-based underbody protective coating, it is a good idea to have the whole of the underframe of the vehicle steam-cleaned, engine compartment included, so that a thorough inspection can be carried out to see what minor repairs and renovations are necessary. Steam-cleaning is available at many garages, and is necessary for the removal of the accumulation of oily grime, which sometimes is allowed to become thick in certain areas. If steam-cleaning facilities are not available, there are some excellent grease solvents available which can be brush-applied; the dirt can then be simply hosed off. Note that these methods should not be used on vehicles with wax-based underbody protective coating, or the coating will be removed. Such vehicles should be inspected annually, preferably just prior to Winter, when the underbody should be washed down, and any damage to the wax coating repaired. Ideally, a completely fresh coat should be applied. It would also be worth considering the use of such wax-based protection for injection into door panels, sills, box sections, etc, as an additional safeguard against rust damage, where such protection is not provided by the vehicle manufacturer.

After washing paintwork, wipe off with a chamois leather to give an unspotted clear finish. A coat of clear protective wax polish will give added protection against chemical pollutants in the air. If the paintwork sheen has dulled or oxidised, use a cleaner/polisher combination to restore the brilliance of the shine. This requires a little effort, but such dulling is usually caused because regular washing has been neglected. Care needs to be taken with metallic paintwork, as special non-abrasive cleaner/polisher is required to avoid damage to the finish. Always check that the door and ventilator opening drain holes and pipes are completely clear, so that water can be drained out. Brightwork should be treated in the same way as paintwork. Windscreens and windows can be kept clear of the smeary film which often appears, by the use of proprietary glass cleaner. Never use any form of wax or other body or chromium polish on glass.

3 Maintenance - upholstery and carpets

Mats and carpets should be brushed or vacuum-cleaned regularly, to keep them free of grit. If they are badly stained, remove them from the vehicle for scrubbing or sponging, and make quite sure they are dry before refitting. Seats and interior trim panels can be kept clean by wiping with a damp cloth. If they do become stained (which can be more apparent on light-coloured upholstery), use a little liquid detergent and a soft nail brush to scour the grime out of the grain of the material. Do not forget to keep the headlining clean in the same way as the upholstery. When using liquid cleaners inside the vehicle, do not over-wet the surfaces being cleaned. Excessive damp could get into the seams and padded interior, causing stains, offensive odours or even rot. If the inside of the vehicle gets wet accidentally, it is worthwhile taking some trouble to dry it out properly, particularly where carpets are involved. *Do not leave oil or electric heaters inside the vehicle for this purpose.*

4 Minor body damage - repair

Note: *For more detailed information about bodywork repair, Haynes Publishing produce a book by Lindsay Porter called "The Car Bodywork Repair Manual". This incorporates information on such aspects as rust treatment, painting and glass-fibre repairs, as well as details on more ambitious repairs involving welding and panel beating.*

Repairs of minor scratches in bodywork

If the scratch is very superficial, and does not penetrate to the metal of the bodywork, repair is very simple. Lightly rub the area of the scratch with a paintwork renovator, or a very fine cutting paste, to remove loose paint from the scratch, and to clear the surrounding bodywork of wax polish. Rinse the area with clean water.

Apply touch-up paint to the scratch using a fine paint brush; continue to apply fine layers of paint until the surface of the paint in the scratch is level with the surrounding paintwork. Allow the new paint at least two weeks to harden, then blend it into the surrounding paintwork by rubbing the scratch area with a paintwork renovator or a very fine cutting paste. Finally, apply wax polish.

Where the scratch has penetrated right through to the metal of the bodywork, causing the metal to rust, a different repair technique is required. Remove any loose rust from the bottom of the scratch with a penknife, then apply rust-inhibiting paint to prevent the formation of rust in the future. Using a rubber or nylon applicator, fill the scratch with bodystopper paste. If required, this paste can be mixed with cellulose thinners to provide a very thin paste which is ideal for filling narrow scratches. Before the stopper-paste in the scratch hardens, wrap a piece of smooth cotton rag around the top of a finger. Dip the finger in cellulose thinners, and quickly sweep it across the surface of the stopper-paste in the scratch; this will ensure that the surface of the stopper-paste is slightly hollowed. The scratch can now be painted over as described earlier in this Section.

Repairs of dents in bodywork

When deep denting of the vehicle's bodywork has taken place, the first task is to pull the dent out, until the affected bodywork almost attains its original shape. There is little point in trying to restore the original shape completely, as the metal in the damaged area will have stretched on impact, and cannot be reshaped fully to its original contour. It is better to bring the level of the dent up to a point which is about 3 mm below the level of the surrounding bodywork. In cases where the dent is very shallow anyway, it is not worth trying to pull it out at all. If the underside of the dent is accessible, it can be hammered out gently from behind, using a mallet with a wooden or plastic head. Whilst doing this, hold a suitable block of wood firmly against the outside of the panel, to absorb the impact from the hammer blows and thus prevent a large area of the bodywork from being "belled-out".

Should the dent be in a section of the bodywork which has a double skin, or some other factor making it inaccessible, from behind, a different technique is called for. Drill several small holes through the metal inside the area - particularly in the deeper section. Then screw long self-tapping screws into the holes, just sufficiently for them to gain a good purchase in the metal. Now the dent can be pulled out by pulling on the protruding heads of the screws with a pair of pliers.

The next stage of the repair is the removal of the paint from the damaged area, and from an inch or so of the surrounding "sound" bodywork. This is accomplished most easily by using a wire brush or abrasive pad on a power drill, although it can be done just as effectively by hand, using sheets of abrasive paper. To complete the preparation for filling, score the surface of the bare metal with a screwdriver or the tang of a file, or alternatively, drill small holes in the affected area. This will provide a really good "key" for the filler paste.

To complete the repair, see the Section on filling and respraying.

Repairs of rust holes or gashes in bodywork

Remove all paint from the affected area, and from an inch or so of the surrounding "sound" bodywork, using an abrasive pad or a wire brush on a power drill. If these are not available, a few sheets of abrasive paper will do the job most effectively. With the paint removed, you will be able to judge the severity of the corrosion, and therefore decide whether to renew the whole panel (if this is possible) or to repair the affected area. New body panels are not as expensive as most people think, and it is often quicker and more satisfactory to fit a new panel than to attempt to repair large areas of corrosion.

Remove all fittings from the affected area, except those which will act as a guide to the original shape of the damaged bodywork (eg headlight shells etc). Then, using tin snips or a hacksaw blade, remove all loose metal and any other metal badly affected by corrosion. Hammer the edges of the hole inwards, in order to create a slight depression for the filler paste.

Wire-brush the affected area to remove the powdery rust from the surface of the remaining metal. Paint the affected area with rust-inhibiting paint, if the back of the rusted area is accessible, treat this also.

Before filling can take place, it will be necessary to block the hole in some way. This can be achieved by the use of aluminium or plastic mesh, or aluminium tape.

Aluminium or plastic mesh, or glass-fibre matting, is probably the best material to use for a large hole. Cut a piece to the approximate size and shape of the hole to be filled, then position it in the hole so that its edges are below the level of the surrounding bodywork. It can be retained in position by several blobs of filler paste around its periphery.

Aluminium tape should be used for small or very narrow holes. Pull a piece off the roll, trim it to the approximate size and shape required, then pull off the backing paper (if used) and stick the tape over the hole; it can be overlapped if the thickness of one piece is insufficient. Burnish down the edges of the tape with the handle of a screwdriver or similar, to ensure that the tape is securely attached to the metal underneath.

Bodywork repairs - filling and respraying

Before using this Section, see the Sections on dent, deep scratch, rust holes and gash repairs.

Many types of bodyfiller are available, but generally speaking, those proprietary kits which contain a tin of filler paste and a tube of resin hardener are best for this type of repair. A wide, flexible plastic or nylon applicator will be found invaluable for imparting a smooth and well-contoured finish to the surface of the filler.

Mix up a little filler on a clean piece of card or board - measure the hardener carefully (follow the maker's instructions on the pack), otherwise the filler will set too rapidly or too slowly. Using the applicator, apply the filler paste to the prepared area; draw the applicator across the surface of the filler to achieve the correct contour and to level the surface. As soon as a contour that approximates to the correct one is achieved, stop working the paste - if you carry on too long, the paste will become sticky and begin to "pick-up" on the applicator. Continue to add thin layers of filler paste at 20-minute intervals, until the level of the filler is just proud of the surrounding bodywork.

Once the filler has hardened, the excess can be removed using a metal plane or file. From then on, progressively-finer grades of abrasive paper should be used, starting with a 40-grade production paper, and finishing with a 400-grade wet-and-dry paper. Always wrap the abrasive paper around a flat rubber, cork, or wooden block - otherwise the surface of the filler will not be completely flat. During the smoothing of the filler surface, the wet-and-dry paper should be periodically rinsed in water. This will ensure that a very smooth finish is imparted to the filler at the final stage.

At this stage, the "dent" should be surrounded by a ring of bare metal, which in turn should be encircled by the finely "feathered" edge of the good paintwork. Rinse the repair area with clean water, until all of the dust produced by the rubbing-down operation has gone.

Spray the whole area with a light coat of primer - this will show up any imperfections in the surface of the filler. Repair these imperfections with fresh filler paste or bodystopper, and once more smooth the surface with abrasive paper. If bodystopper is used, it can be mixed with cellulose thinners, to form a really thin paste which is ideal for filling small holes. Repeat this spray-and-repair procedure until you are satisfied that the surface of the filler, and the feathered edge of the paintwork, are perfect. Clean the repair area with clean water, and allow to dry fully.

The repair area is now ready for final spraying. Paint spraying must be carried out in a warm, dry, windless and dust-free atmosphere. This condition can be created artificially if you have access to a large indoor working area, but if you are forced to work in the open, you will have to pick your day very carefully. If you are working indoors, dousing the floor in the work area with water will help to settle the dust which would otherwise be in the atmosphere. If the repair area is confined to one body panel, mask off the surrounding panels; this will help to minimise the effects of a slight mis-match in paint colours. Bodywork fittings (eg chrome strips, door handles etc) will also need to be masked off. Use genuine masking tape, and several thicknesses of newspaper, for the masking operations.

Before commencing to spray, agitate the aerosol can thoroughly, then spray a test area (an old tin, or similar) until the technique is mastered. Cover the repair area with a thick coat of primer; the thickness should be built up using several thin layers of paint, rather than one thick one. Using 400-grade wet-and-dry paper, rub down the surface of the primer until it is really smooth. While doing this, the work area should be thoroughly doused with water, and the wet-and-dry paper periodically rinsed in water. Allow to dry before spraying on more paint.

Spray on the top coat, again building up the thickness by using several thin layers of paint. Start spraying at one edge of the repair area, and then, using a side-to-side motion, work until the whole repair area and about 2 inches of the surrounding original paintwork is covered. Remove all masking material 10 to 15 minutes after spraying on the final coat of paint.

Allow the new paint at least two weeks to harden, then, using a paintwork renovator, or a very fine cutting paste, blend the edges of the paint into the existing paintwork. Finally, apply wax polish.

Plastic components

With the use of more and more plastic body components by the vehicle manufacturers (eg bumpers. spoilers, and in some cases major body panels), rectification of more serious damage to such items has become a matter of either entrusting repair work to a specialist in this field, or renewing complete components. Repair of such damage by the DIY owner is not really feasible, owing to the cost of the equipment and materials required for effecting such repairs. The basic technique involves making a groove along the line of the crack in the plastic, using a rotary burr in a power drill. The damaged part is then welded back together, using a hot-air gun to heat up and fuse a plastic filler rod into the groove. Any excess plastic is then removed, and the area rubbed down to a smooth finish. It is important that a filler rod of the correct plastic is used, as body components can be made of a variety of different types (eg polycarbonate, ABS, polypropylene).

Damage of a less serious nature (abrasions, minor cracks etc) can be repaired by the DIY owner using a two-part epoxy filler repair material. Once mixed in equal proportions, this is used in similar fashion to the bodywork filler used on metal panels. The filler is usually cured in twenty to thirty minutes, ready for sanding and painting.

If the owner is renewing a complete component himself, or if he has repaired it with epoxy filler, he will be left with the problem of finding a suitable paint for finishing which is compatible with the type of plastic used. At one time, the use of a universal paint was not possible, owing to the complex range of plastics encountered in body component applications. Standard paints, generally speaking, will not bond to plastic or rubber satisfactorily. However, it is now possible to obtain a plastic body parts finishing kit which consists of a pre-primer treatment, a primer and coloured top coat. Full instructions are normally supplied with a kit, but basically, the method of use is to first apply the pre-primer to the component concerned, and allow it to dry for up to 30 minutes. Then the primer is applied, and left to dry for about an hour before finally applying the special-coloured top coat. The result is a correctly-coloured component, where the paint will flex with the plastic or rubber, a property that standard paint does not normally posses.

5 Major body damage - repair

Where serious damage has occurred, or large areas need renewal due to neglect, it means that complete new panels will need welding-in, and this is best left to professionals. If the damage is due to impact, it will also be necessary to check completely the alignment of the bodyshell, and this can only be carried out accurately by a Citroën dealer, using special jigs. If the body is left misaligned, it is primarily dangerous, as the car will not handle properly; secondly, uneven stresses will be imposed on the steering, suspension and possibly transmission, causing abnormal wear, or complete failure, particularly to such items as the tyres.

6 Front bumper - removal and refitting

Removal

Models up to July 1991

1 Unscrew and remove the bumper stay bolt from the side of the chassis member under the wheel arch on each side **(see illustrations)**.

2 Firmly grip the bumper and pull it from the car, detaching it from the location points each side. As it is withdrawn, disconnect the headlight washer hose and the wiring to the auxiliary lights, where applicable.

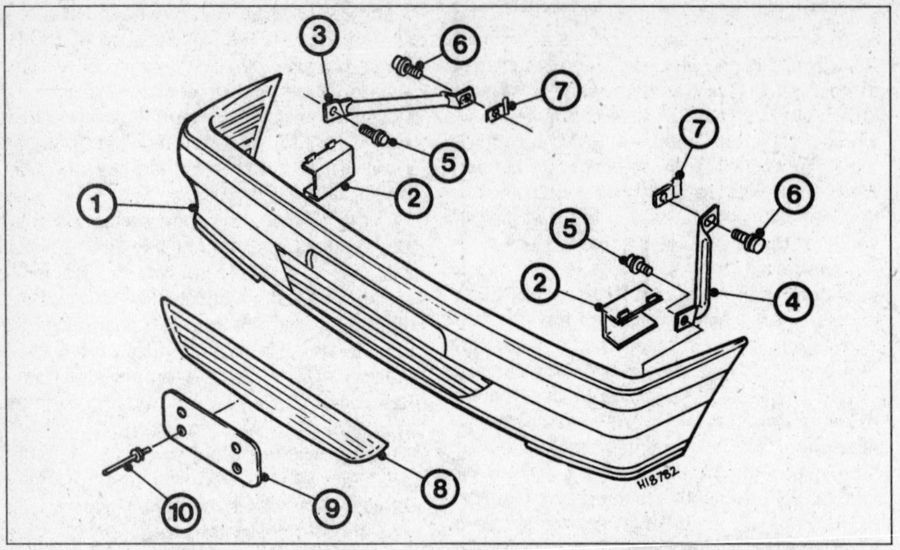

6.1a Front bumper assembly components on models up to July 1991

1 Bumper	*4 Stay (left-hand)*	*8 Grille*
2 Bracket	*5 Self-tapping screw*	*9 Number plate bracket*
3 Stay (right-hand)	*6 Cap screw*	*10 Rivet*
	7 Nut	

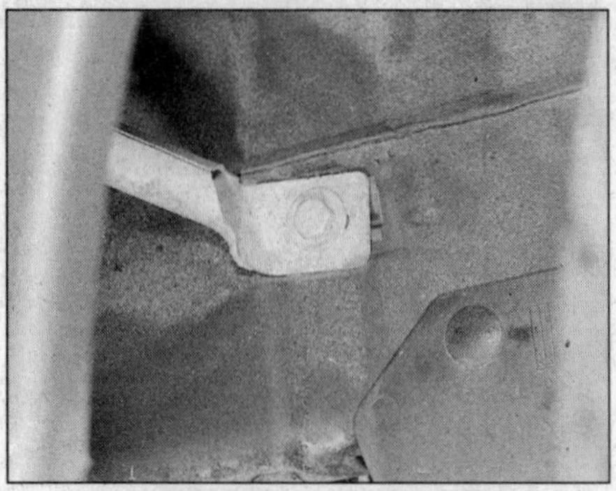

6.1b Front bumper stay bolt (models up to July 1991)

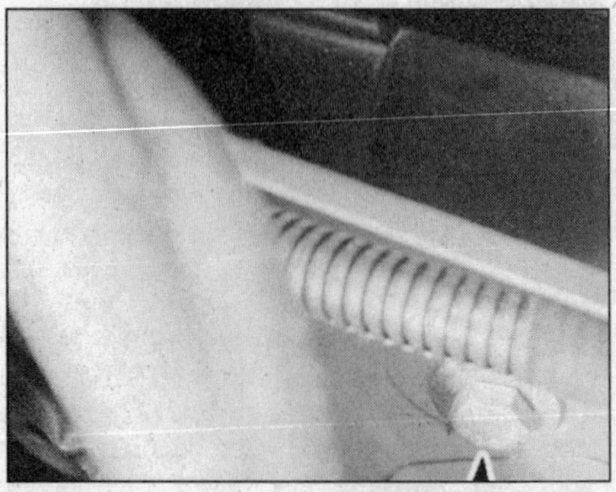

6.7 Front bumper securing bolt (arrowed) - viewed with headlight removed

Models from July 1991 on

3 Disconnect the battery negative lead.

4 Remove both headlights as described in Chapter 12.

5 Remove the auxiliary lights (where applicable) from the front bumper, with reference to Chapter 12.

6 Working in the engine compartment, unscrew the filler neck from the washer fluid reservoir.

7 Reach down through the headlight apertures, and unscrew the two front bumper securing bolts **(see illustration).**

8 Apply the handbrake, then jack up the front of the vehicle and support securely on axle stands (see *"Jacking, towing and wheel changing"*). Remove both front roadwheels.

9 Remove the screws securing the wheel arch liners to the bumper **(see illustration),** then release the securing clips (which are a push-fit), and remove the front wheel arch liners.

10 Unscrew the three bumper lower securing screws from the bottom edge of the bumper.

11 Working under the wheel arch, unscrew the bumper left-hand securing bolt.

12 Working under the right-hand wheel arch, release the securing strap, then move the washer fluid reservoir to one side (take care not to strain the wiring or the fluid hoses). This will provide access to the two bumper right-hand securing bolts (note that the outer bolt can be reached with the reservoir in place). Unscrew the bolts **(see illustrations).**

13 Lift the bumper from the front of the vehicle. Where applicable, disconnect the wiring plugs from the auxiliary lights; note the routing of the wiring, to aid refitting. Similarly, where applicable, disconnect the headlight washer fluid hose.

Refitting

14 Refitting is a reversal of removal. Ensure that the washer fluid reservoir securing strap(s) is/are correctly refitted. Where applicable, also ensure that the auxiliary light wiring and headlight washer hose are correctly routed and connected.

7 Rear bumper - removal and refitting

Removal

1 Open the tailgate. Prise out the plastic "rivets" (items "5" in the accompanying illustration) from either end of the bumper **(see illustration).**

2 Working under the car, unscrew the bumper moulding retaining nuts ("7"), and recover the washers.

3 On some models, a retaining "plug" is moulded into the left-hand side of the bumper, and this is pressed through the body. Working under the car, this plug will be found adjacent

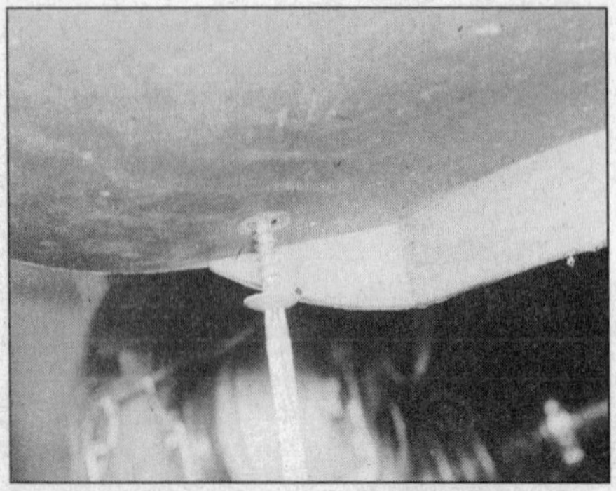

6.9 Removing a wheel arch liner-to-front bumper securing screw

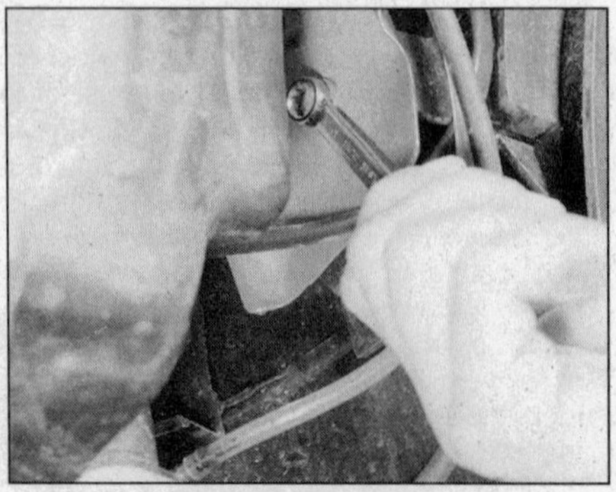

6.12a Unscrewing the front bumper outer . . .

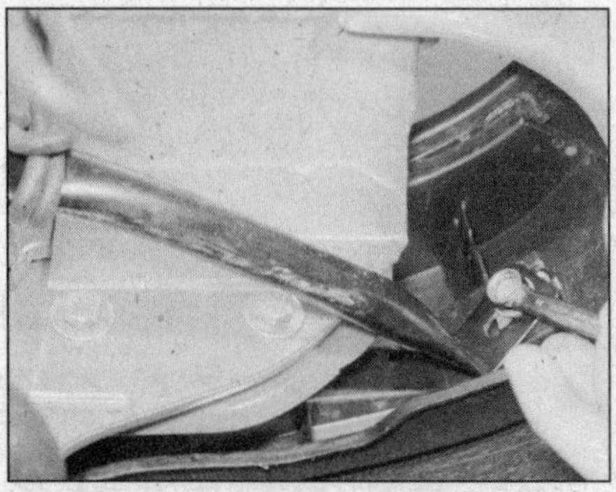

6.12b . . . and inner right-hand securing bolts

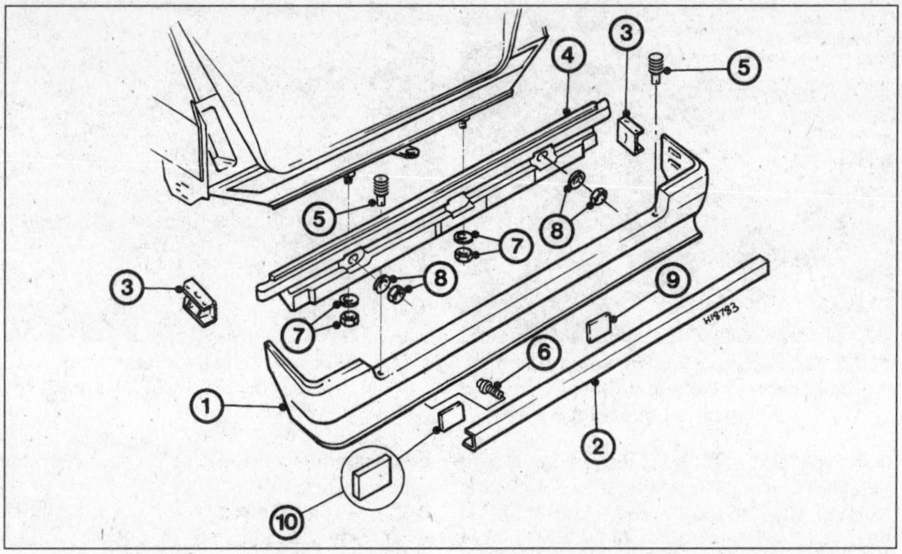

7.1 Rear bumper components

1 Rear bumper moulding (plastic)
2 Tailgate moulding
3 Side retaining bracket
4 Bumper inner member (metal)
5 Plastic "rivet"
6 Self-tapping screw
7 Bumper moulding retaining nuts/washers
8 Bumper inner member retaining nuts/washers
9 Clip
10 Clip (not used in UK)

to the exhaust system rear silencer - prise out the plug, and push it back through the hole in the body. Note that some models may also have a plug on the right-hand side.

4 Carefully withdraw the bumper moulding rearwards from the car, sliding it from the side retaining brackets.

5 If required, the bumper inner member can be removed, after its retaining nuts ("8") are removed.

Refitting

6 Refitting is a reversal of removal.

8.1 Bonnet hinge bolts

8 Bonnet - removal, refitting and adjustment

Removal

1 Open the bonnet, and have an assistant support it. Using a pencil or felt tip pen, mark the outline of each bonnet hinge relative to the bonnet, to use as a guide on refitting **(see illustration)**.

2 Disconnect the windscreen washer supply pipe from its non-return valve. Withdraw the hose from the bonnet, noting its routing.

3 Unscrew the bonnet retaining bolts, and recover the washers. With the help of an assistant, carefully lift the bonnet clear **(see illustration).** Store the bonnet out of the way in a safe place.

4 Inspect the bonnet hinges for signs of wear and free play at the pivots, and if necessary, renew them. Each hinge is secured to the body by a single pivot bolt.

Refitting

5 With the aid of an assistant, offer up the bonnet, and loosely fit the retaining bolts and washers. Align the hinges with the marks made on removal, then tighten the retaining bolts securely. Reconnect the windscreen washer supply pipe, ensuring that it is routed as noted before removal.

6 Adjust the alignment of the bonnet as follows.

Adjustment

7 Close the bonnet, and check for alignment with the adjacent panels. If necessary, slacken the hinge bolts and re-align the bonnet to suit. Once the bonnet is correctly aligned, tighten the hinge bolts securely.

8 Check that the front of the bonnet is level with the front of each wing. If not, it is possible to adjust the height of the bonnet by turning the rubber buffers in the engine compartment front cross panel **(see illustration).**

9 Once the bonnet is correctly aligned, check that it fastens and releases in a satisfactory manner. If adjustment is necessary, slacken the bonnet lock retaining bolts, and adjust the position of the lock to suit. Once the lock is operating correctly, securely tighten its retaining bolts.

9 Bonnet release cable - removal and refitting

Removal

1 Working in the engine compartment, unhook the end of the bonnet release cable from the lock lever. If necessary, unbolt the lock and move it to one side to facilitate this.

2 Where applicable, unscrew the cable securing clip from the front body panel.

3 Working inside the vehicle, remove the securing bolts, and withdraw the bonnet release lever from under the facia **(see illustration).**

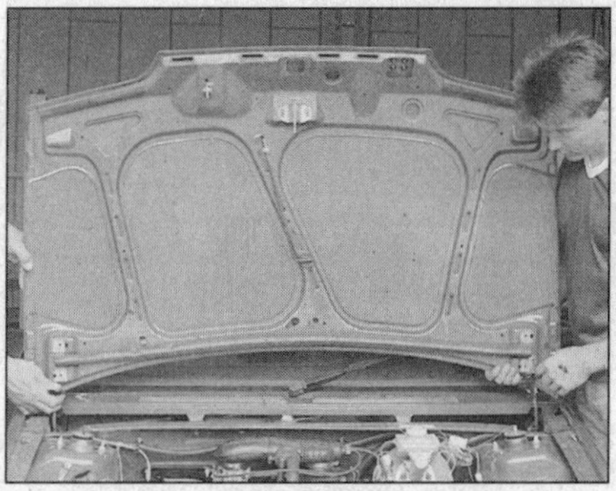

8.3 Removing the bonnet

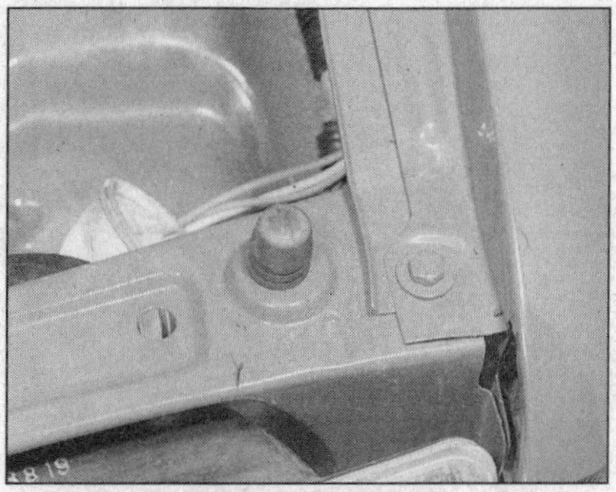

8.8 Adjust the rubber buffers up or down to align the front of the bonnet

9.3 Bonnet release lever and retaining bolts

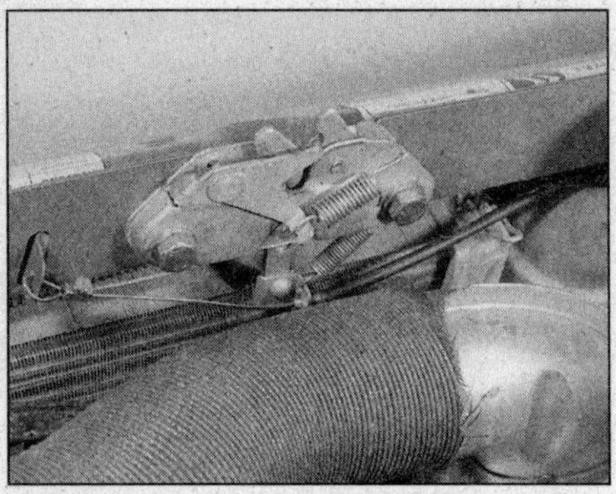

10.2a Bonnet lock showing securing bolts and cable attachment (note early arrangement of cable)

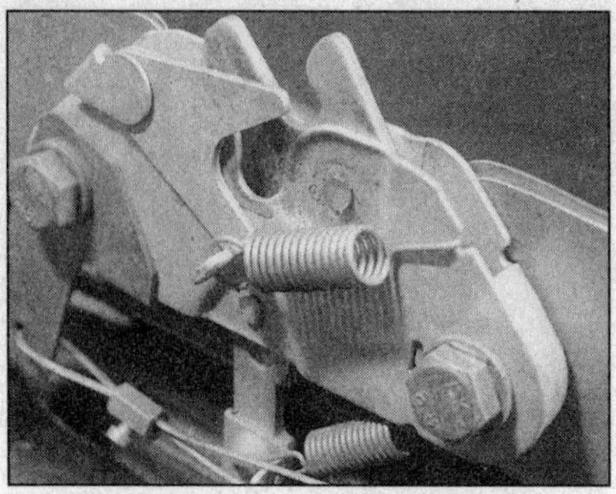

10.2b Bonnet lock showing securing bolts and cable attachment (note later arrangement of cable)

11.4 Door hinge pin (A), check strap roll pin (B) and courtesy light switch (C)

4 Note the routing of the cable, and release it from any clips in the engine compartment, then feed the cable through the bulkhead grommet into the vehicle interior. Note that the cable is integral with the release lever, and cannot be renewed separately.

Refitting

5 Refitting is a reversal of removal, but ensure that the bulkhead grommet is securely located, and make sure that the cable is routed as noted before removal. Check that the release lever operates correctly, and if necessary adjust the clamp position at the lock end of the cable.

10 Bonnet lock - removal and refitting

Removal

1 Open the bonnet, and mark the position of the bonnet lock on the cross panel to facilitate refitting.

2 Unscrew the two securing bolts, and remove the lock assembly from the cross panel **(see illustrations).**

3 Detach the end of the cable from the lock, and where necessary from the cross panel.

Refitting

4 Refitting is a reversal of removal. If necessary, adjust the position of the lock striker on the bonnet and the lock on the cross panel.

11 Door - removal, refitting and adjustment

Front door

Removal

1 The door hinges are welded to both the doors and the body pillars, and removal of the doors is by driving out the hinge pins. Before removing the door, first disconnect the battery negative lead.

2 Open the door and remove the courtesy light switch (Chapter 12, Section 4). This is necessary for access to the door check strap pin.

3 If applicable, remove the trim panel and detach the wiring connections to the electric window motor and/or the door-mounted speaker. On later models (July 1991-on), a multi-pin wiring connector may be located on the inner edge of the door, in which case, disconnect this instead.

4 Using a suitable punch, drive out the roll pin from the door check strap **(see illustration).**

5 Support the door (in the fully-open position) with blocks or a jack. Place a piece of rag between the base of the door and the jack, to protect the paintwork.

6 Drive out the hinge pins, and remove the door.

Refitting and adjustment

7 Refit in the reverse order of removal. When the hinge pins are refitted, close the door and check it for alignment and security in the closed position. To adjust the door for alignment, a special Citroën tool (No 8.1305) or a similar tool will be required. The tool is located over the hinge, and the hinge levered in the required direction to suit. It is unlikely that the tool will be available to the home mechanic, and therefore if adjustment is necessary, the work should be entrusted to a Citroën dealer.

8 Where necessary, the striker on the body pillar may be adjusted to ensure correct closure of the door.

Rear door

9 The procedure is as described previously for the front door. On certain higher-specification models, it will be necessary to remove the door inner trim panel (see Section 12) in order to disconnect any wiring from the components inside the door (no door wiring connector is used). Note the routing of the wiring, release it from any clips inside the door, then feed the wiring harness through the grommet in the front edge of the door.

12 Door inner trim panels - removal and refitting

Front door trim panel

Removal

1 Unscrew and remove the door pocket screws **(see illustrations).**

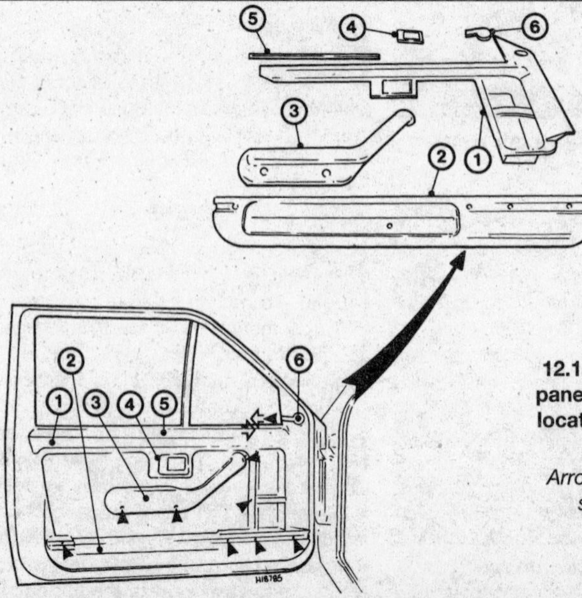

12.1a Front door trim panel components and locations (early model)

Arrows indicate screw securing points

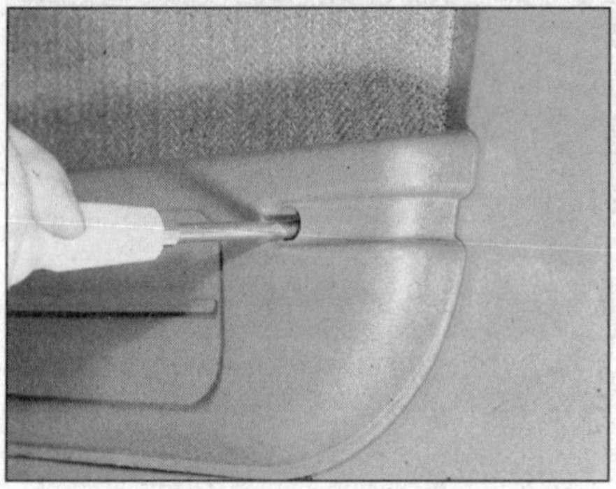

12.1b Door pocket screw removal

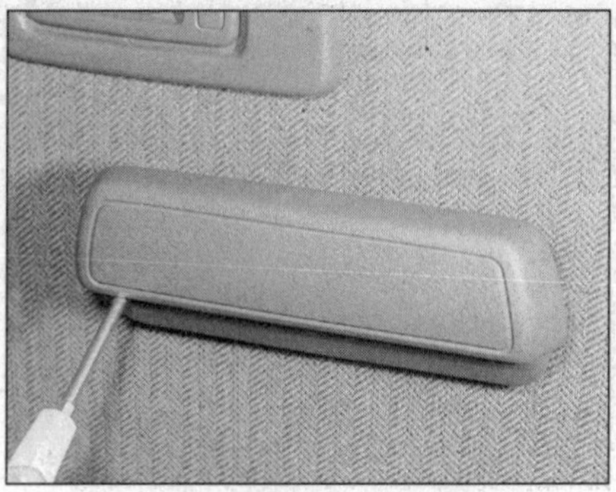

12.2a Door armrest retaining screw removal (early models)

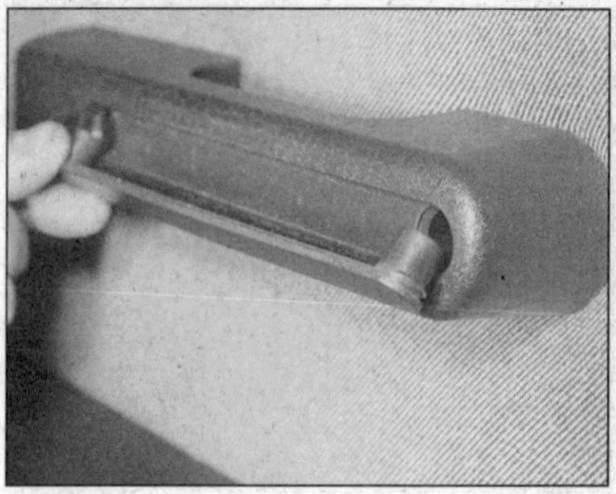

12.2b Removing the plastic cover for access to the armrest screws (later models)

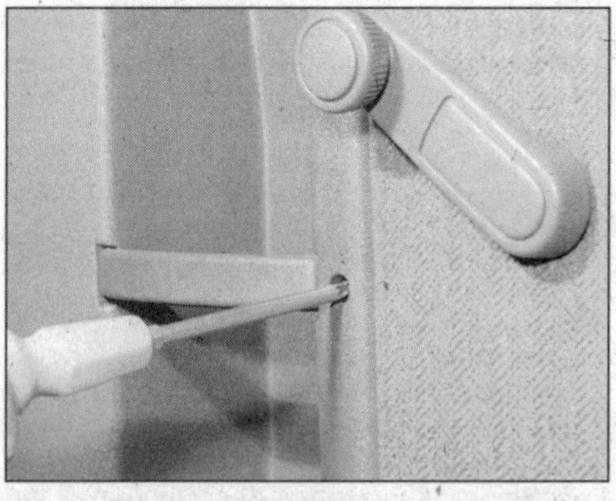

12.3 Inner door trim panel retaining screw location on early models

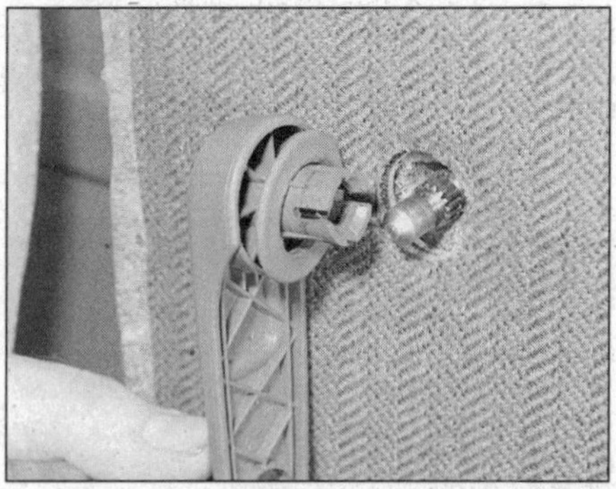

12.4 Window regulator handle removal

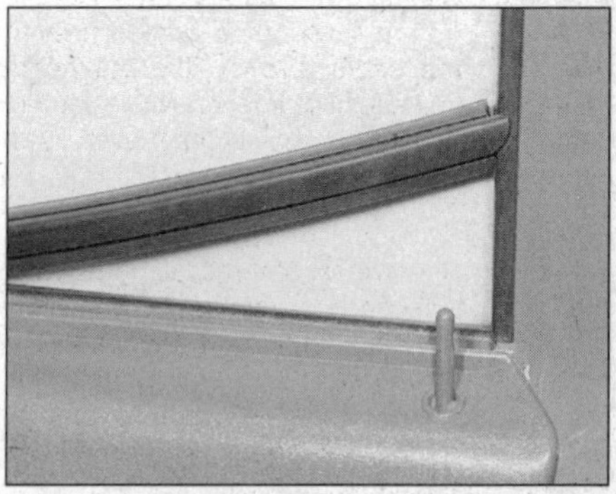

12.5 Removing the door window seal on early models (up to July 1991)

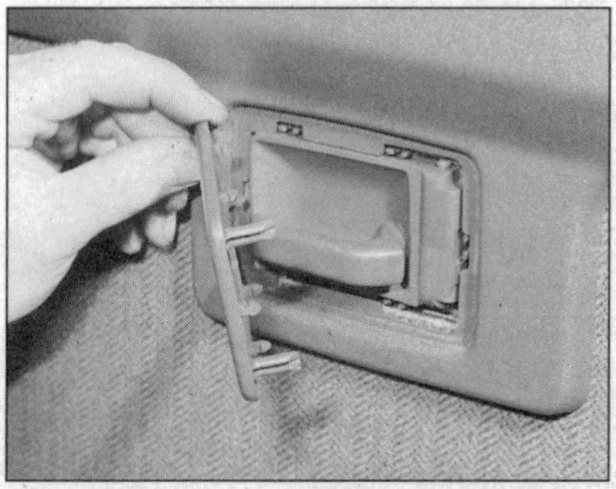

12.6 Removing the interior door handle trim panel

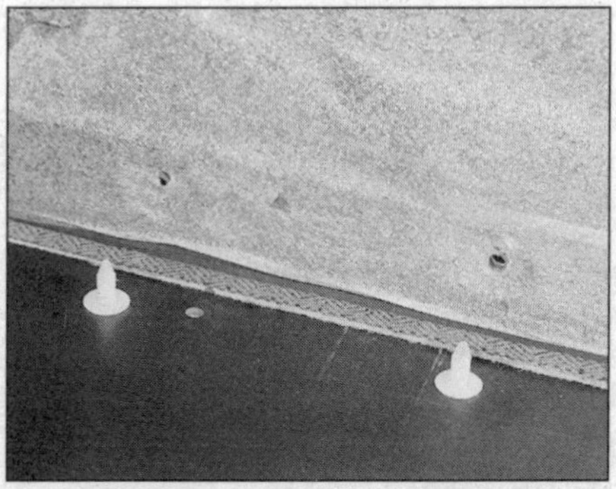

12.7 Door trim removal showing retaining clips

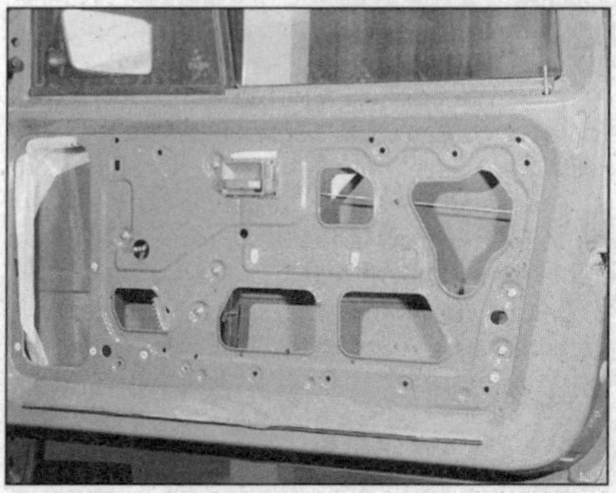

12.8 View of the door with the inner trim panel and insulation sheet removed

2 Undo the retaining screws and remove the armrest - on later models (July 1991-on), it will be necessary to prise out the plastic cover in order to access the screws (see illustrations).

3 On early models (up to July 1991), undo the retaining screw from the door panel. This screw is located just forwards of the window regulator handle (see illustration). This screw is not fitted to later models.

4 To remove the window regulator handle (where applicable), note its fitted position with the window fully raised, then pull it from its shaft (see illustration). Recover the trim disc.

5 On early models, prise free and remove the window seal from the door (see illustration).

6 Remove the trim panel from the door interior handle. To do this, slide the trim panel forwards, then use a screwdriver to prise it out (see illustration).

7 If the main door trim panel incorporates a speaker, on early models, remember to disconnect the wiring as the panel is withdrawn; on later models (July 1991-on), remove the speaker completely as described in Chapter 12. The door trim panel(s) can now be carefully prised free and removed using a wide-bladed screwdriver (see illustration).

8 Access to the inner door components can be made by carefully peeling free the insulation sheet from the door (see illustration). Note that the sheet may be destroyed during removal.

Use a hairdryer to heat the edge of the sealing sheet to ease removal.

Refitting

9 Refit in the reverse order of removal.

Rear door inner trim panel

10 The procedures are very similar to those described for the front door.

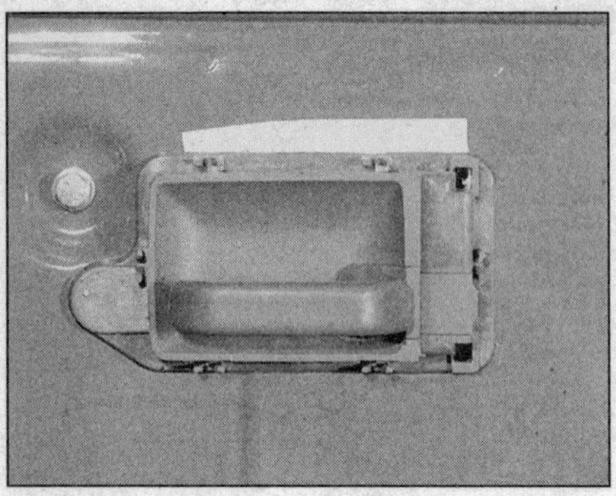

13.2a Front door interior handle - slide it forwards to detach it

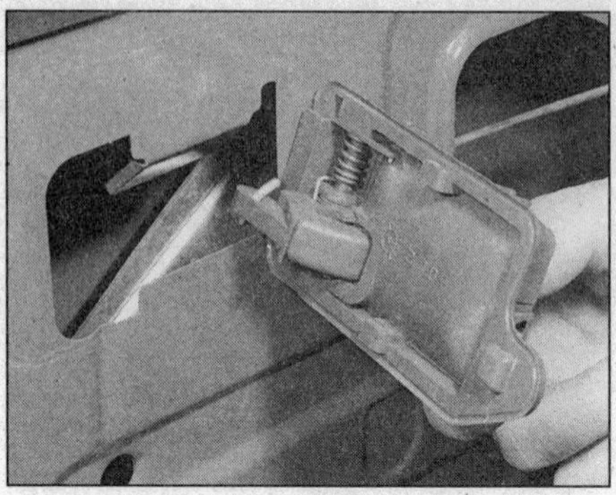

13.2b Removing the front door interior handle

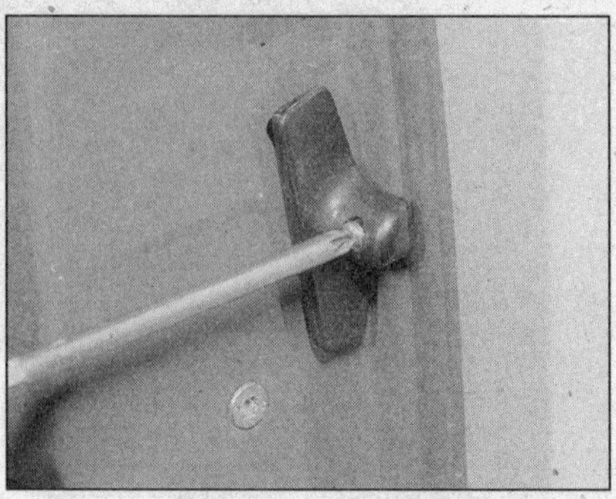

13.8 Removing the exterior door handle button (3-door models)

13 Door handle and lock components - removal and refitting

Interior door handle

Removal

1 Remove the door inner trim panel, as described in Section 12.

2 Slide the handle assembly towards the front of the door, then pull the assembly from the door aperture, and disconnect the link rod (if necessary, release the link rod from the clips on the door) **(see illustrations).**

Refitting

3 Refitting is a reversal of removal, but ensure that the link rod is correctly reconnected, and refit the inner trim panel with reference to Section 12.

Exterior door handle (5-door models)

Removal

4 Remove the interior door handle as described previously.

5 Reach up inside the door, and unscrew the mounting nuts securing the exterior door handle to the door. Withdraw the handle from the outside of the door.

Refitting

6 Refitting is a reversal of removal.

Front door lock (3-door models)

Removal

7 Remove the door inner trim panel, as described in Section 12.

8 With the door open, remove the screw and detach the exterior button from the lock **(see illustration).**

9 Remove the interior door handle as previously described.

10 Detach the locking and remote handle link control rods as necessary.

11 Unscrew the mounting screws, and withdraw the lock from inside the door **(see illustration).**

Refitting

12 Refitting is a reversal of removal, but check the operation of the lock before refitting the interior trim panel.

Front door lock (5-door models)

Removal

13 Remove the door inner trim panel, as described in Section 12.

14 Remove the interior door handle as previously described.

15 On models with central locking, disconnect the battery negative lead, then disconnect the wiring to the actuator, unscrew the mounting screws and disengage the actuator from the lock.

16 Detach the locking and remote handle link control rods as necessary.

17 Unscrew the mounting screws, and withdraw the lock from inside the door.

Refitting

18 Refitting is a reversal of removal, but check the operation of the lock before refitting the interior trim panel.

Front door lock cylinder

Removal

19 Remove the door inner trim panel, as described in Section 12.

20 Working inside the door, pull the securing clip from the rear of the lock cylinder, then remove the lock cylinder from the outside of the door.

Refitting

21 Refitting is a reversal of removal.

Rear door lock

Removal and refitting

22 The procedure is similar to that described previously for the front door lock on 5-door models.

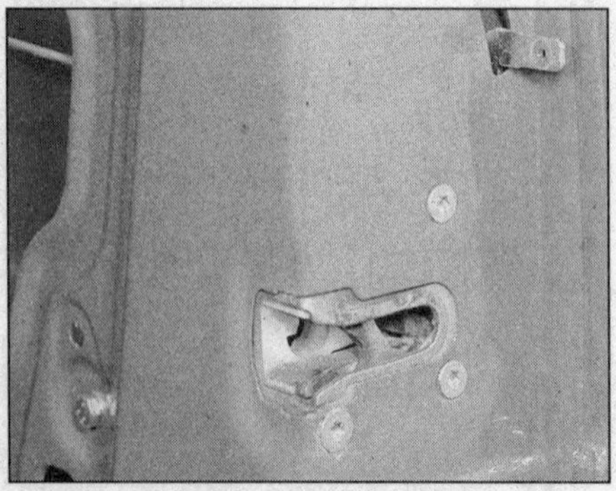

13.11 Door lock retaining screws (3-door models)

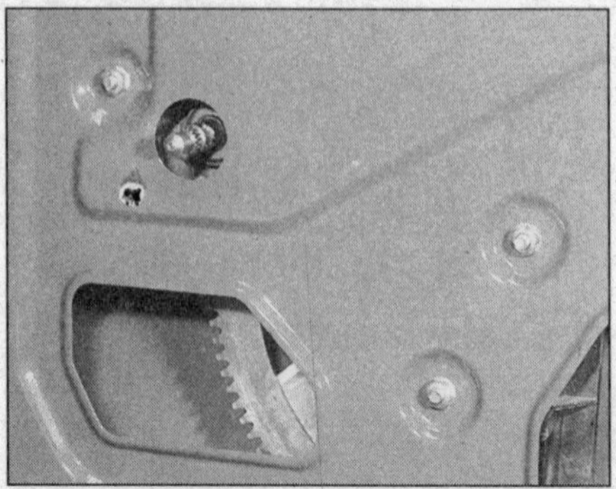

14.2 Window regulator retaining nuts (early models)

14 Door window glass and regulator - removal and refitting

Window regulator

Removal

1 Remove the door inner trim panel and the plastic sealing sheet as described in Section 12.

2 To remove the manual (non-electric) regulator, first unscrew and remove the three regulator-to-door panel retaining nuts **(see illustration).** Then, supporting the window, move it to a suitable access position and unscrew the two regulator-to-window support screws.

3 The procedures for removing the electrically-operated regulator are similar, but also detach the wiring at the block connector.

4 Support the window and withdraw the regulator unit through the door panel access aperture.

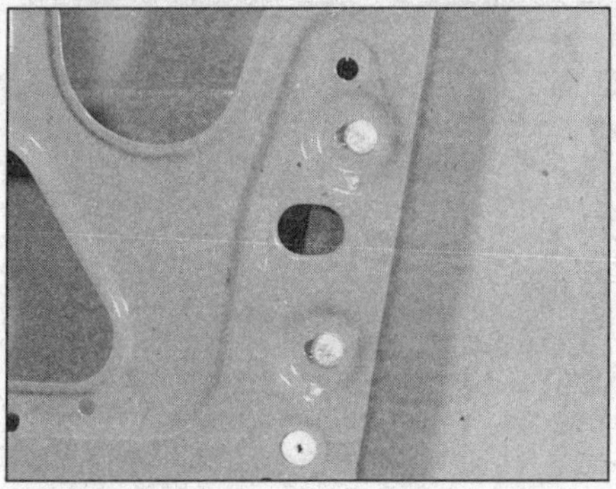

14.6 Door glass channel bolts (early models)

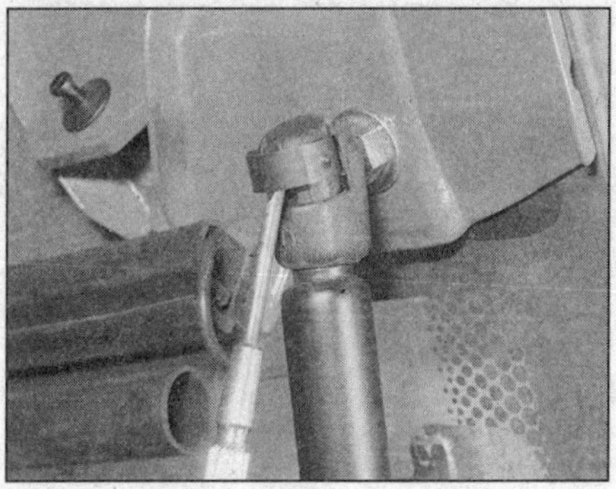

15.7a Prise off the spring clip . . .

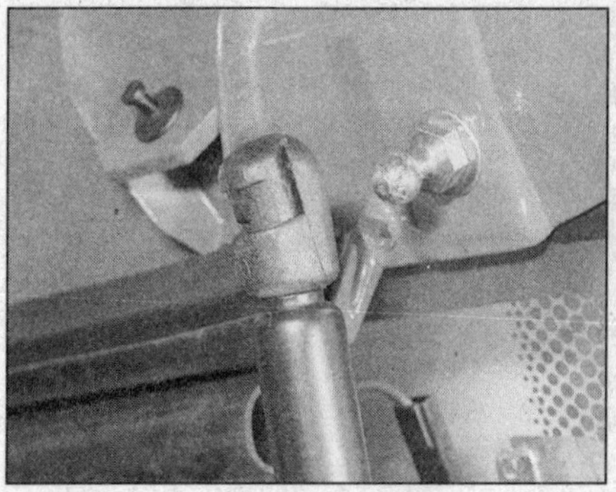

15.7b . . . and pull the support strut from the balljoint

Refitting

5 Refitting is a reversal of the removal procedure.

Door glass

Removal

6 To remove the door glass, first remove the window regulator then unbolt the glass side channels, tilt the glass and withdraw it upwards **(see illustration)**.

7 With the front main door glass removed on 3-door models, pull the quarter glass rearwards and remove it from the door together with its seal.

Refitting

8 Refitting is a reversal of the removal procedure. Check that the window operates smoothly, and if necessary adjust the positions of the side channels as necessary.

15 Tailgate and support struts - removal and refitting

Tailgate

Removal

1 Open the tailgate, and have as assistant support it. Remove the trim panel.

2 Disconnect the struts from the body by prising out the clips and pulling off the sockets.

3 Disconnect the wiring for the heated rear window and (if fitted) the tailgate wiper motor. Also detach the washer tube.

4 Drive out the hinge pins using a suitable drift, and remove the tailgate.

Refitting

5 Refit in the reverse order of removal. Check for satisfactory alignment, but note that it is not possible to adjust the position of the tailgate. Adjust the position of the lock striker plate if necessary, to achieve satisfactory closing.

Support struts

Removal

6 Support the tailgate in the open position, either with the help of an assistant, or using a stout piece of wood.

7 Using a suitable flat-bladed screwdriver, prise off the spring clip, and pull the support strut from its balljoint on the tailgate (see illustrations).

8 Similarly, release the strut from the balljoint on the body, and withdraw the strut from the vehicle.

Refitting

9 Refitting is a reversal of removal, but ensure that the spring clips are correctly engaged.

16 Tailgate lock components - removal and refitting

Removal

1 Open the tailgate and prise free the trim panel for access to the lock components **(see illustration)**.

2 Remove the wiper motor cover, then slide free the retaining clip, disconnect the connecting rod and remove the lock cylinder.

3 To remove the lock, undo the retaining bolts, detach the connecting rod and remove the lock. On central locking models, the actuator is removed in the same manner, but also disconnect the wiring from the actuator unit.

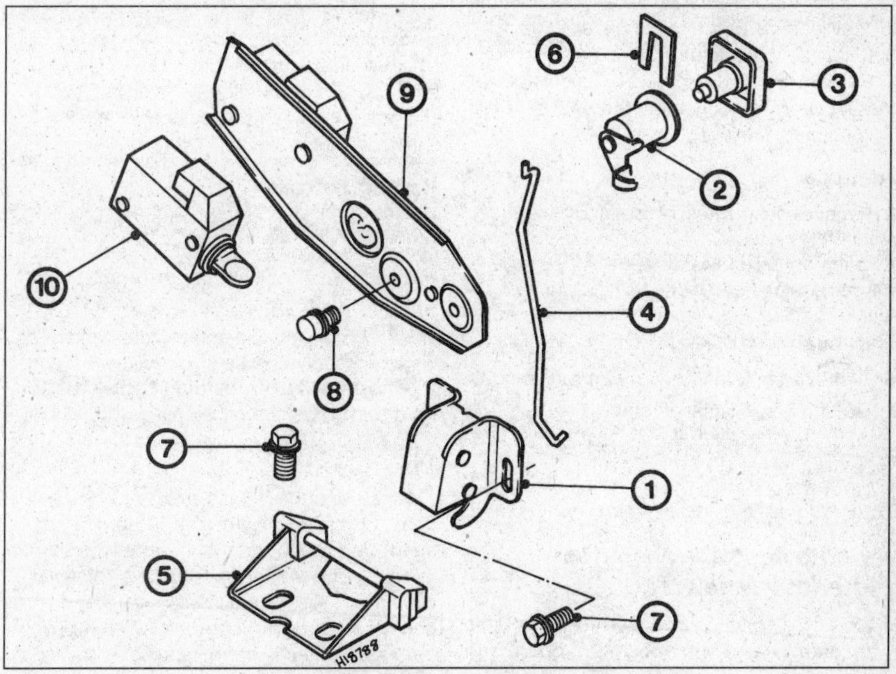

16.1 Typical tailgate lock components

1 Lock
2 Lock cylinder housing
3 Lock cylinder
4 Lock connecting rod
5 Striker
6 Retainer clip (lock barrel)
7 Bolt
8 Bolt
9 Actuator support (central locking)
10 Actuator (central locking)

4 To remove the striker plate, first mark its position on the body to ensure correct refitting. Unscrew the two securing bolts and remove the striker plate from the body.

Refitting

5 Refitting is a reversal of the removal procedure. Adjust the position of the striker plate, if required, so that the tailgate shuts securely.

17 Central locking components - removal and refitting

Note: *Before attempting work on any of the central locking system components, disconnect the battery negative lead. Reconnect the lead on completion of work.*

Electronic control unit

1 At the time of writing, no information was available for the electronic control unit.

Door lock actuator

2 The actuator is located near the door lock assembly, and can be removed after removing the trim panel (see Section 12).

Tailgate lock actuator

Removal

3 Open the tailgate.
4 Remove the tailgate trim panel.
5 If necessary, to improve access, remove the lock cylinder as described in Section 16.
6 Disconnect the actuator wiring connector.
7 Remove the securing screws and withdraw the actuator, disconnecting the operating rod as the actuator is withdrawn.

Refitting

8 Refitting is a reversal of removal.

Remote control receiver unit (where applicable)

Removal

9 Remove the interior light with reference to Chapter 12, Section 6.
10 Release the receiver unit and remove it.

Refitting

11 Refitting is a reversal of removal.

Remote control transmitter batteries - renewal

12 Using a small screwdriver, carefully prise the two halves of the transmitter apart, and remove the two batteries, noting which way round they are fitted.
13 Fit the two new batteries, ensuring that they are fitted the correct way round; the battery and transmitter terminals are marked "+" and "-" to avoid confusion. Clip the transmitter back together.

18 Electric window components - removal and refitting

Window switch

1 Refer to Chapter 12, Section 4.

Window regulator motor

2 The regulator motor is bolted in position, and access to it is obtained through the inner door panel aperture in a similar manner to that described for the manual regulator type.
3 Removal and refitting details for the regulator motor assemblies are given in Section 14.

19 Exterior mirror - removal and refitting

Removal

1 Remove the door inner trim panel as described in Section 12.
2 On early models (up to July 1991), using a socket through the holes in the door inner skin, unscrew the mirror mounting bolts then remove the mirror from the outside of the door **(see illustration).**
3 On later models (July 1991 on), it is necessary to remove the inner moulding and control knob first before the mirror is withdrawn from the outside.
4 The mirror glass may be removed on later models as follows. Locate the spring clip which secures the bottom edge of the glass, then use a suitable screwdriver to prise the clip apart. Remove the glass and recover the spring clip if it is loose.

Refitting

5 Refitting is a reversal of removal. If necessary, renew the gasket and sealing washers. When refitting the mirror glass, push it into position until the spring clip locks into the groove.

20 Windscreen, tailgate and fixed windows - general information

These areas of glass are secured by the tight fit of the weatherstrip in the body aperture, and on later models are bonded in position with a special adhesive. Renewal of such fixed glass is a difficult, messy and time-consuming task, which is considered beyond the scope of the home mechanic. It is difficult, unless one has plenty of practice, to obtain a secure, waterproof fit. Furthermore, the task carries a high risk of breakage; this applies especially to the laminated glass windscreen. In view of this, owners are strongly advised to have this sort of work carried out by one of the many specialist windscreen fitters.

19.2 Exterior mirror retaining bolts (early model)

21 Opening rear quarter windows - removal and refitting

Removal

1 Open the window.
2 Support the glass, then working inside the vehicle, remove the screws securing the glass panel to the hinges and the handle. Withdraw the panel, taking care not to damage the surrounding paintwork. Where applicable, recover the plastic nuts and the trim from the panel.
3 The handle or hinges may be removed by unscrewing the securing screws.
4 If necessary, the weatherstrip may be removed from the body aperture.

Refitting

5 Refitting is a reversal of removal. If the weatherstrip has been removed, clean the contact surfaces before refitting it. Take care not to overtighten the glass panel securing screws (it is easy to strip the threads of the plastic nuts).

22 Sunroof - general information

1 A manual tilt-type sunroof may be fitted, depending on model.
2 Removal of the sunroof glass is straightforward. Turn the knob to fully open the sunroof.
3 Press simultaneously the two red buttons at the lock end of the glass, and push the sunroof upwards.
4 From the outside of the sunroof, disconnect the glass from the lock by lifting the latch.
5 Raise the sunroof vertical and lift it upwards from the hinges. The sunroof may be stored in the special cover supplied in the boot of the car when new.
6 Refitting is a reversal of the removal procedure.

23 Body exterior fittings - removal and refitting

Wheel arch liners

1 The wheel arch liners are secured by a combination of self-tapping screws, and push-fit clips. Removal is self-evident, and normally the clips can be released by pulling the liner away from the wheel arch.

Body trim strips and badges

2 The various body trim strips and badges are held in position with a special adhesive tape. Removal requires the trim/badge to be heated, to soften the adhesive, and then cut away from the surface. Due to the high risk of damage to the vehicle paintwork during this operation, it is recommended that this task should be entrusted to a Citroën dealer.

24 Seats - removal and refitting

Front seat

Removal

1 Unclip and detach the trim panel from the inboard side seat runner.

2 Move the seat fully to the rear, then unscrew and remove the socket-head retaining bolts at the front using a 5 mm Allen key.

3 Move the seat forwards, then unscrew and remove the rear retaining bolts **(see illustration).** Remove the seat from inside the car.

Refitting

4 Refitting is a reversal of the removal procedure.

Rear seat

Removal

5 To remove the backrest, tilt it forwards about 45°, and lift it from its pivot brackets as shown **(see illustration).**

6 To remove the seat squab, lift it at the front edge and release it from its location.

Refitting

7 Refitting is a reversal of the removal procedure.

25 Seat belt components - general

1 The seat belts do not normally require any attention, apart from periodically checking their condition and security.

2 Typical mounting points are shown in the accompanying illustrations. Prise off the cover for access to the upper mounting bolt **(see illustrations).**

3 Access to the mountings is obtained after the removal of the appropriate trim panel. Note the locations and fitted sequence of bolts, nuts, spacers and washers, as applicable.

4 Whenever the belt is removed and refitted, check it for satisfactory operation on completion by gripping the webbing and pulling it sharply - the inertia reel must lock. Tighten all mountings securely, or to the specified torque, where given.

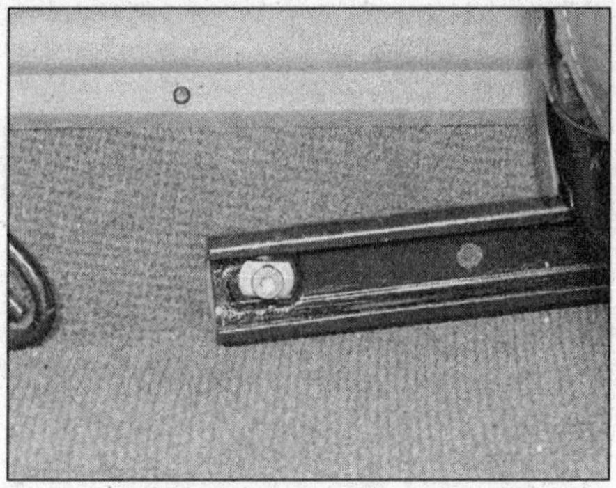

24.3 Front seat runner rear retaining bolt

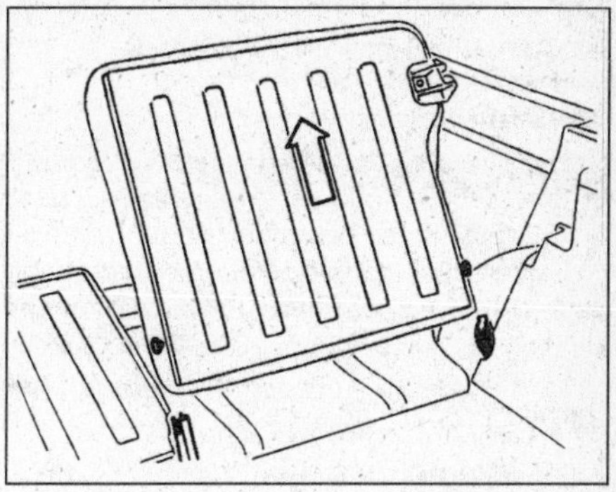

24.5 Rear seat backrest removal

26 Interior trim panels - removal and refitting

Door trim panels

1 Refer to Section 12.

Parcel shelf end supports (early models)

2 Prise free the two clips securing the shelf support on its outboard edge, then undo the two retaining screws from the inboard end **(see illustration).**

3 Withdraw the shelf support from the car.

Other interior trim panels

4 Removal of the trim panels is straightforward, but care must be taken to avoid damaging the panels or breaking the securing clips.

5 To remove the luggage compartment trim panels, first remove the rear seat as described

25.2a Prise off the cover (arrowed) for access to the upper mounting bolt

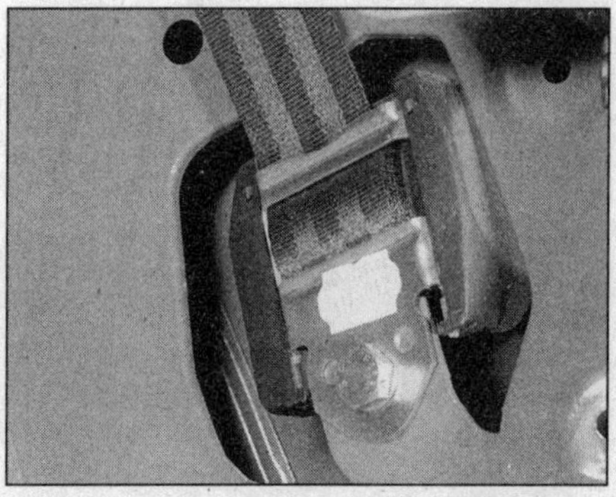

25.2b Front seat belt inertia reel and mounting location (trim removed)

25.2c Rear seat belt inertia reel and mounting location (trim removed)

26.2 Parcel shelf retaining bolt

earlier. Move the front seats forwards for access to the centre pillar trim panels.

Carpets

6 The passenger compartment floor carpet is in one piece, and is secured at its edges by screws or various types of clips.

7 Carpet removal and refitting is reasonably straightforward, but time-consuming, due to the fact that all adjoining trim panels must be removed first, as must components such as the seats and centre console.

Headlining

8 The headlining is clipped to the roof, and can be withdrawn only once all fittings such as the grab handles, sunvisors, sunroof (if fitted), windscreen, centre and rear pillar trim panels, and associated panels have been removed. The door, tailgate and sunroof aperture weatherstrips will also have to be prised clear.

9 Note that headlining removal requires considerable skill and experience if it is to be carried out without damage, and is therefore best entrusted to an expert.

27 Centre console - removal and refitting

Removal

1 Remove the oddment bin from the centre console, then unscrew the two upper retaining screws.

2 Release the gear lever gaiter from its floor mounting, and slide it up the lever to allow access to the console floor mounting screws.

3 Undo the screws and remove the console. As it is withdrawn, detach the wiring connectors from the console-mounted switches, noting their positions for correct refitting.

Refitting

4 Refitting is a reversal of removal.

28 Facia assembly - removal and refitting

Note: *The following procedure is for models manufactured before June 1991, but the procedure for later models is very similar.*

Removal

1 Disconnect the battery negative lead.

2 Remove the right and left-hand parcel shelves and the central console as previously described.

3 Remove the face level ventilation grilles by releasing the securing clip on the side of each and pulling them free **(see illustration).** Do not lose the clips.

4 Remove the steering wheel and column as described in Chapter 10.

5 Remove the following with reference to Chapter 12:

a) Instrument panel.
b) Radio.
c) Windscreen wiper motor.
d) Fusebox.

6 Remove the heater control panel as described in Chapter 3.

7 Prise free and remove the centre switch panel **(see illustration).**

8 Where applicable, disconnect the choke cable from the carburettor as described in Chapter 4A.

9 Where necessary, open the glovebox then remove the securing screws and withdraw the glovebox from the facia.

10 Unscrew and remove the facia retaining screws, one on each side, two on the heater unit (front and bottom) and two underneath the heater unit **(see illustration).**

11 Partial withdrawal of the facia unit is now possible, but for full removal, disconnect the wiring loom and connections. As they are disconnected, note their respective routings.

Refitting

12 Refitting is a reversal of the removal procedure, but note the following additional points:

a) Ensure that all wiring connections are correctly and securely made. Route the looms as noted during removal.
b) Where applicable, reconnect the choke cable with reference to Chapter 4A.
c) Refit the steering wheel and column as described in Chapter 10.
d) On completion, check for satisfactory operation of all components.

28.3 Removing a ventilation grille from the facia

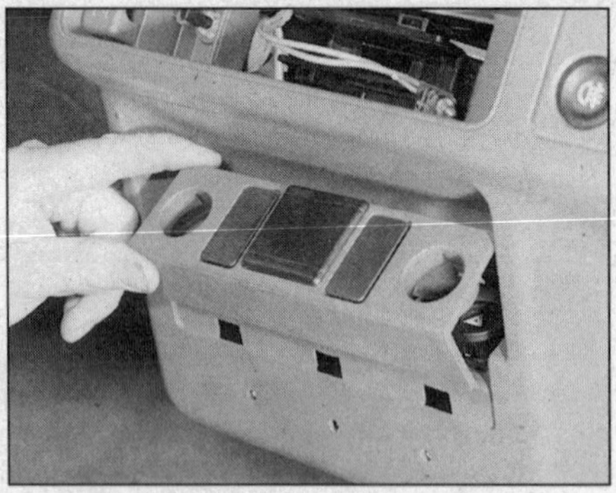

28.7 Removing the switch panel trim

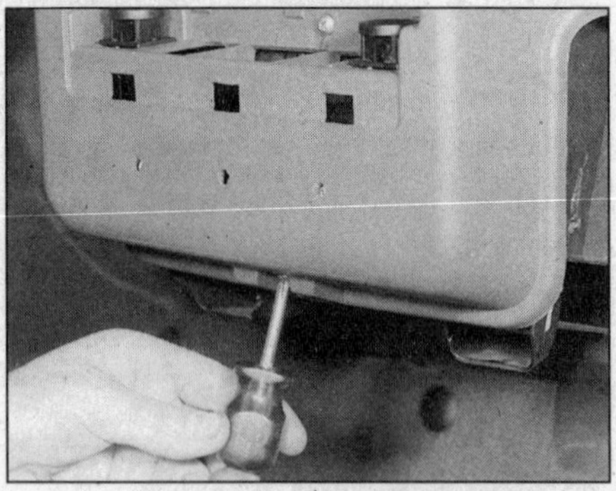

28.10 Removing a facia lower retaining screw

Chapter 12 Body electrical systems

Contents

Degrees of difficulty

Easy, suitable for novice with little experience	**Fairly easy,** suitable for beginner with some experience	**Fairly difficult,** suitable for competent DIY mechanic	**Difficult,** suitable for experienced DIY mechanic	**Very difficult,** suitable for expert DIY or professional

Specifications

Bulbs

Bulbs	Wattage
Headlight (E2 type bulb)	40/45
Headlight (H4 type bulb)	55/60
Front sidelight	5
Front driving/foglight (H3 type bulb)	55
Front direction indicator light	21
Direction indicator side repeater light	5
Stop-light/tail light	21/5
Tail light	5
Direction indicator light	21
Rear foglight	21
Reversing light	21
Rear number plate light	5
Map reading light	5
Glovebox light	5
Interior light	5
Cigar lighter	1.2
Ashtray	1.2
Heater controls	1.2
Instrument panel warning/illumination	1.2

Fuses (models up to July 1991)

No	Rating (amps)	Circuit(s) protected
1	10	Heated rear window and warning light
2	30	Windscreen and tailgate wash/wipe, stop-lights, interior spotlight (GT models)
3	30	Instrument panel warning lights, instrument lighting, fuel gauge, cigar lighter illumination, heater control lighting and blower motor. Electric window motor relay, heated rear window relay, heated rear window relay, direction indicators, clock (+ ignition switch), water level indicator
4	25	Front auxiliary lights (GT models), central door locking
5	30	Radiator cooling fan, carburettor heating
6	10	Hazard warning lights
7	10	Reversing lights, tachometer, oil level control unit, dim-dip lights relay
8	20	Interior light, radio, clock, tailgate wiper park position feed, boot light, cigar lighter
9	30	Electric window motors, carburettor heater
10	20	Horn
11	5	Rear foglight and warning light
12	5	RH sidelight, RH rear lights. Switch illumination for rear foglight, hazard warning lights, heated rear window and tailgate wiper switches
13	5	LH sidelight, LH rear lights. Number plate light, sidelight warning light

Fuses (July 1991-on models)

No	Rating (amps)	Circuit(s) protected
1	30	Heater blower, recycling and air conditioning switches
2	30	Wash/wipe, instrument panel, radio, lights-on audible warning, stop-lights, tailgate wiper delay, 4x4 switch
3	30	Indicators, cooling fan relay, heated rear screen switch, electric window relay, induction heating
4	25	Central locking
5	30	Heated rear window
6	10	Hazard warning lights
7	10	Reversing light, instrument panel and lighting, coolant level, ABS, dim-dip
8	20	Interior light, radio, clock, rear wiper, boot light, radio
9	30	Electric window motors
10	20	Horn
11	5	Rear foglight
12	5	RH front sidelight, RH rear light, illumination of control switches, cigar lighter, ashtray and radio
13	5	LH front sidelight, LH rear light, number plate light, sidelight warning light

Supplementary fuses (in engine compartment)

No	Rating (amps)	Circuit(s) protected
1	30	Radiator cooling fan
2	10	Front foglight
3	30	Air conditioning relay
4	-	Unused
5	15	ABS
6	-	ABS

1 General information and precautions

General information

The body electrical system consists of all lights, wash/wipe equipment, interior electrical equipment, and associated switches and wiring.

The electrical system is of the 12-volt negative earth type. Power to the system is provided by a 12-volt battery, which is charged by the alternator (see Chapter 5A).

The engine electrical system (battery, alternator, starter motor, ignition system - petrol engine models, pre-heating system - Diesel engine models, etc) is covered separately in Chapter 5.

Precautions

Before carrying out any work on the electrical system, read through the precautions given in *"Safety first!"* at the beginning of this manual, and in Chapter 5.

If the radio/cassette player fitted to the vehicle has an anti-theft security code (as does the unit fitted as standard), refer to *"Radio/cassette unit anti-theft system - precaution"* at the start of this manual before disconnecting the battery.

Prior to working on any component in the electrical system, the battery negative lead should first be disconnected, to prevent the possibility of electrical short-circuits and/or fires.

2 Electrical fault-finding - general information

Note: *Refer to the precautions given in "Safety first!" and in Section 1 of this Chapter before starting work. The following tests relate to testing of the main electrical circuits, and should not be used to test delicate electronic circuits (such as anti-lock braking systems), especially not those where an electronic control unit is used.*

General

1 A typical electrical circuit consists of an electrical component, any switches, relays, motors, fuses, fusible links or circuit breakers related to that component, and the wiring and connectors which link the component to both the battery and the chassis. To help to pinpoint a problem in an electrical circuit, wiring diagrams are included at the end of this manual.

2 Before attempting to diagnose an electrical fault, first study the appropriate wiring diagram, to obtain a more complete understanding of the components included in the particular circuit. The possible sources of a fault can be narrowed down by noting whether other components related to the circuit are operating properly. If several components or circuits fail at one time, the problem is likely to be related to a shared fuse or earth connection.

3 Electrical problems usually stem from simple causes, such as loose or corroded connections, a faulty earth connection, a blown fuse, a melted fusible link, or a faulty relay (refer to Section 3 for details of testing relays). Visually inspect the condition of all fuses, wires and connections in a problem circuit before testing the components. Use the wiring diagrams at the end of this Chapter to determine which terminal connections will need to be checked, in order to pinpoint the trouble-spot.

4 The basic tools required for electrical fault-finding include a circuit tester or voltmeter (a 12-volt bulb with a set of test leads can also be used for certain tests); a self-powered test light (or continuity tester); an ohmmeter (to measure resistance); a battery and set of test leads; and a jumper wire, preferably with a circuit breaker or fuse incorporated, which can be used to bypass suspect wires or electrical components. Before attempting to locate a problem with test instruments, use the wiring diagrams to determine where to make the connections.

5 To find the source of an intermittent wiring fault (usually due to a poor or dirty connection, or damaged wiring insulation), a "wiggle" test can be performed on the wiring. This involves wiggling the wiring by hand, to see if the fault occurs as the wiring is moved. It should be possible to narrow down the source of the fault to a particular section of wiring. This method of testing can be used in conjunction with any of the tests described in the following sub-Sections.

6 Apart from problems due to poor connections, two basic types of fault can occur in an electrical circuit - open-circuit, or short-circuit.

7 Open-circuit faults are caused by a break somewhere in the circuit, which prevents current from flowing. An open-circuit fault will prevent a component from working, but will not cause the relevant circuit fuse to blow.
8 Short-circuit faults are caused by a "short" somewhere in the circuit, which allows the current flowing in the circuit to "escape" along an alternative route, usually to earth. Short-circuit faults are normally caused by a breakdown in wiring insulation, which allows a feed wire to touch either another wire, or an earthed component such as the bodyshell. A short-circuit fault will normally cause the relevant circuit fuse to blow.

Finding an open-circuit

9 To check for an open-circuit, connect one lead of a circuit tester or voltmeter to either the negative battery terminal or a known good earth.
10 Connect the other lead to a connector in the circuit being tested, preferably nearest to the battery or fuse.
11 Switch on the circuit, bearing in mind that some circuits are live only when the ignition switch is moved to a particular position.
12 If voltage is present (indicated either by the tester bulb lighting or a voltmeter reading, as applicable), this means that the section of the circuit between the relevant connector and the battery is problem-free.
13 Continue to check the remainder of the circuit in the same fashion.
14 When a point is reached at which no voltage is present, the problem must lie between that point and the previous test point with voltage. Most problems can be traced to a broken, corroded or loose connection.

Finding a short-circuit

15 To check for a short-circuit, first disconnect the load(s) from the circuit (loads are the components which draw current from a circuit, such as bulbs, motors, heating elements, etc).
16 Remove the relevant fuse from the circuit, and connect a circuit tester or voltmeter to the fuse connections.
17 Switch on the circuit, bearing in mind that some circuits are live only when the ignition switch is moved to a particular position.
18 If voltage is present (indicated either by the tester bulb lighting or a voltmeter reading, as applicable), this means that there is a short-circuit. If voltage is present with the switch in its off position, then there is a short circuit between the fuse and the switch.
19 If no voltage is present, but the fuse still blows with the load(s) connected, this indicates an internal fault in the load(s).

Finding an earth fault

20 The battery negative terminal is connected to "earth" - the metal of the engine/transmission unit and the car body - and most systems are wired so that they only receive a positive feed, the current returning via the metal of the car body. This means that the component mounting and the body form part of that circuit. Loose or corroded mountings can therefore cause a range of electrical faults, ranging from total failure of a circuit, to a puzzling partial fault. In particular, lights may shine dimly (especially when another circuit sharing the same earth point is in operation), motors (eg wiper motors or the radiator cooling fan motor) may run slowly, and the operation of one circuit may have an apparently-unrelated effect on another. Note that on many vehicles, earth straps are used between certain components, such as the engine/transmission and the body, usually where there is no metal-to-metal contact between components, due to flexible rubber mountings, etc.
21 To check whether a component is properly earthed, disconnect the battery, and connect one lead of an ohmmeter to a known good earth point. Connect the other lead to the wire or earth connection being tested. The resistance reading should be zero; if not, check the connection as follows.
22 If an earth connection is thought to be faulty, dismantle the connection, and clean back to bare metal both the bodyshell and the wire terminal or the component earth connection mating surface. Be careful to remove all traces of dirt and corrosion, then use a knife to trim away any paint, so that a clean metal-to-metal joint is made. On reassembly, tighten the joint fasteners securely; if a wire terminal is being refitted, use serrated washers between the terminal and the bodyshell, to ensure a clean and secure connection. When the connection is remade, prevent the onset of corrosion in the future by applying a coat of petroleum jelly or silicone-based grease, or by spraying on (at regular intervals) a proprietary ignition sealer, or a water-dispersant lubricant.

3 Fuses and relays - general information

Fuses

1 Fuses are designed to break a circuit when a predetermined current is reached, in order to protect the components and wiring which could be damaged by excessive current flow. Any excessive current flow will be due to a fault in the circuit, usually a short-circuit (see Section 2).
2 On early models (up to July 1991), the fuses are located beneath a cover on top of the facia panel, between the instrument panel and the windscreen. On later models (July 1991 on), the fuses are located behind a cover on the right-hand side of the facia on right-hand drive models, or the left-hand side of the facia on left-hand drive models.
3 For access to the fuses, use a coin or screwdriver to turn the cover retaining screw(s), then withdraw the cover **(see illustrations)**. If required, the fusebox on early models may be removed by sliding it towards the centre to release it, then lifting it clear.
4 Additional fuses are located in an auxiliary fusebox in the engine compartment, attached to a bracket on the left-hand suspension turret **(see illustration)**.
5 A blown fuse can be recognised from its melted or broken wire.
6 To remove a fuse, first ensure that the relevant circuit is switched off.
7 Using the plastic tool provided in the fusebox, pull the fuse from its location.
8 Spare fuses are provided in the blank terminal positions in the fusebox.
9 Before renewing a blown fuse, trace and rectify the cause, and always use a fuse of the correct rating. Never substitute a fuse of a higher rating, or make temporary repairs using wire or metal foil; more serious damage, or even a fire, could result.

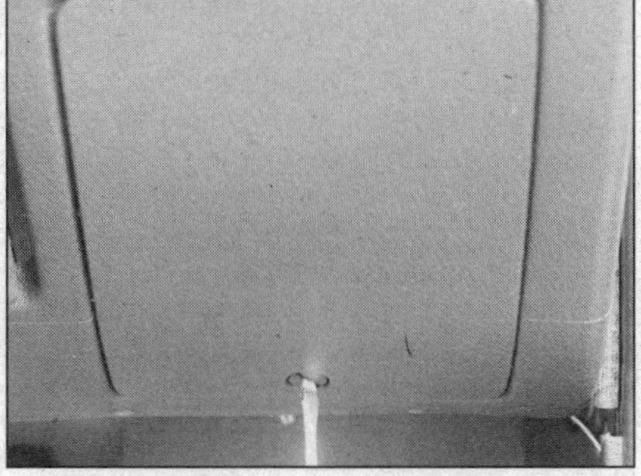

3.3a Release the retaining screw and remove the cover . . .

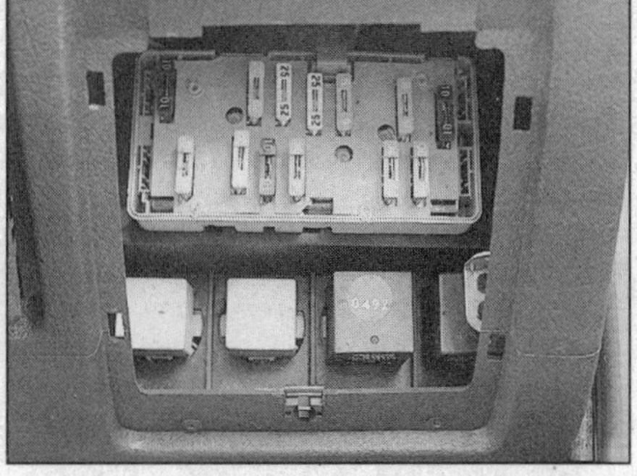

3.3b . . . for access to the fuses (later model shown)

3.4 Auxiliary fusebox in the engine compartment (cover opened)

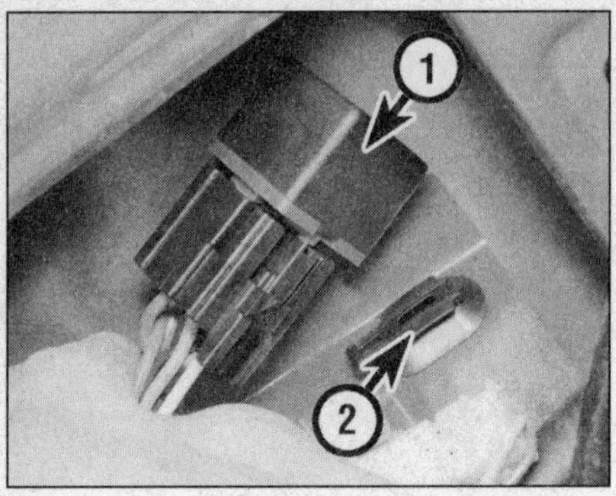

3.13a Rear wiper motor relay (1) and securing clip (2)

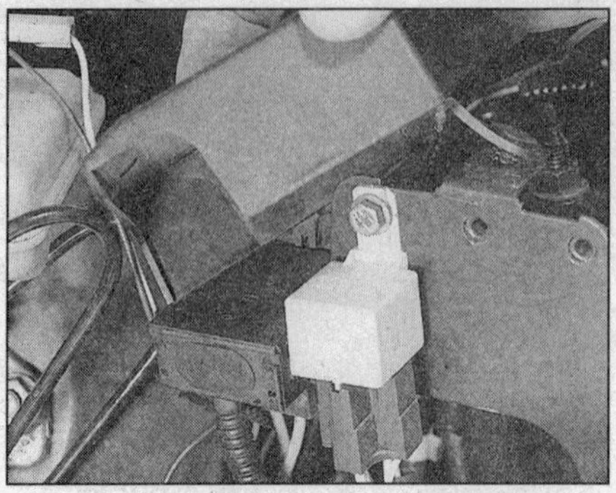

3.13b Relays located in auxiliary fusebox - carburettor model shown

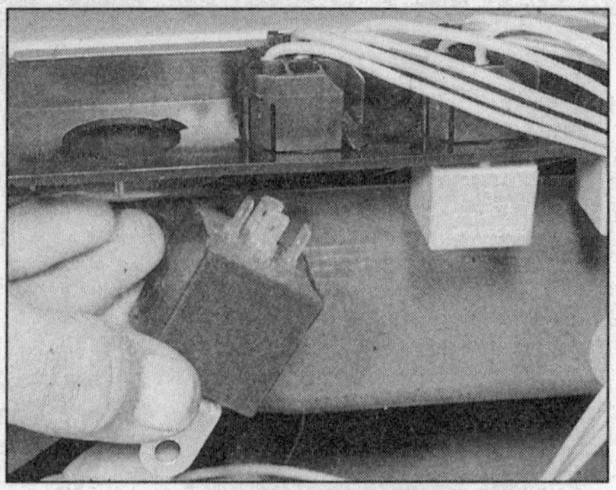

3.15 Removing a relay

10 On later models, the fuses are colour-coded as follows. Refer to the wiring diagrams for details of the fuse ratings and the circuits protected:

Colour	Rating
Orange	*5A*
Red	*10A*
Blue (auxiliary fusebox)	*15A*
Yellow	*20A*
Clear or White	*25A*
Green	*30A*

11 The radio/cassette player has an in-line fuse located in the wiring behind the unit.

Relays

12 A relay is an electrically-operated switch, which is used for the following reasons:

a) A relay can switch a heavy current remotely from the circuit in which the current is flowing, allowing the use of lighter-gauge wiring and switch contacts.

b) A relay can receive more than one control input, unlike a mechanical switch.

c) A relay can have a timer function - for example, the intermittent wiper relay.

13 Most of the relays are located next to the main fusebox, either on top of the facia or on the right-hand or left-hand side of the facia panel (according to model). The rear wiper motor relay is located in the tailgate, behind the tailgate trim panel. On some models, additional engine-related relays are located in an auxiliary fusebox mounted on the left-hand side of the engine compartment **(see illustrations)**.

14 If a circuit or system controlled by a relay develops a fault, and the relay is suspect, operate the system. If the relay is functioning, it should be possible to hear it "click" as it is energised. If this is the case, the fault lies with the components or wiring of the system. If the relay is not being energised, then either the relay is not receiving a main supply or a switching voltage, or the relay itself is faulty. Testing is by the substitution of a known good unit, but be careful - while some relays are identical in appearance and in operation, others look similar but perform different functions.

15 To remove a relay, first ensure that the relevant circuit is switched off. The relay can then simply be pulled out from the socket, and pushed back into position **(see illustration)**.

16 On UK models, a dim-dip headlight system may be fitted. With this system, if the sidelights are switched on with the engine running, the headlights will also be illuminated at reduced output. The resistor for this system is located on the front right-hand side of the front engine compartment crossmember, and is accessed by first removing the radiator grille **(see illustration)**.

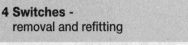

4 Switches - removal and refitting

Note: *Disconnect the battery negative lead before removing any switch, and reconnect the lead after refitting the switch.*

Ignition switch/steering column lock

1 Refer to Chapter 10.

Steering column combination switches

2 Remove the steering wheel as described in Chapter 10.

3 Remove the steering column shroud securing screws. Unclip and lift off the upper shroud, then withdraw the lower shroud.

4 Remove the securing screws, and withdraw the relevant switch from the housing on the steering column. Where applicable, note the location of the insulating foam around the switch body.

5 Disconnect the wiring plug(s) from the rear of the switch.

6 Refitting is a reversal of removal, ensuring that, where applicable, the insulating foam is positioned around the switch as noted before removal.

Facia-mounted pushbutton switches

7 On early models, remove the relevant trim panel, then depress the plastic clips on the rear of the switch in order to remove it from the panel. On models from June 1991 onwards, use a screwdriver to carefully prise the switch from the facia **(see illustrations)**. Where necessary, protect the surrounding trim using card or a pad of cloth.

8 Disconnect the wiring from the rear of the switch.

3.16 Headlight dim-dip resistor, located on the right-hand side of the engine compartment front crossmember

4.7a Use a screwdriver to prise the switch from the facia

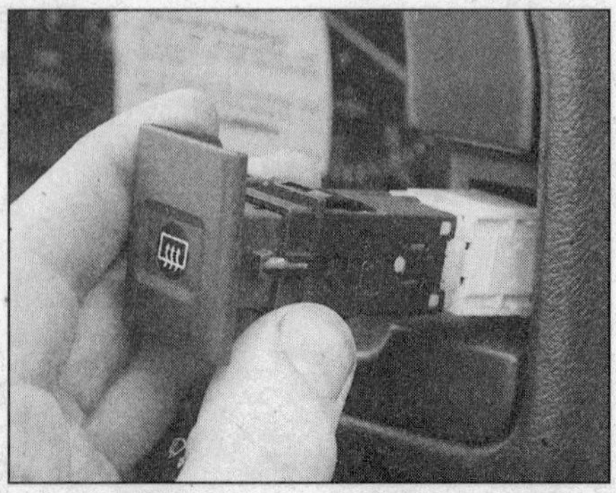

4.7b Removing a switch from the facia

9 Refitting is a reversal of removal. On early models, refit any trim panels removed before pressing the switch into position until the clips engage.

Heater blower motor switch

10 Remove the heating/ventilation control panel as described in Chapter 3.
11 Remove the switch from the panel.
12 Refitting is a reversal of removal.

Courtesy light switches

13 Open the door, then where necessary prise the rubber gaiter from the switch.
14 Remove the securing screw, then withdraw the switch from the door pillar **(see illustration)**. Disconnect the wiring connector as it becomes accessible.

> **HAYNES HINT** *Tape the wiring to the door pillar, to prevent it falling back into the door pillar. Alternatively, tie a piece of string to the wiring, to retrieve it.*

15 Refitting is a reversal of removal, ensuring (where applicable) that the rubber gaiter is correctly seated on the switch.

Glovebox and luggage compartment light switches

16 Open the glovebox, or the tailgate, as applicable, then carefully prise the switch from its location and disconnect the wiring connector.
17 Refitting is a reversal of removal.

Centre console-mounted switches

18 Using a suitable flat-bladed screwdriver, carefully prise the switch from the panel on the centre console.
19 Disconnect the switch wiring connectors.
20 Refitting is a reversal of removal.

Electric window switches

21 On early models (up to July 1991), the electric window switches are located on a panel over the centre console. On later models, they are located in the door pockets.
22 To remove the switch on early models, unclip and remove the lower facia panel for access to the switches. The heater unit, and possibly other adjacent fittings, are likely to impair access. Loosen off the two screws (one each side) and remove the console, then undo the two heater retaining screws. Raise the facia, pivoting it upwards to give the required access to the switches. Release the switch from the panel and detach the wiring connectors.
23 On later models, carefully prise the switch out of the door pocket using a screwdriver, and disconnect the wiring. On some models, the switch wiring connector may be located inside the door, in which case it will be necessary to remove the door trim panel and the plastic sealing sheet for access, as described in Chapter 11.
24 Refitting is a reversal of removal. Where applicable, refit the door inner trim panel with reference to Chapter 11, and use a new sealing sheet.

5 Bulbs (exterior lights) - renewal

General

1 Whenever a bulb is renewed, note the following points:

a) Disconnect the battery negative lead before starting work.
b) Remember that, if the light has just been in use, the bulb (and its holder) may be extremely hot.
c) Always check the bulb contacts and holder, ensuring that there is clean metal-to-metal contact between the bulb and its live contact(s) and earth. Clean off any corrosion or dirt before fitting a new bulb.
d) Wherever bayonet-type bulbs are fitted, ensure that the live contact(s) bear firmly against the bulb contact.
e) Always ensure that the new bulb is of the correct rating, and that it is completely clean before fitting it; this applies particularly to headlight/foglight bulbs (see following paragraphs).

Headlight

2 Open the bonnet, then working at the rear of the headlight assembly, release the securing clip, and lift up the headlight rear cover (where fitted) **(see illustration)**.
3 Pull the wiring plug from the rear of the bulb **(see illustration)**.
4 Press together the ends of the bulb retaining clip, and release it from the rear of the light **(see illustration)**.
5 Withdraw the bulb **(see illustration)**.
6 When handling the new bulb, use a tissue or clean cloth, to avoid touching the glass with the fingers; moisture and grease from the skin can cause blackening and rapid failure of this type of bulb. If the glass is accidentally touched, wipe it clean using methylated spirit.
7 Install the new bulb, ensuring that its locating tabs are correctly located in the light unit cut-outs. Secure the bulb in position with the retaining clip, and reconnect the wiring connector plug.

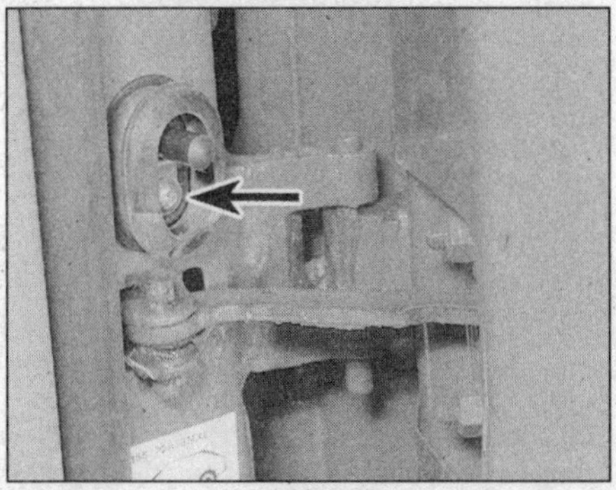
4.14 Door courtesy light switch retaining screw (arrowed)

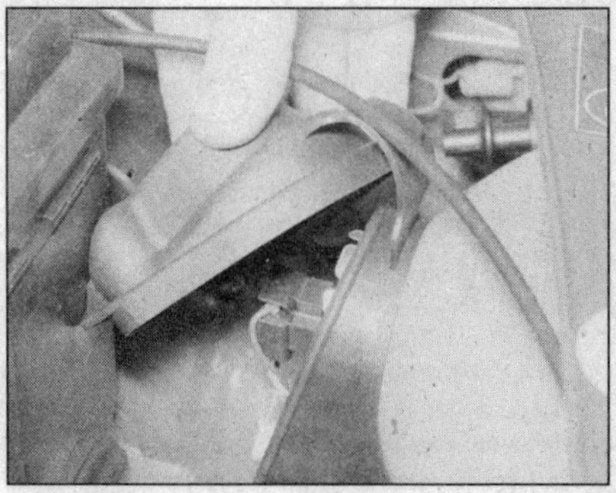
5.2 Lift up the headlight rear cover . . .

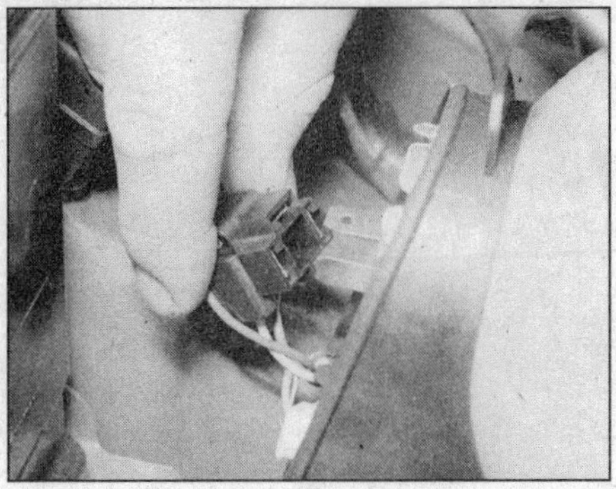
5.3 . . . pull the wiring plug from the bulb . .

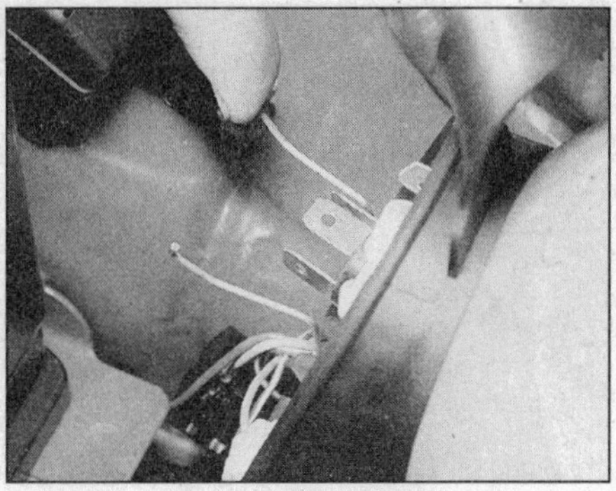
5.4 . . . release the retaining clip . . .

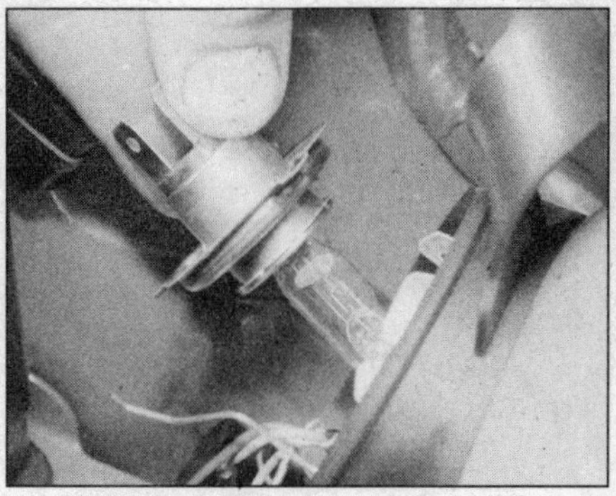
5.5 . . . and withdraw the bulb

12

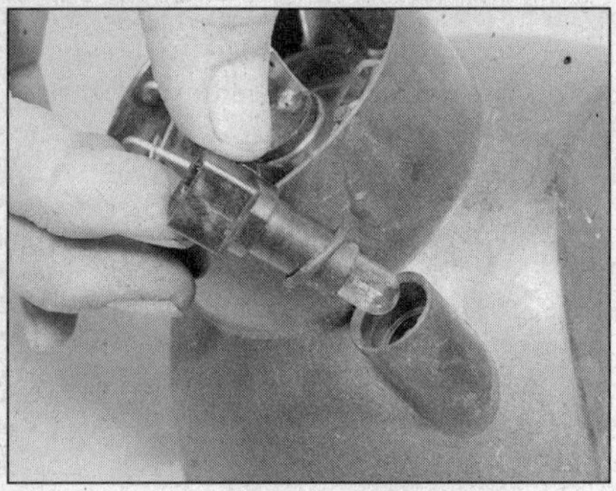

5.10 Sidelight bulb and holder removal from headlight

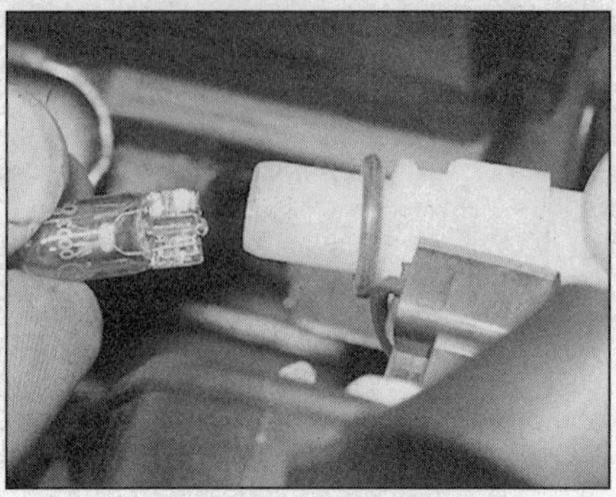

5.11 Removing a sidelight bulb

5.13 Front indicator light bulb and holder removal

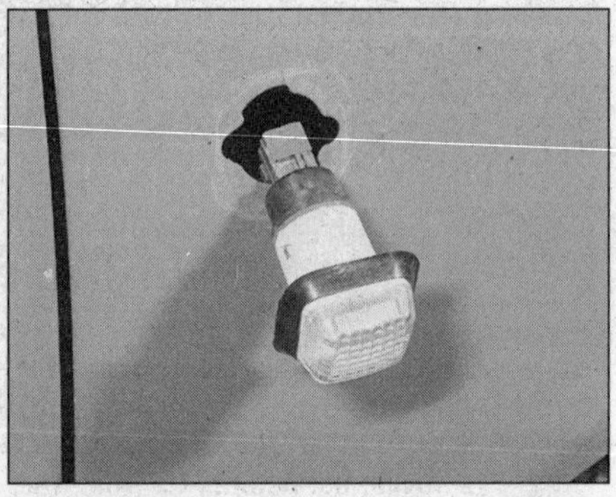

5.16 Removing the side repeater light from the wing panel

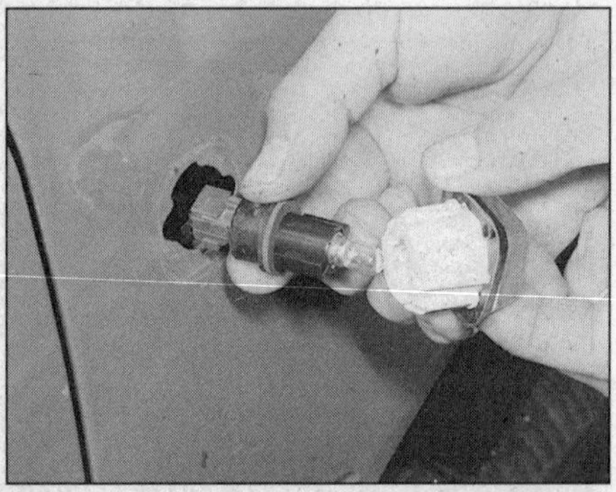

5.18 Disconnecting the bulbholder from the side repeater lens

8 Push the headlight rear cover (where applicable) back into position, ensuring that it is correctly seated on the rear of the light unit.

Front sidelight

9 Proceed as described in paragraph 2.

10 Pull the bulbholder, complete with wiring connections, from the headlight unit **(see illustration)**.

11 Pull the push-fit bulb from the bulbholder **(see illustration)**.

12 Fit the new bulb using a reversal of the removal procedure, ensuring that the bulbholder sealing ring (where applicable) is in good condition.

Front direction indicator

13 Open the bonnet, and working at the front wing behind the direction indicator light, twist the bulbholder and withdraw it from the rear of the light unit **(see illustration)**.

14 Depress and twist the bulb to remove it from the bulbholder.

15 Refitting is a reversal of removal.

Front direction indicator side repeater

16 On early models (up to July 1991), twist the light unit through 45° and withdraw it from the wing panel **(see illustration)**.

17 On later models, push the unit towards the rear of the vehicle to disengage it from the wing panel.

18 Twist the bulbholder and remove it from the light unit, then pull out the push-fit bulb **(see illustration)**.

19 Refitting is a reversal of removal.

Front driving lights/foglights

20 Working at the front of the light unit, remove the two securing screws, and withdraw the glass, surround and reflector assembly.

21 Disconnect the bulb wiring connector.

22 Release the spring clip, and remove the bulb from the rear of the light unit.

23 When handling the new bulb, use a tissue or clean cloth, to avoid touching the glass with the fingers; moisture and grease from the skin can cause blackening and rapid failure of this type of bulb. If the glass is accidentally touched, wipe it clean using methylated spirit.

24 Install the new bulb, ensuring that its locating tabs are correctly located in the light unit cut-outs. Secure the bulb in position with the retaining clip, and reconnect the wiring connector.

25 Refit the glass, surround and reflector assembly, and tighten the securing screws.

Rear light cluster

26 Open the tailgate, unscrew the two wing nuts, and then withdraw the light unit and lens from the body. If necessary, detach the wiring connectors **(see illustration)**.

27 Release the retaining clip, and separate the holder from the light unit **(see illustrations)**.

28 Refitting is a reversal of removal.

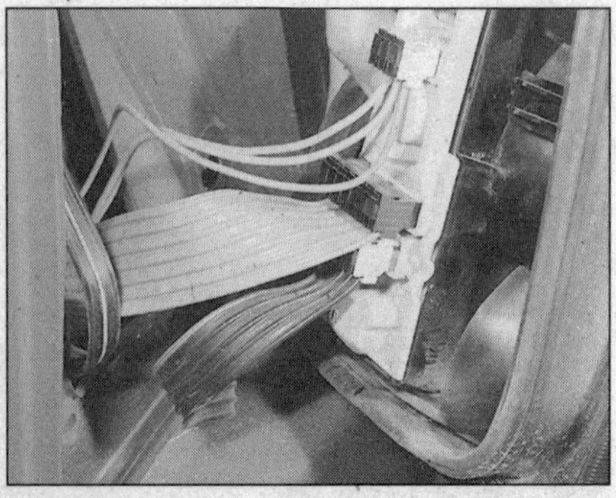

5.26 Rear light cluster removal, showing wiring connectors

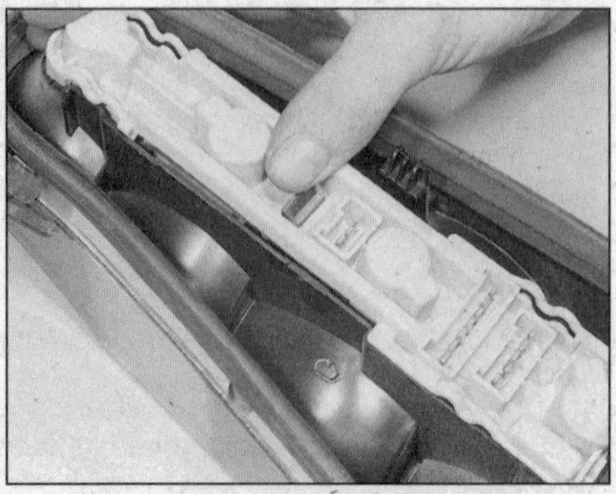

5.27a Release the retaining clip . . .

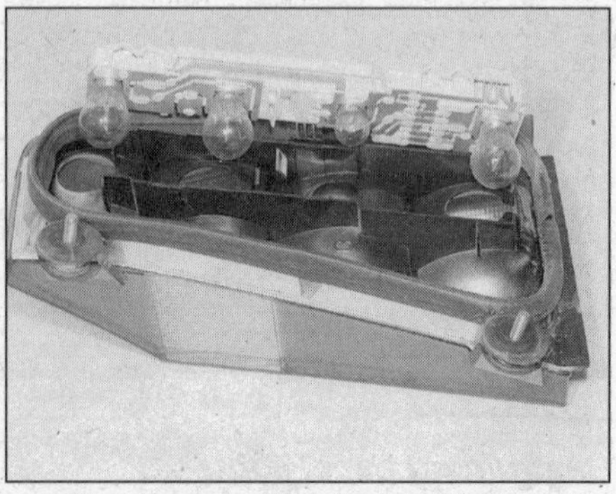

5.27b . . . to detach the bulbholder from the light unit

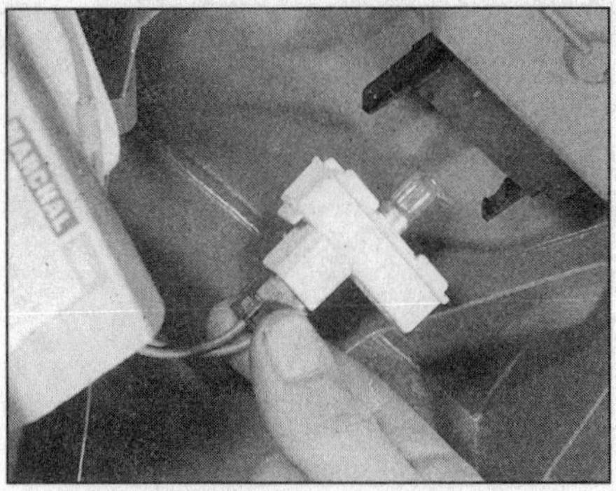

5.30 Rear number plate light bulbholder removal

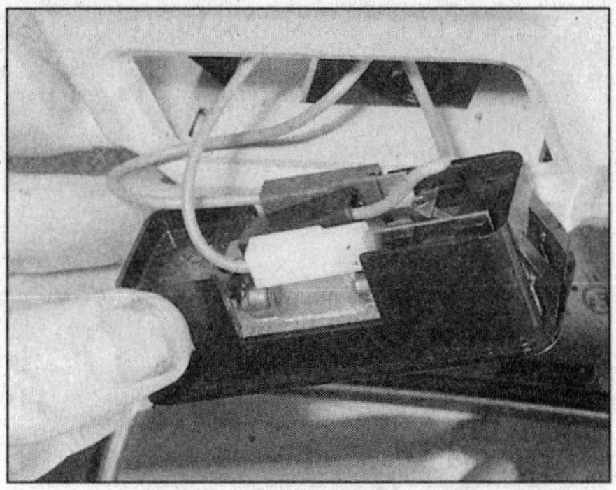

6.2 Courtesy light removal

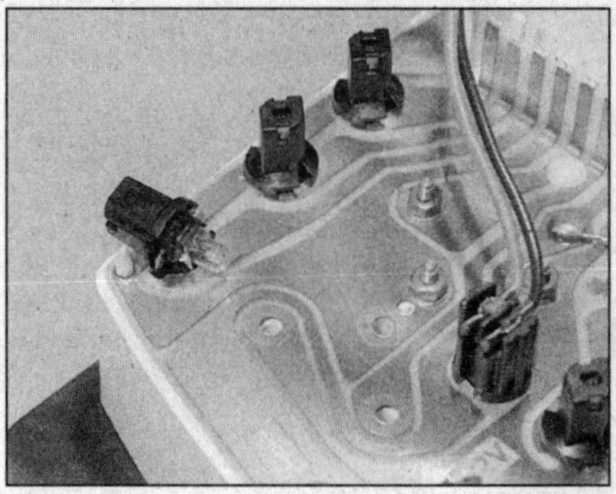

6.7 Instrument panel bulb and holder removal

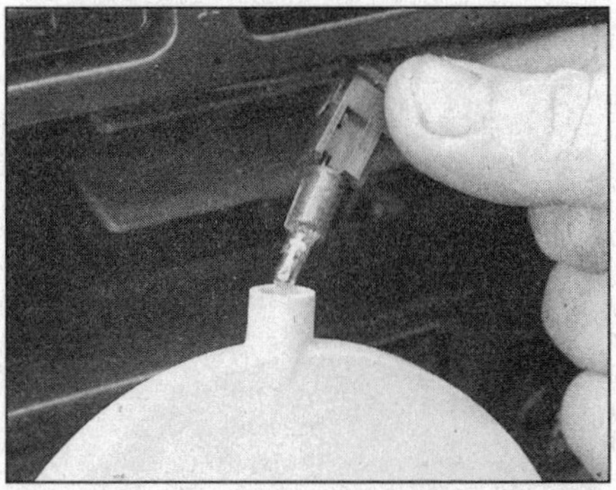

6.11 Removing the heater control panel illumination bulb

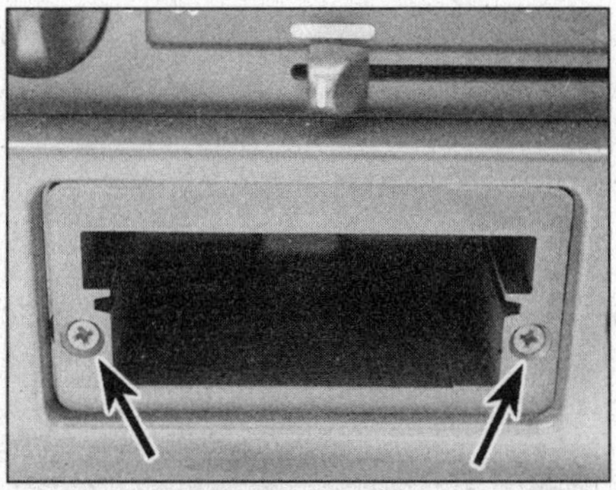

6.16 Ashtray housing retaining screws (arrowed)

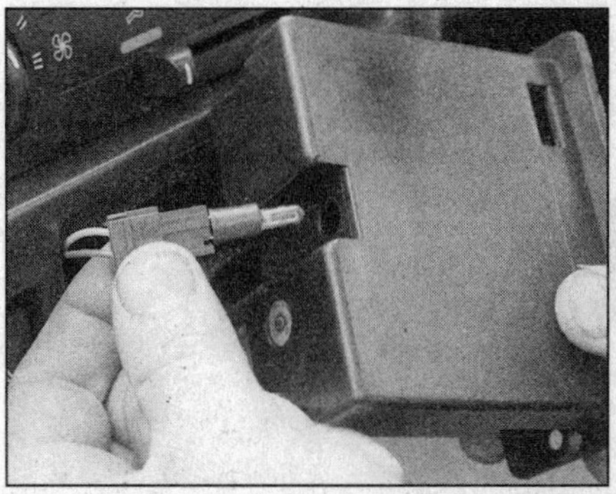

6.17 Removing the bulbholder from the rear of the ashtray housing

Rear number plate light

29 Open the tailgate, then remove the inner cover panel for access to the light unit.

30 Prise open the black retainer clips, and withdraw the bulbholder **(see illustration)**.

31 Depress and twist the bulb to remove it.

32 Refitting is a reversal of removal.

6 Bulbs (interior lights) - renewal

General

1 Refer to Section 5, paragraph 1.

Courtesy light

2 Carefully prise the light unit from its location. If a reading light is fitted, this can be removed in the same manner **(see illustration)**.

3 Remove the festoon or bayonet type bulb from the terminals in the light unit.

4 Refitting is a reversal of removal. If a festoon type bulb is fitted, make sure that the bulb contacts hold the bulb securely; bend them slightly if necessary.

Glovebox and luggage compartment lights

5 The procedure is similar to that for the courtesy light.

Instrument panel lights

6 Remove the instrument panel as described in Section 9.

7 Twist the relevant bulbholder anti-clockwise, and withdraw it from the rear of the panel **(see illustration)**.

8 All bulbs are integral with their holders.

9 Refit the bulbholder to the rear of the instrument panel, then refit the instrument panel as described in Section 9.

Heater control panel illumination bulb

10 Remove the control panel as described in Chapter 3.

11 Pull the bulbholder from the rear of the panel **(see illustration)**.

12 The bulb is a push fit in the bulbholder.

13 Fit the new bulb using a reversal of the removal procedure.

Switch illumination bulbs

14 All the facia switches are fitted with illumination bulbs, and some also have a bulb to show when the circuit concerned is operating. The bulbs are an integral part of the switch assembly, and cannot be obtained separately. Bulb renewal will therefore require renewal of the complete switch assembly.

Ashtray illumination bulb

15 Remove the ashtray from its location in the facia.

16 Unscrew the two crosshead screws, and withdraw the ashtray housing from the facia **(see illustration)**.

17 Pull the bulbholder from the housing, then disconnect the wiring **(see illustration)**. It is not possible to separate the bulb from the bulbholder.

18 Refitting is a reversal of the removal procedure.

7 Exterior light units - removal and refitting

Note: *Disconnect the battery negative lead before removing any light unit, and reconnect the lead after refitting.*

Headlight

Removal

1 To remove a headlight unit, grip and pull the unit outwards from the front to disengage it from the two inboard adjusters, then pull it towards the centre to disengage it from the single outer adjuster **(see illustration)**. Where

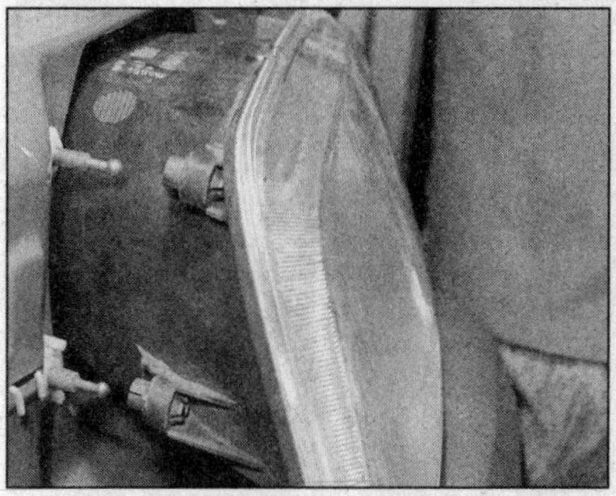

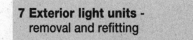

7.1 Headlight unit removal

applicable, also disconnect it from the headlight level adjustment unit.

2 Remove the rear cover (where applicable), then detach the wiring connectors and remove the unit.

3 If desired, the balljoint and adjuster units (and the electric adjuster motor, where applicable) can be removed from the body after twisting the unit itself (or the locking collar, as applicable) to release the unit from the aperture in the body.

Refitting

4 Refitting is a reversal of removal, ensuring that the headlight balljoints are correctly engaged. Have the beam alignment checked by a suitably-equipped garage at the earliest opportunity.

Front direction indicator light

Removal

5 Remove the headlight unit as described above.

6 Release the side retainer, then press the retainer tab on the other side using a thin-bladed screwdriver and withdraw the unit **(see illustrations)**. Disconnect the bulbholder.

7 Refitting is a reversal of the removal procedure.

Front direction indicator side repeater light

Removal

8 On early models (up to July 1991), twist the light unit through 45° and withdraw it from the wing panel. On later models, push the unit towards the rear of the vehicle to disengage it from the wing panel.

9 Withdraw the light unit from the wing panel, and disconnect the wiring plug **(see illustration)**. Tape the wiring to the wing panel, to prevent it falling back into the hole.

Refitting

10 Refitting is a reversal of removal.

Front driving light/foglight

Removal

11 Trace the wiring back from the light unit, and disconnect the wiring connector (usually located in the engine compartment, behind the headlight unit). Note the routing of the wiring, to aid refitting.

12 Note the alignment of the light unit, for use when refitting, so that the light aim is not lost - make some removable alignment marks between the light unit and the bumper if wished. Working up behind the front bumper, unscrew the nut and recover the washer from the light mounting stud. Note that the light will be free to pivot once the nut has been loosened.

13 Withdraw the light unit from the bumper.

Refitting

14 Refitting is a reversal of removal, ensuring that the wiring is routed correctly. Check the aim of the light (aligning any marks made prior to removal) before finally tightening the securing nut.

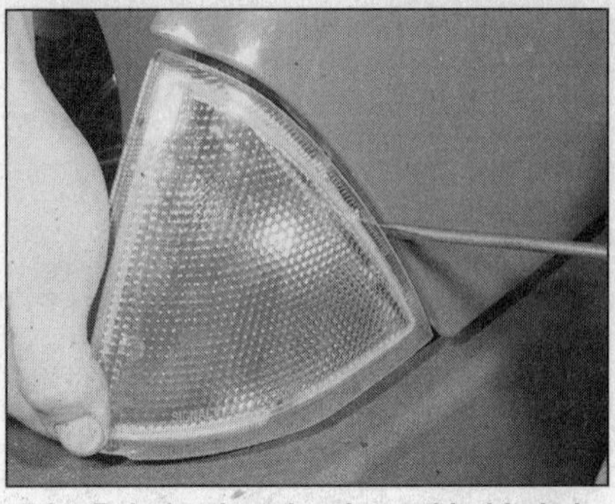

7.6a Release the tab using a thin-bladed screwdriver . . .

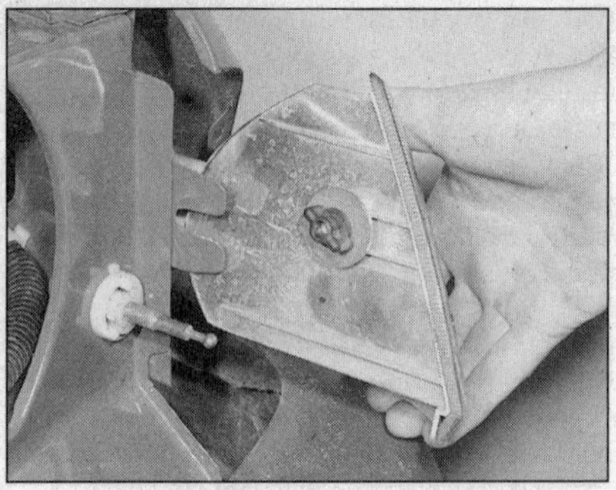

7.6b . . . then withdraw the unit

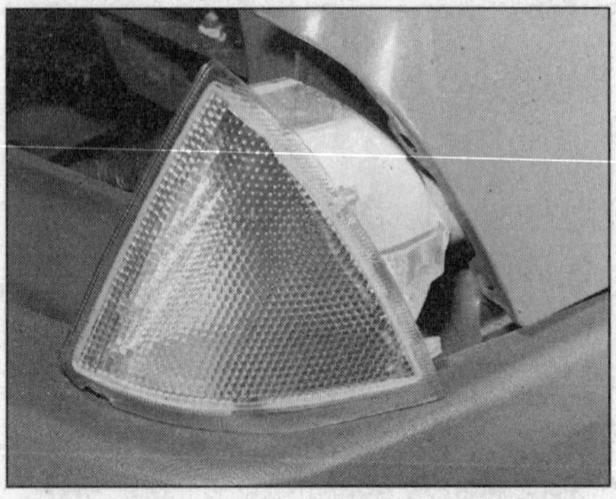

7.6c Front direction indicator, showing location pegs and slots in wing

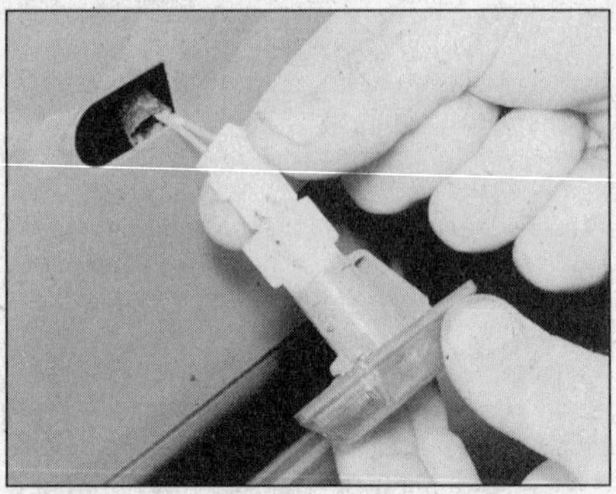

7.9 Removing a front direction indicator side repeater light

Rear light cluster

Removal

15 Open the tailgate.

16 Where applicable, prise the plastic cover from the rear of the light unit.

17 Either unclip the bulbholder or disconnect the wiring plug from the rear of the unit.

18 Unscrew the two wing nuts, and withdraw the light unit from the body.

Refitting

19 Refitting is a reversal of removal, but check the condition of the seals on the rear of the light assembly. If necessary, these seals may be obtained separately.

Rear number plate light

Removal and refitting

20 The procedure is described in Section 5.

8 Headlight beam alignment - general information

1 Accurate adjustment of the headlight beam is only possible using optical beam-setting equipment, and this work should therefore be carried out by a Citroën dealer or suitably-equipped workshop.

2 All models are equipped with headlight beam adjustment, which allows the aim of the headlights to be adjusted to compensate for the varying loads carried in the vehicle. Certain models have a switch on the facia, which enables beam adjustment via electric adjuster motors located in the rear of the headlight assemblies. Models not equipped with electric headlight adjusters have levers located on the rear of the headlight units (in the outer top corner) in the engine compartment. The switch or levers, as applicable, should be positioned according to the load being carried in the vehicle.

9 Instrument panel - removal and refitting

Removal

1 Disconnect the battery negative lead.

Models up to July 1991

2 Remove the steering wheel as described in Chapter 10. On GT models, it may not be strictly necessary to remove the steering wheel, but this will in any case provide more working room.

3 Remove the fusebox inspection panel (see Section 3), and reach down through the aperture to detach the speedometer cable from the instrument panel. Also disconnect the two wiring block connectors from the panel.

4 On GT models, use a screwdriver to carefully prise off the surround from the face of the instrument panel. Take care not to damage the surrounding trim panel.
5 Release the retaining clips using a suitable flat-bladed tool (or electrician's screwdriver) inserted between the edge of the panel and the facia surround. On non-GT models, there are two clips along the top edge and two along the bottom edge; GT models have only two retainers along the bottom edge. As the clips are released, simultaneously pull the instrument panel from the recess in the facia and remove it **(see illustrations)**.

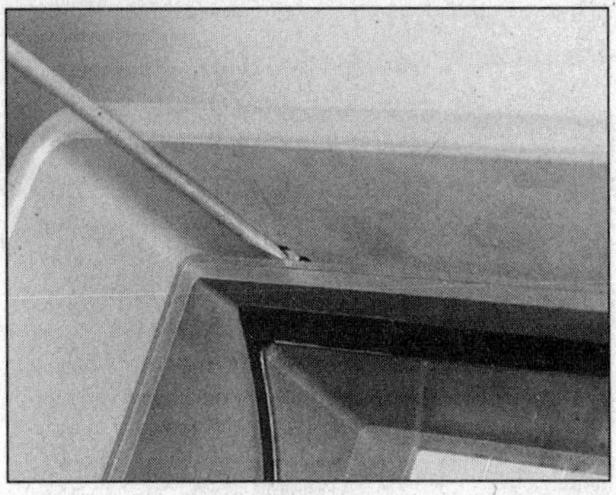

9.5a Releasing the retaining clips on the instrument panel

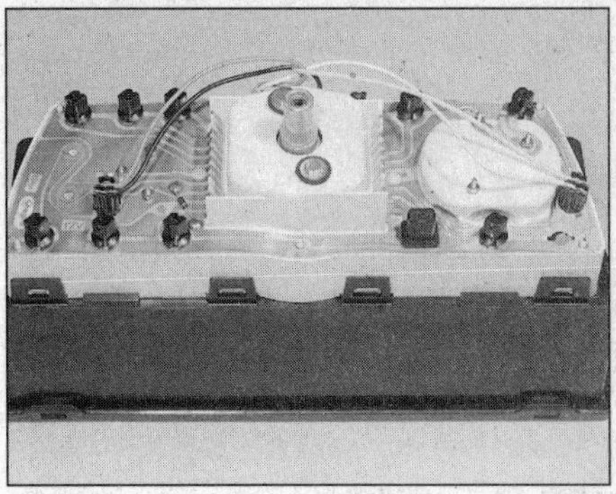

9.5b Instrument panel removed from the facia

Models from July 1991 onwards

6 Remove the steering wheel as described in Chapter 10.
7 Prise the two switches out of the instrument panel surround using a screwdriver, then disconnect the wiring plugs.
8 Remove the upper and lower steering column shrouds. Unscrew the two screws securing the bottom of the surround to the facia panel, and the two remaining screws securing the top of the surround. Remove the surround.
9 Release the instrument panel from the facia, and withdraw it sufficiently to disconnect the wiring plugs and speedometer cable. Remove the panel from the car.

Refitting

All models

10 Refitting is a reversal of removal, but make sure that the speedometer cable and wiring plugs are correctly connected. Check the operation of the instruments and warning lights on the panel.

10 Instrument panel components - general

1 Individual components (ie speedometer, tachometer, printed circuit etc) are available separately from Citroën, and their removal is straightforward. Small and medium-size screwdrivers and a pair of pliers are the only tools required to remove the instruments.

11 "Lights on" warning system - general information

1 Later vehicles covered by this manual are fitted with a "lights-on" warning system. The purpose of this system is to inform the driver that the lights have been left switched on, once the ignition switch has been turned off - the buzzer will sound when a door is opened. The system consists simply of a buzzer unit which is connected to the door courtesy light switches.
2 The buzzer unit is located with the relays (see Section 3).

12 Cigarette lighter - removal and refitting

Removal

Models up to July 1991

1 Access to the cigar lighter is poor. Even with the adjacent grille and the radio unit removed, it is still difficult to reach and release the retaining clips from the underside. It may well be found necessary to at least partially remove the facia, with reference to Chapter 11.
2 When suitable access is gained to the rear of the unit, disconnect the element wire and the illumination bulb wire, then compress the retaining clips and withdraw the cigarette lighter **(see illustration)**.

Models from July 1991 onwards

3 Remove the ashtray from its location in the facia.
4 Unscrew the two crosshead screws, and withdraw the ashtray housing from the facia (see illustration 6.16).
5 Access can now be gained to the rear of the unit, through the ashtray aperture. Disconnect the wiring, release the retaining clips, and withdraw the unit from the facia.

Refitting

6 Refitting is a reversal of removal.

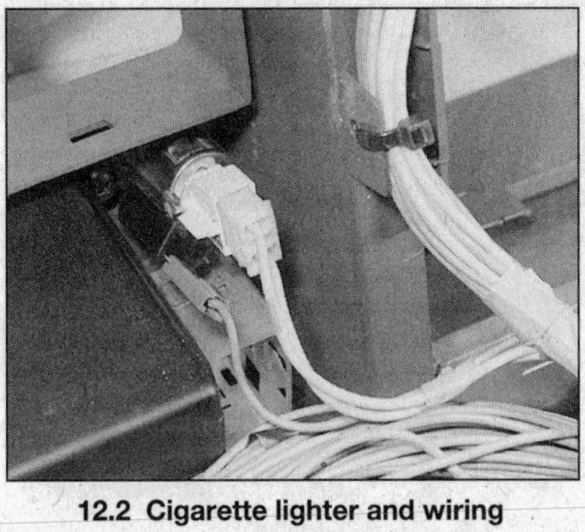

12.2 Cigarette lighter and wiring connectors

13 Horn - removal and refitting

Removal

1 The horn is attached to the inside of the front chassis member on the right-hand side **(see illustration)**. Access is best achieved from the underside of the car. If necessary, apply the handbrake then jack up the front of the car and support it on axle stands.
2 Unscrew the mounting bracket retaining bolt and (where necessary) disconnect the earth wire, then disconnect the horn feed wire. Remove the horn.

Refitting

3 Refitting is a reversal of the removal procedure.

14 Speedometer cable - removal and refitting

Removal

1 On some models, the speedometer cable is in two sections, and these may be separated by unscrewing the ferrule located in front of the bulkhead **(see illustration)**. Each section of the cable is available separately.

13.1 Horn location and wiring connections

12

14.1 On some models, the speedometer cable may be separated into two sections by unscrewing the ferrule (arrowed)

14.3 Speedometer cable-to-instrument panel connection viewed through the fusebox aperture - models up to July 1991

15.2 Wiper arm spindle nut

2 Disconnect the speedometer cable from the transmission by extracting the rubber retainer, and pulling the cable from the pinion housing. It will be necessary to remove the inlet air ducting first in order to gain access.

3 On early models (up to July 1991), to disconnect the speedometer cable at the instrument panel end, remove the fusebox as described in Section 3, then working through the aperture in the top of the facia, detach the cable from the speedometer **(see illustration)**. On later models, it will be necessary to remove the instrument panel completely, with reference to Section 9.

4 Release any clips, then withdraw the cable through the bulkhead and remove it from the engine compartment side.

Refitting

5 Refitting is a reversal of the removal procedure.

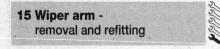

15 Wiper arm - removal and refitting

Removal

1 Operate the wiper motor, then switch it off so that the wiper arm returns to the at-rest ("parked") position.

> **HAYNES HiNT** *Stick a piece of tape along the edge of the wiper blade, to use as an alignment aid when refitting.*

2 Where applicable, lift up the wiper arm spindle nut cover, then slacken and remove the spindle nut **(see illustration)**. Lift the blade off the glass, and pull the wiper arm off its spindle. If necessary, the arm can be levered off the spindle using a suitable flat-bladed screwdriver.

Refitting

3 Ensure that the wiper arm and spindle splines are clean and dry, then refit the arm to the spindle, aligning the wiper blade with the tape.

4 Refit the spindle nut, tighten it securely, and where applicable, clip the cover back into position.

16 Windscreen wiper motor and linkage - removal and refitting

Removal

1 Disconnect the battery negative lead.

2 Remove the wiper blades and arms, as described in Section 15.

3 Open the bonnet, then remove the air intake cowl and deflector as follows. Unscrew the cowl retaining screws and nuts, and then withdraw the cowl. Undo the three retaining screws, and remove the deflector shield for access to the wiper motor **(see illustrations)**.

4 Disconnect the wiring plug from the motor **(see illustration)**. If necessary, remove the screw retaining the wiring clip to the bulkhead.

5 Unscrew the mounting screws, and slide the wiper motor unit from the scuttle **(see illustration)**.

6 To remove the wiper motor from its support bracket, first undo the nut securing the connector arm to the drive spindle **(see illustration)**; mark the relative positions of the arm and spindle, then detach the arm.

7 Unscrew the three retaining bolts, and

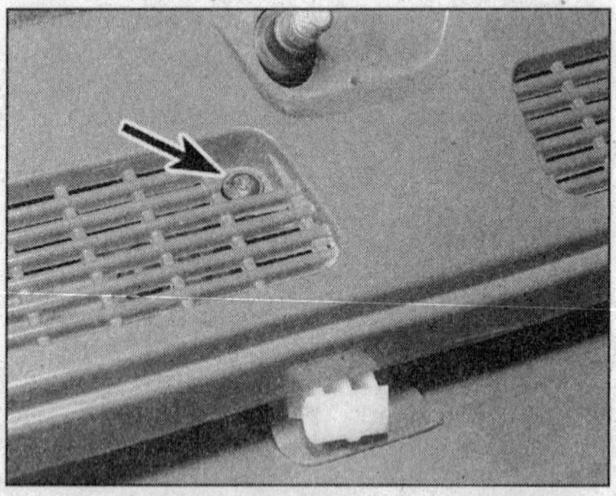

16.3a Cowl retaining screw (arrowed)

16.3b Unscrew and remove the nut and flat washer . . .

16.3c . . . and remove the deflector shield

16.4 Windscreen wiper motor and wiring plug

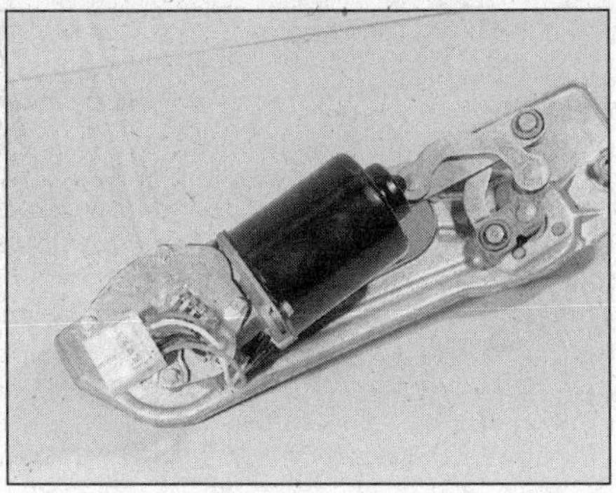

16.5 Windscreen wiper motor and support bracket

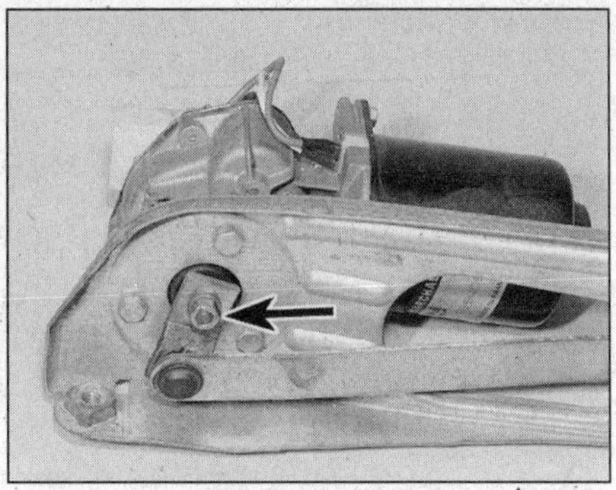

16.6 Windscreen wiper motor connector arm-to-spindle nut (arrowed)

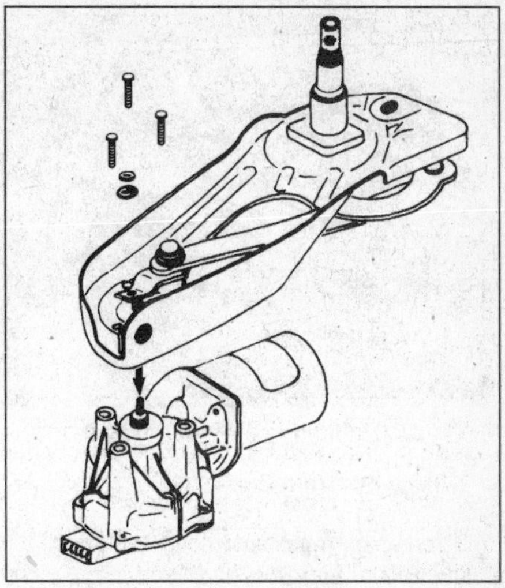

16.7 Removing the wiper motor from its support bracket

separate the motor from the support bracket **(see illustration)**.

Refitting

8 Refitting is a reversal of the removal procedure.

17 Tailgate wiper motor - removal and refitting

Removal

1 Disconnect the battery negative lead.

2 Remove the tailgate wiper arm, as described in Section 15.

3 Recover the spindle dust cover, then unscrew the trim disc and lift off the grommet cover.

4 Open the tailgate.

5 Carefully prise free the trim cover clips, and remove the cover from the inside of the tailgate.

6 Disconnect the wiper motor wiring, then undo the mounting bolts and remove the wiper motor assembly from the tailgate **(see illustration)**.

Refitting

7 Refitting is a reversal of removal. Check the condition of all seals, and renew them if necessary. Make sure that the wiper arm is located correctly on the arm to provide the correct parked position.

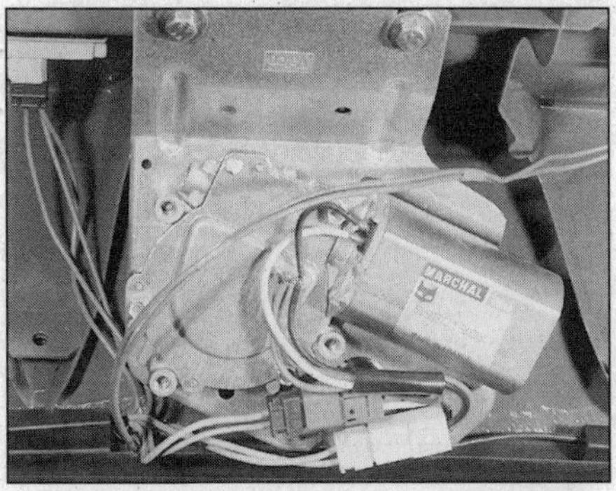

17.6 Tailgate wiper motor and mounting plate

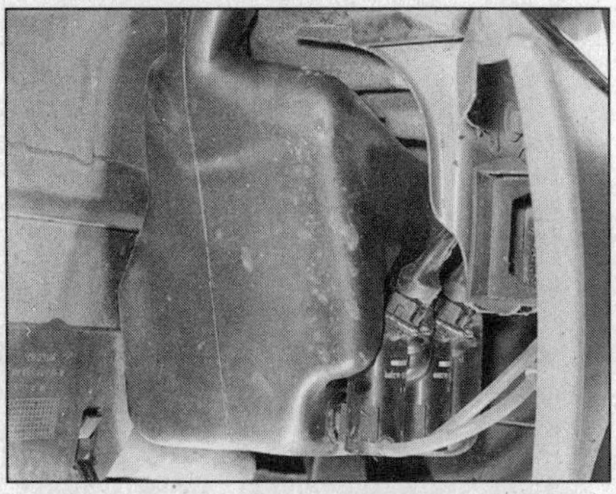

18.1 Windscreen/tailgate washer system reservoir and pump location under the right-hand front wing

18 Windscreen/tailgate washer system components - removal and refitting

Washer fluid reservoir

Removal

1 The reservoir is located under the right-hand front wing **(see illustration)**. On later models (July 1991-on), it is concealed by the wheel arch liner.

2 Disconnect the battery negative lead.

3 Working in the engine compartment, unscrew the filler neck from the top of the reservoir **(see illustration)**.

4 Apply the handbrake, then jack up the front of the vehicle and support securely on axle stands (see *"Jacking, towing and wheel changing"*).Remove the right-hand roadwheel.

5 Remove the screw securing the front of the wheel arch liner to the bumper, then release the securing clips (which are a push fit), and withdraw the liner from under the wheel arch.

6 Release the securing strap from the reservoir, then lower the reservoir from the wheel arch **(see illustration)**.

7 Disconnect the washer pump wiring plug(s) **(see illustration)**. Disconnect the fluid hose(s)

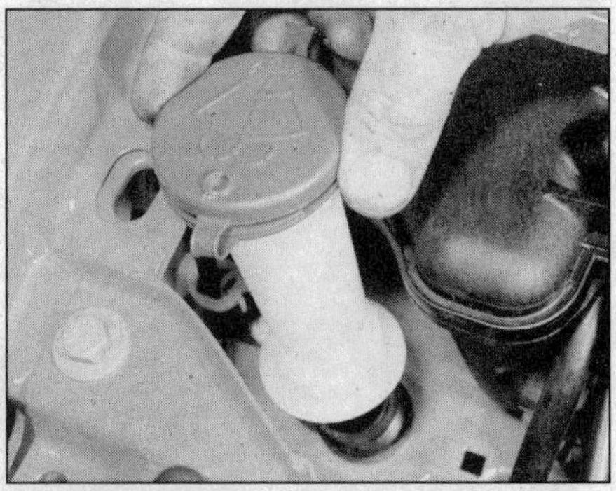

18.3 Unscrew the filler neck from the washer fluid reservoir

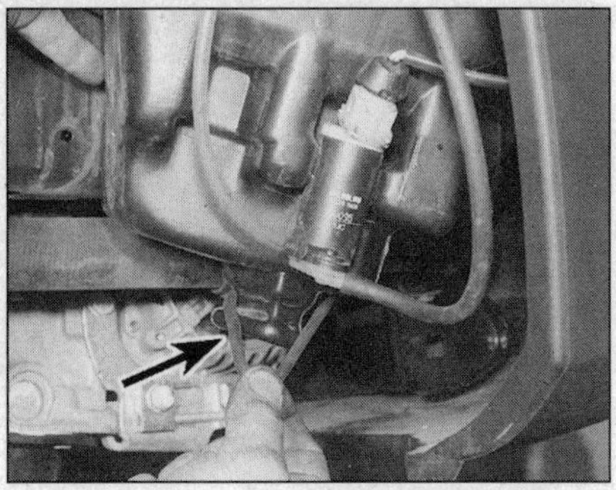

18.6 Releasing the securing strap (arrowed)

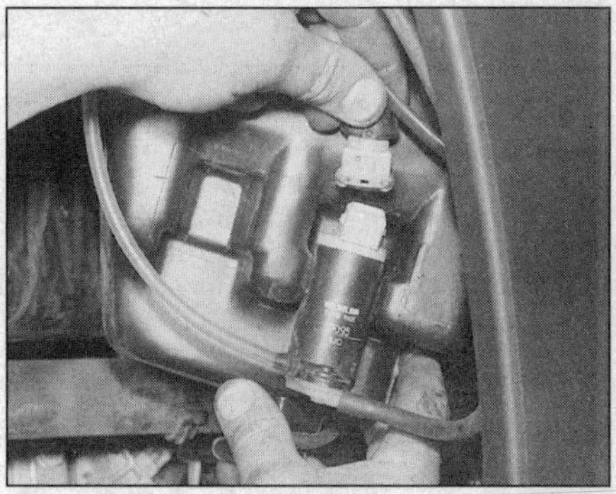

18.7 Disconnecting the wiring plug(s) and the hose(s)

18.10 Removing a washer fluid pump

from the pump(s) - be prepared for fluid spillage - then withdraw the reservoir.

Refitting

8 Refitting is a reversal of removal.

Washer pump(s)

Removal

9 Remove the fluid reservoir as described previously in this Section.

10 The washer pump(s) is/are a push fit in the reservoir **(see illustration)**.

Refitting

11 Refitting is a reversal of removal, but check the condition of the mounting grommet in the reservoir, and renew if necessary.

Windscreen washer jet

12 Carefully prise the washer nozzle from the bonnet (take care not to damage the paintwork), and disconnect the fluid hose.

13 Refitting is a reversal of removal. Adjust the aim of the washer jet (if necessary) using a pin in the washer nozzle.

Tailgate washer jet

14 Carefully prise the washer jet from the tailgate (take care not to damage the paintwork), and disconnect the fluid hose **(see illustration)**.

15 Take care not to allow the hose to drop back into the tailgate - tape it to the tailgate if necessary.

16 Refitting is a reversal of removal. Adjust the aim of the washer jet (if necessary) using a pin in the washer nozzle.

19 Headlight washer system components - removal and refitting

Washer fluid reservoir

1 Proceed as described in Section 18 for the windscreen/tailgate washer fluid reservoir.

Washer pump

2 Remove the fluid reservoir with reference to Section 18.

3 The washer pump is a push fit in the reservoir.

4 Refitting is a reversal of removal.

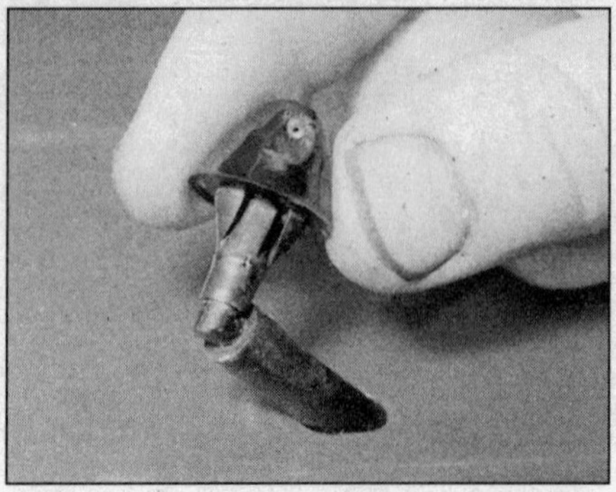

18.14 Removing the tailgate washer jet

Washer jets

5 Remove the front bumper as described in Chapter 11.

6 Working behind the bumper, disconnect the fluid hose from the rear of the washer jet.

7 Prise off the securing clip (or unscrew the securing nut and washer, as applicable), then withdraw the washer jet from the top of the bumper.

8 Refitting is a reversal of removal. Refit the bumper with reference to Chapter 11.

20 Radio/cassette player - removal and refitting

Note: *Refer to "Radio/cassette unit anti-theft system - precaution" at the start of this manual, before proceeding.*

Removal

1 On most models, a radio (or radio/cassette) is fitted as standard equipment, and is located in the central facia. On models where a radio is not fitted during production, an aperture is provided in the central facia, blanked off with a finisher panel.

2 Irrespective of whether a radio is fitted from new or not, most cars are fitted with "pre-radio equipment", comprising a roof-mounted aerial and coaxial aerial cable, normal interference suppression and radio connection wiring harnesses (including speaker wiring on some models). Speaker housings are either located in each front door panel or the rear quarter panels.

3 To remove an early standard unit, disconnect the battery negative lead, pull off the radio control knobs and unscrew the mounting nuts. The surround can then be withdrawn and the radio removed, after disconnecting the aerial and wiring.

4 On later models, the radio fixing is by means of concealed side clips, access to which is gained by inserting special release tools through the slotted holes in the front face of the unit each side. These tools may be provided with the vehicle when new (if so, they will be in the glovebox) but if not, they can be obtained from your Citroën dealer. Insert the tools into the release access holes each side, release the clips and withdraw the radio.

5 When the radio is withdrawn sufficiently, disconnect the wiring plugs and the aerial lead, and withdraw the unit.

Refitting

6 Refit in the reverse order of removal. Check that the wiring is positioned correctly behind the radio, to allow space for the unit to be pushed into position. Make sure that the radio is fully engaged with its retaining clips, where applicable.

21 Speakers - removal and refitting

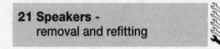

Front door-mounted speakers - 5-door models

1 Disconnect the battery negative lead.

2 On early models (up to July 1991) it is necessary to remove the trim panel with reference to Chapter 11 and disconnect the wiring, then unscrew the mounting screws and remove the speaker from the inner face of the trim panel **(see illustrations)**.

3 On later models (July 1991 on) prise off the speaker cover, then unscrew the mounting screws and withdraw the speaker sufficiently to disconnect the wiring **(see illustrations)**.

4 Refitting is a reversal of removal.

Rear speakers - 3-door models

5 Disconnect the battery negative lead.

6 Remove the rear quarter trim panel as described in Chapter 11, Section 26 **(see illustration)**.

7 Disconnect the wiring from the speaker, then unscrew the mounting screws and withdraw the speaker.

8 Refitting is a reversal of removal.

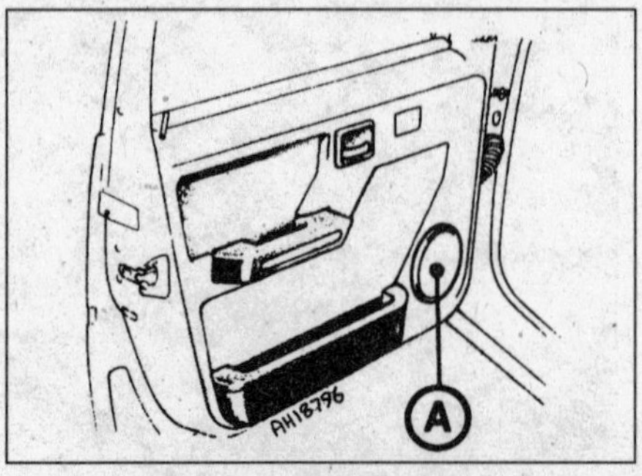

21.2a Speaker unit location (A) in the front door panel (5-door model)

21.2b Speaker and mounting screws

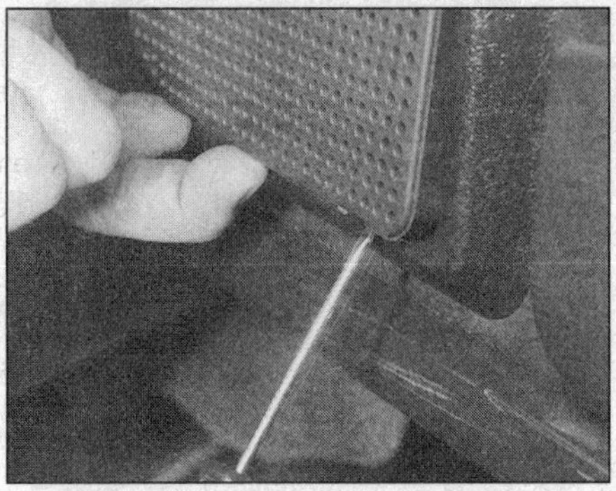
21.3a Prise off the speaker cover . . .

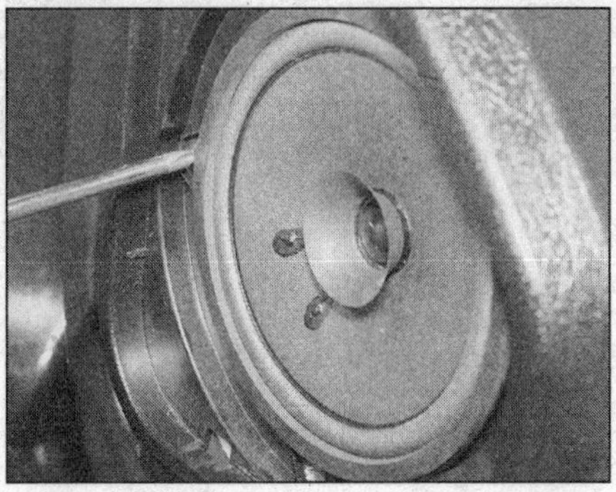
21.3b . . . unscrew the mounting screws . . .

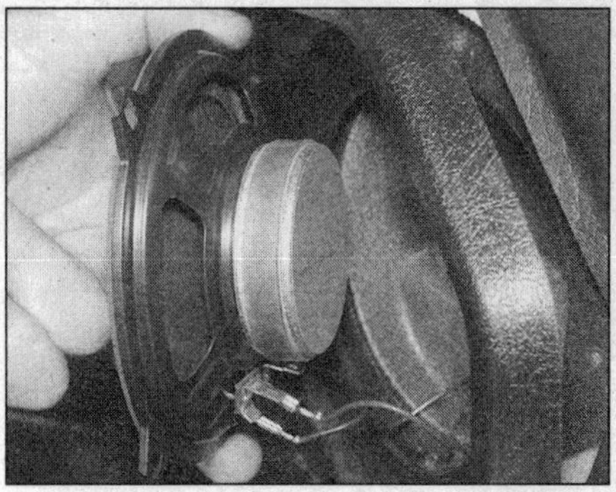
21.3c . . . and withdraw the speaker in order to disconnect the wiring

22 Radio aerial - removal and refitting

Removal

1 Remove the radio as described in Section 20, and disconnect the aerial connection - this is usually a thick coaxial cable..
2 Remove the courtesy light with reference to Section 6.
3 Unscrew the two retaining screws and remove the courtesy light panel **(see illustration)**.
4 Unscrew the aerial retaining nut and the earth lead nut **(see illustration)**.
5 Attach a length of string to the radio end of the aerial lead. The string must be at least as long as the aerial lead, so that when the lead is pulled through the body channels, the string temporarily takes its place. The string can subsequently be reattached, to redirect the lead through the channels during the refitting procedure.
6 Detach and remove the parcel shelf or trim panel (as applicable) on the passenger side.
7 Detach the trim from the windscreen pillar on the passenger side. Also carefully detach the headlining at the leading edge on the passenger side.
8 Remove the aerial from the roof, and withdraw the lead and string, feeding them through the various body channels. When the string emerges through the hole in the roof panel, untie it from the radio end of the aerial lead, and leave it in place in the car.

Refitting

9 Refitting is a reversal of the removal procedure. Use the string to pull the aerial lead through into the radio aperture, then untie it. Ensure that the lead connections are secure, and that the earth lead connection is clean.

23 Heated front seat components - general information

1 Certain models may be equipped with heated front seats. The seats are heated by electrical elements built into the seat cushions.
2 For access to the heating elements, the seats must be dismantled. This work should be entrusted to a Citroën dealer.
3 The heated seat switches are mounted in the centre console. Removal and refitting details are given in Section 4.

24 Wiring diagrams - explanatory notes

The wiring diagrams in this manual represent typical examples of those available. To assist you in using the diagrams, refer to the accompanying table of notes and the symbols used **(see illustrations)**; the following is an explanation of the various letters and their use, in conjunction with the wiring diagram keys:

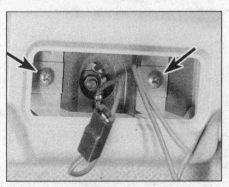

22.3 Interior roof light panel fixing screws (arrowed)

22.4 Aerial retaining nut and earth lead

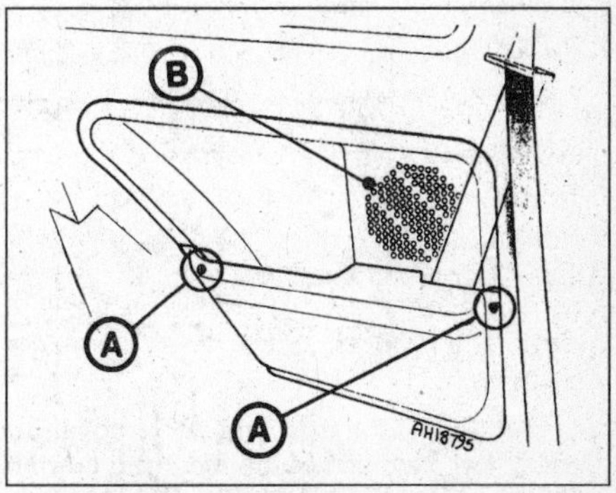

21.6 Rear side panel and retaining screws (A) on 3-door models. Remove the screws for access to the speaker (B)

a) **Large numbers -** identify the various components.
b) **Capital letters printed in the middle of a wire -** indicate which harness the wire is located in.
c) **Small letters located at the connection points -** indicates the colour of either the wire itself, or of the marking on the wire. If the letter has a line drawn above it, then this shows it indicates the colour of the wire itself; if there is no line above the letter, it indicates the colour of the marking on the wire.
d) **Connecting blocks -** The first number and letter(s) inside the box indicates the size and colour of the connecting block. The second letter (where applicable) and last number gives the exact location of the relevant wire in that connecting block; the letter indicates which row the wire is situated in, and the number denotes its location in that row. For example:
3 Bl 2 - shows that the wiring connector is blue in colour, and contains three wiring channels, the wire shown in the diagram being located in the second channel of the connector.
15 V A 2 - shows that the wiring connector is green in colour, and contains fifteen channels. The A shows that the wire shown in the diagram is in the upper row of the connector, and the 2 shows it to be in the second channel of that row.

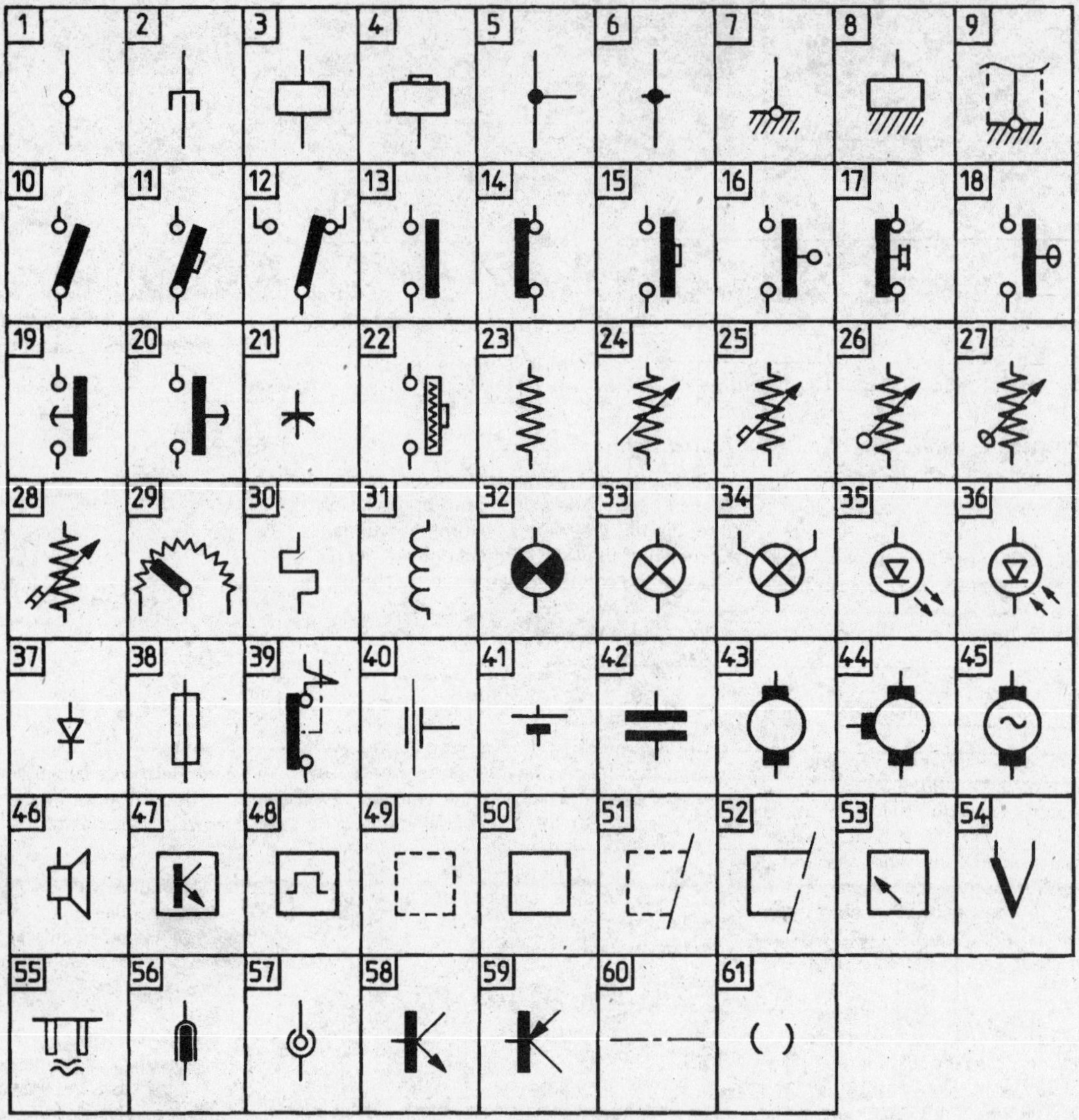

24.1a Key to symbols used in wiring diagrams

1 *Socket connection*
2 *Pin connection*
3 *Connector connection*
4 *Connector connection with index (for differentiation)*
5 *Junction not to be dismantled (splice)*
6 *Junction not to be dismantled (with other connection possibilities)*
7 *Socket earthing*
8 *Connector earthing*
9 *Part body earth connection*
10 *Switch (non-automatic return)*
11 *Manual switch*
12 *Selector switch*
13 *Switch on at-rest (automatic return)*
14 *Switch off at-rest (automatic return)*
15 *Manual contact switch*
16 *Mechanical contact switch*
17 *Pressure contact switch*
18 *Thermal switch*
19 *Contact delayed on opening*
20 *Contact delayed on closing*
21 *Friction contact switch*
22 *Manual contact switch (cigar lighter) with resistance*
23 *Resistance*
24 *Rheostat*
25 *Manual rheostat*
26 *Mechanical rheostat*
27 *Temperature rheostat (thermistor)*
28 *Pressure rheostat*
29 *Rheostat*
30 *Shunt*
31 *Coil (relay-solenoid)*
32 *Warning light*
33 *Light bulb*
34 *Double-filament light bulb*
35 *Light-emitting diode (LED)*
36 *Photo-diode*
37 *Diode*
38 *Fuse*
39 *Thermal circuit breaker*
40 *Screening*
41 *Battery cell*
42 *Suppressor*
43 *Motor*
44 *Two-speed motor*
45 *Alternative power generator*
46 *Sound equipment (horn, loudspeaker)*
47 *Electronic control unit*
48 *Delay unit*
49 *Part framing (with its circuit diagram)*
50 *Part framing (without its circuit diagram)*
51 *Part extract*
52 *Part extract*
53 *Indicator*
54 *Thermocouple*
55 *Electrodes*
56 *Oxygen sensor*
57 *Supply socket*
58 *NPN transistor*
59 *PNP transistor*
60 *Connection indicating line*
61 *No extremity*

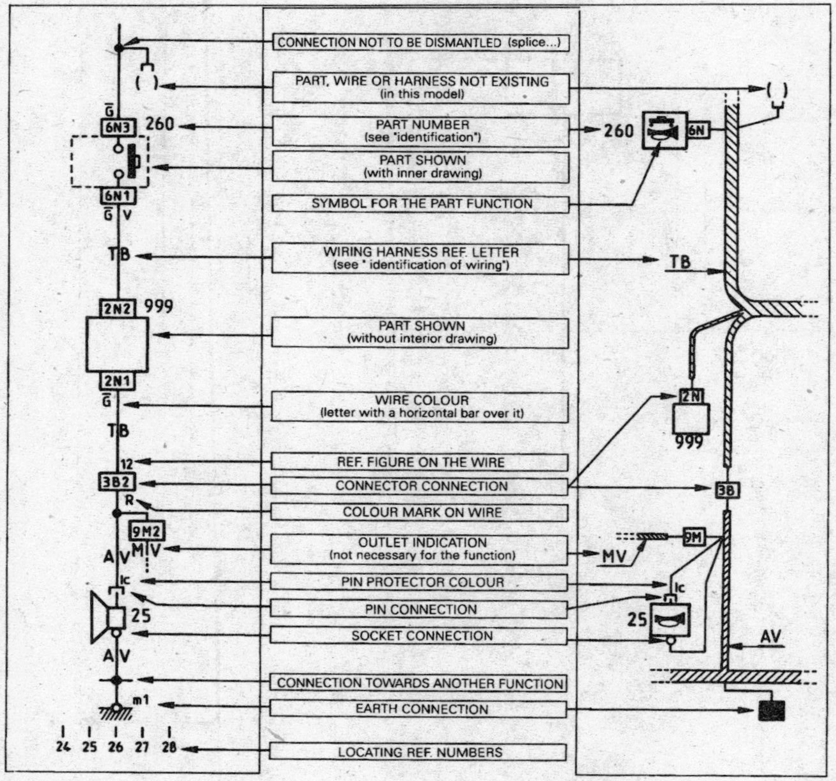

24.1b Notes on the use of wiring diagrams

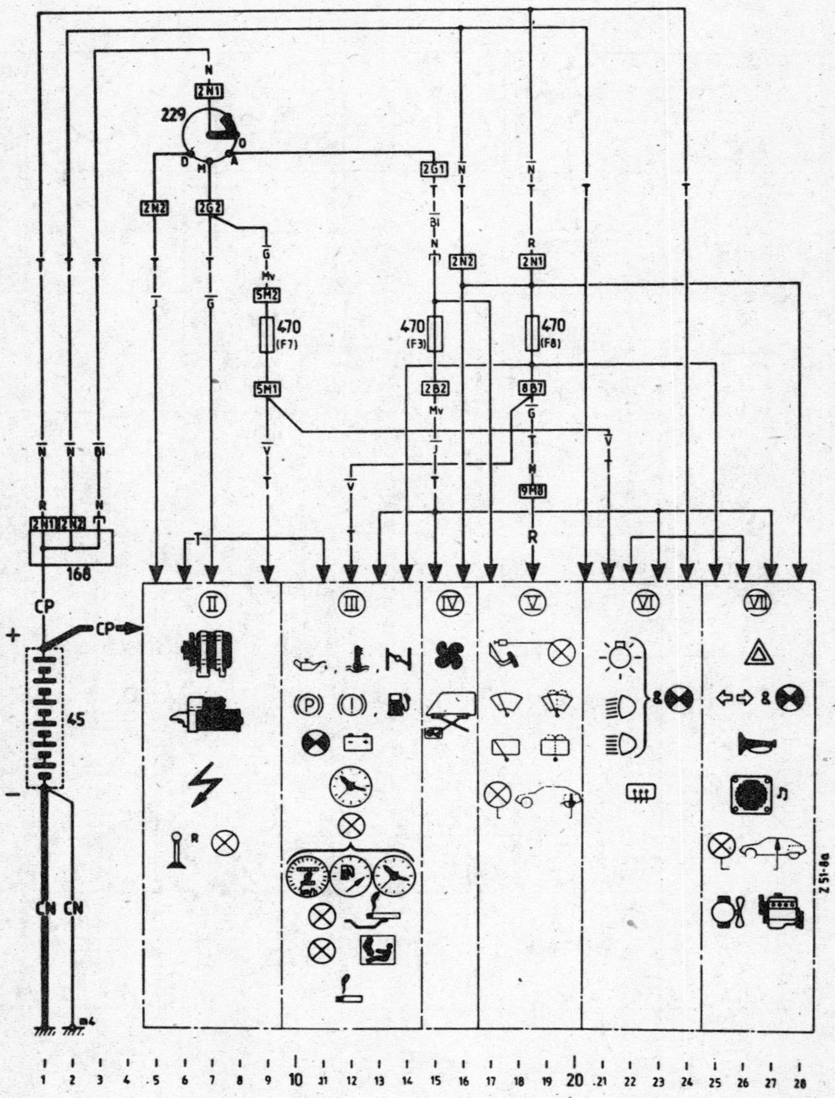

Typical wiring diagram for models up to July 1991 (except GT) - circuit 1

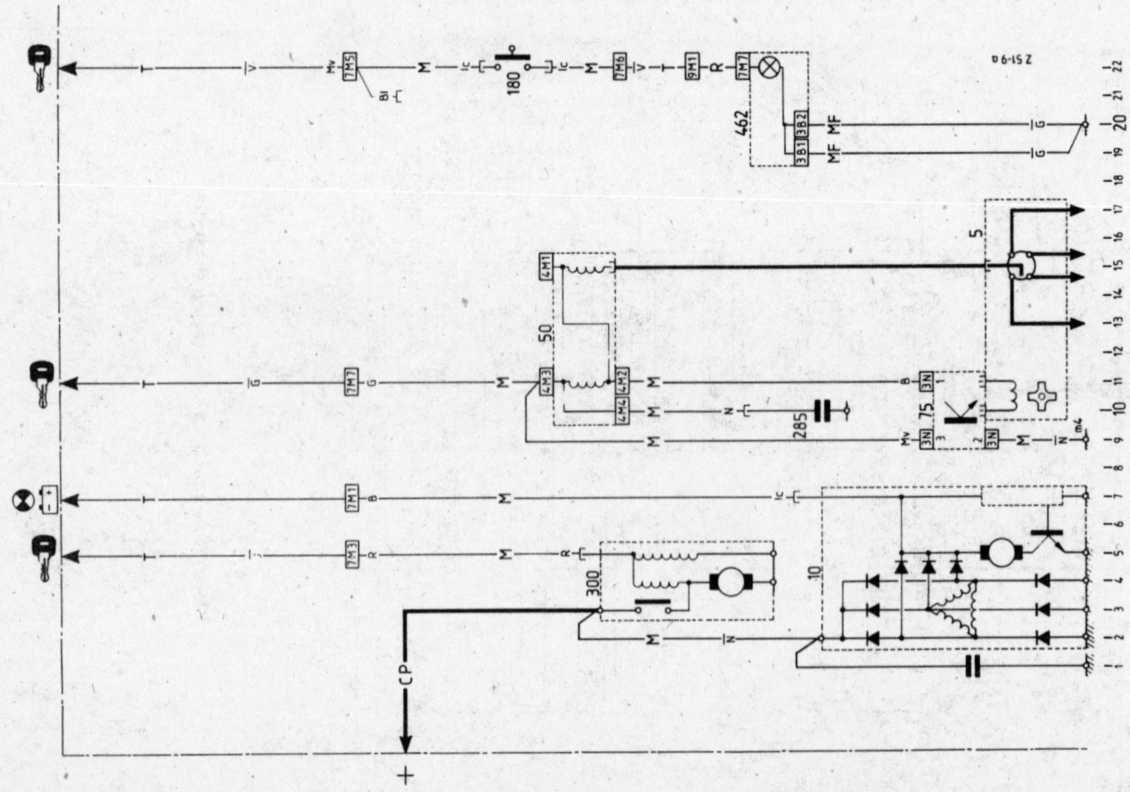

Typical wiring diagram for models up to July 1991 (except GT) - circuit 2

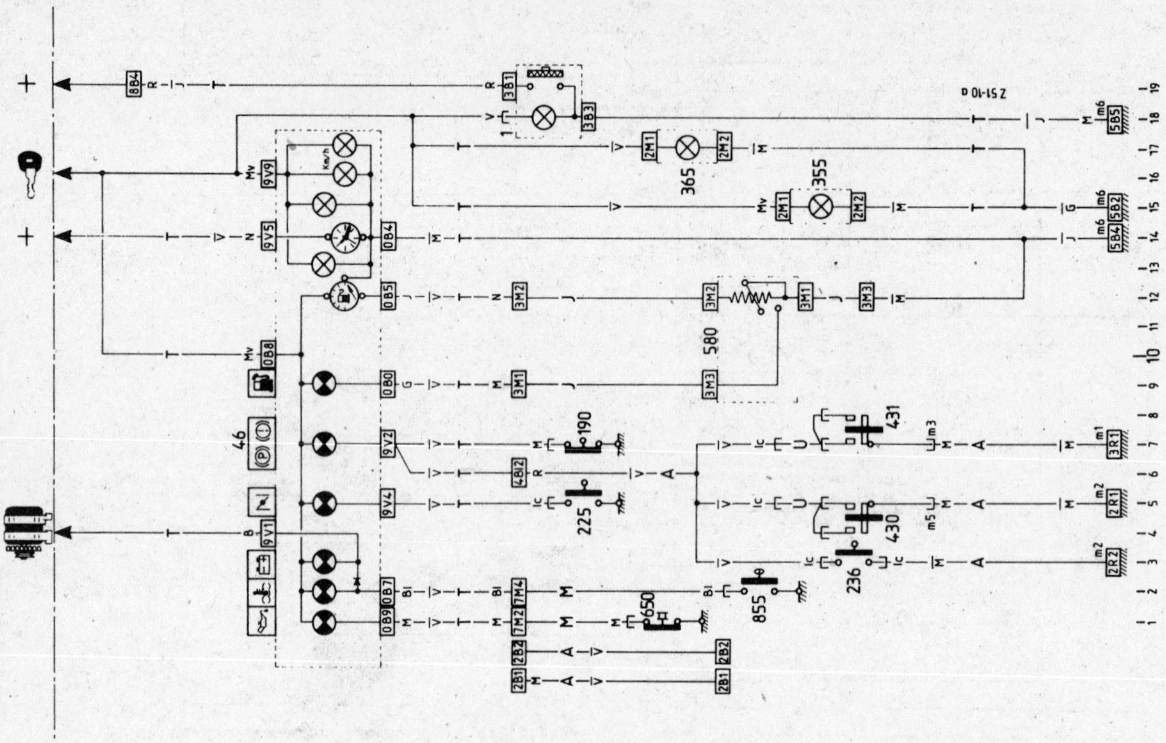

Typical wiring diagram for models up to July 1991 (except GT) - circuit 3

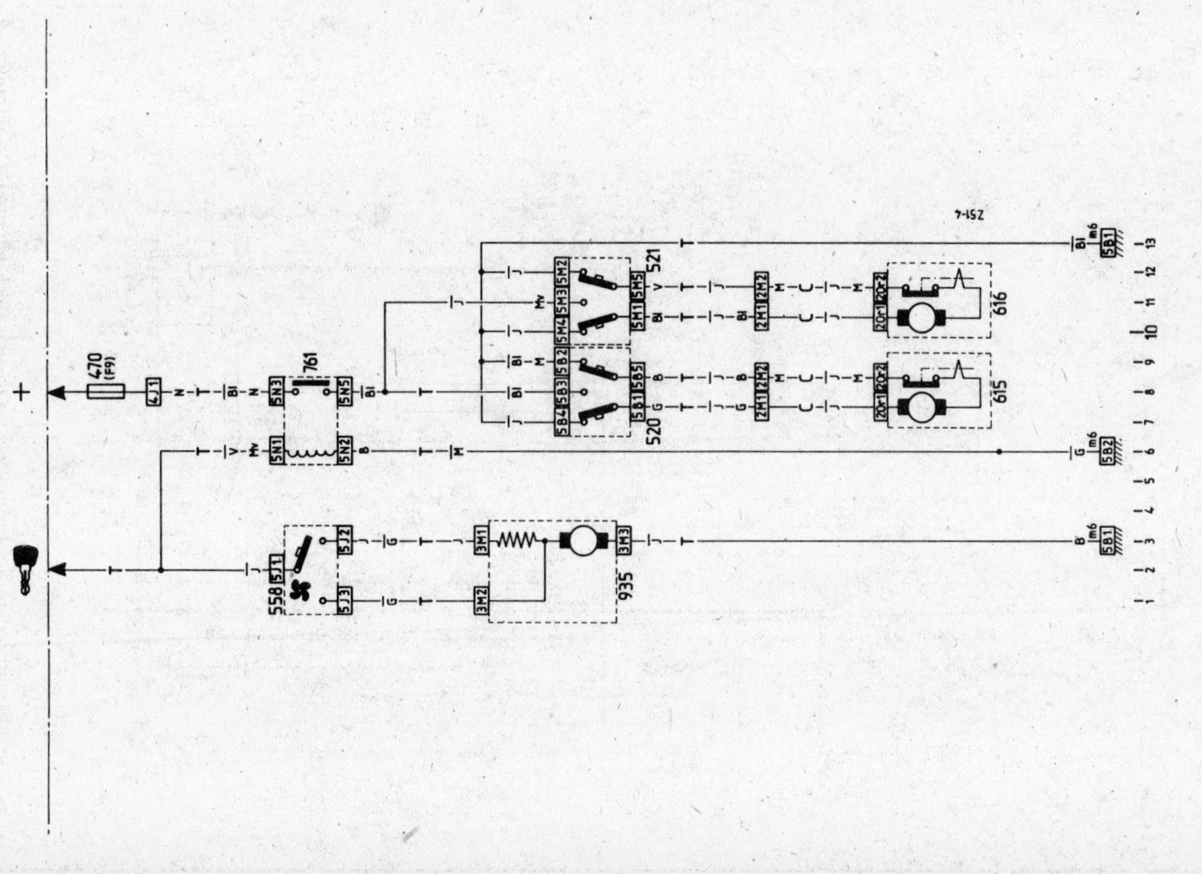

Typical wiring diagram for models up to July 1991 (except GT) - circuit 4

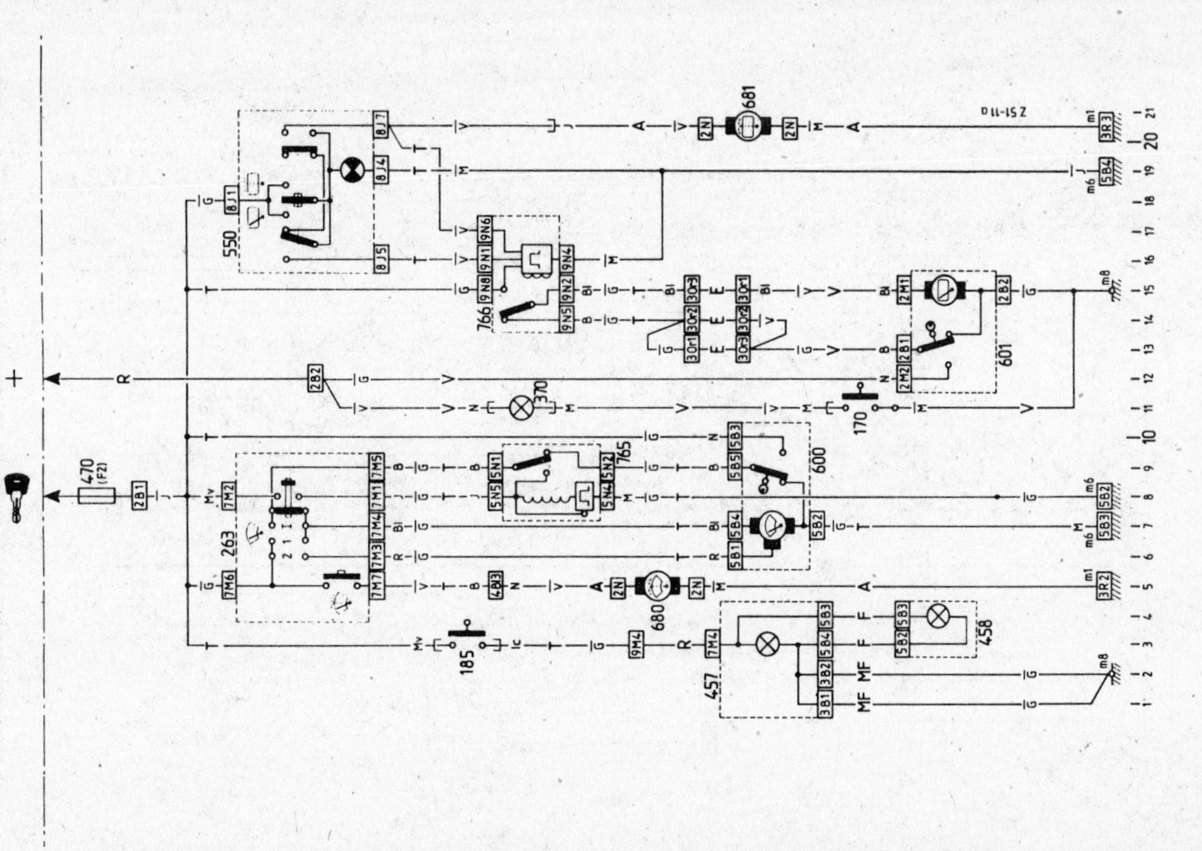

Typical wiring diagram for models up to July 1991 (except GT) - circuit 5

WD

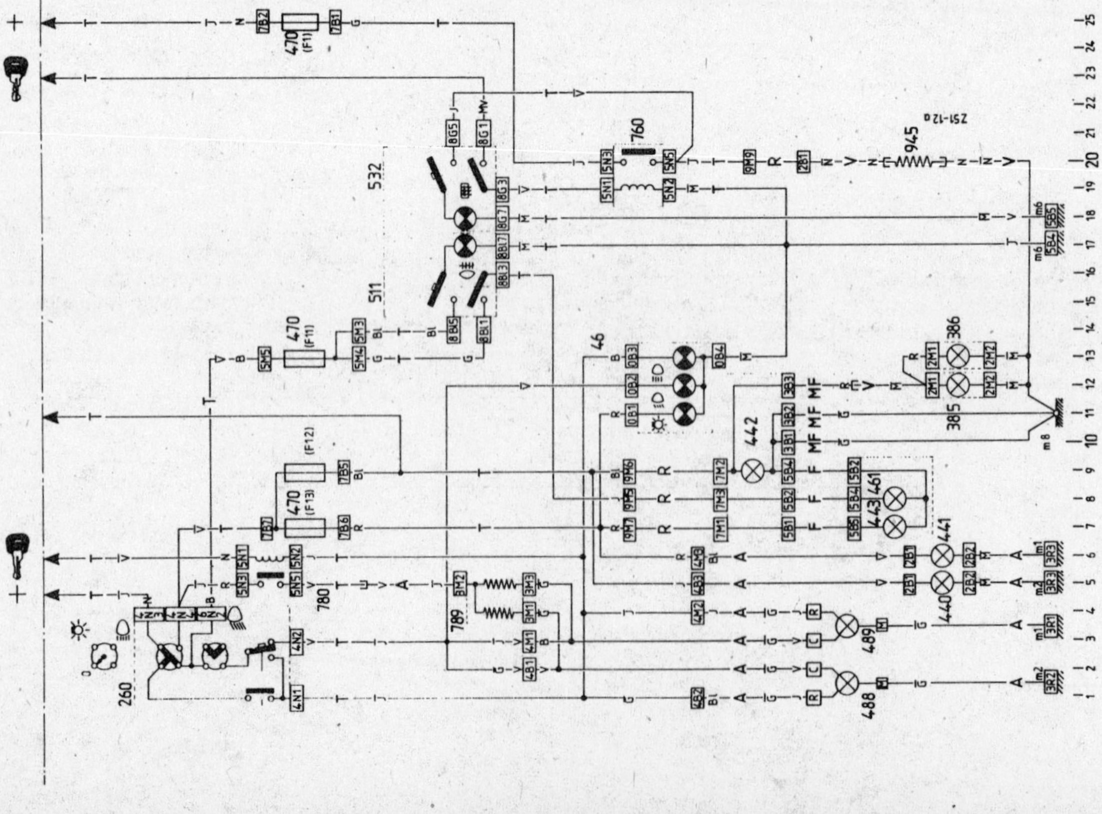

Typical wiring diagram for models up to July 1991 (except GT) - circuit 6

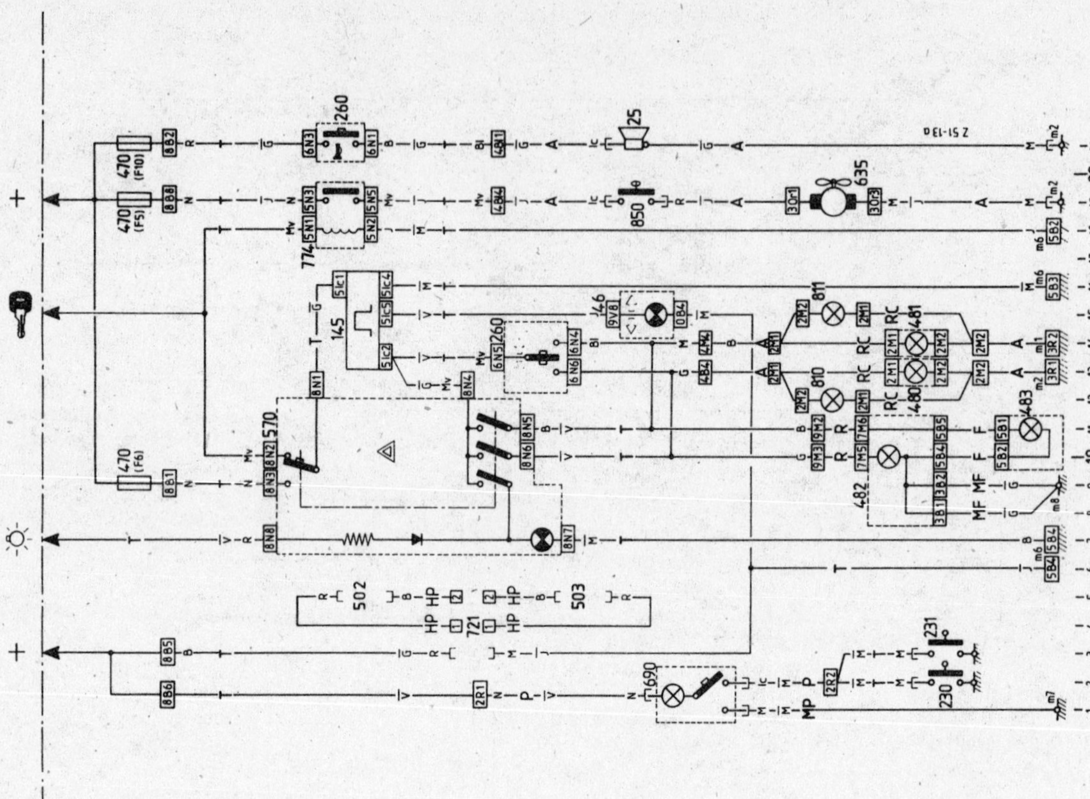

Typical wiring diagram for models up to July 1991 (except GT) - circuit 7

Key to wiring diagram for models up to July 1991 (except GT)

Not all items fitted to all models

No	Description
1	Cigar lighter
5	Ignition distributor
10	Alternator
25	Horn
45	Battery
46	Instrument panel
50	Ignition coil
55	Anti-pollution control unit
70	Monitoring unit (for horn, indicators, headlights)
75	Ignition module
84	Water level indicator unit
85	Oil level control unit
90	Central door lock control unit
130	TDC sensor
140	Distance sensor
145	Direction indicator unit
168	Battery connector
170	Tailgate switch
180	Reversing light switch
185	Stop-light switch
190	Handbrake switch
225	Choke warning light switch
229	Ignition switch
230	Door switch (LH, front)
231	Door switch (RH, front)
236	Brake hydraulic fluid level switch
237	Coolant level switch
260	Lighting/direction indicator/horn switch
263	Windscreen wiper/washer switch
285	Coil suppressor
300	Starter motor
302	Flowmeter
331	Main actuator
332	Idling actuator
333	Carburettor float chamber venting solenoid
334	Canister electro-valve
336	Ignition distributor vacuum electro-valve
337	Butterfly opener electro-valve
355	Heater control lighting
365	Ashtray lighting
370	Boot lighting
385	LH rear No. plate lighting
386	RH rear No. plate lighting
430	LH front brake caliper
431	RH front brake caliper
440	LH front sidelight
441	RH front sidelight
442	LH tail light
443	RH tail light
445	LH rear light
446	RH rear light
457	LH stop-light
458	RH stop-light
460	LH rear foglight
461	RH rear foglight

No	Description
462	LH reversing light
463	RH reversing light
470	Fuses
480	LH front direction indicator
481	RH front direction indicator
482	LH rear direction indicator
483	RH rear direction indicator
486	LH front auxiliary light
487	RH front auxiliary light
488	LH main and dipped beams
489	RH main and dipped beams
502	LH rear speaker
503	RH rear speaker
511	Rear foglight switch
512	Front auxiliary light switch
520	LH front window switch
521	RH front window switch
532	Heated rear screen switch
535	Driver's heated seat switch
536	Passenger's heated seat switch
546	Map reading light switch
550	Tailgate wipe switch
558	Heater fan switch
570	Hazard warning switch
580	Fuel gauge
600	Windscreen wiper motor
601	Tailgate wiper motor
615	LH front window motor
616	RH front window motor
625	LH front door lock motor
626	RH front door lock motor
627	LH rear door lock motor
628	RH rear door lock motor
629	Tailgate lock motor
635	Radiator cooling fan motor
640	Clock
650	Engine oil low pressure switch
660	On-board computer
680	Windscreen washer pump
681	Tailgate washer pump
682	Headlight washer pump
688	Throttle butterfly position potentiometer
690	Courtesy light
695	Map reading light
720	Diagnostic socket
721	Radio connections
728	Carburettor heater
729	Anti-pollution relay
736	Additional main beams relay
737	Headlight dipped beam relay
755	Headlight washer relay
760	Heated rear screen relay
761	Front window motor relay
765	Windscreen wiper motor relay
766	Tailgate wiper motor relay
767	Electric cooling fan timer relay
768	Electric cooling fan control relay
769	Electric cooling fan power relay

No	Description
774	Radiator cooling fan relay
780	Dim-dip lights relay (UK only)
789	Dim-dip lights resistance (UK only)
795	Instrument lighting rheostat
810	LH side repeater
811	RH side repeater
822	LH heated seat
823	RH heated seat
833	Lambda probe (catalytic converter models)
835	Engine oil level sensor
840	Water temperature sensor
843	Oil temperature sensor
850	Cooling fan thermal switch
853	Air temperature switch
855	Engine coolant thermal switch
935	Blower motor
945	Heated rear screen

Harness code

A	Front
AE	Driving school
B	Water level indicator unit
C	Door
D	Emission control
CK	On carburettor
CN	Battery negative cable
CP	Battery positive cable
E	Tailgate window wiper
F	Rear light cluster inter-connection
HP	Speakers
J	Fuel gauge
K	Piloted carburation
M	Engine
MF	Light earth
MP	Interior lighting earth
P	Interior lighting
PR	Rear door
R	Rear
RC	Direction indicator repeater
SC	Heated seat
T	Instrument panel
TC	Carburettor warning light
U	Brake pad wear
V	Tailgate

Colour code

B	White
Bl	Blue
G	Grey
Ic	Transparent
J	Yellow
M	Brown
Mv	Mauve
N	Black
Or	Orange
R	Red
V	Green

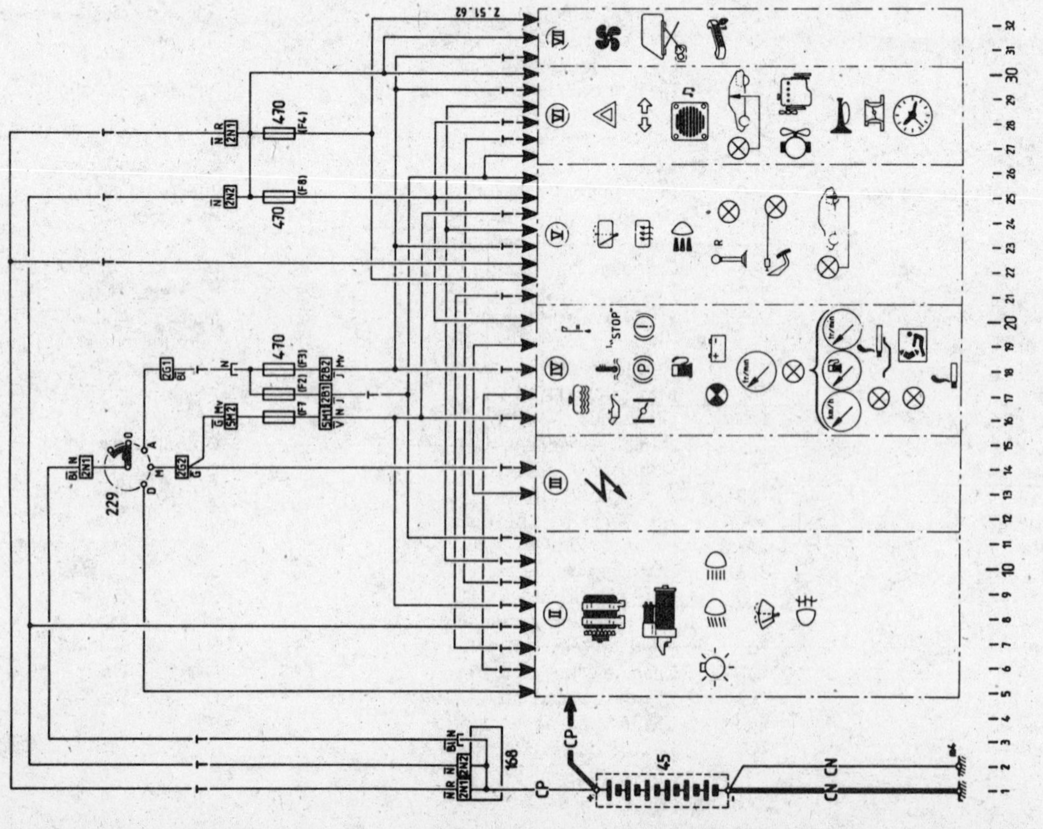

Typical wiring diagram for GT models up to July 1991 - circuit 1

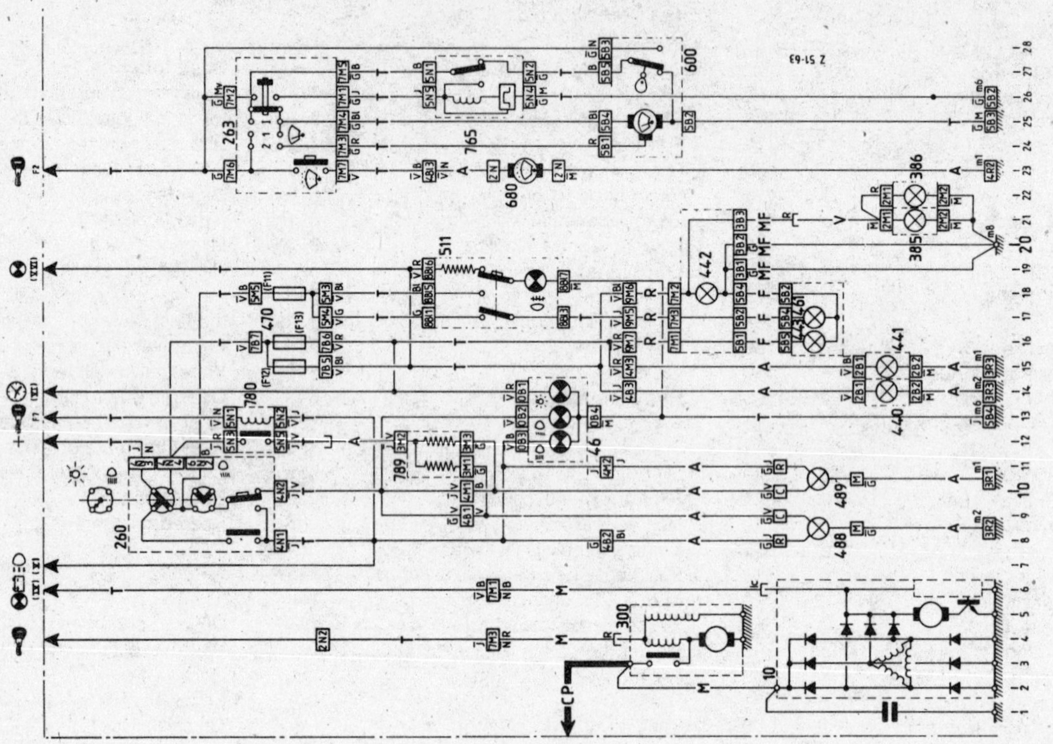

Typical wiring diagram for GT models up to July 1991 - circuit 2

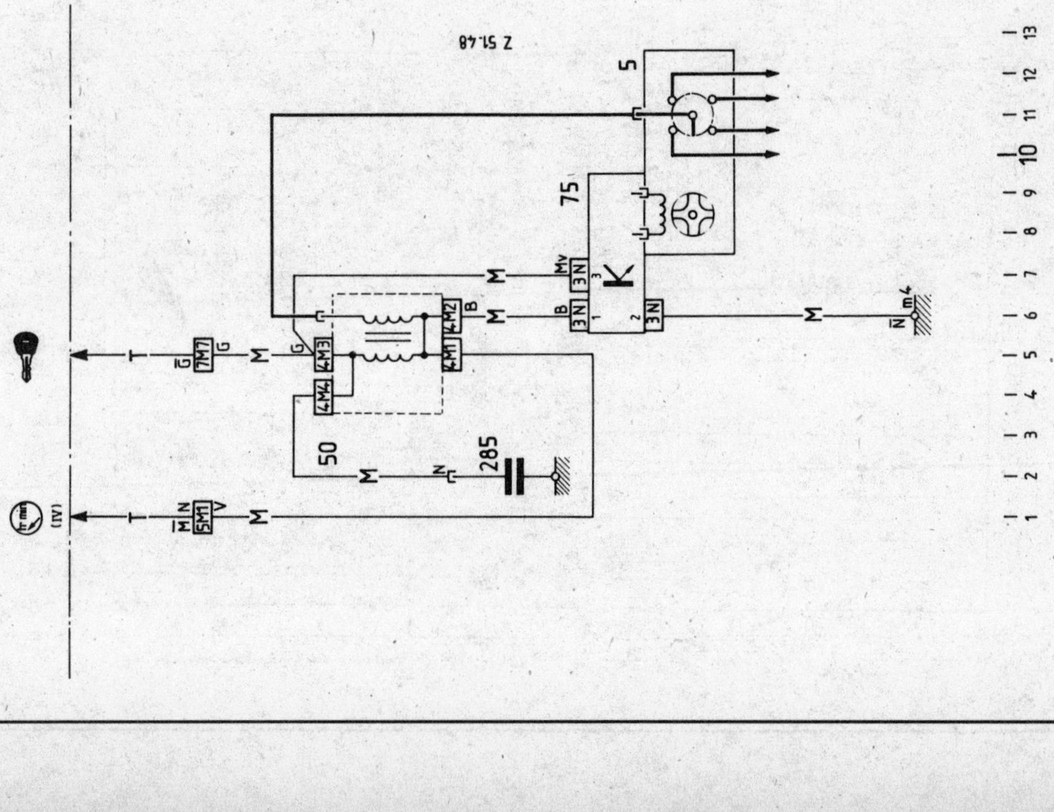

Typical wiring diagram for GT models up to July 1991 - circuit 3

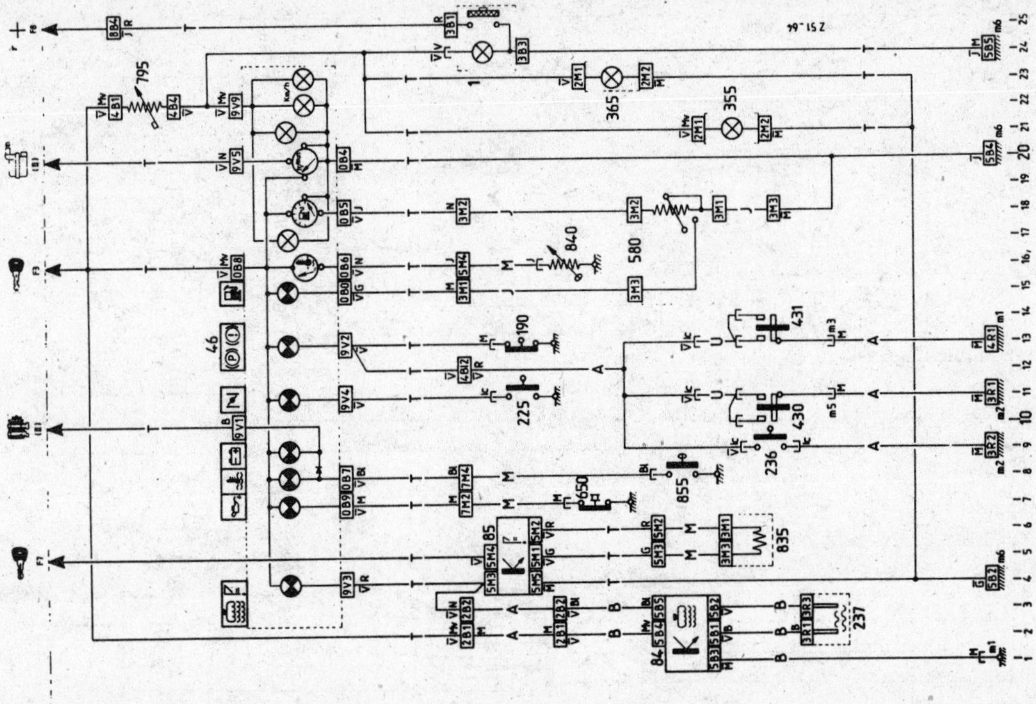

Typical wiring diagram for GT models up to July 1991 - circuit 4

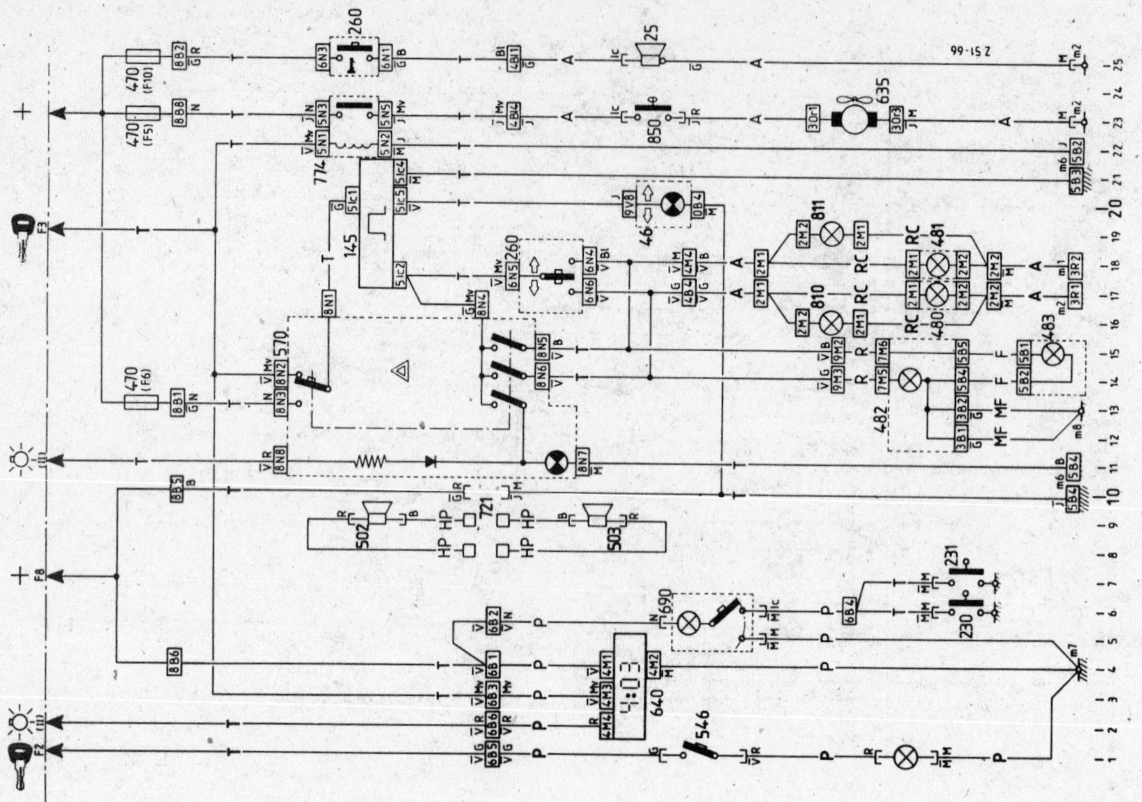

Typical wiring diagram for GT models up to July 1991 - circuit 6

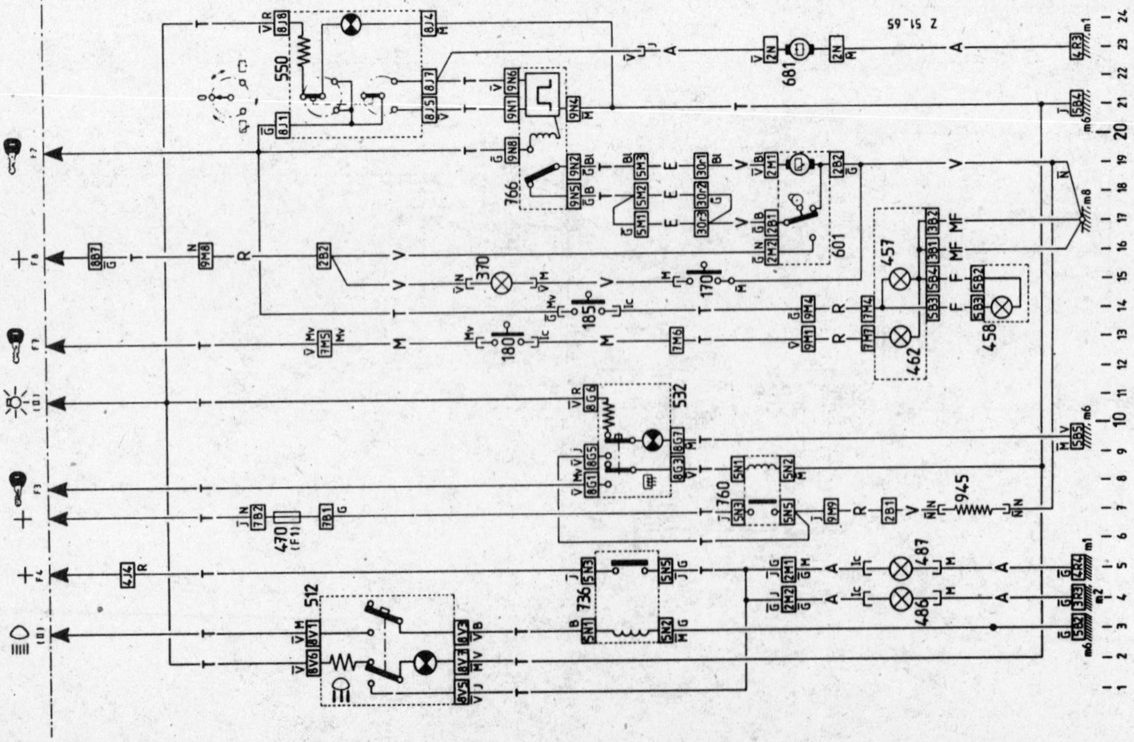

Typical wiring diagram for GT models up to July 1991 - circuit 5

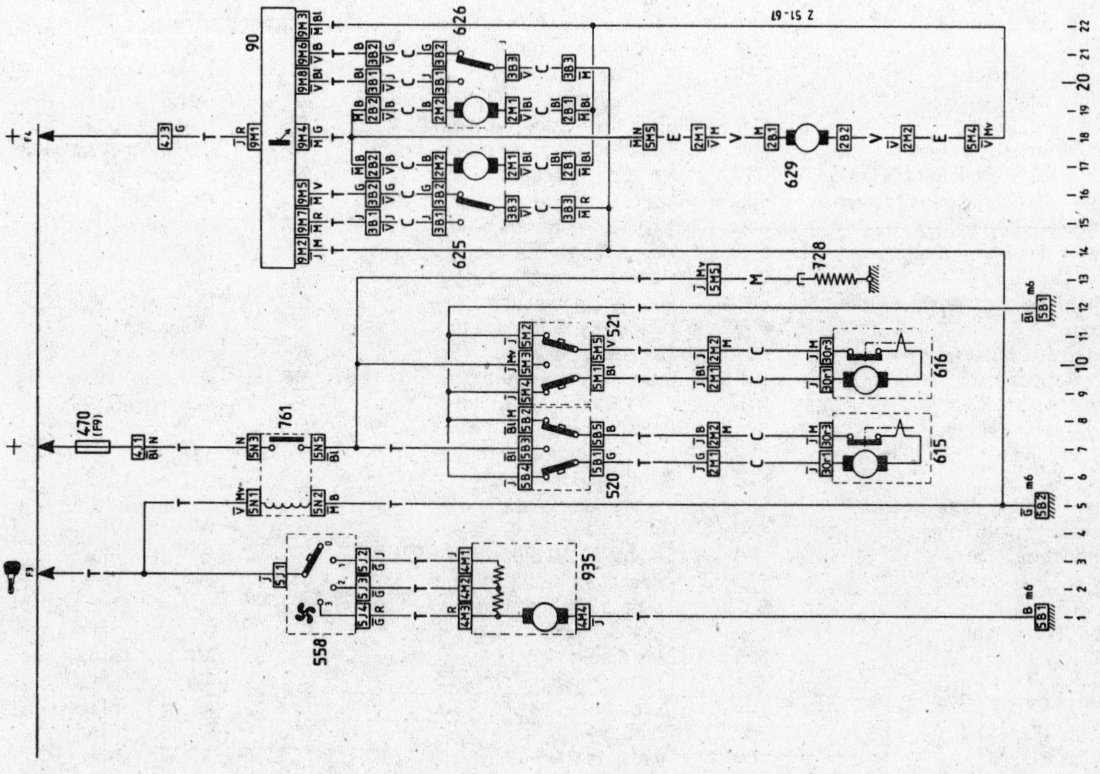

Typical wiring diagram for GT models up to July 1991 - circuit 7

Key to wiring diagram for GT models up to July 1991

Not all items fitted to all models

No	Description
1	Cigar lighter
5	Distributor
10	Alternator
25	Horn
45	Battery
46	Instrument panel
50	Ignition coil
75	Ignition module
84	Water level indicator unit
85	Oil level control unit
90	Door locking control unit
145	Direction indicator unit
168	Battery connector
170	Boot light switch
180	Reversing light switch
185	Stop-light switch
190	Handbrake switch
225	Starter motor switch
229	Ignition switch
230	Interior light switch (front LH door)
231	Interior light switch (front RH door)
236	Hydraulic brake fluid level switch
237	Coolant level switch
260	Lighting/direction indicator/horn switch
260	Lighting/direction indicator/horn switch
263	Windscreen wash/wipe switch
285	HT coil suppressor
300	Starter motor
355	Heater control lighting
365	Ashtray lighting
370	Boot light
385	LH rear number plate lighting
386	RH number plate lighting
430	LH front brake caliper
431	RH front brake caliper
440	Front LH sidelight
441	Front RH sidelight
442	LH tail light
443	RH tail light
457	LH stop-light
458	RH stop-light
461	RH rear foglight
462	LH reversing light
470	Fuses F7, F2, F3, F8, F4
470	Fuses F12, F13, F11
470	Fuse F1
470	Fuses F6, F5, F10
470	Fuse F9
480	Front LH direction indicator
481	Front RH direction indicator
482	Rear LH direction indicator
483	Rear RH direction indicator
486	LH front auxiliary light
487	RH front auxiliary light
488	LH headlight main and dipped beams
489	RH headlight main and dipped beams
502	Provision for rear LH speaker
503	Provision for rear RH speaker
511	Rear foglight switch
512	Front auxiliary light switch
520	Front LH window motor switch
521	Front RH window motor switch
532	Heated rear screen switch
546	Map reading light switch
550	Tailgate wash/wipe switch
558	Heater fan switch
570	Hazard warning switch
580	Fuel tank gauge unit
600	Windscreen wiper motor
601	Tailgate wiper motor
615	Front LH window motor
616	Front RH window motor
625	Front LH door lock motor
626	Front RH door lock motor
629	Boot door lock motor
635	Engine cooling fan
640	Clock
650	Engine oil low pressure switch
680	Windscreen washer pump
681	Tailgate washer pump
690	Courtesy light
695	Map reading light
721	Electrical supply for radio
728	Carburettor heater
736	Front auxiliary lights relay
760	Heated rear screen relay
761	Electric window motor relay
765	Windscreen wiper motor relay
766	tailgate wiper motor relay
774	Radiator cooling fan relay
780	Dim-dip lights relay (UK only)
789	Dim-dip lights resistance (UK only)
795	Instrument lighting rheostat
810	LH side repeater light
811	RH side repeater light
835	Engine oil level sensor
840	Water temperature sensor
850	Cooling fan thermal switch
855	Engine coolant thermal switch
935	Heater fan
945	Heated rear screen

Harness code

A	Front
B	Water level indicator unit
C	Door
CN	Battery negative cable
CP	Battery positive cable
E	Tailgate wiper
F	Rear light interconnection
HP	Speakers
J	Gauge
M	Engine
MF	Light earth
P	Interior light
R	Rear
RC	Direction indicator repeater
T	Instrument panel
U	Brake pad wear
V	Tailgate

Colour code

B	White
Bl	Blue
G	Grey
Ic	Transparent
J	Yellow
M	Brown
Mv	Mauve
N	Black
Or	Orange
R	Red
V	Green

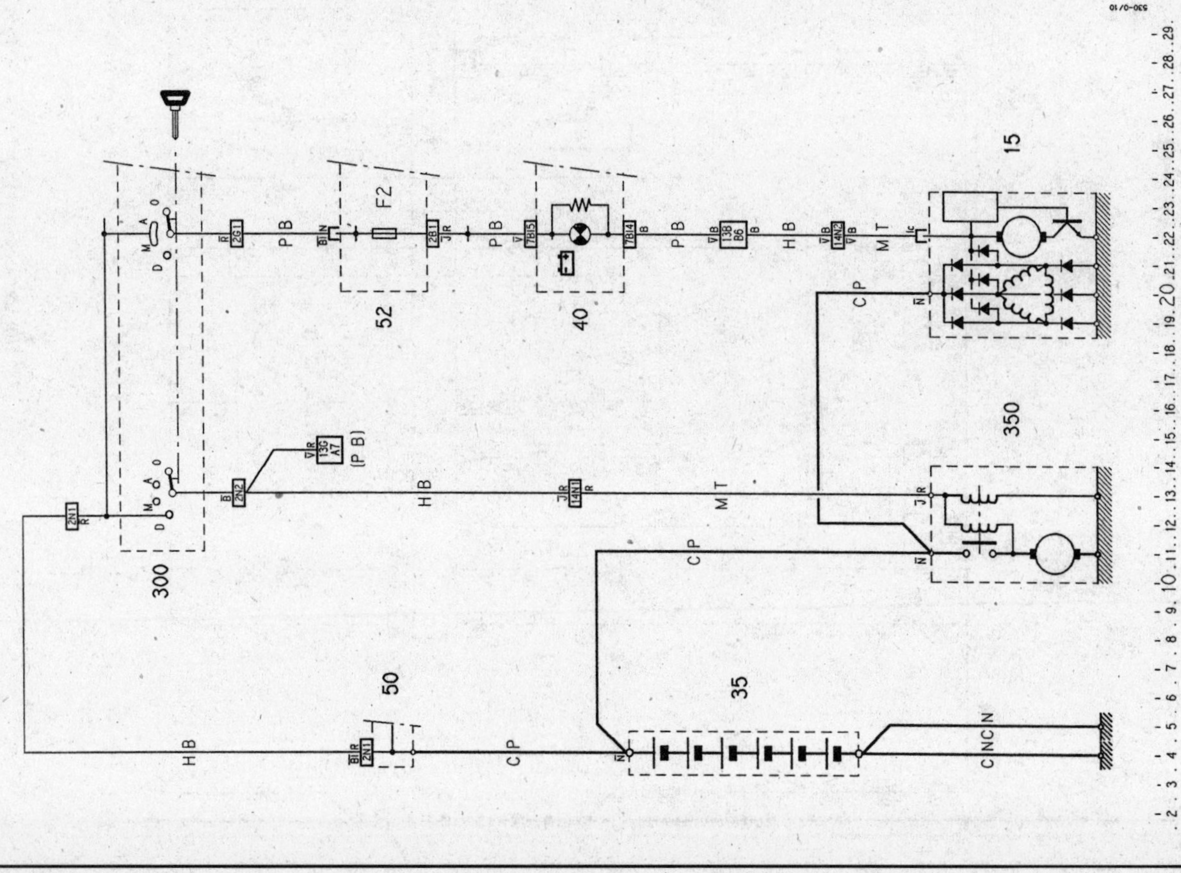

Starting and charging systems - all models from July 1991 on

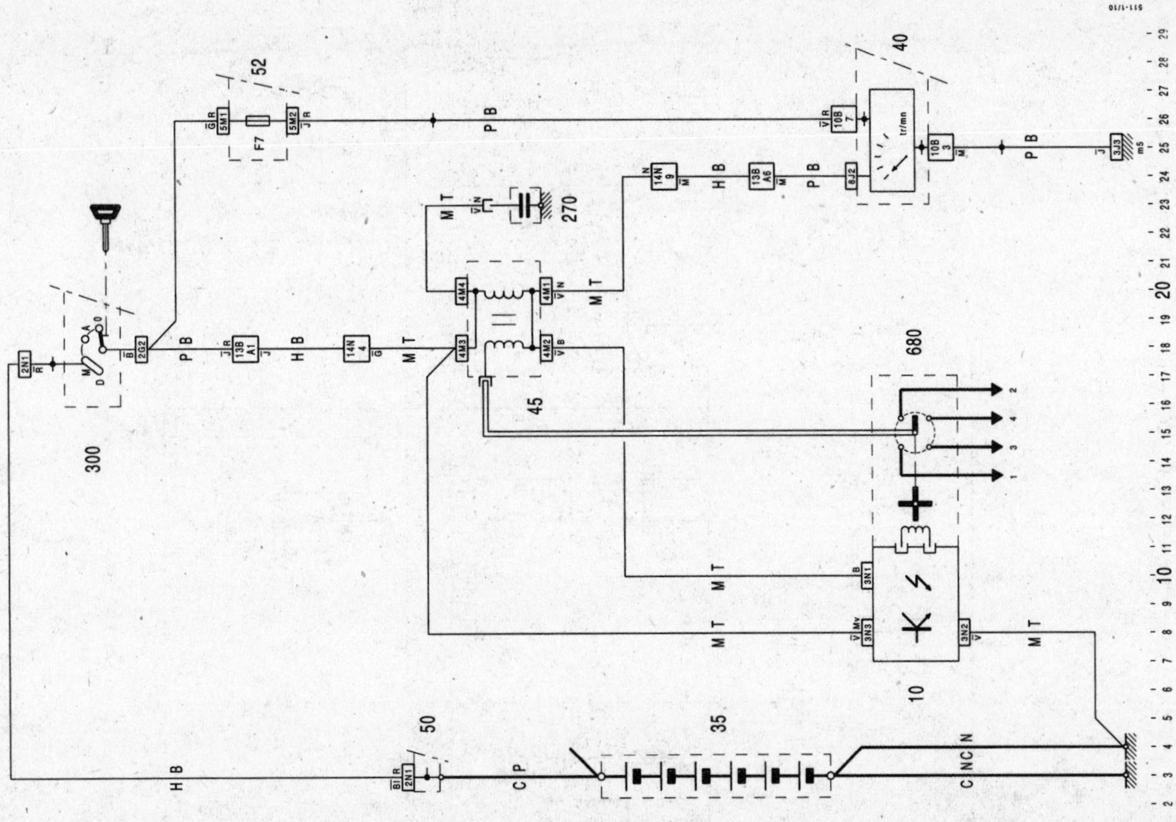

Engine electrical systems - 954 cc/1124 cc (C1A/H1A) engines, from July 1991 on

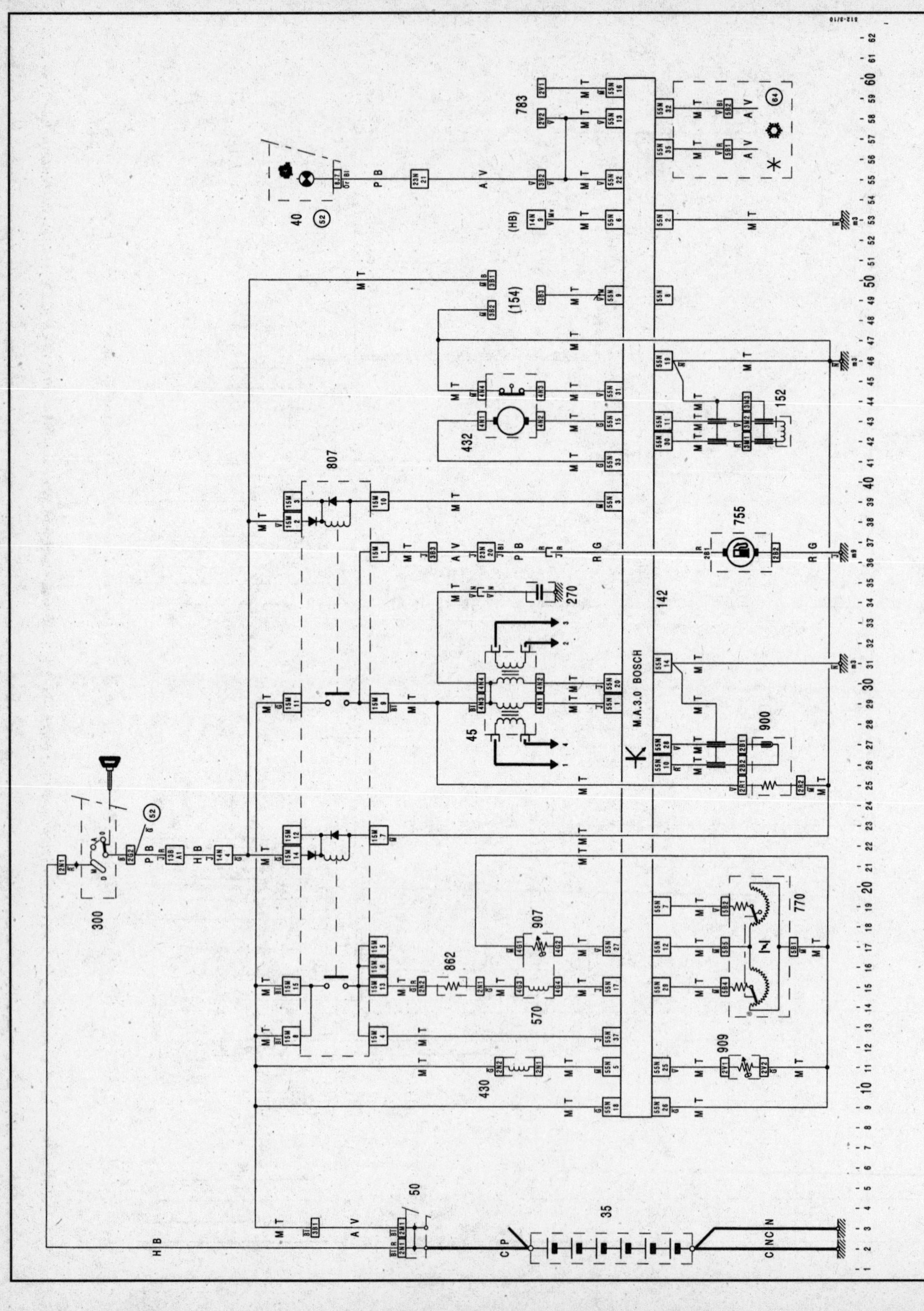

Engine electrical systems - 954 cc (CDZ/CDY) engines, from July 1991 on

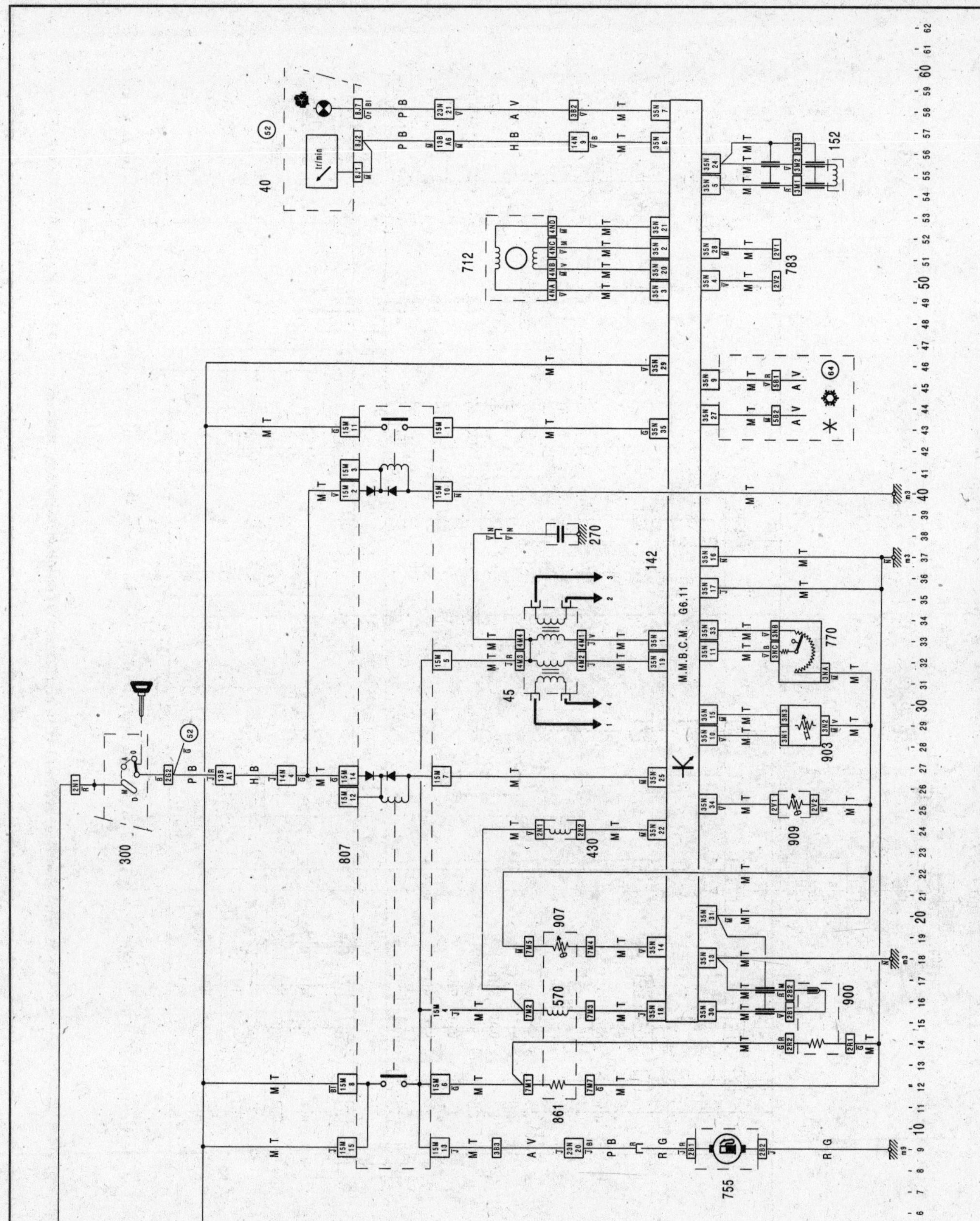

Engine electrical systems - 1124 cc (HDZ/HDY) engines, from July 1991 on

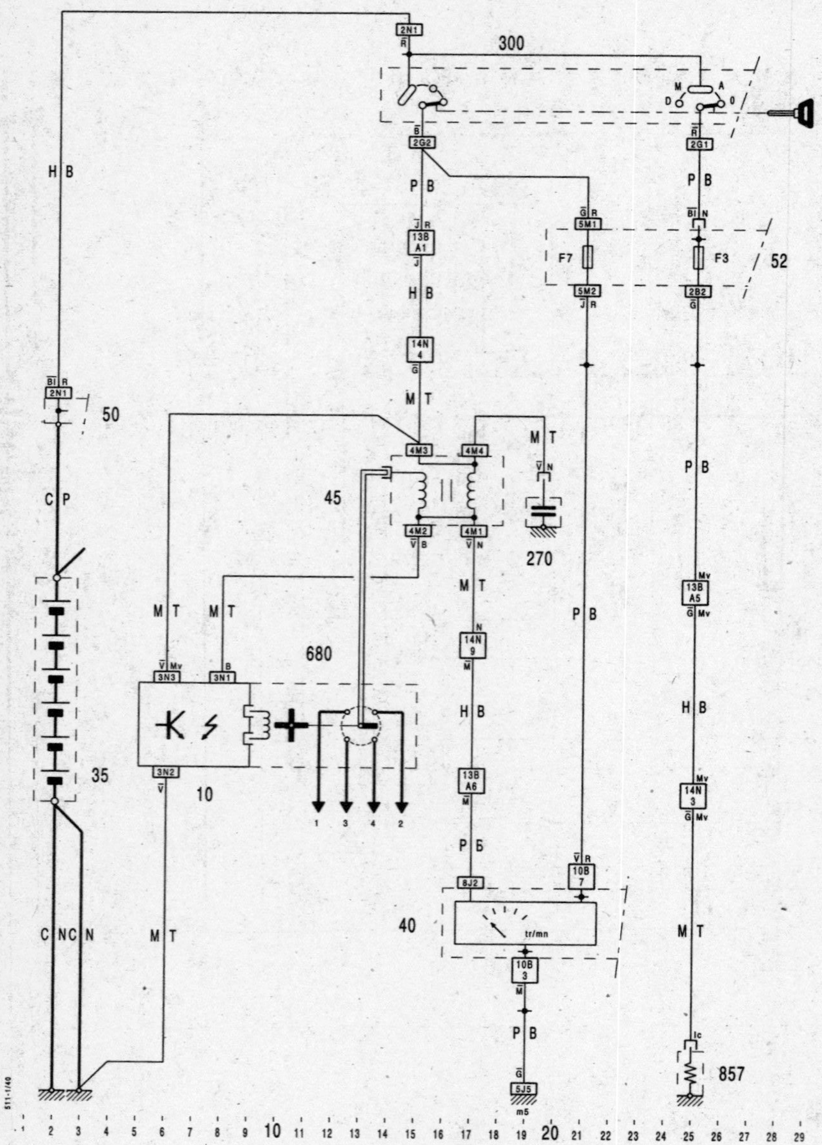

Engine electrical systems - 1360 cc (K2A) engines, from July 1991 on

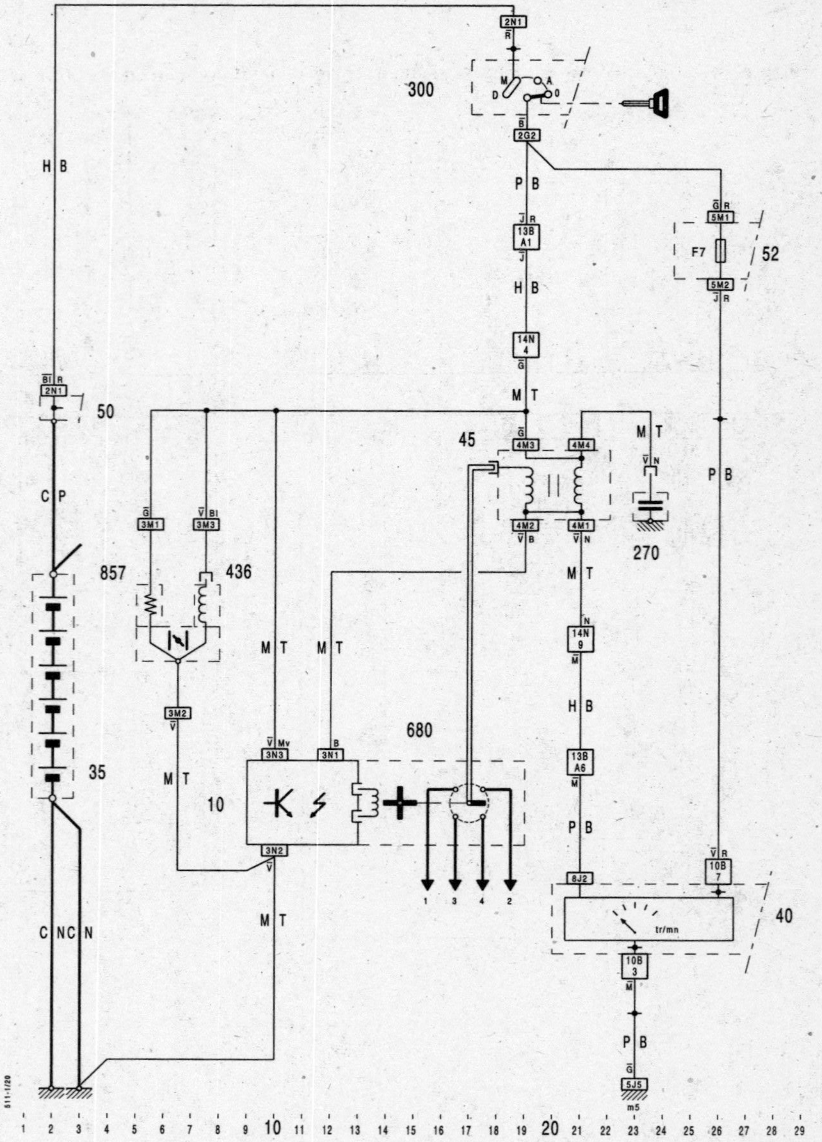

Engine electrical systems - 1360 cc (K2D) engines, from July 1991 on

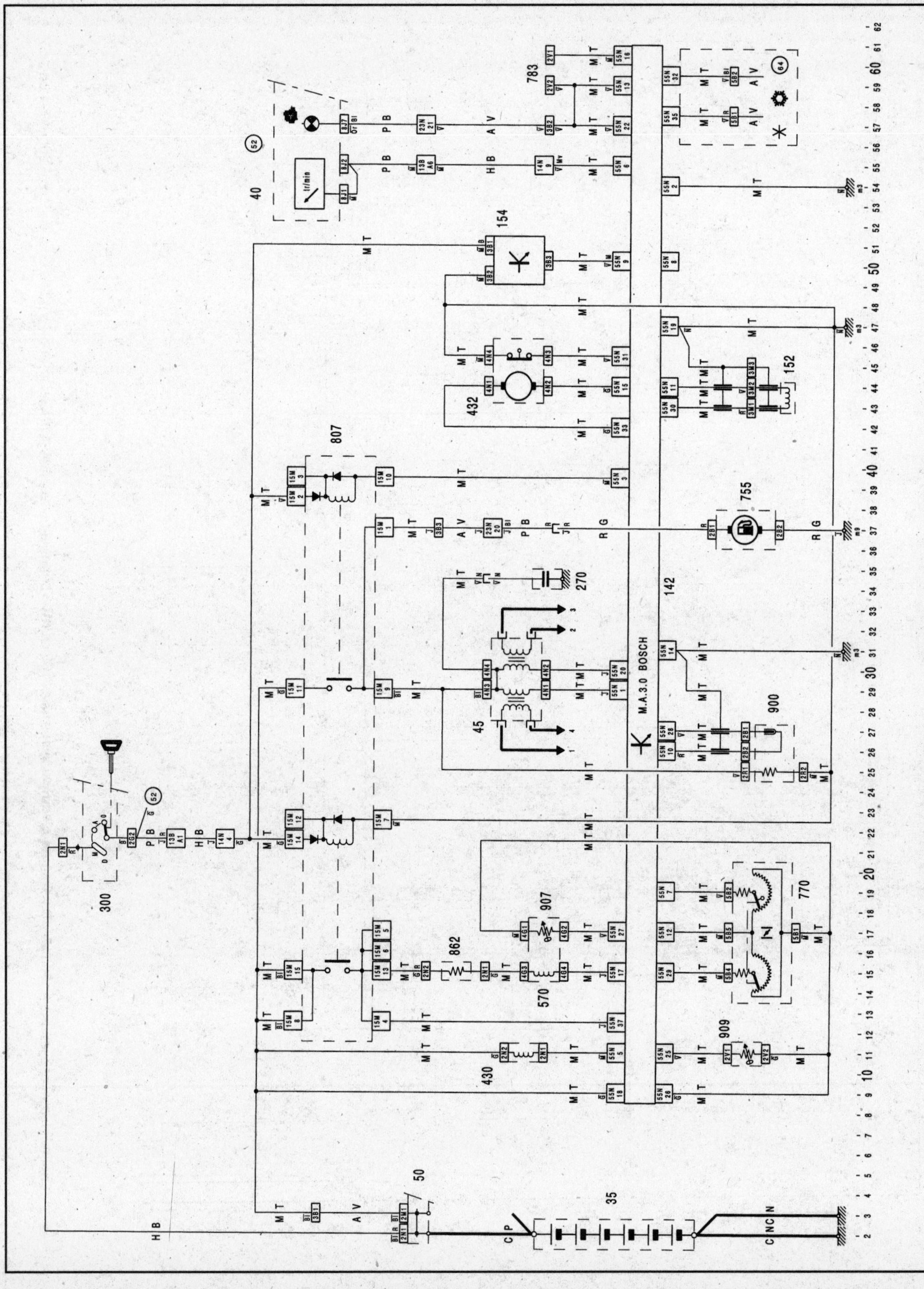

Engine electrical systems - 1360 cc (KDX) engines, from July 1991 on

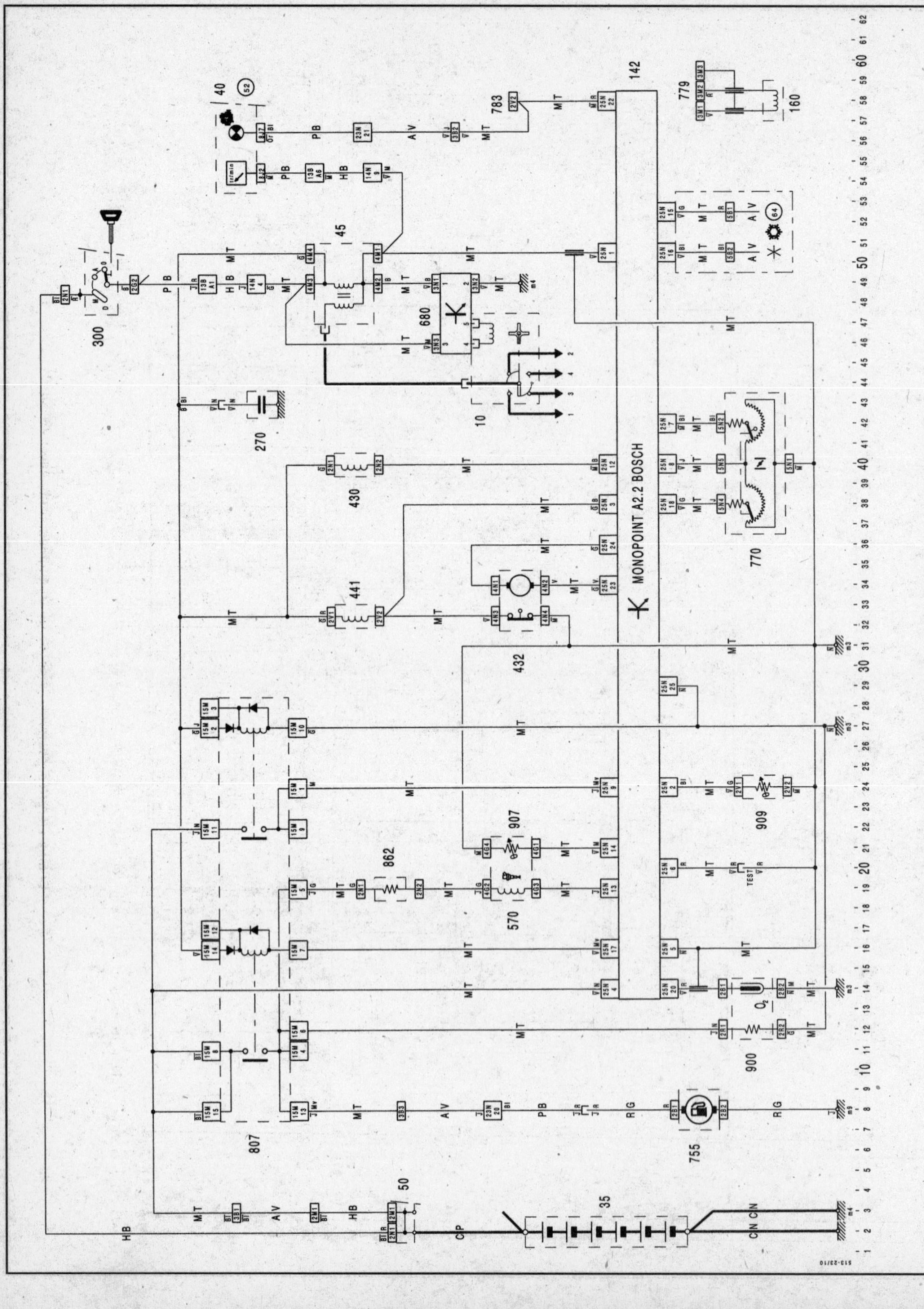

Engine electrical systems - 1360 cc (KDY) engines, from July 1991 on

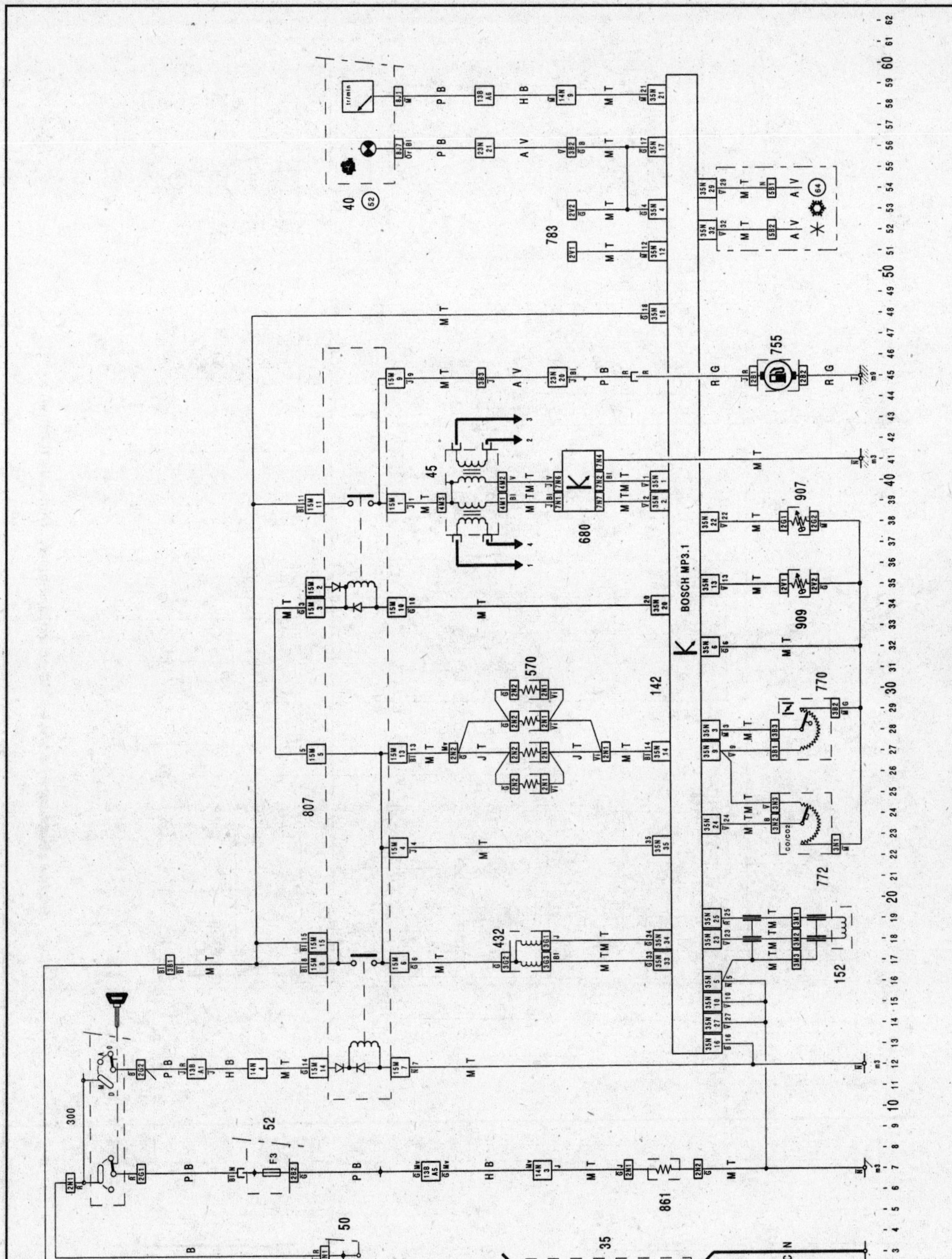

Engine electrical systems - 1360 cc (K6B) engines, from July 1991 on

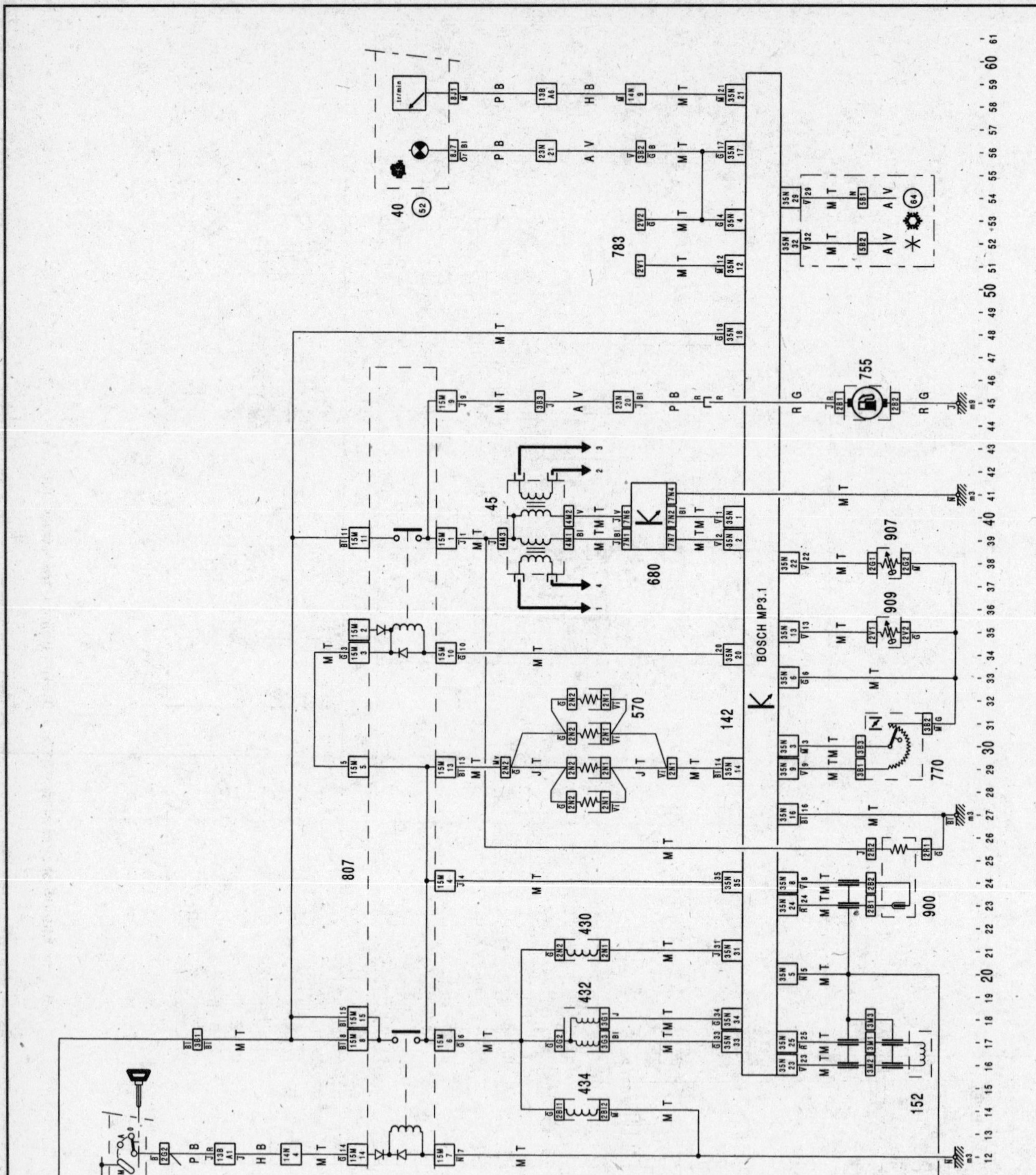

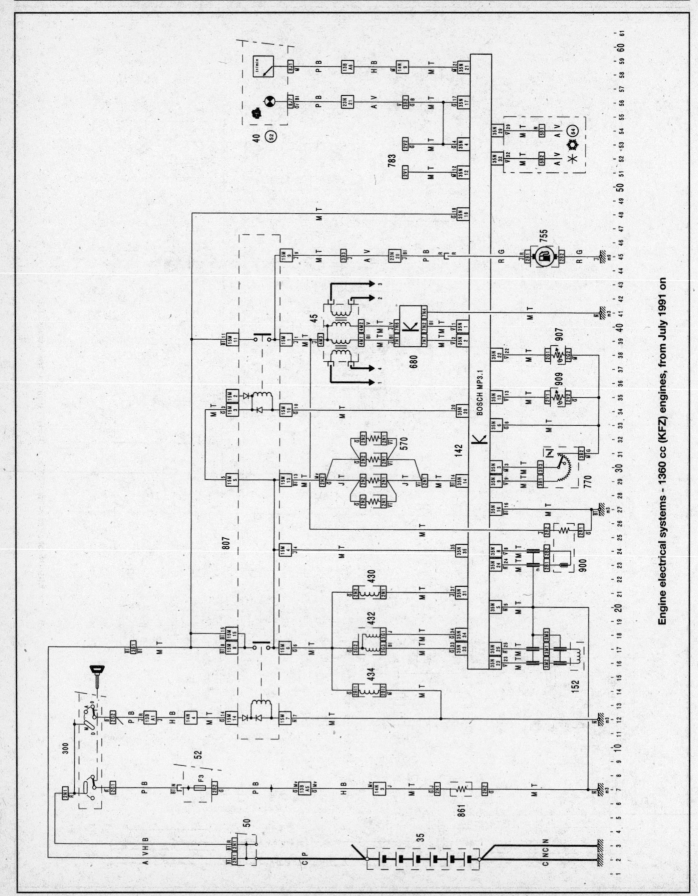

Engine electrical systems - 1360 cc (KFZ) engines, from July 1991 on

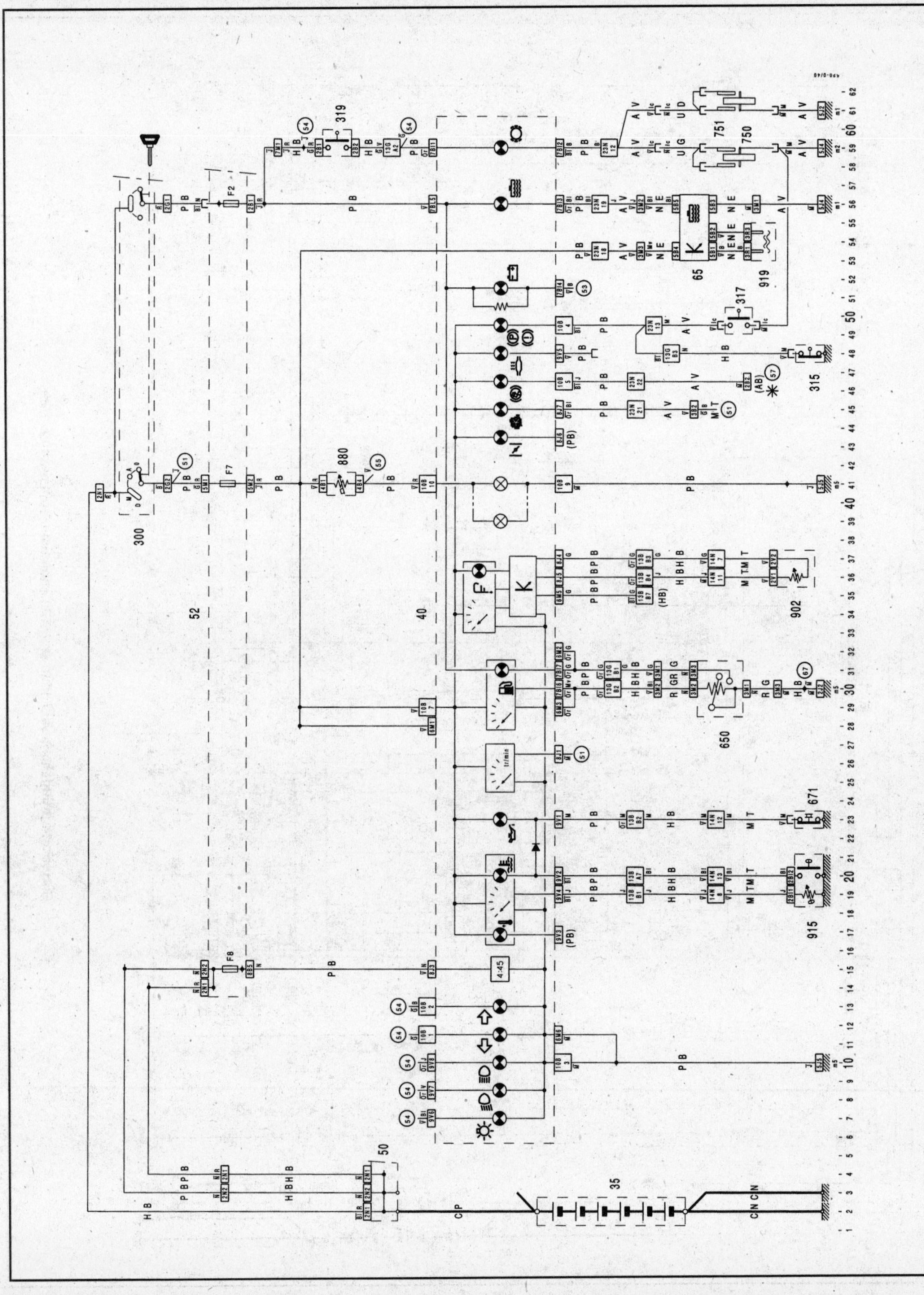

Engine electrical systems - 1360 cc (K9A) Diesel engines

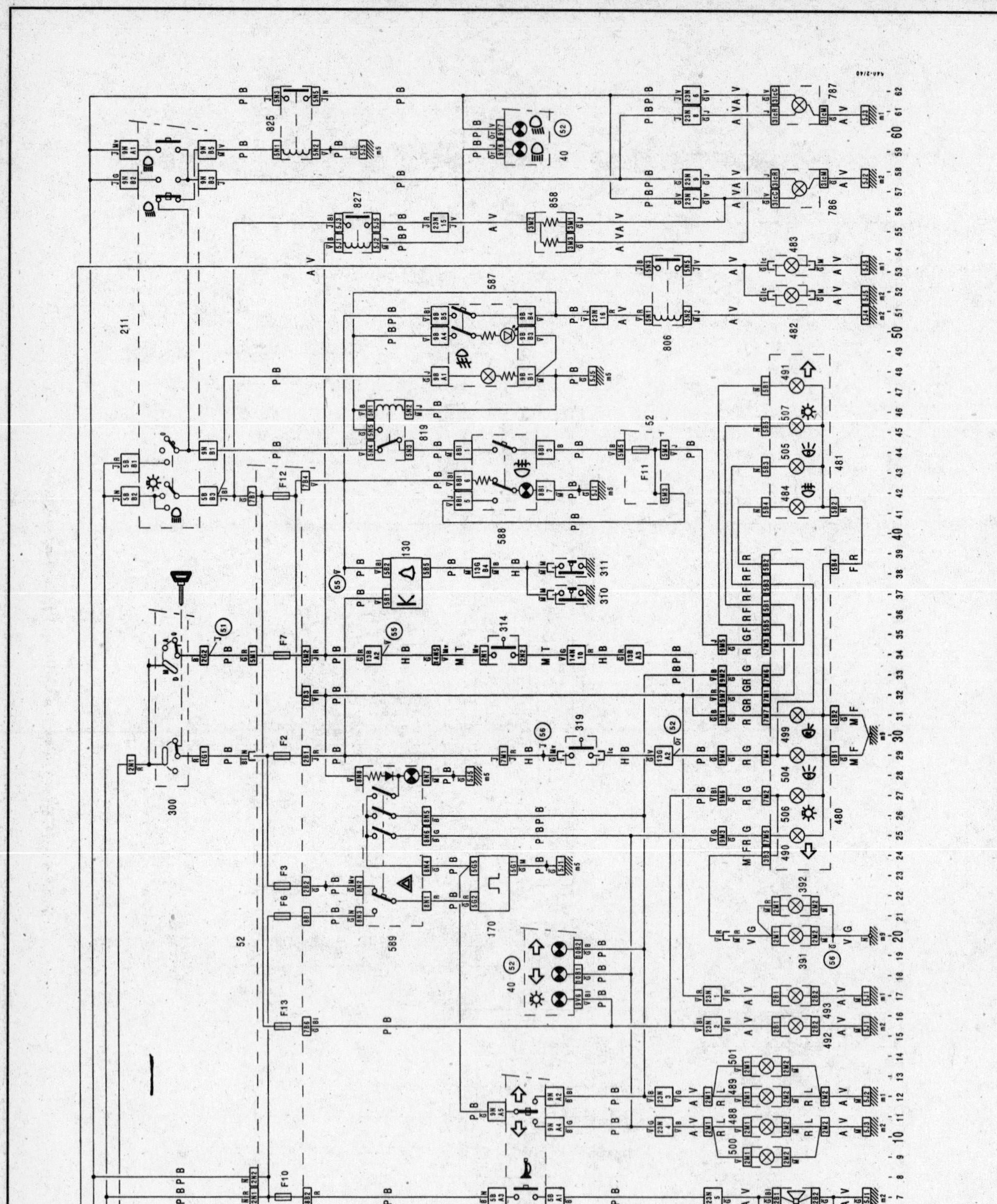

Exterior lighting, including "dim-dip" (UK models) - from July 1991 on

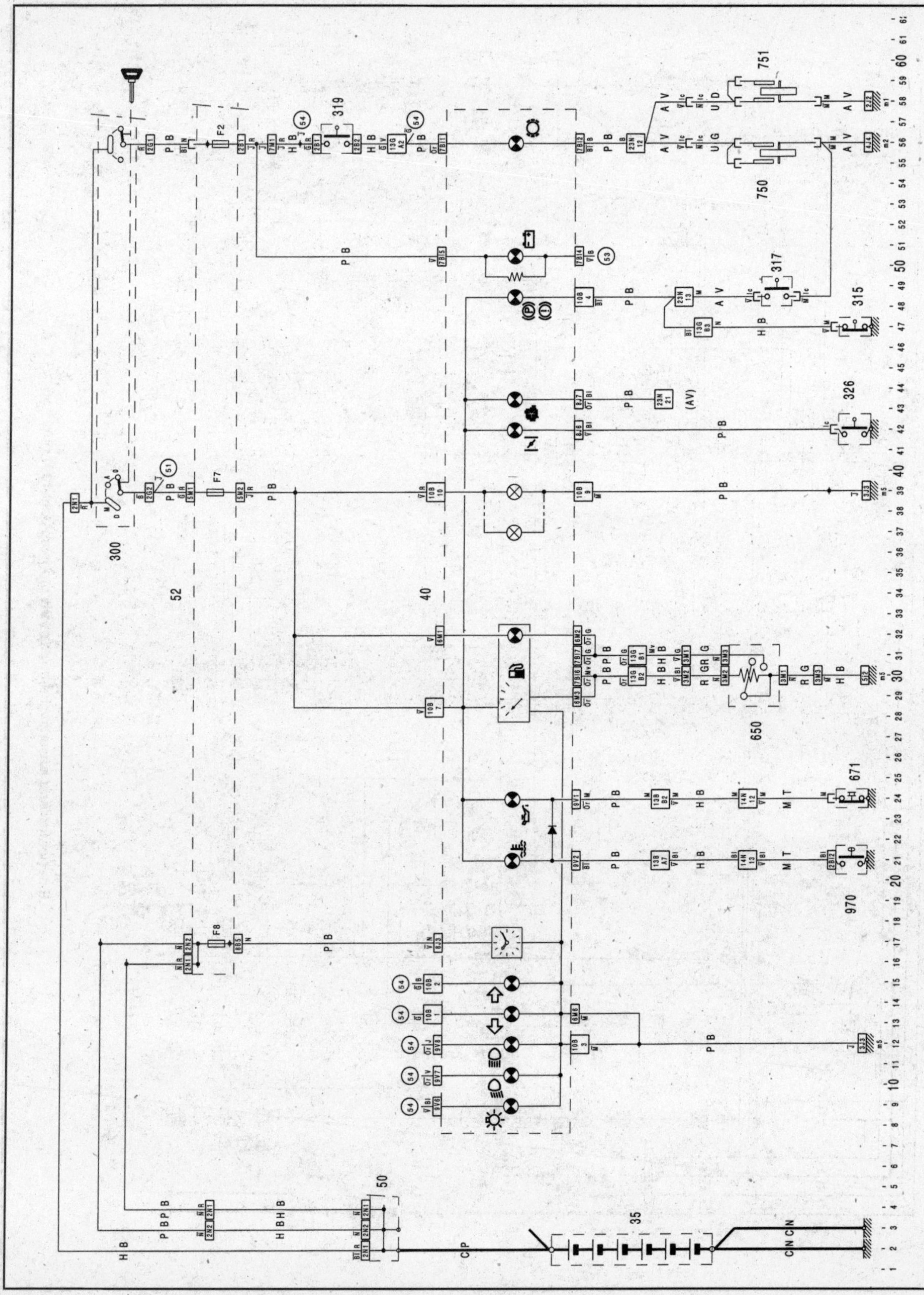

Instrument panel (low-series models) - from July 1991 on

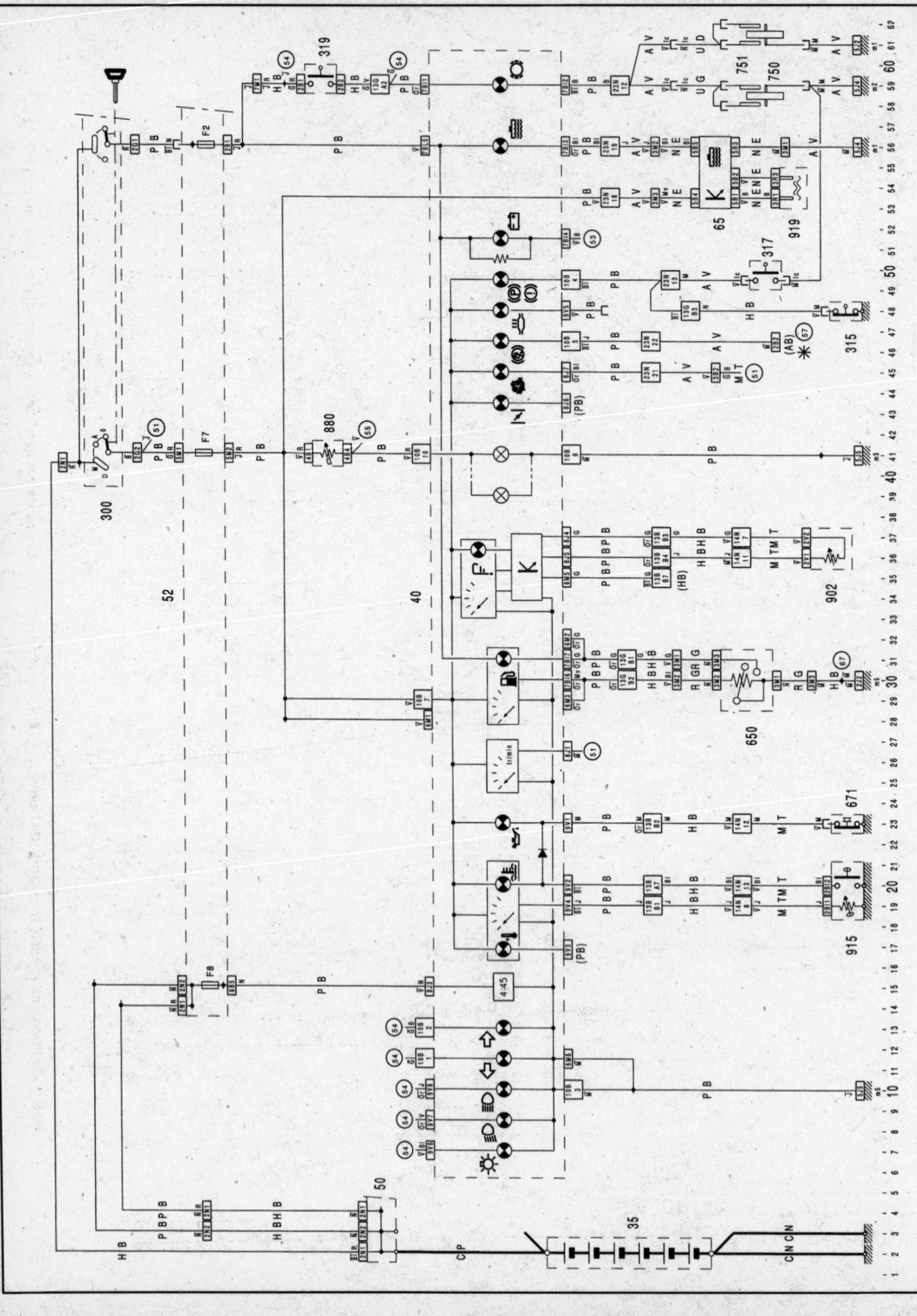

Instrument panel (high-series models) - from July 1991 on

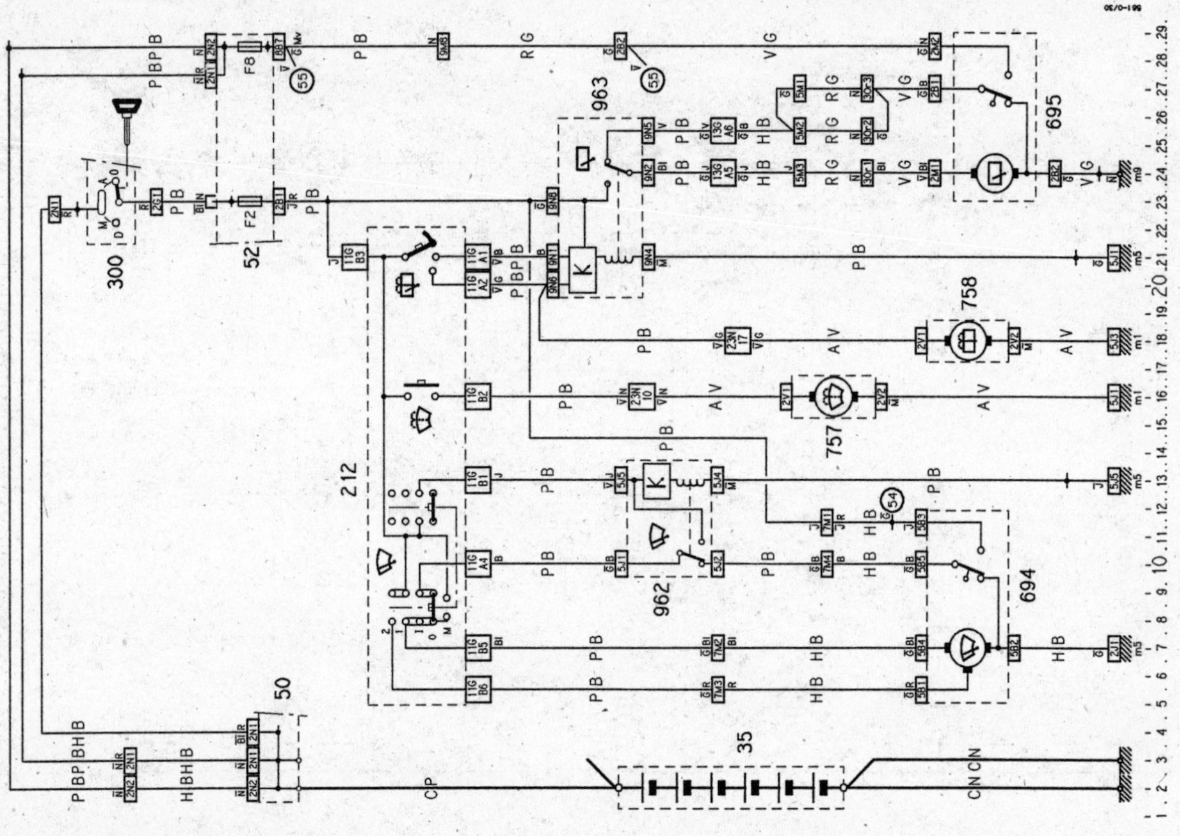

Windscreen and tailgate wipers - all models from July 1991 on

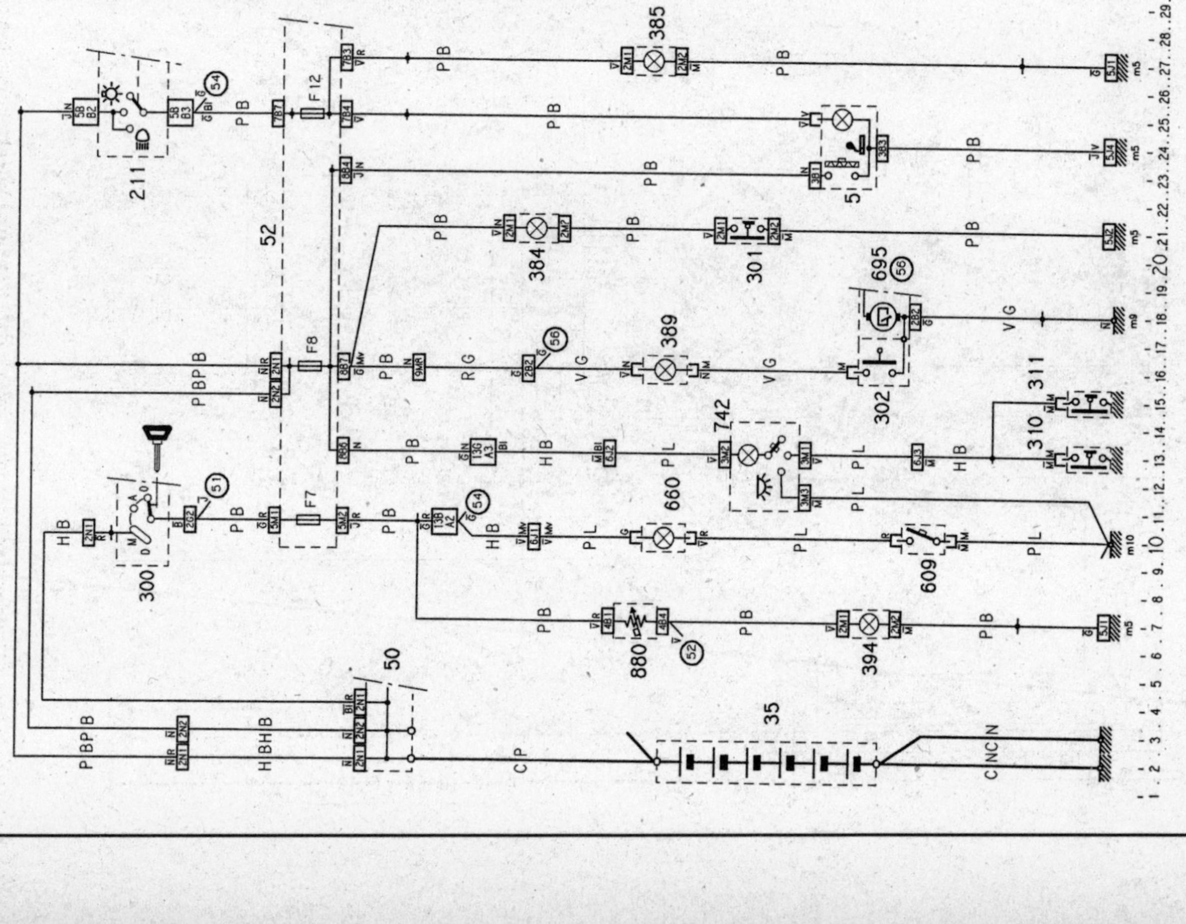

Interior lighting - all models from July 1991 on

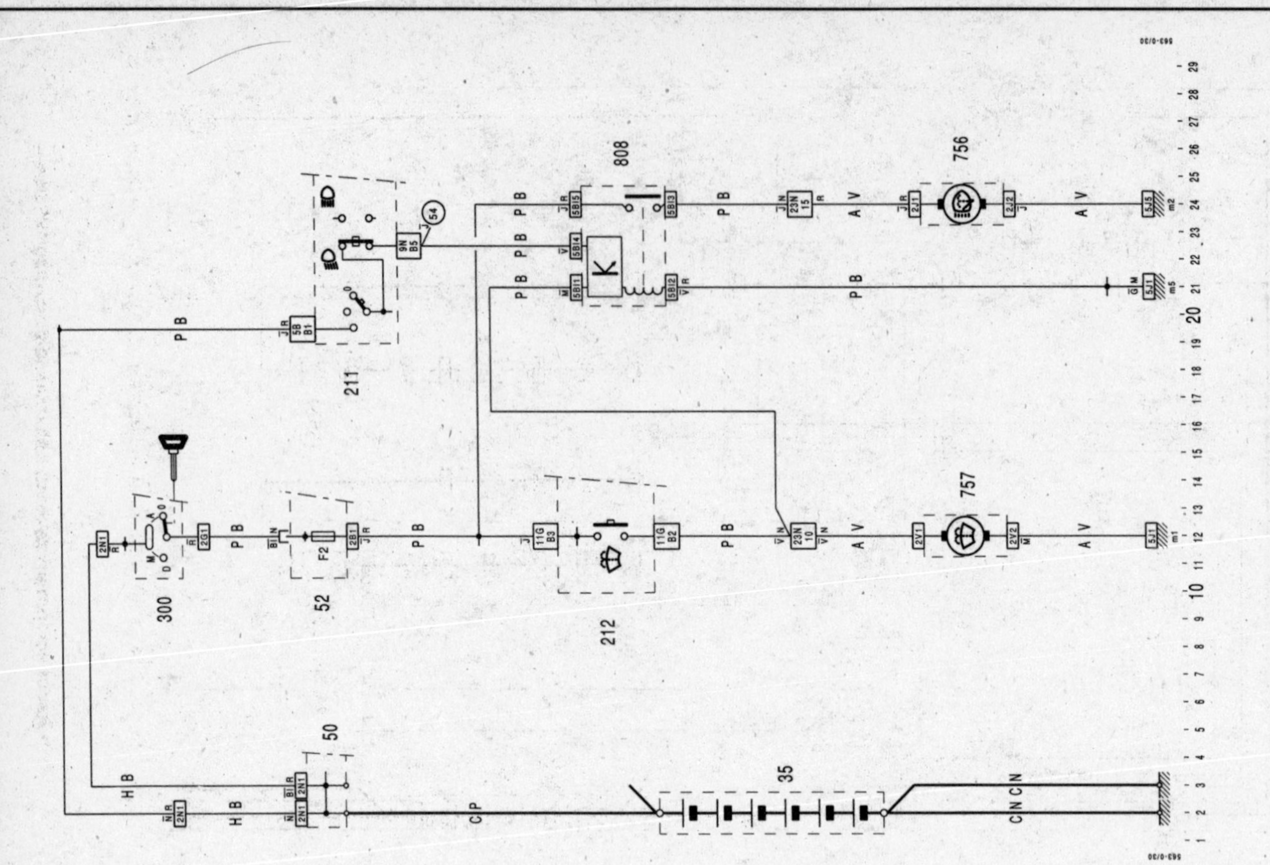

Headlight washers - all models from July 1991 on

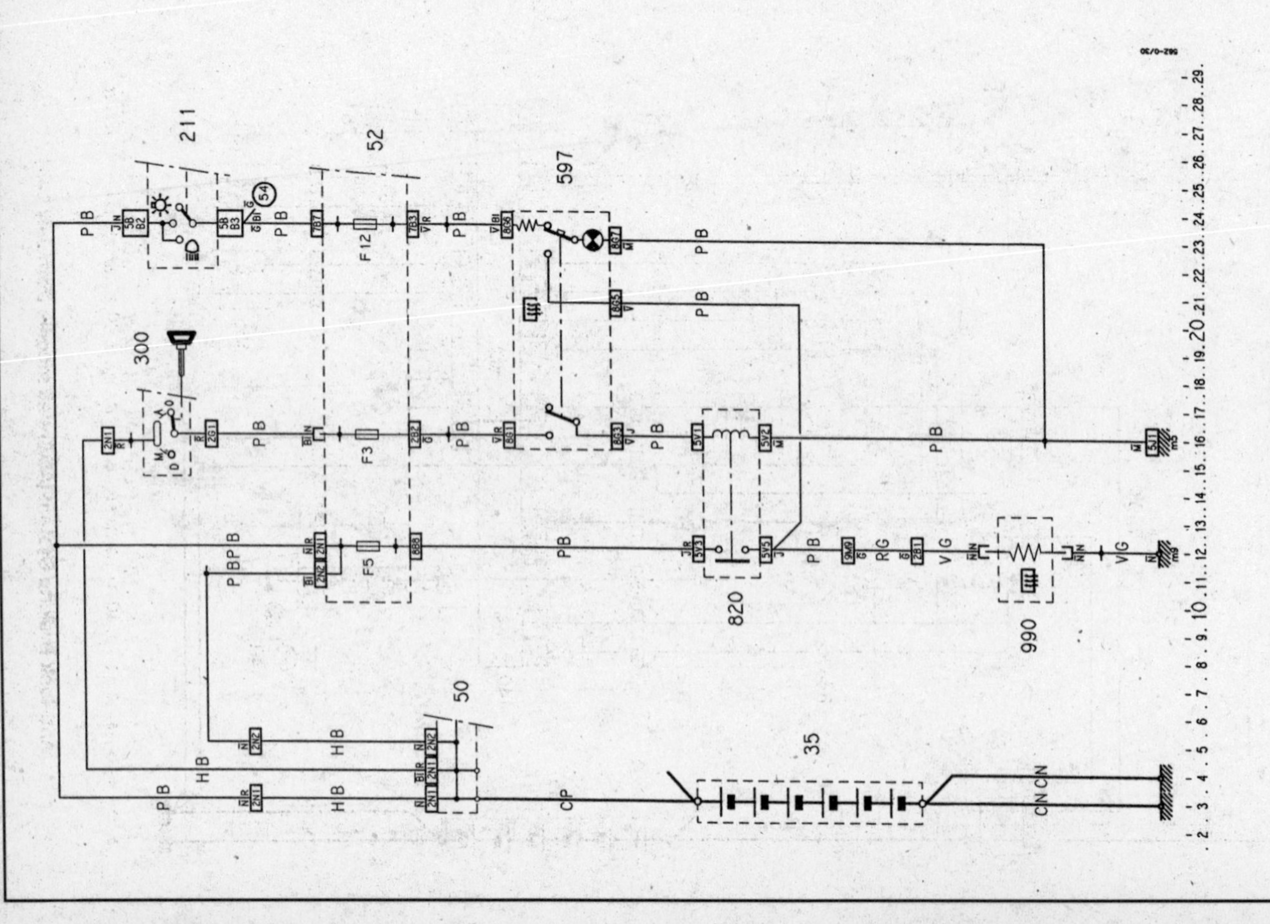

Heated rear window - all models from July 1991 on

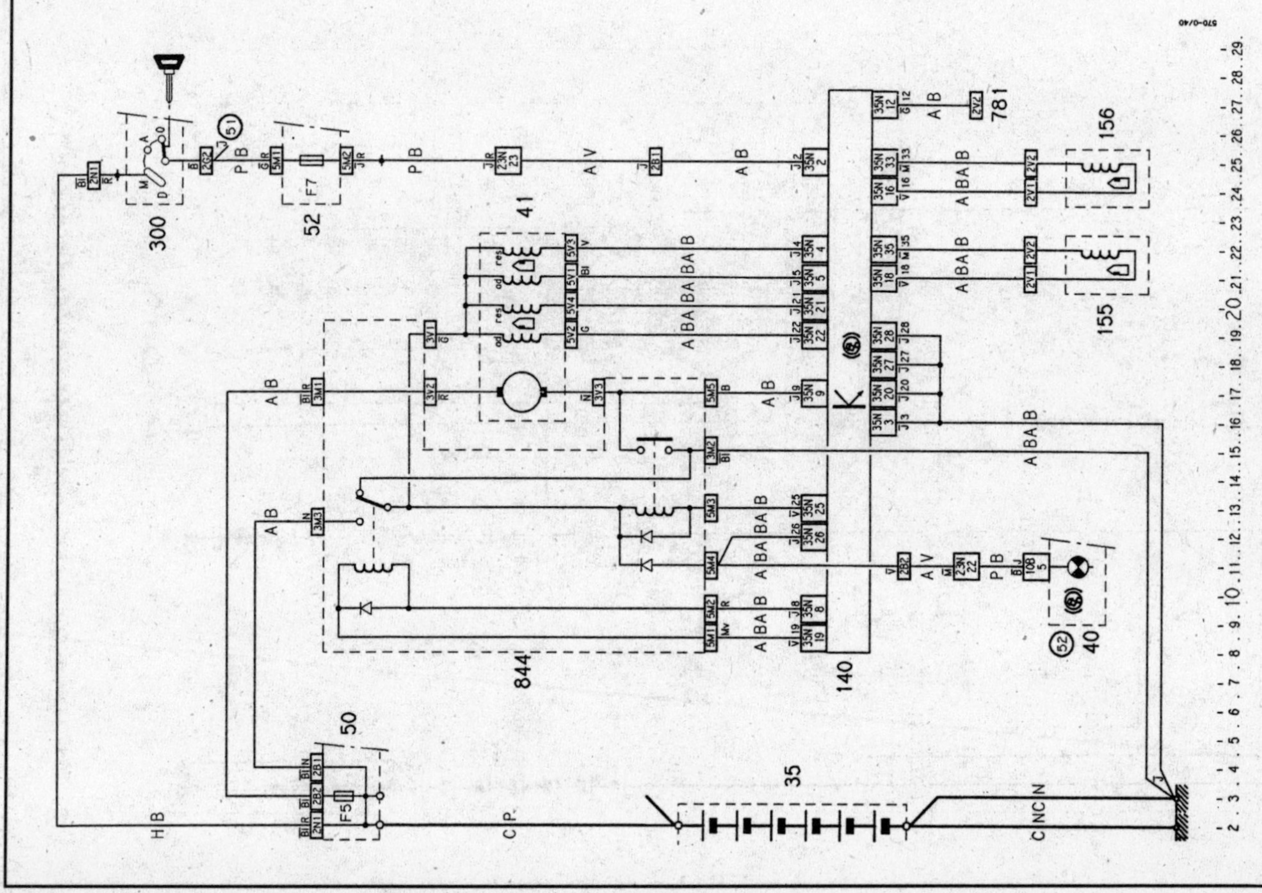

Anti-lock Braking System (ABS) - all models from July 1991 on

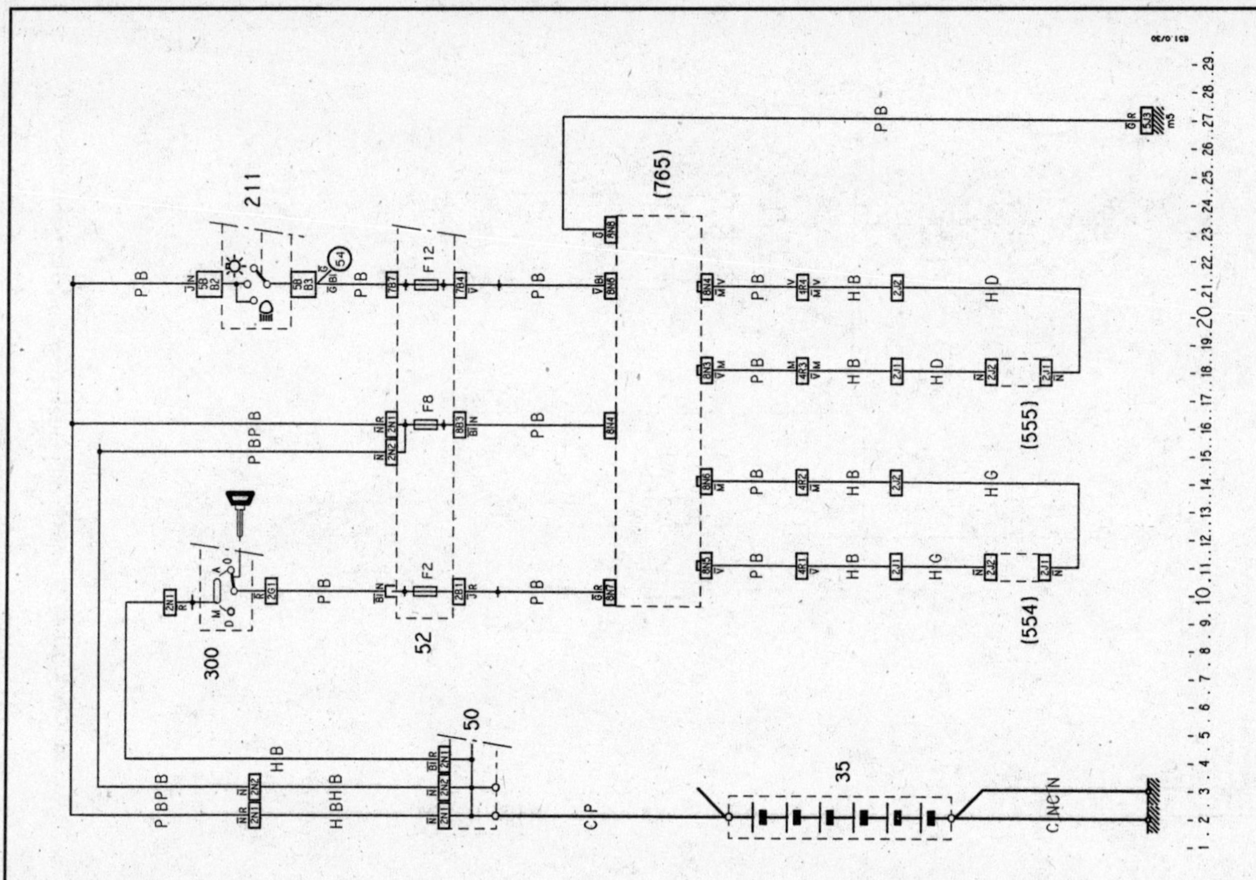

Radio equipment (typical) - all models from July 1991 on

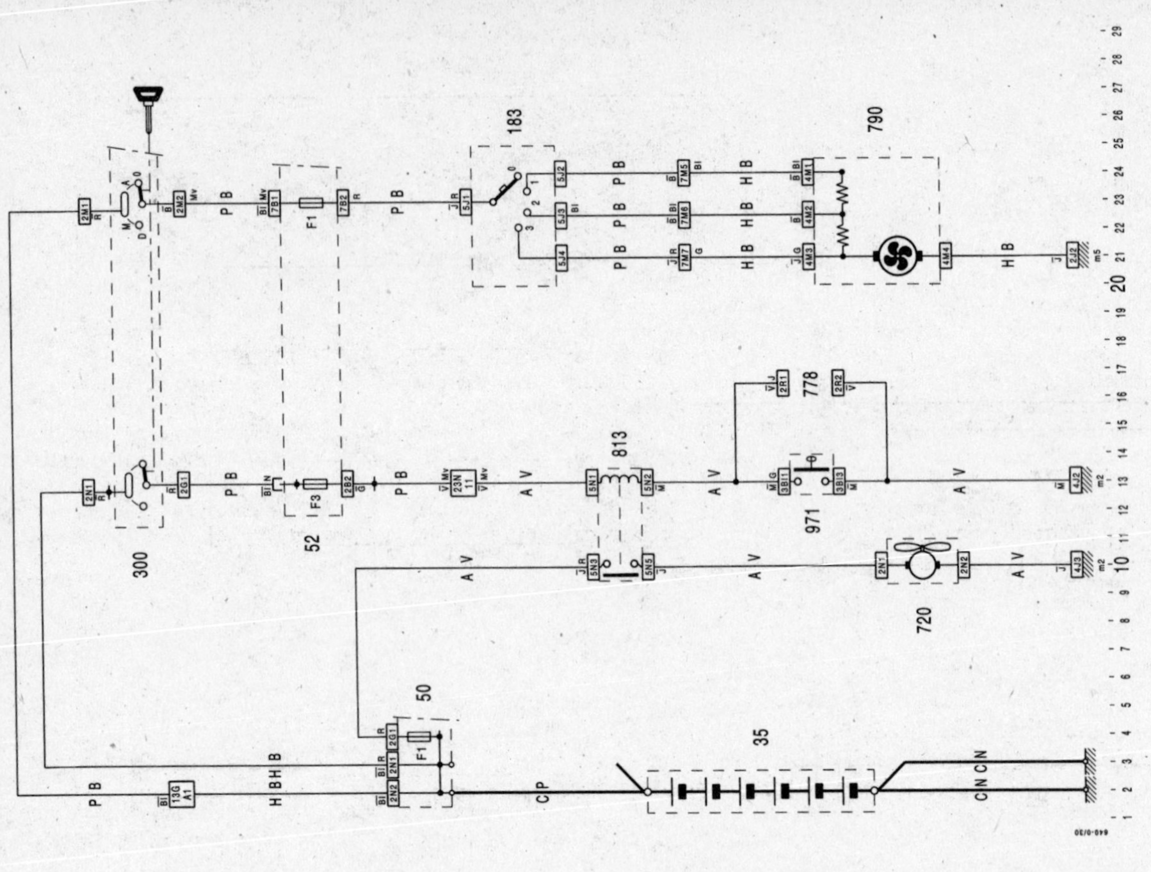

Air conditioning, heater blower and engine cooling fan - all models from July 1991 on

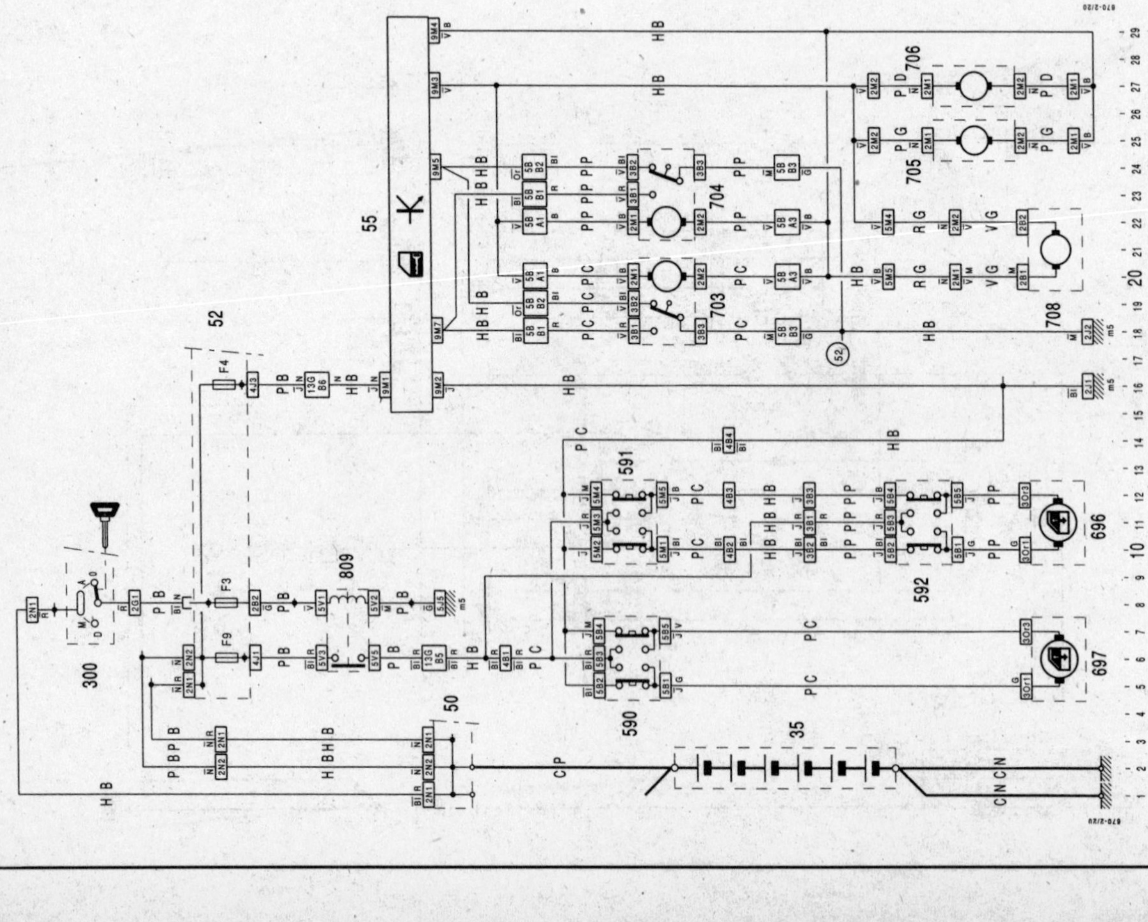

Electric windows and central locking system (typical) - all models from July 1991 on

Key to wiring diagrams - all models from July 1991 on

Not all items fitted to all models

No	Description
5	Front cigar lighter
10	Ignition distributor
15	Alternator
20	LH horn
35	Battery
40	Instrument cluster
41	Hydraulic valve block (ABS)
45	Ignition coil
50	Supply connector box
52	Junction box
53	Water temperature control unit
55	Central door locking control unit
58	Remote control door locking receiver (PLIP)
59	Pre-heater (glow plugs) control unit
61	Catalytic converter control unit
63	Additional fusebox
65	Water level control unit
100	Spark plugs
101	Glow plugs
130	Lights-on warning buzzer
140	Anti-lock braking system ECU
141	Air conditioning ECU
142	Fuel injection ECU
144	Exhaust gas recirculation ECU
152	Engine speed sensor
154	Distance sensor
155	LH front wheel sensor (ABS)
156	RH front wheel sensor (ABS)
160	TDC sensor
170	Flasher unit
183	Air blower control
184	Air conditioning control
186	Cooled air blower motor control
187	Driving school instructor select switch
211	LH steering column switch
212	RH steering column switch
254	Air horn compressor
255	Air con. compressor driving clutch
270	HT coil suppressor
300	Ignition switch
301	Glovebox light switch
302	Boot light switch
305	Driver's door locking switch
306	Passenger's door locking switch
307	LH rear door closing switch
308	RH rear door closing switch
310	LH front door pillar switch
311	RH front door pillar switch
312	LH rear door pillar switch
313	RH rear door pillar switch
314	Reversing light switch
315	Handbrake switch
317	Hydraulic fluid level switch
318	Throttle butterfly switch
319	Stop-light switch
322	Atmospheric pressure switch
326	Starter motor switch
350	Starter motor
384	Glovebox lighting
385	Front ashtray illumination
389	Boot light
391	Number plate LH light
392	Number plate RH light
394	Heater control illumination
429	Fuel cut-off solenoid (stop solenoid)
430	Canister discharge solenoid
431	Fast idling solenoid
432	Idling actuator
434	Canister solenoid
437	Exhaust gas recirculation solenoid
441	Vacuum advance solenoid
443	Injection timing correction solenoid
480	LH rear light
481	RH rear light
482	LH front auxiliary light
483	RH front auxiliary light
484	Rear foglight
488	LH front direction indicator
489	RH front direction indicator
490	LH rear direction indicator
491	RH rear direction indicator
492	LH sidelight
493	RH sidelight
499	Reversing light
500	LH direction indicator repeater
501	RH direction indicator repeater
504	LH stop-light
505	RH stop-light
506	LH tail light
507	RH tail light
540	Fuse
554	LH rear speaker
555	RH rear speaker
570	Injector
582	Refrigerated air switch
587	Front auxiliary light switch
588	Rear foglight switch
589	Hazard warning light switch
590	Driver's window switch
591	Passenger's window switch (on driver's door)
592	Passenger's window switch (on passenger's door)
597	Heated rear window switch
601	Driver's heated seat switch
602	Passenger's heated seat switch
609	Map reading light switch
610	Differential locking switch
612	Flashing light/air horn switch
650	Fuel gauge
660	Map reading light
671	Engine oil pressure switch
680	Ignition module
694	Windscreen wiper motor
695	Tailgate wiper motor
696	LH front window motor
697	RH front window motor
703	Driver's door locking motor
704	Passenger's door locking motor
705	LH rear door locking motor
706	RH rear door locking motor
708	Tailgate locking motor
711	Air recycling motor
712	Idling control stepper motor
714	ABS hydraulic pump motor
715	LH headlight adjustment device motor
716	RH headlight adjustment device motor
720	Radiator cooling fan
742	Courtesy light
750	LH front brake pads sensor
751	RH front brake pads sensor
755	Fuel pump
756	Headlight washer pump
757	Windscreen washer pump
758	Rear screen washer pump
765	Radio set
770	Throttle spindle potentiometer
772	Mixture adjustment potentiometer
775	Pressure switch
777	Flashing light plug
778	Radiator cooling fan test plug
779	TDC sensor plug
781	ABS diagnostic socket
783	Injection diagnostic socket
786	Headlight: LH main and dipped beams
787	Headlight: RH main and dipped beams
790	Air blower motor
791	Cooled air blower motor
798	Injection timing cut-off relay
804	Air conditioning relay
805	Compressor cut-off relay (temperature)
806	Front auxiliary light relays
807	Injection double relay
808	Headlight washer relay
809	Front window relay
813	Radiator cooling fan relay
819	Rear foglight relays
820	Heated rear window relay
821	Air conditioning supplementary relay
822	Compressor cut-off relay (injection)
825	Headlight dipped beam relay
827	Dim-dip relay (UK only)
843	Air horn compressor relay
844	ABS main relay

(continued opn next page)

Key to wiring diagrams - all models from July 1991 on

Not all items fitted to all models

(continued from previous page)

No	Description
857	Carburettor base heating resistance
858	Dipped beams resistance (dim-dip)
859	Air blower speed resistor
861	Inlet air heating resistance
862	Injector additional resistance
880	Instrument lighting rheostat
900	Oxygen sensor
902	Engine oil level sensor
903	Injection air pressure sensor
907	Injection air temperature sensor
909	Injection water temperature sensor
910	Water temp. sensor (control unit)
911	Water temp. sensor (gauge)
912	Evaporator temperature sensor
915	Water temperature switch sensor
917	Catalytic converter temperature sensor
919	Engine coolant level sensor
962	Windscreen intermittent wipe timer
963	Tailgate intermittent wipe timer
970	Coolant temp. warning thermal switch
971	Cooling fan thermal switch (radiator)
990	Heated rear window

Harness code	
AB	Anti-lock braking system (ABS)
AC	Cigar lighter
AE	Driving school
AL	Electrical feed
AV	Front
BR	Cooled air control unit
CA	Cooled air control
CL	Console
CN	Negative cable
CP	Positive cable
FR	Rear lights
GA	Flashing light/air horn
HB	Interior
HD	RH rear speaker
HG	LH rear speaker
JT	Injectors
LA	Interference suppression connection
MF	Rear light earth
MT	Engine (and injection)
NC	Ribbon connectors (driver's side)
PB	Dashboard
PC	Driver's door
PD	RH rear door
PG	LH rear door
PL	Interior light
PP	Passenger's door
RD	RH rear
RG	LH rear
RL	Direction indicator side repeater
SC	Heated seats
UD	RH brake pad wear
UG	LH brake pad wear
VD	RH side tailgate
VG	LH side tailgate

Colour code	
B	White
Bl	Blue
G	Grey
Ic	Clear/transparent
J	Yellow
M	Brown
Mv	Purple
N	Black
Or	Orange
R	Red
Ro	Pink
V	Green
Vi	Lilac

Tools and Working Facilities

Introduction

A selection of good tools is a fundamental requirement for anyone contemplating the maintenance and repair of a motor vehicle. For the owner who does not possess any, their purchase will prove a considerable expense, offsetting some of the savings made by doing-it-yourself. However, provided that the tools purchased meet the relevant national safety standards and are of good quality, they will last for many years and prove an extremely worthwhile investment.

To help the average owner to decide which tools are needed to carry out the various tasks detailed in this manual, we have compiled three lists of tools under the following headings: *Maintenance and minor repair*, *Repair and overhaul*, and *Special*. Newcomers to practical mechanics should start off with the *Maintenance and minor repair* tool kit, and confine themselves to the simpler jobs around the vehicle. Then, as confidence and experience grow, more difficult tasks can be undertaken, with extra tools being purchased as, and when, they are needed. In this way, a *Maintenance and minor repair* tool kit can be built up into a *Repair and overhaul* tool kit over a considerable period of time, without any major cash outlays. The experienced do-it-yourselfer will have a tool kit good enough for most repair and overhaul procedures, and will add tools from the *Special* category when it is felt that the expense is justified by the amount of use to which these tools will be put.

Maintenance and minor repair tool kit

The tools given in this list should be considered as a minimum requirement if routine maintenance, servicing and minor repair operations are to be undertaken. We recommend the purchase of combination spanners (ring one end, open-ended the other); although more expensive than open-ended ones, they do give the advantages of both types of spanner.

- ☐ *Combination spanners:*
- ☐ *Metric - 8, 9, 10, 11, 12, 13, 14, 15, 17 & 19 mm*
- ☐ *Adjustable spanner - 35 mm jaw (approx)*
- ☐ *Spark plug spanner (with rubber insert) - petrol models*
- ☐ *Spark plug gap adjustment tool - petrol models*
- ☐ *Set of feeler gauges*
- ☐ *Brake bleed nipple spanner*
- ☐ *Screwdrivers:*
  Flat blade - approx 100 mm long x 6 mm dia
  Cross blade - approx 100 mm long x 6 mm dia
- ☐ *Combination pliers*
- ☐ *Hacksaw (junior)*
- ☐ *Tyre pump*
- ☐ *Tyre pressure gauge*
- ☐ *Oil can*
- ☐ *Oil filter removal tool*
- ☐ *Fine emery cloth*
- ☐ *Wire brush (small)*
- ☐ *Funnel (medium size)*

Repair and overhaul tool kit

These tools are virtually essential for anyone undertaking any major repairs to a motor vehicle, and are additional to those given in the *Maintenance and minor repair* list. Included in this list is a comprehensive set of sockets. Although these are expensive, they will be found invaluable as they are so versatile - particularly if various drives are included in the set. We recommend the half-inch square-drive type, as this can be used with most proprietary torque wrenches. If you cannot afford a socket set, even bought piecemeal, then inexpensive tubular box spanners are a useful alternative.

The tools in this list will occasionally need to be supplemented by tools from the *Special* list:

- ☐ *Sockets (or box spanners) to cover range in previous list (including Torx sockets)*
- ☐ *Reversible ratchet drive (for use with sockets)* **(see illustration)**
- ☐ *Extension piece, 250 mm (for use with sockets)*
- ☐ *Universal joint (for use with sockets)*
- ☐ *Torque wrench (for use with sockets)*
- ☐ *Self-locking grips*
- ☐ *Ball pein hammer*
- ☐ *Soft-faced mallet (plastic/aluminium or rubber)*
- ☐ *Screwdrivers:*
  Flat blade - long & sturdy, short (chubby), and narrow (electrician's) types
  Cross blade - Long & sturdy, and short (chubby) types
- ☐ *Pliers:*
  Long-nosed
  Side cutters (electrician's)
  Circlip (internal and external)
- ☐ *Cold chisel - 25 mm*
- ☐ *Scriber*
- ☐ *Scraper*
- ☐ *Centre-punch*
- ☐ *Pin punch*
- ☐ *Hacksaw*
- ☐ *Brake hose clamp*
- ☐ *Brake/clutch bleeding kit*
- ☐ *Selection of twist drills*
- ☐ *Steel rule/straight-edge*
- ☐ *Allen keys (inc. splined/Torx type)* **(see illustrations)**
- ☐ *Selection of files*
- ☐ *Wire brush*
- ☐ *Axle stands*
- ☐ *Jack (strong trolley or hydraulic type)*
- ☐ *Light with extension lead*

Special tools

The tools in this list are those which are not used regularly, are expensive to buy, or which need to be used in accordance with their manufacturers' instructions. Unless relatively difficult mechanical jobs are undertaken frequently, it will not be economic to buy many of these tools. Where this is the case, you could consider clubbing together with friends (or joining a motorists' club) to make a joint purchase, or borrowing the tools against a deposit from a local garage or tool hire specialist. It is worth noting that many of the larger DIY superstores now carry a large range of special tools for hire at modest rates.

The following list contains only those tools and instruments freely available to the public, and not those special tools produced by the vehicle manufacturer specifically for its dealer network. You will find occasional references to these manufacturers' special tools in the text of this manual. Generally, an alternative method of doing the job without the vehicle manufacturers' special tool is given. However, sometimes there is no alternative to using them. Where this is the case and the relevant tool cannot be bought or borrowed, you will have to entrust the work to a franchised garage.

- ☐ *Valve spring compressor* **(see illustration)**
- ☐ *Valve grinding tool*
- ☐ *Piston ring compressor* **(see illustration)**
- ☐ *Piston ring removal/installation tool* **(see illustration)**
- ☐ *Cylinder bore hone* **(see illustration)**
- ☐ *Balljoint separator*
- ☐ *Coil spring compressors (where applicable)*
- ☐ *Two/three-legged hub and bearing puller* **(see illustration)**

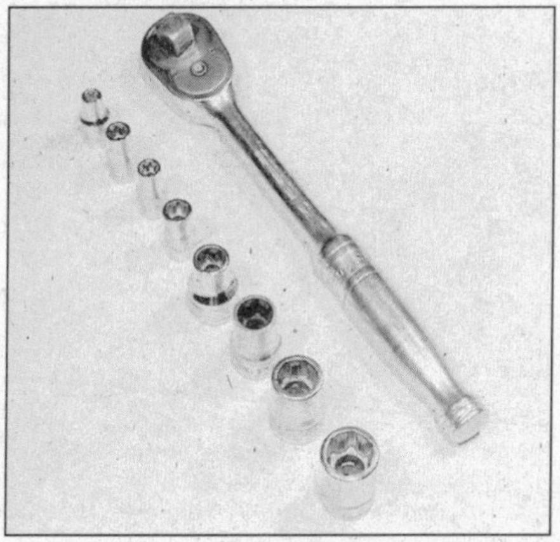

Sockets and reversible ratchet drive

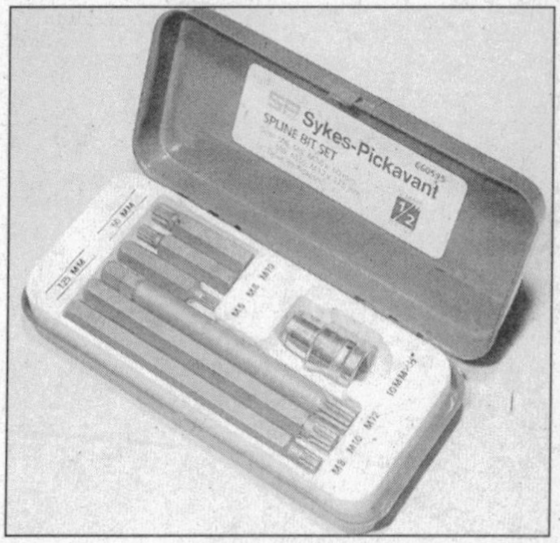

Spline bit set

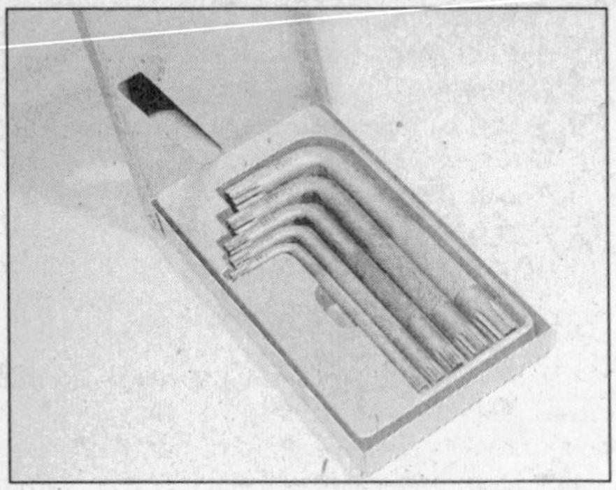

Spline key set

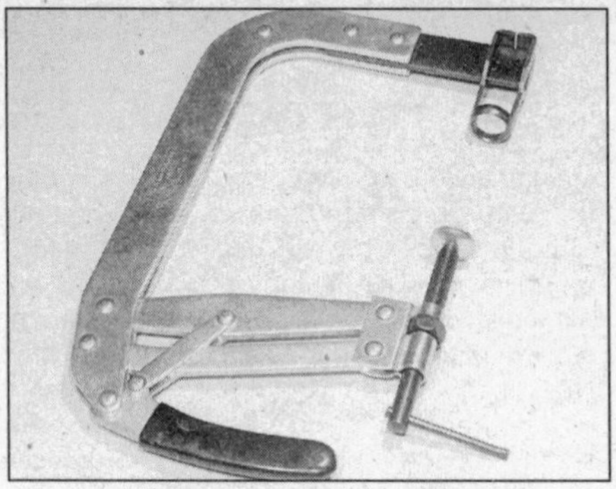

Valve spring compressor

Piston ring compressor

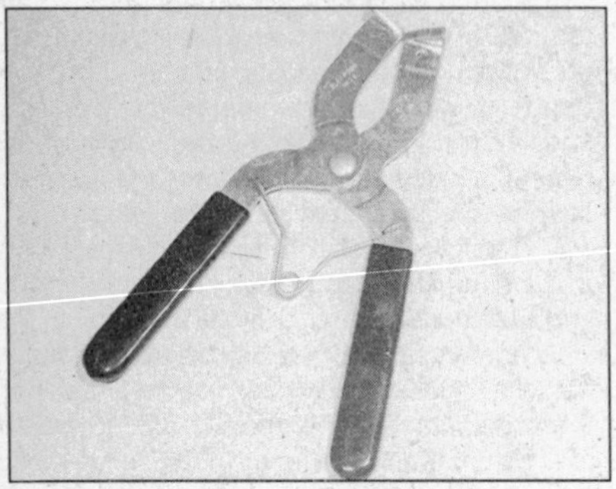

Piston ring removal/installation tool

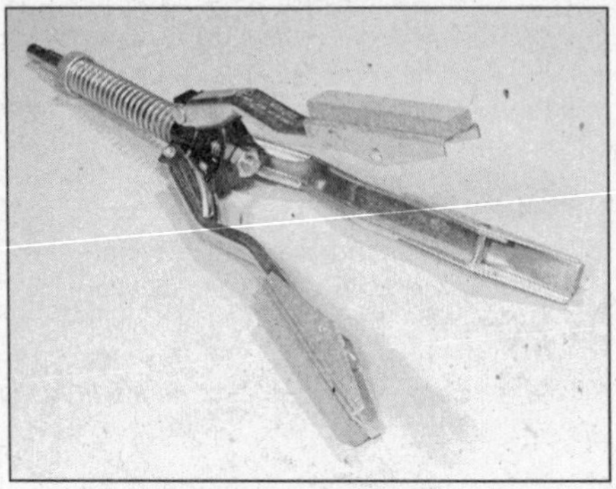

Cylinder bore hone

Three-legged hub and bearing puller

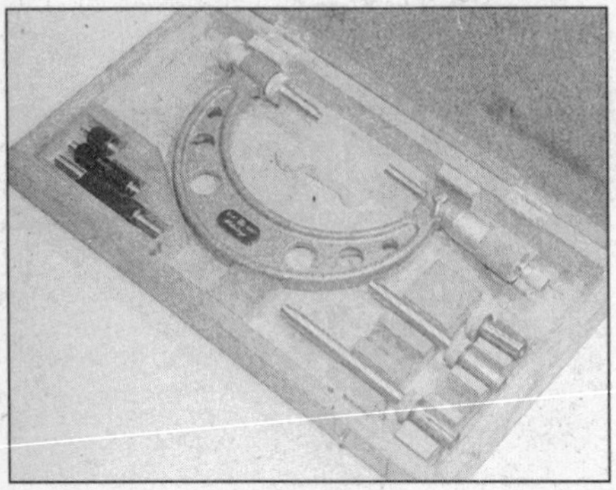

Micrometer set

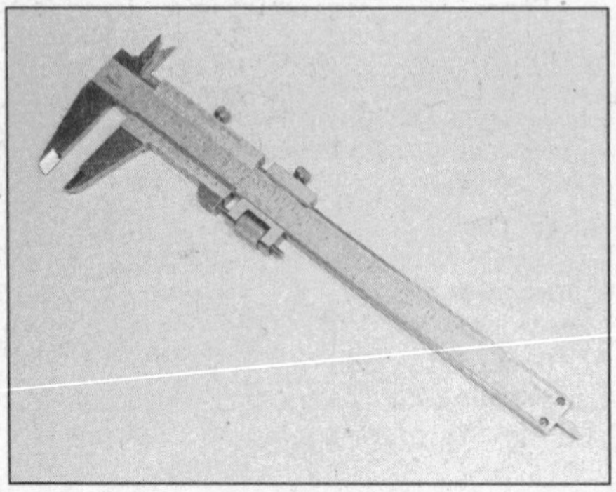

Vernier calipers

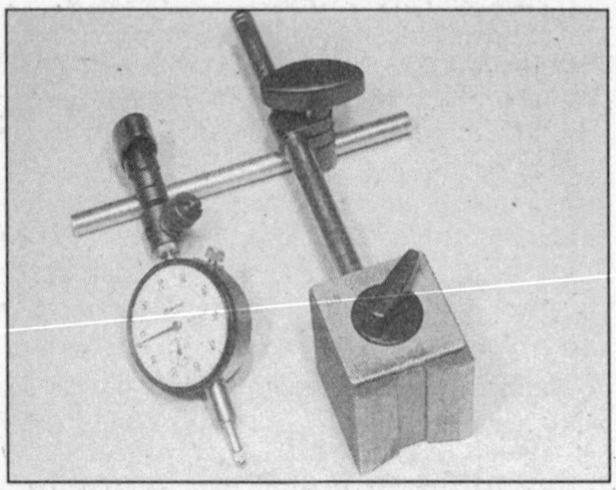

Dial test indicator and magnetic stand

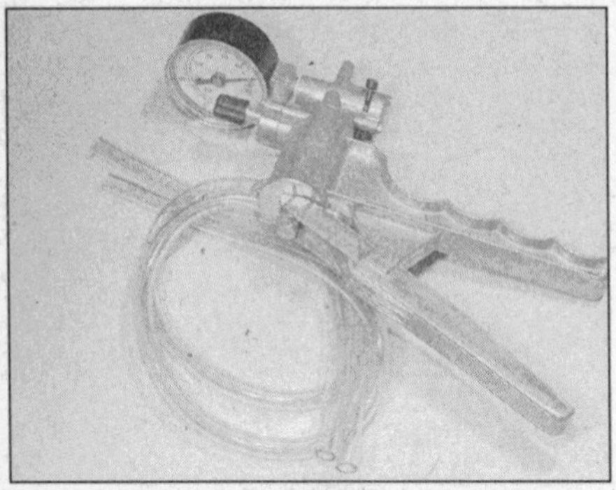

Vacuum pump and gauge

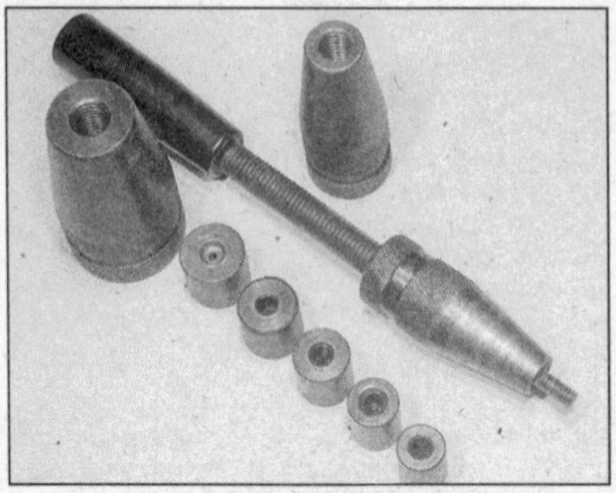

Clutch plate alignment set

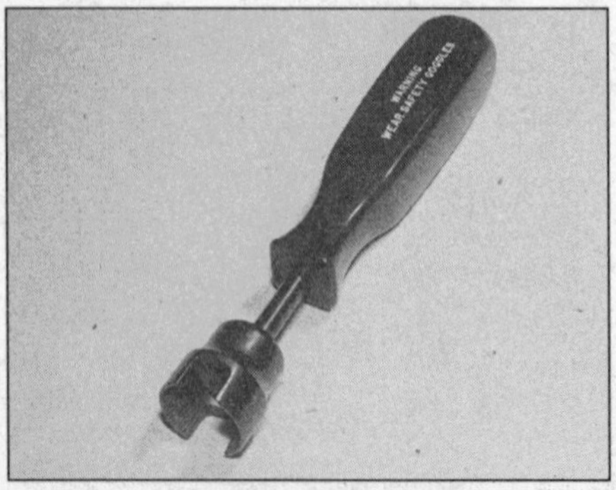

Brake shoe steady spring cup removal tool

- ☐ *Impact screwdriver*
- ☐ *Micrometer and/or vernier calipers* **(see illustrations)**
- ☐ *Dial gauge* **(see illustration)**
- ☐ *Stroboscopic timing light - petrol models* **(see illustration)**
- ☐ *Dwell angle meter/tachometer*
- ☐ *Universal electrical multi-meter*
- ☐ *Cylinder compression gauge* **(see illustration)**
- ☐ *Hand-operated vacuum pump and gauge* **(see illustration)**
- ☐ *Clutch plate alignment set* **(see illustration)**
- ☐ *Brake shoe steady spring cup removal tool* **(see illustration)**
- ☐ *Bush and bearing removal/installation set* **(see illustration)**
- ☐ *Stud extractors* **(see illustration)**
- ☐ *Tap and die set* **(see illustration)**
- ☐ *Lifting tackle*
- ☐ *Trolley jack*

Buying tools

For practically all tools, a tool factor is the best source, since he will have a very comprehensive range compared with the average garage or accessory shop. Having said that, accessory shops often offer excellent quality tools at discount prices, so it pays to shop around.

Remember, you don't have to buy the most expensive items on the shelf, but it is always advisable to steer clear of the very cheap tools. There are plenty of good tools around at reasonable prices, but always aim to purchase items which meet the relevant national safety standards. If in doubt, ask the proprietor or manager of the shop for advice before making a purchase.

Care and maintenance of tools

Having purchased a reasonable tool kit, it is necessary to keep the tools in a clean and serviceable condition. After use, always wipe off any dirt, grease and metal particles using a clean, dry cloth, before putting the tools away. Never leave them lying around after they have been used. A simple tool rack on the garage or workshop wall for items such as screwdrivers and pliers is a good idea. Store all normal spanners and sockets in a metal box. Any measuring instruments, gauges, meters, etc, must be carefully stored where they cannot be damaged or become rusty.

Take a little care when tools are used. Hammer heads inevitably become marked, and screwdrivers lose the keen edge on their blades from time to time. A little timely attention with emery cloth or a file will soon restore items like this to a good serviceable finish.

Working facilities

Not to be forgotten when discussing tools is the workshop itself. If anything more than routine maintenance is to be carried out, some form of suitable working area becomes essential.

It is appreciated that many an owner-mechanic is forced by circumstances to remove an engine or similar item without the benefit of a garage or workshop. Having done this, any repairs should always be done under the cover of a roof.

Wherever possible, any dismantling should be done on a clean, flat workbench or table at a suitable working height.

Any workbench needs a vice; one with a jaw opening of 100 mm is suitable for most jobs. As mentioned previously, some clean dry storage space is also required for tools, as well as for any lubricants, cleaning fluids, touch-up paints and so on, which become necessary.

Another item which may be required, and which has a much more general usage, is an electric drill with a chuck capacity of at least 8 mm. This, together with a good range of twist drills, is virtually essential for fitting accessories.

Last, but not least, always keep a supply of old newspapers and clean, lint-free rags available, and try to keep any working area as clean as possible.

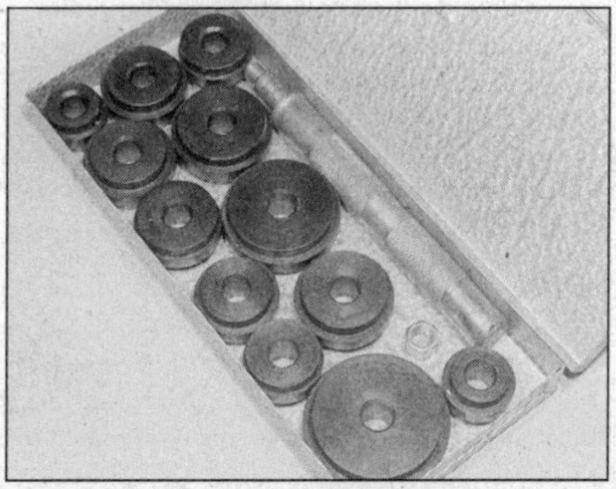

Bush and bearing removal/installation set

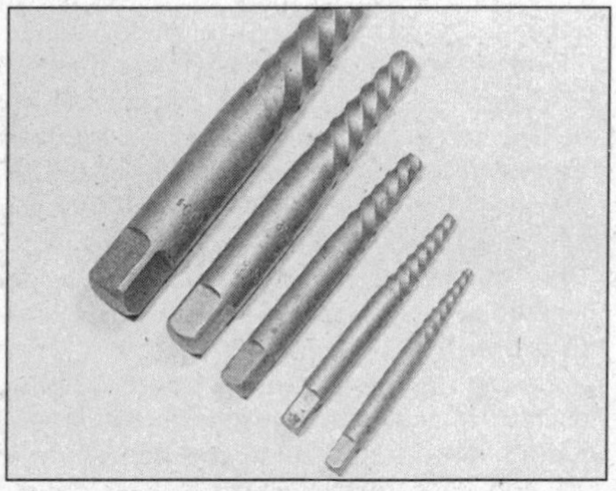

Stud extractor set

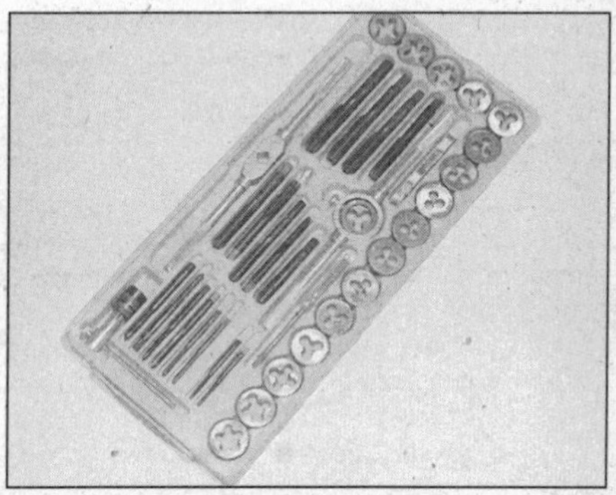

Tap and die set

General Repair Procedures

Whenever servicing, repair or overhaul work is carried out on the car or its components, it is necessary to observe the following procedures and instructions. This will assist in carrying out the operation efficiently and to a professional standard of workmanship.

Joint mating faces and gaskets

When separating components at their mating faces, never insert screwdrivers or similar implements into the joint between the faces in order to prise them apart. This can cause severe damage which results in oil leaks, coolant leaks, etc upon reassembly. Separation is usually achieved by tapping along the joint with a soft-faced hammer in order to break the seal. However, note that this method may not be suitable where dowels are used for component location.

Where a gasket is used between the mating faces of two components, ensure that it is renewed on reassembly, and fit it dry unless otherwise stated in the repair procedure. Make sure that the mating faces are clean and dry, with all traces of old gasket removed. When cleaning a joint face, use a tool which is not likely to score or damage the face, and remove any burrs or nicks with an oilstone or fine file.

Make sure that tapped holes are cleaned with a pipe cleaner, and keep them free of jointing compound, if this is being used, unless specifically instructed otherwise.

Ensure that all orifices, channels or pipes are clear, and blow through them, preferably using compressed air.

Oil seals

Oil seals can be removed by levering them out with a wide flat-bladed screwdriver or similar implement. Alternatively, a number of self-tapping screws may be screwed into the seal, and these used as a purchase for pliers or some similar device in order to pull the seal free.

Whenever an oil seal is removed from its working location, either individually or as part of an assembly, it should be renewed.

The very fine sealing lip of the seal is easily damaged, and will not seal if the surface it contacts is not completely clean and free from scratches, nicks or grooves.

Protect the lips of the seal from any surface which may damage them in the course of fitting. Use tape or a conical sleeve where possible. Lubricate the seal lips with oil before fitting and, on dual-lipped seals, fill the space between the lips with grease.

Unless otherwise stated, oil seals must be fitted with their sealing lips toward the lubricant to be sealed.

Use a tubular drift or block of wood of the appropriate size to install the seal and, if the seal housing is shouldered, drive the seal down to the shoulder. If the seal housing is unshouldered, the seal should be fitted with its face flush with the housing top face (unless otherwise instructed).

Screw threads and fastenings

Seized nuts, bolts and screws are quite a common occurrence where corrosion has set in, and the use of penetrating oil or releasing fluid will often overcome this problem if the offending item is soaked for a while before attempting to release it. The use of an impact driver may also provide a means of releasing such stubborn fastening devices, when used in conjunction with the appropriate screwdriver bit or socket. If none of these methods works, it may be necessary to resort to the careful application of heat, or the use of a hacksaw or nut splitter device.

Studs are usually removed by locking two nuts together on the threaded part, and then using a spanner on the lower nut to unscrew the stud. Studs or bolts which have broken off below the surface of the component in which they are mounted can sometimes be removed using a proprietary stud extractor. Always ensure that a blind tapped hole is completely free from oil, grease, water or other fluid before installing the bolt or stud. Failure to do this could cause the housing to crack due to the hydraulic action of the bolt or stud as it is screwed in.

When tightening a castellated nut to accept a split pin, tighten the nut to the specified torque, where applicable, and then tighten further to the next split pin hole. Never slacken the nut to align the split pin hole, unless stated in the repair procedure.

When checking or retightening a nut or bolt to a specified torque setting, slacken the nut or bolt by a quarter of a turn, and then retighten to the specified setting. However, this should not be attempted where angular tightening has been used.

For some screw fastenings, notably cylinder head bolts or nuts, torque wrench settings are no longer specified for the latter stages of tightening, "angle-tightening" being called up instead. Typically, a fairly low torque wrench setting will be applied to the bolts/nuts in the correct sequence, followed by one or more stages of tightening through specified angles.

Locknuts, locktabs and washers

Any fastening which will rotate against a component or housing in the course of tightening should always have a washer between it and the relevant component or housing.

Spring or split washers should always be renewed when they are used to lock a critical component such as a big-end bearing retaining bolt or nut. Locktabs which are folded over to retain a nut or bolt should always be renewed.

Self-locking nuts can be re-used in non-critical areas, providing resistance can be felt when the locking portion passes over the bolt or stud thread. However, it should be noted that self-locking stiffnuts tend to lose their effectiveness after long periods of use, and in such cases should be renewed as a matter of course.

Split pins must always be replaced with new ones of the correct size for the hole.

When thread-locking compound is found on the threads of a fastener which is to be re-used, it should be cleaned off with a wire brush and solvent, and fresh compound applied on reassembly.

Special tools

Some repair procedures in this manual entail the use of special tools such as a press, two or three-legged pullers, spring compressors, etc. Wherever possible, suitable readily-available alternatives to the manufacturer's special tools are described, and are shown in use. Unless you are highly-skilled and have a thorough understanding of the procedures described, never attempt to bypass the use of any special tool when the procedure described specifies its use. Not only is there a very great risk of personal injury, but expensive damage could be caused to the components involved.

Environmental considerations

When disposing of used engine oil, brake fluid, antifreeze, etc, give due consideration to any detrimental environmental effects. Do not, for instance, pour any of the above liquids down drains into the general sewage system, or onto the ground to soak away. Many local council refuse tips provide a facility for waste oil disposal, as do some garages. If none of these facilities are available, consult your local Environmental Health Department for further advice.

With the universal tightening-up of legislation regarding the emission of environmentally-harmful substances from motor vehicles, most current vehicles have tamperproof devices fitted to the main adjustment points of the fuel system. These devices are primarily designed to prevent unqualified persons from adjusting the fuel/air mixture, with the chance of a consequent increase in toxic emissions. If such devices are encountered during servicing or overhaul, they should, wherever possible, be renewed or refitted in accordance with the vehicle manufacturer's requirements or current legislation.

OIL CARE FOLLOW THE CODE

OIL BANK LINE
0800 66 33 66

Note: It is antisocial and illegal to dump oil down the drain. To find the location of your local oil recycling bank, call this number free.

Introduction

The vehicle owner who does his or her own maintenance according to the recommended service schedules should not have to use this section of the manual very often. Modern component reliability is such that, provided those items subject to wear or deterioration are inspected or renewed at the specified intervals, sudden failure is comparatively rare. Faults do not usually just happen as a result of sudden failure, but develop over a period of time. Major mechanical failures in particular are usually preceded by characteristic symptoms over hundreds or even thousands of miles. Those components which do occasionally fail without warning are often small and easily carried in the vehicle.

With any fault-finding, the first step is to decide where to begin investigations. Sometimes this is obvious, but on other occasions, a little detective work will be necessary. The owner who makes half a dozen haphazard adjustments or replacements may be successful in curing a fault (or its symptoms), but will be none the wiser if the fault recurs, and ultimately may have spent more time and money than was necessary. A calm and logical approach will be found to be more satisfactory in the long run. Always take into account any warning signs or abnormalities that may have been noticed in the period preceding the fault - power loss, high or low gauge readings, unusual smells, etc - and remember that failure of components such as fuses or spark plugs may only be pointers to some underlying fault.

The pages which follow provide an easy-reference guide to the more common problems which may occur during the operation of the vehicle. These problems and their possible causes are grouped under headings denoting various components or systems, such as Engine, Cooling system, etc. The Chapter and/or Section which deals with the problem is also shown in brackets. Whatever the fault, certain basic principles apply. These are as follows:

Verify the fault. This is simply a matter of being sure that you know what the symptoms are before starting work. This is particularly important if you are investigating a fault for someone else, who may not have described it very accurately.

Don't overlook the obvious. For example, if the vehicle won't start, is there fuel in the tank? (Don't take anyone else's word on this particular point, and don't trust the fuel gauge either!) If an electrical fault is indicated, look for loose or broken wires before digging out the test gear.

Cure the disease, not the symptom. Substituting a flat battery with a fully-charged one will get you off the hard shoulder, but if the underlying cause is not attended to, the new battery will go the same way. Similarly, changing oil-fouled spark plugs (petrol models) for a new set will get you moving again, but remember that the reason for the fouling (if it wasn't simply an incorrect grade of plug) will have to be established and corrected.

Don't take anything for granted. Particularly, don't forget that a "new" component may itself be defective (especially if it's been rattling around in the boot for months), and don't leave components out of a fault diagnosis sequence just because they are new or recently-fitted. When you do finally diagnose a difficult fault, you'll probably realise that all the evidence was there from the start.

1 Engine

Engine fails to rotate when attempting to start

- ☐ Battery terminal connections loose or corroded (Chapter 1).
- ☐ Battery discharged or faulty (Chapter 5A).
- ☐ Broken, loose or disconnected wiring in the starting circuit (Chapter 5A).
- ☐ Defective starter solenoid or switch (Chap-ter 5A).
- ☐ Defective starter motor (Chapter 5A).
- ☐ Starter pinion or flywheel ring gear teeth loose or broken (Chapters 2A/B and 5A).
- ☐ Engine earth strap broken or disconnected (Chapter 5A).

Engine rotates, but will not start

- ☐ Fuel tank empty.
- ☐ Battery discharged (engine rotates slowly) (Chapter 5A).
- ☐ Battery terminal connections loose or corroded (Chapter 1).
- ☐ Ignition components damp or damaged - petrol models (Chapters 1 and 5B).
- ☐ Broken, loose or disconnected wiring in the ignition circuit - petrol models (Chapters 1 and 5B).
- ☐ Worn, faulty or incorrectly-gapped spark plugs - petrol models (Chapter 1).
- ☐ Preheating system faulty - Diesel models (Chapter 5C).
- ☐ Choke mechanism incorrectly adjusted, worn or sticking - carburettor petrol models (Chapter 4A).
- ☐ Faulty fuel cut-off solenoid - carburettor petrol models (Chapter 4A).
- ☐ Fuel injection system fault - fuel-injected petrol models (Chapter 4B/C).
- ☐ Stop solenoid faulty - Diesel models (Chapter 4D).
- ☐ Air in fuel system - Diesel models (Chapter 4D).
- ☐ Major mechanical failure (eg camshaft drive) (Chapter 2A/B).

Engine difficult to start when cold

- ☐ Battery discharged (Chapter 5A).
- ☐ Battery terminal connections loose or corroded (Chapter 1).
- ☐ Worn, faulty or incorrectly-gapped spark plugs - petrol models (Chapter 1).
- ☐ Preheating system faulty - Diesel models (Chapter 5C).
- ☐ Choke mechanism incorrectly adjusted, worn or sticking - carburettor petrol models (Chapter 4A).
- ☐ Fuel injection system fault - fuel-injected petrol models (Chapter 4B/4C).
- ☐ Other ignition system fault - petrol models (Chapters 1 and 5B/C).
- ☐ Fast idle valve incorrectly adjusted - Diesel models (Chapter 4D).
- ☐ Low cylinder compressions (Chapter 2A/B).

Engine difficult to start when hot

- ☐ Air filter element dirty or clogged (Chapter 1).
- ☐ Choke mechanism incorrectly adjusted, worn or sticking - carburettor petrol models (Chapter 4A).
- ☐ Fuel injection system fault - fuel-injected petrol models (Chapter 4B/C).
- ☐ Low cylinder compressions (Chapter 2A/B).

Starter motor noisy or excessively-rough in engagement

- ☐ Starter pinion or flywheel ring gear teeth loose or broken (Chapters 2A/B and 5A).
- ☐ Starter motor mounting bolts loose or missing (Chapter 5A).
- ☐ Starter motor internal components worn or damaged (Chapter 5A).

Engine starts, but stops immediately

- ☐ Loose or faulty electrical connections in the ignition circuit - petrol models (Chapters 1 and 5B).
- ☐ Vacuum leak at the carburettor/throttle body or inlet manifold - petrol models (Chapter 4A/B/C).
- ☐ Blocked carburettor jet(s) or internal passages - carburettor petrol models (Chapter 4A).
- ☐ Blocked injector/fuel injection system fault - fuel-injected petrol models (Chapter 4B/C).

Engine idles erratically

- ☐ Air filter element clogged (Chapter 1).
- ☐ Vacuum leak at the carburettor/throttle body, inlet manifold or associated hoses - petrol models (Chapter 4A/B/C).
- ☐ Worn, faulty or incorrectly-gapped spark plugs - petrol models (Chapter 1).
- ☐ Uneven or low cylinder compressions (Chapter 2A/B).
- ☐ Camshaft lobes worn (Chapter 2A/B).
- ☐ Timing belt incorrectly tensioned (Chapter 2A/B).
- ☐ Blocked carburettor jet(s) or internal passages - carburettor petrol models (Chapter 4A).
- ☐ Blocked injector/fuel injection system fault - fuel-injected petrol models (Chapter 4B/C).
- ☐ Faulty injector(s) - Diesel models (Chapter 4D).

Engine misfires at idle speed

- ☐ Worn, faulty or incorrectly-gapped spark plugs - petrol models (Chapter 1).
- ☐ Faulty spark plug HT leads - petrol models (Chapter 1).
- ☐ Vacuum leak at the carburettor/throttle body, inlet manifold or associated hoses - petrol models (Chapter 4A/B/C).
- ☐ Blocked carburettor jet(s) or internal passages - carburettor petrol models (Chapter 4A).
- ☐ Blocked injector/fuel injection system fault - fuel-injected petrol models (Chapter 4B/C).
- ☐ Faulty injector(s) - Diesel models (Chapter 4D).
- ☐ Distributor cap cracked or tracking internally - petrol models (where applicable) (Chapter 1).
- ☐ Uneven or low cylinder compressions (Chapter 2A/B).
- ☐ Disconnected, leaking, or perished crankcase ventilation hoses (Chapter 4E).

Engine misfires throughout the driving speed range

- ☐ Fuel filter choked (Chapter 1).
- ☐ Fuel pump faulty, or delivery pressure low - petrol models (Chapter 4A/B/C).
- ☐ Fuel tank vent blocked, or fuel pipes restricted (Chapter 4A/B/C).
- ☐ Vacuum leak at the carburettor/throttle body, inlet manifold or associated hoses - petrol models (Chapter 4A/B/C).
- ☐ Worn, faulty or incorrectly-gapped spark plugs - petrol models (Chapter 1).
- ☐ Faulty spark plug HT leads - petrol models (Chapter 1).
- ☐ Faulty injector(s) - Diesel models (Chapter 4D).
- ☐ Distributor cap cracked or tracking internally - petrol models (where applicable) (Chapter 1).
- ☐ Faulty ignition coil - petrol models (Chapter 5B).
- ☐ Uneven or low cylinder compressions (Chapter 2A/B).
- ☐ Blocked carburettor jet(s) or internal passages - carburettor petrol models (Chapter 4A).
- ☐ Blocked injector/fuel injection system fault - fuel-injected petrol models (Chapter 4B/C).

Engine hesitates on acceleration

- ☐ Worn, faulty or incorrectly-gapped spark plugs - petrol models (Chapter 1).
- ☐ Vacuum leak at the carburettor/throttle body, inlet manifold or associated hoses (Chapter 4A/B/C).
- ☐ Blocked carburettor jet(s) or internal passages - carburettor petrol models (Chapter 4A).
- ☐ Blocked injector/fuel injection system fault - fuel-injected petrol models (Chapter 4B/C).
- ☐ Faulty injector(s) - Diesel models (Chapter 4D).

Engine stalls

- ☐ Vacuum leak at the carburettor/throttle body, inlet manifold or associated hoses (Chapter 4A/B/C).
- ☐ Fuel filter choked (Chapter 1).
- ☐ Fuel pump faulty, or delivery pressure low - petrol models (Chapter 4A/B/C).
- ☐ Fuel tank vent blocked, or fuel pipes restricted (Chapter 4).
- ☐ Blocked carburettor jet(s) or internal passages - carburettor petrol models (Chapter 4A).
- ☐ Blocked injector/fuel injection system fault - fuel-injected petrol models (Chapter 4B/C).
- ☐ Faulty injector(s) - Diesel models (Chapter 4D).

Engine lacks power

- ☐ Timing belt incorrectly fitted or tensioned (Chapter 2A/B).
- ☐ Fuel filter choked (Chapter 1).
- ☐ Fuel pump faulty, or delivery pressure low - petrol models (Chapter 4A/B/C).
- ☐ Uneven or low cylinder compressions (Chapter 2A/B).
- ☐ Worn, faulty or incorrectly-gapped spark plugs - petrol models (Chapter 1).
- ☐ Vacuum leak at the carburettor/throttle body, inlet manifold or associated hoses - petrol models (Chapter 4A/B/C).
- ☐ Blocked carburettor jet(s) or internal passages - carburettor petrol models (Chap-ter 4A).
- ☐ Blocked injector/fuel injection system fault - fuel-injected petrol models (Chapter 4B/C).
- ☐ Faulty injector(s) - Diesel models (Chapter 4D).
- ☐ Injection pump timing incorrect - Diesel models (Chapter 4D).
- ☐ Brakes binding (Chapters 1 and 9).
- ☐ Clutch slipping (Chapter 6).

Engine backfires

- ☐ Timing belt incorrectly fitted or tensioned - petrol models (Chapter 2A).
- ☐ Vacuum leak at the carburettor/throttle body, inlet manifold or associated hoses - petrol models (Chapter 4A/B/C).
- ☐ Blocked carburettor jet(s) or internal passages - carburettor petrol models (Chapter 4A).
- ☐ Blocked injector/fuel injection system fault - fuel-injected petrol models (Chapter 4B/C).

Oil pressure warning light illuminated with engine running

- ☐ Low oil level, or incorrect oil grade (Chapter 1).
- ☐ Faulty oil pressure sensor (Chapter 5A).
- ☐ Worn engine bearings and/or oil pump (Chapter 2C).
- ☐ Excessively high engine operating temperature (Chapter 3).
- ☐ Oil pressure relief valve defective (Chapter 2A/B).
- ☐ Oil pick-up strainer clogged (Chapter 2A/B).

Engine runs-on after switching off

- ☐ Excessive carbon build-up in engine - petrol models (Chapter 2C).
- ☐ Excessively high engine operating temperature - carburettor petrol models (Chapter 3).
- ☐ Faulty fuel cut-off solenoid - carburettor petrol models (Chapter 4A).
- ☐ Faulty stop solenoid - Diesel models (Chapter 4D).

Engine noises

Pre-ignition (pinking) or knocking during acceleration or under load

- ☐ Ignition timing incorrect/ignition system fault - petrol models (Chapters 1 and 5B).
- ☐ Incorrect grade of spark plug - petrol models (Chapter 1).
- ☐ Incorrect grade of fuel - petrol models (Chapter 1).
- ☐ Vacuum leak at carburettor/throttle body, inlet manifold or associated hoses - petrol models (Chapter 4A/B/C).
- ☐ Excessive carbon build-up in engine - petrol models (Chapter 2C).
- ☐ Blocked carburettor jet(s) or internal passages - carburettor petrol models (Chapter 4A).
- ☐ Blocked injector/fuel injection system fault - fuel-injected petrol models (Chapter 4B/C).

Whistling or wheezing noises

- ☐ Leaking inlet manifold or carburettor/throttle body gasket - petrol models (Chapter 4A/B/C).
- ☐ Leaking exhaust manifold gasket or pipe-to-manifold joint (Chapter 4).
- ☐ Leaking vacuum hose (Chapters 4, 5B and 9).
- ☐ Blowing cylinder head gasket (Chapter 2A/B).

Tapping or rattling noises

- ☐ Worn valve gear or camshaft (Chapter 2A/B).
- ☐ Ancillary component fault (water pump, alternator, etc) (Chapters 3, 5A, etc).

Knocking or thumping noises

- ☐ Worn big-end bearings (regular heavy knocking, perhaps less under load) (Chapter 2C).
- ☐ Worn main bearings (rumbling and knocking, perhaps worsening under load) (Chapter 2C).
- ☐ Piston slap (most noticeable when cold) (Chapter 2C).
- ☐ Ancillary component fault (water pump, alternator, etc) (Chapters 3, 5A, etc).

2 Cooling system

Overheating

- ☐ Insufficient coolant in system (Chapter 1).
- ☐ Thermostat faulty (Chapter 3).
- ☐ Radiator core blocked, or grille restricted (Chapter 3).
- ☐ Electric cooling fan or thermoswitch faulty (Chapter 3).
- ☐ Pressure cap faulty (Chapter 3).
- ☐ Ignition timing incorrect/ignition system fault - petrol models (Chapters 1 and 5B).
- ☐ Inaccurate temperature gauge sender unit (Chapter 3).
- ☐ Airlock in cooling system (Chapter 1).

Overcooling

- ☐ Thermostat faulty (Chapter 3).
- ☐ Inaccurate temperature gauge sender unit (Chapter 3).

External coolant leakage

- ☐ Deteriorated or damaged hoses or hose clips (Chapter 1).
- ☐ Radiator core or heater matrix leaking (Chapter 3).
- ☐ Pressure cap faulty (Chapter 3).
- ☐ Water pump seal leaking (Chapter 3).
- ☐ Boiling due to overheating (Chapter 3).
- ☐ Core plug leaking (Chapter 2C).

Internal coolant leakage

- ☐ Leaking cylinder head gasket (Chapter 2A/B).
- ☐ Cracked cylinder head or cylinder bore (Chapter 2).

Corrosion

- ☐ Infrequent draining and flushing (Chapter 1).
- ☐ Incorrect coolant mixture or inappropriate coolant type (Chapter 1).

3 Fuel and exhaust systems

Excessive fuel consumption

- ☐ Air filter element dirty or clogged (Chapter 1).
- ☐ Choke cable incorrectly adjusted, or choke sticking - carburettor petrol models (Chapter 4A).
- ☐ Fuel injection system fault - fuel injected petrol models (Chapter 4B/C).
- ☐ Faulty injector(s) - Diesel models (Chapter 4D).
- ☐ Ignition timing incorrect/ignition system fault - petrol models (Chapters 1 and 5B).
- ☐ Tyres under-inflated (Chapter 1).

Fuel leakage and/or fuel odour

- ☐ Damaged or corroded fuel tank, pipes or connections (Chapter 4).
- ☐ Carburettor float chamber flooding (float height incorrect) - carburettor petrol models (Chapter 4A).

Excessive noise or fumes from exhaust system

- ☐ Leaking exhaust system or manifold joints (Chapters 1 and 4).
- ☐ Leaking, corroded or damaged silencers or pipe (Chapters 1 and 4).
- ☐ Broken mountings causing body or suspension contact (Chapter 1).

4 Clutch

Pedal travels to floor - no pressure or very little resistance

- ☐ Broken clutch cable (Chapter 6).
- ☐ Incorrect clutch cable adjustment (Chapter 6).
- ☐ Broken clutch release bearing or fork (Chapter 6).
- ☐ Broken diaphragm spring in clutch pressure plate (Chapter 6).

Clutch fails to disengage (unable to select gears).

- ☐ Incorrect clutch cable adjustment (Chapter 6).
- ☐ Clutch disc sticking on gearbox input shaft splines (Chapter 6).
- ☐ Clutch disc sticking to flywheel or pressure plate (Chapter 6).
- ☐ Faulty pressure plate assembly (Chapter 6).
- ☐ Clutch release mechanism worn or incorrectly assembled (Chapter 6).

Clutch slips (engine speed increases, with no increase in vehicle speed).

- ☐ Incorrect clutch cable adjustment (Chapter 6).
- ☐ Clutch disc linings excessively worn (Chapter 6).
- ☐ Clutch disc linings contaminated with oil or grease (Chapter 6).
- ☐ Faulty pressure plate or weak diaphragm spring (Chapter 6).

Judder as clutch is engaged

- ☐ Clutch disc linings contaminated with oil or grease (Chapter 6).
- ☐ Clutch disc linings excessively worn (Chapter 6).
- ☐ Clutch cable sticking or frayed (Chapter 6).
- ☐ Faulty or distorted pressure plate or diaphragm spring (Chapter 6).
- ☐ Worn or loose engine or gearbox mountings (Chapter 2A/B).
- ☐ Clutch disc hub or gearbox input shaft splines worn (Chapter 6).

Noise when depressing or releasing clutch pedal

- ☐ Worn clutch release bearing (Chapter 6).
- ☐ Worn or dry clutch pedal bushes (Chapter 6).
- ☐ Faulty pressure plate assembly (Chapter 6).
- ☐ Pressure plate diaphragm spring broken (Chapter 6).
- ☐ Broken clutch disc cushioning springs (Chapter 6).

5 Manual transmission

Noisy in neutral with engine running

- ☐ Input shaft bearings worn (noise apparent with clutch pedal released, but not when depressed) (Chapter 7).*
- ☐ Clutch release bearing worn (noise apparent with clutch pedal depressed, possibly less when released) (Chapter 6).

Noisy in one particular gear

- ☐ Worn, damaged or chipped gear teeth (Chapter 7).*

Difficulty engaging gears

- ☐ Clutch fault (Chapter 6).
- ☐ Worn or damaged gear linkage (Chapter 7).
- ☐ Incorrectly-adjusted gear linkage (Chapter 7).
- ☐ Worn synchroniser units (Chapter 7).*

Jumps out of gear

- ☐ Worn or damaged gear linkage (Chapter 7).
- ☐ Incorrectly-adjusted gear linkage (Chapter 7).
- ☐ Worn synchroniser units (Chapter 7).*
- ☐ Worn selector forks (Chapter 7).*

Vibration

- ☐ Lack of oil (Chapter 1).
- ☐ Worn bearings (Chapter 7).*

Lubricant leaks

- ☐ Leaking differential output oil seal (Chapter 7).
- ☐ Leaking housing joint (Chapter 7).*
- ☐ Leaking input shaft oil seal (Chapter 7).*

**Although the corrective action necessary to remedy the symptoms described is beyond the scope of the home mechanic, the above information should be helpful in isolating the cause of the condition, so that the owner can communicate clearly with a professional mechanic.*

6 Driveshafts

Clicking or knocking noise on turns (at slow speed on full-lock).

- ☐ Lack of constant velocity joint lubricant, possibly due to damaged gaiter (Chapter 8).
- ☐ Worn outer constant velocity joint (Chapter 8).

Vibration when accelerating or decelerating

- ☐ Worn inner constant velocity joint (Chapter 8).
- ☐ Bent or distorted driveshaft (Chapter 8).

7 Braking system

Note: *Apart from checking the condition of all pipe and hose connections, any faults occurring on the anti-lock braking system should be referred to a Citroën dealer for diagnosis.*

Vehicle pulls to one side under braking

- ☐ Worn, defective, damaged or contaminated front brake pads or rear brake shoes on one side (Chapters 1 and 9).
- ☐ Seized or partially-seized front brake caliper or rear wheel cylinder piston (Chapters 1 and 9).
- ☐ A mixture of brake pad/shoe lining materials fitted between sides (Chapters 1 and 9).
- ☐ Front brake caliper mounting bolts loose (Chapter 9).
- ☐ Rear brake backplate mounting bolts loose (Chapter 9).
- ☐ Worn or damaged steering or suspension components (Chapters 1 and 10).

Noise (grinding or high-pitched squeal) when brakes applied

- ☐ Brake pad or shoe friction lining material worn down to metal backing (Chapters 1 and 9).
- ☐ Excessive corrosion of brake disc or drum. (May be apparent after the vehicle has been standing for some time (Chapters 1 and 9).

Excessive brake pedal travel

- ☐ Inoperative rear brake self-adjust mechanism (Chapters 1 and 9).
- ☐ Faulty master cylinder (Chapter 9).
- ☐ Air in hydraulic system (Chapters 1 and 9).
- ☐ Faulty vacuum servo unit (Chapter 9).

Brake pedal feels spongy when depressed

- ☐ Air in hydraulic system (Chapters 1 and 9).
- ☐ Deteriorated flexible rubber brake hoses (Chapters 1 and 9).
- ☐ Master cylinder mounting nuts loose (Chapter 9).
- ☐ Faulty master cylinder (Chapter 9).

Excessive brake pedal effort required to stop vehicle

- ☐ Faulty vacuum servo unit (Chapter 9).
- ☐ Disconnected, damaged or insecure brake servo vacuum hose (Chapter 9).
- ☐ Primary or secondary hydraulic circuit failure (Chapter 9).
- ☐ Seized brake caliper or wheel cylinder piston(s) (Chapter 9).
- ☐ Brake pads or brake shoes incorrectly fitted (Chapters 1 and 9).
- ☐ Incorrect grade of brake pads or brake shoes fitted (Chapters 1 and 9).
- ☐ Brake pads or brake shoe linings contaminated (Chapters 1 and 9).

Judder felt through brake pedal or steering wheel when braking

- ☐ Excessive run-out or distortion of front discs or rear drums (Chapters 1 and 9).
- ☐ Brake pad or brake shoe linings worn (Chapters 1 and 9).
- ☐ Brake caliper or rear brake backplate mounting bolts loose (Chapter 9).
- ☐ Wear in suspension or steering components or mountings (Chapters 1 and 10).

Brakes binding

- ☐ Seized brake caliper or wheel cylinder piston(s) (Chapter 9).
- ☐ Incorrectly-adjusted handbrake mechanism (Chapter 9).
- ☐ Faulty master cylinder (Chapter 9).

Rear wheels locking under normal braking

- ☐ Rear brake shoe linings contaminated (Chapters 1 and 9).
- ☐ Faulty brake pressure regulator (Chapter 9).

8 Suspension and steering

Vehicle pulls to one side

- ☐ Defective tyre (Chapter 1).
- ☐ Excessive wear in suspension or steering components (Chapters 1 and 10).
- ☐ Incorrect front wheel alignment (Chapter 10).
- ☐ Accident damage to steering or suspension components (Chapter 1).

Wheel wobble and vibration

- ☐ Front roadwheels out of balance (vibration felt mainly through the steering wheel) (Chapters 1 and 10).
- ☐ Rear roadwheels out of balance (vibration felt throughout the vehicle) (Chapters 1 and 10).
- ☐ Roadwheels damaged or distorted (Chapters 1 and 10).
- ☐ Faulty or damaged tyre (Chapter 1).
- ☐ Worn steering or suspension joints, bushes or components (Chapters 1 and 10).
- ☐ Wheel bolts loose (Chapters 1 and 10).

Excessive pitching and/or rolling around corners, or during braking

- ☐ Defective shock absorbers (Chapters 1 and 10).
- ☐ Broken or weak spring and/or suspension component (Chapters 1 and 10).
- ☐ Worn or damaged anti-roll bar or mountings (Chapter 10).

Wandering or general instability

- ☐ Incorrect front wheel alignment (Chapter 10).
- ☐ Worn steering or suspension joints, bushes or components (Chapters 1 and 10).
- ☐ Roadwheels out of balance (Chapters 1 and 10).
- ☐ Faulty or damaged tyre (Chapter 1).
- ☐ Wheel bolts loose (Chapters 1 and 10).
- ☐ Defective shock absorbers (Chapters 1 and 10).

Excessively-stiff steering

- ☐ Lack of steering gear lubricant (Chapter 10).
- ☐ Seized track rod end balljoint or suspension balljoint (Chapters 1 and 10).
- ☐ Incorrect front wheel alignment (Chapter 10).
- ☐ Steering rack or column bent or damaged (Chapter 10).

Excessive play in steering

- ☐ Worn steering column intermediate shaft universal joint (Chapter 10).
- ☐ Worn steering track rod end balljoints (Chapters 1 and 10).
- ☐ Worn rack-and-pinion steering gear (Chapter 10).
- ☐ Worn steering or suspension joints, bushes or components (Chapters 1 and 10).

Tyre wear excessive

Tyres worn on inside or outside edges

- ☐ Tyres under-inflated (wear on both edges) (Chapter 1).
- ☐ Incorrect camber or castor angles (wear on one edge only) (Chapter 10).
- ☐ Worn steering or suspension joints, bushes or components (Chapters 1 and 10).
- ☐ Excessively-hard cornering.
- ☐ Accident damage.

Tyre treads exhibit feathered edges

- ☐ Incorrect toe setting (Chapter 10).

Tyres worn in centre of tread

- ☐ Tyres over-inflated (Chapter 1).

Tyres worn on inside and outside edges

- ☐ Tyres under-inflated (Chapter 1).

Tyres worn unevenly

- ☐ Tyres/wheels out of balance (Chapter 1).
- ☐ Excessive wheel or tyre run-out (Chapter 1).
- ☐ Worn shock absorbers (Chapters 1 and 10).
- ☐ Faulty tyre (Chapter 1).

9 Electrical system

Note: *For problems associated with the starting system, refer to the faults listed under "Engine" earlier in this Section.*

Battery will not hold a charge for more than a few days

- ☐ Battery defective internally (Chapter 5A).
- ☐ Battery terminal connections loose or corroded (Chapter 1).
- ☐ Auxiliary drivebelt worn or incorrectly adjusted (Chapter 1).
- ☐ Alternator not charging at correct output (Chapter 5A).
- ☐ Alternator or voltage regulator faulty (Chapter 5A).
- ☐ Short-circuit causing continual battery drain (Chapters 5A and 12).

Ignition/no-charge warning light remains illuminated with engine running

- ☐ Auxiliary drivebelt broken, worn, or incorrectly adjusted (Chapter 1).
- ☐ Alternator brushes worn, sticking, or dirty (Chapter 5A).
- ☐ Alternator brush springs weak or broken (Chapter 5A).
- ☐ Internal fault in alternator or voltage regulator (Chapter 5A).
- ☐ Broken, disconnected, or loose wiring in charging circuit (Chapter 5A).

Ignition/no-charge warning light fails to come on

- ☐ Warning light bulb blown (Chapter 12).
- ☐ Broken, disconnected, or loose wiring in warning light circuit (Chapter 12).
- ☐ Alternator faulty (Chapter 5A).

Lights inoperative

- ☐ Bulb blown (Chapter 12).
- ☐ Corrosion of bulb or bulbholder contacts (Chapter 12).
- ☐ Blown fuse (Chapter 12).
- ☐ Faulty relay (Chapter 12).
- ☐ Broken, loose, or disconnected wiring (Chapter 12).
- ☐ Faulty switch (Chapter 12).

Windscreen/tailgate washers inoperative, or unsatisfactory in operation

One or more washer jets inoperative

- ☐ Blocked washer jet (Chapter 1).
- ☐ Disconnected, kinked or restricted fluid hose (Chapter 12).
- ☐ Insufficient fluid in washer reservoir (Chapter 1).

Washer pump fails to operate

- ☐ Broken or disconnected wiring or connections (Chapter 12).
- ☐ Blown fuse (Chapter 12).
- ☐ Faulty washer switch (Chapter 12).
- ☐ Faulty washer pump (Chapter 12).

Washer pump runs for some time before fluid is emitted from jets

- ☐ Faulty one-way valve in fluid supply hose (Chapter 12).

Electric windows inoperative, or unsatisfactory in operation

Window glass will only move in one direction

- ☐ Faulty switch (Chapter 12).

Window glass slow to move

- ☐ Regulator seized or damaged, or in need of lubrication (Chapter 11).
- ☐ Door internal components or trim fouling regulator (Chapter 11).
- ☐ Faulty motor (Chapter 11).

Window glass fails to move

- ☐ Blown fuse (Chapter 12).
- ☐ Faulty relay (Chapter 12).
- ☐ Broken or disconnected wiring or connections (Chapter 12).
- ☐ Faulty motor (Chapter 11).

Instrument readings inaccurate or erratic

Instrument readings increase with engine speed

- ☐ Faulty voltage regulator (Chapter 12).

Fuel or temperature gauges give no reading

- ☐ Faulty gauge sender unit (Chapters 3 and 4).
- ☐ Wiring open-circuit (Chapter 12).
- ☐ Faulty gauge (Chapter 12).

Fuel or temperature gauges give continuous maximum reading

- ☐ Faulty gauge sender unit (Chapters 3 and 4).
- ☐ Wiring short-circuit (Chapter 12).
- ☐ Faulty gauge (Chapter 12).

Windscreen/tailgate wiper inoperative, or unsatisfactory in operation

Wiper fails to operate, or operate very slowly

- ☐ Wiper blade stuck to screen, or linkage seized or binding (Chapters 1 and 12).
- ☐ Blown fuse (Chapter 12).
- ☐ Cable or cable connections loose, broken or disconnected (Chapter 12).
- ☐ Faulty relay (Chapter 12).
- ☐ Faulty wiper motor (Chapter 12).

Wiper blade sweeps over too large or too small an area of the glass

- ☐ Wiper arm incorrectly positioned on spindle (Chapter 1).
- ☐ Excessive wear of wiper linkage (Chapter 12).
- ☐ Wiper motor or linkage mountings loose or insecure (Chapter 12).

Wiper blade fails to clean the glass effectively

- ☐ Wiper blade rubber worn or perished (Chapter 1).
- ☐ Wiper arm tension spring broken, or arm pivot seized (Chapter 12).
- ☐ Insufficient windscreen washer additive to adequately remove road film (Chapter 1).

Horn inoperative, or unsatisfactory in operation

Horn operates all the time

- ☐ Horn contacts permanently bridged or horn push stuck down (Chapter 12).

Horn fails to operate

- ☐ Blown fuse (Chapter 12).
- ☐ Cable or cable connections loose, broken or disconnected (Chapter 12).
- ☐ Faulty horn (Chapter 12).

Horn emits intermittent or unsatisfactory sound

- ☐ Cable connections loose (Chapter 12).
- ☐ Horn mountings loose (Chapter 12).
- ☐ Faulty horn (Chapter 12).

Central locking system inoperative, or unsatisfactory in operation

Complete system failure

- ☐ Blown fuse (Chapter 12).
- ☐ Faulty relay (Chapter 12).
- ☐ Broken or disconnected wiring or connections (Chapter 12).
- ☐ Faulty control unit (Chapter 11).

Latch locks but will not unlock, or unlocks but will not lock

- ☐ Faulty master switch (Chapter 12).
- ☐ Broken or disconnected latch operating rods or levers (Chapter 11).
- ☐ Faulty relay (Chapter 12).
- ☐ Faulty control unit (Chapter 11).

One solenoid/motor fails to operate

- ☐ Broken or disconnected wiring or connections (Chapter 12).
- ☐ Faulty solenoid/motor (Chapter 11).
- ☐ Broken, binding or disconnected latch operating rods or levers (Chapter 11).
- ☐ Fault in door latch (Chapter 11).

Index

Note: *References throughout this index relate to Chapter•page number*